Encyclopaedia of Indian Coins

(Ancient Coins of Northern India, up to *circa* 650 AD)

Encyclopaedia of Indian Coins

(Ancient Coins of Northern India, up to *circa* 650 AD)

Vol. I

Prashant Srivastava

AGAM KALA PRAKASHAN
DELHI

First Published 2012

ISBN : 978 -81-7320-118-9

Published by:
Dr. Agam Prasad, M.A., Ph.D., Diploma in Museology
For **Agam Kala Prakashan**
34, Central Market, Ashok Vihar
Delhi - 110 052
Tel.: 27212195, 65688806-7 Fax: 91-11-27212195
Email: agambooks@gmail.com, agambook@yahoo.com
www.agamkala.com

Composed by:
Aman Printographics
Mobile: 9891395309

Printed by:
Chawla Offset
Delhi-110 052

Printed in India

Contents

For my wife
Dr Nidhi Srivastava

...pṛithivī tvam
(*Bṛihadāraṇyakopanishad* IV. 4. 20)

Preface

Coins form one of the important sources of the history of ancient India; in fact, for certain periods, like those of the Indo-Greeks, the Śaka-Pahlavas, and the Western Kshatrapas, monetary issues are almost the only source of our information. In the Preface of his *magnum opus*, *The Indo-Greeks* (Oxford, 1957), A K Narain very aptly remarks, 'For certain periods of Indian history the historian has to be a numismatist'.

Several years back, the Numismatic Society of India launched an ambitious scheme of publishing corpuses of Indian coins, from the earliest times to the modern period, in ten volumes, each volume being of between four hundred and five hundred pages, and having illustrations of coins arranged in twenty to twenty-five plates. Unfortunately, only Volume IV, that is A S Altekar's *The Coinage of the Gupta Empire* (Varanasi, 1957), saw the light of day. A N Lahiri, in his individual capacity, published a *Corpus of Indo-Greek Coins* (Calcutta, 1965). Tribal coins were dealt with, first by K K Dasgupta, in his *A Tribal History of Ancient India—A Numismatic Approach* (Calcutta, 1974), and, recently, by Devendra Handa, in *Tribal Coins of Ancient India* (New Delhi, 2007). R C Senior produced the masterly work, *Indo-Scythian Coins and History* (Lancaster, Pennsylvania, London, 2001), in three volumes. However, a concise A-Z encyclopaedia of the coins of ancient India remains a *desideratum*. Hence, the present *Encyclopaedia of India Coins*.

I am well aware that, as early as nineteenth century, while preparing the work, *The Coins of the Mohammadan States of India* (London, 1885), Stanley Lane-Poole had realized, 'To be a general numismatist is beyond the powers of one man'. That is why, for the present work, I have confined myself to the ancient coins of northern India, up to *circa* 650 AD, and further encyclopaediae of the ancient coins of southern India, and the early mediaeval coins of northern India, might be prepared some time in the future.

Even then, in preparing an encyclopaedia of this limited size, I have had to be selective, and, very often, not necessarily out of choice. Still, I am open to charges of ignorance for what I have had to omit. I have also tried to be concise, yet explicit. To avoid repetition, cross referencing has been resorted to, other relevant entries in the *Encyclopaedia* being indicated by means of an asterisk (*). However, I must admit that certain entries (for example, V'ima Takshuma) have exceeded the size limit I had set for each entry, either because some recent material appeared to deserve more detailed handling, or the entries formed some of my favourite subjects; in some cases, for example, those of the Indo-Greek and Śaka-Pahlava rulers, coins form the most important (and, very often, the only) source of our information about them, and, hence, I had, perforce, to give their political history in brief. Also, in a work of this nature, it has not always been possible to avoid repetition altogether.

In the A-Z encyclopaedia, there are some references at the end of each entry. They represent only those books, monographs, and research papers, which had a direct bearing on the subject, and which I have had occasion to consult during the writing of that particular entry. In cases, where more than one publications of a scholar were available on the same subject, I have usually referred to his latest work, and not burdened the reader with the earlier one(s), unless it was otherwise deemed necessary. As a result, the specialist would find many omissions, for which I would crave his indulgence.

An Introduction, in the beginning, deals with such aspects of ancient Indian numismatics, as the origin and antiquity of coinage in India, and the authority to issue coins. This is followed by the A-Z encyclopaedia. In this, the issuers—kings/queens, dynasties, tribes, etc, and the devices—deities, symbols, etc, have been introduced briefly, mostly at the beginning of the respective entry, before dealing with the numismatic aspects. However, it was felt that the introduction of the political background of certain issuers, mostly kings, of the mythological background of certain deities, and the significance of certain symbols, deserves a somewhat fuller treatment, either by virtue of their importance, or their obscurity, even at the cost of some repetition. This has been done, again in an alphabetical order, in the Appendix, 'More About Some Issuers and Devices', which comes after the A-Z Encyclopaedia. All such entries in the body of the A-Z Encyclopaedia, as having a companion entry in the Appendix, have been indicated by means of a cross (†), placed at the end of the entry. A Select Bibliography is given at the end for the benefit of those who wish to pursue further reading.

I am indebted to the University Grant Commission for extending adequate financial assistance for the present work in the form of a major research project grant.

I also wish to thank my first readers, my mentor, Professor Kiran Kumar Thaplyal, and my father, Shri Priyonath Srivastava, who went through the truly rough drafts, and offered some valuable suggestions.

The Indian Institute of Research in Numismatic Studies, Nashik, provided some coin photographs for research purposes. For this, I express my gratitude to Dr Amiteshwar Jha, Shri

Danish Moin, Shri Rehan Ahamad, and other members of the staff at the Institute, and, above all, to Shri (now Dr) K K Maheshwari. I wish to put on record, my thanks to Dr Ram Chandra Tiwari, Dr Rakesh Tewari, Shri I P Pandey, Dr S N Upadhyaya, Dr Anita Chaurasia, and the photographer, Shri Sharada Prasad Tripathi, of the State Museum, Lucknow, for providing some of the photographs illustrating the *Encyclopaedia*.

Professor S P Shukla, formerly of the Kurukshetra University, Dr R S Bisht, former Joint Director-General of the Archaeological Survey of India, and Dr Abhay Kumar Singh, Reader in Ancient History and Culture, M J P Rohilkhand University, Bareilly, provided some study material, for which I am beholden to them.

For providing facilities of study, I wish to thank the librarian and staff of the Tagore Library, University of Lucknow, Lucknow; Central Archaeological Library, New Delhi; National Museum, New Delhi; the Indian Institute of Research in Numismatic Studies, Nashik; American Institute of Indian Studies, Gurgaon; State Museum, Lucknow; State Archaeological Organization, Uttar Pradesh, Lucknow; etc.

As always, my deepest gratitude goes to my parents, Smt Pushplata Srivastava and Shri Priyonath Srivastava, who have been a constant source of inspiration; and to my wife, and my daughters, Pratichi and Purvi, for bearing with me. My sister, Monica, and her family provided me hospitality during my stays at Delhi in connection with this work. My heartfelt thanks to her, to Naveen, and the whole family.

In the end, I thank Dr Agam Prasad of Agam Kala Prakashan, Delhi, and his staff, especially Shri A.K. Pandey, for their cooperation in bringing out this *Encyclopaedia* in its present form.

25 July 2011. **Prashant Srivastava**

Abbreviations

Br	Brāhmī
Gr	Greek
k	king
Kh	Kharoshṭhī
l	left
ld	legend
obv	obverse
Pkt	Prakrit
r	right
rev	reverse
Skt	Sanskrit

Introduction

Origin of coinage in India

In the primitive stages, the needs of human beings were simple and were supplied mostly by nature—the trees and plants provided fruits and roots, and the animals, meat to feed them; the leaves and barks of trees and animal skins covered their bodies; the natural caves gave them shelter from the elements and enemies. But as man settled down and society came into existence, occupations became specialized. What man could not himself produce, he had to obtain from others. This gave birth to the barter system. But barter system requires a double coincidence. Of the two persons participating in the transaction, what one person requires must be in excess with the second person, and the latter must be desirous of the commodity that is in excess with the former. Also, it was always not easy to determine the relative value of the various commodities. To do away with these difficulties, a certain commodity was adopted as a medium of exchange. In vedic India, cow seems to have served this purpose. Ten cows are mentioned as the cost of [an image of] *Indra. The wealth of a person has been calculated in cows. Battles were often fought to appropriate the animal wealth of other tribes.

But such a medium of exchange cannot have its submultiples. One could not pay half, or one-fourth, or one-eighth of a cow. This difficulty was overcome by the introduction of metal as medium of exchange. Dividing a lump or piece of metal does not adversely affect its intrinsic value. Each transaction, however, required the use of scales and weights to weigh the metal, and also provision had to be made for the testing of the purity of the metal. Gradually, to get rid of these problems, metallic pieces of definite weight, and more or less definite shape and size, came to be issued by recognized authorities, each piece bearing a device, or a legend, or both, identifying the issuing authority, and testifying to the metallic purity and weight of the piece. Such metallic pieces are termed coins. The earliest coins were perhaps manufactured by the Lydians or the Greek settlers of Asia, around 700 BC. These were of electrum, a natural alloy of gold and silver, which was later on replaced by gold.

Regarding the origin of coinage in India, Altekar rightly observes, 'The origin of the coinage in ancient India is shrouded in considerable obscurity. The evidence available to decide the question is scanty, dubious and capable of different interpretations.' Widely divergent views have been expressed by scholars as to the origin of coinage in India.

H H Wilson suggested that the Indians learnt the art of coinage from the Bactrians and the Romans. James Prinsep, too, felt that there was no coinage in India prior to the advent of Alexander. These two scholars would, thus, place the antiquity of Indian coinage somewhere in the fourth century BC, or even later. Kennedy was of the view that the Indian punch marked coins were copied from the Babylonian coins *circa* sixth century BC, and this seems to have the support of V A Smith, who said that Indian coinage began around the seventh century BC as a result of foreign maritime trade. John Allan believed that the idea of coinage was suggested in India by the Iranian *sigloi*, in the late fifth or early fourth century BC, although the punch marked coins are entirely different from the Achaemenian coins. He opined that the Nanda rulers of the third quarter of the fourth century BC, who were famous for their great wealth, were, perhaps, the first to issue coins in India. J-A Decourdemanche, too, believed that the punch marked coins are simply an Indian variety of the coinage of the Achaemenians.

For establishing that the Indians borrowed the art of coinage from others, three conditions must be fulfilled : (i) the date of beginning of coinage in that area must be earlier than its introduction in India; (ii) there should be sufficient similarity in shape, size, weight, etc, between the earliest coins of India and those of that region; and (iii) there should be evidence of the Indians coming into contact with people of that region, prior to the introduction of coinage in India.

There is no resemblance between Greek coins on the one hand, and the *punch marked coins, which represent the earliest known coinage of India, on the other. The design, fabric, symbols of the most ancient coins of India—the punch marked coins, 'bear no trace of the conventionalities of the Greek art'. Also, as Altekar observes, had the Indians learnt the art of coining money from the Greeks, 'the earliest coins would have been nothing short of coins of full die-struck maturity'. Even the weight standard is different. While the Greek **drachm* weighs 67.2 grains, the Indian **paṇa* weighs about 56 grains. Greek coins bear legend, while the punch marked coins are anepigraphous. Busts of kings and figures of deities, seen on Greek coins, are not to be met with on punch marked coins, which bear symbol(s) on one side or both the sides. Besides, there is clear literary evidence to show that coins were already in circulation in India at the time of Alexander's invasion. According to Quintus Curtius Rufus, Omphis, the king of Taxila, presented 80 talents of *signati argenti*, 'marked silver', to the Macedonian invader. It has been agreed upon that by the pieces of marked silver, punch marked coins were meant. This literary evidence is corroborated by archaeological sources. A coin hoard from the Bhir mound at Taxila contained 1055 common type of punch marked coins, 33 *bent bar pieces, two *tetradrachms* of Alexander, one of Philip Aridaeus, and an Achaemenian *siglos*. Of these, the *siglos* was 'well worn', while the coins of

Alexander and Philip were in 'mint condition'. Some of the punch marked coins bear double obverse, showing that they had become so worn out that symbols had to be punched on them a second time, and in some cases, even the latter devices had become blurred. Philip died in 317 BC, and so the hoard would have been buried in the last quarter of the fourth century BC. The worn out condition of the punch marked coins shows that they must have been in circulation for at least a couple of centuries before they were interred. This renders untenable the theory that the Indians learnt the art of coinage from the Greeks.

There is some similarity between the Babylonian *shekels* and the Indian *paṇas*. For instance, both of them bear punch marks; both are flat; both are anepigraphous; both have no definite shape or size; both follow some standard of weight. The Jātaka stories, taken by some scholars as depicting life of sixth-fifth centuries BC, refer to Indian merchants visiting Bāveru, which is identified with Babylonia. There is also a view that silver was imported from Babylonia. This led Kennedy to propose a Babylonian origin for Indian coinage. But the symbols punched on *shekels* differ from those on *paṇas* in nature and character. The *shekel* weighs 132 grains, while a standard punch marked coin weighs about 56 grains. No Babylonian *shekel* has so far been found in India. The most important point that goes against the Babylonian theory is that the antiquity of the *shekel* does not go back beyond 525 BC, while coinage had been introduced in India anterior to that date. Therefore, the theory of Kennedy cannot be entertained.

According to Decourdemanche, the punch marked coins form an Indian variety of the Achaemenian *sigloi*, the former being issued with Indian symbols for circulation in India. But, as Altekar queries, 'why should Achaemenian rulers issue coins with Hindu symbols, when none such existed in the country before their advent ? How could they think of a shape for their Indian currency so totally dissimilar from their own *sigloi* ?' Decourdemanche believed that the weight of punch marked coins conforms to the metric system connected with the talent. But actually, the weight of a *paṇa* is based on the *raktikā* seed (*abrus precatorius*), each of which weighs, on an average, 1.8 grains. The weight of a *siglos* is 86.45 grains, and seems to have no connection whatsoever with the weight of the *paṇa*, that is 56 grains. The Achaemenian coins carry the figure of the archer king, running or kneeling to the right; no such depiction is to be seen on punch marked coins, which bear a number of symbols. The punch marked coins are believed to have originated about the sixth century BC in the *madhyadeśa*, and there could hardly have been any Persian (Achaemenian) influence in that area at that time.

Thus, there is no similarity between the punch marked coins, the earliest available coins of India, and the Greek/Graeco-Bactrian, Babylonian, and Iranian coins, as to warrant that these punch marked coins were inspired by them, and, hence, most of the Indian scholars, and a number of European ones, too, do not subscribe to the view that Indian coinage owes its origin to foreigners—Greeks or Bactrians, Babylonians, Iranians. E J Rapson suggests that the punch marked coins were developed independently of any foreign influence. Edward Thomas states that the '[d]esigns, treatment and die-devices (of ancient Indian coins), evince independent thought.' Further, various stages in the evolution of coinage—barter system, cow, gold dust, pieces of metal without stamp (in the vedic age), and, finally, metallic pieces of fixed weight bearing devices as mark of authority, are discernible in India, and no abrupt introduction of a new technique is seen. Hence, the theory of indigenous origin of coinage in India seems to be the most acceptable. Cunningham, who places the punch marked coins as early as 1000 BC, too, does not accept the various theories regarding the foreign origin of Indian coinage. D R Bhandarkar, S K Chakrabortty, A S Altekar, and others are staunch advocates of the theory of the indigenous origin of Indian coins.

In recent years, the theory of the foreign (Graeco-Iranian) origin of Indian coinage has been revived by scholars like M K Dhavalikar and Joe Cribb. Most of the punch marked coins are in silver. Dhavalikar expresses surprise over the sudden introduction of a full-fledged silver coinage in India, when all the ancient religious texts refer to the monetary use of gold only. Unstamped bar-shaped silver ingots were used in central Asia, which was under Iranian influence, and Dhavalikar suggests that the origin of the Indian bent bars may be traced to this Iranian practice.

Cribb's theory may be summed up as follows : The cup-shaped coins and the early series of regular punch marked coins share 'characteristics of design and technology', and as there is no evidence to show that the latter were the precursor of the former, the early series of regular punch marked coins may be derived from the cup-shaped coins. The so-called bent bars and the cup-shaped coins have the same style of punch; have the punches arranged in a similar pattern; have the same curved form of flan; have a denomination system, which includes fractional coins; besides, the lower denomination of the cup-shaped coins are 'exact matches in form' to the bent bars. The bent bars, thus, share the features of cup-shaped coins, but do not show the features found on the early series of regular punch marked coins derived from the cup-shaped ones, indicating that the bent bars might be earlier than the cup-shaped coins and served as the prototypes for the latter. Therefore, the bent bar coins and the cup-shaped coins represent the earliest phase of Indian coinage, from which all the features of the regular punch marked coins of the Ganga region were evolved. The Chaman-i-Hazouri hoard contains Greek coins, mostly datable to the fifth century BC; one Iranian imitation of an Athenian coin dated between 390 BC and 350 BC; and a group of locally made adaptations of Greek coins, 'which seem to provide a missing link between Greek coinage and the bent bars', the smaller denominations of bent bars being indistinguishable from 'the smaller denominations of these local adaptations of Greek coinage'. The Gandhāra coins of the Chaman-i-Hazouri hoard are all short and broad bent bars. On the contrary, except for a few specimens which are broad, most of the Gandhāra coins of the Taxila hoard, which was deposited after 323 BC, are narrower, showing that the Chaman-i-Hazouri hoard is earlier than the Taxila hoard, and that the bent bars developed from the broad to narrower shape during the period separating the deposit of the two hoards. The lower denominations of the 'imitations' of Greek coins, resemble the lower denominations of punch marked coins of Gandhāra and the Ganga region. But they were meant to be 'imitations' of Greek coins in the hoard, as most of them were struck as units, halves, or quarters of Greek or Iranian coinage standards. The standard of the Iranian *shekel* (around 185 grains) was adopted for the Gandhāra coins and for more than half of the 'imitations' of the Greek coins in the Chaman-i-Hazouri hoard. John Allan had also suggested that the bent bars were struck as double the weight of the silver coins struck by the Achaemenian rulers. The discovery of contemporary forgeries of the local coins of Gandhāra at Kauśāmbī shows that these coins were available as prototypes in the Ganga region. On the basis of the above, Cribb suggests that Indian coinage was evolved from the Graeco-Iranian coins. He feels that it would be easy to explain the sudden use of silver for minting coins in India, if it be accepted that 'the whole concept of the monetary use of silver could have been introduced from outside of the sub-continent', the idea coming from the Achaemenian territory, 'being suggested by the *sigloi*' (which have been regarded by some as Graeco-Persian coins).

The Greek and Iranian coins were manufactured by the die-striking process. On the contrary, the bent bars, the cup-shaped coins, and the punch marked coins were manufactured by the punching method. Regarding the Indian 'imitations' of the Greek coins from the Chaman-i-Hazouri hoard, Cribb himself says that they were mostly made by the same method as the local Gandhāra punch marked coins. Now, if the Indians had learnt the art of minting coins by first imitating the Graeco-Iranian coins, why did they not adopt the die-striking method used in the manufacture of these Graeco-Iranian coins, and evolved a whole new (punch marking) method for manufacturing the imitations of these coins ? Further, to accept Cribb's theory of Graeco-Iranian origin of Indian coinage, one also has to believe with him, that coinage in India originated in the early fourth century BC, although most of the scholars favour the sixth century BC as the date for the origin of coinage in India.

It is likely that the Indians had evolved their coinage, independent of any foreign influence, and manufactured their coins—bent bar coins, cup-shaped coins and regular punch marked coins, by the punching method. When they had occasion to manufacture 'imitations' of Graeco-Iranian coins, they adopted the punching method for that too, instead of using the die-striking method by which the Graeco-Iranian coins were manufactured (Allan 1936; Altekar 1953; D R Bhandarkar 1984; Chakrabortty 1931; Cribb 2005; Cunningham 1971b; Decourdemanche 1912; Dhavalikar 1975; S R Goyal 1995b; P L Gupta 2004; Mitchiner 1973; Prinsep 1858; Rapson 1897; Smith 1972; Prashant Srivastava 2010; Wilson 1971).

Antiquity of coinage in India

Most of the scholars are of the view that in the age of the Harappan culture, 'coinage was yet to be evolved'. But in 1926, a silver vase was unearthed in the DK area of Mohenjodaro, which contained pieces of jewellery and some flat silver objects. These silver pieces were regarded by

K N Dikshit as 'precursors of punch marked coins of later times'. D D Kosambi also regarded the weights of three of the silver pieces as corresponding to the mean of the class D weight from Mohenjodaro and Harappa, and representing 'the beginning of a coinage system'. This, however, has not been accepted by most of the scholars.

A passage in the *Ṛigveda* refers to Rudra as wearing a **nishka*, which is *viśvarūpa* in form. This *viśvarūpa* form is understood to mean that probably the *nishka* had numerous symbols marked upon it. It has been suggested that in this context, *nishka* was a gold coin bearing symbols, and was occasionally used as an ornament, either singly or several of them strewn together in a necklace. It may, however, be mentioned that scholars have pointed out that *viśvarūpa* is also used in various contexts for a chariot, cattle, plant, etc. In another passage of the same text, there is an account of the sage, Kakshīvat by name, receiving ten horses and ten *nishkas* from King Bhavya. The *Atharvaveda* refers to the gift of 300 horses, 10,000 cows, 10 necklaces, and 100 *nishkas*. It has been noted in this connection that a gift of ten, or a hundred ornaments (if *nishkas* are taken to mean necklaces) would be rather curious. For no one person, or even the members of his family, would need so many pieces of the same ornament to be worn on the body. It would be reasonable to infer that *nishka* was an article of a definite weight and value, if not of a definite size and shape. If it had symbols or devices on it, it could well be a coin-token, if not a coin. Any reference to the use of *nishka* in commercial transactions in the *Ṛigveda* would have provided conclusive evidence to this fact. But we have no such reference in the said text. Also, nowhere in the *Ṛigveda* is there any reference to the issue of *nishkas* under any recognized authority. Therefore, it seems more reasonable to infer that, primarily, *nishka* was an ornament of a specific weight, which gradually gave place to a coin denomination of that weight. Manu, Yājñavalkya, and Vishṇu give the weight of a *nishka* as 320 *rattīs*.

Incidentally, a passage in the *Ṛigveda* depicts Indra as being requested to bestow upon a worshipper *manās* of gold. The term *mina* denoted a silver or gold ingot of a fixed weight in Babylonia. Could the *manā* of the *Ṛigveda* be the Sanskrit pronunciation of the Babylonian *mina*, and denote a gold coin ? But even if the vedic Indians knew of the *mina*, later total disappearance of the term *manā* from Indian language and literature would tend to show that *manā* 'as a regular weight or coin was foreign to Vedic India'.

Explicit information about the coinage of the period is wanting in the later saṁhitās, brāhmaṇas, and the upanishads. The *Pañchaviṁśabrāhmaṇa* refers to a silver *nishka* as an ornament of the vrātyas. *Nishka* is also mentioned in the *Gopathabrāhmaṇa* in connection with the challenge of Uddālaka Āruṇi, who travelled with a *nishka* attached to his banner, declaring that it would be given to the person who would defeat him in debate. A king is seen in the *Chhāndogyopanishad*, offering his daughter, 1,000 cows, a horse, a chariot, a village, and a single *nishka* to a sage to learn from him an esoteric doctrine.

In vedic literature, *nishka* is always mentioned in connection with charity or as a prize. It is to be noted that the typical ornaments, like *khādi* and *rukma*, are never mentioned in the context of charity. This would show that *nishka* in that period was not just an ordinary ornament. It was a piece of well defined weight and had some purchasing value, but not probably a regular coin, as its multiples and submultiples do not find mention in the vedic literature, as also the authority responsible for its issue.

Another gold piece, round in shape, was the **śatamāna* mentioned in later vedic literature. There is a reference to two *śatamānas* attached to the wheel of the royal chariot being offered as *dakshiṇā* to the officiating priest at the time of the *rājasūya yajña*. The **suvarṇa* was, in later times, a gold coin of 80 *rattīs*. It is difficult to say if it was a coin or a piece of gold weighing 80 *rattīs* in the period of the brāhmaṇas as well. In the *Bṛihadāraṇyakopanishad*, it is told that at the time of the *bahudakshiṇā yajña*, Janaka organized a philosophical debate. It was declared that the winner was to receive a thousand cows, with 10 *pādas* attached to the horns of each cow. This *pāda* could be a coin or a metallic (gold ?) piece equal to a quarter of some standard coin—a *nishka*, a *śatamāna*, or a *suvarṇa*. In the *Taittirīyabrāhmaṇa*, there is an account of each chariot racer receiving one **kṛishṇala*.

In later vedic literature, *nishka*, *śatamāna*, *suvarṇa*, and *pāda* are mentioned, always in connection with the fee paid to the priests on auspicious occasions, and never as ornaments. It is not mentioned whether or not they bore any mark or device on their surface. It has been suggested that they might have been used as currency, but as things were very cheap, the occasions when transactions were made with the help of gold currency would have been very rare indeed, and usually barter was in vogue. Silver and copper currencies, which would have been required for smaller transactions, are nowhere mentioned in the literature of the period.

While earlier literature referred to gold pieces only in the context of generous gifts, the literature of the period from about the sixth century BC refers to coins in connection with ordinary commercial transactions. Thus, in the *Ashṭādhyāyī*, articles worth one, two, and three *nishka(s)* are called *naishkikaṁ*, *dvi-naishkikaṁ*, and *tri-naishkikaṁ*, respectively, while terms like *naishka-śatika* and *naishka-sāhassrika* denoted persons worth a hundred and a thousand *nishkas*, respectively. The term *nishka* also occurs in the Jātaka literature. Thus, in the *Bhūridattajātaka*, the *bodhisattva* earns a hundred *nishkas* a day, and in the *Kuhakajātaka*, a person misappropriates a deposit of a hundred *nishkas* placed with him. *Pāda*- or Quarter-*nishka* is referred to by Patañjali. The *Udayajātaka* refers to gold **māshakas*. Whether these *māshakas* were gold coins weighing about 1/16 of a *suvarṇa*, or 'small medallic pieces' of the same weight used for preparing necklaces, is not certain. *Śatamāna* as a gold coin is mentioned by both Pāṇini and Kātyāyana. Pāṇini explains *śātamāna* as an object purchased for a *śatamāna*. Some scholars opine that *śatamāna* literally means a *māna* (standard) of hundred, and might have weighed a hundred *rattīs*. But Manu and Yājñavalkya refer to it as of 320 *rattīs*. Some scholars suggest that *mañjāḍī* weighing about 3.2 *rattīs* was the *māna*.

There is also evidence from the *Maitrāyaṇīsaṁhitā* of the *Yajurveda*, the *Śatapathabrāhmaṇa*, and the *Kātyāyanaśrautasūtra* to show that silver *śatamāna* existed side by side with a gold one.

About the middle of the sixth century BC, silver *śatamānas* appear to have been introduced into circulation. V S Agrawala identifies the silver *bent bar coins, weighing about 175 grains (= 100 *rattīs*) as silver *śatamāna*. But S R Goyal has pointed out that *śatamāna* in the *Śatapathabrāhmaṇa* (as also in Sāyaṇa's commentary) is referred to as round in shape, and not as long which is the case with the bent bar pieces. Altekar likens some Kosala coins weighing between 75 and 79 grains with *arddha-śatamāna*, the coins from the Paila hoard weighing 44 grains with *pāda-śatamāna*, and the Sonepur silver punch marked coins weighing 21 grains with *pādārddha-śatamāna* or **śāṇa*. According to the *Mahābhārata*, eight *śāṇas* constitute a *śatamāna*. Later on, however, this silver *śatamāna* and its submultiples were replaced by the silver **kārshāpaṇa* currency.

Kārshāpaṇa and its submultiples are mentioned quite frequently in the *Ashṭādhyāyī* and the *Tripiṭaka*. The former text refers to *kārshāpaṇa*, **arddha-kārshāpaṇa*, **pāda-kārshāpaṇa*, **dvi-māshaka* (one-eighth *kārshāpaṇa*), and **māsha* (one-sixteenth *kārshāpaṇa*). The coin is referred to as *kahāpaṇa* in the *Vinayapiṭaka*, the *Majjhimanikāya*, and the *Aṅguttaranikāya*. While the *Vinayapiṭaka* also refers to *pāda-kahāpaṇa*, the Jātaka tales refer to *arddha-kārshāpaṇa*, *pāda-kārshāpaṇa*, **chatur-māshaka*, *tri-māshaka*, **dvi-māshaka*, *eka-māshaka*, and **arddha-māshaka*. Most of these coin denominations have been identified with the actual specimens found. Thus, silver currency was quite well-established at the time of Pāṇini, the *Tripiṭaka*, and the Jātaka literature.

The dates of Pāṇini, the Jātaka literature, and the śrautasūtras are controversial. As ten of the *janapadas* mentioned by Pāṇini belong to the list of the *śoḍasha mahājanapadas*, some scholars place him as early as 'the early phase of the age of the sixteen *mahājanapadas*, ie 7th-6th century BC', although the generally accepted date for him is the fifth century BC. The generally favoured date for the *Tripiṭaka* is *c* 450 BC, while the śrautasūtras may be placed about a century earlier. There are references to a well established system of currency in these texts dating between *c* 600 BC and *c* 450 BC. However, some recent writers on the subject, accepting the view that the *nirvāṇa* of the Buddha should be dated *c* 400 BC or even later, suggest that India's first coins were issued as late as *c* 350 BC. Bhandarkar's view that coinage was in vogue amidst the vedic Aryans as early as the middle of the third millennium BC, is regarded as untenable by a vast majority of scholars. Even Cunningham's view that the antiquity of coinage in India may be taken as far back as 1000 BC is not substantiated by literary or archaeological evidence.

The theory of placing the beginning of coinage in India in the sixth century BC seems to be supported by archaeological evidence as well. No punch marked coins are available from strata lower than those of the Northern Black Polished Ware. Even with the Northern Black Polished Ware (sixth century BC to first century BC), the punch marked coins at sites, like Atranjikhera,

Kauśāmbī, Rajghat, Rupar, Hastinapur, etc, are found in strata later than the earliest phase of the Northern Black Polished Ware. It is felt that the economy of the post-Harappan chalcolithic and other cultures (like the Painted Grey Ware culture) 'was not sufficiently developed to need or support a gold coinage'. From about the sixth century BC, which is marked by the widespread use of iron, the use of Northern Black Polished Ware, and the beginning of the second urbanization, the atmosphere for the introduction of coinage was there, and silver and copper punch marked coins were issued.

Silver was scarce in India, while silver punch marked coins are abundant. Silver could have been brought from Afghanistan, or Iran, or even Babylonia, as a result of trade. This metal is not referred to in the *Ṛigveda*, and only rarely in early vedic literature, showing that it was not much in use in that period. Though some scholars have tried to show that silver was not scarce in India, it could hardly have been enough to meet the need of issuing huge quantities of punch marked coins, and had to be imported from elsewhere. In fact, the *Periplus* and a few other Greek works mention the import of silver in India. There is also a suggestion that the term *kārshāpaṇa* is of Iranian origin. It is quite likely that silver was imported into India from Iran at the time of the rise of Achaemenian imperialism and the beginning of the rise of Magadhan imperialism in the sixth century BC. Some scholars have expressed doubts regarding the presence of coinage before 700 BC anywhere in the world (Allan 1936; Altekar 1953; Bechert 1995; D R Bhandarkar 1984; Bopearachchi and Pieper 1998; Chakrabortty 1931; Cribb 2005; Cunningham 1971b; Decourdemanche 1912; Dhavalikar 1975; S R Goyal 1995b; P L Gupta 2004; Prinsep 1858; Rapson 1897; Smith 1972; Wilson 1971).

Authority for issuing coins in ancient India

The point as to whether coinage was introduced in India by the state or by private individuals and institutions, is a controversial one. *Nishka*, *śatamāna*, *suvarṇa*, and *pāda* are mentioned in the later vedic literature almost invariably in connection with honoraria paid by kings to priests. This has led scholars like Altekar to propose that it is 'quite probable that they might have been usually manufactured in the royal treasury by a royal officer', and that these pieces 'may have been issued both by kings as well as by rich merchants dealing in bullion'.

The earliest available coins of India, that is the punch marked coins, are anepigraphous. As such, it is difficult to ascertain as to who issued these coins. But a vast majority of scholars are of the view that in the early period, the state 'was undertaking only a few functions, and coinage is not likely to have been one of them'. The adoption of coinage would have greatly facilitated commercial transactions, and might have initially been introduced by the merchant community. Later on, the state saw the advantages of the coinage system, and gradually took over the function of issuing coins. But, as has been remarked by several scholars, the right to issue coins was never zealously guarded by the state in ancient India.

Innumerable coins bearing names and title(s), or simply names, of the kings have been found from all over the subcontinent. But apart from the king, we have coins issued in the names of subkings, commander-in-chief of the imperial forces, feudatories, and others. Sometimes, coins were issued conjointly by a king and his subordinate ruler(s) or officer(s), and even by two or more subordinate rulers.

The coins of the Śaka-Pahlavas provide some examples of coins issued in the names of various authorities, either with the king or independently. *Spalirises, the brother of *Vonones, issued coins as a subordinate ruler, for, on these coins he does not assume any sovereign titles. Vonones issued a number of coins with his subordinate rulers, like *Spalahora and *Spalagadama. *Orthagnes struck coins conjointly with his subordinate ruler, *Gondopharnes and the latter's subordinate in the administrative hierarchy, namely *Guḍa. *Azes II issued coins with his **stratega* (= Greek, **strategos*, 'commander-in-chief of the imperial forces'), *Aśpavarman. Among the examples of coins issued by two subordinate rulers may be counted those struck conjointly by *Spalyris with Spalagadama, and by Spalirises with *Azes I. Among the *Western Kshatrapas, both the **mahākshatrapa* and the **kshatrapa* issued coins.

That feudatories could issue coins in the times of the *Imperial Guptas seems probable from one interpretation of lines 23-24 of the Allahabad pillar inscription of *Samudragupta, according to which the *Daivaputrashāhishāhānushāhi Śaka-muruṇḍa* and the inhabitants of Ceylon and other islands requested the Gupta monarch to permit them to issue coins bearing the **garuḍa* insignia of the Imperial Guptas.

The royal bride in ancient India was usually to be a queen-consort, and she had no authority in the matter of issuing coins. But in very rare instances, she was a queen-regnant, and could, in that capacity, issue coins. *Agathokleia, the dowager queen of the *Indo-Greek ruler, *Menander I, issued coins conjointly in her own, and her son *Strato I's, name. Among the Śaka-Pahlavas, *Machene, as regent, issued coins (of which only one specimen is known thus far) with her minor son, *Maues. We have joint coins of king and queen, as of the Indo-Greek queen, *Kalliope, with *Hermaios, and possibly of the Imperial Gupta queen, *Kumāradevī, with *Chandragupta I.

Sometimes, two rulers entered into an alliance and issued joint coins. This appears to be the case with the joint issue of *Lysias of the family of *Euthydemos, and *Antialkidas of the rival family of *Eukratides. Tarn regards the Lysias-Antialkidas coins as issued by Lysias alone and referring to, but not expressing, a *rapprochement*, 'probably a treaty of permanent peace' between the two Indo-Greek factions, in view of the Śaka menace. Rapson and Gardner, however, regard this type of coin as a joint type; Narain takes it as a mule.

Among the republican states, coins were issued mostly in the name of the *gaṇa* (republic); in some instances, an ambitious head of the republic (*gaṇapramukha*, at times, referred to as **rājan*, 'king', or **mahārāja*, 'great king'), introduced his name as well on the coins issued by the republic. Thus, we have *Ārjunāyana coins bearing the legend *Ārjunāyanānāṁ*, '[Coin] of the Ārjunāyanas', and *Mālava coins bearing the legend **Mālavagaṇasya*, '[Coin] of the Mālava *gaṇa*', showing that these coins were issued in the name of the republic. We also have *Kuṇinda coins bearing the legend, *Rājñaḥ Kuṇindasa Amoghabhūtisa mahārājasa*, which could mean both '[Coin] of King *Amoghabhūti, Great King of the Kuṇindas', and '[Coin] of King Amoghabhūti, Great King, and of the Kuṇindas'. K P Jayaswal concludes from this that these coins were 'struck in the name of the king and the political community'. The *Audumbara coins bearing the legend mentioning the name of the republic and its head, too, seem to fall in the same category.

Certain Kuṇinda coins bear the legend *Bhagavata-Chatreśvara-mahātmanaḥ*, and certain *Yaudheya coins bear the legend *Bhagavata-svāmino-Brahmaṇya-Yaudheya* or *Bhagavata-svāmino-Brahmaṇya-devasya-Kumārasya*. This has led scholars like J N Banerjea to conclude that the Kuṇindas and the Yaudheyas had dedicated their state to *Śiva and *Kārttikeya, respectively, and the coins were issued in their respective names in the capacity of a sovereign ruler. K K Dasgupta points out that even to this day, at Malan in Kulu *tehsil* near the old Kuṇinda territory, Jamlu, the tutelary deity of the village, is regarded as 'the ultimate authority and the source of power in the political, judicial and religious spheres'. But some scholars find it hard to accept this view as the deities have been given no royal titles on these coins.

Sometimes, coins were also issued by *janapadas*, as is clear from their legends and findspots. Of these, we have some examples in the coins bearing the legend, *Majhamikāya-Śibi-janapadasa*, showing that they were issued in the name of 'the Country (or Nation) of the *Śibis of Mādhyamikā', and the coins with the legend, *Rājaña-janapadasa*, 'of the country of the *Rājanya tribe'. Quite interesting are the coins issued by guilds [*Guild coins] and cities [*City coins] (Allan 1936; Altekar 1953; D R Bhandarkar 1984; Chakrabortty 1931; Cribb 2005; Cunningham 1971b; Decourdemanche 1912; Dhavalikar 1975; S R Goyal 1995b; P L Gupta 2004; Bela Lahiri 1974; Bela Lahiri 1976; Prinsep 1858; Rapson 1897; Smith 1972; Thaplyal 1996; Wilson 1971).

A

Abdagases. *Śaka-Pahlava k; nephew of *Gondopharnes; *c* first century AD. He seems to have started his career as a subordinate of Gondopharnes, perhaps in western Gandhāra, and assumed sovereignty after the death of his uncle on some territories, like Arachosia, Seistan, and Takshaśilā, of the empire formerly ruled by Gondopharnes. He issued coins in silver and copper/bronze. Some of his silver coins show debasement. The good quality silver coins and the copper/bronze coins show bust of the king, usually diademed, on the obv. The rev of the good quality silver coins has the figure of king seated as an archer, while that of the copper/bronze coins has the figure of *Nike, or thundering *Athena. For his debased silver coins, Abdagases chose the obv device of horseman king; the rev has *Zeus standing, sometimes holding out Nike on his r hand. On the good quality silver coins, the Gr ld occupies the rev. But on all his other types, the obv ld is in Gr, and the rev ld in Pkt, written in the Kh script. In the Gr ld, besides **basileus*, **basileuontos basileon*, and *basileos basileon megalos*, Abdagases also uses the additional titles of **soter*, **epiphanes*, and **dikaios*. In the rev Kh ld, he is **maharaja*, **maharaja rajatiraja*, **tratara*, **dhramiä*, etc. The form of his name occurring in the Kh ld is *Avadagasa* (Cunningham 1971a; Gardner 1971; Jenkins and Narain 1957; Marshall 1975; B N Mukherjee 1969a; Rapson 1987; Senior 2001; Sircar 1980b; Tarn 1980; Whitehead 1914).†

Abdagases

Abdagases hoard. The *provenance* of this hoard is not known for sure. The rulers represented in this hoard include *Azes I (posthumous coin), *Azes II with some **Apracharaja*, *Gondopharnes, and *Abdagases (Senior 2001).

Abhedaka. See Ābhīraka.

Ābhīraka. *Kshaharāta k. He seems to be the earliest known Kshaharāta Kshatrapa. His copper coins have been found from the Kachchh and Junagarh regions of Gujarat. These bear the figure of *Nike to the r on the obv, while the rev has a capital consisting of a *lion and a *wheel. The legends on these coins, in both Greek and Br, seem to give the name of his family as Kshaharāta, and his title as **kshatrapa*. The name on the coins is not very clear, and had earlier been read as Aghudaka or Abhedaka. But R C Senior has now read it as Ābhīraka. The use of Nike as a coin device by him seems to place him before *Bhūmaka. This is supported by the find of a coin of Ābhīraka, which was counterstruck by Bhūmaka (Jha and Rajgor 1994; Mitchiner 1976; Rajgor 1988-89; Rajgor 1991; Senior 2001).

Achyu[ta]. *Pañchāla k. This ruler has been identified with Achyuta, who is mentioned in the Allahabad pillar inscription of *Samudragupta as one of the rulers of northern India defeated by that Gupta emperor. This seems to be supported by the palaeography of the coin ld. One type of Achyu[ta] coins shows the bust of the king and the ld *Achyu[ta]* on either side of it; the other type bears a **chakra* and the ld *Achyu[ta]* on both sides. Some scholars take the two types as belonging to two different kings. *Chakra* is also met with on the coins of the *Nāga kings, and there is a suggestion that he might have belonged to the Nāga family. However, the symbol is also seen on the rev of the coins of the early Pañchāla rulers, like *Damagupta and *Vaṅgapāla. In the context of the Pañchāla coins, the *chakra* may stand for the *Sudarśanachakra* of Vishṇu (Allan 1936; Bela Lahiri 1974; Pieper 2005; Smith 1972).

Ādimūla-Kāhāvaṇa. Coin denomination. Mentioned in the **Aṅgavijjā*, this coin denomination is used to denote the original **kārshāpaṇa*, as distinguished from the new coins of the same name, designated as **bāla-kāhāvaṇa* and **ṇava-kāhāvaṇa*. Another name for the *ādimūla-kāhāvaṇa* in the same text is **purāṇa*. It would have been the traditional Indian silver coin of 32 *rattīs* (V S Agrawala 1957).

Æ. Abbreviation. This is the symbol for **aes*, and is used as the abbreviation for copper or bronze coinage (Junge 1984).

Aegis. Symbol. This is *Athena's peculiar shield or breastplate adorned with the *Gorgon's head to frighten off her foes. The goddess, and also her divine father, *Zeus, are often shown bearing the shield, *aegis*, on the coins of the *Indo-Greeks and the *Śaka-Pahlavas. This peculiar shield, as a device, appears, perhaps for the first time, on the coins of the Indo-Greek rulers, *Antimachos II and *Polyxenos. On the coins of the latter, the *aegis* is radiate, and has the depiction of Gorgon's head. The device seems to have been copied, on a copper type, by the *Śaka-Pahlava ruler, *Maues (Bopearachchi 1993; Bopearachchi and Pieper 1998; Bopearachchi and Rahman 1995; Gardner 1971; Graves 1955; Jenkins and Narain 1957; Kerenyi 1951; A N Lahiri 1965; Marshall 1975; Narain 1957a; Rose 1958; Senior 2001; Whitehead 1914;).

Aes. Metal for coins. It is the Latin for bronze, and should be used for bronze coinage in the strict sense. But it is also used for copper coinage. Bronze was used for minting the first coins of the Roman times, and, as such, *aes* in a wider sense stands for money also. It is abbreviated as **Æ* (Junge 1984).

Agathokleia. *Indo-Greek queen-regent; wife of *Menander I; mother of *Strato I; *c* second century BC. Most of the scholars regard her as the daughter of *Demetrios I, and a sister of *Agathokles. Earlier scholars, like Cunningham and Gardner, described her as the wife of Strato I, but Prinsep, and, following him, Rapson, Smith, Brown, Tarn, Narain, A N Lahiri, B N Mukherjee, and others regard her as the mother of Strato I, who, on the death of her husband, Menander I, assumed the regency of the kingdom during the minority of her son. There are some anepigraphous *staters* with the helmeted bust of *Athena (or of Agathokleia herself) on the obv, and a horned Indian owl with the Gr letter, *A*, on the rev. Scholars like Whitehead, Altekar, and Narain attribute these *staters* to Menander, but A N Lahiri's attribution of this type to Agathokleia seems to be more convincing. She seems to have issued these coins immediately on assuming regency, and avoided mentioning her full name on them. She struck joint coins with *Strato I. These coins are in gold, silver,

Agathokleia and Strato I

Agathokleia and Strato I

and copper. The gold coins are struck on the Attic standard, while the silver and copper coins are struck on the Indian standard. All the coins are die-struck pieces. The gold and silver coins are round in shape, while the copper ones are square in shape. The earlier silver types have the diademed bust of the queen and the ld **Bassilisses Agathokleias*, sometimes with the additional epithet of **theotropos*; the rev of some such coins has a diademed warrior holding shield and lance, while others have naked *Herakles seated on rock and holding club. The rev Kh ld on all these coins is **Maharajasa* **tratarasa* **dhramikasa Stratasa*. Later, she seems to have delegated greater powers to her son, and issued silver coins with the jugate busts of both of them and the ld *Basileos soteros Stratonos kai Agathokleias* on the obv. The rev has thundering Athena, and the Kh ld mentioning both of them, but later on, only Strato I. A bronze coin in the British Museum collection has the bust of Agathokleia on the obv and 'bow and quiver, with strap' on the rev. Both the obv and the rev legends refer to Strato I alone. From the non-mention of Agathokleia in the legends on this type, it is surmised that she now possessed only nominal power in the government, or had altogether ceased to wield any power and Strato I depicted her bust on the coin merely out of respect for his mother, than out of any other considerations (Bopearachchi 1993; Bopearachchi and Pieper 1998; Bopearachchi and Rahman 1995; Cunningham 1970; Gardner 1971; A N Lahiri 1965; Marshall 1975; Narain 1957a; Rapson 1906; Rapson 1987; Senior 2001; Prashant Srivastava 1996a; Tarn 1980; Whitehead 1914).†

Agathokles. *Indo-Greek k; son of *Demetrios I; *c* second century BC. There is a possibility that, on the death of Demetrios I, he ruled over Arachosia and Drangiana, conjointly with his elder brother, *Pantaleon; the two brothers together expanded their sway by conquering Kabul and western Gandhāra. Agathokles issued coins in silver, copper and cupro-nickel; some of them are based on the Attic standard, and some on the Indian standard. All the coins are die-struck pieces. Most of his coins are round in shape, though the square shape is not unknown; the coin with *stūpa* on the obv, has an irregular shape. His normal silver coinage usually bears the diademed bust of the king to the r on the obv, but the copper and cupro-nickel coins bear the bust of *Dionysos; the square silver type bears the figure of a *panther; as mentioned earlier, an irregular shaped copper type has the representation of a *stūpa* on the obv. The rev mostly has Zeus holding out *Hekate, but on some coins, panther has also been depicted. The square silver type has *Yakshiṇī Aśvamukhī on the rev, and the irregular shaped copper type has a *tree-in-railing on the rev. Six coins of Agathokles from the *Ai Khanum hoard bear the figure of *Balarāma on the obv, and that of *Vāsudeva-Kṛishṇa on the rev. Agathokles is known to have struck at least six types of commemorative coins, all *tetradrachms*, in honour of Alexander, Antiochos of Syria, *Diodotos I, *Euthydemos I, Demetrios I, and Pantaleon; there are indications that he commemorated both the Diodoti. Tarn regards these pieces as 'pedigree coins' through which Agathokles tried to gain the support of the Greeks of Bactria against his Eukratid rival(s). But Narain feels that these coins were struck by Agathokles to commemorate his occupation of parts of Gandhāra, including Takshaśilā. However, recent writers on the subject, like R C Senior, seem to support the view that these are pedigree coins, 'intended as propaganda in a civil conflict'. These commemorative coins bear the head of the commemorated king to the r on the obv, and a Gr ld mentioning his name. It is to be noted that the title of **basileus* is never used with the name of the commemorated king, most probably because they had ceased to be king before these coins were issued; instead, he is given some additional epithet, like *tou Philippou* for Alexander, **nikator* for Antiochos, **soteros* for Diodotos I, **theos* for Diodotos II (or *theos* for Diodotos I, and *soteros* for Diodotos II, as suggested by Senior), *theos* for Euthydemos I, **aniketos* for Demetrios I, and *soteros* for Pantaloen. Except for the use of *aniketos* for Demetrios (albeit, perhaps, the second ruler of this name), none of the commemorated kings is known to have ever assumed the epithet given to him on these commemorative coins. Agathokles himself does not use the title of *basileus* when he mentions himself as the commemorator on the rev, perhaps out of regard for the commemorated kings who have not been given the title of *basileus*; instead he uses the epithet of **dikaios*, and the ld begins with **basileuontos*, 'during the reign'. The rev type of these commemorative coins is usually, but not necessarily, the *canting type of the commemorated king. Thus, we have enthroned *Zeus, holding out *eagle on the rev of the type issued in memory of Alexander, thundering Zeus with eagle at

Agathokles

his l foot on the rev of the types issued in memory of Antiochos and Diodotos I, naked *Herakles bearing a club seated on a rock on the rev of the type issued in memory of Euthydemos I, standing Herakles crowning himself with his r hand on the rev of the type issued in memory of Demetrios I, and enthroned Zeus holding out *Hekate on the rev of the type issued in memory of Pantaleon. The coins struck on the Attic standard, including the commemorative coins, bear ld only in Gr. The coins struck on the Indian standard have a Gr ld on the obv, and a Pkt ld, mostly written in the Kh script, on the rev. On the square silver type bearing the figure of Yakshiṇī Aśvamukhī, the Pkt ld is engraved in the Br script. Besides the title of *basileus*, Agathokles also assumed the epithet *dikaios* on some of his coins. On the square silver type, *basileus* is rendered into Pkt as **rajañe* in the Br ld. The Pkt form of the name of the king is Agathukleya on the square silver coins, and Akathukreya on the irregular shaped copper coins (Bopearachchi 1993; Bopearachchi and Pieper 1998; Bopearachchi and Rahman 1995; Cunningham 1970; Gardner 1971; A N Lahiri 1965; Marshall 1975; Narain 1957a; Rapson 1987; Senior 2001; Sircar 1980a; Prashant Srivastava 1996a; Tarn 1980; Whitehead 1914). †

Aghudaka. See *Ābhīraka.

Agni. Vedic fire god. Chief among the terrestrial deities in the vedic period, being celebrated in as many as 200 hymns of the *Ṛigveda*, Agni the fire god was the most closely associated with human life than any other god. He is frequently given the epithets, *gṛihapati*, 'lord of the house', and *atithi*, 'guest'. He is described variously as the son of Asura, or of Dyaus (and Pṛithivī), or of Tvashṭṛi (and Āpaḥ). He was born in the highest heaven, but was brought from thence by Mātariśvan, and established on earth in the form of sacrificial fire by the Atharvan priests. He is the intermediary between the worshipper and the worshipped, and acts as a *dūta*, 'messenger', between the two. But his most important function is that of a *purohita*, 'domestic priest'. It is believed that the earliest anthropomorphic representation of Agni appears on the coins of the *Pañchāla ruler, *Agnimitra. The deity stands facing on a railed platform between two pillars. His r hand is raised; the l hand is in the *kaṭihasta mudrā*. Banerjea feels that 'some object (a sword or a club ?) seems to project downwards from his hip'. Five flames issue from his head, probably representing his hair. Cunningham, Allan, and others identify this deity as Agni. But some scholars point out that it is difficult to find any characteristic attribute of the Indian fire god, except for the fire flames represented as his hair. Bazin Foucher identifies the deity on these coins of Agnimitra as the representation of Ādi Nāga, the presiding deity of Ahichchhatra, the capital city of Pañchāla, on the basis of the similarity between this representation and that on the rev of the coins of *Bhūmimitra of Pañchāla. It must, however, be pointed out that while the latter holds a snake in the hand, no such object is visible in the hands of the former. Again, Richard Burn has pointed out that the five lines issuing from the head of the deity 'are not identical on the two coins, those of Agnimitra ending in sharper points than those of Bhūmimitra', something which would appear natural when it is seen that the five lines are fire flames in the former case, and serpents in the latter. Thus, the identification of the deity on the rev of the coins of Agnimitra with Agni seems quite plausible. Again, the general practice of representing a deity, anthropomorphically or symbolically, on the rev of the Pañchāla coins, with the issuer having the name of the deity as a component of his own name, would support this identification. One type of the coins of Agnimitra has, on the rev, an elaborate symbol, identified as an *agni vedikā* or fire altar, 'with three flames coming out of it'. Thus, on this type, Agni seems to be represented symbolically. There is also a suggestion that the deity on the coin of the Pañchāla ruler, *Phalgunīmitra, be identified as Agni. The basis for this suggestion is, probably, the fact that the hair of this deity is represented by five flames. Cunningham regards this figure as 'the constellation Phalgunī personified'. The iconography of Phalgunī is not known, and, as such, it is difficult to argue in favour or against the view of Cunningham, though the peculiar numismatic tradition regarding the rev device of the Pañchāla coins would apparently support Cunningham's identification. But as regards the identification of this deity as Agni, it must be pointed out that one would expect Agni to be represented as a male, while the deity on the rev of the coins of Phalgunīmitra is female. *Hephaistos, the Greek counterpart of the Indian Agni, and **Athsho*, the Zoroastrian counterpart of this Indian deity, also find representation on ancient Indian coins. **Pharro*, depicted on their coins by the *Kushāṇa rulers, too, seems to have some association with fire (Allan 1936;

Banerjea 2002; R G Bhandarkar 1928; Sukumari Bhattacharji 1970; Bhaskar Chattopadhyay 1977; Cunningham 1971b; Darmesteter 1974; Griswold 1999; Hillebrandt 1999; Hopkins 1915; Kothari and Morrison 1990; Macdonell 1897; Rao 1985; Prashant Srivastava 1993b; S K Srivastava 1989; Wilkins 2006). †

Agnimitra. *Kauśāmbī k. He seems to be earlier than the homonym known from the *Pañchāla series, and both should be regarded as different from the Śuṅga ruler, Agnimitra. His coins, issued in copper, have a *bull to the r, *Ujjain symbol, etc, on the obv; the rev has a *tree-in-railing, a *triangular-headed symbol, and an uncertain symbol, and the name of the issuer in the genitive. The style, execution, and combination of symbols on his coins also connect him with *Praushṭhamitra, *Jyeshṭhamitra, and *Bahasatimita II, and some coins of all these four rulers are countermarked with the *nandipada-triśūla* (Allan 1936; Altekar 1942b; Bopearachchi and Pieper 1998; Bela Lahiri 1974).

Agnimitra. *Pañchāla k. He seems to have followed *Bhānumitra and *Sūryamitra, as a female figure obliterates the three Pañchāla symbols on the coins of all these three Pañchāla kings. Bela Lahiri places Agnimitra in the eleventh chronological position among the Pañchāla rulers known from coins. The deity, *Agni, on the coins of Agnimitra stands on a platform between two pillars, and his hair is represented like five flames of Agni. One scholar, however, takes them to be the representation of the hoods of Ādināga, the presiding deity of Ahichchhatrā. But one type has, on the rev, an elaborate symbol, identified as an *agnivedikā* or fire altar, 'with three flames coming out of it' (Allan 1936; Bopearachchi and Pieper 1998; Kothari and Morrison 1990; Bela Lahiri 1974; Prashant Srivastava 1993b).

Agra. Tribe. The earliest mention of this tribe is to be found in the *Ashṭādhyāyī* of Pāṇini. Other references are met with in Baudhāyana and Patañjali, the *Mahābhārata, Mahāmāyūrī, Chāndravyākaraṇa,* the *Kāśikā*, and the *Sarasvatīkaṇṭhābharaṇa*. Yāska, in his Nirukta, refers to a teacher named Āgrāyaṇa. The Classical writers refer to the Agalassoi in the neighbourhood of the Siboi, in the context of the invasion of India by Alexander, and this tribe has been identified by some scholars with the Agras of Indian literature and coins; the Greek form of the name has been regarded as the rendering of Skt *Agrāsaḥ*. The chief city of the Agras seems to be Agrodaka, which is mentioned in the *Mahāmāyūrī* and has been identified with Aggalapura of the *Vinayapiṭaka* and with modern Agroha, about 14 miles from Hissar in Haryana, from where a hoard of 51 Agra coins has been found in the course of excavations in 1938-39. According to a local tradition, the city of Agroha was founded by one *Rājā* Agra (later named Agrasena), from whom the Agravālas claim their descent. The Agras issued die-struck coins in copper, barring one in silver; they are mostly rectangular or square in shape, although the round shape is not altogether unknown. On the basis of palaeography, and the similarity of these coins with those of the *Rājanyas, the Agra coins are placed in the second-first centuries BC, or even a little earlier. The weight of these coins ranges from 13 to 119.5 grains, and it is not possible to identify any of these weights with some submultiple of the Indian *paṇa* standard. The Agra coins had earlier been divided into four classes—(i) '*Tree-in-railing : *Bull' type; (ii) 'Tree-in-railing : *Lion' type; (iii) 'Tree-in-railing : Composite animal with bull's body and owl's head or with two heads, one each of an elephant and a lion' type; and (iv) 'Tree-in-railing : *Lakshmī' type. However, recently, three more classes of Agra coins have been reported. These include (v) 'Tree-in-railing: Six-arched hill' type; (vi) 'Tree-in-railing : Pillared temple' type; and (vii) 'Tree-in-railing : **Chakra* and *lion' type. These classes present several varieties. For instance, Lakshmī on the rev of some specimens of Class IV is seen standing to front with lotus stalks in both her hands; on other specimens of the same class, she stands on a five-arched hill with elephants annointing her; some other coins of this class have the goddess standing on a lotus seat with her hands on hip; still other specimens of Class IV have the goddess represented symbolically by a *tulasī* plant flanked by two elephants holding inverted pitchers in their trunks. The animal on the rev is sometimes shown within a rayed circle, perhaps to indicate its sanctity. All these coins bear a Br ld on the obv, and on some coins of Classes I and II, the same ld is repeated on the rev. On most of the coins, the ld is *Agodaka* (or *Agodake*) *Agāchajanapadasa*, '[coin] of the *Agratyajanapada* [issued from, or current at] Agrodaka'. Agra or Agrātya seems to be name of the tribe as well as the *janapada*.

But on some coins, there is a different ld, which has been read by Barnett as *Agāchamitra-padābhishṭhāyināṁ* or *Agāchamitrapadāb hishṭhāyinaḥ,* and interpreted as '[coin] of the rulers (or ruler) of the Allied State of the Agāchas'. On this basis, it has been suggested that the Agras had formed some confederacy with other tribes, like the Rājanya, *Vṛishṇi, and *Mālava, to tackle the problem posed by foreign rule in northwestern India. Sircar, however, taking Agrātyamitra (literally, 'friend of the Agrātyas) as tutelary deity, translates the ld as '[This is the coin] of those who dwell at the feet of Agrātyamitra'. But Agrātyamitra as name of a deity is not known (Allan 1936; Chakrabortty 1931; Cunningham 1971b; K K Dasgupta 1974; Handa 2007a; Jayaswal 1988; Marshall 1975; Mitchiner 1975-1976; Smith 1972).

Agrarāja. *Kauśāmbī k. He is identified with Āgaraju of a Bharhut inscription, and may be placed in the mid-first century BC. The inscription refers to him as the son of Viśvadeva, and the father of Dhanabhūti. His coins seem to connect him with *Bahasatimita II and others, like *Praushṭhamitra, *Jyeshṭhamitra, and *Agnimitra, and there is a possibility that he ruled over the southern parts of Kauśāmbī, while *Bahasatimita II and others were ruling over the northern parts. He issued copper coins, with a *bull to the l before a *dhvajastambha* on the obv; the rev has a *tree-in-railing, the *Ujjain symbol, and the *taurine symbol. The ld, *Agarajasa*, occurs on the rev, within a square incuse, which seems to point towards an early date for him. Altekar earlier read the rev ld as *Śuṅgarajasa*, but later corrected it as *Agarajasa* (Altekar 1942a; Altekar 1942b; K D Bajpai 1960; Bopearachchi and Pieper 1998; Bela Lahiri 1974; Sircar 1986).

Ahuramazda. Supreme Avestan deity. He is the supreme godhead in the religion of Zoroaster. His name literally means 'the Lord of high Knowledge' or 'the Wise Lord'. It is quite clear from the *Avesta* that he is the 'Heaven God', the creator. But the attribute most closely associated with him is *asha*, that is morality, which is the Avestan equivalent of *ṛita*. Thus, Ahuramazda is the supreme guardian of moral law. Ahuramazda seems to correspond to the vedic Asura-*Varuṇa and the Greek *Ouranos. The figure of Ahuramazda appears on the coins of the *Kushāṇa rulers, *Kanishka I and *Huvishka. On the rev of the gold coin of the former, the deity is shown riding a horse with two heads, and the ld reads *Mazdooano*. On the rev of the gold coins of Huvishka, bearded and nimbate Ahuramazda stands with a sceptre in the l hand and a garland in the r hand, and the ld reads *Woromozdo*. It has been observed that the representation of Ahuramazda on Kushāṇa coins is not in proportion to his hieratic importance in Avestan religion, and this has been compared with the rare appearance of the *Buddha on ancient Indian coins (Altekar 1952b; Barton 1990; Sukumari Bhattacharji 1970; Cunningham 1971a; Darmesteter 1974; Noss 1949; Rosenfield 1967; Prashant Srivastava 2007d; Stein 1888). †

Huvishka

Ai Khanum hoards. The first Ai Khanum hoard of 677 silver *punch marked coins and six bilingual coins of *Agathokles was found in 1970 by the French excavators in the ancient Greek city of Ai Khanum, near the Oxus valley, on the borders of Afghanistan and the former USSR. The hoard seems to have been hidden *c* 145 BC. Two further hoards from the same site were published in 1975 and 1980, and their composition is quite similar to the fourth hoard from Ai Khanum. The second hoard, found in 1973, comprised 63 silver coins, and the rulers represented include *Agathokles, *Antimachos I, *Apollodotos, *Demetrios I, *Diodotos I, *Diodotos II, *Eukratides I, *Euthydemos I, and *Euthydemos II. The third hoard, found in 1973-1974, comprised 142 silver coins. The rulers represented include Agathokles, Antimachos I, Demetrios I, Diodotos I, Diodotos II, Euthydemos I, Euthydemos II, and Eukratides I. The rulers represented in the fourth hoard of around 1,000 coins of the *Indo-Greek rulers, struck on the Attic standard, include Agathokles, Antimachos I, Apollodotos, Demetrios I, Diodotos, Eukratides I, Euthydemos I, Euthydemos II, *Pantaleon; there are also two coins of Macedonia in this hoard, one of which belongs to the city of Akanthos, and the other to the city of Paros (Audouin and Bernard 1973; Bopearachchi 1993; Bopearachchi 1994; Bopearachchi and Rahman 1995; Holt 1980; Narain 1973; Petitot-Biehler 1975).

Ajavarman. *Ayodhyā k. He seems to be among the earliest of the Ayodhyā kings who issued round die-struck coins, as his coins bear a square incuse, and as a symbol on the obv of his coins connects him with the Ayodhyā kings known from the square cast coins. The obv of his coins bears a *bull to the l before a symbol, and the ld *Ajavarmasa*, while the rev has a **nandipada* within a square (Bela Lahiri 1974; Smith 1972).

Ajuna. *Parataraja k.

Akhnoor hoard 1. This hoard was discovered at Akhnoor in Kashmir. The rulers represented include *Apollophanes, *Strato I, Strato I with *Strato II, *Zoilos II, and *Azes I (Senior 2001).

Akhnoor hoard 2. This hoard was discovered at Akhnoor in Kashmir. The rulers represented in this hoard include *Apollophanes, *Strato I, Strato I with *Strato II, *Rañjuvula, and Bhadrayaśa (Senior 2001).

Almora

Almora. Initially, only three coins, one each of *Haradatta, *Śivadatta, and *Śivapālita, and a fourth one on which the name is taken as *Mṛigabhūti, were found in Almora. The obv of the coins of the first two kings shows in the centre, a circle joined by a curved line, a stag or *bull before a *tree-in-railing, and the name of the king in Br. Śivapālita's coin shows an additional device on the obv, a human figure. The rev of the first three coins shows 'an altar surmounted by a triangle-headed standard with a **nandipada* symbol on its face'. Rapson, on the basis of the similarity of device (identifying the animal as stag), considers the rulers as belonging to a branch of the *Kuṇinda tribe; and this has been accepted by scholars like J C Powell-Price, Bela Lahiri, and M P Joshi. The name Mṛigabhūti reminds one of the Kuṇinda, *Amoghabhūti. Later on, Almora coins bearing the names of other rulers, like Panadatta (Parṇadatta ?), Śivarakshita, Vijayabhūti, Gomitra, Āseka (Aśoka ?), and Jayaghosha, have also been reported. Of these, only Vijayabhūti used the title of **rājan*. The so-called tree symbol is somewhat similar to one of the three *Pañchāla symbols. Taking the Almora symbols as Buddhist, Powell-Price opined that a group of Buddhist kings ruled at Pañchāla, Almora, and the country of the Kuṇindas. This view, however, looks far-fetched. Similarity of complex *nandipada* symbol on Pañchāla and *Ayodhyā coins and the find of the coin of one Śivapālita at Śrāvastī made some scholars, like P L Gupta and Michael Mitchiner, to consider Almora coins as belonging to the

Ayodhyā series. However, there is a difference in the depiction of the *nandipada* on Almora and Ayodhyā coins; the coin of Śivapālita of Almora and that of Śrāvastī differ considerably, and the *nandipada* does not occur on the latter. Besides, Śrāvastī coins are smaller in size and are of silver-coated copper. P L Gupta modified his stance after the discovery of a much better specimen, bearing the name of Vijayabhūti, from Almora, and located the rulers issuing these coins in some 'hilly region'. K K Dasgupta, after discussing various aspects of the Almora coins, concludes that in style, fabric, size, and weight (some coins are known to weigh variously 327, 281, and 304 grains), these coins form a class apart. These Almora coins have variously been placed between first century BC and second century AD by Rapson; in the second-first centuries BC by Allan; and in the first century AD by D C Sircar. Probably, *Kanishka I overthrew this dynasty (Allan 1936; K K Dasgupta 1974; Handa 2007a; M P Joshi 1989; Bela Lahiri 1974; Mitchiner 1975-1976; Powell-Price 1945; Rapson 1987; Sircar 1980d).

Altar or ***Garuḍa*** **type.** Copper. This type of copper coins was issued by the *Imperial Gupta ruler, *Kumāragupta I. On the obv of this type occurs an uncertain figure, identified as an altar by some, and as a **garuḍa* by others; below the figure is the ld *Śrī-Ku*. The rev bears the goddess seated on a stool or on a couchant *lion, with probably a stalked lotus in both her hands. Some scholars express the possibility of these coins being the issues of *Kumāragupta II (Allan 1914; Altekar 1957; P L Gupta 1998; Smith 1972).

Amoghabhūti series. *Kuṇinda coins. Issued in both silver and copper, the coins of this series have been divided into two classes. Class I has, on the obv, a deer with **śrīvatsa* between horns, and a square **stūpa* (?) surmounted by an umbrella above the animal; *Lakshmī is seen standing holding a flower in her r hand beside the deer; there are also some other symbols. The Br ld reads *Rājñaḥ Kuṇindasa* (or *-sya*) *Amoghabhūtisa* (or *-sya*) *Mahārājasa* (or *-sya*). The rev has a collection of symbols, like **svastika*, **nandipada*, six-arched *hill, *tree-in-railing, **jayadhvaja*, and *undulating line, in various combinations, and the Kh ld *Raña Kuṇindasa Amoghabhutisa Maharajasa*. Class II is mostly similar to Class I, the main difference being the absence of the Kh ld on the rev. The legends have been taken to mean '[coin] of great King Amoghabhūti, the Kuṇinda king' or '[coin] of Amoghabhūti *mahārāja, rājā of the Kuṇindas'. To P L Gupta, the occurrence of the titles *rājan and mahārāja together appears curious, and he suggests that rājñaḥ may be mistake for Rājanaḥ and standing for the *Rājanya tribe that might have been allied to the Kuṇindas. But maharaja and rajatiraja occur together on *Śaka-Pahlava coins. It seems to signify that the office of rājan was held by Mahārāja Amoghabhūti. On the basis of the difference of type, fabric, etc, Jayaswal considers Amoghabhūti ('of unfailing prosperity') as a title held by several Kuṇinda chiefs between c 150 BC and 100 AD. K K Dasgupta suggests that such coins were issued by a king or by kings bearing the title Amoghabhūti without giving the name of the king. Smith is of the view that the coins with the name Amoghabhūti continued to be manufactured long after the reign of that king. But, according to Allan, the Amoghabhūti coins were not issued over such a long period, and seem to be the issues of one king only. He feels that the coins in coarse fabric might have been later imitations. The view of P L Gupta, that since both Amogha and Bhūti stand for *Śiva, the coins might have been issued by the Kuṇindas in the name of that deity, seems to be less convincing. The coins of this series, also bearing the name of *Prajāpati Akhya, have been regarded as forged ones (Allan 1936; Chakrabortty 1931; Cunningham 1971b; K K Dasgupta 1974; P L Gupta 1988; Handa 2007a; Jayaswal 1988; M P Joshi 1989; K K Maheshwari 1978; Marshall 1975; Mitchiner 1975-1976; Smith 1972).

Kuṇinda

Amphitrite. Greek goddess, '*the* mistress and proprietress of the sea'. She was one of the 50 Nereides or daughters of Neraios. She was married to *Poseidon, and bore him a son, *Triton, and a daughter, Rhodos. On the coins of *Maues and of *Azes bearing the figure of *Poseidon of the obv, the rev has a female figure standing facing between two vines, which she grasps with her hands. She is identified variously as Maenad, Bacchante, India, and *yakshī. But she could also be identified as Amphitrite, the wife of Poseidon, especially when her divine spouse is seen on the obv of these coins. On some coins of this type, issued by Maues, the goddess' r hand is extended towards a small figure whose posterior half resembles that of a fish, and this figure might be identified as *Triton, the son of Amphitrite and Poseidon, appearing, respectively, on the rev and obv

Maues

Azes I

of the coins (Bopearachchi 1993; Bopearachchi and Pieper 1998; Bopearachchi and Rahman 1995; Bhaskar Chattopadhyay 1977; Cunningham 1971a; Gardner 1971; Graves 1955; Kerenyi 1951; Marshall 1975; Rose 1958; Prashant Srivastava 1993a; Prashant Srivastava 2007c; Whitehead 1914). †

Amreli hoard 1. This hoard of 1,400 silver coins, mainly of the *Kārddamaka Kshatrapas, was discovered in district Amreli of Gujarat. Reportedly, six rulers are represented in this hoard, but the names of only four—*Vijayasena, *Rudrasiṁha II, *Rudrasena I, and *Viśvasena, are mentioned. There is a suggestion that *Rudrasena II and *Īśvaradatta are, perhaps, also represented in this hoard (Bhowmik 1965; Jha and Rajgor 1994).

Amreli hoard 2. This hoard of around 300 silver and potin coins of the *Kārddamaka rulers was discovered in the excavations conducted at the site in Gujarat, some time before 1945. The rulers represented by the silver coins in the hoard include *Vijayasena, *Rudrasena II, *Viśvasiṁha, *Bhartṛidāman, and Svāmi *Rudrasena III. *Rudrasena I is represented by the potin currency in the hoard. Around 56 silver, potin, lead, and silver-coated copper coins of the Kārddamaka rulers are also reported in the course of excavations conducted at the site in 1952-1953. The silver coins belong to *Vīradāman, the potin coin to *Rudrasena I, the lead coins to *Rudrasena II, and the two silver-coated copper coins, probably to *Dāmajadaśrī III. The dates on some lead coins are illegible (Jha and Rajgor 1994; S R Rao 1966).

Amyntas. *Indo-Greek k; son of *Antialkidas (?); early first century BC. After the death of *Apollodotos, he regained the territories his father had lost of Apollodotos, and also overthrew *Theophilos, *Peukolaos, and *Diomedes, thus occupying the regions to the north of the Hindukush, the Pushkalāvatī region, the Kabul valley, and western Gandhāra. He appears to have issued the two types of his double-*decadrachms*, and assumed the title of **niketoros*, to commemorate the re-establishment of the authority of his family. He issued coins in silver and copper; some of them are based on the Attic standard, and some on the Indian standard. All the coins are die-struck pieces. The silver coins are all round in shape, while the copper ones are square. The obv of his coins usually bears the

Amyntas

bust of the king to the r, wearing various types of headdresses, like smooth helmet, *kausia*, Medusa helmet, and Phrygian cap. On some coins, the bust of the king is shown to the l, thrusting javelin. On one copper type, the bearded male bust, wearing a Phrygian cap, on the obv, has been identified as that of 'Zeus-Mithra'. The rev of most of the types bears the figure of enthroned *Zeus holding out Athena-Nike. Others have the figure of *Athena standing with spear and shield, or thundering to the l with **aegis* over her left arm. Besides his normal coinage, Amyntas also struck some victory medals in the form of two types of Attic double-*decadrachms* (above), known from the *Qunduz hoard. These bear the diademed bust of the king, wearing smooth helmet, to the r. The rev of one type has the figure of enthroned Zeus holding out Athena-Nike, while that of the other has enthroned *Demeter, bearing **cornucopiae*. The coins struck on the Attic standard bear ld only in Gr. The coins struck on the Indian standard have a Gr ld on the obv, and a Pkt ld, written in the Kh script, on the rev. Besides the title of **basileus*, Amyntas assumed the epithet **nikatoros*. These are rendered into Pkt as **maharaja* and **jayadhara*. The Pkt form of the name of the king, as met with on coins, is Amita (Bopearachchi 1993; Bopearachchi and Pieper 1998; Bopearachchi and Rahman 1995; Cunningham 1970; Gardner 1971; A N Lahiri 1965; Marshall 1975; Narain 1957a; Rapson 1987; Senior 2001; Sircar 1980a; Prashant Srivastava 1996a; Tarn 1980; Whitehead 1914). †

Anamitra. *Pañchāla k. The rev of the coins of Anamitra, *Śivanandiśrī, *Śrīnandi, *Varuṇamitra, *Vasusena, and *Yugasena does not bear the anthropomorphic or symbolic representation of any divinity, as is the usual case with the Pañchāla series, and, on this basis, it has been suggested that they might have ruled at a later period, when the practice of representing a deity alluding to the name of the issuing king on the rev of the coin had become lax. Bela Lahiri places Anamitra in the twenty-fourth chronological order among the Pañchāla rulers known from coins. The obv of the coins of Anamitra bear a symbol, which is somewhat similar to that appearing on some coins of *Agnimitra and *Indramitra; the rev symbol is shaped like the Br letter *ya* (K D Bajpai 1966; Bela Lahiri 1974).

Anantadevī. *Imperial Gupta queen. She was the consort of *Kumāragupta I, and the mother of *Pūrugupta. She seems to have belonged to the Nāga family. Her figure occurs on the obv of the *King-and-Queen type, and the rev of the **Aśvamedha* type of Kumāragupta I; she is, perhaps, also represented on the obv of the **Apratigha* type of Kumāragupta I (Altekar 1957; Prashant Srivastava 2004b).

Kumāragupta I : *Aśvamedha* type

Aṇḍikā. Coin denomination (?). Mentioned in sources, like the *Bakhshali manuscript, it weighs 1¼ *rattī* (R C Agrawala 1954b).

Aṅgavijjā. Text. This Pkt text, of unknown authorship, forms part of the Jaina canon. It seems to have been compiled *c* third-fourth centuries AD, and retouched some time later, perhaps in the Gupta period. Although it deals primarily with 'prognostication on the basis of bodily signs and other physical objects', it is valuable as a source of the cultural history of the period. It mentions, in all, 22 coin denominations : (1) **suvaṇṇa-māsaka*, (2) **rayaya-māsaka*, (3) **dīnāra-māsaka*, (4) **ṇāṇa-māsaka*, (5) **kāhāpaṇa*, (6) **khattapaka*, (7) **purāṇa*, (8) **sateraka*, (9) **suvaṇṇa-kākaṇī*, (10) **māsaka-kākaṇī*, (11) **suvaṇṇa-guñja*, (12) **dīṇāri*, (13) **ādimūla-kāhāvaṇa*, (14) **uttama-kāhāvaṇa*, (15) **majjhima-kāhāvaṇa*, (16) **jahaṇṇa-kāhāvaṇa*, (17) **bāla-kāhāvaṇa*, (18) **ṇāṇaka*, (19) **māsaka*, (20) **addha-māsaka*, (21) **kākaṇī*, and (22) **aṭṭhā* (V S Agrawala 1957).

Aniketos. Title. Meaning 'invincible', this title was first adopted by *Demetrios. Tarn suggests that the adoption of this title by him might have something to do with the fact that Alexander was hailed as *aniketos* at Delphi. On the coins of Demetrios, the title is rendered into Pkt as **aparajita*. Three other Indo-Greek kings, *Artemidoros, *Lysias, and *Philoxenos, who use this title, render it into Pkt as **apaḍihata*. While *aparajita* means 'unconquered', *apaḍihata* (= Skt, *apratihata*) means 'irresistible', and there is a suggestion that the two renderings indicate defensive and offensive roles, respectively (Cunningham 1970; Gardner 1971; A N Lahiri 1965; Marshall 1975; Narain 1957a; Tarn 1980; Whitehead 1914).

Antialkidas

Antialkidas

Antialkidas

Antialkidas. *Indo-Greek k; son of *Heliokles II (?); last quarter of the second century BC. He seems to have retrieved the fallen fortunes of his family, and established his sway over the Kabul valley, western Gandhāra, and Takshaśilā. He is mentioned in the Besnagar *garuḍa* pillar inscription of the time of King Bhāgabhadra, and the language of the inscription gives the indication that the seat of his power was Takshaśilā. He sent an envoy, Heliodoros, to the court of that Indian ruler, and in the inscription the envoy uses the title of *trātāra* (Pkt equivalent of the Greek title **soteros*) for Bhāgabhadra, leading to the inference that the Indian king might have saved Antialkidas from some enemy. Narain, however, believes that towards the close of his reign, the authority of Antialkidas was confined to the Takshaśilā region alone, with *Apollodotos occupying almost all his territories to the west of the river Indus, and *Strato I ruling over the Jammu-Sialkot region to the east of the river Jhelum. Beleaguered by these problems, Antialkidas might have sought the help of Bhāgabhadra, but to no avail. He ruled up to *c* 100 BC, when he was, perhaps, overthrown by Apollodotos. Senior, however, places his reign from *c* 127 BC to 120 BC. Antialkidas issued coins in silver and copper; some of them are based on the Attic standard, and some on the Indian standard. All the coins are die-struck pieces. The silver coins are all round in shape; the copper ones are known in both round and square shapes. On most of the silver types, there is the depiction of the diademed bust of the king to the r, sometimes wearing a helmet or *kausia*. But sometimes, the bust of the king, thrusting javelin, is shown to the l. One type of square copper coins has the bust of the king, but the rest of the copper types have the bust of *Zeus, thundering, or with thunderbolt over the r shoulder. The rev of the silver types is mostly occupied by the figure of enthroned Zeus Nikephoros, sometimes with the forepart of an *elephant beside it, towards which *Nike is extending a wreath; on one type, however, enthroned Zeus does not hold out Nike. On two types, Zeus is shown walking beside an elephant carrying Nike. On the rev of the copper types, the most common device is the palms and **pilei* of the *Dioskuri, but one type has an elephant to the r, with a wreath in its upraised trunk. The coins struck on the Attic standard bear ld only in Gr. The coins struck on the Indian standard have a Gr ld on the obv, and a Pkt ld, written in the Kh script, on the rev. Besides the title of **basileus*, Antialkidas assumed the epithet **nikephoros*. These are rendered into Pkt as **maharaja* and **jayadhara*, respectively. There is a square bronze coin bearing the bust of *Herakles with club over shoulder, to the r, and the name of *Lysias with the epithet **aniketos*, on the obv, and *palms and **pilei*, and the name of Anticalkidas, with the epithet **jayadhara*, on the rev. Another bronze piece, in the American Numismatic Society, has the name of Antialkidas in Gr on the obv, and that of Lysias in Kh on the rev. These coins are regarded by some scholars as joint issues of the two kings, and Tarn suggests that this shows a *rapprochement* between the rival Indo-Greek families in view of the *Śaka-Pahlava menace. But Narain regards this piece as a 'mule'. Antialkidas also restruck a coin of Lysias. The Pkt form of the name of the king, as met with on coins, is Aṁtiālikita (Bopearachchi 1993; Bopearachchi and Pieper 1998; Bopearachchi and Rahman 1995; Cunningham 1970; Gardner 1971; A N Lahiri 1965; Marshall 1975; Narain 1957a; Rapson 1987; Senior 2001; Sircar 1980a; Prashant Srivastava 1990c; Tarn 1980; Whitehead 1914). †

Antialkidas

Antimachos I. *Indo-Greek k; son or close relative of *Diodotos II; early second century BC. He was earlier regarded as one of the three original founders of the Indo-Greek kingdom, and described, variously, as a son or a close relative of *Diodotos II, a son of *Euthydemos I, a Sogdian with a Greek name, etc. There is a suggestion that he might have risen to power by 'eliminating' *Euthydemos II. He moved from eastern Bactria, and gradually occupied the Kabul valley, upper Indus valley, parts of Paropamisadae, and, perhaps, also Takshaśilā for some time. He eventually annexed the whole of Bactria, and even conquered Margiana. He issued silver and copper coins, all of which were struck on the Attic standard. All the coins are die-struck pieces. The silver coins are all round; most of the copper coins, too, are round, but one copper type is square or rectangular in shape. He is believed to be the first Indo-Greek king to issue square coins after the Indian model. The obv of the silver type usually bears the diademed bust of the king to the r, wearing *kausia*, while the rev has the standing figure of *Poseidon, holding a long trident in his r hand, and palm bound with fillet under his left arm. The obv of the round copper type has *elephant on the obv, and winged *Nike on the rev. However, the rectangular copper type has a winged *thunderbolt on the rev. Besides his normal coinage, Antimachos I also issued two types of commemorative coins, one each in memory of *Diodotos I and *Euthydemos I, respectively. The obv of these Attic *tetradrachms* has the figure of the commemorated king, and his name, along with an epithet—**soteros* for the former and **theos* for the latter. It is to be noted that the title of **basileus* is never used with the name of the commemorated king, most probably because they had ceased to be king before these coins were issued; instead, he is given the additional epithet. Neither of the two commemorated kings is known to have ever assumed the epithet given to him on these commemorative coins. The rev of the type issued in memory of Diodotos I bears the figure of thundering *Zeus with *eagle at his l foot, while that of the type issued in memory of Euthydemos bears the figure of naked *Herakles holding club, seated on a rock. In the rev ld, Antimachos I himself does not use the title of *basileus* when he mentions himself as the commemorator, perhaps out of regard for the commemorated kings who have not been given the title of *basileus*; instead he uses the epithet of **theos*, and the ld begins with *basileuontos*, 'during the reign'. A round copper type of Antimachos I has the figure of elephant to the r on the obv, and winged Nike, bearing *palm and wreath, standing to the l on the prow of a ship. This is believed by some scholars to be a victory medal, issued by Antimachos I to commemorate some naval victory. The legends engraved on the coins of Antimachos I are all in Gr. Besides the title of *basileus*, he uses the epithet *theos* on all his coins, except for the square copper ones, which has led Tarn to the conclusion that this type was, perhaps, not issued by Antimachos I. There are also some crude coins in the name of Antimachos I, which may be *Śaka-Pahlava issues (Bopearachchi 1993; Bopearachchi and Pieper 1998; Bopearachchi and Rahman 1995; Cunningham 1970; Gardner 1971; A N Lahiri 1965; Marshall 1975; Narain 1957a; Rapson 1987; Senior 2001; Sircar 1980a; Tarn 1980; Prashant Srivastava 1996a; Whitehead 1914). †

Antimachos II. *Indo-Greek k; brother of *Menander I (?); *c* third quarter of the second century BC. He seems to have started his career as a subking of Menander I in the Swat valley, but was later transferred to northern Arachosia by *Agathokleia during her regency, where, for a short while, he set himself up as an independent king; Osmund Bopearachchi, however, suggests that Menander I succeeded Antimachos II. There seem to be some indications of the extension of his authority over western Gandhāra-Paropamisadae region. Antimachos II issued silver and copper coins, all struck on the Indian standard. All the coins are die-struck pieces. The silver coins are all round, and the copper ones are all square. The obv of the silver type has winged *Nike, bearing *palm and fillet, standing to the l, while the rev has the figure of king prancing on a horse to the r. Coins bearing an *aegis* on the obv, and palm and wreath on the rev, are known in both silver and copper. The obv of the coins in both the metals bears a Gr ld, while the Pkt ld on the rev is engraved in the Kh script. He modified the disposition of the ld on his silver coins. Besides the title of **basileus*, Antimachos II also assumed the title of **nikephoros*. These are rendered into Pkt as **maharaja* and **jayadhara*, respectively. The Pkt form of the name of the king, as met with on coins, is Aṁtimakha (Bopearachchi 1993; Bopearachchi and Pieper 1998; Bopearachchi and Rahman 1995; Cunningham 1970; Gardner 1971; A N Lahiri 1965; Marshall 1975; Narain 1957a; Rapson 1987; Senior 2001; Sircar 1980a; Tarn 1980; Whitehead 1914). †

Antimachos II

Antimachos II

Apaḍihata. Title. It is the Pkt rendering of **aniketos*, and used by *Artemidoros, *Lysias, and *Philoxenos. Its Skt equivalent is *apratihata*. **Aparajita* (Skt, *aparājita*) is also used on *Indo-Greek coins as the Pkt rendering of *aniketos*. The connotations of *aparājita* and *apratihata* differ from each other by shade only, with the former meaning 'unconquered', and the latter 'irresistible'. On this basis, it has been suggested that *aparajita* indicates the defensive role of the adopter, while *apaḍihata* indicates the offensive role of the adopter (Cunningham 1970; Gardner 1971; A N Lahiri 1965; Marshall 1975; Narain 1957a; Tarn 1980; Whitehead 1914).

Aparajita. Title. It is the Pkt rendering of **aniketos*, and used by *Demetrios. Its Skt equivalent is *aparājita*. [**Apaḍihata*] (Cunningham 1970; Gardner 1971; A N Lahiri 1965; Marshall 1975; Narain 1957a; Tarn 1980; Whitehead 1914).

Apollo. Greek solar god. This son of Leto by *Zeus, and the twin of *Artemis, was the third greatest deity, besides Zeus and *Athena, in the Greek pantheon. Immediately after his birth, he had to fight

Apollodotos

and vanquish several enemies, like the giant Tityos, Pythos, the gragoness Delphyne, Phegyas, and the Kyklopes. He also had a dispute with *Herakles, which was settled by their father, Zeus. He had several love affairs, most of which 'ended tragically'. From his oracular shrine at Delphi, Apollo proclaimed the will of his father, while seated on the **tripod lebes*. Later on, he was recognized as the sun god, *Helios. The representation of Apollo was quite popular on *Indo-Greek and *Śaka-Pahlava coins. The bust of the deity is to be found on the obv of the copper coins of Indo-Greek rulers, like *Euthydemos, *Eukratides, and *Strato I. On some coins, we see the depiction of Apollo, standing, usually with a bow in his l hand and an arrow in his r hand. Such a depiction may be seen on the coins of the Indo-Greek rulers, *Apollodotos, Strato I, Eukratides, and Euthydemos, and the Śaka-Pahlava ruler, *Maues. While the deity is naked on the coins of Apollodotos and Eukratides, he wears chlamys and boots on those of Strato I, and has a halo behind his head on the coins of Euthydemos. On some coins of Apollodotos, *Dionysios, *Hippostratos, and *Zoilos, Apollo is shown dressed in chlamys and boots; he stands with a quiver at his back, and holds an arrow in both his hands; his bow rests on the ground before him. On a type of Zoilos occurs a similar depiction, but with a small elephant in the field. Seated Apollo, holding out his bow in l hand, may be seen on the obv of the square copper coins of Apollodotos. On most of these coins, the rev bears the **tripod lebes*, the characteristic symbol of Apollo (Bopearachchi 1993; Bopearachchi and Pieper 1998; Bopearachchi and Rahman 1995; Bhaskar Chattopadhyay 1977; Cunningham 1971a; Gardner 1971; Graves 1955; Kerenyi 1951; A N Lahiri 1965; Marshall 1975; Rose 1958; Prashant Srivastava 2006b; Prashant Srivastava 2007c; Whitehead 1914). †

Zoilos II

Apollodotos. *Indo-Greek k; son of *Menander (?); latter half of the second century BC. On the basis of the amendation in a statement of Justin suggested by Bayer, a number of scholars express the possibility of the existence of two Indo-Greek kings named Apollodotos, but Narain feels that the numismatic evidence does not support such a hypothesis. Subsequent writers on the subject, however, still believe in the existence of two Apollodoti. Apollodotos is believed to have started his career as a subking or joint king of his younger brother, *Strato I, initially ruling over the

Apollodotos

Swat valley. He helped Strato I in recovering western Gandhāra, the Kabul valley, the Ghazni area; he also seems to have overthrown *Antialkidas in Takshaśilā. Perhaps encouraged by these successes, he declared his independence, and might have even replaced Strato I. The *provenance* of his coins shows that, at least for some time, he ruled over almost the whole of the kingdom of his father, although he later lost some territories in the Swat valley and the Hazara region, and perhaps also Takshaśilā, to *Maues. Apollodotos issued coins in both silver and copper. He used the Attic standard for some of his silver types; the rest of his silver types and all his copper types are struck on the Indian standard. All the coins are die-struck pieces. The coins of both the metals are to be found in round as well as square shapes. The diademed bust of the king, so common on the obv of most of the Indo-Greek coins, is somewhat rare, though not unknown, on the obv of the coins of Apollodotos, as most of his silver coins bear the figure of an *elephant. Naked and lauriate *Apollo, bearing bow and arrow, is seen standing to front on the obv of one square silver type. The most common rev device for his silver coins is the humped *bull; but one type, bearing the bust of the king on the obv, has the thundering *Athena, with **aegis* over her left arm, sometimes holding out *Nike on her r hand, on the rev, while the square silver type with the Apollo obv, has the **tripod lebes* on the rev. The obv of the copper types of Apollodotos is mostly occupied by the figure of Apollo standing; only on one type is the god shown as seated. Most of these types have the *tripod lebes* on the rev; one square copper type, having no Gr ld, has the royal diadem on the rev. One square copper type, attributed to Apollodotos, has a the figure of a humped bull to the r on the obv, and *tripod lebes* on the rev. By far, the 'Elephant : Bull' type is the most common silver type for Apollodotos. The coins of Apollodotos mostly bear the Gr ld on the obv, and the Pkt ld, written in the Kh script, on the rev. Besides the title of **basileus*, Apollodotos uses the epithet **soteros* on most of his coins. On some types, he uses the epithet **philopator*, besides *soteros*. On the round silver type bearing the bust of the king on the obv and thundering Athena on the rev, he uses *soteros*, *philopator*, and **megas*. It is interesting to note that while the former is rendered into Pkt as **maharaja*, and the latter, as **tratara*, *megas* and *philopator* are not rendered into Pkt on the coins of Apollodotos. There is no Gr ld on the square copper coins of the 'Apollo standing

Apollodotos

Apollodotos

r : Royal diadem' type, while the square copper coins of 'Humped bull : *Tripod lebes*' type are anepigraphous. The Pkt form of the name of the ruler, as met with on coins, is Apaladata (Bivar 1970; Bopearachchi 1993; Bopearachchi and Pieper 1998; Bopearachchi and Rahman 1995; Cunningham 1970; Gardner 1971; Jenkins 1959; A N Lahiri 1965; Marshall 1975; Narain 1957a; Rapson 1987; Sircar 1980a; Tarn 1980; Whitehead 1914).†

Apollophanes. *Indo-Greek k; scion of the family of *Apollodotos (?); early first century BC. He appears to have ruled over the Jammu-Sialkot region in the interval between the two phases of the reign of *Strato I; Osmud Bopearachchi associates him with western Punjab. Strato I seems to have regained his authority by overthrowing him. He is known to have issued only silver coins, struck on the Indian standard. All the coins are die-struck pieces. They are all round in shape. The obv bears the diademed bust of the king to the r, sometimes in a smooth helmet. The rev has thundering *Athena, with **aegis* on her left arm. The obv has the Gr ld, while the rev has the Pkt ld, engraved in the Kh script. Besides the title of **basileus*, Apollophanes also assumed the epithet **soteros*. These are rendered into Pkt as **maharja* and **tratara*, respectively. The Pkt form of the name of the ruler, as met with on coins, is Apalavina (Bopearachchi 1993; Bopearachchi and Pieper 1998; Bopearachchi and Rahman 1995; Cunningham 1970; Gardner 1971; A N Lahiri 1965; Marshall 1975; Narain 1957a; Rapson 1906; Rapson 1987; Sircar 1980a; Tarn 1980; Whitehead 1914).†

Apracharaja. Title. This title was used on coins and in inscriptions by members of a ruling family of the Swat valley. It appears for the first time in the Shinkot Bajaur relic casket inscriptions of the time of *Menander, Viyakamitra, and Vijayamitra. N G Majumdar renders this title into Skt as *a-pratyag-rāja*, and translates it into English as one who has no royal adversary'. He compares this title with **apaḍihata* and **apratihatachakra*, occurring on the coins of the *Śaka-Pahlava ruler, *Gondopharnes, and of *Rañjuvula and *Sasan. D C Sircar translates it as 'a king having no equal, that is an unrivalled king'. He further says that as Viyakamitra was, very probably, a feudatory of *Menander, *apracharaja* appears to be a feudatory title. But Sten Konow points out that it is 'unlikely that a vassal chief could use such a title'. An alternative suggestion is that *apracharaja* stands for *a-prāchya-rāja*, 'king of the west'. There is also the suggestion of D C Sircar that *apracharaja* should be taken to convey the sense of 'a king who is not equal to the *Mahārāja*', a title which seems to go well with the feudatory status of Viyakamitra. Vijayamitra is also styled *apracharaja*, and he, too, served as a feudatory under the *Śaka-Pahlavas. But his overlord is not mentioned in the Shinkot Bajaur relic casket inscription, or in the other inscriptions of the Apracha family mentioning Vijayamitra. *Apracharaja* might also have been taken as a family name. But in the inscriptions, when a member of this family is mentioned as *kumāra* or **stratega* or both, he is not styled as *apracharaja*; when the same person is referred to as *apracharaja*, he is no longer referred to as *kumāra/stratega*. A case in point is Vishṇuvarman. He is called *kumāra* in the reliquary inscription of the time of *Kumāra* Vishṇuvarman, and *stratega* in the reliquary inscriptions of the time of *Kharaösta and Indravarman. But in the Indravarman reliquary inscription of Azes year 63, he is styled *apracharaja*, and not *kumāra* or *stratega*. This would suggest that *apracharaja* was a title of office, and not a family name (for references, see Prashant Srivastava 2007a).

***Apratigha* type.** Gold. The significance of the obv composition of this new type of *Kumāragupta I is very controversial. The type was termed the *Pratāpa* type by some scholars, but *Apratigha* type seems to be more correct. The obv has a male figure in the centre, dressed in *dhotī*, and with hands joined in the *namaskāra* pose. To the r is a female figure, shown arguing with him. To the l is another male figure holding a **garuḍadhvaja*. The ld on the obv has not yet been satisfactorily read. The rev has *Lakshmī seated on a lotus bloom, with a stalked lotus in her r hand; the l hand is on the waist. The rev ld *Apratighaḥ*, 'invincible', gives the type its name. Various scholars have tried to interpret the obv composition as the *Buddha being worshipped by two women; as king in the company of his two wives; as a sage being consulted by the king and queen; as the scene of the *dhyānabhaṅga* of *Śiva by *Pārvatī; as Kumāragupta consulting his parents; as king being requested by his queen and his heir-apparent or general not to the renounce the world; etc (Ashvini Agrawal 1989; Allan 1914; Altekar 1957; R D Banerji 1933; S R Goyal 2005; P L Gupta 1998; K P Jayaswal 1933; Smith 1972;

Kumāragupta I : *Apratigha* type

Prashant Srivastava 1987; Prashant Srivastava 1996a; Thaplyal, forthcoming).

Apratihatachakra. Title. This title, which means 'one whose wheel cannot be stopped', was assumed on coins by *Gondopharnes, *Rañjuvula, and *Sasan, among the *Śaka-Pahlavas (Gardner 1971; Jenkins and Narain 1957; Marshall 1975; Rapson 1975; Senior 2001; Whitehead 1914).

AR. Abbreviation. This is the symbol for *argentum*, the Latin for silver, and is commonly used as an abbreviation for silver coinage (Junge 1984).

Archebios

Archebios

Archebios. *Indo-Greek k; son of *Eukratides II (?); third quarter of the second century BC or early first centuries BC. He ruled over the territories of Kabul and Ghazni to the south of the Hindukush, parts of western Gandhāra, and, perhaps, also the Takshaśilā region. He issued one silver type based on the Attic standard; the rest of his silver types, and all his copper types are struck on the Indian standard. All the coins are die-struck pieces. All his silver coins are round in shape, as also one copper type. The rest of the copper types are square in shape. The obv of all the silver types bears the diademed bust of the king, sometimes wearing a smooth helmet or Medusa helmet. The bust is generally to the r, but when the king is shown thrusting a javelin, his bust is to the l. The rev of all the silver types has thundering *Zeus to front, bearing a long sceptre. The round copper type has winged *Nike, bearing wreath and palm, standing to the l on the obv, and an *owl to the r on the rev. Among the square copper types, one has an *elephant to the r on the obv, and an owl to the r on the rev. The other has the bust of Zeus, with a long sceptre over his left shoulder, on the obv, and palms and **pilei* on the rev. A third type of square copper coins has the helmeted bust of the king to the r on the obv, and palms and *pilei* on the rev. The silver type struck on the Attic standard has only a Gr ld, on the rev. The rest of the silver types, and all the copper types, have a Gr ld on the obv, and a Pkt ld, written in the Kh script, on the rev. Besides the title of **basileus*, Archebios assumed the epithets, **dikaios* and **nikephoros*. These are rendered into Pkt as **maharaja*, **dhramika*, and **jayadhara*, respectively. The Pkt form of the name of the ruler, as met with on coins, is Arkhebiya (Bopearachchi 1993; Bopearachchi and Pieper 1998; Bopearachchi and Rahman 1995; Cunningham 1970; Gardner 1971; A N Lahiri 1965; Marshall 1975; Narain 1957a; Rapson 1987; Senior 2001; Sircar 1980a; Tarn 1980; Whitehead 1914).†

Archer type. Copper. This type was first issued in copper by *Chandragupta II in the *Imperial Gupta dynasty. The nimbate king standing to the l, with a bow in his l hand, and an arrow in his r hand, is depicted on the obv; there is the vertical ld *Chandra* under the king's left arm. The rev has *Lakshmī seated on a lotus bloom, holding a noose in her r hand and a lotus in the left; to the r is the Br ld, *Śrī-Vikramaḥ*. *Kumāragupta I also issued this type of copper coins. The obv of his coins resembles that of his father's coins of this type, but there is no ld under the king's left arm. The rev has the figure of **garuḍa*, with the ld *Śrī Kumāraguptaḥ* below it (Allan 1914; Altekar 1957; P L Gupta 1998; Smith 1972).

Archer type. Gold. The Archer type of gold coins was first introduced by *Samudragupta among the *Imperial Guptas in an attempt at Indianizing his *Standard type, as the king as his own standard bearer does not go well with Indian etiquette. The obv of this type shows the nimbate king standing with a bow in his l hand, and either holding an arrow in the r hand or offering oblations at an altar with this hand. On the left is the **garuḍadhvaja*. Under of the left arm of the king is the vertical ld, *Samudra*. The circular ld reads *Apratirathaḥ vijitya kshitiṁ sucharitair-* (or *avanīśo-*) *divaṁ jayati*. The rev has an enthroned goddess, with a *pāśa* in her r hand and a **cornucopiae* in the left; the ld is *Apratirathaḥ*. This type seems so popular among the Imperial Guptas, that all the successors of Samudragupta who struck coins, with the exception of *Rāmagupta and *Bhānugupta, issued Archer type of coins. This type was the most popular type of *Chandragupta II. The obv has the archer king, as on the coins of his father. The vertical ld below the king's arm is *Chandra*; the circular ld reads *Devaśrī-mahārājādhirāja Śrī-Chandraguptaḥ*. The rev bears the figure of *Lakshmī seated on a throne or a lotus bloom. She holds a *cornucopiae* or lotus in her l hand; the r hand has a *pāśa*, or is empty. The ld on the rev is *Śrī-Vikramaḥ*. These coins are divided into two classes, on the basis of the seat of the goddess on

Samudragupta : Archer type

Samudragupta : Archer type

Chandragupta II : Archer type

Chandragupta II : Archer type

Kumāragupta I : Archer type

the rev. The coins of this type show a pleasing variety. This variety is missing on the coins of this type issued by his son, *Kumāragupta I, although he issued a large number of these coins. The obv has the archer king, as on the prototype. The circular ld on various specimens reads *Mahārājādhirāja Śrī-Kumāraguptaḥ*, or *Vijitāvaniravanipatiḥ Kumāragupto divaṁ jayati*, or *Jayati mahītalaṁ Śrī-Kumāraguptaḥ sudhanvī*, etc. Lakshmī on the rev is seated on a lotus bloom, with a *pāśa* in her r hand and a lotus in the left. But on some specimens of this type, she scatters coins with, or holds a flower in, her r hand. The rev ld is *Śrī-Mahendraḥ*. The coins of this type of Kumāragupta I are divided into four classes, on the basis of the vertical ld in the field on the obv. Class I has *Kumāra* under the king's left arm; Class II has *Kumāra* outside the bow; Class III has just *Ku* under the king's left arm; and Class IV has neither *Kumāra* nor *Ku* in the field. The Archer type formed the most popular type of *Skandagupta, too. His coins of this type have been divided into two varieties, on the basis of their weight, some coins being of an average weight of 132 grains, and others, of about 144 grains. The obv shows the archer king, with a *garuḍadhvaja* behind his r hand. There is the vertical ld, *Skanda*, under his left arm. The circular ld on the lighter variety of this type reads *Jayati mahītalaṁ Skandaguptaḥ sudhanvī*, and that on the heavier variety probably reads *Parahitakārī-rājā jayati divaṁ Śrī-Kramādityaḥ*. The rev of this type of Skandagupta has nimbate Lakshmī seated on a lotus, with a *pāśa* in her r hand and a lotus in her l hand. The rev ld on the coins of the lighter variety is *Śrī-Skandaguptaḥ*, and that on the heavier variety, *Kramādityaḥ*. The Archer type of *Ghaṭotkachagupta has the royal archer on the obv, with *garuḍadhvaja* behind the r arm. There is the vertical ld *Ghaṭo* under his left arm. The circular ld is illegible, only traces of its characters being visible. The rev is similar to that of the same type of Skandagupta, above. The rev ld is *Kramādityaḥ*. On the obv of the Archer type of *Kumāragupta II, the royal archer has the *garuḍadhvaja* behind his r arm, and the Br letter *Ku* above a crescent below his left arm. The circular ld is almost illegible, and is, perhaps, *Mahārājādhirāja-Śrī-Kumāragupta*. The rev has Lakshmī seated on a lotus bloom, with a *pāśa* in her r hand, and a lotus in the left. The rev ld is *Kramāditya*. The same type of *Budhagupta has, on the obv, the vertical ld *Budha* under the archer king's left arm on some coins, but this ld is missing on other coins of this type issued by him. The circular ld is mostly lost, and begins in *Para*.... The rev has Lakshmī seated on lotus, with *pāśa* and lotus, and the rev ld reads *Śrī-Vikrama*. The Archer type of *Vainyagupta has the vertical ld *Vainya* under the left arm of the archer king on the obv, and the circular ld is indistinct. The rev is similar to that of the same type of Skandagupta, and the ld here is *Dvādaśādityaḥ*. The Archer type of *Narasiṁhagupta is similar to the same type of Skandagupta, but the *garuḍadhvaja* on the obv is on the left, and there is the vertical ld *Nara* under the king's left arm. The circular ld is illegible. The rev ld is *Bālādityaḥ*. Some coins of this type are of relatively purer metal than the others; these latter coins do not bear any circular ld on the obv. The Archer type of *Kumāragupta III is quite similar to the same type of Kumāragupta II (above), but the rev ld is *Śrī-Kramādityaḥ*, instead of simply *Kramāditya*. The metal of the coins of Kumāragupta III shows signs of relative debasement, and the style, execution, and palaeography are also different from those of the coins of Kumāragupta II. Chandragupta III is also believed to have issued Archer type of coins, which are heavier in weight than the same type of coins of Chandragupta II. *Vishṇugupta also issued Archer type of coins, on the obv of which is shown the archer king, with a *garuḍadhvaja* on the left, and the vertical ld *Vishṇu* under his left arm. There are no traces of any circular ld. On the rev, Lakshmī is seated on lotus, with a *pāśa* in her r hand, and a lotus in her left. The rev ld is *Śrī-Chandrāditya*. Some Archer type of coins of *Samāchāradeva are also available, which show some additional features. The king stands on the obv, with a bow in his l hand, and offering oblations with the r. There is a bull standard behind his r hand. The ld below his left arm is *Samā-*; there is the letter *cha* between the king's feet, and, probably, *ra* above the bull, making the whole ld *Samāchāra*. The rev device is similar to that of the same type of Skandagupta; the rev ld is *Śrī-Narendravinīta*. The Archer type coins were also issued by the Gauḍa king, *Jaya[nāga]. The obv shows the nimbate king standing left, and holding a bow in his l hand and arrows in his r hand. There is a *chakradhvaja* behind the r hand of the king, on the basis of which Altekar labels this type as the *Chakradhvaja* type. The vertical ld under the left arm of the king read *Jaya*; the circular ld is not clear. The rev device of *Gajalakshmī is remarkable, in that there is only one elephant, to the l, annointing the goddess. The rev ld reads *Śrī-Prakāṇḍayaśasāḥ*

Kumāragupta I : Archer type

Skandagupta : Archer type

Budhagupta : Archer type

Narasiṁhagupta : Archer type

Vishṇugupta : Archer type

(Ashvini Agrawal 1989; Allan 1914; Altekar 1957; R D Banerji 1933; S R Goyal 2005; P L Gupta 1998; K P Jayaswal 1933; Smith 1972; Thaplyal, forthcoming).

Arddha-kākaṇī. Coin denomination. Also known as **ashṭabhāga-māshaka*, it was a copper coin, mentioned in the *Arthaśāstra* of Kauṭilya, and equal to 1/132 of a **kārshāpaṇa*, and thus weighing 0.62 *rattī*. But such a coin would have been too small in size, and would have been a 'nominal coin', the actual payment being made, not in coins, but in *cowries*. S K Chakrabortty, on the authority of Kauṭilya who speaks of the *paṇa*, half-*paṇa*, quarter-*paṇa*, and one-eighth-*paṇa* as silver coins, and **māshaka*, half-*māshaka*, **kākaṇī*, and half-*kākaṇī* as copper coins, suggests that, in states where bimetallism was the practice, such coins were submultiples of the silver *kārshāpaṇa* 'in value only and not in weight', and would have had a weight in copper valued at 1/132 of a silver *kārshāpaṇa*. The coin would, thus, have had a weight heavier than 0.62 *rattī* (D R Bhandarkar 1984; Chakrabortty 1931; Sircar 1952; Sircar 1968).

Arddha-kārshāpaṇa. Coin denomination. It was half of a **kārshāpaṇa*. The silver *arddha-kārshāpaṇa* would have weighed 16 *rattīs*, while the copper *arddha-kārshāpaṇa*, 40 *rattīs* (V S Agrawala 1953; D R Bhandarkar 1984; Chakrabortty 1931).

Arddha-māshaka. Coin denomination. It was 1/32 of a **kārshāpaṇa*, and the copper *arddha-māshaka* would have weighed 2½ *rattīs*. The coin denomination occurs in texts like the **Ashṭādhyāyī* and the *Arthaśāstra*, and in the **Aṅgavijjā* as *addha-māsaka*, where the context again seems to indicate that it was a copper coin, 2.5 *rattīs* in weight (V S Agrawala 1953; V S Agrawala 1957; D R Bhandarkar 1984; Chakrabortty 1931; Sircar 1952; Sircar 1968).

Ardhanārīśvara. Androgynous form of *Śiva. On the rev of a coins of a later *Kushāṇa ruler, *Kanishka III, occurs the figure of Śiva. But, according to some scholars, the left breast of this figure is quite developed, and should be identified as the Ardhanārīśvara form of this deity. However, this suggestion is not acceptable to a large number of scholars on the grounds that the label inscription reads *Oesho*, and not *Ommo-Oesho*, which should have been the case had this representation been intended for Śiva-Ardhanārīśvara. Secondly, the figure holds **triśūla* and *pāśa* in its two hands. Had the figure been intended for Śiva-Ardhanārīśvara, the left (female) hand of the deity would have been shown holding some attribute associated with *Umā, like lotus, mirror, parrot, or sceptre (O P Singh 1968; M N P Tiwari and Savita Sharma 1983).

Ardha-paṇa. Coin denomination. Mentioned in the *Arthaśāstra* of Kauṭilya, it was a silver coin and a submultiple of the **paṇa*, being one-half of it (Sircar 1952; Sircar 1968).

Ardochsho. Avestan goddess, Ashi Vanguhi. The ld *Ardochsho* on *Kushāṇa coins seems to represent the Avestan female divinity ('angel') Ashi Vanguhi, later known as Ashishang, 'good truth'. She is described as a daughter of *Ahuramazda and a sister of the Amcsha Spentas, 'good spirits'. She is associated with prosperity and wisdom, and is praised in the *Ashi Yasht*. She granted wealth, victory, and progeny to her worshippers like Zoroaster and Kava Vishtaspa. Some scholars relate her to Ardvi Sūra Anāhita, and regard her as a local goddess of water and moisture in eastern Iran. On Kushāṇa coins, the goddess labelled *Ardochsho* may be seen both standing and enthroned. On the rev of some gold coins of *Kanishka I, the nimbate figure of *Ardochsho* is seen standing holding a **cornucopiae*. But the standing deity on the coins of *Huvishka may sometimes be seen holding a wreath in addition to the *cornucopiae*. Enthroned *Ardochsho* on some coins of Kanishka I holds a *cornucopiae* in one hand and a wreath in the other, but on others, she holds a flower in the r hand, and a wheat-stem in the left, a feature which connects her with corn, like *Demeter. On the rev of some copper coins of *Vāsudeva I, the enthroned deity holds a *cornucopiae* in her l hand, and a fillet in her r hand. This deity played a significant role in the numismatic history of ancient India for at least five centuries after the Kushāṇas (Bhaskar Chattopadhyay 1967; Bhaskar Chattopadhyay 1977; Cunningham 1971a; Darmesteter 1974; Gardner 1971; Rosenfield 1967; Stein 1888; Whitehead 1914).†

Kanishka I

Huvishka

Huvishka

Kanishka III

Vāsudeva II

Ārjunāyana. Tribe. The Ārjunāyanas find mention in the *Gaṇapāṭha* of Pāṇini, the Allahabad pillar inscription of

*Samudragupta, the *Bṛihatsaṁhitā, Chāndravyākaraṇa, Kāśikā, Sarasvatīkaṇṭhābharaṇa*, and the *Abhidhānachintāmaṇi*. On the basis of the information supplied by the *Mahāmāyūrī*, this tribe is placed between eastern Punjab and western Uttar Pradesh. Cunningham places their territory in north Rajasthan to the north of Malwa and south of Madradeśa, Smith in Bharatpur and Alwar region, and Allan in Delhi-Jaipur-Agra triangle. Handa procured two coins of the tribe from the ancient mounds of Nohar and Dhanasia in the Ganganagar district of Rajasthan, and, on this basis, regards the Ārjunāyanas as the western neighbours of the *Agras.The tribal name connects them with Arjuna, the Pāṇḍava hero. Except for one silver coin, all Ārjunāyana coins (which are very rare) are in copper, and round in shape. Following Allan, these coins have been divided into two classes. Class I has, on the obv, human figure in between *yūpa* and *tree-in-railing and the Br ld *Ārjunāyanānāṁ*, and on the rev, *bull, standing. Class II has two varieties : (i) on the obv, humped bull standing facing an altar within railing, and the ld, *Ārjunāyanajayaḥ*, and on the rev, tree-in-railing and *elephant with trunk upraised, and (ii) on the obv, humped bull, standing facing sacrificial altar and Br ld *Ajunayanāṁ jaya…*, and on the rev, traces of the upraised trunk of an elephant. The last component of the Br ld on these coins has been read variously as *Damarudasa* or *Bhadrarāmasa*, which have been regarded as the name of the chief of the tribe in the genitive. But Handa reads it as *Bhadrārāmasa* and regards it as the genitive form of a place name, which he proposes to identify with modern Bhadra (Bhādarā), 'a tahsil town in district Sri Ganganagar of Rajasthan', an ancient site. A recently discovered silver coin with bull facing *yūpa* and the ld mentioning the name of the tribe on the obv, and traces of an elephant with upraised trunk on the rev, is interesting. The two coins reported by Handa from the Ganganagar district bear a tree-in-railing on the obv and the figure of a *lion on the rev. The human figure may be that of a deity, probably *Lakshmī due to the similarity of the figure with that of Lakshmī on Mathurā coins. The bull before sacrificial altar may represent *śūlagava* sacrifice mentioned in the gṛihyasūtras. It has been pointed out that in metal, shape, size, weight, ld, devices, and chronology, the Ārjunāyana coins closely resemble *Rājanya coins. The Ārjunāyanas seem to have started issuing their coins in *c* first century BC, and their coinage ceased with their accepting the suzerainty of *Kanishka I. There is a view that Ārjunāyana coins were issued after *Huvishka when the *Kushāṇa power was on the decline. The Ārjunāyans continued to be a political power till they came to owe allegiance to Samudragupta (*c* 350 AD), as per the testimony of the Allahabad pillar inscription of that ruler (Nisar Ahmad 1993; Allan 1936; Chakrabortty 1931; Cunningham 1971b; K K Dasgupta 1974; P L Gupta 1977; Handa 2007a; Jayaswal 1988; Marshall 1975; Mitchiner 1975-1976; Smith 1972).

Artemidoros. *Indo-Greek k; subking of *Apollodotos; early first century BC. After starting his career as a subking, he seems to have asserted his independence for a short while. He has been associated, variously, with the Pushkalāvatī, Peshwar, or the Takshaśilā regions. R C Senior has read a Gr ld meaning 'Artemidoros, son of the king of kings, Maues', on a coin, and, on this basis, as also on the basis of the similarity of devices, suggested that Artemidoros was a son of *Maues. He issued silver and copper coins, all struck on the Indian standard. All the coins are die-struck pieces. The silver coins are all round in shape. The copper coins are mostly square in shape, but one type is round. The obv of the silver coins bears the diademed bust of the king to the r, sometimes wearing a smooth helmet. On some specimens, the bust of the king to the r, and thrusting javelin, is seen from the back. The rev of these coins mostly has the figure of *Artemis, standing clad in skins; she is shown drawing a bow, and has a quiver at her back. However, one silver type has the wreath- and palm-bearing winged *Nike, standing to the r, as the rev device. One silver type, struck on the Indian standard, also has the king on prancing horse to the r. The square copper coins have, on the obv, the figure of standing Artemis, drawing an arrow from the quiver at her back on one type, or holding out a bow on the other. The rev of these coins has the figure of a humped *bull to the r. The round copper type has a male figure standing to front on the obv, and a *panther to the r on the rev, All the coins of Artemidoros bear the Gr ld on the obv, and the Pkt ld, written in the Kh script, on the rev. Besides the title of **basileus*, Artemidoros assumed the epithet **aniketos*. These are rendered into Pkt as **maharaja* and **apaḍihata*, respectively. Artemidoros is known to have restruck the joint coins of *Hermaios with *Kalliope. The Pkt form of the name of the ruler, as met with on coins, is Atrimitora (Bopearachchi 1993; Bopearachchi 1994;

Bopearachchi and Pieper 1998; Bopearachchi and Rahman 1995; Cunningham 1970; Gardner 1971; A N Lahiri 1965; Marshall 1975; Narain 1957a; Rapson 1987; Senior 2001; Sircar 1980a; Tarn 1980; Whitehead 1914).†

Artemis. Greek goddess, associated with hunting and wild beasts. She was the daughter of Leto by *Zeus, and a twin of *Apollo. Like her brother, she is an archer. The Greeks assimilated her to a 'pre-Greek mistress of wild beasts'. She is famous as a virgin huntress, the 'goddess of plant life', and 'the physician goddess of animals', and has lunar traits. On coins, she is always shown as standing, usually with either a torch in her hands, or bow and arrows. On the rev of some coins of *Diodotos, the goddess, clad in *himation*, is seen running to the r. She holds a torch in both her hands, and has a quiver at her shoulder; her hound is seen running beside her. When shown with her bow and arrow, she is mostly depicted as drawing an arrow from her quiver, as on some coins of *Demetrios, *Artemidoros, and *Peukolaos. On the obv of some coins of the *Śaka-Pahlava king, *Maues, Artemis is represented with a veil round her head. It may be remarked that the torch in the hands of the Artemis indicates her lunar character, while the bow and arrow and quiver reveal her character as a huntress (Bopearachchi 1993; Bopearachchi and Pieper 1998; Bopearachchi and Rahman 1995; Bhaskar Chattopadhyay 1977; Cunningham 1971a; Gardner 1971; Graves 1955; Kerenyi 1951; A N Lahiri 1965; Marshall 1975; Rose 1958; Prashant Srivastava 2007c; Whitehead 1914).†

Arthapatirāja. *Nala k.

Arthaśāstra. Text on statecraft by Kauṭilya; *c* fourth century BC, with several revisions. Kauṭilya refers to some gold and silver coins and weights. His **suvarṇa* weighs 80 *rattīs*, the **suvarṇa-māsha* weighing 5 *rattīs*, and these gold weights are the same as given by Manu, Yājñavalkya, and Vishṇu. But the *Arthaśāstra* does not seem to state clearly that the *suvarṇa* was a gold coin current at the time. The **dharaṇa* of Kauṭilya weighs 1,408 *gaurasarshapas*, which would make it about 145.14 grains, and this is much more than the weight of the standard Indian silver coin of 32 *rattīs* prescribed by authorities like Manu, Yājñavalkya, and Vishṇu. The *Arthaśāstra* refers to the standard silver coin as **paṇa*, and its submultiples were **ardha-paṇa*, **pāda-paṇa*, and **ashṭabhāga-paṇa*. The copper coins mentioned in the text include **māshaka*, **ardha-māshaka*, **pāda-māshaka* or **kākaṇī*, and **ashṭabhāga-māshaka* or **ardha-kākaṇī* (P L Gupta 1960; Kangle 2000; Sircar 1952; Sircar 1968).[†]

Arya.... *Kulūta chief. He ruled in the first-second centuries AD, and issued the Class III of *Kulūta coins, on which the ld is hardly legible, but the initial part of the name of the chief has been read by Allan as *Arya*... (Allan 1936; Chakrabortty 1931; Cunningham 1971b; K K Dasgupta 1974; Handa 2007a; Jayaswal 1988; Marshall 1975; Smith 1972).

Āryyasoma/Jayasoma (?). *Vṛishṇi general (?).

Āseka (Aśoka ?). *Almora k.

Ashaeichsho. Avestan, Asha Vahishta. The ld *Ashaeichsho* on *Kushāṇa coins stands for the Iranian Amesha Spenta, Asha Vahishta, which later became Ardavahishta. He presides over fire, 'the mightiest of physical elements'. He is believed to be the impersonation of the sunlight, and on this ground, is compared with the vedic Savitṛi. *Asha* in the original name of the deity is the Avestan term for moral order, and is the same as the vedic *ṛita*. On some gold coins of *Huvishka, the rev has the depiction of the radiate figure of the deity standing to the l. His r hand is extended, while the left one rests on the hilt of the sword tied to his waist. From the ld, *Ashaeichsho*, it is clear that he is to be identified with Asha Vahishta (Bhaskar Chattopadhyay 1977; Darmesteter 1974; Gardner 1971; Rosenfield 1967; Stein 1888).

Huvishka

Ashṭabhāga-māshaka. Coin denomination. Mentioned in the *Arthaśāstra* of Kauṭilya, it was a copper coin and a submultiple of the **māshaka*, being one-eighth of it. It was also known as **ardha-kākaṇī* (Sircar 1952; Sircar 1968).

Ashṭabhāga-paṇa. Coin denomination. Mentioned in the *Arthaśāstra* of Kauṭilya, it was a silver coin and a submultiple of the **paṇa*, being one-eighth of it (Sircar 1952; Sircar 1968).

Ashṭādhyāyī. Text on Skt grammar by Pāṇini; *c* fifth century BC. Some significant numismatic data is furnished in the Ārhīya section of this text, when the relevant sūtras refer to articles as *tena krītam*, 'purchased with that' and *tad-arhati*, 'worth that'. The coin denominations in various metals mentioned in this text include **nishka*, **suvarṇa*, **suvarṇa-māshaka*, **śatamāna*, **śāṇa*, **kārshāpaṇa*, with its various submultiples like **ardha-kārshāpaṇa* or *bhāga*, **pāda-kārshāpaṇa*, **dvi-māshaka*, **māsha*, **ardha-māsha*, **kākaṇi*, **viṁśatika*, **triṁśatika*, and *rūpa* (V S Agrawala 1953).†

Azes II and Aśpavarman

Aśpavarman. *Apracha chief. Aśpavarman, the son of Indravarman, is known to have served the Śaka-Pahlava rulers as **strategos*. He is known from some copper coins, which have the horseman king and the name of *Azes [II] on the obv, and armed *Athena and the name of Aśpavarman on the rev. The rev Kh ld describes Aśpavarman as 'son of Indravarman' and **stratega*, which is believed to be the Pkt equivalent of *strategos*. Thus, on these coins, Aśpavarman appears as serving under Azes II as his *strategos*. We also have his joint coins with *Gondopharnes. These coins, in billon, have horseman king and a corrupt Gr ld mentioning Gondopharnes on the obv; the rev has *Zeus standing with sceptre and the Kh ld describing Aśpavarman as 'son of Indravarman' *stratega*, and *tratara*. It appears that when Gondopharnes invaded the kingdom of Azes II, *Strategos* Aśpavarman sided with the invader, and when Azes II had been defeated, the victorious invader rewarded Aśpavarman by allowing him to continue as *strategos*. He also added the Takshaśilā region to the charge of Aśpavarman, as per numismatic and epigraphic evidence. For, Aśpavarman is also known from a silver saucer inscription found in a deposit buried beneath the floor of a room in Block 'D', Stratum III, at Sirkap, Taxila (Cunningham 1971a; Gardner 1971; Jenkins and Narain 1957; Marshall 1975; B N Mukherjee 1969; Senior 2001; Sircar 1980b; Prashant Srivastava 1996a; Prashant Srivastava 2007a; Tarn 1980; Whitehead 1914).

Aśpavarman hoard. This hoard of over 1,000 coins, was discovered somewhere in the Swat region, and was disposed of in Germany. Most of the coins in this hoard are associated with *Aśpavarman.

There are also some posthumous issues in the name of *Azes I, one coin of *Azes II with *Indravasu, some coins of *Gondopharnes with *Sasan, and, reportedly, also some worn coins of Gondopharnes alone, and of *Abdagases (Senior 2001).

Aśvaghosha. *Kauśāmbī k. He may be identifed, on palaeographical grounds, with the homonym, whose inscription of year 40 occurs on the Aśokan pillar at Kauśāmbī. Some scholars, like Vögel, take the numeral 40 in the epigraph as a date in the Śaka era, in which case the date would come to (78+40 =) 118 AD. However, according to others, the coin should better be placed before *Kanishka I (accession, 78 AD), and therefore the year 40 should be regarded as the regnal year of that king. Allan places him in the second century BC, and Bela Lahiri, about the beginning of the first century AD. He issued copper coins, both round and square in shape, with a *bull to the r and an uncertain symbol on the obv; the rev has a *tree-in-railing with some uncertain symbols, and name of the issuer in the genitive. The square coins are of comparatively thin fabric, and the square shape and thin fabric connect him with *Parvata, *Īśvaramitra, *Rāḍhamitra, and *Priyamitra (Allan 1936; Altekar 1942b; Bopearachchi and Pieper 1998; Bela Lahiri 1974).

Aśvaka. Tribe. The *Mahābhārata* mentions Aśvaka and Aśmaka as variants of the name of the same tribe living in the northwest. The Aśvakas of coins are, in all probability, identical with the Assakenoi, who, according to the classical writers, offered a tough resistance to Alexander. The Assakenoi territory has been located in the Swat valley and its city, Massaga, is identical with Maśkāvatī of Pāṇini's *Ashṭādhyāyī*. The find of Aśvaka coins at Taxila may indicate that they, at least some of them, had migrated there, or the presence of these coins may be due to trade contacts. It is difficult to say if the Aśvakas had any connection with the Aśmakas of the Godavari region (referred to as *dākshiṇātyas* in Pāṇini). A few coins found near Taxila bear the device of a pile of balls, *crescent-on-hill, a human figure, and a *taurine, and the Br ld *Vaṭasvaka* in the characters of *c* third or second century BC. Cunningham is inclined to include these coins under Taxila coins. *Vaṭāśvaka* as the name of a tribe is not known. Bühler rendered *Vaṭasvaka* into Skt as *Vaṭāśvakaḥ*, 'the Aśvaka tribe of the *vaṭa* or fig tree clan'. Allan takes the ld in the singular and as a place name. *Vaṭa* also means a *cowrie*-shell, which, like coin, was a medium of exchange, and hence, *Vaṭasvaka* may be equal to Skt *Aśvakānāṁ vaṭaḥ*, 'the coin of the Aśvakas'. However, examples of tribes drawing their name from the tree are known in the case of the Aśvatthas and the *Audumbaras. The weight of the Aśvaka coins ranges between 135 and 146 grains, which is very near to the weight of **kārshāpaṇa* (80 *rattīs*) (Allan 1936; Chakrabortty 1931; Cunningham 1971b; K K Dasgupta 1974; Handa 2007a; Jayaswal 1988; Marshall 1975; Mitchiner 1975-1976; Smith 1972; Prashant Srivastava 2007a).

Samudragupta : *Aśvamedha* type

Samudragupta : *Aśvamedha* type

Kumāragupta I : *Aśvamedha* type

***Aśvamedha* type.** Gold. When *Samudragupta performed the *aśvamedha* as a fitting *finale* to his victories in Āryāvartta and the Dakshiṇāpatha, he issued the *Aśvamedha* type of coins, most probably to be given away as *dakshiṇā* to the officiating priests and the brāhmaṇas. The obv has the scene of the horse sacrifice, the uncaparisoned sacrificial horse being shown before the *yūpa*. There is a crescent above the back of the horse in some cases. Beneath the horse, there is the Br letter *si* (for *siddhaṁ*). On some specimens is a pedestal (for the officiating priest ?) beneath the horse. The circular ld read *Rājādhirājaḥ pṛithivīmavitvā* (or *vijitya*) *divaṁ jayatyāhṛita-vājimedhaḥ*. The rev has the queen standing in front of an ornamental *sūchī*. She holds a *chāmara* over her r shoulder in her r hand, and a towel in her l hand, hanging by her side. The ld on the rev is *Aśvamedha-Parākramaḥ*. This type of Samudragupta is regarded as one of the best specimens of Indian numismatic art. These coins are the only available contemporary evidence of the performance of the horse sacrifice by Samudragupta. The type was continued by his grandson, *Kumāragupta I. The obv and rev devices of his coins of this type are quite similar to those of Samudragupta, but on some coins, the horse on the obv is caparisoned. The circular ld, according to Altekar, reads *Devojitaśatruḥ Kumāraguptodhirājā*. The rev ld is *Śrī-Aśvamedha-Mahendraḥ*. Artistically, these coins of Kumāragupta I are of an inferior quality to those of Samudragupta. Apart from a stone figure of a horse, bearing the name of *Mahendrāditya*, presently housed in the State Museum, Lucknow, the *Aśvamedha* type of coins of Kumāragupta I are the only source of our information regarding the performance of the horse sacrifice by this ruler (Ashvini Agrawal 1989; Allan 1914; Altekar 1957; R D

Banerji 1933; S R Goyal 2005; P L Gupta 1998; K P Jayaswal 1933; Smith 1972; Prashant Srivastava 1996a; Thaplyal, forthcoming).

Atakatakā. Guild. *Takshaśilā. Guild coins.

Athena. Greek goddess of war. This most important Greek deity after *Zeus, has as her mother Metis, 'wise counsel'. Athena was actually the Father's daughter, as she was born from the head of her father, Zeus. Her most notable aspect was that of a victorious war goddess. The *thunderbolt in her hand seems to indicate that some of the functions of Zeus might have been discharged to a certain extent by Athena. The bust of Athena is found on the obv of some joint coins of *Agathokleia and *Strato I, as also on the obv of some copper coins of *Menander I. Besides the bust of Athena, the goddess is also shown as standing or seated on coins. When depicted as standing, she sometimes holds a long spear in one of her hands, and her peculiar shield, the **aegis*, may be seen on the other arm, as on the coins of *Demetrios, *Diodotos, Menander, *Amyntas, *Vonones with *Spalahora, *Azes I, and *Gondopharnes. On the rev of some coins of Strato I, the goddess holds spear and shield, and has *Nike standing on her outstretched r hand. A similar depiction, but with Athena seated, may be seen on the rev of some coins of *Theophilos. On some coins of Azes I, Athena is shown standing with her spear on her back, and her shield on her left arm, while she crown herself with her r hand. On some coins of Azes I, Gondopharnes, and *Rañjuvula, the goddess is depicted as standing, but she holds a thunderbolt in one hand, instead of the spear; the *aegis* is seen on the other arm, as before. Even more interesting is the representation of Athena hurling her thunderbolt with her r hand, while she holds her shield on her left arm. Such a depiction may be seen on the coins of Menander, Strato I, *Nikias, Amyntas, *Apollodotos, *Apollophanes, *Dionysios, *Epander, *Polyxenos, *Zoilos, and *Azilises, as also on the joint coins of Agathokleia with Strato I, and Azes I with Azilises. On the rev of some double-*decadrachms* of Amyntas, a shield-bearing goddess is shown standing on the outstretched r hand of enthroned *Zeus. This goddess has been identified as 'Athena-Nike' by some scholars. [*Owl, *Pallas] (Bopearachchi 1993; Bopearachchi and Pieper 1998; Bopearachchi and Rahman 1995; Bhaskar Chattopadhyay 1977; Cunningham

Menander

Menander

Menander

Azes

Strato I

Azes II and Aśpavarman

Huvishka

1971a; Gardner 1971; Graves 1955; Kerenyi 1951; A N Lahiri 1965; Marshall 1975; Rose 1958; Prashant Srivastava 2007c; Whitehead 1914).†

Athsho. Avestan fire god. The ld *Athsho* (the variant *Athosho* occurs on a gold coin of *Huvishka) on *Kushāṇa coins seems to be used for the name of the Avestan fire god Ātar. At several places in the *Avesta*, Ātar is mentioned as the son of *Ahuramazda. He is the source of royal glory (Kavaem Khvareno). In Iranian mythology, he accompanies the chariot of the sun. He defends the world against all evils. His characteristic attribute is the tongs, which, according to a passage in the Vendidad, is required for tending the fire of Ahuramazda. On Kushāṇa coins, the deity labelled as *Athsho* is usually shown as a bearded and diademed deity, standing with a wreath in his r hand and tongs in the left. Such a depiction may be seen on some gold and copper coins of *Kanishka I and some copper coins of Huvishka. On the rev of a variety of the gold coins of Huvishka, *Athsho* stands with a hammer and tongs in his hands, and flames are shown as issuing from his shoulders. The representations of *Athsho* on Kushāṇa coins remind one of *Hephaistos. Like the Greek god, *Athsho* also holds tongs in one of his hands. In some representations, he also carries the smith's hammer. But the flames of fire issuing from the shoulders of *Athsho* on some coins of Huvishka show that while Hephaistos was the Greek counterpart of the vedic Tvashṭṛi, *Athsho* was primarily the god of fire who also discharged the functions of the divine smith like Hephaistos, and this is symbolized by the hammer and tongs in his hands. Incidentally, the figure of *Athsho* with flaming shoulders is reminiscent of the images of *Agni from Mathurā, which are datable to the Kushāṇa period (Bhaskar Chattopadhyay 1977; Darmesteter 1974; Gardner 1971; Graves 1960; Rosenfield 1967; Stein 1888; Whitehead 1914).

Aṭṭhā. Coin denomination. It occurs in the **Aṅgavijjā*, where the context seems to indicate that it was a copper coin weighing five-eighth of a *rattī*. This has been identified with the **arddha-kākaṇī* of the *Arthaśāstra* of Kauṭilya. V S Agrawala takes the existence of such minute coins as 'for granted' (V S Agrawala 1957).

Attic standard. A gold standard, based on a unit (**stater*) of 130 grains, was current throughout the Greek world. This seems to have been standardized to 134.4 grains by Athens, and became known as the Attic standard or the Euboic-Attic standard. This Attic standard was adopted by Alexander and his successors, including the Seleukids of Syria. These Seleukids passed it on to the *Indo-Greeks (Gardner 1918; Hill 1906; A N Lahiri 1965).

Attock hoard. This hoard of 693 *Indo-Greek coins was discovered in the village of Attock, between Peshawar and Taxila. The rulers represented in this hoard include *Amyntas, *Antialkidas, *Lysias, *Menander I, and *Zoilos I (Bopearachchi 1994).

***AU*.** Abbreviation. This is the symbol for *aurum*, the Latin for gold, and is commonly used as an abbreviation for gold coinage (Junge 1984).

Audumbara : Dharaghosha

Audumbara : Dharaghosha

Audumbara. Tribe. Audumbara, a *tadddhita* form of *udumbara*, means people connected with the fig tree (*udumbara*) or a country where fig trees grow in abundance. The Audumbaras are referred to in the *Gaṇapāṭha* of Pāṇini, which locates them near Jalandhar. Besides, they are also mentioned in the *Mahābhārata, Bṛihatsaṁhitā, Vishṇupurāṇa*, and the Sanchi inscriptions. In the *Chāndravyākaraṇa*, the *Kāśikā* and the *Vaijayantī*, the Audumbaras are referred to as one of the sections of the Śālvas. Patañjali refers to them as kshatriyas, Jayaswal takes them as of Aryan origin, while Przyluski regards them as speakers of Austro-Asiatic languages. The Adamviras or Admeras, a section of the Johiya Rajputs, as also Gujarat brāhmaṇas of Audumbara caste and Viśvāmitra *gotra*, are taken as reminiscent of the Audumbaras. Audumbara coins have been found from the Pathankot-Gurdaspur region, and a few other sites of Punjab, and at Irippal, district Kangra, and a few other sites of Himachal Pradesh. The tribe seems to have occupied Kangra, Gurdaspur, Hoshiarpur areas. Pliny's reference to Odombeores in Kuchchh region suggests that some of them might have migrated there from Punjab and Himachal Pradesh. The coins of this tribe are divided into two classes. Class I comprises copper coins, which bear, on the obv, *tree-in-railing, forepart of an *elephant, and *undulating line below, and on the rev, storeyed *temple and trident-battleaxe; on some coins of *Śivadāsa and *Rudradāsa, Devendra Handa reports the figure of a *lion also on the obv. The obv has a Kh ld, mentioning the name of the chief along with the titles of **rañа* (= Skt, **rājña*) and *mahadeva* (= Skt, *mahādeva*); the rev has a Br ld mentioning the name of the tribe, sometimes accompanied by the name of the issuing chief. The four chiefs represented by this class are Śivadāsa, Rudradāsa, *Dharaghosha, and *Mahādeva. Class II comprises silver coins, which show four varieties. The first variety has humped *bull and *lotus flower on the obv, and *elephant and *trident on the rev; the second variety has humped bull, **chakra*, and **nandipada* on the obv, and elephant and trident on the rev; the third variety has a peculiar symbol on the obv, and a standing figure holding trident-battleaxe on the rev; the fourth variety has *Viśvāmitra on the obv, and trident-battleaxe and tree-in-railing on the rev. The first two varieties bear a Kh ld on the obv reading *Bhagavata Mahadevasa rajarañа*, and a Br ld on the rev reading *Bhagavata Mahadevasa rajaraja*. The third variety has the ld, in Br, only on the rev, which reads *Bhagavata Mahadevasa*. There is some controversy regarding the attribution of the coins bearing such legends [*Mahādeva]. The obv Kh ld on the fourth variety refers to Dharaghosha with the titles of *rañа* and *mahadeva*, and the additional ld *Viśpamitra*; the rev refers to the king with the same titles, and also mentions the tribal name. On palaeographical grounds, the coins of Class I are placed in the second or first century BC, while those of Class II at the end of the first century BC or the beginning of the first century AD, on the basis of the *Indo-Greek influence on them. The copper coins weigh between 31 and 46 grains, while the silver coins weigh about 40 grains and seem to be based on the weight standard of the Indo-Greek coins of roughly 36 grains. On the basis of the weights of the three known silver coins of the tribe, Devendra Handa feels that they might represent one-fourth of the weight of the Persian *siglos* of 160 grains, a denomination adopted by this tribe for trade with its western neighbours. There is a suggestion that the tree appearing on the coins of this tribe within a railing, may be identified as *udumbara* or fig tree. The storeyed temple on the Audumbara coins is accompanied by a trident-battleaxe, which has led to the suggestion that it is a Śaiva temple. The names of chiefs like Śivadāsa and Rudradāsa, and the devices of trident, trident-battleaxe, and bull, attest to the Śaiva affiliations of the tribe. Some round copper coins, belonging variously to Ajamita (Āryamitra), Mahimita (Mahīmitra), Bhānumita (Bhānumitra), and Mahabhutimita (Mahābhūtimitra), have been included by Cunningham in the Audumbara series on the basis that they were found along with them. But others, like Jagannath, A M Shastri, Nisar Ahmad, and Michael Mitchiner, regard them as later in date and unconnected with the Audumbaras, mainly on the grounds that these coins bearing *mitra*-ending names are different from the Audumbara coins as regards the fabric, shape, devices, legends, etc. The rulers mentioned on these coins have been labelled by scholars like Nisar Ahmad and Devendra Handa as 'the Mitras of Punjab' (Nisar Ahmad 1977; Allan 1936; Chakrabortty 1931; Cunningham 1971b; K K Dasgupta 1974; Handa 2007a; Jayaswal 1988; Marshall 1975; Mitchiner 1975-1976; A M Shastri 1964; A M Shastri 1972; Smith 1972).

***Aureus*.** Coin denomination. Gold coins, the *aurei*, were issued in large numbers during campaigns of Sulla against Mithridates in Asia Minor *c* 87 BC, mainly to pay the troops. These gold coins were first copied by Julius Caesar in Gaul, and then issued regularly by him in Rome. It, thus, became the principal gold denomination of ancient Rome from the first century BC, till it was superseded by the **solidus* of the Roman emperor, Constantine the Great, in the early years of the fourth century AD. An *aureus* was equal to 25 *denarii* in value [**denarius*] (Junge 1984).

Aurihar hoard. This hoard of 543 silver *punch marked coins, belonging to the Magadha and Kosala *janapadas*, was found in 1952 at Aurihar in the Ghazipur district of Uttar Pradesh. Most of these coins are presently in the State Museum, Lucknow, some in the Patna Museum, and a few in the Bharat Kala Bhavan, Varanasi (Rajgor 2001).

Autokratoros. Title. Meaning 'king absolute', this title is regarded as 'the trade mark of a military usurper', and adopted by *Theophilos among the *Indo-Greeks, and *Gondopharnes among the *Śaka-Pahlavas. Outside of India, this title was also used by Sulla of Rome, and the Arsakid rulers, Sinatrukes and Phraates IV (Cunningham 1970; Gardner 1971; A N Lahiri 1965; Marshall 1975; Narain 1957a; Tarn 1980; Whitehead 1914; Wroth 1903).

Avantivarman. *Maukhari k; son of *Śarvavarman; *c* end of the sixth century AD to beginning of the seventh century AD. He is referred to as *parameśvara* in one inscription, but a Nalanda seal accords him full imperial titles. There are suggestions that the Later Gupta king, Mahāsenagupta, and *Śaśāṅka of Gauḍa, served him as his feudatories. His coins have been found in the *Bhitaura hoard. They are all in silver, and weigh around 36 grains. They are all of the **Madhyadeśa* type of the Imperial Gupta silver coins, with the royal head to the r and the date of issue on the obv, and a fan-tailed *peacock with the Br ld reading *Vijitāvaniravanipati Śrī-Avantivarman divaṁ jayati* on the rev. The dates on the various coins of Avantivarman have been read as 67, 71, 25 by R Burn; 57, 70, 25 by Brown; and 17, 57, 260 by Dikshit. N G Majumdar is of the view that the dates on these coins have generally totally disappeared and it is not possible to the read them (Richard Burn 1906; D Devahuti 1964; Pires 1934; Thaplyal 1985).[†]

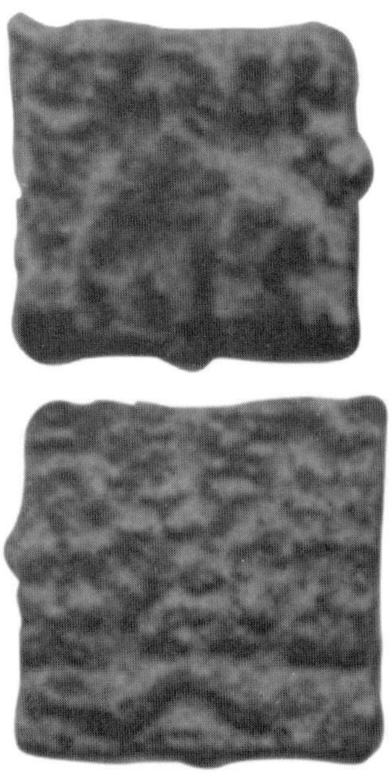

Ayodhyā

Ayodhyā. The coins of the kings of Ayodhyā have been divided into two distinct series: (i) square cast coins, and (ii) round die-struck coins. The former generally bear the figure of a *bull, rarely an *elephant, before a symbol on the obv, and a group of symbols in different combinations on the rev. The rulers known from the coins of Series I are (alphabetically), *Dhanadeva, *Jyeshṭhadatta, *Mūladeva, *Naradatta, *Poṭhadeva (Praushṭhadeva), *Śivadatta, *Vāyudeva, and *Viśākhadeva, although some scholars would place Naradatta and Śivadatta of Ayodhyā coins among the rulers of *Mathurā. Dhanadeva may be identical with the homonym of Ayodhyā stone inscription, who has been referred to therein as sixth in descent from Pushyamitra. Coins of Dhanadeva, Vāyudeva, and Viśākhadeva have similarity of device—*Gajalakshmī, standing, while Śivadatta's coins show Gajalakshmī, sitting. Praushṭhadeva and Mūladeva, known from bull type of coins alone, are to be placed earlier than Dhanadeva. Bela Lahiri proposes the following chronological order—Praushṭhadeva, Mūladeva, Vāyudeva, Dhanadeva, Viśākhadeva, Śivadatta, Naradatta, and Jyeshṭhadatta. The rule of the kings who issued square cast coins could be dated from the middle of the first century BC to the second half of the first century AD. Their rule seems to have terminated with the conquest of this region by *Kanishka I. The series of round die-struck coins seems to have been issued when the *Kushāṇa rule over the region slackened after Kanishka. These coins bear a bull on the obv, and a *cock or a **nandipada* on the rev. The kings known are (alphabetically), *Ajavarman, *Āyumitra, *Devamitra, *Kumudasena, *Mādhavavarman, *Saṅghamitra, *Satyamitra, and *Vijayamitra. According to Bela Lahiri, of these rulers, Kumudasena, Ajavarman, and Mādhavavarman seem to be earlier as is indicated by the presence on their coins of a square incuse, which is characteristic of the earliest die-struck coins of India. Curiously, of the Ayodhyā kings, Kumudasena alone has the title of **rājan* on his coins. On the basis of the forms of the letter *ma* on the coins, Bela Lahiri suggests the following order of succession of the other rulers—Saṅghamitra, Vijayamitra, Devamitra, Satyamitra, and Āyumitra. The coins of this series may be placed between *c* 150 AD and the end of the third century AD, the latter date marking the beginning of the *Imperial Gupta period. It seems that the rule of the local dynasty of Ayodhyā was brought to an end by one of early Imperial Gupta rulers, for the puranic evidence shows that *Chandragupta I exercised authority over Sāketa. The bull, common to both the series, is a characteristic local device. From some seals discovered at Rajghat are known Dhavasena, his son Vishṇumitra, and the latter's son Saṅghamitra, and also one Vijayamitra and his son Śivamitra. Saṅghamitra and Vijayamitra of these seals may be identical with the homonyms of coins (Allan 1936; Bopearachchi and Pieper 1998; Bela Lahiri 1974; Mitchiner 1975-1976; Smith 1972).

Ayodhyā

Ayodhyā. City coins. The early, uninscribed coins from Ayodhyā, like the local *Takshaśilā coins, bear the device of steelyard. Allan believes that they could be city coins of Ayodhyā, and he dates them to *c* 200 BC. Some coins in the Allahabad Museum bear legends, which have been read, variously, as *Ajudhe*, *Ajadhe*, or *Ajidhe*, and these have been considered as issues of the city of Ayodhyā. However, it is well to note that such coins have not been obtained at Ayodhyā, and the reading of the legends is doubtful (Bela Lahiri 1974; Bela Lahiri 1976; J P Singh 1971).

Āyumitra. *Ayodhyā k. He is placed after *Saṅghamitra, *Vijayamitra, *Devamitra, and *Satyamitra by Bela Lahiri on the basis of a comparative study of the letter *ma* occurring in the coin legends. But on the basis of a coin bearing the names of Devamitra and Āyumitra, it seems more likely that Āyumitra came immediately after Devamitra. It has been proposed that he should be placed towards the end of the third or the beginning of the fourth century AD. His coins are all in copper, and bear the figure of a *bull before a spear on the obv, along with the name of the issuer in the genitive. The rev has a *cock on a post to the r, and a tree. Allan renders his name as Āryamitra (Allan 1936; Bela Lahiri 1974; Smith 1972; Prashant Srivastava 1992b; Prashant Srivastava 1996a).

Azes. Two *Śaka-Pahlava kings (?). A large number of coins bearing the name of Azes have come to the light. From the fact that on some coins, the name of Azes occurs in Gr on the obv, and of *Azilises (Ayalisha) in Kh on the rev, while on some others, the order is reversed, it has been suggested that there were two Śaka-Pahlava kings bearing the name Azes. Of these, the elder, that is *Azes I, associated his son, Azilises, in government, perhaps in his old age, and the latter, in his turn, associated his own son, *Azes II, in government towards the close of his reign. The issue of the existence of two kings named Azes is a contentious one, and needs to be addressed in some detail, as it has a bearing on the history and coinage of the Śaka-Pahlava rulers. Whitehead, on the contrary, is of the view that there might have been two kings named Azilises, and only one Azes. His argument is that as the 'best didrachms of Azes compare unfavourably with the fine silver coins of Azilises', hence, Azilises preceded Azes. However, in view of the fact that the coins of Azilises do not show any great difference in style and execution, while the same cannot be said of the coins bearing the name of Azes, there is greater likelihood of there being two rulers named Azes. Scholars like Ernst Herzfeld and J E van Lohuizen de Leeuw suggested that Azes, Azilises, Aya, and Ayilisha (the last two being the Pkt forms of Azes and Azilises, respectively) are the different names of one and the same king. But this view has not been taken seriously by scholars. Sten Konow was earlier of the view that there was only one Azes. But later on, he accepted the theory of the existence of two kings named Azes. Jenkins has shown that some coins bearing the name of Azes are of fine quality silver, bear the obv device of horseman king with spear, and have the early form of the

Kh letter *sa* in the rev ld; other coins bearing the name of Azes are in debased silver, bear the obv device of horseman king with whip, and have the late form of the Kh letter *sa*. He ascribes the former coins to Azes I, and the latter to Azes II. R C Senior has recently pleaded the case for a single king named Azes. He regards all the joint issues in the name of Azes/Azilises or Azilises/Azes as 'mules'. He says that 'mules', by their very nature, are extremely rare, while joint coins should be more prolific and produced from several dies. But he himself admits that the Azilises/Azes copper coins are 'more problematic since more than one die is known and so far no coin exists with an Azes obv (ie, no coin of this type known of Azes alone)'. He has tried to explain away this problem by suggesting a number of possibilities and 'unusual' situations. The evidence of coin hoards, too, has been cited, but it cannot be said to be conclusive. For instance, the *Nul Guniar hoard, which has coins of both the 'King mounted with spear' and 'King mounted with whip' types of Azes, but no coins of Azilises, has been taken as confirmation of the suggestion that Azilises did not intervene between Azes I and Azes II series of coins. It is further argued that all the coins were patinated to the same extent, showing that they were deposited 'within a short period of issue'. But should such conclusions be drawn on the basis of a hoard of mere 11 coins ? Would the patination become markedly different within a period of, say, some 20 years ? The stratified evidence of the Azes coins from Taxila also supports the existence of two kings bearing the name of Azes. The occurrence of the early form of the Kh letter *sa* on the coins of Azes found in the lower strata, when compared with the occurrence of the later form of the same letter on the Azes coins from the upper strata, also indicates the existence of two Azes. Moreover, the coins of Azilises themselves show no debasement, and, as such, the debased coins of Azes [II] cannot be placed before him. The view of R C Senior that Azilises started ruling at the same time as Azes, and predeceased the latter, is difficult to accept. But the most clinching evidence in favour of the existence of two kings named Azes is as follows : The dates of Vijayamitra are available from several inscriptions. The Shinkot-Bajaur relic-casket inscriptions refer to his regnal year 5. Then, there is the Indravarman reliquary inscription of Azes year 63, which mentions year 25 of Vijayamitra. A third inscription, the Prahodia inscription, is reported to refer to year 32 of Vijayamitra, and this may be the reason for identifying *apracharaja* whose regnal year 25 is mentioned in the Indravarman reliquary inscription, with Vijayamitra. Finally, there is the so-called 'Bhagamoya' inscription of year 77 of Azes, which also mentions Vijayamitra. If Azes year 63 of the Indravarman relic-casket inscription, is regnal year 25 of Vijayamitra, then Azes year 77 of the 'Bhagamoya' inscription will make regnal year 39 of Vijayamitra. This shows that Vijayamitra must have ruled for 39+ years. The era of Azes is generally identified with Vikrama *saṁvat* commencing 58 BC. On this basis, year 63 of Azes, mentioned in the Indravarman relic casket inscription, comes to 5 AD. This is believed to be the 25th regnal year of Vijayamitra. Hence, Vijayamitra would have started ruling *c* 20 BC. The 'Bhagamoya' inscription shows that he was ruling in Azes year 77, ie, 19 AD. We have joint coins to show that Azes had Indravasu, the son of Vijayamitra, as his subordinate ruler, and Aśpavarman, the son of Vijayamitra's nephew, Indravarman as his *strategos*. If there were only one Azes, this would mean that he survived, not only Vijayamitra, but also received the services of Vijayamitra's son, Indravasu, and of Aśpavarman, the son of Vijayamitra's nephew, Indravarman. According to the 'Bhagamoya' inscription, Vijayamitra was ruling in Azes year 77. To have Aśpavarman serve under him, Azes would require an exceptionally long reign of 77+ years. But if we accept the existence of two kings named Azes, this problem would be solved. We would have an Azes whose year is mentioned in these records, and a second king of that name as overlord of Indravasu and Aśpavarman. Azes I would have been dead at the time of the issue of the Indravarman reliquary inscription of Azes year 63 (= 5 AD), for this epigraph refers to the era as *maharajasa Ayasa atidasa*, 'of the *Maharaja* Aya deceased'. It is quite possible that Azes I was not alive even in the early years of the reign of Vijayamitra. R C Senior seems to be right when he suggests on numismatic grounds, that Vijayamitra asserted himself immediately after the death of Azes, *c* 20 BC (Gardner 1971; Herzfeld 1932; Jenkins 1955; Konow 1929; Konow 1933; van Lohuiaen de Leeuw 1949; N G Majumdar 1928-1929; Marshall 1975; B N Mukherjee 1969a; Senior 2001; Sircar 1980b; Prashant Srivastava 1996a; Prashant Srivastava 2005b; Prashant Srivastava 2007a; Tarn 1980; Whitehead 1914).

Azes I. *Śaka-Pahlava k; son of *Spalirises; first century BC. He started his career as a junior subordinate of *Vonones, while his father, Spalirises, was the senior subordinate ruler. Numismatic evidence shows that later on, Azes I succeeded, not his father, Spalirises, in Arachosia, but *Maues in India. Azes I extended Śaka-Pahlava sway towards eastern Punjab. He is regarded as one of the great rulers of ancient India, who unified a great part of northwestern India. As a junior subordinate ruler under Vonones, Azes I issued some silver coins bearing horseman king and the name of Spalirises as **basileus* **megalos* on the obv; the rev has *Zeus standing with thunderbolt and sceptre and the name of Azes [I] as **maharaja* **mahata*, on which neither Spalirises nor Azes I uses the sovereign title of 'king of kings'. As an independent ruler, Azes I issued both silver and copper coins. The most common obv device, on both the silver and copper issues, is horseman king with spear. Some other silver types have *Zeus standing with spear, or the same deity standing with thunderbolt. The rev devices on silver coins include standing *Nike holding wreath and palm, Zeus holding sceptre, Zeus with thunderbolt, thundering *Athena, and a goddess holding palm and lamp. One silver type from the Gandhāra region has an enthroned city goddess, holding an indistinct object in her r hand on the obv, and standing *Hermes holding 'torque' and **caduceus* on the rev. The obv devices on copper coins include *Poseidon trampling on a river god, male deity (*Śiva ?) holding trident and club, *Hephaistos standing with hammer and tongs, etc. Interestingly, one copper type shows king riding a camel on the obv. The rev devices include Poseidon holding trident, *Amphitrite between two vines, and *Herakles seated on rock or standing and crowning himself. One recently reported square copper type has, on the obv, the depiction of a deity, holding, perhaps, a dolphin, in his r hand, and a trident-topped sceptre in his l hand, and seated on an object, which has been tentatively identified by R C Senior as a river goddess. Senior suggests that the seated deity may be identified as Poseidon. The rev of this coin has a turreted female deity, with her arm around the stem of a tree-in-railing. Animals like humped *bull, *elephant, and *lion are also seen on the obv as well as the rev. The obv ld is in Gr, and has the titles **basileos basileon megalos* for Azes. The rev ld is in Pkt and the script used is Kh. On most of the coins, Azes assumes the titles **maharaja rajaraja mahata* on the rev. But on one copper

Azes I

Azes I

type, he has only *maharaja mahata* as his titles. Towards the end of his rule, he associated his son, *Azilises, in government, issued joint coins with him. These bear horseman king and the name of Azes [I] on the obv, and lamp- and palm-bearing goddess and the name of Azilises on the rev. The form of his name in the rev Pkt ld is *Aya* (Cunningham 1971a; Gardner 1971; Jenkins and Narain 1957; Marshall 1975; B N Mukherjee 1969; Senior 2001; Senior 2003; Sircar 1980b; Prashant Srivastava 1996a; Tarn 1980; Whitehead 1914).[†]

Azes II

Azes II. *Śaka-Pahlava k. He started his career as a junior co-ruler of his father, *Azilises, and issued at least three types of joint coins with him. Both the silver types bear the figure of horseman king and the name of Azilises on the obv. The rev ld refers to Azes [II]. The first type has *Athena thundering on the rev, while the second type has *Zeus Nikephoros standing. The third type is in copper, and has *Herakles crowning himself and the name of Azilises on the obv; the rev has horse walking r, and the name of Azes [II]. Ultimately, Azes II succeeded his father to the throne and issued his independent coinage. He also struck joint coins with *Indravasu, and with *Aśpavarman. Both these types of joint coins have horseman king and the name of Azes [II] on the obv, and Athena holding spear and shield on the rev. The rev ld of the coins struck in association with Indravasu refers to him as 'son of Vijayamitra' and **apracharaja*. The coins issued by Azes II in association with Aśpavarman refer to the latter as 'son of Indravarman' and **stratega* in the rev ld. Thus, Aśpavarman served under Azes II as his commander-in-chief. The coins of Azes II are in silver, copper, and billon. The most common obv device, for both silver and copper issues, is horseman king with whip. The rev of the various silver types has *Athena standing (sometimes crowning herself), Zeus Nikephoros, Zeus standing with sceptre, city-goddess standing (sometimes with **cornocopiae*), and *Poseidon standing with trident. On some copper types, the obv has the king seated on cushions, and holding an *aṅkuśa* in his r hand. Other obv devices on copper coins include *Hermes standing, enthroned city goddess holding **cornucopiae*, a female deity standing and holding flower in her r hand (*Lakshmī ?), *elephant, *bull, and *lion. The rev devices include Zeus Nikephoros, Athena standing, Hermes standing with **caduceus*, standing city goddess,

Azes II

Azes II

Azes II

bull, lion, etc. The billon type has the horseman king with whip on the obv, and a city goddess, holding a *cornucopiae*, on the rev. The obv Gr ld refers to Azes II as *basileos basileon megalos*. The rev Pkt ld in the Kh script usually has *maharaja rajaraja mahata* as the titles of Azes II, but on one silver type, the additional title *dhramiä* has been used. There is a possibility that Gondopharnes invaded the kingdom of Azes II, and defeated him. The form of the name of Azes II in the Pkt ld is Aya (Bopearachchi and Rahman 1995; Cunningham 1971a; Gardner 1971; Jenkins and Narain 1957; Marshall 1975; B N Mukherjee 1969a; Rapson 1987; Raychaudhuri 1982; Senior 2001; Sircar 1980b; Prashant Srivastava 1996a; Tarn 1980; Whitehead 1914).†

Azes II

Azilises. *Śaka-Pahlava k; son of *Azes I; end of the first century BC to beginning of the first century AD. He seems to have started his career as a junior co-ruler of his father, Azes I, whom he ultimately succeeded; R C Senior, however, regards him as the '*sole* successor' of *Maues in Hazara, a view which is difficult to accept. He ruled over the extensive territories, like the Hazara-Kashmir region, and parts of western Gandhāra, which had earlier been under the authority of Maues and Azes I. The depiction *Herakles seated on some of his coins might be indicative of his hold over parts of southern Afghanistan, while that of *Gajalakshmī on the rev of one of his silver types might be indicative of the extension of his sway up to Mathurā in the east. His silver coins issued in association with Azes I bear horseman king and the name of Azes [I] on the obv, and lamp- and palm-bearing goddess and the name of Azilises on the rev. On succeeding his father, Azilises issued his independent coinage in both silver and copper. The most common obv device, for both the silver and copper issues, is the figure of king on horseback, holding a spear or a whip. Other obv devices on silver coins include *Zeus Nikephoros, standing or enthroned, and Zeus standing beside city goddess. The rev devices on his silver issues include the *Dioskuri mounted, either singly or in pair, Dioskuri standing side by side, Zeus standing with sceptre, *Gajalakshmī, and king standing with spear and sword. The obv devices on copper coins include Zeus Nikephoros standing, Herakles standing with club and lion's skin, male deity (*Śiva?) holding club and standing beside *Nike, *Lakshmī seated on an elephant and flanked by two elephants, *Hephaistos standing

Azilises

Azilises

Azilises

Azilises

with hammer and tongs, *Indra on elephant, enthroned city goddess, etc. On one copper type, the king is armed and stands on the ground. The rev devices include Athena thundering, goddess holding palm and/or lamp, Herakles seated on rock, Zeus standing beside city-goddess, etc. Some animals, like *elephant, *bull, *horse, and *lion, may be seen on either of the two sides of the coins. In the obv Gr ld, Azilises uses the titles **basileos basileon megalos*. The rev Pkt ld in the Kh script mostly has **maharaja rajatiraja* (or *rajaraja*) *mahata*, but on at least three copper types occur the titles *maharaja mahata* only. Towards the end of his reign, Azilises seems to have associated his son, *Azes II, in government as a junior co-ruler, and issued at least three types of joint coins with him. Both the silver types bear the figure of horseman king and the name of Azilises on the obv. The rev ld refers to Azes [II]. The first type has *Athena thundering on the rev, while the second type has *Zeus Nikephoros standing. The third type is in copper, and has *Herakles crowning himself and the name of Azilises on the obv; the rev has *horse walking r, and the name of Azes [II]. R C Senior, however, regards these joint issues as 'mules'. The form of the name of Azilises in the Pkt ld is Ayilisha (Cunningham 1971a; Gardner 1971; Herzfeld 1932; Jenkins and Narain 1957; van Lohuizen de Leeuw 1949; Marshall 1975; B N Mukherjee 1969a; Senior 2001; Sircar 1980b; Prashant Srivastava 1996a; Prashant Srivastava 2007a; Tarn 1980; Whitehead 1914).[†]

B

Babyal hoard. This hoard of over 500 silver *punch marked coins bearing a *triskeles* like symbol, was discovered in 1992 at Babyal near Rohtak in Haryana (Rajgor 2001).

BACRI hoard. Ths hoard of over 2,000 *Kuṇinda and *Yaudheya circular, die-struck copper coins, was reportedly found in the Mandi district in the Kangra region of Himachal Pradesh. It is presently housed in the Birla Archaeological and Cultural Research Institute, Hyderabad, and contains a number of interesting coins (Handa 2007a; A M Shastri 1984).

Bahasatimita I. *Kauśāmbī k. The name of this ruler is rendered into Skt as Bṛihaspatimitra by some scholars, and as Bṛihatsvātimitra by others. Some coins, bearing the name Bahasatimita, have been cast in moulds, while others are die-struck pieces. The difference in the type, fabric, and palaeography of the coin legends of the two series has led to the suggestion that Bahasatimita of the cast coins should be distinguished from that of the die-struck coins, and that the former (Bahasatimita I) should be identified with the homonym known from the Mora brick inscription, and the latter (*Bahasatimita II), with the homonym known from the Pabhosa inscription. Bela Lahiri places Bahasatimita I towards the end of the second century BC. His coins bear, on the obv, *horse to the r, **nandipada*, etc, and the ld *Bahasatimitasa*; the rev has an *elephant to the r, *tree-in-railing, *Ujjain symbol, etc (Allan 1936; Bopearachchi and Pieper 1998; Bela Lahiri 1974).

Bahasatimita II. *Kauśāmbī k. He is identified with the homonym known from the Pabhosa inscription, which describes him as a great grandson of *Vaṅgapāla of Ahichchhatrā. Bela Lahiri considers the possibility of Bṛihaspatimitra of the *Pañchāla series and the homonym of the Kauśāmbī coins being identical. The identification of Bahasatimita of the Kauśāmbī coins with the homonym mentioned in the Hathigumpha inscription as the king of Magadha defeated by Khāravela, has been suggested; the depiction of **nandipada* on the Hathigumpha inscription of Khāravela, and the same symbol being countermarked on the coins of Bahasatimita, is taken by K P Jayaswal as indicative of Khāravela's victory of the Kauśāmbī king. But, as Bela Lahiri points out, the following points go against this view: (i) the same symbol is also countermarked on the coins of *Praushṭhamitra, *Agnimitra, and *Jyeshṭhamitra of Kauśāmbī; (ii) no coin of Bahasatimita has been found in Magadha; and (iii) countermarking Kauśāmbī coins by Khāravela would mean his rule over Kauśāmbī, which does not seem to have been the case. It may also be mentioned that, on the Kauśāmbī coins, *nandipada* as a symbol occurs on the coins of *Rāmamitra, and may be, as Bela Lahiri suggests, it was he who counterstruck the coins of these four kings. As the Pabhosa inscription, assigned to the second half of the first century BC, probably refers to him as a former king, he is ascribed to *c* 50 BC. His coins bear, on the obv, *bull to the r, *Ujjain symbol, etc, while the rev has a *tree-in-railing in the centre, *undulating line, and another symbol, and the ld mentioning the name of the king in the genitive. The style, execution, and combination of symbols on his coins also connect him with *Praushṭhamitra, *Agnimitra, and *Jyeshṭhamitra II, and some coins of all these four rulers are countermarked with the *nandipada-triśūla* (Allan 1936; Altekar 1942a; Bopearachchi and Pieper 1998; Bela Lahiri 1974).

Bahasatimitra (=Bṛihaspatimitra or Bṛhatsvātimitra). *Pañchāla k. Nothing much is known about this ruler. Smith mentions his name as a ruler of Pañchāla, but does not describe his coin type (Bela Lahiri 1974; Smith 1972).

Bajaur hoards. Two hoards were reported from the Bajaur region in 1942. These comprised the coins of *Antimachos II, *Apollodotos, and *Menander I, in abundance, along with a limited number of the coins of *Zoilos I—just one coin in the first hoard, and four in the second. The second hoard also contained 700 *punch marked coins, including some *bent bars. A third hoard of 800 *Indo-Greek coins also comes from the same area. The rulers represented in this hoard include Antimachos II, Apollodotos, and Menander I (Bopearachchi 1994; Haughton 1946; Rajgor 2001).

Bakhshali manuscript. It is an ancient treatise on mathematics, written on birch bark in the *Śārada script, discovered in 1881 at Bakhshali near Mardan. It has been dated to the third or fourth century AD by A F R Hoernle, but G R Kaye regards it as not earlier than the ninth or tenth century AD on numismatic and other grounds. Besides coins, it also deals with weights and measures. It refers to **stater*, **dramma*, **dīnāra*, **raktikā*, **aṇḍikā*, **dhānaka*, **kākinī* (**kākaṇī*), *māśaka* (= **māshaka*), and **śāṇa*, which are all regarded as coin denominations (R C Agrawala 1954b).

Balabhūti. *Mathurā k. He issued some coins with *Lakshmī holding lotus in her r hand and the ld *Rājñaḥ Balabhūtisa* on the obv, and three *elephants with riders on the rev. Some of his coins show a standing figure with an uncertain object in the r hand and the same ld on the obv, and tree-in-railing on the rev. Allan expresses the possibility that the issuer of this second type might belong to a dynasty different from that of the issuer of the first type (Allan 1936; Bela Lahiri 1974).

***Bāla-kāhāvaṇa*.** Coin denomination. Mentioned in the **Aṅgavijjā*, it seems to be a silver coin of about 20 *rattīs* issued from the time of *Eukratides I onwards. The prefix *bāla*, 'young', was added to *kāhāvaṇa* to distinguish this **kārshāpaṇa* struck on the reduced standard, from the original *kārshāpaṇa* weighing 32 *rattīs*. These latter coins now came to be designated **ādimūla-kāhāvaṇa* or **purāṇa* (V S Agrawala 1957).

Balarāma. Vaishṇava deity. This son of Vasudeva and Rohiṇī, and the elder brother of *Vāsudeva-Kṛishṇa, is one of the five deified heroes of the Yādava-Sātvata-Vṛishṇi clan, one of the four *vyūhas* worshipped by the followers of Bhāgavata sect, and is sometimes regarded as one of the incarnations of *Vishṇu; according to one view, while Vāsudeva-Kṛishṇa was a full manifestation of Vishṇu, Balarāma was a partial *avatāra* of that deity. Vögel is of the view that the worship of Balarāma in Bhāgavatism is the result of the assimilation of a nāga deity in that cult. He has the plough (*hala*) as his attribute, which hints at his association with agriculture. Six coins issued by the *Indo-Greek ruler, *Agathokles, were discovered in the course of excavations at Ai Khanum, on the border of Afghanistan and the former USSR, by Paul Bernard. These coins bear, on the rev, the figure of Vāsudeva-Kṛishṇa. The obv has the figure of a helmeted male deity, dressed in *dhotī* and *uttarīya*, and wearing 'strange half-boots having curved sole-ends'. According to Bernard, he holds a *gadā* in his r hand, while in his l hand, he holds a strange instrument which ends in a 'Z' shape, and looking 'somewhat between an *aṅkuśa* and a *hala'*. A sword in a sheath hangs on a cross belt at his left. Bernard proposes to identify this figure, either as that of the king represented as a *chakravartin*—although he is not very keen about this identification—or of *Śiva. But A K Narain identifies this figure with Balarāma, as he feels that it is actually shown bearing a *muśala* and a *hala*, the two attributes associated with that deity. Incidentally, this accords well with the description of the deity as given in the *Vaikhānasāgama*, which says that he should be shown holding a *muśala* in his r hand, and a *hala* in his l hand. On the obv of a square copper type of the *Śaka-Pahlava ruler, *Maues, there occurs the figure of an Indian deity walking to the l, who, according to the R C Senior, holds a club in his r hand, and a 'plough' over his left shoulder. Senior identifies this deity as 'Bala-Kṛishṇa', by which he seems to mean a syncretic deity, Balarāma-Vāsudeva-Kṛishṇa. This representation would be interesting, if the identification proposed by Senior is correct, as such a syncretic form of Balarāma and Vāsudeva-Kṛishṇa is, perhaps, not known from any other source. Although there seems to be no doubt that the object in the upraised r hand of the deity on the coin is a club, the presence of the plough on the left should of the deity, as suggested by Senior, is open to doubt. On the rev of the coins of Agathokles (above), the plough in the upraised l hand of Balarāma is quite clear, the deity holding it by its pole. However, on the obv of the type of Maues, the l hand of the deity depicted hangs down and appears to touch the thigh; it does not seem to be holding any object. From the illustration produced by Senior, the curved object over the left

Fig.1: Balarāma

shoulder of the deity seems to be surmounted by something, which would be difficult to explain if the curved object is taken to be a plough. A similar curved object, though somewhat smaller in size, is also seen over the r shoulder. The pole of the 'plough' is also not visible on the coin. On the whole, nothing definite can be said about the object over the left shoulder of the deity, or about the identity of the deity himself. Senior reports the occurrence of a similar deity holding a female divinity in one hand on some types of Azilises. On some round copper coins, of uncertain provenance, occurs a device, which is described by Allan as 'bushy tree in railing'. But J N Banerjea proposes to identify it as a column surmounted by a fan-palm capital, similar to those discovered at Besnagar and Pawaya. This may have some connection with Balarāma, who has a fan-palm for his banner and is, consequently, called *Tāladhvaja* (Allan 1936; Banerjea 2002; Sukumari Bhattacharji 1970; S R Goyal 1986; T R R Iyengar 2003; Narain 1973; Senior 2001; Sircar 1971; Sircar 1986; Wilkins 2006).[†]

Fig.2: 'Bala-Kṛishṇa'?

Balavāhana/Balavighna (?). *Vṛishṇi general (?).

Baldwin hoard. This hoard, perhaps from Akhnoor or Jammu, was reported by Michael Mitchiner. The rulers represented in this hoard include *Strato I and *Rañjuvula; there is also a posthumous *Azes I coin (Mitchiner 1975-1976; Senior 2001).

Bamnala hoard. This hoard of 21 *Imperial Gupta gold coins was found in 1940 at the village Bamnala, district Nimar (Madhya Pradesh). The rulers represented in this hoard are *Samudragupta, *Chandragupta II, and Kumāragupta I (Altekar 1957).

Bargama hoard. This mixed hoard of the local *punch marked coins of the Magadha *janapada*, and of another *janapada* the identity of which is not certain, was discovered about a century ago from the village Bargama in the Shahdol district of Madhya Pradesh. It is originally said to have comprised some 2,500-3,000 coins, but parts of the hoard have been disposed off at intervals. A study of some 186 coins from this hoard, all conforming to the **kārshāpaṇa* weight standard, shows that 68 of these coins are the local punch marked coins of the Magadha *janapada*, and bear five symbols. The remaining 118 coins in the study have four symbols punched on them, and these have been attributed, variously and generally tentatively, to Kaliṅga *janapada*, Chedi *janapada*, or Kosala/Dakshiṇa Kosala *janapada* (Sharad Sharma and B P Verma 2001-2002).

Barwani hoard. This hoard of silver *punch marked coins of the Imperial series was found around 1943 in the village Pati in the former Barwani state in Madhya Pradesh. Initially, it was reported to comprise 3,450 coins, but at present, the hoard, now in the National Museum, New Delhi, is reported to consist of 3,420 coins only. It is believed to be the largest hoard of silver punch marked coins found so far in northern India (P L Gupta 1992).

Basileos basileon megalos. Title. Literally meaning 'king of kings, the great', this apparently 'Scythian' or 'Iranian' title was assumed by sovereign *Śaka-Pahlava rulers, the subordinate ones using the title of **basileus* and **maharaja*. In Pkt, it was rendered as **maharaja rajatiraja* (or *rajaraja*) *mahata*. The title of *basileos basileon* is believed to have been first used on coins by the Arsakid ruler, Mithridates II, *c* 109 BC. The Śaka-Pahlava rulers, who assumed this title on coins, are *Maues, *Azes I, *Azilises, *Azes II, *Vonones, *Gondopharnes, *Abdagases, and *Pakores. Interestingly, on the coins of Maues, the title has been rendered into Pkt as *rajatiraja mahata* only (Gardner 1971; Marshall 1975; Rapson 1987; Senior 2001; Tarn 1980; Whitehead 1914; Wroth 1903).

Basileuontos. This term was first used for themselves in the rev ld by *Agathokles and *Antimachos I on their commemorative coins, and there has been a lot of debate over the exact import of this term. De Bartholomaei is of the view that it denotes a title superior to **basileus*. Droysen, however, argued that it denotes a subordinate position, and is inferior to *basileus*. The view of Droysen is supported by Cunningham. The title of *basileuontos* occurs on a coin of Arsakes XII of Parthia, who served under his father as a subordinate king. If this coin was issued during the lifetime of the father of Arsakes XII, as Cunningham supposes, it must, of necessity, be a title inferior to *basileus*. Cunningham renders it as lieutenant. However, in two Ptolemaic epigraphs, the Rosetta Stone and the Tanaitic inscription, the term *basileuontos* appears simply to mean 'during the reign'.

It is now accepted by most of the scholars that *basileuontos* on the commemorative coins of Agathokles and Antimachos I, too, occurs in this very sense. Agathokles and Antimachos I themselves do not use the title of *basileus* when they mention themselves as the commemorators on the rev of these coins, perhaps out of regard for the commemorated kings who have not been given the title of *basileus*; instead they use the epithets of **dikaios* and **theos*, respectively, and the ld, in both the cases, begins with *basileuontos*, 'during the reign'. Interestingly, the term appears also on the coin of *Mamvadi (For references, see Prashant Srivastava 1996a; also Senior 2001).

Basileuontos basileon. Title. This title was assumed by the *Śaka-Pahlava ruler, *Abdagases, and by the *Apracha ruler, Sapedana, on some of their coins. The import of this title is uncertain (Gardner 1971; Marshall 1975; Rapson 1987; Senior 2001; Tarn 1980; Whitehead 1914).

Basileus. Title. Meaning 'king', this title was borne by all the Indo-Greek kings, and following them, by the *Śaka-Pahlava and the early *Kushāṇa kings as well. In the Kh ld, *basileus* is generally rendered as **maharajasa*, but as *rajañe* on some coins of *Pantaleon and *Agathokles, and *rajasa* on *drachms* issued on the Indian standard by *Eukratides. Besides *basileus*, some Indo-Greek kings took one or more epithet(s) also. In the *Śaka-Pahlava period, it became the title of subordinate rulers, and was assumed by *Maues, *Abdagases, and *Sanabares (Cunningham 1970; Gardner 1971; A N Lahiri 1965; Marshall 1975; Narain 1957a; Tarn 1980; Whitehead 1914).

Basilissa. Title. Meaning 'queen', this title was first adopted by the *Indo-Greek queen-regent *Agathokleia, and later by the *Śaka-Pahlava queen-regent *Machenes (Cunningham 1970; Gardner 1971; A N Lahiri 1965; Marshall 1975; Narain 1957a; Tarn 1980; Whitehead 1914).

Basti hoard. This hoard of 11 *Imperial Gupta gold coins was discovered in 1887 in Basti (Uttar Pradesh). Only 10 of these coins could be recovered, all of which belong to *Chandragupta II (Altekar 1957).

Samudragupta : Battle-axe type

Samudragupta : Battle-axe type

Battle-axe type. Gold. This type of *Samudragupta was produced by replacing the standard in the hand of the king on his *Standard type, with a battle-axe, just as his *Archer type was produced by replacing the standard with a bow. The obv has the nimbate king, standing with a battle-axe in the l hand, while the r hand is on waist akimbo. Before the king is a dwarf attendant looking up at him. There is a crescent standard between the two. The circular ld reads *Kṛitāntaparaśu jayatyajitarājajetājitaḥ*. The rev bears the enthroned figure of *Lakshmī, with a *pāśa* in her r hand, and a **cornucopiae* or lotus bud in her l hand. The ld on the rev is *Kṛitāntaparaśuḥ*. The type is divided into two classes on the basis of the relative position of the king and the attendant. Interestingly, the epithet *Kṛitāntaparaśu* is used for Samudragupta in some inscriptions of his successors (Ashvini Agrawal 1989; Allan 1914; Altekar 1957; R D Banerji 1933; S R Goyal 2005; P L Gupta 1998; Smith 1972; Thaplyal, forthcoming).

Bayana hoard. This hoard of apparently 2,100 *Imperial Gupta gold coins was discovered in 1946 in the village Hullanpur near Bayana (Rajasthan). Of these, only 1,821 coins could be recovered. This is the biggest hoard of Imperial Gupta gold coins known so far. The rulers represented in the hoard are *Chandragupta I, *Samudragupta, *Kācha, *Chandragupta II, *Kumāragupta I, and (*Skandagupta) Kramāditya (Altekar 1955; Altekar 1957; B Ch Chhabra 1986).

Bent bar

Bent bars. These coins, a class of the silver *punch marked coins, are local to northwestern India, particularly the Gandhāra region. They are so called because the specimens, which were available earlier, were in the form of bars, bent into a concave shape when marks were punched on them. But later on, such specimens came to the light, which are not bent, and as such, the name of bent bars is no longer an apt one. Scholars now prefer to call them wheel marked coins, as these coins bear the mark(s) of wheel on the concave side. These coins are of two types : (i) larger, with two wheel marks on the concave side (the obv), the convex (rev) side being blank, and (ii) smaller, with only one wheel mark, and representing lower denomination. Smith dates these bent bars between 600 BC and 500 BC. Chakrabortty regards them as weights, and not as coins.

Allan considers the bent bars of the full-sized variety as representing double-*siglos* of 172 grains, and those of the smaller variety, its lower denomination. But the Persian *siglos* was an oval globule with the figure of the king punched on it, while the blank of the bent bars was chipped from a long bar, and impressed with the device by a punch. Further, a *siglos* weighed 86 grains, and this would make a double-*siglos* 172 grains in weight; the average weight of a full bent bar is 179.6 grains, to which, margin should be given to wear and tear. This fits better with the view of V S Agrawala and others that the full sized bent bars represent the **śatamāna* currency of 100 **rattī* (about 180 grains) unit. It must, however, be pointed out that Manu gives the weight of a *śatamāna* as 320 *rattīs*. Allan is of the opinion that the *signati argenti*, 'coined silver money', presented by the king of Taxila to Alexander, refer to the bent bars. It is difficult to say which agency (kings or guilds) issued the bent bars (Allan 1936; Pratipal Bhatia 1989; Chakrabortty 1931; Cribb 2005; Cunningham 1971b; Mitchiner 1973; Rajgor 2001; Smith 1972).

Bhabua hoard 1. This hoard of 90 silver *punch marked coins, mostly belonging to the Kāśī *janapada*, was discovered in 1953 at Bhabua in the Rohtas district of Bihar (Rajgor 2001).

Bhabua hoard 2. This hoard of 450 silver *punch marked coins was discovered in 1981 at Bhabua in the Rohtas district of Bihar. Some of the coins in the hoard belong to the Kāśī *janapada* (Rajgor 2001).

Bhabua hoard 3. This hoard of 90 silver *punch marked coins of the Kāśī *janapada* was discovered in 1991 at Bhabua in the Rohtas district of Bihar (Rajgor 2001).

Bhadrā. Deity. On the rev of the coins of the *Pañchāla ruler, *Bhadraghosha, occurs the figure of a female divinity, standing facing on a lotus bloom. The iconographic features of this goddess are not clear, as is usual on the Pañchāla series, and Allan proposes to identify her as Bhadrā, 'in allusion to the name of Bhadraghosha'. It may be pointed out that in the Pañchāla series, there is the tradition of depicting on the rev of the coin, a divinity in anthropomorphic or symbolic form, who name usually forms a component of the name of the issuer. J N Banerjea suggests that this Bhadrā may be *Lakshmī, or, alternatively, *Durgā who is associated with *Vāsudeva-Kṛishṇa and *Balarāma as their sister Subhadrā or Ekānaṁśā (Allan 1936; Banerjea 2002; Dasgupta 1974).

Bhadraghosha. *Pañchāla k. The appearance of the rev symbol of *Vaṅgapāla on the coins of Bhadraghosha and *Phalgunīmitra is taken to indicate that they ruled after Vaṅgapāla. Bela Lahiri places Bhadraghosha in the eighth chronological position among the Pañchāla kings known from coins. He seems to be associated with *Bhānumitra and *Sūryamitra, because on some coins of all these three kings, the second Pañchāla symbol is counterstruck by the third one. The female deity represented on the rev of his coins is recognized as *Bhadrā (Allan 1936; Bela Lahiri 1974).

Bhadramagha. *Magha k.

Bhadramukha. Dynasty. *Kārddamaka.

Bhadrayaśa. *Śaka-Pahlava (?) k. He is known from a few coins in silver, bearing the diademed bust of the king and a blundered Gr ld, quite similar to that on the coins of *Zoilos, on the obv, and thundering *Athena and a Kh ld referring to Bhadrayaśa as **maharaja* and **tratara* on the rev. Hoard evidence seems to suggest that he ruled over parts of Hazara-Kashmir region after *Strato I. He might have preceded or succeeded *Rañjuvula in that area. He might be identical with the homonym, mentioned in a Jaina inscription from Mathurā (B N Mukherjee 1969a; Senior 2001).

Bhāga. Coin denomination. This is mentioned as another name for **ardha-kārshāpaṇa* in the **Ashṭādhyāyī* (V S Agrawala 1953).

Bhāgabhadra. Śuṅga (?) k. Mentioned in the Besnagar *garuḍa* pillar inscription of the time of Bhāgabhadra, he is generally identified with the Śuṅga ruler, Bhāgavata, referred to in the puranic lists. Dinkar Rao has published a rectangular copper coin, with blank rev, obtained from a footpath coin dealer at Delhi. The obv of the coin has a big symbol, perhaps a **svastika*, and a ld, restored by Rao as *Suṅgo Bhadasa*, which he interprets as *Śuṅgaḥ Bhadrasya*, and ascribes this coin to the Śuṅga ruler, Bhāgabhadra. But, in his editorial note on Rao's paper, P L Gupta has doubted the reading of the ld as restored by Rao, and the attribution of this coin to the Śuṅga ruler, Bhāgabhadra (Dinkar Rao 1977).

Bhāgila. City coins. Five coins from Hoshangabad district (Madhya Pradesh), bearing the ld *Bhāgilāya*, in *c* second century BC characters, are taken to be city coins, as Bhāgila appears to be the name of a city, not far from Sanchi (Bela Lahiri 1974; Bela Lahiri 1976; J P Singh 1971).

***Bhaṁmaka* (?).** Coin denomination (?). A small Kh inscription, discovered by Aurel Stein on a wall painting of an ancient shrine in Chinese Turkestan, is said to refer to a painter, Tita (= Titus) by name, who received 300 *bhaṁmakas* for executing that fresco. Stein regards this *bhaṁmaka* as denoting 'some monetary value', and he identifies it with the Skt *bharman*, which, according to Monier-Williams, denotes a 'coin' as well as 'gold'. But R C Agrawala points out that the first two letters, read as *bha* and *ma*, respectively, are not very clear in the inscription, and he proposes to the read the word as **nāṇaka* (R C Agrawala 1954a; Monier-Williams 2005; Stein 1921).

Bhānugh[osha]. *Yaudheya (?) chief. His name is reported to occur on some copper coins from the *Chakkar hoard. K K Maheshwari regards him as a Yaudheya chief, but P L Gupta associated him with the family of the Varsha *gaṇa* (P L Gupta 1987; P L Gupta 1988; Handa 2007a; K K Maheshwari 1978).

Bhānugupta *Prakāśāditya*. *Imperial Gupta k; son of Pūrugupta; early sixth century AD. He is known from the Eran pillar inscription of *Gupta era 191 (= 510 AD), which records that Goparāja, an ally of Bhānugupta, died fighting, most probably the *Hūṇas. The result of the battle is not known from this inscription, although there are indications that Bhānugupta succeeded in worsting his adversaries. R C Majumdar suggested the possibility of the division of the Gupta empire among three Imperial Gupta rulers, with Bhānugupta ruling over of the western provinces, *Vainyagupta over the eastern provinces, and *Narasiṁhagupta over the rest of the territories. The

Bhānugupta :
Horseman-lion-slayer type

Bhānugupta :
Horseman-lion-slayer type

Bhānugupta : Archer type

attribution of the *Horse-rider-lion-slayer type of gold coins, bearing the ld *Śrī-Prakāśāditya*, has long been the subject of debate among scholars, because the name of the issuing king in the obv ld could not be properly read. This Prakāśāditya was variously identified with Pūrugupta, Yaśodharman of Malwa, or *Budhagupta. But the name of the issuing king has been read as Bhānugupta in the obv ld of a coin of this type from the Safipur *tehsil* (District Unnao, Uttar Pradesh). This put to an end all the controversies regarding the identity of Prakāśāditya, and the attribution of these coins. Incidentally, with the identification of Prakāśāditya with Bhānugupta, the find of these coins from Rampur, Shahjahanpur, Kanauj, Hardoi, Unnao, and Varanasi in Uttar Pradesh, would render untenable the view that the authority of Bhānugupta was confined only to the western provinces of the Gupta empire (Ashvini Agrawal 1989; Allan 1914; Altekar 1957; R D Banerji 1933; Fleet 1888; S R Goyal 2005; P L Gupta 1998; K P Jayaswal 1933; R C Majumdar 1988; K S Shukla 1980; Smith 1972; Prashant Srivastava 1996a; Thaplyal, forthcoming).†

Bhānumitra. *Pañchāla k. He seems to be associated with *Bhadraghosha and *Sūryamitra, because on some coins of all these three kings, the second Pañchāla symbol is counterstruck by the third one. Bela Lahiri places him in the ninth chronological position among the Pañchāla kings known from coins. The rev of his coins bears the solar disc on a pedestal between two pillars (Allan 1936; Bela Lahiri 1974).

Bhānuva. *Yaudheya chief. His name, sometimes with the title **rājña*, occurs on Class V of the *Yaudheya coins. P L Gupta suggests that his full name might be Bhānuvarman. K K Maheshwari expresses the possibility that the name might have been *Bhānugh[osha] (Allan 1936; K K Dasgupta 1974; P L Gupta 1987; P L Gupta 1988; Handa 2007a; K K Maheshwari 1978).

Bharsar hoard. This hoard of 160 coins was discovered in 1851 at Bharsar near Varanasi (Uttar Pradesh). Details of only 32 of these coins are known. The *Imperial Gupta rulers represented in this hoard are *Samudragupta, *Chandragupta II, *Kumāragupta I, *Skandagupta and (*Bhānugupta) Prakāśāditya. Allan records that of the 160 coins of this hoard, only 90 could be recovered. Out of these 90 coins, 71 belonged to Chandragupta II (Allan 1914; Altekar 1957).

Bhartṛidāman. *Kārddamaka k. He was the son of *Rudrasena II, and started his career as a **kshatrapa* in the year 200, perhaps under his father. Later on, he ruled as **mahākshatrapa*, and the coins issued by him in that capacity bear the dates of *Śaka year 204-217. The stone inscription from Mewasa in the Kachchh district of Gujarat has been referred to his reign. All his coins are of the *Kārddamaka silver type (Jha and Rajgor 1994; Mirashi 1982; Mitchiner 1976; Rapson 1975; Raychaudhuri 1972; Senior 2001; Sircar 1980e).

Bhavadatta. *Mathurā k. He issued coins, which show *Lakshmī with lotus in her r hand and some symbols on the obv; and three *elephants with riders on the rev. The rev device is degenerate (Allan 1936; Bela Lahiri 1974).

Bhavadattarāja. *Nala k.

Bhavanāga. *Nāga k. He is known not only from coins, but also from Vākāṭaka records which describe him as the maternal grandfather of Rudrasena I. This would place Bhavanāga at the end of the third or the beginning of the fourth century AD, quite near *Gaṇapatināga. On some coins, he is given the title of *adhirāja*, showing his exalted position, and it is likely that he performed some of the ten *aśvamedhas* ascribed to the Bhāraśiva Nāgas. He is associated with *Bṛihasaptināga and *Devanāga by the use of the 'Trident' type. He also issued the 'Bull' type of coins. He assumed the title of **mahārāja-śrī* on coins (Bela Lahiri 1974; H V Trivedi 1957).

Bhavavarman. *Vemaki chief.

Bhimajhunasa. *Parataraja k.

Bhīmanāga. *Nāga k. He is associated with *Vasunāga, *Skandanāga, and *Bṛihaspatināga by the use of the 'Peacock' type. He seems to be earlier than the other three rulers on the grounds that the ld on the rev of his coins is engraved in two straight lines, as against the custom of writing it in a circular fashion so common on Nāga coins. He is among the few Nāga rulers who did not issue the 'Bull' type of coins, although a coin of this type has doubtfully been attributed to him. He assumed the title of **mahārāja* on coins (Cunningham 1967; Bela Lahiri 1974; H V Trivedi 1957).

Bhīmavarman. *Magha k.

Bhir Mound hoard. This hoard of 1,167 silver *punch marked coins was found in 1924 from the Bhir Mound at Taxila. It includes 1,055 regular silver *punch marked coins, 33 *bent bars, and 79 'minute' coins, together with two coins of Alexander, and one coin of Philip Aridaeus (Walsh 1975; Rajgor 2001).

Bhitaura haord. This hoard of 531 coins was found in an earthen pot in the village of Bhitaura near Faizabad (Uttar Pradesh). Of these 531 coins, one is a gold piece of the Later Indo-Scythian type, 522 silver coins, and eight copper coins. The copper coins all belong to Pratāpāditya II of Kashmir. Three of the 522 silver coins are *Ādivarāha drammas*, while one is of uncertain type. The remaining 518 silver coins are all of the **Madhyadeśa* type of *Imperial Gupta silver coins, that is bearing the royal head to the r and the date of issue on the obv, and a fan-tailed *peacock and the Br ld *Vijitāvaniravanipati-śrī*-(name of issuer) *divaṁ jayati* on the rev. The names, and in many cases also the date, on 192 of these coins are lost; 284 coins bear the name Śrī Śīlāditya (generally identified with *Harsha); nine bear the name Śrī Pratāpaśīla (generally identified with *Prabhākaravardhana); 32 are *Maukhari coins; and one belongs to a king named Harśa (not Harsha) (Richard Burn 1906; D Devahuti 1964).

Bhūmaka. *Kshaharāta k. He is one of the earliest known **kshatrapas*, who was appointed by the Kushāṇa ruler to administer the southwestern parts of the empire, although doubts have recently been expressed from certain quarters regarding his subordinate status. Sylvain Lévi's view, that Bhūmaka should be identified with Ysāmotika, the father of *Chashṭana, as *ysama* is the Śaka word for the earth (Skt, *bhūmi*), does not seem to be convincing. The find of his coins from the coastal regions of Gujarat, parts of Malwa, and the Ajmer region of Rajasthan give us an idea of the territories under his rule. He issued coins in copper, lead, and an alloy of copper and lead. The obv of his round coins in all the metals and the alloy bears an arrow on the left, and thunderbolt on the r, and a discus in the centre. The obv ld in Kh reads *Chhaharadasa Chhatrapasa Bhumakasa*. The rev has capital of a pillar surmounted by a *lion and a *wheel. The Br ld on the rev reads *Kshaharātasa Kshatrapasa Bhūmakasa*. But one copper coin in the collection of the Mathurā Museum, rectangular in shape, has an arrow and a thunderbolt and no ld on the obv, while the rev has a four-spoked wheel in the centre and the Br ld *Kshaharātasa Bhūmakasa* (Jha and Rajgor 1994; Mirashi 1982; Mitchiner 1976; Rapson 1975; Raychaudhuri 1972; Senior 2001; A M Shastri 1995; Sircar 1980e).[†]

Bhūmimitra. *Pañchāla k. He is placed immediately after *Agnimitra, in the twelfth chronological position among the Pañchāla rulers known from coins, mainly because the deity on the rev of his coins resembles that on the coins of Agnimitra. Cunningham identifies the deity on the coins of Bhūmimitra as the earth goddess, but Allan takes it as 'King of Nāgas representing the Earth', as the hair are represented by five nāgas, and there is a snake in the hand of the figure (Allan 1936; Bela Lahiri 1974).

Pañchāla : Bhūmimitra

Bījakosha. It is generally believed that the goddess on the rev of the early *Imperial Gupta coins (*Simhavāhinī Devī*, *Lakshmī) holds a **cornucopiae* in one of her hands, on the grounds that this goddess was modelled after **Ardochsho* of the *Kushāṇa coins who usually holds this attribute, and *cornucopiae* as a symbol of plenty and prosperity suits Lakshmī. But as early as 1885, Theobald had noticed that the alleged *cornucopiae* depicted on Imperial Gupta coins is markedly different from the *cornucopiae* seen in the hands of *Demeter, **Ardochsho*, and others on *Indo-Greek, *Śaka-Pahlava, and Kushāṇa coins, in that while the latter is shown overflowing with fruits and grains, the former seems to be closed by a convex line decorated with pellets or dots. But, a *cornucopiae* 'can never have a lid on its mouth'. There is a suggestion that when the device of *Ardochsho* of Kushāṇa coins was being Indianized by the Imperial Gupta mint-masters, in order to transform *Ardochsho* into the Lakshmī, the *cornucopiae* in the hand of the goddess on Kushāṇa

Samudragupta : Standard type

Samudragupta : Lyrist type

Chandragupta II : Archer type

Samudragupta : Archer type

coins was replaced by a *bījakosha* (lotus seed chamber), which is not only known in India as a source of wealth, but is also similar in shape to a *cornucopiae*. Thus, by giving a slightly different form to this attribute of the goddess, the idea of plenty and prosperity was conveyed 'through an approximately similar drawing', and this became an apt attribute for Lakshmī, the Indian goddess of wealth. A further development of the motif was the replacement of the *bījakosha* by a stalked lotus in the hand of the goddess on later coins (V S Agrawala 1955; Allan 1914; Altekar 1957; Sohoni 1957; Prashant Srivastava 2007e).

Billon. Metal (alloy) for coins. Some amount of alloy was required to impart the necessary hardness to the metal used for the manufacture of coins; some amount might have remained due to the difficulty in separating the metals. But the deliberate use of mixed metals, like *potin, billon, and *brass, for coinage was, perhaps, 'the result of conscious attempt at depreciation promoted by avarice or due to financial stress'. Billon is described thus in the *Encyclopaedia Britannica* : 'it is silver with a great proportion of alloy', but others hold that it is a mixture of copper, pewter, lead, and 'a little silver'. In the third century AD, the Roman emperors minted extensively in billon. The *Indo-Greek ruler, *Strato I, is known to have struck billon coins also (Cunningham 1970; Junge 1984; A N Lahiri 1965).

Bimetallism. Bimetallism is a currency system, in which two metallic standards are adhered to at one and the same time, like gold and silver, or silver and copper. The working of this system is very difficult, since it requires constant revaluation of metal to the fluctuations in the relative values of the two metals involved. The ratio between two metals varies, with the change in the value of either metal, and if the weight of the coin of one of the two metals is kept constant, the weight of the other would have to be varied. The situation is further complicated if a third metallic standard is introduced, as, for example, the introduction of gold coinage by the *Kushāṇas [trimetallism]. This may account, to some extent, for the variations in the weight of some existing specimens from the weight of the theoretic standard coins (D R Bhandarkar 1984; Chakrabortty 1931; Junge 1984).

Bizago. Deity. See *Kārttikeya.

Blank. *Flan.

Boar. Symbol. Boar is associated in Indian mythology with *Vishṇu, who is known to have incarnated as a *varāha*. But the device of a boar's head appearing on the obv of one of the copper types of *Menander, does not seem to have Vaishṇava affiliations (A N Lahiri 1965).

Boddo. *Buddha, Śākyamuni.

Bow and quiver. Symbol. These weapons appear on the rev of a copper type of the *Indo-Greek ruler, *Strato I, having the bust of *Apollo on the obv (Bopearachchi 1993; Bopearachchi and Pieper 1998; Bopearachchi and Rahman 1995; A N Lahiri 1965).

Bow case and club. Symbol. These weapons were a quite common device on the coins of the Arsakids, and their appearance on the rev of a copper type of the *Indo-Greek ruler, Zoilos I, seems to suggest his conquest of certain Arsakid territories. Marshall is of the view that the depiction of the bow-in-case on a type of the *Śaka-Pahlava ruler, *Maues, seems to indicate his fealty to the Arsakid ruler, Mithridates II, although there are some difficulties, chronological and otherwise, in accepting this (Bopearachchi 1993; Bopearachchi and Pieper 1998; Bopearachchi and Rahman 1995; Cunningham 1970; Cunningham 1971a; Gardner 1971; Jenkins and Narain 1957; A N Lahiri 1965; Marshall 1975; Senior 2001; Whitehead 1914).

Brahmamitra. *Kanauj k. His coins are not known from Kanauj, and he has been regarded as a ruler of Kanauj only on the basis of the general similarity of his coins with that of *Vishṇudeva, in that they all bear three symbols on the obv. However, only the *tree-in-railing on the obv is common with the coin of Vishṇudeva; the other two symbols on the coins of Brahmamitra are the *Ujjain symbol, and the *triangular-headed symbol. The rev of the coins of Brahmamitra is not very clear. K D Bajpai regards him as identical with *Brahmamitra known from *Kauśāmbī coins, but this is not likely as the coins of the two rulers named Brahmamitra are quite different from each other. Bela Lahiri proposes to identify him with *Brahmamitra of *Mathurā, whose coins, too, bear the Ujjain symbol. She feels that Brahmamitra of Mathurā might have extended his sway towards Kanauj. Bela Lahiri assigned him to the first century BC (Allan 1936; K D Bajpai 1964; Bela Lahiri 1974).

Brahmamitra. *Mathurā k. He issued coins, which show *Lakshmī with lotus in her r hand and some symbols on the obv; and three *elephants with riders on the rev. Powell-Price considers him as a *Pañchāla ruler, rather than a king of Mathurā. But his coins show features of the Mathurā coins, which are quite different from the Pañchāla coins, and also the name Brahmamitra is not met with in the Pañchāla series. Some scholars take him as identical with the homonym known from *Kanauj coins (Allan 1936; Bela Lahiri 1974).

Brāhmī. Script. The name Brāhmī, which occurs at the top of the lists of scripts in some Buddhist and Jaina texts, was used for the first time by Bühler for the script in which most of the Aśokan inscriptions are engraved. Although the Harappan Indians were using a writing system in the third millennium BC, there is no clear relationship between the Harappan and the Br scripts. While some scholars believe that a system of writing was current among the vedic Indians, others take the antiquity of writing in India in the post-Harappan period variously to the eighth century BC, or the sixth century BC, or the fifth century BC, or the time of Aśoka (third century BC). The origin of the Br script, too, is a subject of debate among scholars, with some of them subscribing to the theory of indigenous origin, and others, to that of foreign origin. While Edward Thomas suggests a Dravidian origin of the Br script, Cunningham, Dawson, Lassen, Ojha, and R B Pandey believe in the vedic origin of that script, and Shamasastry derives its characters from Tantric signs and symbols. Among the advocates of the foreign origin of the Br script, Greek inspiration or influence has been suggested by Prinsep, F Max Müller, Senart, de Rochette, Wilson, and Halevy. But, it appears that the Br script had come into existence much before the earliest cultural contacts between the Indians and the Greeks. In 1806, Jones suggested a Semitic origin of the Br script, and this has been supported by a number of scholars. Some, like Benfey, Weber, Bühler, and Jensen, regard Br as a derivative of the Phoenician script; Deecke, Taylor, and Sethe advocate a south Semitic origin of Br; while Diringer holds that the early Aramaic script served as the prototype for the Br script. Rhys Davids suggests that the Br characters might have been derived from a pre-Semitic system of writing, from which both the north and south Semitic scripts also originated. Dani also feels that some 11 characters of Br may be based on north Semitic and early Phoenician characters, and the 'idea may have been brought from further afield'. To this, L Gopal objects : 'But if only idea was needed for the creation of the Br script there is no need for a cumbersome exercise to derive the forms of only 11 out of 46 letters from n. Semitic and early Phoenician scripts. The Indian *varṇa-mālā* was in existence well before Pāṇini, and even before Yāska. To create a script on the basis of the *varṇa-mālā* with the help of simple geometrical signs—angle, triangle, hook, dash and dot—was not a difficult task.' Br script is written from left to the r, except for a few rare cases where the writing is in the boustrophedon method. Aśokan Br does not show any regional differentiation, the differences in the forms of letters being due to scribes. But later, all the Indian, and many of the south-east Asian scripts, developed from Br due to factors like 'regional cultures, personal mannerisms, efforts at speed, beautification and decoration and the writing materials and the tools'. In the period second century BC to first century AD, the four broad regional variations of Br were the eastern, north-western, Deccan and south Indian. The Br of *c* 350 AD was classified by Bühler into nine north Indian, and five south Indian styles. Dani classified the regional scripts into four geographical groups, with three regional scripts in the north Indian group, two in the Gujarat, Rajasthan and central Indian group, one in the Deccan group, and three in the south Indian group (Bühler 1904; Dani 1997; Diringer 2005; L Gopal and T P Verma 1989; Ojha 1959; R B Pandey 1953).

Brass. Metal (alloy) for coins. Some amount of alloy was required to impart the necessary hardness to the metal used for the manufacture of coins; some amount might have remained due to the difficulty in separating the metals. But the deliberate use of mixed metals, like *potin, *billon, and brass, for coinage was, perhaps, 'the result of conscious attempt at depreciation promoted by avarice or due to financial stress'. Brass is an alloy of copper and zinc, usually in the proportion of 2 : 1 or 4 : 3, and was used for minting coins by the *Rājanyas, as also by the *Yaudheyas, three of whose brass coins are reported in the Indian Museum, Calcutta. It was used for manufacture of coins by the *Imperial Guptas also, as pointed out by C D Chatterjee. Interestingly, some Chinese coins, though said to be struck in bronze, actually contain 30% zinc, and are, thus, brass coins (C D Chatterjee 1957; Junge 1984; Smith 1972).

Bṛihaspatināga. *Nāga k. He is believed to have succeeded Skandanāga, as he issued both 'Peacock' and 'Trident' type of coins, thus connecting the two groups of kings who used these two types, respectively. He has been given the credit for introducing the 'Trident' type among the Nāgas. Besides, he also issued the 'Bull' and 'Wheel' types of coins. He was followed by Devanāga and *Bhavanāga, perhaps in this very order. He assumed the title of **mahārāja* on coins (Cunningham 1967; Bela Lahiri 1974; H V Trivedi 1957).

Bṛihatsaṁhitā. Text. The work on astrology by Varāhamihira, dated to the beginning of the sixth century AD, refers to two coin denominations as **kārshāpaṇa* and **rūpaka*, while giving the list of prices of precious stones and pearls in chapters 79-82 and chapter 30, respectively. In the case of precious stones, the prices have been specified, but the coin denomination is not mentioned, and it is the commentator, Bhaṭṭotpala, who says that the *kārshāpaṇas* are meant. But in the case of pearls, the prices have been specified in *kārshāpaṇa* and *rūpaka*. A M Shastri is of the view that these two terms imply one and the same coin denomination. Incidentally, this is supposed to be the earliest reference to the coin denomination, *rūpaka* (A M Shastri 1967).

Bronze. Metal for coins. It is an alloy of copper and tin, and was commonly used for the manufacture of coins in ancient times. Often, it is difficult to distinguish between bronze and copper coins. Working in bronze has a long tradition, and this metal was adopted for coinage quite early, not only in India, but elsewhere as well. Chinese bronze coinage has an unbroken history for almost

3,000 years, and before turning to *silver, the Roman also issued bronze coins for about 300 years. It was used to mint coins, both by the indigenous and foreign rulers of ancient India [**Æ*, **aes*] (D R Bhandarkar 1984; Chakrabortty 1931; Junge 1984; A N Lahiri 1965).

Buddha, Maitreya. The Future Buddha. According to the Buddhist belief, when the *Śākyamuni Buddha, then a *bodhisattva*, was leaving the Tuśita heaven for the Sahā world, he removed his crown, and placing it on the head of Maitreya, prophesied that he shall be the next 'to obtain supreme and perfect Enlightenment'. On the rev of two copper coins of the *Kushāṇa ruler, *Kanishka I, occurs a seated figure, with the l hand in lap and the r hand raised up in the *varadamudrā* on one coin, and with both hands raised in front of breast on the other coin. Part of the rev ld has been read as *Boudo* by Cunningham, on which basis, he identified the figure as that of the *Śākyamuni Buddha. B N Mukherjee read the ld as *Ametobou*, and identified the figure as that of the *dhyānī* Buddha, Amitābha. But Joe Cribb read the ld on these coins as *Metrauo Boudo*, which he later modified to *Metrago Boudo*, and suggested that these two coins of Kanishka I bear the figure of Maitreya Buddha. This suggestion of Cribb has the support of scholars, like J C Huntington, Martha Carter, and K D Bajpai (K D Bajpai 1989; Martha Carter 1998; Cribb 1980; Cribb 1999-2000; Cunningham 1971a; Foucher 2003; Huntington 1993; B N Mukherjee 1987).

Buddha, Śākyamuni. Deified human being; founder of Buddhism; *c* sixth-fifth centuries BC. The Buddha, born Siddhārtha, was the son of the Śākya, Śuddhodana, and his Koliya wife, Māyādevī. Although he was brought up in all luxury, at the age of 29, he renounced the world, and after an effort of six years, attained *saṁbodhi*, thus becoming the Buddha, 'the enlightened one'. He delivered his first sermon at Sarnath near Vārāṇasī, and spent the next 45 years of his life in preaching his doctrine, mainly in eastern Uttar Pradesh and Bihar. He taught the Four Great Truths (*chatvāri ārya satyāni*, and the Middle Path (*majjhimapratipadā*). He entered the *parinirvāṇa* at Kuśīnārā *c* 483 BC, at the age of 80 years. In early art, the Buddha was represented symbolically. In human form, he is represented for the first time, perhaps on the coins of *Kanishka I. Attempts have

Kanishka I

been made to identify the seated king on a coin type of *Maues as the Buddha, but without much success. Whitehead and Smith are of the view that the figure of the Buddha appears on some coins of *Kujula Kadphises, who is known from numismatic sources to have assumed the title of *sachadhramathida*, 'steadfast in true law', (Buddhism ?). But on some of these coins, the figure, which has been identified as the Buddha, is shown holding sceptre or a weapon in one of his hands, a feature not usually associated with the Buddha, and there is a suggestion that the depiction is that of the seated king. But the label inscriptions on some gold and quite a few copper coins of Kanishka I leave little ground for any uncertainty regarding the identification of the deity depiction on them with the Buddha. On the rev of two gold coins, one from Ahin-Posh near Jalalabad in Afghanistan and the other from Rajgadh in western Madhya Pradesh, the nimbate Buddha stands to front. His r hand is extended forward either in the *abhayamudrā* or held in front of the chest, while the l hand, perhaps, holds his begging bowl. The head of the Buddha resembles a *śaṅkha*. The ld beside the figure reads *Boddo*. On some copper coins occurs the figure of the Buddha, with his r hand, perhaps, in the *vyākhyānamudrā*, while the l hand holds his begging bowl. The ld on these coins reads *Sakayamo Boddo*, 'Śākyamuni Buddha'. On some other specimens of the same ruler, the Master is seated with his hands raised in front of his chest; according to some scholars, he is here shown in the *dharmachakrapravarttanamudrā*, 'the posture of the turning of the wheel of law'. On a recently reported gold coin of *Huvishka, the standing figure of the Buddha and the ld *Boddo* appear on the rev, indicating the continuance of the tradition of depicting the Buddha on coins during his reign. There is a single-lined halo surrounding the head and the entire body of the Buddha, except for his feet. His r hand is raised to the level of his chest; the l hand holds the end of his cloak at the level of his waist. There is also a suggestion that the *lion appearing on some ancient Indian coins might be regarded as the theriomorphic representation of the Buddha, who is also known as Śākyasiṁha. The *wheel on some coins of the *Indo-Greek ruler, *Menander, has been identified as the Buddhist **dharmachakra*, and symbolically represents the Buddha (K D Bajpai 1989; Coomaraswamy 2003; Cribb 1999-2000; Cunningham 1971a; Foucher 2003; Gardner 1971; Handa 2005-2006; Marshall 1975; Rosenfield 1967; Smith 1972; Tarn 1980; Whitehead 1914).[†]

Budhagupta *Vikramāditya.* *Imperial Gupta k; son of Pūrugupta; last quarter of the fifth century AD. The find of his inscriptions and seals from such far flung places as Sarnath and Rajghat (District Varanasi), Paharpur (District Rajshahi), Damodarpur (District Dinajpur), Eran (District Sagar), Nandanpur (District Monghyr), and Nalanda would suggest that his empire extended from the Himalayas in the north to at least eastern Malwa in the south, and from eastern Punjab in the west to Bengal in the east. There are indications that towards the end of his reign, there was a decline in the power and prestige of the Imperial Guptas; the Eran region seems to have been lost to the Hūṇas, some time after his reign. He was, perhaps, the last Imperial Gupta to issue coins both in gold and silver. He issued *Archer type of gold coins, which are divided into two classes, the first of which has the ld *Budha* under the king's arm on the obv, and the ld *Śrī-Viramaḥ* on the rev; the vertical ld *Budha* is not met with on the coins of Class II. Budhagupta issued silver coins of the **Madhyadeśa* type only (Ashvini Agrawal 1989; Allan 1914; Altekar 1957; R D Banerji 1933; Fleet 1888; S R Goyal 2005; P L Gupta 1998; K P Jayaswal 1933; Smith 1972; Thaplyal 1972; Thaplyal, forthcoming).†

Budhagupta : Archer type

Bull. Symbol. It is generally believed that the bull was originally worshipped independently, 'without any human or divine master to the ride him', since the neolithic period in (southern) India; the bull was sometimes associated with the mother goddess as her consort. But later this cult was absorbed by Śaivism, and *Śiva 'displaced the Primeval Bull who was the fecundative power of the archetypal feminine deity'. On ancient Indian coins, the bull, with or without hump, may be seen as standing or recumbent, and such representations usually have Śaiva affiliations, although it cannot be altogether ruled out that on some of these coins, for instance on the coins of the *Rājanya *janapada* and the *Agra tribe, where the beast appears within a rayed circle on the rev, that the bull, in itself, was worshipped as a divinity. The figure of the standing bull, sometimes before a *taurine symbol, or a couchant bull before a fish-like symbol, appears on the *punch marked coins. Humped bull is also seen on the coins of such tribal republics as the *Audumbara, *Ārjunāyana, *Mālava, Rājanya, *Śibi, *Uddehika, *Vemaki, and *Yaudheya,

Punch marked coin

Vemaki

Diomedes

Apollodotos

Uncertain ascription

Kauśāmbī

Skandagupta

and *janapadas* as *Ayodhyā, *Eran, *Kanauj, and *Kauśāmbī. A single bull, or two bulls face to face, appear on some coins of *Taxila. On some of these coins, the bull stands before a *yūpa*, the device perhaps representing the performance of the *śūlagava* sacrifice. Again, on some others, the humped bull has a crescent on its head, and seems to the represent *Śiva *Śaśāṅkaśekhara*. On some *Ujjayinī coins, the bull stands beside Śiva, looking up at the deity, as described in the *Matsyapurāṇa*. The figure of a bull before a **liṅgaṁ* occurs on the rev of some Ārjunāyana coins. Some coins of the same tribe, as also some coins of *Gomitra of *Mathurā, have the device of a bull standing before a *tree-in-railing. The animal on the *Nāga coins is usually recumbent. The *Indo-Greeks, *Śaka-Pahlavas, *Kushāṇas, and the *Hūṇas, also issued coins with the bull device in northwestern India. While on the coins of *Apollodotos, *Artemidoros, *Diomedes, *Epander, *Maues, *Azes, *Azilises, *Kujula Kadphises, and *Mihirakula, the bull may be seen as an independent device, sometimes with Śaiva affiliation, on the coins of *Vāsudeva I and some of his successors, the animal is depicted beside Śiva. A gold piece, perhaps of Indo-Greek or Śaka-Pahlava origin, has the figure of a bull, with the legends *tauros* and *ushabhe* above and below the device, on one side, and the figure of the city goddess of Pushkalāvatī (**Pakhalavadi-devada*, identified as Ambā), on the other. The bull device also occurs on the coins of some *Imperial Gupta rulers, like *Skandagupta. It may also be added here that in the *Vishṇudharmottarapurāṇa*, the bull is associated with *Kārttikeya, and the beast appearing on the rev of some Yaudheya coins, bearing the figure of Kārttikeya on the obv, may be seen in this light. Very often, the bull device on one side of the coin, is combined with the *elephant device on the other side, as, for example, on some tribal, Indo-Greek, and Śaka-Pahlava coins (Allan 1936; Altekar 1957; Banerjea 1968; Banerjea 2002; R G Bhandarkar 1928; Sukumari Bhattacharji 1970; Bopearachchi 1993; Bopearachchi and Pieper 1998; Bopearachchi and Rahman 1995; Chakrabortty 1931; Mahadev Chakravarti 1994; Bhaskar Chattopadhyay 1977; Cunningham 1971a; K K Dasgupta 1974; Gardner 1971; Handa 2007a; Kosambi 1965; Macdonell 1897; Marshall 1975; O'Flaherty 1975; R B Pande 1988; Rao 1985; Senior 2001; Prashant Srivastava 2004b; Prashant Srivastava and Deepak Tiwari 1994).†

Bullion. This is uncoined metal, mostly gold or silver, shaped variously as a bar, plate, ingot, etc. It is still the 'preferred currency' for government reserves and large scale international monetary transactions (Junge 1984).

Buner casket hoard. This hoard was found in a bronze casket from Buner in the Swat region. The rulers represented in this hoard include *Azes I with *Aśpavarman and *Abdagases; there are two posthumous coins of Azes I, and a silver **denarius* of the Roman emperor, Tiberius (Senior 2001).

Buner hoard. This hoard was discovered at Nawagai in Buner in the Swat region. The rulers represented in this hoard include *Azes I, *Azilises, and *Azes II (Senior 2001).

Bust, royal. Device. The depiction of the royal bust was quite common on the coins of the *Indo-Greeks; the *Śaka-Pahlavas start depicting the device from the time of *Orthagnes onwards; even some *Kushāṇa rulers depicted the bust of the king on the obv of their coins. The silver coins of the *Western Kshatrapas, the *Imperial Guptas, the *Pushpabhūtis, the *Maukharis, etc, also bear the royal bust on the obv. Often, an attempt has been made at a realistic portraiture of the king, especially on the Indo-Greek coins. Some Indo-Greek coins show the depiction of conjugate busts of two persons, one male and the other female. But portraiture of the king, realistic or otherwise, on coins is very rare among the ancient Indian rulers of indigenous origin, the depiction of the bust of the king on such coins usually being the result of the impact of foreign numismatic traidition (Allan 1914; Allan 1936; Altekar 1957; Gardner 1971; A N Lahiri 1965; Rapson 1975; Smith 1972; Prashant Srivastava 1998b; Whitehead 1914)

Menander

V'ima Kadphises

Bust type. Copper. Among the *Imperial Guptas, the Bust type was issued in copper by *Chandragupta II. The obv bears the bust of the king, sometimes shown with a flower in the r hand; on some specimens occurs the ld *Śrī-Vikramāditya*. The rev has **garuḍa*-with-outstretched-wings, standing on an altar; below its figure is the ld **Mahārāja Chandraguptaḥ*, or simply *Chandragupta* (Allan 1914; Altekar 1957; P L Gupta 1998; Smith 1972).

C

Maues

Caduceus. Symbol. *Zeus was forbidden by his mother, Rhea, to marry. At this, he sought to rape his mother, who turned herself into a serpent. Then, Zeus coupled with Rhea in the form of a serpent, both 'entwined in an indissoluble knot', and this became the emblem of *Hermes—the *caduceus*, his magic staff. In art, this *caduceus* is usually seen in the hand(s) of this Greek god. As an independent device, it appears on the coins of the *Indo-Greek ruler, *Demetrios, and the *Śaka-Pahlava ruler, *Maues (Bopearachchi 1993; Bopearachchi and Pieper 1998; Bopearachchi and Rahman 1995; Gardner 1971; Graves 1955; Kerenyi 1951; A N Lahiri 1965; Pinsent 1969; Rose 1958; Schroder nd; Senior 2001; Whitehead 1914).

Kujula Kadphises

Camel. Symbol. In Indian mythology, this animal is associated with Śukra. A two-humped Bactrian camel, which appears on the obv of a copper type of *Menander, seems to be a novel numismatic feature introduced by this *Indo-Greek ruler himself, and apparently had no connection with Śukra (Bopearachchi 1993; Bopearachchi and Pieper 1998; Bopearachchi and Rahman 1995; Cunningham 1970; Gardner 1971; A N Lahiri 1965; Stutley 2003; Whitehead 1914).

Canting symbol. A symbol, which, by means of a pun, indicates the identity of the issuing person or state, is a canting symbol (Hill 1906).

Canting type. A type, which, by means of a pun, indicates the identity of the issuing person or state, is a canting type (Hill 1906).

Casting coins in moulds. Technique of manufacture of coins. In the casting method of making coins, molten metal was poured into moulds. In the earlier stage, the mould was used to cast blanks, and thereafter, the devices were punched on them. Later on, all the required devices or/and legends were marked in the negative in a single mould. Coin moulds have been found from Eran (*Erakiṇa), *Takshaśilā, *Mathurā, Atranjikhera, Sisupalgarh, Sanchi, Nalanda, Kondapur, Rohtak, Sunet, etc. They are all of burnt clay, except the one from Eran, which is in bronze. Their examination shows that various techniques were used for their manufacture. The moulds from Mathurā, Sisupalgarh, and Kondapur bear the devices, which are met with on the *punch marked coins. Usually, moulds could be used only once, and had to be broken in the process of taking out coins from them. But some moulds could be repeatedly used for this purpose; for example, the bronze mould from Eran. First, moulds were made, with device on one side only, and the other side remained blank. But later on, two separate pieces, both bearing devices and/or ld, were joined together, leaving a cavity for the molten metal to be poured through the hole left on one side. Thus were obtained devices on both the sides of the coins. After the molten metal cooled down, and became solid, the mould was broken, and the coin was taken out of it. In this technique, only one coin could be produced at a time, and the mould could be used only once, and, hence, separate moulds had to be prepared for the manufacture of each coin. Later, other techniques of casting coins were developed, according to which, a large number of coins could be produced at one stretch. The production of coins by this method can be understood on the basis of the evidence of the thousands of *Yaudheya coin moulds, particularly those found at Sunet and Rohtak, which have been scientifically studied by Birbal Sahni, from the point of view of the technique of manufacturing coins. Sunet moulds of the Yaudheyas are single-coin discs, bearing the impression on one side (obv or rev) only. A series of discs was placed, one above the other, so as to make a cylindrical pipe. 'Each pair of discs, when coupled face to face, would have its two exposed sides blank. A number of such pairs were placed parallel to each other, with a layer of plaster…laid between the contiguous pairs…. The whole series was then plastered over on the outside, taking care to the leave open all the channels

Uninscribed cast coin

Uninscribed cast coin

Uninscribed cast coin

Uninscribed cast coin

Uninscribed cast coin

into the sockets.' The Yaudheya coin moulds found at Rohtak reveal a much more complex technique, as shown by Sahni. A series of discs was prepared. A number (eight in the case of Rohtak moulds) of coin moulds were impressed on these discs. Coin models could be of clay, wax, wood, or soapstone. But once the engraving of the originals had been done, and coins prepared, actual coins could be conveniently used as coin models for further manufacturing of coins. The impressions were made on both the sides—obv and rev—of each disc. A thin crust of dark gray dusting powder has been found on blank faces; obviously, this was used to prevent the discs from adhering firmly. The discs were placed one above the other, in a vertical column. 'The coupled faces of the contiguous discs bore the negative impression of the obv and rev devices, respectively, and were so placed as to make the opposing sockets coincide exactly'. The whole pile was plastered over with clay on all the sides, leaving only a funnel-like crater on the top, for receiving the molten metal. Through this crater, the molten metal went vertically down, into the central canal, and after filling it, moved to the coin sockets, arranged in a ring, through horizontal channels radiating from a common shaft. The clay luting bound the disc into a compact pile, and also prevented the leakage of metal. The porous nature of the luting material (because of the presence of husk, etc) allowed the escape of hot gases in advance of the inflowing metal. The metal was allowed to cool down, and the coins were taken out by breaking the moulds. Sahni, after examining the discs carefully, arrived at the conclusion that the radiating channels were made in a single operation by means of a single rayed model, pressed into the clay. However, each coin socket was made separately by pressing in a different coin model at the end of each radiating ray. Neither radial canals, nor the coin sockets, coincide in their positions on the two sides of a disc. As Sahni points out, this technique of manufacturing coins at Rohtak in the first century BC 'was more complex than yet known anywhere in the world', and reflects a high degree of skill and intelligence on the part of their makers and users. The cast coins are all of copper. The technique of metal casting was known to India, since the hoary past, and the manufacturing of early cast coins was independent of any outside inspiration, though it is possible that the complicated method of casting of Yaudheya coins might bear some foreign influence (Chakrabortty 1931; B N Mukherjee and P K D Lee 1988; Sahni 1945).

Chakkar hoard. Discovered in 1970-1971 in the village of Chakkar in the Mandi district of Himachal Pradesh, it consists of 536 coins, of which 484 have been attributed to the *Kuṇindas. The remaining 52 have been ascribed to the *Yaudheyas by K K Maheshwari. But P L Gupta feels that some of these coins, which bear the names of *Bhānugh[osha] and *Jayava[rmā], should be attributed to the family of the Varsha *gaṇa*. Devendra Handa, too, is not in favour of ascribing these coins to the Yaudheyas (P L Gupta 1987; P L Gupta 1988; Handa 2007a; K K Maheshwari 1978).

Chakra. Symbol. This symbol is associated with both *Sūrya and *Vishṇu, and sometimes it is difficult to determine as to which deity the *chakra* represented on the coin is associated with. But the *chakra* on the rev of some *Vṛishṇi coins, although earlier regarded as the Buddhist **dharmachakra* by some scholars, seems to be the *sudarśanachakra* of Vishṇu, the most popular of whose incarnations—*Vāsudeva-Kṛishṇa—being associated with this tribe. The *chakra* on the obv of a type of the *Kulūta Vīrayaśas should also be so identified, as it is quite similar to the *chakra* on the Vṛishṇi coins. A copper type of the *Pañchāla (?) ruler, *Achyu[ta], also bears a *chakra* on the rev. This, too, may be regarded as the *sudarśanachakra* of Vishṇu, one of whose names is Achyuta. But the *chakra* appearing on the *punch marked coins, including the *bent bar coins, and on local and tribal coins, like those of *Kāḍa, *Kauśāmbī, *Takshaśilā, and *Ujjayinī, seems to be associated with *Sūrya, the wheel indicating the solar motion. On some of these coins, the *chakra* is spoked. The rayed sun is quite clear on some *Mālava and *Yaudheya coins. An attempt has been made by Spooner to identify the wheel appearing on ancient Indian coins as a representation of the Zoroastrian deity, Mithra (*Mihira), but this view is not tenable as the Sun god was worshipped all over the world—as *Sūrya, Savitṛi, Pūshan, etc in India; as Shamash among the Semites; as Asura in Assyria; as Arima by the Hittites; as Amon, Ra, and Aton in Egypt. No wonder, representations of the Sun god, often in the form of a wheel, occur in the art of all the ancient races; wheel is also seen on Harappan seals. [**dharmachakra*] (Allan

Punch marked coin

Vemaki

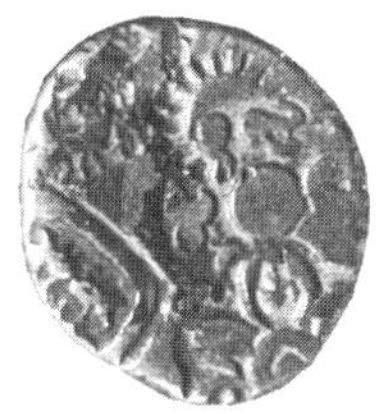

Punch marked coin

Punch marked coin

Punch marked coin

Punch marked coin

1936; Banerjea 2002; Chakrabortty 1931; Bhaskar Chattopadhyay 1977; Cunningham 1971b; K K Dasgupta 1974; Handa 2007a; Savita Sharma 1990).

***Chakra* type.** Copper. The *Chakra* type in copper was first issued by *Chandragupta II among the *Imperial Guptas. This type of his coins has on the obv, a **chakra* on top, and the ld *Chandra-* below it. The rev has a **garuḍa* on top, and the ld *–gupta* below it (Allan 1914; Altekar 1957; P L Gupta 1998; Smith 1972).

Kācha

***Chakradhvaja*.** Symbol. This is a standard surmounted by a *chakra* or wheel, and was earlier known to have occurred only on the obv of the coins of *Kācha. The *Imperial Guptas were devout worshippers of *Vishṇu, and the **chakra* is a characteristic attribute of that deity. Hence, the *chakradhvaja* seems to have Vaishṇava affiliations. Joe Cribb has traced the occurrence of the *chakradhvaja* on a coin of the later *Kushāṇa chief, *Maśra. In Bengal, *Jaya[nāga] depicted the *chakradhvaja* beside the king on the obv of his gold coins. Thus, the *chakradhvaja* is not peculiar to Kācha alone. It occurs on coins, both earlier and later than him (Altekar 1957; Cribb 1985a).

Chakrapurusha. Deity. The obv of the **Chakravikrama* type of *Chandragupta II bears the figure of a crowned deity standing, with a halo in the form of a double-rimmed wheel reaching from the top of his head to his knees. He holds a *gadā* in his l hand hanging by his side. The r hand holds three round objects, which he is offering to the king standing facing him. The issuer of this type was a great devotee of *Vishṇu, and the deity on the obv was identified with Vishṇu. But later, it was pointed out that the depiction of the deity was in 'remarkable conformity' with the description of the Chakrapurusha given in the *Ahirbudhnyasaṁhitā*, and he should be regarded as Chakrapurusha who was the personification of the wheel attribute of Vishṇu, and was often identified with Vishṇu himself. The *prasāda* being offered by the deity to the king, in the form of three round objects, is taken to symbolize the sovereignty of the three worlds, or the three steps, namely *dama*, *tyāga*, and *apramāda* which are believed to lead to immortality, or *prabhuśakti*, *utsāhaśakti*, and *mantraśakti* which together constitute the *kriyāśakti* of the king. Interestingly, according to the *Ahirbudhnyasaṁhitā*, Chakrapurusha was a representation of the *kriyāśakti* of the king (V S Agrawala 1954; Altekar 1957; C Sivaramamurti 1951).

Chakravikrama type. Gold. Known only from one specimen so far, the *Chakravikrama* type is among the most artistic coins of *Chandragupta II. On the obv, *Chakrapurusha is shown with an elaborate nimbus, and holding a *gadā*, while he offers three round objects to the king standing facing him. These three round objects are believed to represent the three constituents of the *kriyāśakti* or power of the king, or, alternatively, the three worlds. On the rev, *Lakshmī stands on a lotus pedestal, with a stalked lotus bud in her l hand; the r hand is pointing at something not visible on the coin. The rev ld, *Chakravikramaḥ*, has been interpreted as 'One whose valour is like that of Chakra, ie Chakrapurusha'. The coin does not mention the name of Chandragupta II, but the component *vikrama* in the rev ld has been taken to show that it was, most probably, issued by that *Imperial Gupta ruler, whose *āditya viruda* was *Vikramāditya*. In 1960, another specimen of the type was reported to exist with Panna Lal, a goldsmith of Shahganj, in the Jaunpur district of Uttar Pradesh. Devendra Handa also referred, perhaps to this very specimen, in the Chandrapur Session of the Numismatic Society of India (2007). The coin is believed to have formed a part of a hoard of around 100 Imperial Gupta coins, from the village of Madan Kola, near Shahganj. However, doubts have been expressed regarding its authenticity (Ashvini Agrawal 1989; Allan 1914; Altekar 1957; R D Banerji 1933; R G Chandra 1960; S R Goyal 2005; P L Gupta 1998; Smith 1972; Thaplyal, forthcoming).

Chandragupta II : *Chakravikrama* type

Chalkon. Coin denomination. According to Cunningham, this was the Greek copper unit, and weighed 67.2 grains. Side by side, Indian *punch marked copper coins weighing 144 grains, were also in circulation. The *Indo-Greek rulers struck their copper coins on the Attic standard in Bactria, and on the Indian standard in their Indian territories. Cunningham further observes that the *chalkon* of the Attic standard of 67.2 was raised to 70 grains in order to make it almost half of an Indian *paṇa*, representing an attempt at unifying the Greek and Indian systems. Indo-Greek copper coins corresponding to 5, 4, 2½, 2, 1, and ½ Bactrian *chalkon*, and 5, 2½, 1¼, 1, ¾, and ½ Indian *paṇa*, are known. Eight *chalkaus* would be equal to an **obol*, and 48 *chalkaus*, to a **drachm* (Cunningham 1970; Frey 1973; Junge 1984; A N Lahiri 1965).

Chalkos. Metal for coins. It is the Greek for copper or bronze, there being no distinction between the two metals, as is also the case with the Latin, **aes* (Cunningham 1970; Junge 1984; A N Lahiri 1965).

Chaman hoard. It was reportedly discovered in 1940, somewhere between Chaman and Kandahar. The rulers represented in this hoard include *Vonones with *Spalahora,, *Spalirises with *Azes I, Azes I alone, Azes I with *Azilises, Azilises, and *Azes II (Senior 2001).

Chaman-i-Hazouri hoard. This hoard was discovered in 1933, along with some fragments of jewellery, at Chaman-i-Hazouri near Kabul in Afghanistan, and was published some 20 years later by Daniel Schlumberger. The actual composition of this hoard is not known for certain, although there are indications that it originally contained 'some hundreds if not thousands' of coins. Schlumberger could report only 30 coins of various Greek city states like Athens, and different cities in Ionia, the Aegean islands, Macedonia, Thrace, and Cyprus, 34 'owls' of Athens and their imitations, eight Achaemenian coins, 14 *bent bars, 29 local silver coins. Dilip Rajgor, however, gives the following composition of this hoard—63 Greek coins, eight Achaemenian coins, one derivative of Athenian coins, 12 bent bars, and 43 Gandhāra coins of the double die type, that is a total of 127 coins (Bopearachchi and Rahman 1995; Rajgor 2001).

Chandigarh hoard. This is a large hoard of copper coins, reported from Chandigarh. The rulers represented in this hoard include *Gondopharnes, *Gondopharnes with *Sasan, and Rañjuvula. There are also a few 'uncertain' pieces (Senior 2001).

Chandragupta I. *Imperial Gupta k; son of Ghaṭotkacha; early fourth century AD. The Imperial Guptas rose to prominence during the reign of Chandragupta I, as revealed by the facts that he was the first ruler of his dynasty to assume the title of **mahārājādhirāja*, and issue gold coins. On these coins, he is associated with the Lichchhavi princess, *Kumāradevī. The importance attached to the Lichchhavi relations has led V A Smith to suggest that Chandragupta I must have gained politically from this matrimonial alliance. The marriage seems to have led to an amalgamation of the Imperial Gupta and Lichchhavi states, which was later inherited by *Samudragupta. On the basis of a puranic passage, it is believed that Chandragupta I ruled over nearly the whole of Bihar and parts of Uttar Pradesh and Bengal. The *Gupta era, commencing 319 AD, is believed to have been founded by Chandragupta I. The *King-and-Queen type, issued in gold, is the only definitely known coin type of Chandragupta I. The reported silver coins of this type seem to be fake. A copper coin, bearing the ld *Lichchhavayaḥ* on the obv, and *Chandragupta* on the rev, is reported from Sanghol, and attributed to Chandragupta I. A *Standard type of coin, attributed by B Ch Chhabra to Chandragupta I, is generally believed to have been issued by *Chandragupta II (Ashvini Agrawal 1989; Allan 1914; Altekar 1957; R D Banerji 1933; Fleet 1888; S R Goyal 2005; P L Gupta 1998; K P Jayaswal 1933; Manmohan Kumar 1978; Smith 1972; Prashant Srivastava 1996a; Thaplyal 1980-1981; Thaplyal, forthcoming).†

Chandragupta I and Kumāradevī

Chandragupta II *Vikramāditya*. *Imperial Gupta k; son of *Samudragupta; last quarter of the fourth century and early years of the fifth century AD. There is literary, epigraphic, and numismatic evidence to show that he killed his elder brother, *Rāmagupta, captured his throne, and married his widow. He is known to have defeated *Rudrasiṁha III, the *Kārddamaka ruler of Gujarat-Kathiawar, and annexed the Kārddamaka kingdom to his empire. It is known from the Udaigiri inscription of Vīrasena Śāba that Chandragupta II had set out 'to conquer the whole world', and his general, Āmrakārddava, claims in his Sanchi inscription to have won many battles. But we have no definite information about any of the military achievements of Chandragupta II. However, if King Chandra of the Mehrauli iron pillar inscription has rightly been identified with Chandragupta II, it may be said that in the east, Chandra/Chandragupta II 'defeated a confederacy of hostile chiefs in Vaṅga', that is eastern Bengal, while in the west, 'having crossed in warfare the seven mouths of the river Sindhu, conquered the Vāhlīkas', that is Bactria (Balkh). There are some indications that he performed the *aśvamedha*, though most of the scholars have reservations about it. He issued coins, not only in gold, but also in silver and copper. If the silver coins of the *King-and-Queen type

Chandragupta II : Archer type

Chandragupta II : Lion-slayer type

Chandragupta II :
Chhatra type

Chandragupta II :
|Horseman type

Chandragupta II :
Chakravikrama type

bearing the name of *Chandragupta I and *Kumāradevī are taken as forgeries, he was the first Imperial Gupta ruler to issue coins in silver. His gold coins are of at least eight types : (i) *Archer type, (ii) Lion-slayer type, (iii) *Horseman type, (iv) **Chhatra* type, (v) *Couch type, (vi) *King-and-Queen-on-Couch type, (vii) *Standard type, and (viii) **Chakravikrama* type. His silver coins resemble the *Kārddamaka silver issues in that the obv has the bust of the king to the r and the date of the issue of the coins (in the *Gupta era). The rev has the *garuḍa* in place of the *crescent-on-hill symbol occurring on the Kārddamaka coins. These are termed the *Western Indian type of Imperial Gupta silver coins. These silver coins are divided into two classes on the basis of the circular ld they bear. One on class, it reads *Śrī-Guptakulasya-mahārājādhirāja Śrī-Chandragupta Vikramāṅkasya*, while on the other, it reads *Paramabhāgavata-mahārājādhirāja Śrī-Chandragupta Vikramāditya*. The first ld ends in the genitive as on the coins of the *Western Kshatrapas, while the second ends in the nominative as on the gold and copper coins of the Imperial Guptas. On this basis, it has been suggested that the class of coins with the first ld was, perhaps, issued earlier than the class of coins bearing the second ld. Great variety is seen in the copper coins of Chandragupta II, the king issuing at least 10 types : (i) **Chhatra* type, (ii) *Standing king type, (iii) *Archer type, (iv) *Bust type, (v) **Chakra* type, (vi) *Vase type, (vii) *Crowned head type, (viii) *Lakshmī type, (ix) *Crescent and *garuḍa* type, and (x) **Jitaṁ Bhagavatā Padmanābhena* type. A recently reported copper type, perhaps from Bangladesh, bears the figure of a standing horse to the r, with a globe in front of its neck, on the obv. The rev has a *garuḍa* with outstretched wings, with the ld *Śrī-Vikrama* below it. The ld seems to associate this type with Chandragupta II (Ashvini Agrawal 1989; Allan 1914; Altekar 1957; R D Banerji 1933; Fleet 1888; S R Goyal 2005; P L Gupta 1998; K P Jayaswal 1933; Rhodes and Saha 2006; A M Shastri 1999-2000; Smith 1972; Prashant Srivastava 1996a; Thaplyal, forthcoming).†

Chandragupta III. *Imperial Gupta k. The *Archer type of gold coins, now ascribed to *Vainyagupta, were earlier regarded as the issues of Chandragupta III due to the Rapson's erroneous reading *Chandra*, instead of the correct reading *Vainya*, under the king's arm on the obv. But there are some Archer type of gold coins bearing ld

Chandra under the king's arm on the obv, and *Śrī-Vikramaḥ* on the rev. Despite the title *Vikrama* on these coins, it is difficult to ascribe them to *Chandragupta II *Vikramāditya*, as the weight of these coins is considerably higher than that of the coins of Chandragupta II. On this basis, some scholars have expressed the possibility of a third Imperial Gupta king bearing the name of Chandragupta (Ashvini Agrawal 1989; Allan 1914; Altekar 1957; S R Goyal 2005; P L Gupta 1998; Smith 1972; Thaplyal, forthcoming).

Chashṭana. *Kārddamaka k; son of Ysā(Ghsā)motika; first half of the second century AD. He is believed to have started his career as a governor of the southwestern provinces of the Kushāṇa empire, especially entrusted with the task of recovering the territories lost to the Sātavāhanas as a result of the defeat of *Nahapāna at the hands of Gautamīputra Sātakarṇi, which task, as per the numismatic evidence, he succeeded in accomplishing to a certain extent. But, recently, doubts have been expressed as to his ever occupying a subordinate position under any political power. On his early coins, he uses the title of **kshatrapa*, but on later coins, he calls himself **mahākshatrapa*. It is not certain whether he ruled before his brother, *Dāmaghsāda I, or after him. He seems to have appointed his son, *Jayadāman, as *kshatrapa* on his own elevation to the position of *mahākshatrapa*. But Jaydāman predeceased Chashṭana, and the former's son, *Rudradāman I, was appointed as heir-apparent. Chashṭana issued coins in silver, copper, and lead. His silver coins bear the bust of the king to the r on the obv. The early silver coins have a crescent to the l and a star to the r. But later on, he added the hill symbol on the rev. This symbol is very common on the Sātavāhana coins, and it has been taken to show that he wrested some territories from the Sātavāhanas. Very soon, the hill symbol, which was originally on an equality with the crescent and the star, became more prominent, and the other two symbols were relegated to a secondary position. The Greek characters on the obv might be the transliteration of the rev Br or Kh ld, as on the obv of the silver coins of *Nahapāna. Two legends appear on the rev—one in Br and the other in Kh, mentioning the name of Chashṭana, usually along with his titles of *rājan* and **kshatrapa*/**mahākshatrapa*, and the name of his father. This silver type introduced by Chashṭana, was continued by all his successors. But the use of the Kh script was discontinued after Chashṭana and Jayadāman. The obv of one type of the copper coins of Chashṭana shows a *horse standing to the r before a *yūpa*. The rev has a *crescent-on-hill, star, and crescent; the rev ld in Br is fragmentary, and refers to his name and his title of *mahākshatrapa*, along with his patronymic. Another type of his copper coins has the crescent and the star on the obv, and the crescent-on-hill symbol on the rev. The obv has a Br ld *Rājño Kshatrapasa Ghsamotikaputrasa Chashṭanasa*, and, perhaps, also a Kh ld. The rev has some corrupt Greek characters. This type is also reported in lead from Malwa (Jha and Rajgor 1994; Mirashi 1982; Mitchiner 1976; Rajgor 1991; Rapson 1975; Raychaudhuri 1972; Senior 2001; Sircar 1980e).†

Kuṇinda : *Chatreśvara* series

***Chatreśvara* series.** *Kuṇinda coins. Issued in copper only, these coins bear, on the obv, the standing figure of *Śiva holding trident-battleaxe in the r hand, while the l hand is on waist with a tiger-skin hanging from the left arm, and the Br ld *Bhagavata Chatreśvara Mahātmanaḥ*. The rev has a *deer, **śrīvatsa*, *tree-in-railing, *hill symbol with a **nandipada* above, hollow square, **jayadhvaja*, and an *undulating line. Śiva on the obv, is usually one-headed; however, recently, some coins bearing the same ld, but with three-headed Śiva seated on an Apasmārapurusha, have been reported. The depiction of the Apasmārapurusha at so early a date is surprising. These coins have been placed a couple of centuries later than the *Amoghabhūti series, and are thus datable to the second or third century AD. In the ld, *Chatreśvara* is taken as a dialectical variant of *Chhatreśvara* (*Chhatra* being one of the names of Śiva in the *Mahābhārata*). M C Joshi prefers *Ch[i]treśvara*, as a *svayambhū liṅga* of that name is under worship in Kumaon, the region which formed a part of the Kuṇinda territory. The obv device—deity holding trident-battleaxe, with tiger-skin hanging from his left arm—clearly shows Śaivite affiliation. The divine (*bhagavata*, not *bhāgavata*, 'devotee of god' as read by some) Chhatreśvara, the great-souled one (*mahātmanaḥ*), was the presiding deity of the Kuṇindas and the coins were issued in his name, like *Yaudheya coins issued in the name of *Kārttikeya, and, perhaps, the tribal state was dedicated to Śiva. The views that Chhatreśvara was the name of a Kuṇinda chief, or that Chhatra was the capital of the Kuṇindas, are less convincing. Devendra Handa doubts the ascription of these coins to the Kuṇindas. He is of the view that the *Yaudheyas wrested the Garhwal region from the Kuṇindas, and issued the coins bearing the name and figure of *Kārttikeya in the plains, and the Chatreśvara series in the Garhwal region. The 'close resemblance' between the Chatreśvara series and some Yaudheya coins has also been noticed by A M Shastri (Allan 1936; Chakrabortty 1931; Cunningham 1971b; K K Dasgupta 1974; Handa 2007a; Jayaswal 1988; M C Joshi 1962; M P Joshi 1989; Marshall 1975; Mitchiner 1975-1976; A M Shastri 1984; Smith 1972).

Chatur-māshaka. Coin denomination. It seems to be a copper coin, weighing 20 *rattīs* (D R Bhandarkar 1984; Chakrabortty 1931).

Chauraṁsa-kāhavaṇa. Coin denomination. Mentioned in the **Aṅgavijjā*, it denoted a square **kārshāpaṇa* (V S Agrawala 1957).

***Chhatra* type.** Copper. This type was issued by *Chandragupta II, and bears on the obv, the figure of the king standing left, with a dwarf parasol-bearer behind him. The rev has the figure of a **garuḍa* with human face and arms, and wings outstretched in the upper half; the lower half has the Br ld **Mahārāja Śrī-Chandraguptaḥ*. This type was continued by *Kumāragupta I, but the manner of engraving the ld on the rev of this type is different from that on his father's coins. On the coins of Kumāragupta I, the ld is in two lines, and reads *Mahārāja Śrī-Kumā-/-ragupta* (Allan 1914; Altekar 1957; P L Gupta 1998; Smith 1972).

Chandragupta II : *Chhatra* type

Chandragupta II : *Chhatra* type

***Chhatra* type.** Gold. First introduced in gold by *Chandragupta II, the *Chhatra* type of coins was continued by *Kumāragupta I and *Skandagupta. The obv of the coins of Chandragupta II has the king offering oblations at an altar. Behind the king is a dwarf parasol bearer, who is sometimes female. The circular ld, on various specimens, is **Mahārājādhirāja Śrī-Chandraguptaḥ*, or *Kshitimavajitya sucharitairdivaṁ jayati Vikramādityaḥ*. The rev has the standing figure of *Lakshmī, generally shown with a *pāśa* in her r hand, and a lotus in her l hand. The rev ld is *Vikramādityaḥ*. The *Chhatra* type of coins of Kumāragupta I are quite rare, and are a close imitation of the coins of the same type of Chandragupta II, above. The circular ld on the obv is incomplete, and reads *Jayati mahītalaṁ*.... The rev ld is *Śrī-Mahendrāditya*. The obv and rev devices of the *Chhatra* type

Kumāragupta I : *Chhatra* type

Skandagupta : *Chhatra* type

of Skandagupta are also quite similar to those on the coins of this type of his grandfather and father, but the altar visible on the obv of the coins of his predecessors, is conspicuous by its absence on his own coins of this type. The incomplete circular ld on the obv reads *Vijitāvani*.... The rev ld is *Kramādityaḥ*, and it is on the basis of this epithet that the type has been ascribed to Skandagupta, although it has been pointed out that several other *Imperial Gupta rulers, like *Ghaṭotkachagupta, *Kumāragupta II and *Kumāragupta III, also assumed this epithet (Ashvini Agrawal 1989; Allan 1914; Altekar 1957; R D Banerji 1933; S R Goyal 2005; P L Gupta 1998; Smith 1972; Thaplyal, forthcoming).

City coins. The city states of Greece are so well known for their political, economic, religious, and social activities. In India, coins of various cities are known. It appears that after the disintegration of the Maurya empire, some cities, which were main trade centres, found it convenient to issue coins as medium of exchange for local transactions. This reflects their autonomy, at least in the economic field, as pointed out by Bela Lahiri. The city coins are all of copper. They are square, or rectangular, or round, and some cities issued coins in more than one of these shapes. Most of the city coins are die-struck; only a few are cast. They bear the figure of an animal, or a deity, or a group of symbols. The metrology of the coins is not uniform, and, hence, their weight standard is difficult to determine. The cities which issued coins are *Ayodhyā, *Vārāṇasī, *Kauśāmbī, *Vidiśā, *Erakiṇa, *Bhāgila, *Kurara, *Ujjayinī, *Tripurī, *Māhishmatī, *Jyeshṭhapura, and, probably, Tagara, almost all of them situated on river banks. Scholars have suggested, for these coins, dates ranging from the end of the third century BC to the beginning of the first century BC. But, probably, the earliest such coins belong to the second century BC. At Ayodhyā and Kauśāmbī, city issues were followed by dynastic ones. It is difficult to ascertain the issuing authority of the coins bearing legends variously as *Kāḍasa*, *Upagoda*, and *Upātikyā*. A gold coin, in all probability, issued by a foreign ruler, bears the figure of a deity, and the ld meaning '*Devatā* of Pushkalāvatī', and another gold coin issued by *Eukratides, bears the figure of a deity, and the ld meaning 'City-deity of Kapiśā', indicating the importance of cities (Bela Lahiri 1974; Bela Lahiri 1976; J P Singh 1971).

Club. Symbol. This was a characteristic attribute of *Herakles, and when it appears, with the thick end up, on the coins of the *Indo-Greek rulers, *Menander and *Theophilos, it seems to indicate the presence of that deified Greek hero (Bopearachchi 1993; Bopearachchi and Pieper 1998; Bopearachchi and Rahman 1995; Cunningham 1970; Cunningham 1971a; Gardner 1971; Graves 1955; Kerenyi 1951; A N Lahiri 1965; Marshall 1975; Rose 1958; Whitehead 1914).

Clustre of dots. Symbol. This symbol is depicted on some ancient Indian coins, like the *punch marked coins, and those of the *Imperial Guptas. Durga Prasad describes it as *vindumaṇḍala* (Allan 1936; Altekar 1957; Bhaskar Chattopadhyay 1977).

Cock. Symbol. In the *Vishṇudharmottarapurāṇa*, cock, the harbinger of the rising sun, is associated with *Kārttikeya. On certain *Yaudheya copper coins, the deity is shown standing on a lotus. As lotus has solar associations, the depiction of Kārttikeya on lotus bloom also might hint at the solar basis of this deity. The *śakti* of Kārttikeya is also said to have been fashioned from a portion of the sun god's glory. A bird is shown represented on some round die-struck inscribed coins of *Ayodhyā. Allan expresses the possibility of the identification of the bird with a **haṁsa*, but most of the scholars regard it as a cock. The depiction of the bird on these coins might, or might not, have some connection with Kārttikeya. Cock also occurs on the rev of some coins of *Sophytes (Allan 1936; Banerjea 2002; Chakrabortty 1931; Bhaskar Chattopadhyay 1977; Gardner 1971; Handa 2007a; Bela Lahiri 1974; Rao 1985).

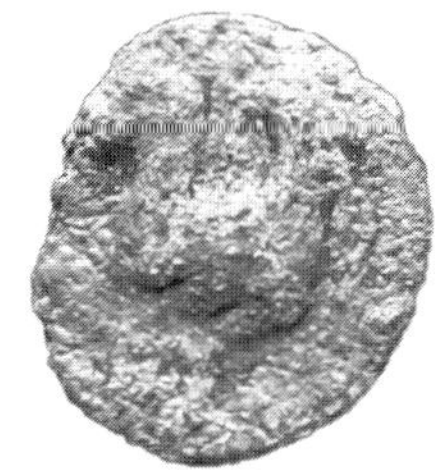

Sophytes

Yaudheya

Coin. It is a piece of metal (or of some other 'convenient material', in exceptional cases), of a definite weight, more or less definite shape and size, issued by a recognized authority to serve as a medium of exchange, and bearing a symbol or a type as a guarantee of the quality and quantity of the metal. It has, or is supposed to have, an intrinsic value, 'more or less nearly approaching the value imposed upon it by the issuing authority'. There is almost a general consensus among scholars that coins were first issued by merchants or their organizations for their own convenience, but when the state saw its advantages, it gradually established its monopoly on this activity (Hill 1906; Thaplyal 1971).

Copper. Metal for coins. Next to gold, copper is believed to have been adopted as medium of exchange. As soon as coinage evolved in India, copper coins began to be issued. D R Bhandarkar has pointed out that copper, in ancient times, was not as cheap as it is in modern times, and, as such, was well suited for purposes of coinage. Copper coins were issued in ancient India, right from the beginning of coinage, throughout the period under study here. Extensive mining of copper did not exist in India, the copper mines worked being those of Rajasthan and Tamilnadu. Consequently, considerable quantities of the metal had to be imported to meet the numismatic and other needs, and there are references in the *Periplus Maris Erythraei* to the western ports of India being engaged in this import in the first century AD. Similar conditions seem to have existed before and after this period as well. It was used to mint coins, both by the indigenous and foreign rulers of ancient India (Altekar 1940; D R Bhandarkar 1984; Chakrabortty 1931; A N Lahiri 1965; Schoff 2001).

Azes II

Huvishka

Cornucopiae. Symbol. In Greek mythology, the *cornucopiae* is generally associated with *Zeus. It is told in some versions that Zeus was fed by Amaltheia, a goat, or by a wet nurse of that name, who used a goat's horn to feed him. Later, Zeus took the horn of the goat, filled it with fruits, flowers, etc, and placed it, along with the goat, among the stars. This horn became the *cornucopiae*, 'the horn of plenty', and was commonly depicted in Greek art as a symbol of prosperity. The *cornucopiae*, as an independent device, is to be seen, for example, on the rev of a copper coin type of the *Indo-Greek ruler, *Theophilos. As the horn of plenty, it came to be associated with *Demeter, the Greek goddess of agriculture, as her characteristic attribute, and we find it occurring as such on the coins of the Indo-Greek rulers, like *Amyntas and *Philoxenos, and the *Śaka-Pahlava ruler, *Azes. On *Kushāṇa coins, the *cornucopiae* is seen in the hand of **Ardochsho*, the Iranian goddess of fortune, who seems to correspond to the Greek Demeter, Roman Fortuna, and the Indian *Lakshmī; sometimes, this attribute is also seen in the hand of **Nana*. Such representations are seen on the rev of the coins of *Kanishka I and *Huvishka. Interestingly, a female deity on the rev of a gold type of Huvishka holds a *cornucopiae* in both her hands, but in the label inscription she is called *Mioro* instead of *Ardochsho*. *Cornucopiae*, the 'horn of plenty', is shown in art as overflowing with fruits, flowers, and corn, but on coins, it is not easy to determine the contents of the *cornucopiae*. Like several other Kushāṇa numismatic elements, the *cornucopiae* in the hand of the goddess, too, is seen on the rev of the early *Imperial Gupta coins. But from the time of *Samudragupta onwards, the depiction of the *cornucopiae* in the hand of the goddess differs considerably from that occurring on the Indo-Greek, Śaka-Pahlava, and Kushāṇa coins, and gradually takes the shape of the **bījakosha* (V S Agrawala 1955; Allan 1914; Altekar 1957; Bopearachchi 1993; Bopearachchi and Pieper 1998; Bopearachchi and Rahman 1995; Cunningham 1970; Cunningham 1971a; Gardner 1971; Kerenyi 1951; A N Lahiri 1965; Rose 1958; Senior 2001; Sohoni 1957; Prashant Srivastava 2007e; Whitehead 1914).†

Samudragupta : Standard type

Samudragupta : Lyrist type

Couch type. Gold. The Couch type of *Chandragupta II is believed to be a modified adaptation of the *Lyrist type of *Samudragupta. Chandragupta II was, probably, not a musician, and, hence, he is not shown playing on the *vīṇā*. On the obv, the king is shown seated on a high backed couch, with a flower in his r hand; the l hand is placed on the couch. The obv circular ld on various specimens reads *Devaśrī-mahārājādhirāja Śrī-Chandraguptasya*, or *–gupta Vikramādityasya*, or **Paramabhāgavata-mahārājādhirāja Śrī-Chandraguptaḥ*. On some specimens, an additional ld, *rūpākṛiti*, occurs below the couch on the obv. This might refer to the figure of the king on the coin, or the beautiful figure; or it might mean 'One who is expert or successful (*kṛitin*) in composing *rūpa*, a variety of [Skt] drama'. The rev has the goddess seated on a throne or couch, with a lotus bloom in one of her hands; the other hand is empty. The rev ld is *Śrī-Vikramaḥ*, or *Vikramāditya* (Ashvini Agrawal 1989; Allan 1914; Altekar 1957; R D Banerji 1933; S R Goyal 2005; P L Gupta 1998; Smith 1972).

Chandragupta II : Couch type

Countermark. It is a small mark placed on a coin, usually by an authority other than the original issuer, giving the coin 'fresh currency' (Hill 1906).

Crescent-and-*Garuḍa* type. Copper. The Crescent-and-*Garuḍa* type of copper coins was struck by the *Imperial Gupta ruler, *Chandragupta II. The obv has, on the top, a crescent, and the ld *Chandra-* below it. The rev bears the figure of a **garuḍa*, and below, under a straight line, is the ld *–gupta* (Allan 1914; Altekar 1957; P L Gupta 1998; Smith 1972).

Uninscribed cast coin

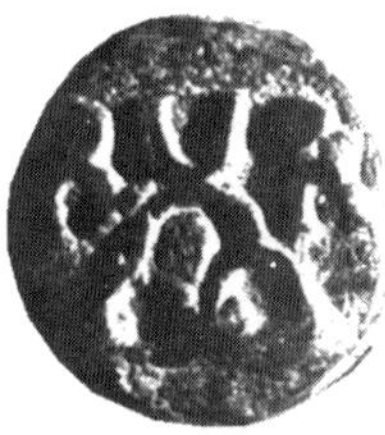
Uninscribed cast coin

Uninscribed cast coin

Uninscribed cast coin

Jīvadāman

Crescent-on-hill. Symbol. This was a very popular symbol on silver and copper punch marked coins, uninscribed cast copper coins, local and tribal coins like those of *Ujjayinī, *Taxila, Tripurī, and the *Kuṇindas, and the coins of the *Kārddamaka Kshatrapas and the 'Bodhi' dynasty. Rapson was of the view that the 'Bodhi' kings ruled over some region that was closely associated with the *Western Kshatrapas in western India. But A M Shastri, on the basis of the discovery of a large number of 'Bodhi' coins from Tripuri in the Jabalpur district of Madhya Pradesh, locates the 'Bodhi' kingdom in that region, where they succeeded the Sātavāhanas, and suggests that the 'Bodhi' kings 'were obviously indebted to the Sātavāhanas for the crescented three-peaked hill'. Most of the scholars regard this symbol as of Śaivite affiliation. For, *Śiva's epithets like *Girīśa*, *Girichara*, *Giritra*, etc, associate him with mountains; his abode is Mount Kailāsa; the hill is surmounted by a crescent, and Śiva has a crescent as an ornament on his forehead. Interestingly, on the obv of the coins of the *Aśvaka tribe, a female worshipper is shown along with piles of offerings, beside a crescent-on-hill, and there is a suggestion that it may represent the female devotee worshipping Śiva in the form of *Girīśa Śaśāṅkaśekhara* [*hill] (Allan 1936; Banerjea 2002; Bhaskar Chattopadhyay 1977; Chakrabortty 1931; Cunningham 1971b; Dasgupta 1974; Handa 2007a; Marshall 1975; Rao 1985; Rapson 1975; Senior 2001; Savita Sharma 1990; A M Shastri 1971; Prashant Srivastava 2007a).

Cross. Symbol. This symbol appears, often in combination with other symbols, like the *tree-in-railing, *crescent-on-hill, *taurine, etc, on the *punch marked coins, the uninscribed cast copper coins, and on the coins of *Taxila and Tripurī. A comparison of the cross with the **svastika* seems to show that the latter is, perhaps, a cross with short horizontal line attached to the ends of the four arms forming the cross. This has led to the view that the *svastika* might have evolved from the cross. There is also a suggestion that the cross symbolically represents *Śiva and Śakti, just like the combined symbol of the **liṅgaṁ* and the *yoni*, although this has not found universal acceptance (Allan 1936; Chakrabortty 1931; Mahadev Chakravarti 1994; Bhaskar Chattopadhyay 1977; Handa 2007a).

Crowned head type. Copper. In the *Imperial Gupta dynasty, *Chandragupta II issued the Crowned head type in copper. This type has the head of the king to the l, bearing an Indian or Persian crown, on the obv. The rev has a nimbate **garuḍa*-with-outstretched-wings, and the ld *Chandragupta* below it (Allan 1914; Altekar 1957; P L Gupta 1998; Smith 1972).

Cup-shaped coins. These coins, a class of silver *punch marked coins and also called saucer-shaped coins, are available in three denominations—full, weighing 48 *rattīs*, and its one-sixth and one-twelfth. The full coins bear four symbols, two of which are constant and almost similar in design, the other two varying and smaller in size. A few small counter-stamps may also be seen, perhaps punched by the bankers. They have been regarded among the earliest monetary issues of India. The one-sixth denomination is represented by elongated and thin coins of 8 *rattīs*, bearing the two constant symbols of the larger coins. These coins first came from the area around Varanasi; later on, such cup-shaped punch marked coins have also been reported from Ayodhyā, the Malla *janapada*, and the Kuntala region. It has recently been suggested that some cup-shaped coins might also have come from the Gandhāra region. All are more or less oval in shape. Some are of relatively pure silver, while others, heavier and of thicker fabric, are of highly alloyed silver. They are made by flattening round globules of silver, which gave them the peculiar cup or saucer shape. Terry Hardaker reports some cup-shaped coins, which he feels come from the Gandhāra region, bearing no punch marks, and having only bankers' marks. These pieces have been struck in the centre 'with the edge of a large blunt punch containing no visible design', perhaps to give the cup shape to the blank. Under normal circumstances, such blanks would then have been marked with symbols. That these pieces bearing no punch marks were in actual circulation seems to be suggested by the 'moderate wear' they show. A N Lahiri thinks that the

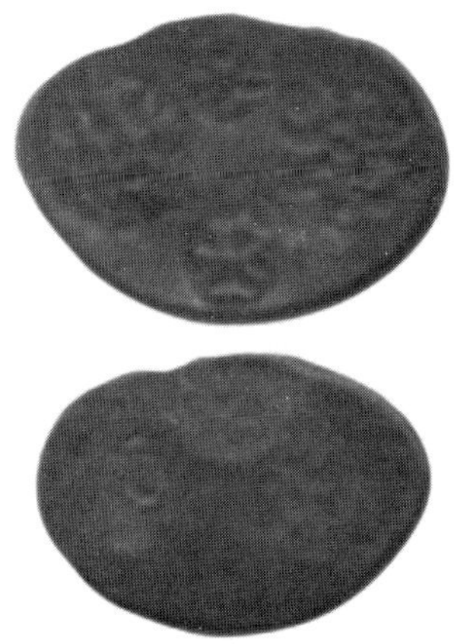
Cup-shaped coin

Cup-shaped coin

common 32 *rattī* coins evolved from the 48 *rattī* local Kāśī-Kosala coins of the cup-shaped type made out of metal globules. But the 32 *rattī kārshāpaṇa* was rarely made by this method of flattening metal globules, and mostly by sheet-cutting method. The number of symbols punched on these common punch marked coins was increased from four (of the cup-shaped coins) to five (Allan 1936; Cribb 1985b; Cribb 2005; P L Gupta 2004; Hardaker 2005-2006; Hirano 1999-2000; A N Lahiri 1971; Rajgor 2001).

D

Dahigaon hoard. This hoard of 36 silver coins of the *Kārddamaka Kshatrapas (26 coins) and the Traikūṭakas (10 coins), was discovered at Dahigaon in the Buldhana district of Maharashtra, in 1958. The rulers represented in the hoard include the Kārddamaka Kshatrapas, *Saṅghadāman or *Yaśodaman II, *Vijayasena, *Dāmajadaśrī (III ?), *Bhartṛidāman, *Viśvasena, and *Rudrasiṁha II; all the 10 Traikūṭaka coins belong to Dahrasena (Jha and Rajgor 1994; Mirashi 1973).

Dāmaghsada I. *Kārddamaka k. R C Senior reports some billon and copper coins bearing the name of Dāmaghsada. The billon issue has a *horse and a Kh ld beginning with *Raño mahachhatrapasa*, on the obv. The rev has a *hill symbol, with a crescent to the l, and a star to the r. The Br ld on this side seems to refer to Dāmaghsada, with the titles of *rājan*, *svāmin*, and *mahākshatrapa*, and as the son of Ysā(Ghā)motika. This would make Dāmaghsada I a brother of *Chashṭana. The copper coins have similar obv and rev devices as the billon issue. The ld, usually on the rev, is in Br. Some coins also have a Greek or Br ld on the obv. The chronological position of Dāmaghsada I is not certain (Senior 2001).

Dāmaghsada II. *Kārddamaka k. Rapson regarded Dāmaghsada, mentioned on certain coins as a son of *Rudradāman I, as the same as *Dāmajadaśrī [I], mentioned on certain other coins as a son of Rudradāman I. But Amiteshwar Jha and Dilip Rajgor regard them as two different rulers, both being sons of Rudradāman I. They suggest that, as the coins of Dāmajadaśrī I are closer to those of Rudradāman

I, and the coins of Dāmaghsada II are closer to those of *Rudrasiṁha I, Dāmajadaśrī I appears to have ruled earlier than Dāmaghsada; Dāmaghsada II might have served as **kshatrapa* under Dāmajadaśrī I, and succeeded him to the office of **mahākshatrapa*. The relative scarcity of his coins seems to indicate a short reign period for him (Jha and Rajgor 1994; Mirashi 1982; Mitchiner 1976; Rapson 1975; Raychaudhuri 1972; Senior 2001; Sircar 1980e).

Damagupta. *Pañchāla k. He seems to be one of the earliest rulers known from Pañchāla coins. There is a restruck coin, involving Vaṅgapāla and Damagupta. Some scholars are of the view that the coin was originally struck by the former, and restruck by the latter. But Bela Lahiri states that the devices of Vaṅgapāla on both the obv and the rev are more prominent than those of Damagupta, and the coin should be regarded as the issue of Damagupta restruck by Vaṅgapāla, which would place Vaṅgapāla later than Damagupta. The rev of a coin of Damagupta has a three-spoked *wheel with *taurines (Dar 1940; K D Bajpai 1953; Bela Lahiri 1974; Prashant Srivastava 1989; Prashant Srivastava 1996a).

Dāmajadaśrī I. *Kārddamaka k. He was the son of *Rudradāman I. He started his career as a **kshatrapa*, and later succeeded his father as **mahākshatrapa*. Rapson regarded *Dāmaghsada as another form of his name, but some scholars are of the opinion that Dāmaghsada was different from Dāmajadaśrī I, both being sons of Rudradāman I, and Dāmaghsada first serving under Dāmajadaśrī I as his *kshatrapa*, and then succeeding him to the office of *mahākshatrapa*. He issued *Kārddamaka silver type of coins. The relative scarcity of his coins seems to indicate his short reign (Jha and Rajgor 1994; Mirashi 1982; Mitchiner 1976; Rapson 1975; Raychaudhuri 1972; Senior 2001; Sircar 1980e).

Dāmajadaśrī II. *Kārddamaka k. He was the son of *Rudrasena I, and served as a **kshatrapa* under his uncle, *Dāmasena, from *Śaka year 154 to 155. He issued coins of the *Kārddamaka silver type (Jha and Rajgor 1994; Mirashi 1982; Mitchiner 1976; Rapson 1975; Raychaudhuri 1972; Senior 2001; Sircar 1980e).

Dāmajadaśrī III. *Kārddamaka k. He was the son of *Dāmasena, and succeeded his brother, *Vijayasena, as **mahākshatrapa* in the *Śaka year 172 or 173 : some scholars regard the reading of Śaka year 172 on his coins as doubtful. His reign lasted till Śaka year 177. He issued coins of the *Kārddamaka silver type (Jha and Rajgor 1994; Mirashi 1982; Mitchiner 1976; Rapson 1975; Raychaudhuri 1972; Senior 2001; Sircar 1980e).

Dāmasena. *Kārddamaka k. He was the son of *Rudrasiṁha I, and ruled as **mahākshatrapa* from *Śaka year 145 to 159. In the year 154, he appointed his nephew, *Dāmajadaśrī II, as his **kshatrapa*. But from year 156 to 160, we find *Vīradāman, the son of Dāmasena, serving as *kshatrapa*. He issued coins of the *Kārddamaka silver type. There are also some potin coins, which bear on the obv, the figure of an *elephant to the r, with a star above to the l, and a crescent to the r. The rev of these coins has a *crescent-on-hill, star, and crescent. There is no ld on these coins, but the dates of issue of the coins—Śaka years 147-158, fall within the reign of Dāmasena as *mahākshatrapa,* and these coins might have been issued during his reign for circulation in the Malwa region (Jha and Rajgor 1994; Mirashi 1982; Mitchiner 1976; Rapson 1975; Raychaudhuri 1972; Senior 2001; Sircar 1980e).

Daric. Coin denomination. It was the gold coin of ancient Iran, struck, perhaps, from the time of Darius I (521-486 BC). It weighed around 129.6 grains, and contained 3% silver alloy. It was a widely diffused gold coin of the ancient world, being accepted throughout the Mediterranean and Black Sea areas, and as far east as India. Twenty **sigloi* were equal to one *daric* in value. There is a suggestion that the *daric* got its name from Darius [I], but some scholars are of the view that it is the Greek form of the Persian *zariq*, 'gold'. Double *darics*, modelled after the *darics*, were issued by the generals and satraps appointed by Alexander in Iran after his conquest of the Achaemenian empire. These bear Gr letters, monograms, and symbols in the field (Junge 1984).

Daska hoards. One hoard in the village of Daska, situated midway between Gujranwala and Sialkot, was discovered in a pot in 1993. Around 300 coins from this hoard are known, and the rulers represented in this hoard include *Amyntas, *Antimachos II, *Apollodotos, *Diomedes, and *Menander I. Another hoard of around 400 coins is also reported from the same village by Aman ur Rahman, but the particulars of this hoard is not known, except for two coins of Amyntas (Bopearachchi 1994; Bopearachchi and Rahman 1995).

Samudragupta : *Aśvamedha* type

Dattadevī. *Imperial Gupta queen. She was the consort of *Samudragupta, and the mother of *Chandragupta II. Her figure appears on the reverse of the **Aśvamedha* type of her husband (Altekar 1957).

Punch marked coin

Kuṇinda

Deer. Symbol. In the Śrīsūkta of the *Ṛigveda*, Śrī is compared to a *hāriṇī*, a female deer, and the deer appearing on the *Amoghabhūti and **Chatreśvara* series of *Kuṇinda coins, as also on the coins of the *Yaudheya tribe, is regarded as the theriomorphic representation of *Lakshmī. On the coins of the Amoghabhūti series, the animal stands beside a female figure, which is identified as Lakshmī by some scholars. But K K Dasgupta feels that if the deer on this series is regarded as the theriomorphic representation of Lakshmī, then it would mean an unnecessary duplication, for the goddess is also represented there in the anthropomorphic form. He is inclined to identify the deer on these coins as Yaksha Ushṭrapāda, who is mentioned in the *Māhāmāyūrī* as the tutelary deity of the Kuṇindas. It has also been suggested that when the deer appears on the *Chatreśvara* series, it has Śaiva affiliations (Allan 1936; Banerjea 2002; Chakrabortty 1931; Bhaskar Chattopadhyay 1977; K K Dasgupta 1974; Handa 2007a; Bela Lahiri 1974; Rao 1985; Savita Sharma 1990).

Azes II

Demeter. Greek goddess of agriculture. She was the daughter of the Titan Kronos and the Titaness Rhea, and a sister of *Zeus, Hades, *Poseidon, Hestia, and Hera. Her name Demeter probably signifies her quality as the Earth-mother. In most of the accounts, Demeter is the wife of Poseidon. She 'despatched Triptolemos (a culture hero) to teach men agriculture'. She has the **cornucopiae* as her characteristic attribute. On the coins of the *Indo-Greeks and the *Śaka-Pahlavas, Demeter is shown as either standing or seated. On the obv of some copper coins of *Philoxenos, as also on some copper of *Azes I, the standing goddess holds a *cornucopiae* in her l hand, while her r hand is upraised or extended. When enthroned, as, for example, on the rev of some double-*decadrachms* of *Amyntas, and on some coins of Azes I, Demeter again holds a *cornucopiae* in her l hand, while her r hand is outstretched (Bopearachchi 1993; Bopearachchi and Pieper 1998; Bopearachchi and Rahman 1995; Bhaskar Chattopadhyay 1977; Cunningham 1971a; Gardner 1971; Graves 1955; Kerenyi 1951; A N Lahiri 1965; Marshall 1975; Rose 1958; Prashant Srivastava 2007c; Whitehead 1914).†

Demetrios I. *Indo-Greek k; son of *Euthydemos I; first half of the second century BC. Scholars have attributed him wide ranging conquests, and there are suggestions that he occupied Aria, Arachosia, Seistan, and the eastern parts of Gedriosia. The conquests of Sogdiana, and perhaps Ferghana, also seem to have been achieved by *Euthydemos II, during his reign. Mainly on the basis of some bilingual coins bearing the name of Demetrios, it was almost universally believed that Demetrios crossed the Hindukush, and occupied the Kabul and the Indus valleys. But scholars, like Macdonald and Narain, seem to be right in ascribing these bilingual coins to *Demetrios II. Demetrios had to face danger of the nomads from the north, and the Imperial Parthians from the west, besides restive elements in Sogdiana, Aria, Drangiana, and India. He, therefore, very wisely desisted from disturbing the powers on the other side of the Hindukush, and, rather, utilized his energies in consolidating the territories he had already conquered. But the subsequent discoveries of his coins from several places in the North West Frontier Province, and the use of the elephant's scalp as his headdress on coins, have led Osmund Bopearachchi to suggest that Demetrios I might have attempted conquests to the south of the Hindukush. He issued coins in silver and copper, based on the Attic standard. All the coins are die-struck pieces. The coins are all round in shape. The silver coins bear the diademed bust of the king to the r, in elephant's scalp, on the obv, and naked *Herakles standing to front and crowning himself with his r hand, on the rev. One copper type has buckler with *Gorgon's head on the obv, and a trident on the rev. A second type has the bust of Herakles to the r, with a club over his left shoulder, on the obv, and radiate standing *Artemis, bearing a bow and drawing an arrow from the quiver at her back,

Demetrios I

on the rev. Another copper type has *elephant's head to the r, with a bell round the neck, on the obv, and **caduceus* on the rev. All these types bear the Gr ld on the rev, in which Demetrios uses the title of **basileus*. Besides this normal coinage, Demetrios I is also believed to have issued a silver type, in Attic *tetradrachms*, in memory of *Diodotos I. This type bears the diademed head of Diodotos I on the obv, and thundering *Zeus, holding **aegis* on his left arm, on the rev. The type makes no mention of Demetrios I, but bears the ld *Diodotou soteros* on the rev. However, it has not been regarded as an issue of Diodotos I himself, because of the conspicuous absence of the royal title of **basileus*. On the basis of the monogram on this type, it has been ascribed to Demetrios I. Recently, another Attic *tetradrachm*, this one in memory of Antiochos *Nikator*, has been reported. It bears the diademed head of the king to the r on the obv; the rev has thundering Zeus, holding *aegis* on his left arm, and with an *eagle at his feet, and the ld *Antiochou Nikatoros*. This type cannot be regarded as the normal issue of Antiochos, primarily because the title of *basileus* is conspicuous by its absence on this coin, too, and secondarily because the rev has the type of *Diodotos, and not of Antiochos II, which was *Apollo seated on *omphalos*. When Diodotos issued coins in the name of Antiochos, he used for him the title *basileus*, and, therefore, it is difficult to the regard it as an issue of Diodotos. The monogram on the rev of this coin is the same as that on the *Diodotou soteros* coin, and seems to connect the type with Demetrios. There are some imitation Demetrios coins, which might have been struck by the *Śaka-Pahlavas (Bopearachchi 1993; Bopearachchi 1994; Bopearachchi and Pieper 1998; Bopearachchi and Rahman 1995; Cunningham 1970; Gardner 1971; A N Lahiri 1965; Macdonald 1987; Marshall 1975; Narain 1957a; Rapson 1987; Senior 2001; Sircar 1980a; Prashant Srivastava 1996a; Tarn 1980; Whitehead 1914).†

Demetrios II. *Indo-Greek k; son of *Antimachos I (?); early second century BC. He is believed to some scholars to be the first Indo-Greek king to issue bilingual coins, the Kh ld on the rev being meant for his Indian subjects. This has led to the inference that Demetrios II was perhaps the first Indo-Greek king to cross the Hindukush, and occupy the Kabul valley. He seems to have assumed the title of **aniketos* after this achievement. He might also have conquered Gandhāra and some of its western territories. When he was busy in these southern ventures, *Eukratides I occupied Bactria. The attempts of Demetrios II to recover this region proved futile, and he also seems to have been killed in his encounter with Eukratides I. Demetrios II would occupy a very important place in the numismatic history of the Indo-Greeks, if he is regarded as the first ruler to issue coins with a Gr ld on the obv, and a Kh ld on the rev of his coins struck on the Indian standard, and the first to give the Pkt equivalent (**aparajita*) of the Greek title (*aniketos*) of the king on coins. He is believed to have issued silver coins struck on both the Attic standard and the Indian standard, and copper coins struck on the Indian standard alone. All the coins are die-struck pieces. The silver coins are round in shape, while the copper coins are square in shape. The obv of his coins is occupied by the bust of the king to the r, and wearing a headdress on the coins struck on the Indian standard—a *kausia* on the silver coins, and an elephant's scalp on the copper coins. The rev of the Attic standard silver coins has the figure of *Athena, standing to the r, and bears spear and shield. The rev of the Indian standard silver type has thundering *Zeus to the front, with a long sceptre in his l hand. The copper type has a winged *thunderbolt on the rev. The coins struck on the Attic standard have only the Gr ld, with the royal title of **basileus*, on the rev. As mentioned earlier, the coins struck on the Indian standard bear a Gr ld on the obv, and the Pkt ld, written in the Kh script, on the rev. On these coins, besides the title of *basileus*, he assumed the epithet *aniketos*. These are rendered into Pkt as **maharaja* and *aparajita*, respectively. The Pkt form of the name of the ruler, as met with on coins, is Dimetriya. The possibility of the existence of a third ruler bearing the name Demetrios has also been expressed by scholars like A N Lahiri and Colin M Kraay (Bopearachchi 1993; Bopearachchi and Pieper 1998; Bopearachchi and Rahman 1995; Cunningham 1970; Gardner 1971; Kraay 1985; A N Lahiri 1965; Macdonald 1987; Marshall 1975; Narain 1957a; Rapson 1987; Sircar 1980a; Prashant Srivastava 1996a; Tarn 1980; Whitehead 1914).†

Denarius. Coin denomination. It was the Roman silver coin, first introduced in 269-268 BC. Its original weight was 70 grains, but after 210 BC and up to the time of Augustus (27 BC – 14 AD), it weighed 60 grains, and after Nero (54-68 AD), it was reduced to 52 grains. One *denarius aureus*, that is the gold *denarius*, was equal to 25 silver *denarii* in value. Apparently, this term was introduced into Indian coinage during the *Kushāṇa rule, and denoted their gold coin. In Indian literary and epigraphic sources, it appears as **dīnāra* (V S Agrawala 1957; C S Gupta 1982).

Denomination. It is the 'name given to any particular coin to denote its value'. It is not necessary for the value or denomination to be stated on the coin itself, particularly in ancient times (Junge 1984).

Deva hoard. This hoard of 54 silver coins was discovered in the Kaira district of Gujarat. The rulers represented in this hoard include the *Kārddamaka Kshatrapas, *Rudradāman I, *Rudrasiṁha I, *Jīvadāman, *Rudrasena I, *Pṛithvīsena, *Dāmasena, *Vīradāman, and *Vijayasena. Three coins belong to *Īśvaradatta, and seven are in a very damaged state and defy all attempts at ascription (Jha and Rajgor 1994; Pandya 1965).

Devamitra. *Ayodhyā k. He is placed after *Saṅghamitra and *Vijayamitra, and before *Satyamitra and *Āyumitra by Bela Lahiri on the basis of a comparative study of the letter *ma* occurring in the coin legends. But on the basis of a coin bearing the names of *Devamitra and Āyumitra, it seems more likely that Devamitra ruled immediately before Āyumitra. His coins are all in copper, and bear the figure of a *bull before a spear on the obv, along with the name of the issuer in the genitive. The rev has a *cock on a post to the r, and a tree (Bela Lahiri 1974; Smith 1972; Prashant Srivastava 1992b; Prashant Srivastava 1996a).

Devanāga. *Nāga k. He is associated with *Bṛihaspatināga and *Bhavanāga by the use of the 'Trident' type, and seems to have ruled between the two. He also issued the 'Bull' and 'Wheel' types of coins. He assumed the title of **mahārāja-śrī* on coins (Cunningham 1967; Bela Lahiri 1974; Smith 1972; H V Trivedi 1957).

Devasenā. *Shashṭhī-Devasenā.

Devavrata. Title. This title means 'steadfast in god (more particularly *Śiva)', and shows the Śaivite inclinations of the *Śaka-Pahlava ruler, *Gondopharnes, as also of *Sasan, the two kings who assumed this title on their coins (Gardner 1971; Jenkins and Narain 1957; Marshall 1975; Senior 2001; Whitehead 1914).

Devnimori hoard. This hoard of 37 or 38 silver coins was discovered during the course of excavations at the site of Devnimori in the Sabarkantha district of Gujarat, in 1960-1961. Of these, 26 coins could not be attributed to any ruler. The rest were issued by the *Kārddamaka rulers, like *Viśvasena, *Bhartṛidāman, *Jīvadāman, and Svāmi *Rudrasena III, though the possibility of the existence of the coins of *Rudrasena II, *Viśvasiṁha, *Rudrasiṁha II, and *Yaśodāman II, has also been expressed (Jha and Rajgor 1994).

Dhanadeva. *Ayodhyā k. Besides his copper coins, he is also known from the Ayodhyā stone inscription, wherein he is referred to as sixth in descent from Pushyamitra Śuṅga, and on this basis, he is placed towards the end of the first century BC. Some of his coins bear the figure of a *bull before a symbol on the obv, and a combination of symbols on the rev. But other coins have a bull to the r on the obv, and a standing figure, identified with *Lakshmī, surrounded by symbols, like the *tree-in-railing, **nandipada*, **svastika*, etc, on the rev. The ld *Dhanadevasa* occurs on the obv of all his coins. The rev type of Lakshmī connects him with other Ayodhyā rulers, like *Vāyudeva, *Viśākhadeva, and *Śivadatta (Allan 1936; Bela Lahiri 1974; Smith 1972).

Dhanadeva. *Kauśāmbī k. He appears to be identical with **Rājan* Dhanadeva of some sealings found at Rajghat near Varanasi. He issued copper coins of the 'Bull : Tree-in-railing' type, after a break in the issue of the local coins of Kauśāmbī due to the *Kushāṇa interregnum. Imitations of his coins are also known, these imitation coins bearing names like *Nava, Mūlahasta (?), and Vishṇuśrī (?). Allan places him in the first century BC-first century AD time-bracket, although Bela Lahiri would place the Dhanadeva group of kings in the early centuries of the Christian era. The peculiar tree on his coins closely resembles that on the coins of *Rajanīmitra, and this might provide a link between the early Kauśāmbī rulers and the Dhanadeva group of kings (Allan 1936; Altekar 1942a; Bela Lahiri 1974).

Dhānaka. Coin denomination (?). Mentioned in sources, like the *Bakhshali manuscript, it weighs 5 *rattīs* (R C Agrawala 1954b).

Dharaghosha. *Audumbara chief. Both copper coins of Class I of *Audumdara coins, and silver coins of Class II of *Audumbara coins, bearing the name of Dharaghosha, are available. On these coins, he uses the titles of **raña* and **mahadeva*. He seems to have ruled towards the end of the first century BC or the beginning of the first century AD. The figure of *Viśvāmitra on his silver coins is interesting (Allan 1936; Chakrabortty 1931; Cunningham 1971b; K K Dasgupta 1974; Handa 2007a; Jayaswal 1988; Marshall 1975; Mitchiner 1975-1976; Smith 1972).

Audumbara : Dharaghosha

Dharaṇa. Coin denomination. It was the name generally used for the standard silver *punch marked coins, also known as **kārshāpaṇa*, each weighing 32 *rattīs*. But lawgivers, like Manu and Yājñavalkya, also refer to a gold *dharaṇa*, weighing 3200 *rattīs*, and, thus, equal to 10 **nishkas* and 40 **suvarṇas* (D R Bhandarkar 1984; Bühler 2001; Chakrabortty 1931).

Dharmachakra. Symbol. The *Indo-Greek ruler, *Menander, depicted a peculiar type of wheel on the obv of some of his copper coins. Tarn is of the view that the purpose of this depiction is to show Menander as a *chakravartin*. But, in view of the facts that Menander's Buddhist leanings are evident from the *Milindapañho*, and that the wheel on his coins bears a close affinity to the *dharmachakra* seen on early Buddhist monuments, like those of Sanchi, the spokes of the *chakra* being provided with terminals outside the rim in the shape of *triratnas*, Marshall, and, following him, a number of other scholars, identify the wheel on the coins of Menander as the Buddhist *dhramachakra*. Although a similar wheel also occurs on the earlier **paṁchanekame* coins of *Taxila, there is a suggestion that the use of the elaborate *chakra* on the obv of the *Kulūta coins of *Vīrayaśas, and on the rev of the coin of the *Vṛishṇis, might have been inspired by the device of these coins of Menander. But keeping in view the affiliation of the Vṛishṇi people with Vāsudeva-Kṛishṇa, whose attribute was the *sudarśanachakra*, the suggestion that the symbol on the Vṛishṇi coin seems to the represent the *sudarśanachakra* of the Vṛishṇi hero, seems to be more appropriate than that of Cunningham and Allan, who regard it as a Buddhist *dharmachakra* (Allan 1936; Chakrabortty 1931; Cunningham 1971b; Gardner 1971; Handa 2007a; A N Lahiri 1965; Marshall 1975; Savita Sharma 1990; Tarn 1980; Whitehead 1914).

Dholera hoard. This hoard of 32 silver coins of the *Kārddamaka Kshatrapas was discovered in the Rajkot district of Gujarat in 1988. The rulers represented in this hoard include *Vijayasena, *Bhartṛidāman, *Viśvasena, *Yaśodāman II, and *Rudrasena III (Jha and Rajgor 1994).

Dhramaṭhida. Title. Meaning 'steadfast in religion', this title was adopted by the *Kushāṇa ruler, *Kujula Kadphises, on his coins; sometimes, this title is preceded by *sacha-*, the whole title now meaning 'steadfast in true religion'. It has been taken by some scholars to indicate the Buddhist leanings of that ruler (Cunningham 1962; Cunningham 1971a; Gardner 1971; Rosenfield 1967; Whitehead 1914).

Dhramiä. Title. **Dhramika.*

Dhramika. Title. It is the Pkt rendering of **dikaios*, and used by *Archebios, *Heliokles, *Menander, *Peukolaos, *Strato I, *Theophilos, and *Zoilos I. Among the *Śaka-Pahlavas, it was assumed by *Abdagases, *Azes II, *Sapedana, *Sapalagadama, and *Sapalahora. The Skt equivalent is *dhārmika* (Cunningham 1970; Gardner 1971; A N Lahiri 1965; Marshall 1975; Narain 1957a; Tarn 1980; Whitehead 1914).

Dhruvadevī. *Imperial Gupta queen. She was married to *Rāmagupta, who agreed to surrender her to the invading Śaka king as per one of the terms of peace. She turned to *Chandragupta II for help. Chandragupta II, disguised as Dhruvadevī, killed the Śaka king, and saved her. Then, he also killed Rāmagupta, occupied his throne, and married his wife. In Imperial Gupta genealogies, Dhruvadevī is mentioned as the *mahādevī* of Chandragupta II, and on a seal from Vaiśālī, as the mother of Govindagupta. There is a suggestion that she might have belonged to the ruling house of Kauśāmbī. Her figure appears on rev of the *King-and-Queen-on-Couch type of Chandragupta II (Ashvini Agrawal 1989; Altekar 1957; D R Bhandarkar 1981; Thaplyal 1997).

Dhruvamitra. *Pañchāla k. He is placed among the later rulers of Pañchāla known from coins, on palaeographical grounds. His coins are associated with those of *Rudragupta at Rohtayya and Ramnagar; the rev device on the coins of these two rulers is the same—a *trident or trident-battleaxe on a pedestal between two pillars. This seems to be the symbolic representation of *Śiva, who is also known as Dhruva and Rudra, the names these two rulers bore, respectively (Allan 1936; Bela Lahiri 1974).

Dhruvamitra. *Uddehika chief. Belonging, perhaps, to the second-first centuries BC, he issued copper coins bearing a **svastika* and *Ujjain symbol and the legends *Sudavapa* and *Dhruvamitasa* on the obv, and indistinct symbols on the rev (Allan 1936; Chakrabortty 1931; Cunningham 1971b; K K Dasgupta 1974; Handa 2007a; Jayaswal 1988; Bela Lahiri 1974; Marshall 1975; Smith 1972).

Die. It is 'the instrument containing the design which, by being impressed, produces the type on a coin'. In ancient times, for single die-struck coins, the die was generally embedded in the anvil, but for double die-struck coins, one die was inserted in the anvil, while the other was inserted in the lower end of the punch. The symbols, devices, legends, etc, desired on the coin in relief and in the positive, were engraved on the die in intaglio and in the negative. The only specimen of ancient Indian coin die available comes from *Eran. It is made of bronze, and is dated to *c* 300 BC. Modern dies are usually made of steel, but ancient dies were of iron or bronze (Hill 1906; Junge 1984; B N Mukherjee and P K D Lee 1988; Thaplyal 1989a).

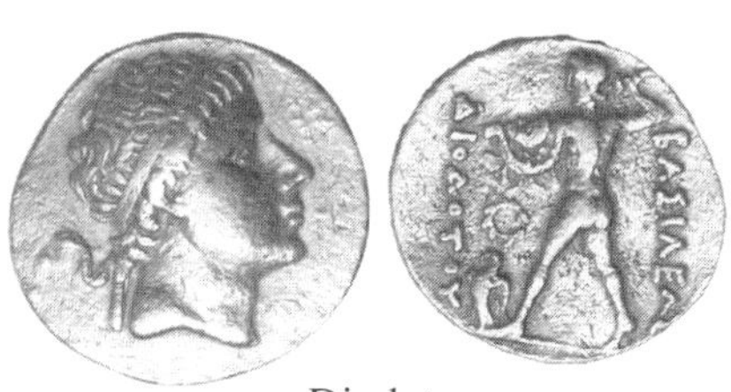
Diodotos

Die-striking method. Technique of manufacture of coins. Although a large number of die-struck coins have been found, so far, no *die has seen the light of day, except for a single specimen from Eran. This is in contrast to the find of a large number of moulds [*Casting coins in moulds]. Under such circumstances, we can only make inferences regarding their characteristic features from the examination of die-struck coins. In the die-striking method, a blank disc, adjusted to the proper size and weight, was heated. While still hot, it was, with the help of tongs, put firmly on the metal anvil with the complete device, or ld, or both, in negative in intaglio form, embedded in or laid on it. Over it was kept a punch. The punch was struck by a hammer, producing a coin of single die-struck variety, showing the device in positive and in relief. If the device or/and ld was also intended on the other side of the coin, then the same was carved in negative on the lower side of the punch that is kept over the blank, with the help of tongs. A blow was (or blows were) given by the hammer over the punch. The coin, thus produced by the double die-struck method, bore obv and rev devices, one from the punch, and the other from the anvil. S K Chakrabortty mentions four stages of die-striking coins. In the first stage, the die covered only two-thirds area of the blank, and the lower face was not stamped. In the second stage, a die was also cut on the anvil. In the third stage, the obv die covered practically the whole face of the metal blank, but the rev die wass smaller than the blank. Finally, in the fourth stage, both the obv and the rev dies covered practically the whole face. The example of the first type is seen in Eran coins, where symbols met with on punch marked type of coins were made by a single die. The impression was made on the metal blank in a semi-molten condition, and the 'impression of the die was left enclosed in a deep incuse square', which is also met with on some coins from other areas like *Pañchāla, *Kauśāmbī, etc. In some double die-struck coins, the obv and rev dies are not parallel to each other. Scholars are divided on the question whether the die-striking method is indigenous in origin, or was introduced as a result of foreign influence. James Prinsep took it as of foreign origin. According to Smith, single die-striking is of indigenous origin, but double die-striking technique was learnt by the Indians from the foreigners. Thomas says that die-striking, and many other matters relating to manufacture of coins, must have been perfected by the Indians before the advent of the Greeks in India. For, had they not done so, they could have not only imitated the technique, but also copied the perfect coins of Alexander, which would have been readily available to them. D R Bhandarkar considers both single and double die-striking as of indigenous origin, and argues that if the Indians knew the single die-striking technique, they themselves, in normal course, would have evolved double die-striking method

Chandragupta I and Kumāradevī

Samudragupta : Archer type

(Chakrabortty 1931; B N Mukherjee and P K D Lee 1988; Prashant Srivastava 2008c).

Dikaios. Title. Meaning 'just', this title was borne by the *Indo-Greek rulers, *Agathokles, *Archebios, *Heliokles, *Menander, *Peukolaos, *Strato I, *Theophilos, and *Zoilos I. Gardner is of the view that the Arsakid ruler, Mithridates I, adopted this epithet in imitation of Agathokles. In Pkt, it has been rendered as **dhramika* or *dhramiä* (Cunningham 1970; Gardner 1971; A N Lahiri 1965; Marshall 1975; Narain 1957a; Tarn 1980; Whitehead 1914).

Huvishka

Dīnāra. Coin denomination. This coin denomination was derived from the Roman **dinarius*. But while the Roman *denarius* was a silver coin, in India, *dīnāra* denoted a gold coin issued first by the *Kushāṇas on the model of the Roman **aureus*, and subsequently by the *Imperial Guptas. References to *dīnāra* occur in Indian literature. In Imperial Gupta epigraphs, the gold coin is termed *dīnāra*, and continued to be termed as such even after *Skandagupta raised the weight of the gold coin to conform to the traditional weight of the Indian **suvarṇa*, that is 80 *rattīs*. It is learnt from the *Gaṇitasārasaṁgraham* that a *dīnāra* was two-thirds of a *suvarṇa*. In the *Bakhshali manuscript, a *dīnāra* is said to be equal to 60 *rattīs* in weight, but this would make the *suvarṇa* of 90 *rattīs*, which seems strange, for, elsewhere in the same manuscript, the weight of the *dīnāra* is given as 80 *rattīs*. In the **Aṅgavijjā*, we have the form *dīṇāri*, which is closer to the original *denarii*. Literary evidence points at the existence of **raupya-dīnāra*, besides gold *dīnāra* (*suvarṇa-dīnāra*) (R C Agrawala 1954b; V S Agrawala 1957; D R Bhandarkar 1984; C S Gupta 1982).

***Dīṇāra-māsaka* (= *Dīnāra-māshaka*).** Coin denomination. This coin denomination, mentioned in the **Aṅgavijjā*, seems to be one-sixteenth of the **dīnāra*, which was the standard gold coin of the *Kushāṇas weighing about 120 grains after the Roman *denarius aureus*. The reference to this coin denomination in the *Aṅgavijjā* is taken to indicate the existence of the submultiples of the *dīnāra*, although no actual specimen of such a submultiple has yet been found (V S Agrawala 1957).

Diodotos I. First *Indo-Greek k; mid-third century BC. Originally a satrap of the Seleukids in Bactria, he rebelled in 256 BC, during the reign of Antiochos II. Not much is known about the subsequent career of Diodotos I, except that, besides Bactria, he also ruled over Margiana and Sogdiana. On the commemorative coins issued by *Demetrios I and *Agathokles in honour of Diodotos I, he is given the title of **soteros*, but it is not known if this title was used by Diodotos I himself in his lifetime. Diodotos I issued coins in gold and silver, all struck on the Attic standard. All the coins are die-struck pieces. All these pieces are round in shape. He experimented with the coinage of Antiochos II, and sometimes substituted his own portrait for those of his erstwhile Seleukid overlord. The obv of one gold type has the diademed head of Antiochos II to the r, while that of the other gold and one silver type has the diademed head of Diodotos I himself to the r. The rev of all the three types bears the figure of thundering *Zeus, with an **aegis* on his left arm and an *eagle in front. All these coins were struck in the name of Antiochos II, and the Gr ld, engraved on the rev, uses the title of **basileus* for the Seleukid monarch (Bopearachchi 1993; Bopearachchi and Pieper 1998; Bopearachchi and Rahman 1995; Cunningham 1970; Gardner 1971; Kovalenko 1995-1996; A N Lahiri 1965; Marshall 1975; Narain 1957a; Newell 1938; Rapson 1987; Sircar 1980a; Prashant Srivastava 1996a; Tarn 1980; Whitehead 1914).†

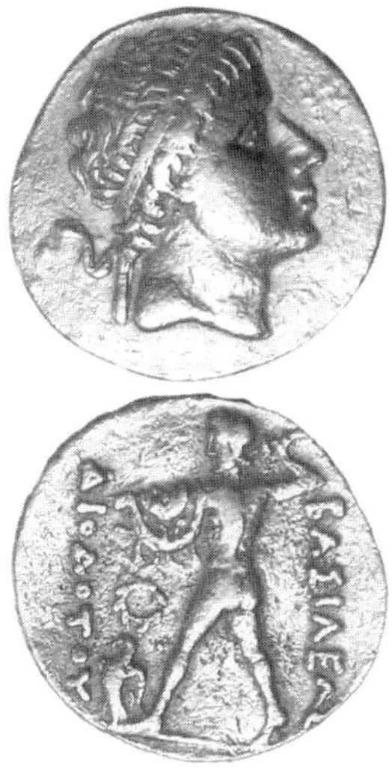

Diodotos

Diodotos II. *Indo-Greek k; son of *Diodotos I; latter half of the third century BC. The Parthians maintained friendly relations with him, for mutual security, as also to foil any attempts on the part of the Seleukids to re-establish their authority over the two breakaway satrapies of Bactria and Parthia. He was able to the retain hold over Bactria and Sogdiana. Polybios seems to suggest that Diodotos II lost his life at the hands of *Euthydemos I. He is believed to be the first Indo-Greek ruler to give his name of the coins. He issued coins in gold, silver, and copper, all struck on the Attic standard. All the coins are die-struck pieces. All his coins are round in shape. One of his silver types has, on the obv, a diademed head to the r, which, according to some scholars, might be identified as that of Antiochos II. But on his second silver type, as well as on the gold type ascribed to him, he depicted the diademed bust of Diodotos to the r, on the obv. The rev of all these types has thundering *Zeus, with an **aegis* on his left arm, standing to the l. The head of Diodotos on these coins 'tends to grow ever younger'. The reason for this might be that Diodotos II first issued coins bearing the (mature) head of his father, and then replaced it with his own (younger) head. One of the copper types of Diodotos II bears the head of the king to the r, wearing a *kausia*, on the obv, while the rev is occupied by the standing figure of *Athena, bearing spear and shield. The other copper type has the lauriate head of Zeus to the r on the obv, and *Artemis, holding a torch in both her hands, running to the r, her hound running beside her, on the rev. Still another copper type has the head of *Hermes to the r on the obv, and standing Athena on the rev. All the types of Diodotos II bear the Gr ld on the rev, and have the title of **basileus* for him (Bopearachchi 1993; Bopearachchi and Pieper 1998; Bopearachchi and Rahman 1995; Cunningham 1970; Gardner 1971; Kovalenko 1995-1996; A N Lahiri 1965; Marshall 1975; Narain 1957a; Newell 1938; Rapson 1987; Sircar 1980a; Prashant Srivastava 1996a; Tarn 1980; Whitehead 1914).†

Diomedes

Diomedes. *Indo-Greek k; son of *Antialkidas; early first century BC. He managed to establish himself in parts of western Gandhāra, apparently after the death of *Apollodotos, *c* 95 BC, and ruled for about 10 years, when he was supplanted by *Amyntas in that region. Diomedes issued coins in silver and copper, all struck on the Indian standard. All the coins are die-struck pieces. The silver coins are all round in shape, while the only known copper type is square in shape. The obv of the silver types is occupied by the diademed bust of the king to the r, sometimes wearing a smooth helmet. But the helmeted bust of the king, when thrusting a javelin, is shown to the l on one type. The rev of these silver types mostly has the mounted *Dioskuri, bearing palms and **pilei*, charging to the r. But on two types, the divine twins are shown standing to the front, the long spears, held in their hands, resting on the ground. The copper type has the Dioskuri standing in a similar manner, but on the obv, while the rev has the figure of a humped *bull to the r. All the types bear the Gr ld on the obv, and the Pkt ld, written in the Kh script, on the rev. Besides the title of **basileus*, Diomedes assumed the epithet *soteros* on his coins. These are rendered into Pkt as **maharaja* and *tratara*, respectively. The Pkt form of the name of the ruler, as met with on coins, is Diyameta (Bopearachchi 1993; Bopearachchi and Pieper

1998; Bopearachchi and Rahman 1995; Cunningham 1970; Gardner 1971; A N Lahiri 1965; Marshall 1975; Narain 1957a; Rapson 1987; Senior 2001; Sircar 1980a; Tarn 1980; Whitehead 1914).†

Dionysios. *Indo-Greek k; scion of the family of *Apollodotos; second decade of the first century BC. He appears to have ruled over the Jammu-Sialkot region in the interval between the two phases of the reign of *Strato I. Dionysios issued at least one silver and three copper types, all struck on the Indian standard. All the coins are die-struck pieces. The silver coins are round in shape; the copper ones are mostly square in shape, but one type is also round in shape. The silver type bears the diademed bust of the king to the r on the obv, and thundering *Athena standing to the l, with an **aegis* on her left arm, on the rev. The obv of all the copper types has the figure of *Apollo standing to the r, bears an arrow in both the hands; the rev mostly has the **tripod lebes*, but on one type, which does not bear any Gr ld and has only the Kh ld on the rev, there is the representation of the royal diadem on the rev. All the coins of Dionysios, barring those of the square copper 'Apollo standing : Royal diadem' type which have no ld on the obv, bear the Gr ld on the obv, and the Pkt ld, engraved in the Kh script on the rev. Besides the title of **basileus*, Dionysios assumed the epithet **soteros* on his coins. These are rendered into Pkt as **maharaja* and **tratara*, respectively. The Pkt form of the name of the ruler, as met with on coins, is Diänisiya (Bopearachchi 1993; Bopearachchi and Pieper 1998; Bopearachchi and Rahman 1995; Cunningham 1970; Gardner 1971; A N Lahiri 1965; Marshall 1975; Narain 1957a; Rapson 1906; Rapson 1987; Sircar 1980a; Tarn 1980; Whitehead 1914).†

Dionysos. Greek god; inventor of wine. An outsider from Thrace and Phrygia, he was accepted in the Greek pantheon as the youngest immortal son of *Zeus. According to some sources, he was born of Persephone, the queen of the underworld, and, as such, had the surname Chthonios, 'the subterranean'. Semele, the name of his mother as given in other versions, seems to be derived from Zemelo, the Phrygian earth goddess, and this connects Dionysos with the earth. He was born from the thigh of Zeus. He is credited with exploits in Egypt, Libya, Syria, and even India. The two brothers, *Pantaleon and *Agathokles, depicted the bust of Dionysos to the r, wearing ivy

Agathokles

wreath and with thyrsos over his left shoulder, on the obv of their bronze and cupro-nickel coins. It may be noted that on the coins of Pantaloen, the bust is that of a young Dionysos (Bopearachchi 1993; Bopearachchi and Pieper 1998; Bopearachchi and Rahman 1995; Bhaskar Chattopadhyay 1977; Cunningham 1971a; Gardner 1971; Graves 1955; Kerenyi 1951; A N Lahiri 1965; Marshall 1975; Rose 1958; Prashant Srivastava 2007c; Whitehead 1914).†

Diomedes

Dioskuri, The. Greek twin gods of sailors, games, and poetry. The twins, Kastor and Pollox (or Polydeukos) were the sons of Leda by *Zeus. The Dioskuri, or *Dios kouroi*, 'sons of Zeus', are believed to be originally the daemons of the morning and evening twilight. There is a tradition that Zeus placed them as stars in the constellation Gemini. Usually, the Dioskuri, charging on horseback and holding spears and palm branches, are depicted together, as on the coins of the *Indo-Greek ruler, *Eukratides, and some other princes of his family like *Diomedes, and on the coins of the *Śaka-Pahlava ruler, *Azilises. But on some silver coins of Eukratides, we find only one of the Dioskuri, charging on horseback. The twin deities, standing side by side, and holding long spears (and sometimes also swords), may be seen on some coins of Eukratides, Diomedes, and Azilises. Some coins of the last mentioned king also bear the figure of just one of the Dioskuri, standing on the ground, with a long spear in his r hand, while his l hand rests on the hilt of a sword. On some gold and silver coins of Eukratides, instead of the anthropomorphic representation of the Dioskuri, we find their characteristic symbols, the palms and **pilei*, representing them (Bopearachchi 1993; Bopearachchi and Pieper 1998; Bopearachchi and Rahman 1995; Bhaskar Chattopadhyay 1977; Cunningham 1971a; Gardner 1971; Graves 1955; Kerenyi 1951; A N Lahiri 1965; Marshall 1975; Rose 1958; Prashant Srivastava 2007c; Whitehead 1914).†

Azilises

Dojaka. Guild. *Takshaśilā. Guild coins.

Dośanasa. Ld. *Takshaśilā. Guild coins.

Drachm. Coin denomination. It is usually derived from the Greek, *drattesthai*, and is believed as representing a 'handful' of **obols*. According to the Attic standard, which was accepted almost universally throughout the Hellenistic world, the *drachm* was the standard silver coin, weighing 67.2 grains, that is half of the weight of a gold **stater* (in the Corinthian system, however, the *drachm* was one-third of the *stater*). The *Indo-Greeks inherited this denomination from the Seleukids, and maintained it in Bactria. *Tetradrachm* (four-*drachm*) and *obol* (one-sixth of a *drachm*) were the common multiple and submultiple, respectively, of the *drachm*; Attic *hemidrachm* (half of a *drachm*) denomination is known for *Antimachos I, *Agathokles, and *Apollodotos; Amyntas issued some Attic double-*decadrachms* (20-*drachm*, weighing about 1300 grains each), which are believed to be the largest available silver coins issued by a ruler of Greek origin anywhere in the world. Twenty *drachms* were equal to one *stater* in value. Some Indo-Greek silver coins weighing around 36 grains, and others weighing around 148 grains, are also known from the time of Eukratides I onwards. Cunningham regarded them as Attic *hemidrachms* and *didrachms* (two-*drachm*), respectively; Gardner suggested that they might have been struck on some Persian standard; von Sallet believed them to be 'reduced *drachms* and *tetradrachms*'. But A N Lahiri is of the opinion that, with the introduction of the Attic *drachms* by the Indo-Greeks in India, silver coins based on two standards, the Attic one of 67.2 grains, and the Indian *dharaṇa* one of 56 grains, circulated side by side. Seeing that the newly-conquered Indians were accustomed to the use of silver coins which were lighter than the copper ones [*punch marked coins], Eukratides introduced in India, 'an arbitrary and hybrid standard of coinage', in which the *drachm* weighed around 36 grains, and the *tetradrachm*, 148 grains, and this was readily adopted by both his Indian and Greek subjects. Realizing the advantage of this new, reduced, standard, most of his successors, as also the *Śaka-Pahlavas, *Western Kshatrapas, *Imperial Guptas, *Hūṇas, *Maukharis, *Pushpabhūtis, and others, struck coins in this standard, which has come to be designated the Indian standard for silver coins [**dramma*, **drakhm*] (Cunningham 1970; Frey 1973; Gardner 1971; Hill 1909; Junge 1984; A N Lahiri 1965; Whitehead 1914).

Drakhma. Coin denomination. This denomination, a form of **drachm*, occurs in the *Niya Kh documents from central Asia, along with several other indigenous and foreign coin denominations.

At some places in these documents, the coin denomination has the form *trakhma* (R C Agrawala 1954a).

Dramma. Coin denomination. This is the Indianized form of **drachm*. Although this coin denomination does not occur in early Skt literature or in inscriptions, on some *Yaudheya coins occurs the ld *Brahmaṇyadevasya dramma*, '*dramma* of Brahmaṇyadeva'. On some coins of the Indo-Sassanian fabric occurs the ld *Śrī dāma*, which appears to be the name of the coin itself as no ruler of this name is known for the period. It is interesting to note that, in the early mediaeval period, the coins of the Gurjara-Pratīhāra ruler, Mihira Bhoja, who assumed the title of *Ādivarāha*, bear the ld *Śrīmadādivarāha dramma*. Some Jaina texts also mention *dramma* as a coin denomination. Besides the Gwalior inscription of Mihira Bhoja, *dramma* is also referred to in the Dadhimata inscription from Gotha-Mangloda near Jodhpur, dated to the seventh century AD, and the Kanheri cave inscription of Pullaśakti, dated Śaka *saṁvat* 765, of the time of Rāshṭrakūṭa Amoghavarsha I. Keilhorn, who edited the latter record, read *kāñchana dramma*, though he was doubtful of the reading of *kāñchana*. This led Altekar to infer that, besides in silver, *dramma* was also struck in gold. However, Mirashi has shown that what has been read as *kāñchana* is actually *ekaṁ*. Further, in the Rāshṭrakūṭa records, different terms have been used for gold and silver coins—*suvarṇa* for the former, and *dramma* for the latter, as in the Cambay plates of Govinda IV. At least ten varieties of *dramma* are known from various epigraphic and literary sources, which belong to a period later than the time frame of this study. It may be mentioned, in passing, that the word *dāma*, which appears to have been derived from *dramma*, came to be used in Hindi, Marathi, and several other modern Indian languages in the sense of value or price (R C Agrawala 1954b; R C Agrawala 1955; Altekar 1967; C S Gupta 1982; Mirashi 1963; Smith 1972).

Dṛiḍhamitra. *Mathurā k. He issued coins, which show *Lakshmī with lotus in her r hand and some symbols on the obv; and three *elephants with riders on the rev (Allan 1936; Bela Lahiri 1974).

Dvi-māshaka. Coin denomination. It seems to be a copper coin, weighing 10 *rattīs* (V S Agrawala 1953; D R Bhandarkar 1984; Chakrabortty 1931).

E

Eagle. Symbol. This bird is closely associated with *Zeus in Greek mythology, and with *Agni and *Sūrya in Indian mythology. On *Indo-Greek coins, eagle may be seen accompanying *Zeus. For instance, on the obv of the coin type issued by *Agathokles to commemorate Alexander, enthroned Zeus is seen holding out an eagle. The bird is also seen perched by the side of the deity on some coins of Agathokles, *Antimachos I, *Demetrios I, and *Diodotos I. In Indian mythology, *Agni and *Sūrya are compared with the eagle [*_Garuḍa_, *_Garuḍadhvaja_] (Bopearachchi 1993; Bopearachchi and Pieper 1998; Bopearachchi and Rahman 1995; Cunningham 1970; Gardner 1971; Graves 1955; Kerenyi 1951; A N Lahiri 1965; Marshall 1975; Rose 1958; Whitehead 1914).†

Diodotos

Electrum. Metal (alloy) for coins. It is a natural or artificial alloy of gold and silver, in which there is more than 20% of silver. The earliest coins of the Greeks, whether in the colonies in western Asia, or in Greece Proper, are electrum pieces. In India, the Sātavāhanas are known to have struck coins in electrum (Hill 1909).

Elios. *Helios.

Elephant. Symbol. This animal is associated with a number of deities, like *Indra, *Lakshmī, and *Zeus. It also seems to be associated with fertility. In Buddhist art, it symbolizes the conception of the *Buddha. Among the *Indo-Greeks, *Demetrios I was the first to use the device of elephant's head on some of his coins, and this was copied by *Menander, and also by *Maues. A similar

Uninscribed cast coin

Maues

Apollodotos

Audumbara : Dharaghosha

Vemaki

Maues

depiction may also be seen on some Ārjunāyana coins. The figure of standing elephant also was popular among the Indo-Greek rulers, a number of whom, like Menander, *Apollodotos, *Antimachos I, *Heliokles, *Lysias, and *Zoilos, used it as a coin device. The device of elephant, standing to the r and holding out wreath in its trunk, was first introduced by *Antialkidas, and it was imitated by Maues, perhaps after his conquest of the Takshaśilā region from the Eukratid princes. The association of the elephant with Takshaśilā is hinted at by Philostratos, in the *Life of Apollonius*, who records that at Taxila, an old elephant, which originally belonged to Poros, and which was dedicated to the temple of the Sun by Alexander, was venerated by the people under the name of Aias. The elephant also appears on three of Allan's nine classes of local coins from Taxila, as also on some coins from *Eran. The elephant device was also used on the *Audumbara, *Uddehika, *Vemaki, *Yaudheya, *Kāḍa, *Ayodhyā, *Kauśāmbī, and *Ujjayinī coins. The device of three elephants appears on the coins of *Mathurā, and that of an elephant with rider, on some coins of the Audumbara tribe. Very often, the device of an elephant on one side of the coin is combined with the *bull device on the other side, as, for example, on some tribal, Indo-Greek, and Śaka-Pahlava coins. The elephant may also be seen as the mount of the king on the *Elephant-rider type and the *Elephant-rider-lion-slayer type of coins of *Kumāragupta I (Allan 1936; Altekar 1957; Banerjea 2002; Bopearachchi 1993; Bopearachchi and Pieper 1998; Bopearachchi and Rahman 1995; Chakrabortty 1931; Bhaskar Chattopadhyay 1977; K K Dasgupta 1974; Gardner 1971; Graves 1955; Handa 2007a; Kerenyi 1951; A N Lahiri 1965; Marshall 1975; Rao 1985; Rose 1958; Senior 2001; Whitehead 1914).†

Kumāragupta I : Elephant-rider type

Elephant-rider type. Gold. This type was introduced by *Kumāragupta I among the *Imperial Guptas, and reminds one of a similar device on the coins of the *Kushāṇa rulers, *V'ima Kadphises and *Huvishka. The obv of this type of Kumāragupta I has the diademed king mounted on a caparisoned elephant marching to the l. He carries a goad in his r hand, while the l hand rests on the waist. Behind the king is seated a parasol bearer. The circular ld reads *Kshataripu Kumāragupto the rājatrātā jayati ripūn*. The rev bears the figure of nimbate *Lakshmī, standing on a lotus bloom, and bearing a lotus creeper with buds and blooms in her r hand, and a **cornucopiae* in her l hand resting on waist. There is a conch in the lower right corner. The rev ld is *Śrī-Mahendragajaḥ*. This type seems to be associated with sport, with the king himself acting as the driver, for he holds an *aṅkuśa* in his hand (Ashvini Agrawal 1989; Allan 1914; Altekar 1957; R D Banerji 1933; S R Goyal 2005; P L Gupta 1998; Smith 1972; Thaplyal, forthcoming).[†]

Kumāragupta I : Elephant-rider type

Elephant-rider-lion-slayer type. Gold. Combining the *Elephant-rider and the *Lion-slayer types, *Kumāragupta I produced a new obv device, the Elephant-rider-lion-slayer type. The king is mounted on a caparisoned elephant, and holds a dagger in his r hand in the posture of attack. Behind him, is a dwarf parasol bearer. The lion is trying to bite the leg of the elephant, while the elephant is trying to trample it. The circular ld has been read as *Kshataripu Kumāragupto the rājatrātā jayati ripūn*. The rev has the nimbate and standing *Lakshmī, with a *peacock beside her, and a stalked lotus in her hand. The rev ld is *Siṅhanihantā Mahendragajaḥ* (Ashvini Agrawal 1989; Allan 1914; Altekar 1957; R D Banerji 1933; S R Goyal 2005; P L Gupta 1998; Smith 1972; Thaplyal, forthcoming).

Kumāragupta I : Elephant-rider-lion-slayer type

Epander. *Indo-Greek k; subking of *Menander I; latter half of the second century BC. He is believed to be a subking of *Menander. His rare coinage does not help us in identifying the province governed by him, but Cunningham places him in the upper Kabul valley. He issued coins in both silver and copper, all struck on the Indian standard. All the coins are die-struck pieces. The silver coins are all round in shape, and the copper ones, of which only one type is known, are square in shape. The obv of the silver coins is occupied by the diademed bust of the king to the r, sometimes in a smooth helmet. The rev has the figure of thundering *Athena, with **aegis* over her left arm. The copper type has winged *Nike, bearing wreath and palm, standing to the r, on the obv, and the figure of a humped *bull to the r on the rev. All the coins have the Gr ld on the obv, and the Pkt ld, written in the Kh script, on the rev. Besides the title of **basileus*, Epander assumed the epithet **nikephoros* on coins. These are rendered into Pkt as **maharaja* and **jayadhara*, respectively. The Pkt form of the name of the ruler, as met with on coins, is Epadra (Bopearachchi 1993; Bopearachchi and Pieper

Epander

1998; Bopearachchi and Rahman 1995; Cunningham 1970; Gardner 1971; A N Lahiri 1965; Marshall 1975; Narain 1957a; Rapson 1987; Senior 2001; Sircar 1980a; Tarn 1980; Whitehead 1914).†

Ephaistos. *Hephaistos.

Epiphanes. Title. Meaning '[god-] manifest', this title was used by the *Indo-Greek rulers, *Plato, *Polyxenos, and *Strato I. This title might have been imitated by Plato from the Seleukid ruler, Antiochos IV, as was done by the Arsakid ruler, Mithridates I. In Pkt, it has been rendered as **prachachha* (Cunningham 1970; Gardner 1878; Gardner 1971; A N Lahiri 1965; Marshall 1975; Narain 1957a; Tarn 1980; Whitehead 1914; Wroth 1903).

Erakilo. *Herakles.

Erakiṇa. City coins. *Eran.

Eran

Eran. This village, in the Sagar district of Madhya Pradesh, was known as Erakiṇa, which was also the name of the *vishaya* in which the ancient town of this name was situated. Important epigraphs belonging to *Samudragupta, *Budhagupta, and *Toramāṇa, and a large number of coins, have been found here showing that it was an important political and trade centre. Here, one witnesses the development from the punch marked system to a fully evolved coin system. The commonest symbol on the punch marked coins is the *Ujjain symbol, depicted in various ways. Other symbols include *tree-in-railing, *elephant, *bull, *horse, *lion, *undulating line, standard, *wheel, *hill, etc. There is also a suggestion that *Kārttikeya may be identified on some coins from Eran. Allan has referred to 15 varieties of uninscribed Eran coins. The coin with the ld *Dhamapālasa* read from right to the l, is taken by Allan as datable to a period not later than the third century BC, but it may actually be of the second century BC. Three coins with different devices and with the ld *Erakanya*, have been found. Of the three coins of this city, one bears, on the obv, 'an archway with crescent above between two crosses, above the inscription *Erakanya*'. The rev shows the *Ujjain symbol, *tree-in-railing, and river. The second bears *bull, *wheel, and the inscription *Erakanya* on the obv, and Ujjain symbol on the rev. The third coin has a *horse and Ujjain symbol on the obv, and the ld *Erak*... between trees-in-railing on the rev. These three coins are regarded as the *city coins of Eran. Some other inscribed coins from Eran have also been reported recently by Pieper, and these bear names like Nārāyaṇamitra and Hastideva, with the title *rājña* (Allan 1936; Bopearachchi and Pieper 1998; Bela Lahiri 1974; Bela Lahiri 1976; Mitchiner 1975-1976; J P Singh 1971).

Euergetes. Title. Meaning 'performer of good deeds', this title was adopted by *Telephos alone, perhaps in imitation of the Seleukid ruler, Antiochos IV, as was the case with the Arsakid rulers, like Mithridates II. In Pkt, it is rendered as **kalanakrama* (Cunningham 1970; Gardner 1878; Gardner 1971; A N Lahiri 1965; Marshall 1975; Narain 1957a; Tarn 1980; Whitehead 1914; Wroth 1903).

Eukratides I. *Indo-Greek k; rival of *Demetrios I; first half of the second century BC. He appears to be the son of *Laodike, a Seleukid princess, and *Heliokles, a general or satrap under Antiochos III. He is believed to be an upstart, who, according to Justin, occupied Bactria, when *Demetrios II was busy in his southern campaigns. The efforts of Demetrios II to regain Bactria proved unsuccessful, and he appears to have lost his life in his encounter with Eukratides I. Justin refers to his wars in Sogdiana, Aria, Arachosia, Drangiana, and India. He also informs us that when he was returning in triumph to Bactria, his son, whom he had left behind in Bactria as his joint king, killed him, 'drove his chariot through his blood', and cast away his corpse. But he does not name this parricide. Eukratides I issued coins in gold, silver, and copper. The gold coins are all struck on the Attic standard. Some types of silver and copper coins are struck on the Attic standard, and some on the Indian standard. It is generally believed that the Indian silver standard of 20 *rattīs* for coins was introduced by Eukratides I, and this was adopted, not only by a number of subsequent Indo-Greek rulers, but also by the *Śaka-Pahlavas, *Western Kshatrapas, *Imperial Guptas, and other political powers, for their silver coinage. All his coins are die-struck pieces. The gold coins are all round in shape. The silver coins are mostly round, but the 'Helmeted bust of the king, left, thrusting javelin : Mounted *Dioskuri' type of silver coins are square in shape. The copper coins are mostly square, but the 'Helmeted bust of the king

Eukratides I

Eukratides I

to the r : Mounted Dioskuri' type of copper coins are round in shape. The gold coins bear, on the obv, the diademed bust of the king to the r, wearing a smooth helmet, and on the rev, mounted Dioskuri to the r, holding spears and palms; one type, however, has the palms and **pilei* of the Dioskuri on the rev. The obv of the silver coins mostly bears the diademed bust of the king to the r, sometimes in a smooth helmet, but on one type, the diademed bust of the king is seen to the l, thrusting javelin. The rev of most of the silver types has mounted Dioskuri charging to the r, bearing spears and palms; but some show the palms and *pilei*, or only one of the Dioskuri, charging, or the Dioskuri standing 'side by side' with spears and swords. The copper types mostly bear the diademed head or bust of the king to the r, sometimes wearing a smooth helmet or *kausia*, but on one type, the diademed bust of the king is seen to the l, thrusting javelin. The rev of the copper types is occupied, variously, by the mounted Dioskuri, or the palms and *pilei*, or wreath- and palm-bearing *Nike standing. One copper type has the diademed bust of the king to the r, wearing a smooth helmet, on the obv, and the enthroned city deity of Kāpiśī and the forepart of an *elephant, on the rev [**Kaviśiye nagara-devata*]. He issued two types of commemorative coins in honour of his parents; both the types are in silver. One type has, on the obv, the diademed and helmeted bust of the king to the r, and the ld *Basileus megas Eukratides*; the rev has the conjugate busts of Heliokles and Laodike to the r, with the Gr ld mentioning their names. The other type is almost similar to the first type, the major difference being that the bust of the king on the obv is to the l, thrusting javelin. Besides his commemorative coins in honour of Heliokles and Laodike, and his normal coinage, Eukratides I also issued some twenty-*stater* pieces, struck on the Attic standard. These are believed to the largest known coins struck by any ruler of Greek origin anywhere in the world. They bear the diademed bust of the king to the r, wearing a smooth helmet, on the obv, and mounted Dioskuri, holding spear and palms, charging to the r, on the rev. The commemorative coins bear Gr legends on both the obv and the rev. The coins in various metals, struck on the Attic standard, bear the Gr ld on the rev. The silver and copper coins, struck on the Indian standard, bear the Gr ld on the obv, and the Pkt ld, written in the Kh script, on the rev. Besides the title of **basileus*, Eukratides I assumed the epithet **megas* on a number of his coins. *Basileus* is mostly rendered into Pkt as **maharaja*, but on one type, bearing the diademed bust of the king in smooth helmet to the r on the obv, and the Dioskuri standing to front on the rev, **raja* is used in place of *maharaja*. *Megas*, in most cases, is not rendered into Pkt in the Kh ld, but in the rev ld where *raja* has been used in place of the usual *maharaja* (above), *mahataka* is given as the Pkt equivalent of *megas*. On one square copper type, **rajadiraja* is used together with *maharaja* in the rev Kh ld. The square copper type, bearing the figure of the city deity of Kāpiśī on the rev, has the Kh ld *Kaviśiye nagara-devata* on that side of the coins. The Pkt form of the name of the ruler, as met with on coins, is Evukratida. The coins of Eukratides I were imitated by the Śaka-Pahlavas, who ousted the Greeks from Bactria (Bopearachchi 1993; Bopearachchi and Pieper 1998; Bopearachchi and Rahman 1995; Cunningham 1970; Gardner 1971; A N Lahiri 1965; Marshall 1975; Narain 1957a; Rapson 1987; Senior 2001; Sircar 1980a; Prashant Srivastava 1996a; Tarn 1980; Whitehead 1914).[†]

Eukratides II. *Indo-Greek k; son of *Heliokles I (?); latter half of the second century BC. He was the governor of the territories to the north of the Hindukush, under Heliokles I, and ruled over Bactria and Badakhshan. During his reign, the *Śaka-Pahlavas of the Jaxartes-Oxus area crossed the river Oxus, and occupied Bactria, which would make Eukratides II the last Indo-Greek king to the rule over Bactria proper. He issued both silver and copper coins, all based on the Attic standard. All the coins are die-struck pieces. These coins are all round in shape. The obv of the silver types has the diademed bust of the king to the r, while the rev has the standing figure of *Apollo, holding bow and arrow. The only known copper type of this ruler has the 'laurelled' head of Apollo to the r on the obv, and a *horse standing to the l on the rev. All the coins of Eukratides II bear the Gr ld, on the rev. Besides the title of **basileus*, he assumed the epithet **soteros* on one of his silver types (Bopearachchi 1993; Bopearachchi and Pieper 1998; Bopearachchi and Rahman 1995; Cunningham 1970; Gardner 1971; A N Lahiri 1965; Marshall 1975; Narain 1957a; Rapson 1987; Sircar 1980a; Prashant Srivastava 1996a; Tarn 1980; Whitehead 1914).[†]

Euthydemos I. *Indo-Greek k; latter half of the third century BC. He might have been a high-ranking military official or a satrap (of

Sogdiana or of Aria and Margiana) under *Diodotos II. Polybios' account suggests that Euthydemos attained kingship of Bactria by 'destroying' the descendants of the original rebels. From this, it has been surmised that he killed Diodotos II and occupied his throne, *c* 235 BC. Around 208 BC, Antiochos III embarked on an expedition to reassert Seleukid authority over Parthia and Bactria, and besieged the capital of Euthydemos I. Ultimately a treaty was agreed upon, after which Antiochos retired to Syria. Euthydemos exercised control over Bactria, Sogdiana, Kabul, Kandahar, Seistan, southern Afghanistan, and adjoining parts of Iran. He issued gold, silver, and copper coins, all struck on the Attic standard. All the coins are die-struck pieces. All these coins are round in shape. The obv of the gold and silver types has the diademed head of the king to the r, while the rev has *Herakles seated on rock and holding a club in his r hand, the weapon resting on the rock in most of the cases, but on the right knee of the hero on one silver type. There is some variety in the devices on the copper types. While the obv of one type has the head of bearded Herakles to the r, that of the second type has the laureate head of *Zeus. The rev has a prancing horse to the r, but on one type, with the head of Herakles on the obv, the rev has the head of a horse. One copper coin of Masson from 'Boghram', reported by Wilson and referred to by Whitehead, bears an indistinct head on the obv, and *Apollo standing and holding bow and arrow on the rev; only the last five letter of the name of the king in the rev ld are legible. A N Lahiri was informed by D W MacDowall that the coin is not housed in the British Museum. All the coins of Euthydemos I bear the Gr ld on the rev, in which he uses the title of **basileus*. On the commemorative coins struck in his honour by *Agathokles and *Antimachos I, he has been given the title of **theos*; on one commemorative coin in his honour, which does not bear the name of the issuer, Euthydemos I is called **megalos*. Some debased coins in the name of Euthydemos seem to have been struck by the Śaka-Pahlavas (Bopearachchi 1993; Bopearachchi and Pieper 1998; Bopearachchi and Rahman 1995; Cunningham 1970; Gardner 1971; A N Lahiri 1965; Marshall 1975; Narain 1957a; Rapson 1987; Senior 2001; Sircar 1980a; Prashant Srivastava 1996a; Tarn 1980; Whitehead 1914; Wilson 1971).†

Euthydemos I

Euthydemos I

Euthydemos I

Euthydemos II. *Indo-Greek k; son of *Euthydemos I; early second century BC. There is a suggestion that he was dispatched by Euthydemos I to conquer territories in the north, and he finally succeeded in occupying the regions as far as Sogdiana, and even Ferghana in its north and north-east, possibly after the death of his father, when *Demetrios had ascended the throne. It was this conquest which enabled him to strike in nickel, Euthydemos II being the first Indo-Greek ruler to issue nickel coins. He seems to have ruled as a joint king or subking of Demetrios, and predeceased him. Euthydemos II issued silver, copper, and cupro-nickel coins, all based on the Attic standard, and all round in shape. All the coins are die-struck pieces. The obv of the silver coins has the diademed bust of the king to the r, and the rev has *Herakles standing, with wreath, club and lion's skin. The cupro-nickel and one copper type has the lauriate head of *Apollo to the r on the obv, and **tripod lebes* on the rev. The other copper types has the head of bearded Herakles to the r on the obv, and a prancing *horse to the r on the rev. All the coins bear the Gr ld on the rev, in which Euthydemos II uses the title of **basileus* (Bopearachchi 1993; Bopearachchi and Pieper 1998; Bopearachchi and Rahman 1995; Cunningham 1970; Gardner 1971; A N Lahiri 1965; Marshall 1975; Narain 1957a; Rapson 1987; Sircar 1980a; Prashant Srivastava 1996a; Tarn 1980; Whitehead 1914).†

Exergue. The field of the coin below the type, separated from the rest of the field either by the lower outline of the type itself or by a line drawn specifically for the purpose, is called the exergue. It usually has features, like the date of issue of the coin, mintmark, or engraver's initial. But on ancient Indian coins, it is generally occupied by the name or epithet of the issuing monarch (Hill 1906; Junge 1984).

F

Fabric. It is the external shape and appearance of the coin, which depends on the technique of its manufacture and the artistic capabilities of the designer. In fact, it is 'the sum…of raw materials and technical processes'. It is distinct from style (Hill 1906; Junge 1984).

Fatuha hoard. This hoard of 46 early *punch marked coins of the Magadha *janapada* was reportedly unearthed in 1997 from Fatuha, about 20 km southeast of Patna city in Bihar. These coins are of the four symbol type (Hirano 2005-2006).

Field. It is that portion of the surface of the coin (and within the border, if there is one), which is not occupied by the type (Hill 1906).

Fire altar. Symbol. Fire worship has occupied an important place in religious life, not only among the Indians, but also among the Zoroastrians of Iran. The fire altar appears on the obv of the *Kushāṇa coins, from the time of *V'ima Kadphises, the king being shown offering oblations in it. This device of the *king sacrificing at an altar was also adopted by the *Imperial Guptas, although on some specimens, the altar seems to take the shape of a **liṅgaṁ* or a **tulasīvṛindāvana*. The rev of the Sassanian coins bears an elaborate fire altar, with or without supporters. Sometimes, the king is shown on one side, and an attendant on the other side, of the fire altar, the two 'acting as guardians of the sacred fire'. The depiction of the fire altar may also be seen on the *Kushāṇo-Sassanian and *Hūṇa coins (Darmesteter 1974; Furdoonjee 1976; Gardner 1971; B B Lal 1997; Macdonell 1897; Upendra Thakur 1967a; Valentine 1993; Whitehead 1914).†

Fish. Symbol. Fishes are regarded as sacred in many parts of the world, because of their silence (like gods), their supposed wakefulness, and their 'fancied perpetual virginity'. The fish is also an auspicious symbol. Further, it is also associated with *Vishṇu as his *matsyāvatāra*, and with Pradyumna, one of the five Vṛishṇivīras, who has the fish as his standard (*mīnadhvaja*). The fish, usually within a tank or in a river, may be seen on some silver *punch marked coins, and the *Ujjayinī, *Uddehika, *Eran, and *Mathurā coins. On the obv of a square copper coin variety from *Taxila, an enclosed standard is seen surmounted by a fish (Allan 1936; Banerjea 2002; Chakrabortty 1931; Bhaskar Chattopadhyay 1977; Cunningham 1971b; K K Dasgupta 1974; Handa 2007a; Bela Lahiri 1974; Rao 1985; Savita Sharma 1990).

Punch marked coin

Flan. It is the shaped piece of metal, which has been fully prepared and checked as to its weight, size, and shape, but which has not yet received the types—symbols, devices, legends, etc, necessary to convert it into a coin. It is also known as a blank (Hill 1906; Junge 1984).

G

Gaḍahara. Tribe. Taking advantage of the weakening authority of the *Kushāṇas, the Gaḍahara tribe seems to have asserted its independence, and issued coins of its own around the fourth century AD. They appear to be of foreign extraction. Their coins, in gold and found in the Punjab and its adjoining regions, bear legends like *Peraya*, *Kirada*, and *Samudra*, along with the tribal name *Gaḍahara*. While the first is regarded as the name of the tribal chief, Kirada is believed by certain scholars to be a variant of the tribal name *Kidāra Kushāṇa, and this variant actually occurs on some of the coins of the Kidāra Kushāṇas. On this basis, it has been suggested that at some stage, the Gaḍaharas might have been subject to the Kidāra Kushāṇas. Samudra on the Gaḍahara coins might be the name of a Gaḍahara chief, but in view of the similarity between this coin type and the coins of the *Imperial Gupta ruler, *Samudragupta, it has been suggested by a number of scholars that this Samudra should be identified with Samudragupta, who might have imposed his authority on the Gaḍaharas. Interestingly, a coin bearing the tribal name *Gaḍahara* and a ld tentatively read as *Chandra*, has been described by Smith. Could the Gaḍaharas have continued under the authority of the Imperial Guptas during the reign of Chandragupta II as well ? The Gaḍahara coins bear the device of *king sacrificing at an altar on the obv, and the figure of seated **Ardochsho* on the rev (Altekar 1986a; Craig Alden Burns 1985b; Cunningham 1962; R C Majumdar 1988; Sircar 1980d; Smith 1893; Smith 1972; Prashant Srivastava 1996a).

Gajalakshmī. Deity. A popular form of the goddess *Lakshmī was Gajalakshmī, also known as Abhishekalakshmī. The *Vishṇudharmottarapurāṇa* states that, in this form, Lakshmī should be shown as flanked by two *elephants, representing the two *nidhis—padma* and *śaṅkha*—and sprinkling the goddess with the contents of two upturned water jars. On ancient Indian coins, both standing and seated Gajalakshmī find representation. On the obv of the coins of *Viśākhadeva of *Ayodhyā, standing Lakshmi is seen being anointed by two elephants, one on either of her sides. A similar depiction may be seen on certain uninscribed coins from *Kauśāmbī. A female divinity standing between two uncertain objects on the rev of some coins of *Vāyudeva of Ayodhyā has also been identified as Gajalakshmī, though this identification is by no means certain. On the rev of a silver type of the *Śaka-Pahlava ruler, *Azilises, there is a beautiful representation of Lakshmī standing facing on a *lotus bloom with stalks and leaves. On each of the two leaves stands an elephant, anointing the goddess. A similar device was also adopted by *Rañjuvula and *Śoḍāsha. Seated Gajalakshmī, with an elephant on her either side anointing her, occurs on the obv of some coins of *Śivadatta of Ayodhyā, and on some coins from *Ujjayinī. On the rev of the gold coins of Śaśāṅka, Lakshmī is seen seated facing on a lotus bloom. She holds a lotus in her l hand, which rests on her knee, while her outstretched r hand is empty. On either side of the goddess is an elephant anointing her. The rev of the gold coins of *Jayanāga represents Lakshmī in a similar fashion, the main differences being that her r hand is not empty and holds a fillet, and the elephant is seen only on the left side, anointing the goddess. (Allan 1914; Allan 1936; Altekar 1957; Banerjea 2002; Chakrabortty 1931; Bhaskar Chattopadhyay 1977; Cunningham 1971a; Cunningham 1971b; K K Dasgupta 1974; Gardner 1971; Handa 2007a; Whitehead 1914).

Ujjayinī

Azilises

Gaṇapatināga. *Nāga k. He ruled over an extensive area, from about the beginning of the fourth century AD to *c* 330 AD when he was 'uprooted' by Samudragupta, as per the evidence of the Allahabad pillar inscription. The largest number of Nāga coins belongs to him. They are of three or four different types, and are known from Padmāvatī, Kāntipurī, Mathurā, and Vidiśā, thus indicating his long reign over an extensive area. The Nāga power seems to have practically ended with him. He assumed the title of **mahārāja-śrī* on coins (Cunningham 1967; Bela Lahiri 1974; Smith 1972; H V Trivedi 1957).

Gaṇeśa. *Śiva; *Hermaios.

Samudragupta :
Tiger-slayer type

Gaṅgā. Deity. Much sanctity is attached to the waters in India since times immemorial. It was believed that Gaṅgā originally flowed in heaven, and when she descended on the earth, *Śiva received her in his matted locks. Since then, Gaṅgā became the second wife of Śiva, the first one being *Umā. The **makara* is associated with Gaṅgā as her mount. On the rev of the *Tiger-slayer type of *Samudragupta, a goddess is shown standing on **makara*, with a *lotus in the l hand; the r hand is outstretched and empty. Smith had suggested her identification with the consort of either *Varuṇa or Kāma, while B N Mukherjee expresses the possibility of her being Yamunā. But most of the scholars identify her as Gaṅgā, more so because the type seems to be associated with Samudragupta's conquest of the Ganga valley. The goddess appears again on the rev of the Tiger-slayer type of *Kumāragupta I, where she holds a stalked lotus in her l hand, while she feeds a *peacock by her r hand. The rev of the *Rhinoceros-slayer type of this ruler bears the figure of Gaṅgā mounted on a *makara*, but there she is shown pointing at some object with the forefinger of her outstretched r hand. The l hand of the goddess is empty and shown hanging down; the lotus, instead of being in the hand of Gaṅgā, is held by the *makara* in its trunk (Altekar 1957; Banerjea 2002; B N Mukherjee 1985; R B Pande 1988; Rao 1985; Prashant Srivastava 1996a).[†]

Kumāragupta I :
Tiger-slayer type

Chandragupta II

Kumāragupta I

Garuḍa. Symbol. The earliest reference to *garuḍa* is to be found in the *Ṛigveda*, where the sun is likened to a golden-winged *garuḍa* (*suparṇo garutmān*). But in later literature, as also in art, he came to be more closely associated with *Vishṇu as his *vāhana*. It is evident from numismatic and epigraphic sources that the *Imperial Gutpas, who were devout worshippers of Vishṇu—they often style themselves **paramabhāgavata*—adopted the *garuḍa* as their royal insignia. The *garuḍa* in theriomorphic form occurs on the silver coins of the *Western Indian type of *Chandragupta II, *Kumāragupta I, and *Skandagupta, as also on some copper coins of Chandragupta II and Kumāragupta I. The bird is also seen on the **Garuḍa*-with-outstretched-wings type of gold coins, struck by the *repousse* method, and ascribed by some scholars to Kumāragupta I and Skandagupta. On these coins, the entire body is that of a bird. But on certain coins of Chandragupta II, the *garuḍa* has human hands. On some copper coins of this ruler, the *garuḍa* has the body of a bird, but the face of a man [**Garuḍadhvaja*, *eagle] (Altekar 1957; Banerjea 2002; Feller 2004; R B Pande 1988; Rao 1985; T P Verma 1991).†

Skandagupta

Garuḍadhvaja. Symbol. This is a banner or standard surmounted by the figure of a **garuḍa*, and has Vaishṇava affiliations. According to a story in the *Mahābhārata*, when *garuḍa* was returning with the pot of abrosia from the capital of *Indra, he met *Vishṇu, and promised to act as his mount and as the device on his standard, which henceforth came to be called the *garuḍadhvaja* because of the device of the *garuḍa* on it. On the Imperial Gupta coins, the *garuḍadhvaja*, in the form of a standard surmounted by the figure of a *garuḍa* (with outstretched wings), occurs on the obv beside the figure of the king. It first appears on the *Standard type of *Samudragupta, and is then seen on a variety of the coins of *Kācha known from the *Bayana hoard, as also on the coins of *Chandragupta II, *Kumāragupta I, *Ghaṭotkachagupta, *Skandagupta, *Kumāragupta II, *Budhagupta, *Vainyagupta, *Narasiṁhagupta, and *Vishṇugupta [*Eagle] (Altekar 1957; Banerjea 2002; Feller 2004; R B Pande 1988; Rao 1985; Raven 1994).†

Skandagupta :
King-and-Female type

Samudragupta :
Standard type

***Garuḍa*-with-*Ku* type.** Copper. This type of copper coins was issued by *Kumāragupta I. The obv has a crescent, with the Br letter *ku* below it. The rev bears a **garuḍa*-with-outstretched-wings on a pedestal (Allan 1914; Altekar 1957; P L Gupta 1998; Smith 1972).

***Garuḍa*-with-outstretched-wings type.** Gold. This type is struck by the **repoussé* method, and resembles the coins of the *Nala and the *Śarabhapurīya dynasties. In the upper half of the obv, is a **garuḍa*-with-outstretched wings; there is a crescent and a **chakra* to the l, and a *chakra* and a *śaṅkha* to the r. In the lower half is the Br ld *Śrī-Mahendrāditya*. The rev is blank. A number of scholars ascribe these coins to some local (*Nala, Śūra, or *Śarabhapurīya ?) ruler of southern Kosala, named Mahendrāditya. Subsequently, similar coins bearing the ld *Śrī-Kramāditya*, were also found, and ascribed, again, to some local ruler (belonging to the Nala, Śūra, or Śarabhapurīya dynasty ?) of southern Kosala. The same type of coins were also issued by Prasannamātra of the Śarabhapurīya dynasty. There is also a suggestion that Śrī-Mahendrāditya and Śrī-Kramāditya may be identified with Mahendrāditya of the *Kathāsaritsāgara*, and his predecessor, respectively. But there are some scholars, like Prayag Dayal and B C Jain, who believe that the Śrī-Mahendrāditya coins were issued by *Kumāragupta I, and Śrī-Kramāditya coins by *Skandagupta, although the palaeography of these coins seems to place these coins in the sixth-seventh centuries AD (Nisar Ahmad 1964; Altekar 1957; B C Jain 1960; Mirsahi 1939; L S Nigam 1987; L S Nigam 1988; T P Verma 1991).

Gaya hoard. This hoard of around 110 local *punch marked coins of the Magadha *janapada* was discovered near Gaya on the Gaya-Jahanabad road in Bihar. It has been remarked that the hoard is significant for bringing to the light new three symbol pattern coins not yet reported, some new four pattern varieties, and some three or four denominations of the earliest phase of the local punch marked coins of the Magadha *janapada*, noticed for the first time (Sharad Sharma and Shinji Hirano 2007).

Ghaṭotkachagupta *Kramāditya*. *Imperial Gupta k; son of *Chandragupta II; first half of the fifth century AD. The newly discovered Ramtek inscription, which shows that he was a son of Chandragupta II, also hints at the strained relationship between Ghaṭotkachagupta and *Kumāragupta I; the former seems to have served the latter as his governor in the Malwa region, and to have rebelled during the reign of Kumāragupta I, but the rebellion was soon crushed, and Ghaṭotkachagupta lost his life. Two coins of Ghaṭotkachagupta are known. One is in the St Petersburg collection, while the other is in Ajit Ghose's collection. Both these coins are of the *Archer type. A **Chhatra* type of gold coin in the *Bayana hoard has the ld *Kramādityaḥ* on the rev. Some scholars, like P L Gupta, ascribe this coin to Ghaṭotkachagupta, who also assumed the epithet, while others, like Altekar, ascribe it to *Skandagupta (Ashvini Agrawal 1989; Allan 1914; Altekar 1957; R D Banerji

1933; Fleet 1888; S R Goyal 2005; P L Gupta 1998; K P Jayaswal 1933; Smith 1972; Thaplyal, forthcoming).†

Gogha hoard 1. This large hoard of around 5,000 silver coins was discovered at Gogha in the Bhavnagar district of Gujarat, some time before 1973. The rulers represented in this hoard include *Apollodotos, *Dionysios, and *Nahapāna (Deyell 1984; Jha and Rajgor 1994; Senior 2001).†

Gogha hoard 2. This hoard, again a large one, comprising around 2,000 silver coins, was discovered at Ghogha in the Bhavnagar district of Gujarat. The rulers represented in this hoard include, besides *Īśvaradatta, the *Kārddamaka Kshatrapas, *Rudradāman I, *Dāmajadaśrī I, *Rudrasiṁha I, *Rudrasena I, *Jīvadāman, *Dāmajadaśrī II, *Pṛithvīsena, *Dāmasena, and *Vijayasena (Jha and Rajgor 1994)

Golakhpur hoard. This hoard of 108 silver *punch marked coins, was found in 1918 at Golakhpur in the Patna District of Bihar. Some coins in this hoard are **kārshāpaṇas* with four symbols, while the rest are *kārshāpaṇas* with five symbols. The hoard is presently housed in the Patna Museum (Rajgor 2001).

Gold. Metal for coins. For ceremonial purposes, the ancient Indians had ranked the various metals in the following order of purity: gold, copper, silver, brass, and iron, and there is a suggestion that this order 'may embody a genuine tradition about the chronological sequence in the use of different metals in this country'. Barring the last, *viz* iron, all these metals, besides some others, were used for the purpose of minting coins in ancient India. R H Inglis-Palgrave is of the opinion that gold first came to be employed in art, most probably, in India or somewhere in the East. Gold was adopted as a theoretical standard of value in ancient India, but so far, no gold coin of indigenous manufacture, contemporaneous to the silver or copper *punch marked coins, has come to the light. The few recently published gold punch marked coins appear forged ones. In fact, except for some golden **darics* and the gold coins of the *Indo-Greeks (rare) and *Kushāṇa rulers, indigenous gold coinage appears in India, for the first time, during the reign of the *Imperial Guptas in

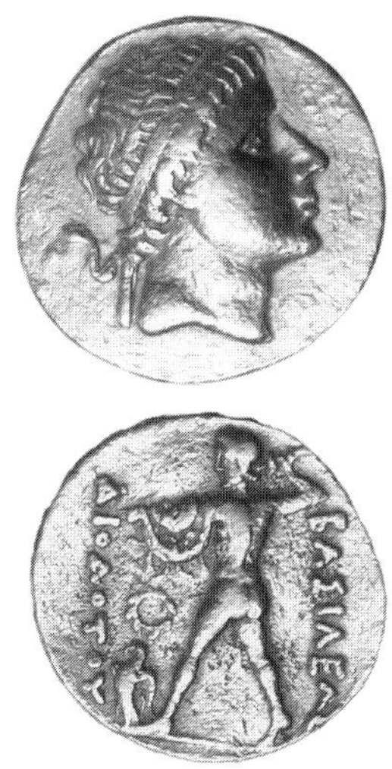

Diodotos

Chandragupta I and Kumāradevī

the fourth century AD, in spite of the comparative abundance of this metal in India, because, as has been observed, the final step towards its evolving into a real coinage 'was perhaps retarded by the high value of the metal'. The fact that Herodotus informs that the Indian area of the Achaemenian empire fetched to it 360 talents of gold dust, also indicates the absence of gold coins in the period. Besides the abundant indigenous supply—from the gold mines 'in Assam, Hyderabad, Mysore and Malabar and from the river washings in the beds of the Indus, the Ganges and the Brahmaputra', some gold was also imported from Tibet, eastern Siberia, and western Asia; gold coins and bullion also flowed into India from the Roman empire at such a rate as to alarm Pliny (Altekar 1940; D R Bhandarkar 1984; Chakrabortty 1931; A N Lahiri 1965; Upadhyaya and Chaturvedi 1972).

Gomitra. *Almora k.

Gomitra. *Kanauj k. He is known from a restruck piece reported by Smith. The obv device of this coin associates him with *Brahmamitra and *Sūryamitra of the Kanauj series. The rev is blurred. The *tree-in-railing seems to connect him with *Vishṇudeva, whose coin also has that symbol on the obv. Bela Lahiri proposes to identify him with *Gomitra of *Mathurā, whose coins, too, bear the *Ujjain symbol. She feels that Gomitra of Mathurā might have extended his sway towards Kanauj. She assigned him to the second century BC on palaeographical grounds (Bela Lahiri 1974; Smith 1972).

Gomitra. *Mathurā k. He issued some coins, which show four symbols on the obv, and tree-in-railing on the rev; others of his coins show *Lakshmī with lotus in her r hand and some symbols on the obv; and three *elephants with riders on the rev. Powell-Price considers him as a *Pañchāla ruler, rather than a king of Mathurā. But his coins show features of the Mathurā coins, which are quite different from the Pañchāla coins, and also the name Gomitra is not met with in the Pañchāla series. Some scholars take him as identical with the homonym known from *Kanauj coins. Allan, on the basis of devices, considers that there were two kings with the name Gomitra. The square coins with four symbols, he assigns to the first of these, and the rectangular coins of the Mathurā type, to the second king of that name (Allan 1936; Bela Lahiri 1974).

Gondermau hoard. This hoard of 51 silver coins was discovered at Gondermau in the Bhopal district of Madhya Pradesh. Of the coins in the hoard, nine are uncertain, while the rest belong to the *Kārddamaka Kshatrapas. The rulers represented in the hoard include *Vijayasena, *Rudrasena II, *Bhartṛidāman, *Viśvasena, *Rudrasiṁha II, and *Rudrasena III (Jha and Rajgor 1994).

Gondopharnes. *Śaka-Pahlava k; son of *Orthagnes (?); first half of the first century AD. He seems to have started his career in Arachosia as a subordinate ruler under *Orthagnes. Later on, he seems to have been sent by his overlord to northwestern India, where he appears to have defeated *Azes II, although there are some scholars, who believe that Gondopharnes succeeded Azes II peacefully. After his successes in northwestern India, he seems to have dissociated himself from the administration of Arachosia, and declared himself independent. Perhaps after the death of Orthagnes, Gondopharnes occupied Arachosia, and allowed Guḍa to continue to serve there as viceroy. He appears to have exercised authority ove the Kabul valley, the Gandhāra region, the Jammu-Pathankot region, etc. He was served, not only by Aśpavarman, but also by the latter's nephew, *Sasan, with whom he issued joint coins, and his own nephew, *Abdagases. He was the last great Śaka-Pahlava ruler. It is clear from the Takht-i-Bahi inscription that he ruled from *c* 19 AD to 46+ AD. However, attempts were made, by scholars like J E van Lohuizen de Leeuw, and, more recently, by R C Senior, to place Gondopharnes in the first century BC. He issued some copper coins with Orthagnes, which bear the bust of the king, and the name of Orthagnes in the obv Gr ld, on the obv, and wreath- and palm-bearing *Nike, and the name of Gondopharnes in the Kh legend, on the rev. On these coins, also associated with the administration of Arachosia is one *Guḍa, a brother of Gondopharnes. Besides his joint coins with Orthagnes, Gondopharnes issued his independent coinage in both silver and copper. The obv of his silver coins is occupied by the diademed bust of the king, or horseman king. One silver type has the figure of *Śiva holding trident and palm; this device, combined with the title **devavrata* for Gondopharnes on this and other types, indicates his Śaivite leanings. The rev of another silver type has the figure of enthroned king being crowned by a female figure (Nike ?), which is interesting. This type has the Gr ld on the rev; otherwise, it occurs on the obv. The rev of some other silver types have *Athena standing with spear and shield, or standing *Zeus. One silver type even has the mounted *Dioskuri on the obv, and winged Nike on the rev; the title **theos* occurs on the obv of this type, while the rev has the name Undophers. The copper coins sometimes show enthroned king on the obv, besides the usual diademed bust of the king, or horseman king, met with on the silver types also; on one copper/billon type, the horseman king is accompanied by a flying female figure holding wreath. The obv of one copper type has *Apollo standing. The rev usually has *Nike standing with wreath and palm, or *Zeus Nikephoros, or Śiva, or Athena, or simply the Gondopharnes symbol. On one copper type with enthroned king on the obv and Nike on the rev, the Gr ld is engraved partly on the obv and partly on the rev. One lead type, attributed to Gondopharnes by R C Senior, has *lion to the r on the obv, and a deity (Athena or Herakles) on the rev. The rev ld seems to mention Guḍa. The titles used by Gondopharnes in the Gr ld are **basileos basileon megalos*, sometimes with the additional title of **autokratoros*. The rev ld is in Pkt in the Kh script. The titles used in the rev ld are **maharaja* **rajaraja* **tratara devavrata*; on one copper type, Gondopharnes is simply *maharaja tratara*. The forms of his name in Gr are Undopheres and Undopherros; in Pkt, they are Gudaphara, Guduphara, and Gudupharna, etc. The joint coin type of Gondopharnes with Aśpavarman has horseman king and a corrupt Gr ld mentioning Gondopharnes on the obv; the rev has Zeus standing with sceptre and the name of Aśpavarman as **stratega*. Gondopharnes issued joint coinage in copper with Sasan. The obv of these joint coins has horseman king and corrupt Gr ld; the rev of one type has Zeus standing with sceptre, and that of another type has Zeus Nikephoros standing. The rev ld might refer to both Gondopharnes and Sasan, or to Sasan alone (Bopearachchi and Rahman 1995; Cunningham 1971a; Gardner 1971; Huxley 1983; Jenkins and Narain 1957; van Lohuizen de Leeuw 1949; Marshall 1975; B N Mukherjee 1969a; Rapson 1987; Senior 2001; Sircar 1980b; Sircar 1986; Prashant Srivastava 1996a;

Prashant Srivastava 2005c; Prashant Srivastava 2007a; Tarn 1980; Whitehead 1914;).†

Gorgon's head. Symbol. The Gorgons were the three daughters of Phorkys, named Stheno, Euryale, and Medousa, of which, the last one was a mortal creature, and she was also taken as a wife by *Poseidon. It is told that Perseus, with the help of *Athena, cut off the head of Medousa with a sickle, and presented the head to Athena. From that time, the Gorgon's head was worn by her, sometimes as a sign on her shield, and sometimes attached to her breast-plate, the **aegis*. A buckler with Gorgon's head is seen on some copper coin types of the *Indo-Greek rulers, *Demetrios I and *Menander (Bopearachchi 1993; Bopearachchi and Pieper 1998; Bopearachchi and Rahman 1995; Gardner 1971; Graves 1955; Kerenyi 1951; A N Lahiri 1965; Marshall 1975; Rose 1958; Whitehead 1914).†

Graeco-Kushāṇa script. Used by the Kushāṇas for their coin legends from the time of *Kanishka I onwards, this script consists mostly of Greek characters, with the addition of some special characters for representing new sounds, like *sh* in *Kushāṇa, Kanishka, *shao, *Athsho, *Ardochsho*, etc.

Guḍa. *Śaka-Pahlava viceroy; brother of *Gondopharnes; first half of the first century AD. When *Gondopharnes was serving under *Orthagnes as his viceroy in Arachosia, he had associated in administration a person named Guḍa, who has been identified as Gad, mentioned in the Syriac version of *The Apocryphal Acts of Judas Thomas, the Apostle*, as a brother of Gondopharnes. Later on, Gondopharnes declared himself independent in northwestern India, and dissociated himself from the administration of Arachosia. During that period, Orthagnes nominated Guḍa to the viceroyalty of that region and issued joint coins with Guḍa alone. It appears that after the death of Orthagnes, Gondopharnes occupied Arachosia, and allowed his brother to continue as viceroy there. All the coins mentioning him, whether struck conjointly with Orthagnes or Gondopharnes, are in copper, and bear the diademed bust of the king on the obv, and wreath- and palm-bearing *Nike on the rev. On the coins, where he is an associate of Gondopharnes serving under Orthagnes, his name is usually in the nominative, while the titles in the rev ld and the name of Gondopharnes are in the genitive, suggesting that these titles qualify Gondopharnes alone. On the coins, which he issued as the viceroy of Orthagnes in Arachosia, the titles **maharaja rajatiraja mahata* have been used for him. In the rev ld of the coins he issued as viceroy of Gondopharnes in Arachosia, he is *maharaja*, 'the victorious general', etc. The forms of his name met with on his coins are Guḍa, Gaḍa, Gada, Guḍana, Gudana, Gaḍaṇa, Gadana, etc (Cunningham 1971a; Gardner 1971; Jenkins and Narain 1957; Marshall 1975; B N Mukherjee 1969a; Rapson 1987; Senior 2001; Sircar 1980b; Prashant Srivastava 1996a; Tarn 1980; Whitehead 1914).

Guild coins. Guilds seem to have had the authority to issue coins in ancient India, and there is even a suggestion that as the adoption of coinage would have greatly facilitated commercial transactions, coinage might initially have been introduced by commercial and trade organizations or by the merchants in their individual capacity. Although in ancient India, coins issued by individual merchants are not known for certain, we do have examples of guild coins from places like *Kauśāmbī and *Takshaśilā (J P Singh 1971; Thaplyal 1996).

Gupta *saṁvat*. This era, beginning 319 AD, was popular in northern, western, and parts of eastern India, during the fourth to sixth centuries AD, and continued to be in use even after the decline of the *Imperial Guptas, among the Maitrakas of Valabhī, who were originally feudatories of the Imperial Guptas; the last known record dated in this era is the Veraval inscription of year 945 (= 1264 AD). Due to its use by the Maitrakas of Valabhī, the era also came to be known as Valabhī *saṁvat*, and Alberuni uses both the names for that era. The founder of the era is not known for certain, and the credit has been given, generally to *Chandragupta I, but to Gupta, Ghaṭotkacha, or *Samudragupta, by some scholars. As per Fleet's calculations, based mainly on Alberuni's statement that Gupta and Valabhī eras are identical and started 241 years after the commencement of the *Śaka *saṁvat*, the Gupta era began on the first day of the bright fortnight of the month of Chaitra in 319 AD. When designated as the Gupta *saṁvat*, the year begins in the month of Chaitra, and the month is *pūrṇimānta*; when designated as the Valabhī *saṁvat*, the year begins in the month of Kārttika, and the month is *amānta*. The dates on the silver coins of the Imperial Guptas are in the Gupta *saṁvat* (Fleet 1888; Salomon 1998; Sircar 1965; Thaplyal, forthcoming).

H

Hagāmasha

Hagāmasha. Śaka satrap. He was a **kshatrapa* of *Mathurā. He seems to have started his career as a subordinate of his elder brother, *Hagāna, with whom he issued joint coins in copper, bearing a peculiar **vajra* (?) symbol and some other symbols, with the Br ld referring to both the brothers as *kshatrapa*; the rev shows a *horse standing. Later, he issued his independent coins, showing that he succeeded Hagāna. These coins are all in copper. The obv has *Lakshmī standing holding a flower in her r hand, flanked by symbols. The Br ld on the obv reads *Khatapasa Hagāmashasa*. The rev has a horse standing to the l. As his coins are stylistically quite close to the issues of *Śoḍāsha, he might have preceded or succeeded the latter (Allan 1936; K D Bajpai 1976; Cunningham 1971b; Senior 2001; Sircar 1968; Sircar 1980b; Smith 1972; Prashant Srivastava 1996a).

Hagāna. Śaka satrap. Known only from the joint coins he issued with his brother, *Hagāmasha, he was a **kshatrapa* of *Mathurā. As the name of Hagāna appears before that of Hagāmasha in the obv ld of their joint coins, the former seems to be the elder of the two brothers. The joint coins, issued in copper, bear on the obv a peculiar **vajra* (?) symbol, along with some other symbols. The Br ld mostly reads *Khatapana Hagānasa Hagāmashasa* in three lines. The rev shows a *horse standing. On numismatic grounds, John Allan placed him before *Śoḍāsha, but recent writers on the subject, like Michael Mitchiner and R C Senior, would date him after Śoḍāsha (Allan 1936; K D Bajpai 1976; Cunningham 1971b; Senior 2001; Sircar 1968; Sircar 1980b; Smith 1972; Prashant Srivastava 1996a).

Hajatriä. *Śaka-Pahlava k. This ruler, known from coins as a son of *Kharaösta, might be identical with Hayuära mentioned in the Mathurā lion capital inscription of the time of *Rañjuvula and *Śoḍāsha. He might have issued some posthumous Azes coins, and seems to have ruled over some territories to the north of Takshaśilā, perhaps in Hazara. Only copper coins bearing his name are known, all square in shape. The obv bears the figure of horseman king holding whip, and a corrupt Gr ld. The rev has a seated deity, and a Kh ld referring to Hajatriä as a **kshatrapa* and son of Kharaösta (Senior 2001; Sircar 1986).

Hajipur hoard. This hoard of 22 *Imperial Gupta gold coins was found in 1893 near Kunahra Ghat in the Bazar of Hajipur (Bihar). Only 14 of these coins could be recovered. The rulers represented in this hoard are *Chandragupta I, *Samudragupta, and *Chandragupta II (Allan 1914; Altekar 1957).

Haṁsa. Symbol. *Haṁsa* (swan/goose) is associated with several deities, like Brahman, Kubera, *Varuṇa, and *Vishṇu, but it is most intimately connected with *Sarasvatī as her mount. Its rare appearance on ancient Indian coins may be seen on the rev of the **Rājalīlā* type of *Samāchāradeva, where the bird is seen by the side of Sarasvatī, craning its neck up, and trying to pluck a leaf from a lotus stalk near it (Allan 1914; Altekar 1957; Banerjea 2002; Bhaskar Chattopadhyay 1977; Rao 1985; Vögel 1962).

Haradatta. *Almora k. He is known from one base silver coin, bearing on the obv, a symbol comprising a curved line ending a circle to its right, in the centre, and a *bull before a *tree-in-railing. The rev has an elaborate symbol, regarded by some scholars as an altar bearing a conventional **nandipada* on its façade, and surmounted by a *triangular-headed symbol, while others associate it with some Greek tradition. The Pkt ld on the obv has the name of the issuer in the genitive (Allan 1936; Handa 2007a; M P Joshi 1989; Bela Lahiri 1974).

Hare. Symbol. The hare on a crescent is seen on some coins of *Vishṇudeva of *Kanauj (Allan 1936; Chakrabortty 1931; Bela Lahiri 1974).

Harsha. *Pushpabhūti k; son of *Prabhākaravardhana; first half of the seventh century AD. He ascended the throne of Thaneshwar on the death of his elder brother, Rājyavardhana II. Immediately before his accession, *Śaśāṅka, together with Devagupta of Malwa, had invaded the *Maukhari kingdom of Grahavarman, to whom Harsha's sister, Rājyaśrī was married, killed him, occupied his capital Kanauj, and imprisoned Rājyaśrī. Rājyavardhana had succeeded in worsting Devagupta, but had himself been killed by Śaśāṅka. On becoming king, Harsha rescued his sister. According to Hiuen-tsang, the vacant throne of Kanauj was offered to Harsha, and he later transferred his capital from Thaneshwar to Kanauj. There is no clear evidence to suggest that Harsha ever defeated Śaśāṅka. Harsha was 'king of Magadha' in 641 AD, and he had conquered Utkal and Ganjam regions of Orissa by 643 AD. He had also defeated a Maitraka ruler of Valabhī. His conquests of Sindh and Nepal (allegedly hinted at in the *Harshacharita*), and of Kashmir and southern India, are doubtful. Harsha invaded the territories of the Chālukya ruler, Pulakeśin II, but was defeated in battle. Harsha is said to have founded the Harsha era, commencing 606 AD, with his accession. In the *Bhitaura hoard, there are 284 silver coins of the **Madhyadeśa* type of the *Imperial Guptas, issued in the name of *Śrī-Śīlāditya*, and nine coins of the same type, but issued in the name of *Śrī-Pratāpaśīla*. Hoernle ascribed all these coins to King Pratāpaśīla Śīlāditya of Kashmir. But Richard Burn and D Devahuti suggest that the *Śrī-Śīlāditya* coins should be ascribed to Harsha, who is styled Śīlāditya, not only in the *Harshacharita*, but also by Hiuen-tsang; the *Śrī-Pratāpaśīla* coins have been ascribed by them to Prabhākaravardhana. The silver coins issued by Harsha weigh around 36 grains. They bear the bust of the king to the r, and the date of issue on the obv, and a fan-tailed *peacock with the Br ld *Vijitāvaniravanipati Śrī-Śīlāditya divaṁ jayati* on the rev. The dates range from year 1 to 33. Harsha is also believed to have struck a gold coin, weighing 113.5 grains, from Farrukhabad district of Uttar Pradesh. It bears a five-line Br ld on the obv—*Paramabha-/ṭṭāraka Mahārā-/jādhirāja Parame-/śvara Śrī Mahārā-/ja Harshadevaḥ.*

The rev has nimbate *Śiva and *Pārvatī, seated on Nandin, to the r. The palaeography of the coin ld is similar to that of the Madhuban and Banskhera inscriptions of Harsha, and the titles used for him on the coin are also found in the Banskhera inscription and the Nalanda seal of that king. The Śaivite leanings of Harsha are mentioned in the *Harshacharita*; the *maṅgalācharaṇa* of two of the works, *Ratnāvalī* and *Priyadarśikā*, ascribed to Harsha, are in praise of Śiva and Pārvatī. Hence, there are valid grounds for ascribing this gold coin to Harsha (K D Bajpai 1976; Richard Burn 1906; D Devahuti 1964; D Devahuti 2001; Pires 1934; Thaplyal 1985).†

Hazara hoard(s). H L Haughton collected some coins in northwestern India, from places like Abbottabad, and Amankot and Baffa near Abbottabad. It is possible that these coins might have come from several hoards. The rulers represented in these hoards include *Azilises and *Azes II (Haughton 1943; Haughton 1958; Senior 2001).

Hekate. Greek goddess of fertitlty, and queen of the ghosts. She was the daughter of the star goddess Asteria and of Perses the son of Eurybia. Her mother was a sister of Leto, which makes Hekate a cousin of *Apollo and *Artemis. She was allowed by *Zeus to continue to enjoy the threefold honour she earlier enjoyed under the Titans. Hekate is a goddess of fertility, and helped women at childbirth. She is a grim goddess, associated with the underworld as queen of the ghosts, and in this capacity, she is also the goddess of magic, and of the cross-roads where three paths meet. She is never depicted alone on coins. When the three-headed goddess appears on the rev of the coins of some *Indo-Greek rulers, like *Pantaleon and *Agathokles, she is always shown standing on the outstretched r hand of *Zeus. On the coins of Agathokles, Hekate holds torches in both her hands (Bopearachchi 1993; Bopearachchi and Pieper 1998; Bopearachchi and Rahman 1995; Bhaskar Chattopadhyay 1977; Cunningham 1971a; Gardner 1971; Graves 1955; Kerenyi 1951; A N Lahiri 1965; Marshall 1975; Rose 1958; Prashant Srivastava 2007c; Whitehead 1914).†

Heliokles. Seleukid general or satrap (?). He was the father of *Eukratides I, who married the Seleukid princess, *Laodike, and, together with his wife, was commemorated by his son on two types of coins. [*Eukratides I] (Bopearachchi 1993; Bopearachchi and Pieper 1998; Bopearachchi and Rahman 1995; Cunningham 1970; Gardner 1971; A N Lahiri 1965; MacDowall 2003-2004; Marshall 1975; Narain 1957a; Rapson 1987; Senior 2001; Sircar 1980a; Prashant Srivastava 1996a; Tarn 1980; Whitehead 1914).

Heliokles I

Heliokles I

Heliokles I. *Indo-Greek k; son of *Eukratides I; latter half of the second century BC. He ascended the throne of Bactria, perhaps after removing his brother, the parricide (?) *Plato. Besides Bactria, his authority extended over the territories of Badakshan and Sogdiana. During his reign, the Arsakids wrested the outlying Indo-Greek provinces, and Mithridates I seems to have conquered territories as far east as Aria. If the suggestion that the monolingual coins, bearing the name of Heliokles, be attributed to Heliokles I, and the bilingual ones, to Heliokles II, be accepted, Heliokles I issued both silver and copper coins, all struck on the Attic standard. All the coins are die-struck pieces. They are all round in shape. The obv of all the silver coins bears the diademed bust of the king to the r, sometimes in Medusa helmet. The rev of one type has *Zeus standing to the front, holding the *thunderbolt in his r hand and a long sceptre in his l hand. But on the rev of the silver type, on the obv of which the bust of the king is shown in Medusa helmet, there is the figure of enthroned Zeus Nikephoros. The obv of both the types of his copper coins has a crude male bust to the r. The rev of one type has standing Zeus, as on one silver type, above, while that of the other copper type has a prancing *horse to the l. The Gr ld on all these coins appears on the rev. On the copper coins of 'Crude bust : Prancing horse' type, the Gr ld is 'blundered'. There is a suggestion that some of these crudely struck copper pieces might be imitations of the types of Heliokles I by the nomads (Kushāṇas or Yueh-chichs ?) in the territories to the north of Termez, to the north of the river Oxus, and along its tributaries. Besides the title of **basileus*, Heliokles I assumed the epithet **dikaios* on his coins (Bopearachchi 1993; Bopearachchi and Pieper 1998; Bopearachchi and Rahman 1995; Cunningham 1970; Gardner 1971; A N Lahiri 1965; MacDowall 2003-2004; Marshall 1975; Narain 1957a; Rapson 1987; Senior 2001; Sircar 1980a; Prashant Srivastava 1996a; Tarn 1980; Whitehead 1914).†

Heliokles II. *Indo-Greek k; son of *Heliokles II (?); end of the second century BC or early first century BC. On the basis of the marked contrast between the portrait of Heliokles on the monolingual coins, and that on the bilingual coins, Gardner has expressed the possibility of the existence of two Indo-Greek kings named Heliokles, and this is supported by a number of scholars, with the monolingual coins being attributed to *Heliokles I and the bilingual ones to Heliokles II. He seems to have come to power after his nephew, *Archebios. He ruled over the Kabul and Ghazni regions, and parts of western Gandhāra where his coins are quite numerous. It is generally believed that he expanded his dominions at the expense of *Strato I, then a minor. If the suggestion that all the bilingual coins bearing the name of Heliokles be attributed to the second ruler of that name is accepted, Heliokles II issued both silver and copper coins, all based on the Indian standard. All the coins are die-struck pieces. The silver coins are all round in shape, while the copper ones are all square in shape. The obv of the silver coins is occupied by the diademed bust of the king. On one type, the bust of the king is to the r; on another type, too, the bust faces the right, but it is shown wearing Medusa helmet. On the obv of two silver types, the diademed bust of the king is to the l, thrusting javelin, the king shown wearing a smooth helmet on one type. The rev of all the silver types has the figure of *Zeus, standing and holding the thunderbolt in his r hand and a long sceptre in his l hand. The obv of most of the copper coins has the diademed bust of the king to the r, sometimes bearded; while the rev has an *elephant to the l. But some copper coins are of the 'Elephant : Humped *bull' type. On the coins of Heliokles II, the Gr ld occurs on the obv, while the Pkt ld, written in the Kh script, appears on the rev. Besides the title of **basileus*, Heliokles assumed the epithet **dikaios* on his coins. These are rendered into Pkt as **maharaja* and **dhramika*, respectively. The Pkt form of the name of the ruler, as met with on coins, is Heliyakreya (Bopearachchi 1993; Bopearachchi and Pieper 1998; Bopearachchi and Rahman 1995; Cunningham 1970; Gardner 1971; A N Lahiri 1965; Marshall 1975; Narain 1957a; Rapson 1987; Senior 2001; Sircar 1980a; Tarn 1980; Whitehead 1914).†

Heliokles II

Helios. Greek sun god. *Apollo was a Greek solar deity, but Helios was the sun god himself. A Titan himself, Helios was the son of

Plato

Telephos

Kanishka I

Kanishka I

the Titan Hyperion and the Titaness Theia, and he had two sisters, *Selene and Eos, 'dawn'. His wife is variously called Perse, Persies, and Neaira. From Neaira, he had two daughters— Lampetia and Phaethousa, and two sons—Aiestes and Phaethon. The Greeks saw in the sun, a ball of fire, an eye, a spoked wheel, but 'the most commanding and persistent likeness which they saw was that of a chariot and horses'. On the obv of some coins of the *Indo-Greek ruler, *Plato, we find radiate Helios, dressed in *chiton* and *chlamys*, riding a quadriga; he holds a sceptre in his r hand. Some other coins of Plato have the figure of radiate Helios standing to front. He holds a sceptre in his l hand, and an uncertain object, identified as callipers by some scholars, in his outstretched r hand. Incidentally, the callipers in the hand of Helios seem to indicate his function as the measurer of time, and there is a suggestion that this figure may be identified as "Helios-Mithra'. On the obv of some copper coins of *Philoxenos, radiate Helios is seen standing, dressed in *chiton*, *himation*, and boots. He holds a long sceptre in his outstretched r hand. The *Śaka-Pahlava rulers do not seem to have depicted Helios on their coins, but some gold and copper coins of the *Kushāṇa ruler, *Kanishka I, bear the standing figure of a deity, with a rayed halo round his head. He is dressed in a long tunic, and his r hand is extended, while the left one rests on his hip. This figure is called *Elios* (= Helios) in the label inscription accompanying it, but it resembles the representation of the Zoroastrian deity, *Mihira, found on Kushāṇa coins, to a great extent (Bopearachchi 1993; Bopearachchi and Pieper 1998; Bopearachchi and Rahman 1995; Bhaskar Chattopadhyay 1977; Cunningham 1971a; Gardner 1971; Graves 1955; Kerenyi 1951; A N Lahiri 1965; Marshall 1975; Rose 1958; Rosenfield 1967; Prashant Srivastava 2007c; Stein 1888; Whitehead 1914).†

Hephaistos. Greek 'god of subterranean fire', and master craftsman. He was, according to Homer, the son of *Zeus and Hera, but according to Hesiod, he was especially Hera's son. The name, Hephaistos, means 'quivering flame', or simply 'fire', and Hephaistos was the 'god of subterranean fire'. He was a master-craftsman, and an incomparable worker in metals. The representation of Hephaistos is not met with on *Indo-Greek coins. The deity is seen standing to front, with a sceptre in his r hand, and tongs and hammer in his l hand, on the obv of some copper coins of the *Śaka-Pahlava rulers, *Azes I and *Azilises. On the rev of some gold coins of the *Kushāṇa ruler, *Kanishka I, we find the figure of a bearded deity, standing with a wreath in his r hand, and tongs in his l hand resting on hip. According to Cunningham, the label inscription accompanying the figure describes it as that of Hephaistos, although the representation is somewhat different from the usual depiction of the Greek deity of that name in art (Bopearachchi 1993; Bopearachchi and Pieper 1998; Bopearachchi and Rahman 1995; Bhaskar Chattopadhyay 1977; Cunningham 1971a; Gardner 1971; Graves 1955; Kerenyi 1951; Marshall 1975; Rose 1958; Prashant Srivastava 2007c; Whitehead 1914).†

Herakles. Greek deified hero. He was the son of Amphitryon and Alkmene, though Homer describes *Zeus as his father. His very name, which means 'Hera's glory', suggests his close association with Hera. He was born in Thebes. Though originally purely human, he was eventually admitted to Olympus, and became 'the object of cult, though only rarely as a god, mostly as a kind of very superior hero'. As a 'subduer of monsters', he slew the Nemean lion, the giant Porphyrion, the Lernaean hydra, and Skylla the wild bitch. He also had conflicts with deities, like *Apollo and *Triton. His twelve labours for King Eurystheos of Tiryns won him great fame. He was adopted as a coin device by the *Indo-Greeks, *Śaka-Pahlavas, and the *Kushāṇas. Among the Indo-Greek rulers, the Euthydemids favoured this, while the Eukratids seem to have avoided it. The bearded bust of Herakles, often accompanied by his characteristic attributes like the club and the lion's skin, appears on the obv of the copper coins of *Euthydemos I, *Demetrios, *Euthydemos II, *Lysias, *Strato I, *Theophilos, and *Zoilos I. The figure of Herakles, often naked, may be seen standing, with club and lion's skin in his l hand and crowning himself with his r hand, on some coins of Demetrios, *Agathokles, Lysias, and Theophilos; also on some coins of the Śaka-Pahlava ruler, *Azes I, and the joint coins of *Vonones with *Spalahora, Vonones with *Spalagadama, and *Azilises with *Azes II; and on the rev of some copper coins of the Kushāṇa ruler, *Huvishka, although in the last case, the crown is not actually visible on the coin and the action has to be assumed from the pose of the r hand of Herakles. On some other coins of

Euthydemos I

Lysias

Zoilos I

Spalyris and Spalagadama

Euthydemos

Huvishka

Theophilos, and also on the rev of some gold and copper coins of Huvishka, Herakles, wearing an ivy wreath, stands to front, with club and lion's skin. A young standing Herakles with his attributes may be seen on the rev of some coins of Euthydemos II. On some coins of Zoilos I, naked Herakles stands facing front. He holds a wreath in his outstretched r hand, and club and lion's skin in his l hand. On his left shoulder is seen *Nike standing and crowning him. On the obv of a type of the Śaka-Pahlava ruler, *Maues, Herakles, standing facing front, has a club and lion's skin in his l hand, while his r hand is placed on hip akimbo. The lion on the rev of this type might or might not represent the Nemean lion killed by Herakles. On the obv of some coins of Azilises, Herakles stands to front, with a diadem in his r hand, and a club and lion's skin in his l hand. Herakles standing facing front, with a club in his r hand and lion's skin in his l hand, is seen on the rev of a coin, which bears the name of a ruler, doubtfully read as *Phseigacharis. On the rev of some copper coins of the Kushāṇa ruler, *Kujula Kadphises, Herakles stands to front, with his r hand resting on a club; a lion's skin is seen over his left arm. The rev of a type of *Rañjuvula has Herakles standing facing front. The club and lion's skin are seen in his l hand, while his r hand is advanced. Naked and bearded Herakles is sometimes seen seated on a rock (often covered with the lion's skin), with his l hand resting on the rock, and his r hand grasping a club, which rests on his right knee or on the rock itself. Such a depiction may be seen on some coins of Euthydemos I, *Antimachos I, and Agathokles, as also on the joint coins of *Agathokleia and Strato I; also on some joint coins of the Śaka-Pahlava rulers, *Spalyris with Spalagadama, as well as on the independent coins of Azes I and of Azilises. It is worthy of note that on the Śaka-Pahlava coins, while the figure of standing Herakles crowning himself is well executed, that of seated Herakles is quite crude and inferior in execution (Bopearachchi 1993; Bopearachchi and Pieper 1998; Bopearachchi and Rahman 1995; Bhaskar Chattopadhyay 1977; Cunningham 1971a; Gardner 1971; Graves 1955; Kerenyi 1951; A N Lahiri 1965; Marshall 1975; Pinsent 1969; Rose 1958; Rosenfield 1967; Prashant Srivastava 2007c; Whitehead 1914).†

Heraos

Heraos. *Kushāṇa k. The reading of the name of this predecessor of *Kujula Kadphises on coins is doubtful, and some scholars suggest it to be Miaos. Cunningham regards him as the father of Kujula Kadphises, and Tarn as his grandfather. Tarn also suggests that Heraos was not a full king, as he is referred to on his coins as *tyrannountos*. There is a possibility that he married a daughter or sister of the *Indo-Greek ruler, *Hermaios. Heraos issued silver coins bearing the diademed bust of the king on the obv, and equestrian king being crowned by flying *Nike on the rev. The ld, on the rev, reads *Tyrannountos Eraou* (?) *Korshanou Sanab*. Tarn feels that the portrait of the king on the obv of these coins resembles that on some of the coins of *V'ima Kadphises. One recently reported type has the diademed bust of the king to the r on the obv, while the rev has a 'soldier' standing to the r, and the Gr ld *Eiarou Koshshanou*. The coins of Heraos mostly come from Bactria north of the Caucasus (Bopearachchi and Pieper 1998; Cunningham 1971a; Gardner 1971; Marshall 1975; Rosenfield 1967; Prashant Srivastava 1996a; Tarn 1980; Whitehead 1914).

Heraos

Hermaios

Hermaios. *Indo-Greek k; son of *Amyntas; first half of the first century BC. The *provenance* of the coins of Hermaios shows his hold over an extensive dominion, comprising the Paropamisadae, some regions to the north of the Hindukush, upper Arachosia, and perhaps even eastern Gandhāra and Takshaśilā. But towards the end of his reign, Hermaios lost most of his provinces to *Azes I. Hermaios also lost the regions to the north of the Hindukush to the Yueh-chihs. He issued independent coins in both silver and copper. One silver type is struck on the Attic standard, while the rest of the silver types and all the copper coins are based on the Indian standard. All the coins are die-struck pieces. The silver coins are round in shape, and the copper ones are square in shape. The obv of the silver coins is mostly occupied by the diademed bust of the king to the r, sometimes wearing a smooth helmet, but one type has the diademed and helmeted king mounted on a prancing horse to the r. The rev of all the silver types has the enthroned figure of *Zeus-Mithra, holding sceptre and callipers in his hands. The obv of the copper coins has 'Bearded male bust r., radiate, wearing Phrygian cap', while the rev has a prancing horse to the r. The male bust on the obv has been identified as that of 'Zeus-Mithra' by Osmund

Hermaios

Hermaios

Hermaios and Kalliope

Bopearachchi. The view that the Indian deity, Gaṇeśa, appears on a coin of Hermaios, has not been generally accepted. The silver type struck on the Attic standard has the Gr ld on the rev. The rest of the coins, all struck on the Indian standard, have the Gr ld on the obv, and the Pkt ld, written in the Kh script, on the rev. There seems to have been an alliance between the descendants of *Eukratides and those of *Menander against the Śaka-Pahlavas and the Yueh-chihs, during the reign of Amyntas, and perhaps as a result of this alliance, *Kalliope, a princess of the family of Menander and a daughter of *Hippostratos, was married to Hermaios. Hermaios and Kalliope, are known to have issued joint coins in silver, based on the Indian standard. These joint coins, round in shape, bear the conjugate busts of Hermaios and Kalliope to the r on the obv. The rev has the helmeted and diademed king mounted on a prancing horse to the r. The Gr ld on the obv and the Kh ld on the rev, both mention the names of the king and the queen, but the titles of **basileus* and **soteros*, rendered into Pkt as **maharaja* and **tratara*, are used only for Hermaios. R C Senior has referred to a rare joint issue of Hermaios and Kalliope, on which the device of king mounted on a prancing horse occupies the obv, replacing the conjugate busts of the king and the queen. These joint coins seem to show that, following the death of Hippostratos, Hermaios and Kalliope might have jointly ruled over some territories previously ruled by Hippostratos. On his normal coinage, too, like the joint coins with Kalliope, besides the title of *basileus*, Hermaios assumed the epithet *soteros*. These are rendered into Pkt as *maharaja* and *tratara*, respectively. There are some posthumous coins issued in the name of Hermaios; these have been ascribed, variously, to the *Śaka-Pahlavas or the Yueh-chihs (that is the *Kushāṇas). There are also some coins on which the name and/or portrait of Hermaios is associated with the *Kushāṇa ruler, *Kujula Kadphises. On some coins of this type, the obv has the head of the king, resembling that of a Roman emperor. On these coins, the epithet *sterossu* is used for Hermaios on the obv, and sometimes, when the name of Hermaios is mentioned on the rev also, **rajaraja* and **mahata* are used for him in the rev ld. There are some coins on which the name and/or portrait of Hermaios is associated with the *Kushāṇa ruler, *Kujula Kadphises. The suggestion of scholars like Percy Gardner, V A Smith, R B Whitehead, and Alberto M Simonetta, that Kujula Kadphises began his career as a subordinate ally of the *Indo-Greek ruler and later displaced him, as also that of other scholars like, Cunningham, Whitehead, Smith, and initially also Rapson, that in view of the *Śaka-Pahlava menace, Hermaios formed an alliance with the Kushāṇa ruler and they issued these coins conjointly, and then Kujula Kadphises immediately succeeded Hermaios, on the basis of these coins, can no longer be entertained in view of the strong evidence indicating an interval of at least 70 years between the end of the reign of Hermaios and the accession of Kujula Kadphises. These might have been propaganda coins, or posthumous Hermaios coins, issued by Kujula Kadphises. The Pkt form of the name of the ruler, as met with on coins, is Heramaya (Bopearachchi 1993; Bopearachchi 1994; Bopearachchi and Pieper 1998; Bopearachchi and Rahman 1995; Cribb 1982; Cunningham 1970; Dobbins 1970; Gardner 1971; A N Lahiri 1965; Macdonald 1987b; Marshall 1975; Narain 1957a; Rapson 1987; Senior 1995; Senior 2001; Simonetta 1958; Sircar 1980a; Smith 1972; Prashant Srivastava 1990b; Prashant Srivastava 1996a; Tarn 1980; Whitehead 1914).†

Hermes. Greek messeanger of the gods, and god of magic. Born of a nymph named Maia, Hermes was one of the youngest sons of *Zeus. Immediately after his birth, he made a lyre from out of a tortoise shell, and stole 50 cows of *Apollo from Peiria. This led to a conflict between them, but their father reconciled them. Hermes is a master-thief, and the god of all forms of magic and trickery. As a traveller, he was the spirit of the *herms*, the piles of stones, which, in ancient Greece, marked paths, boundaries, and also holy places. He was the Psychopompos, 'the conductor of souls', and sometimes acted as the messenger of gods. The *Indo-Greek rulers do not appear to have favoured Hermes as a coin device. The appearance of Hermes on the coins of the *Śaka-Pahlava ruler, *Maues, is doubtful. On one coin type of this ruler, on the rev occurs a male figure standing facing, with his r hand on his hip. He wears *himation* and *petasos*. The identification of this figure with Hermes is not certain due to the absence of the **caduceus*, his characteristic attribute, which helps in the definite identification of the deity on the coins of *Azes I. On one type of Azes I, Hermes is shown standing to the l on the rev. His *chlamys* is shown flying. His r hand is raised, while the *caduceus* is held in his l hand. On another type of Azes, he is depicted in the

Azes II

same manner, but on the obv. On a type of *Kharaösta, housed in the British Museum, the male figure, standing facing towards the left, has been identified with Hermes (Bopearachchi 1993; Bopearachchi and Pieper 1998; Bopearachchi and Rahman 1995; Cunningham 1971a; Gardner 1971; Graves 1955; Jenkins and Narain 1957; Kerenyi 1951; Marshall 1975; Rose 1958; Prashant Srivastava 2006a; Prashant Srivastava 2007c; Whitehead 1914).†

Uninscribed cast coin

Hill. Symbol. This symbol, made of a varying number of arches, was identified as a *stūpa* or a *chaitya* by some early scholars like Theobald and Spooner, but was later on regarded as a hill on the grounds that various birds and animals are often shown surmounting it and sometimes trees are shown growing at its crest, which would seem more apt for a hill rather than a *chaitya*. Marshall regards the hill as a symbol of Mesopotamian origin. It is symbolic of strength, vigour, and vitality. Spooner also pointed out that in Jaina art, the emblem of a hill symbolizes the presence of a *Tīrthaṅkara*, but J N Banerjea associates the hill with *Śiva, who bears the epithets of *Girīśa*, *Giritra*, and *Girichara*, and has Mount Kailāsa as his abode. The peaks were worshipped as the *svayambhūliṅga* of Śiva. The hill symbol occurs on ancient Indian coins in a variety of forms—one-arched, three-arched, six-arched, etc. Sometimes a crescent [*Crescent-on-hill], parasol, *peacock, some quadruped like *bull or *deer, or tree, is seen atop the hill. Such varieties of the symbol may be seen on the *punch marked coins; on the *Eran, *Kauśāmbī, *Kuṇinda, *Rājanya, *Ujjayinī, *Yaudheya, *Śibi, and *Taxila coins; and on the coins of the *Kulūta ruler Vīrayaśas, and of *Viśākhadeva and *Naradatta of *Ayodhyā (Allan 1936; Banerjea 2002; Chakrabortty 1931; Mahadev Chakravarti 1994; Bhaskar Chattopadhyay 1977; K K Dasgupta 1974; Handa 2007a; Savita Sharma 1990).

Hippostratos. *Indo-Greek k; son of *Nikias; first half of the first century BC. Hippostratos seems to have succeeded Nikias in western Gandhāra. Whitehead has placed him in the Peshawar and Hazara regions, but, according to Narain, this seems doubtful in view of the scarcity of his coins at Takshaśilā. He, however, might have controlled some territories to the east of the river Indus. Osmund Bopearachchi regards him as the last Indo-Greek king to the rule over western

Punjab, including Takshaśilā and Pushkalāvatī. He issued silver and copper coins, all based on the Indian standard. All the coins are die-struck pieces. The silver coins are round in shape, while the copper ones are mostly square and rarely round in shape. The obv of the silver types has the diademed bust of the king to the r. The rev of the silver coins is mostly occupied by the figure of the king mounted on a prancing horse to the r, but one type, has *Demeter (?), bearing *cornucopiae*, standing to the l. Two copper types have *Apollo, holding an arrow in both his hands, standing to the r, on the obv, and *tripod lebes* on the rev, the difference between the two types being that while one is round, the other is square in shape. One copper type has *Triton, holding dolphin and rudder in his hands, on the obv, and Demeter (?), bearing *cornucopiae*, standing to the l, on the rev. The obv of yet another copper type bears a radiate and helmeted deity (*Zeus ?) enthroned and holding a diadem and a long sceptre in his hands, while the rev has a *horse walking to the l. All the coins bear the Gr ld on the obv, and the Pkt ld, written in the Kh script, on the rev. Besides the title of **basileus*, Hippostratos assumed the epithet **soteros* on his coins. These are rendered into Pkt as **maharaja* and **tratara*, respectively. However, on some coins, the rev ld also has *jayamta*, or **mahata jayamta*, along with *maharaja* and *tratara*. It is to be noted that there is no Greek equivalent for *jayamta* and *mahata* in the obv ld. The Pkt form of the name of the ruler, as met with on coins, is Hipustrata (Bopearachchi 1993; Bopearachchi and Pieper 1998; Bopearachchi and Rahman 1995; Cunningham 1970; Gardner 1971; A N Lahiri 1965; Marshall 1975; Narain 1957a; Rapson 1987; Senior 2001; Sircar 1980a; Prashant Srivastava and Prachi Srivastava 1993; Tarn 1980; Whitehead 1914).†

Hippostratos

Hippostratos

Hirañasame. Ld. *Takshaśilā. Guild coins.

Hoards. It is a collection of artifacts, which were buried, usually 'with the intention of retrieving them at a later date when the threat of danger had passed', or abandoned deliberately. Coins hoards form one of the various categories of hoards. These coin hoards may come to the light as a result of archaeological excavations, or as chance finds. In the latter case, it is often very difficult to ascertain their *provenance*. Further, it is very rare to see such a hoard in its entirety, for the finders and coin dealers tend to dispose them off 'as quickly and expensively as possible'. Coin hoards help, not only in reconstructing the sequence of rulers represented in each hoard, but also the sequence and development of coin types, and the location of mints.

Uninscribed cast coin

Uninscribed cast coin

Hollow cross. Symbol. This symbol may be seen on some uninscribed cast copper coins, and also on some coins of *Taxila (Allan 1936; Chakrabortty 1931; Savita Sharma 1990).

Uninscribed cast coin

Hagāmasha

Horse. Symbol. This animal is the symbol of speed and strength, especially military strength of kings and warriors in general; it is also sometimes associated with the mother goddess as her consort. It is associated with a number of deities, like *Indra, *Sūrya, Kubera, Revanta, and Kalkin. In Buddhism, the horse denotes the renunciation of the *Buddha. It is one of the seven treasures of a *chakravartin*. In Greek mythology, the horse is associated with *Poseidon, who has the epithet *hippios*. In the *Avesta*, the horse is associated with *Ahuramazda. On ancient Indian coins, the horse may be seen as an independent device, as on the *punch marked coins, and on the coinage of *Kāḍa, *Kauśāmbī, *Eran, *Mathurā, *Rājanya, *Taxila, *Ujjayinī, etc; it is generally difficult to associate the depiction of the horse on these various coins with any one of these deities with any amount of certainty. But on a Kāḍa coin, on which the horse appears on the rev, a rayed circle is depicted on the obv, while on some Ujjayinī coins, a horse is represented just below a solar symbol on the obv. In such cases, the solar association of the horse cannot very well be doubted. The head of a bridled horse, curiously with the horns of a bull, appears on some coins of the *Indo-Greek ruler, *Demetrios I, and may have been copied from the coins of Seleukos I. However, the appearance of the device of a horse's head on a coin type of the *Śaka-Pahlava ruler, *Hyrkodes, might have been the result of Arsakid, rather than of Seleukid, influence. The depiction of the device of standing or prancing horse is seen on the coins of *Euthydemos I, *Euthydemos II, *Menander, *Hermaios, *Eukratides II, and *Hippostratos among the Indo-Greeks, and *Azilises among the *Śaka-Pahlavas. Although there is a suggestion that the depiction of the horse device on the coins of the Euthydemi "may have something to do with the 'heavenly horses' in Ferghana", efforts to conquer which region were initiated by Euthydemos II during the reign of Euthydemos I, and success was achieved during the reign of Demetrios I, yet it is more likely that the horse on the coins of the Euthydemi, as also on those of the other Indo-Greek rulers, is associated with Poseidon. The depiction of a horse standing before a *yūpa*, as seen on the coins of *Vishṇudeva of *Kanauj, and of the *Kārddamaka ruler, *Chashṭana, and the **Aśvamedha* type of *Samudragupta and *Kumāragupta I, symbolizes the performance of the *aśvamedha.* A recently reported copper type, attributed to *Chandragupta II on the basis of the ld, also bears the figure of a standing horse, and may be associated with the horse sacrifice. The horse may also be seen on coins as the mount of deities and kings, as well as drawing chariots (Allan 1936; Altekar 1952; Altekar 1957; Banerjea 2002; R G Bhandarkar 1928; Sukumari Bhattacharji 1970; Bopearachchi 1993; Bopearachchi and Pieper 1998; Bopearachchi and Rahman 1995; Chakrabortty 1931; Bhaskar Chattopadhyay 1977; Cunningham 1971a; Darmesteter 1974; Gardner 1971; Handa 2007a; Kerenyi 1951; A N Lahiri 1965; Bela Lahiri 1974; Macdonell 1897; Narain 1957a; R B Pande 1988; Rao 1985; Rapson 1975; Rhodes and Saha 2006; Rose 1958; Senior 2001; Whitehead 1914).†

Euthydemos I

Horseman type. Gold. This was one of the novel types introduced by *Chandragupta II. The coins of this type are divided into two classes, on the basis of the direction of the horse. The obv has the horseman king wearing *dhotī* and sash, holding a bow or a sword in most cases, but sometimes unarmed. The ld reads **Paramabhāgavata*-**mahārājādhirāja Śrī-Chandraguptaḥ*. The rev has the goddess seated on a wicker stool, with a *pāśa* in her r hand, and a lotus in the left. The ld is *Ajitavikramaḥ*. This type was continued by his son, *Kumāragupta I. His coins of this type was divided into two classes, on the basis of the rev motif : on Class I, the goddess is seated alone; on Class II, she is seen feeding a *peacock. The obv has the horseman king, holding a bow, and sometimes with a sword by his side. There is a great variety in the obv ld, with the different coins bearing *Prithivītalāmbaraśaśi Kumāragupto jayatyajitaḥ*, or *Guptakulavyomaśaśi jayatyajeyo'jitamahendraḥ*, or *Kshitipatirajito vijayī Kumāragupto jayatyajitaḥ*, etc. The rev has *Lakshmī seated

Chandragupta II : Horseman type

Kumāragupta I : Horseman type

Kumāragupta I : Horseman type

on a wicker stool. On Class I, she has a flower or *pāśa* in her r hand; on Class II, she feeds a peacock with this hand. The l hand has a stalked lotus. The rev ld reads *Ajitamahendraḥ*. *Skandagupta appears to be the last *Imperial Gupta ruler to issue this type of coins. The equestrian king on the obv does not carry any weapon. The circular ld is undecipherable. The rev is similar to that of the coins of this type issued by Chandragupta II. The rev ld, according to Altekar, is *Kramādita*, and it is on its basis that this type has been attributed to Skandagupta (Ashvini Agrawal 1989; Allan 1914; Altekar 1957; R D Banerji 1933; S R Goyal 2005; P L Gupta 1998; Smith 1972; Thaplyal, forthcoming).

Bhānugupta : Horseman-lion-slayer type

Bhānugupta : Horseman-lion-slayer type

Horse-rider-lion-slayer type. Gold. The Horse-rider-lion-slayer type of *Bhānugupta is a combination of the *Horseman and the *Lion-slayer types of the *Imperial Guptas. The obv has the king mounted on horseback and hunting a rampant *lion, with a sword. A **garuḍadhvaja* is seen above the horse's head. On one specimen, the circular ld has been read as *Vijita* (or *–tya*) *vasudhāṁ divaṁ jayati Bhānugu[pta]*. The rev has seated *Lakshmī, with a *pāśa* (?) in her r hand, and a lotus in her l hand. The rev ld is *Śrī-Prakāśāditya*. There is a view that this type was issued by Bhānugupta to commemorate his victory over the Hūṇas (Altekar 1957; V S Pathak 1988-89; K S Shukla 1980; Prashant Srivastava 2004a).

Hugli hoard. This hoard of 13 *Imperial Gupta gold coins was found in 1883 near Hugli (West Bengal). The rulers represented are *Samudragupta, *Chandragupta II, and *Kumāragupta I (Altekar 1957).

Hūṇa. Coins, general features. The Hūṇas were a nomadic tribe, inhabiting the northern shores of the Caspian Sea, from where they spread over Asia and Europe. Around the middle of the fifth century AD, a branch of the Hūṇas, known as Ye-tha, Ephthalites, or Hephthalites, advanced towards both Iran and India, and, crossing the Hindukush, occupied Gandhāra. But their efforts to enter further into India were rendered unsuccessful by *Skandagupta. The Hūṇas brought about the downfall of the Iranian empire, and, after destroying the later *Kushāṇa rulers of northwestern India, they again invaded India. Coins reveal the names of about a dozen rulers of Hūṇa origin, who ruled over parts of Punjab, Kashmir, and Afghanistan. These include, besides the significant ones like *Toramāṇa and *Mihirakula, chiefs like *Lae-lih, *Rāmānīla/Ramanila, and *Khiṅgila. Mihirakila was defeated by both Yaśodharman of Mandasor and [*Narasiṁhagupta] Bālāditya. The latter defeat crushed the power of the Hūṇas in India. The *Maukharis and the *Pushpabhūtis also claim to have worsted the Hūṇas. For their coinage, the Hūṇas used silver and copper. There are some gold coins, imitations of *Imperial Gupta gold *Archer type, which are believed by some scholars to have been struck by Hūṇa chiefs. Altekar, after examining the Hūṇa coins, came to the conclusion that the Hūṇas crudely imitated the coins of their conquered territories, like the Sassanian type of coinage in Afghanistan, Kushāṇa type in Kashmir, and Imperial Gupta type in the rest of their Indian territories (Altekar 1986b; Biswas 1973; Cunningham 1962; Cunningham 1967; R C Majumdar 1988; Upendra Thakur 1967a; Upendra Thakur 1967b;).†

Huvishka

Huvishka. *Kushāṇa k; successor of *Vāsishka; first half of the second century AD. He seems to have started his career as a junior co-ruler of *Vāsishka, and later succeeded him as an independent ruler. His inscriptions are dated between 106 and 138 AD. Kanishka II of the Ara inscription of 119 AD seems to have ruled as his junior co-ruler, although there are suggestions that there were two Kushāṇa kings bearing the name of Huvishka, with Huvishka I ruling before Kanishka II, and Huvishka II ruling after him. On the basis of the Mat *devakula* inscription, which seems to indicate that V'ima was the grandfather of Huvishka, A L Basham regards Huvishka I as the son of Kanishka I; there is a possibility that Huvishka II was the son and successor of Kanishka II. But the present state of our knowledge precludes any definite conclusions in this matter. Huvishka apparently ruled over most of the territories brought under Kushāṇa sway by Kanishka I. He issued coins in gold, silver, and copper. These may be classified according to the metal of the coin and the obv device. Huvishka is not known to have used the device of *king sacrificing at an altar, so popular among the Kushāṇa rulers from the time of *V'ima Kadphises onwards. Some of his gold coins bear the obv device of nimbate and helmeted bust of the king on clouds, holding a sceptre in the r hand and a spear in the left. The rev depicts, variously, **Ardochsho,* **Ashaeichsho,* **Athsho,*

Huvishka

Huvishka

Huvishka

Huvishka

Huvishka

**Mao*, **Miiro*, **Nana*, **Oanindo*, **Oachsho*, *Śiva, **Pharro*, **Shaoreoro*, etc. Some other gold coins have the same device on the obv, the difference being that an *aṅkusa* is seen in the l hand of the king, instead of the spear. The rev of these coins bears variously *Ardochsho*, **Oron*, **Lrooaspo*, **Manaobago*, **Mao*, *Miiro*, *Nana*, Śiva, *Pharro*, **Riom*, **Sarapo*, *Kārttikeya as *Maaseno* or *Skando-Komaro*, *Bizago*, *Maaseno*, etc. Sometimes, with this obv device, we have two divinities on the rev, standing side by side—*Mao-Miiro*, *Umā-Śiva, *Nana*-Śiva, etc. On still other gold coins, the obv has a similar device, but the king holds a mace in the r hand and a spear in the l hand. The rev of these coins is occupied variously by figures of *Erakilo* (*Herakles), **Zero*, *Nana*, *Uoromozdo* (*Ahuramazda), Nike etc. On a recently reported gold coin of Huvishka, the obv has the helmeted bust of the king to the l, with a flower-like object in his r hand and a spear in his l hand, while the rev bears the standing figure of the *Buddha and the ld *Boddo* on the rev. Some gold coins of Huvishka bear the obv device of king seated cross-legged on clouds, holding a sceptre in the r hand and a bird-topped standard or a spear in the left. On the rev of these coins may be seen the figures of deities like *Nana*, Herakles, etc. Huvishka also issued gold coins with the figure of king riding an elephant on the obv, and *Ardochsho* on the rev. The silver coins of Huvishka, very few in number, bear a diademed and helmeted bust of the king, holding a mace in the r hand, on the obv; and Śiva and *Nana* standing side by side on the rev. The king riding an elephant may also be seen on the obv of some of the copper coins of Huvishka, while the rev of these coins bears, variously, the figures of Herakles, **Oado*, *Pharro*, *Athsho*, *Ardochsho*, Śiva, *Miiro*, etc. On some other copper coins, king is seated cross-legged on clouds on the obv, and the figure of *Mao* occupies the rev. Still other copper coins have the obv device of king seated on a low seat, while the rev has the figure of *Miiro*. Great variety is seen in the representation of the divinities on the rev of the coins of Huvishka. Thus, on his coins, *Miiro* is seen in 21 different postures and with different attributes; *Pharro* in 18; *Mao* in 11; and *Ardochsho* in nine. While *Kanishka I depicted on his coins, only Śiva and the Buddha, the list of Indian divinities on the coins of Huvishka is fuller with Umā, and Kārttikeya in the different forms of Skanda-Kumāra, Viśākha, and Mahāsena, also finding a place on the rev. The obv of the coins of Huvishka invariably bears the ld **Shaonanoshao Ooeshki Koshano*; the rev inscription gives the name of the deity represented (Altekar 1952b; Basham 1957; Cunningham 1971a; Gardner 1971; Handa 2005-2006; Marshall 1975; von Mitterwallner 1986; Rosenfield 1967; Sircar 1980c; Whitehead 1914).

Hvavamira. *Parataraja k.

Hyrkodes

Hyrkodes. *Kushāṇa (?) k. He is believed to belong to the period when the Kushāṇa power was on the rise. His coins, in silver, come from the 'Bactrian side of the Caucasus', and bear the diademed bust of the king on the obv, with the ld *Yrkodou*. The rev of some of his coins bears a spearman with flames issuing from his shoulders and the ld, perhaps reading *Makarou Ardethrou*; other coins have the forepart of a bridled horse, a device seemingly borrowed from the Seleukids (Cunningham 1971a; Gardner 1971; Marshall 1975; Rosenfield 1967; Senior 2001; Tarn 1980; Whitehead 1914).

I

Chandragupta I and Kumāradevī

Samudragupta : Archer type

Samudragupta : Lyrist type

Imperial Gupta. Coins, general features. The Imperial Guptas began ruling towards the close of the third century AD, somewhere in eastern Uttar Pradesh and Bihar, or in Bengal. The first two rulers, Gupta and Ghaṭotkacha, are styled **mahārāja*, perhaps denoting their feudatory status. *Chandragupta I, the son and successor of Ghaṭotkacha, is the first **mahārājādhirāja*, that is sovereign ruler, the first king of his dynasty to issue to coins, and, perhaps, also the founder of the *Gupta era. His rise to prominence seems to be linked to his marriage with the Lichchhavi princess, *Kumāradevī. This marriage led to the amalgamation of the Gupta and the Lichchhavi states, which was later inherited by *Samudragupta. He brought almost the whole of northern India under his rule, and even made a bid for supremacy in the south. After the shameful *Rāmagupta interregnum, we find *Chandragupta II on the throne. He defeated the *Kārddamaka Kshatrapas of Kathiawar, and is also believed to have led military expeditions to Bengal and Bactria. His son and successor, *Kumāragupta I, proved himself to be an able administrator, and he kept intact the vast empire he inherited from his ancestors. But towards the close of his reign, he had to face internal troubles, as well as the onslaught of the *Hūṇas. However, the Hūṇa invasion was repulsed by his son, *Skandagupta, perhaps while he was still a prince. After Skandagupta, a number of Imperial Gupta rulers, like Pūrugupta, *Kumāragupta II, *Budhagupta, *Vainyagupta, *Bhānugupta, *Narasiṁhagupta, *Kumāragupta III, and *Chandragupta III, are known from various sources—epigraphic, numismatic, and sygillographic. But their order of succession is not known for sure. *Vishṇugupta, who reigned around the middle of the sixth century AD, is the last known Imperial Gupta king. The Imperial Guptas were the first Indian rulers of indigenous origin to issue gold coins, and their significant monetary issues are mostly in that metal. Initially, they seem to have followed the standard of the Roman **dinarius aureus* of 122.9 grains, and the coins of Chandragupta I and Samudragupta weigh, on an average, 120 grains. But the weight goes on increasing during the successive reigns, till it approximated the traditional weight of the Indian **suvarṇa* of 80 *rattīs* (about 144 grains). The increase in the weight of the Imperial Gupta gold coins corresponds to depreciation in the purity of the gold. If the silver coins of the *King-and-Queen type of Chandragupta I and Kumāradevī are taken as fake, Chandragupta II was the first Imperial Gupta ruler to issue silver coins after his conquest of Kathiawar. These silver coins follow the weight standard of the Kārddamaka Kshatrapa coins of 36 grains. Rāmagupta seems to be the first ruler of his family to issue coins in copper, although, on the basis of a copper coin from Sanghol, reportedly bearing the ld *Lichchhavayaḥ* on the obv, and *Chandragupta* on the rev, it has been suggested that Chandragupta I might have been the first Imperial Gupta ruler to issue coins in copper. As the weights of the copper coins range from 18 to 89 grains, it is extremely difficult to determine the standard they followed. Certain brass and lead coins have also been ascribed to the Imperial Guptas. The Imperial Gupta coins are die-struck pieces; only the **Garuḍa*-with-outstretched-wings type, ascribed by some scholars to Kumāragupta I and Skandagupta, were manufactured by the **repoussé* technique. They are all round in shape. The obv of the gold coins is occupied by the figure of the king in various postures; only on the **Aśvamedha* type, the obv has the scene of the horse sacrifice in place of the royal figure. The king is usually shown standing, holding a standard, or some weapon, alone, or in the company of his queen or some deity or a parasol-bearer. Sometimes, he may be riding a horse or an elephant. On some coins, he is shown indulging in his favourite hobby, like playing on the lyre or hunting wild beasts. Thus, we have **Apratigha*, *Archer, **Aśvamedha*, *Battle-axe, **Chakravikrama*, **Chhatra*, *Couch, *Elephant-rider, *Elephant-rider-lion-slayer, *Horseman, *Horse-rider-lion-slayer, *Kārttikeya, King-and-Queen, *Lion-slayer, *Lyrist, *Rhinoceros-slayer, *Standard, *Swordsman, and *Tiger-slayer types of gold coins. The rev is usually occupied by

Chandragupta II : Archer type

Samudragupta : Standard type

Chandragupta II : Lion-slayer type

Kumāragupta I : *Aśvamedha* type

Chandragupta II : Lion-slayer type

Kumāragupta I : Kārttikeya type

Budhagupta : Archer type

Vishṇugupta : Archer type

the figure of some deity—*Lakshmī, **Siṁhavāhinī Devī*, *Gaṅgā, or *Kārttikeya. But the *Aśvamedha* type has the figure of the chief queen on the rev, instead of the figure of some deity. The silver coins are of two types, namely the *Western India type showing the royal bust on the obv and **garuḍa* on the rev, and the **Madhyadeśa* type with the royal bust on the obv and fan-tailed *peacock on the rev. The devices of the gold and silver types are often copied on the copper coins, and we have *Altar or **Garuḍa*, *Archer, *Bust, **Chakra*, **Chhatra*, *Crescent-and-*Garuḍa*, *Crowned head, **Garuḍa*-with-*ku*, *Jitaṁ Bhagavatā-Padmanābhena*, **Kalaśa*, *King's head, *Lakshmī, *Peacock, *Standing king, and *Vase type of copper coins. Initially, under the *Kushāṇa influence, the Imperial Gupta kings are shown wearing central Asian dress—long coat, trousers, and long boots. But gradually, this dress was replaced by the Indian *dhotī*. The male deities always wear *dhotī*. Goddesses and queens are shown wearing *sārī*, *cholī*, and an upper garment. Both male and female figures wear necklace, ear rings, armlets, rings, etc; the females wear, in addition to these, also bangles, girdle, and anklets. Among the animals represented on Imperial Gupta coins, the horse and the elephant are seen as the mount of the king; horse also occurs independently on the *Aśvamedha* type. Tiger, lion, and rhinoceros are shown as the prey of the royal hunter. The *Siṁhavāhinī Devī* has the lion as her mount. The birds represented on these coins include *garuḍa*, the royal insignia of the *Imperial Guptas, and the *peacock. The ld on both the obv and the rev is in Skt, written in the *Br script. The obv has a circular ld, usually metrical; sometimes, the personal name of the king is written vertically under his left arm on the obv, which is reminiscent of the Chinese style of writing. The rev ld is shorter, and usually gives the title(s) and/or name of the issuing king. The gold coins of the Imperial Guptas bear on the rev, 'a small geometric type of drawing…consisting of a circle or parallelogram, usually hanging down from a line with a number of prongs or dots above it'. Similar symbols are also seen on Kushāṇa coins, but there, they represent monograms of individual kings, while they do not seem to have the same significance on the Imperial Gupta coins, and Altekar seems to be right when he concludes that probably 'early Gupta mint-masters regarded these symbols on their prototype as merely decorative elements which they were free to diversify in any artistic way they liked'. Initially, the Imperial

Gupta coins show considerable Kushāṇa influence—their weight is based on the Kushāṇa gold coins; the king wears the Kushāṇa type of dress; the deity bearing the **cornucopiae* on the rev seems to be modelled after **Ardochsho*. But the Gupta mint masters gradually Indianized the coinage, and, in course of time, traces of foreign influence almost vanished from the coins (Ashvini Agrawal 1989; Allan 1914; Altekar 1954; Altekar 1957; R D Banerji 1933; C D Chatterji 1957; Fleet 1888; S R Goyal 1995a; S R Goyal 2005; C S Gupta 1983; P L Gupta 1998; Manmohan Kumar 1978; Prashant Srivastava 1996a; Thaplyal, forthcoming).

Chandragupta II : Archer type

Incuse fabric. It is that form of coin, in which the type on one side is impressed in intaglio, instead of in relief (Hill 1906).

Incuse impression. The sunk impression—square, oblong, triangular, or circular, depending on the shape of the die—made on the flan by the upper die (Hill 1906).

Indo-Greek. Coins, general features. Around the middle of the third century BC, Bactria, under its satrap, *Diodotos I, asserted its independence of the Seleukid emperor, Antiochos II. By the time an attempt could be made by the Seleukids to reassert their authority over Bactria, *Diodotos II, the son and successor of Diodotos I, had been supplanted by *Euthydemos I. Besides Diodotos I, Diodotos II, and Euthydemos I, coins reveal the existence of around three dozen Indo-Greek kings and queens—*Agathokleia, *Agathokles, *Amyntas, *Antialkidas, *Antimachos I, *Antimachos II, *Apollodotos, *Apollophanes, *Archebios, *Artemidoros, *Demetrios I, *Demetrios II, *Diomedes, *Dionysios, *Epander, *Eukratides I, *Eukratides II, *Euthydemos II, *Heliokles I, *Heliokles II, *Hermaios, *Hippostratos, *Kalliope, *Lysias, *Menander I, *Menander II, *Nikias, *Pantaleon, *Peukolaos, *Philoxenos, *Plato, *Polyxenos, *Strato I, *Strato II, *Telephos, *Theophilos, *Thrason, *Zoilos I, and *Zoilos II. The Indo-Greek rule seems to have come to an end sometime around the middle of the first century BC. The fact that so many Indo-Greek rulers have to be placed within less than two centuries goes to show that there were several Indo-Greek principalities in northwestern India, and that they were often engaged in internecine struggles. However, in view of the emerging

Diodotos

Agathokleia and Strato I

Menander

Menander

Hippostratos

Lysias

Antialkidas

Heliokles

Eukratides

*Śaka-Pahlava menace, the rival Indo-Greek ruling families seem to have made an attempt at *rapprochement*, but with no success, and soon, their territories were occupied by the Śaka-Pahlavas. The Indo-Greeks are known to have struck coins in gold, silver, copper, cupro-nickel, lead, and billon. The standard denomination of gold was the **stater*, that of silver was **drachm*, and that of silver was **chalkon*. According to Cunningham, the cupro-nickel coin weighing 134.4 grains, was the *obolos*. The gold, and silver, and cupro-nickel coins are mostly round in shape, while the copper coins in Bactria are round, while those in the Indian territories are square. The coins are all die-struck. As a rule, the Indo-Greek coins, with a few exceptions, bear, on the obv, the realistic head or bust of the king to the r, and, on the rev, the figure or emblem of some deity. The royal bust is absent on the bilingual drachms of Apollodotos, Antimachos II, and Telephos. Conjugate busts appear on some coins of Agathokleia with Strato I, of Hermaios with Kalliope, and on the coins struck by Eukratides I in memory of his parents, Heliokles and *Laodike. The royal head and bust is invariably shown as wearing a diadem, the 'old Asiatic symbol of royalty'. The deities appearing on Indo-Greek coins are mostly from the Greek pantheon—*Apollo, *Artemis, *Athena, *Demeter, *Dionysios, the *Dioskuri, *Hekate, *Helios, *Herakles, *Hermes, *Nike, *Poseidon, *Triton, and *Zeus. Emblems of deities include the **aegis* of Athena, the **tripod lebes* of Apollo, the palms and **pilei* of the Dioskuri, *the *caduceus* of Hermes, and the *thunderbolt of Zeus. Some Indian deities, like *Balarāma and Vāsudeva-Kṛishṇa, also make their appearance on Indo-Greek coins. Animals like *boar, *bull, *camel, *elephant, *horse, and *panther, birds like *eagle and *owl, and sea creatures like dolphin, are find depiction on Indo-Greek coins. In case of the Indo-Greek coins in Bactria, the name and title(s) of the issuing monarch appear on the rev in Gr. But in case of the Indo-Greek coins in the Indian territories, they appear in Gr on the obv, and the literal Pkt translation of this obv Gr ld, usually written in the Kh script, appears on the rev; the rare use of the Br script, in place of the Kh, to write the Pkt ld may be seen, for instance, on some coins of Agathokles. **Basileus* and **maharaja* are the most common titles. Some Indo-Greek rulers also assumed additional epithets, like **aniketos*/**apaḍihata*, **autokratoros*, **dikaios*/**dhramika*, **theos*, **megas*/**mahata*, **nikatoros*/ **jayadhara*, **soteros*/**tratara*, *philopatoros/*priyapita*, etc. The transfer of the Gr ld from the rev to the obv affected the size of the royal bust. The Indo-Greek coins also bear *monograms, the exact significance of which has baffled scholars. Indo-Greek coins are generally very artistic, particularly those issued in Bactria. With the shifting of Greek rule from Bactria to northwestern India, the 'rare gold *staters* and the splendid *tetradrachms* of Bactria' all but disappear. The Indo-Greek dies seem to have been engraved by Greek artists, or by Indian artists trained in the Greek traditions, although, as Marshall writes, 'the engravers…were no slavish copyists of Western models, but were giving free and spontaneous expression to their own ideas' (Bopearachchi 1993; Bopearachchi and Pieper 1998; Bopearachchi and Rahman 1995; C J Brown 1999; Cunningham 1970; Deb 1934; Gardner 1971; A N Lahiri 1965; Marshall 1936; Marshall 1975; Narain 1957a; Narain 1973; Narain 1993; Rapson 1987; Tarn 1980; Whitehead 1914).

Diodotos

Plato

Hermaios

Indra. Vedic god of 'power and valour'. He is believed to be the greatest of the vedic gods. He is one of the 11 atmospheric deities, the god of 'power and valour', and 'the lord of all that moves and breathes'. He is the wielder of the **vajra*, fashioned by Tvashṭṛi or Uśanas from the bones of Dadhyañch. This *vajra*, Indra used to kill the demon Vṛitra. Later, with the rise in the popularity and prominence of the puranic triad of Brahmā, *Vishṇu, and *Śiva, Indra, one of the supreme deities of the vedic pantheon, was reduced to the position of the 'chief of the minor gods', and, finally, was transformed into one of the eight *dikpālas* or guardian deities of the eight quarters of the universe. On the rev of the coins of the *Pañchāla ruler, *Indramitra, appears a deity standing facing on a pedestal on some specimens, or inside a 'domed shrine' on others. He holds an uncertain object in his r hand. On the basis of the statement of Allan, that the deity depicted on the rev of the Pañchāla series, has the name, which 'forms as a rule a component of the issuer's name', the deity on the rev of these coins of Indramitra has been identified as Indra, and the depiction has been regarded as one of the earliest anthropomorphic representations of the deity available. But there are some scholars who find it difficult to accept this identification on the grounds that no characteristic attribute of Indra, like the **vajra* or the *elephant mount, is here associated with the figure of the deity. The *Indo-Greek rulers do not seem to have favoured Indra as a coin device, although there are suggestions that on some of their coins, Indra appears in the garb of *Zeus, and that the elephant occurring on Indo-Greek, as well as other series of coins, might represent Indra theriomorphically. Among the *Śaka-Pahlava rulers, Indra appears only on some coins of *Azilises. On these coins, the deity is shown standing facing front, on his elephant. In his l hand is held a bow. To the r and left of Indra, are depicted foreparts of other elephants. It is seen that the attribute in the hand of Indra on this type, too, that is a bow, does not match with the iconographic description of the deity as given in the ancient Indian texts. However, bow and arrows as attributes of Indra are described in the *Ṛigveda*. Moreover, it is seen that even while constructing images of Indra, the artists sometimes gave him attributes, which are not found associated with him in any known iconographic text. For instance, *akshamālā* and *kamaṇḍalu* are seen in the front right and front l hand, respectively, of an image of Indra illustrated by T A G Rao. Similarly, a two-armed image from the Lakshmaṇa temple at Khajuraho, with one of its hands in the *abhaya* pose and holding a *ghaṭa* in the other hand, is described as an image of Indra on the basis of its *vāhana*, the elephant. *Pāśa* is found in one of the four hands of another image of Indra in the same temple at Khajurao. Even serpent and lotus bloom may be seen in the hands of some images of Indra at Khajuraho. Some scholars are of the view that the elephant, *lion, and *thunderbolt, appearing on some ancient Indian coins, might be regarded as theriomorphic or symbolic representations of Indra (Allan 1936; Banerjea 2002; Sukumari Bhattacharji 1970; Hillebrandt 1999; Macdonell 1897; R B Pande 1988; Rao 1985; Prashant Srivastava 1996b; Prashant Srivastava 2007b; Wilkins 2006).[†]

Indramitra. *Pañchāla k. He seems to be near in time to *Agnimitra, because on some of the coins, the first two Pañchāla symbols are replaced by a new one. Bela Lahiri places Indramitra in the thirteenth chronological position among the Pañchāla rulers known from coins. Since the coins of Agnimitra and Indramitra are quite common in the Kosala region, the extension of Pañchāla authority in that direction might have been achieved during their time. The deity, *Indra, on the rev of some coins of Indramitra, is shown standing on a pedestal, and on others, inside a domed shrine (Allan 1936; Bela Lahiri 1974).

Indravasu. *Apracha k. He is known both from coins and an inscription. Some copper coins bear the figure of horseman king on the obv and standing armed *Athena on the rev. B N Mukherjee has read the name of *Azes [II] as *Azzou* on the obv of at least two of such coins. The rev Kh ld was earlier read as *Vijayamitraputrasa Itravarmasa apracharajasa*, and it was suggested that these coins were issued by Azes II and his subordinate ruler Indravarman, the son of Vijayamitra who ruled over the Swat valley as per the testimony of the Bajaur relic casket inscription mentioning Viyakamitra and Vijayamitra. Marshall found eight coins of this type during the excavations at Taxila, and read *Iṁdravasasa* in place of *Itravarmasa* in the rev ld on these coins. But he identified this Iṁdravasa with Indravarman, the father of *Aśpavarman. However, some time back, R C Senior correctly read *Itravasusa* in place of *Itravarmasa* or *Iṁdravasasa* on these coins. The name of **Apracharaja* Indravasu also occurs in the reliquary inscriptions of the time of *Kharaoasta and Indravarman. Indravasu is mentioned as *apracharaja* on the joint coins with Azes II, and in the reliquary inscriptions of the time of Kharaösta and Indravarman, he shares this title with his father, Vijayamitra. It seems that, following the Śaka-Pahlava tradition of co-rule in which both the senior and the junior co-rulers assumed equivalent titles, as in the case of the joint coins of *Azes I with *Azilises, and of Azilises with Azes II, Indravasu ruled for some time as the co-ruler of Vijayamitra. He also seems to have served as a subordinate of the Śaka-Pahlava ruler, Azes II, as per the testimony of their joint coins. Vijayamitra is mentioned as ruling in later inscriptions also, while in the Indravarman reliquary inscription of Azes year 63, we find Vishṇuvarman co-ruling as *apracharaja* with *Apracharaja* Vijayamitra. From this, it appears that Indravasu predeceased his father, some time before Azes year 63 (= 5 AD), the date of the Indravarman reliquary inscription. The rarity of the coins of Indravasu suggests a short career for him (Cunningham 1971a; B N Mukherjee 1969a; Senior 1996; Senior 2001; Marshall 1975; Salomon 1996; Prashant Srivastava 2007a; Prashant Srivastava 2007g).

Indravasu hoard. This hoard of around 25 coins comes from somewhere in the Swat region. The rulers represented in this hoard include *Azes I (posthumous issues), *Azes II, Azes II with *Indravasu, Azes II with *Aśpavarman, *Gondopharnes with *Sasan, and *V'ima Takshuma (Senior 2001).

Irippal hoard. This hoard of 363 coins was discovered at Irippal in the Kangra district, now in Himachal Pradesh. On 103 of these coins, the name of the issuer was read variously as *Śivadāsa, Rudradāsa, and Dharaghosha, all believed to be *Audumbara chiefs. The ld on the rest of the coins could not be deciphered, and as such, their attribution is not certain (R D Banerji 1914; Handa 2007a).

Īśānavarman. *Maukhari k; son of Īśvaravarman; mid-sixth century AD. The main source of information regarding his reign is his Haraha inscription, which records his victory over the Andhras (Vishṇukuṇḍins), Śūlikas (Chālukyas ?), and Gauḍas, before ascending the throne. Emboldened by these conquests, he asserted independence from the *Imperial Guptas, and assumed the title of **mahārājādhirāja*. He might have also defeated the *Hūṇas. But the Later Gupta king, Kumāragupta, is known to have defeated him, and probably extended the boundaries of his principality up to Prayāga. Some scholars identify the Maukhari ruler defeated by the Later Gupta king, Dāmodaragupta, also with Īśānavarman. He issued silver coins of the **Madhyadeśa* type of the Imperial Guptas, with the royal head to the r and the date of issue on the obv, and a fan-tailed *peacock with the Br ld reading *Vijitāvaniravanipati Śrī-Īśānavarman divaṁ jayati* on the rev. Their average weight is around 36 grains. They have been found in the *Bhitaura hoard. Rapson read the dates on the coins of this Maukhari ruler as 54, 55; Cunningham as 55 or 155; Smith as 54; Fleet as 40, 60, 70; and Dikshit as 245, 257, etc. N G Majumdar is of the view that the dates on these coins have generally totally disappeared and it is not possible to the read them (Richard Burn 1906; D Devahuti 1964; Pires 1934; Thaplyal 1985).[†]

Īśvaradatta. Ābhīra (?) k. The coins of one **Mahākshatrapa* Īśvaradatta, have been found in several hoards of *Kārddamaka coins, and these bear a close affinity to the coins of the Kārddamaka

Kshatrapas. However, he cannot be regarded as a Kārddamaka ruler, mainly on the bases of the facts that his name does not appear to fit in with those of the Kārddamaka rulers, and that he dates his coins in his regnal years while the Kārddamaka Kshatrapas date their issues in the *Śaka era. On this basis, it has been proposed that he was an interloper, who either usurped the Kārddamaka throne, or ruled simultaneously with some Kārddamaka ruler after wresting some of his territories from him. Mirashi is of the view that Īśvaradatta ruled over northern Maharashtra, and wrested some parts of Malwa and Saurashtra from the Kārddamaka Kshatrapas. He issued silver coins, which have been found in several hoards of *Kārddamaka coins, and which bear the bust of the king to the r on the obv, and the *crescent-on-hill, with a crescent to the l, star to the r, and *undulating line below, on the rev. The Br ld on the rev reads *Rājño mahākshatrapasa Īśvaradattasa*, with *varshe prathame* or *varshe dvitīye* on various coins. There have also been attempts to read a date, year 154 or 164, on one of his coins. The coins of Īśvaradatta have been divided into two classes on the basis of the presence or absence of the date in numerals on the obv of the coin (For references, see Jha and Rajgor 1994).†

Īśvaramitra. *Kauśāmbī k. He issued copper coins, both round and square in shape. The square coins are of comparatively thin fabric, and the square shape and thin fabric connect him with *Aśvaghosha, *Parvata, *Rāḍhamitra, and *Priyamitra. This may be taken as a ground to place him, in time, near Aśvaghosha, who, perhaps, ruled towards the beginning of the first century AD. His coins, both round and square ones, bear the ld *Īśaramitasa* in two lines on the obv. The round coins bear the traces of a few dots on the rev, while the square coins have a *yūpa* or a *tree-in-railing. He is the only early ruler of Kauśāmbī to use the title of **rājan* on his (square) coins (K D Bajpai 1953; Bopearachchi and Pieper 1998; Bela Lahiri 1974).

J

Jahaṇṇa-kāhāvaṇa. Coin denomination. Although it is difficult to ascertain as to which coin is implied by this coin denomination (= Skt, *jaghanya-kārshāpaṇa*) mentioned in the **Aṅgavijjā*, it possibly refers to copper (**kārshāpaṇa* ?) coins [**majjhima-kāhāvaṇa*, **uttama-kāhāvaṇa*] (V S Agrawala 1957).

Jarīva. *Hūṇa chief. Cunnigham has published some copper coins, which bear the ld *Shāhi Jara* or *Shāhi Jari*. One coin has the half-length figure of the king to the l and the ld *Shāhi Jara* on the obv, and seated goddess on the rev. Three other coins have enthroned king holding trident and an uncertain object with the ld *Shāhi Jara* on the obv, and enthroned goddess with **cornucopiae* and an uncertain object on the rev. One coin has the king standing with spear in the l hand, and the ld *Shāhi Jari* on the obv, and seated goddess holding *cornucopiae* on the rev. He ascribes these coins to a Hūṇa ruler, whose name he suggests as 'Jara [?]'. A Hūṇa chief, named Jarīva, is known from a Nalanda sealing, which describes him as a **mahārāja* and grandson of *Lavkhāṇa. It has been suggested that these coins may be regarded as issued by him. As his name occurs in the sealing from Nalanda, it has been suggested that Jarīva ruled over that region. But sealings can travel to distant places, and the coins of Jari/Jarīva have been found in Punjab and Kashmir, thereby showing that he would have ruled over these regions, rather than over Nalanda (Altekar 1986b; Biswas 1973; Cunningham 1962; Cunningham 1967; R C Majumdar 1988; Upendra Thakur 1967a; Upendra Thakur 1967b; Thaplyal 1972).

Jaüla. Title. The title *Jaüla*, and its variants, like *Jabula*, *Janabula*, and *Jabūvlaḥ*, occur on the coins of the *Hūṇa chief, *Toramāṇa; his Kura inscription has *Jaūvla*. Although his son and successor, *Mihirakula, does not use this title on coins, it occurs as *Saho Zobol* in the two Uruzgan inscriptions from Afghanistan. The title also occurs on the *Kushāṇo-Sassanian coins. Some scholars suggest that *Jaüla* or *Zabol* refers to the region in the upper reaches of the rivers Helmand and Arghandab in Afghanistan, which was known to the Arabs as Zābulistān. The branch of the Hūṇas, to which Toramāṇa apparently belonged, settled for some time in this region before their arrival into India, and due to this association, the branch came to be known by the name of the Zabula area (Biswas 1973; A D H Bivar 1954; Upendra Thakur 1967b).

Jayadāman. *Kārddamaka k. He was the son of *Chashṭana, and served his father as a **kshatrapa*. On his coins, he uses the titles of **rājan*, *kshatrapa* and *svāmin*, but no source refers to him as **mahākshatrapa*. From this, it has been inferred that he probably predeceased his father. This is corroborated by the Andhau inscription of Śaka year 52 (130 AD), in which we find *Rudradāman I, the son of Jayadāman, assisting Chashṭana in administration. Earlier, it was believed that Jayadāman issued only copper coins. But now, it is known that Jayadāman, too, issued silver coins. These bear the bust of the king to the r and a corrupt marginal Gr ld on the obv; the rev has the *crescent-on-hill, crescent, and star, and legends in both Br and Kh, both of which seem to mention his name with the titles of *rājña* and *kshatrapa*. The copper coins, rectangular in shape, bear the figure of a humped *bull to the r, before a trident-battle-axe, and some meaningless Greek characters on the obv. The rev has a crescent-on-hill, star, and crescent, and the Br ld *Rājño kshatrapasa svāmi Jayadāmasa*. There is another copper coin with the figure of an *elephant on the obv and the *Ujjain symbol on the rev. The ld on this piece is almost illegible. Only the Br letter *ya* can be read, and on this basis, the coin is hesitantly ascribed to Jayadāman by some scholars. But others regard it as a local coin of *Ujjayinī (Jha and Rajgor 1994; Mirashi 1982; Mitchiner 1976; Rapson 1975; Raychaudhuri 1972; Senior 2001; Sircar 1980e).

Antimachos II

Jayadhara. Title. It is the Pkt rendering of both **nikatoros* and **nikephoros*, and used by *Amyntas, *Antialkidas, *Antimachos II, *Archebios, and *Epander (Cunningham 1970; Gardner 1971; A N Lahiri 1965; Marshall 1975; Narain 1957a; Tarn 1980; Whitehead 1914).

Jayadhvaja. Symbol. *Triangular-headed symbol.

Jayaghosha. *Almora k.

Jayagupta. *Pañchāla k. He seems to be near in time to *Indramitra and *Prajāpatimitra, because all the three of them show the divinity on the rev of their coins as standing within a domed shrine. Bela Lahiri places Jayagupta in the seventeenth chronological position among the Pañchāla rulers known from coins. The deity on the coins of Jayagupta is indistinct, and her identification with Jayā is based on the analogy of the name of the issuer (Allan 1936; Bela Lahiri 1974).

Jayamagha (?). *Magha k.

Jayamitra. *Pañchāla k. He seems to be near in time to *Indramitra and *Vishṇumitra, because all the three of them show the divinity on the rev of their coins as standing on a pedestal. Bela Lahiri places Jayamitra in the fifteenth chronological position among the Pañchāla rulers known from coins. The deity on the coins of Jayamitra is indistinct, and her identification with Jayā is based on the analogy of the name of the issuer (Allan 1936; Bela Lahiri 1974).

Jayaṁta. Title. This title, the Greek equivalent of which is not available on any coin, was adopted by *Hippostratos among the *Indo-Greeks. It also appears on the joint coins of *Azes II with *Aśpavarman, and on the coin of an unidentified king in the Punjab Museum collection (Cunningham 1970; Gardner 1971; A N Lahiri 1965; Marshall 1975; Narain 1957a; Tarn 1980; Whitehead 1914).

Jaya[nāga]. Gauḍa k. Known from some gold coins from Bengal, the full name of this ruler is not definitely known as yet. Allan earlier suggested that it was Jaya[gupta], but later proposed that it might be Jaya[nāga]. He regards him as identical with *Mahārājādhirāja paramabhāgavata Śrī Jayanāgadeva of the Vappaghoshavaṭa grant issued from Karṇasuvarṇa, and this identification has found favour with Altekar. On palaeographical grounds, and also on the basis of the information of the *Āryamañjuśrīmūlakalpa* that *Śaśāṅka was followed by a king named Nāga, Jaya[nāga] has been placed in the period *c* 640 to 650 AD, as a successor of Śaśāṅka. As he was a *mahārājādhirāja*, he must have been 'a ruler of some consequence'. His Vaishṇava leanings are indicated by the title of *paramabhāgavata* used for him in the Vappaghoshavaṭa grant (above). He issued gold coins of the *Archer type of the *Imperial Guptas. The obv shows the nimbate king as an archer, with a *chakradhvaja* placed behind his right arm, on which basis Altekar is inclined to the label it as the *Chakradhvaja* type. Under his left arm is the vertical ld, *Jaya*. The rev device of *Gajalakshmī is remarkable in that there is only one elephant anointing the goddess. Incidentally, this device also seems to connect Jaya[nāga] with Śaśāṅka. The rev ld on these coins read *Śrī Prakāṇḍayaśasāḥ* (Allan 1914; Altekar 1957).

Jayasa/Jiyasa (?). *Vṛishṇi general (?).

Jayasoma/Āryyasoma (?). *Vṛishṇi general (?).

Jayava[rmā]. *Yaudheya (?) chief. His name is reported to occur on some copper coins from the *Chakkar hoard. K K Maheshwari regards him as a Yaudheya chief, but P L Gupta associated him with the family of the Varsha *gaṇa* (P L Gupta 1987; P L Gupta 1988; Handa 2007a; K K Maheshwari 1978).

Jessore hoard. This hoard from Muhammadpur near Jessore (Bangladesh) is reported in the *Journal of the Asiatic Society of Bengal* in 1852. The gold coins in this hoard include one later imitation of the *Imperial Gupta coins, one coin of *Śaśāṅka, and one of *Samāchāradeva. The hoard is also said to consist of the silver coins of *Chandragupta II, *Kumāragupta I, and *Skandagupta, though doubts have been expressed over this issue (Altekar 1957).

***Jitaṁ Bhagavatā Padmanābhena* type.** Copper. The obv of this type bears a two line Br ld *Jitaṁ Bhagavatā/Padmanābhena*. The rev has a *kalpavṛiksha* in an ornamental form. The piece does not bear the name of the issuer. But the script is of the Gupta period, and the piece is dedicated to Padmanābha (*Vishṇu). On this basis, K D Bajpai ascribes this piece to *Chandragupta II, who was a Vaishṇava, and suggests that it was issued by the *Imperial Gupta ruler after his victory over eastern Malwa; his alternative suggestion is that the piece might have been a token. But some others scholars regard it as a temple medal (Ashvini Agrawal 1989; K D Bajpai 1971; S R Goyal 2005; P L Gupta 1998; Prashant Srivastava 1996a).

Jīvadāman

Jīvadāman. *Kārddamaka k. He was the son of *Dāmajadaśri * I. Rapson read the date of year 1[00] on a silver coin of Jīvadāman, and believed that upon the death of Dāmajadaśrī I (whom he regarded as identical with *Dāmaghsada), there was to be a struggle for succession between Jīvadāman and his uncle, *Rudrasiṁha I, in which he was initially successful, and we find him ruling as **mahākshatrapa* in *Śaka year 1[00]. But during Śaka year 103-110, and 113-118, Rudrasiṁha I issued coins as *mahākshatrapa*, showing that Jīvadāman had been worsted and removed from the position of *mahākshatrapa*. But in Śaka year 119-120, Jīvadāman is again found issuing coins as *mahākshatrapa*. He seems to have either wrested power from Rudrasiṁha I, or succeeded to the position after the death of the latter. However, Amiteshwar Jha and Dilip Rajgor doubt the reading of year 1[00] on the coin of Jīvadāman, and suggest that there was no struggle between him and Rudrasiṁha I, and that Rudrasiṁha I served as a **kshatrapa* under Dāmaghsada II and had a 'smooth elevation' to the office of *mahākshatrapa*. They also read the dates of year 100 to 102 on a number of coins mentioning Rudrasiṁha I as *mahākshatrapa*. Jīvadāman issued *Kārddamaka silver type of coins. If he ruled as *mahākshatrapa* in the year 1[00], then he would be the first Kārddamaka ruler to give the date of the issue of the coin, which is mentioned in the *Śaka era. But, if he did not rule before Rudrasiṁha I, as suggested by Jha and Rajgor, then this credit would go to the Rudrasiṁha I. Jīvadāman also issued potin coins, which bear the figure of a humped *bull to the r, and some Greek characters on the obv; the rev has a *crescent-on-hill, star, crescent, and curved line, and a Br ld mentioning only his name and titles and not those of his father. The date of year 119 has been reported on some of these potin coins (Jha and Rajgor 1994; Mirashi

1982; Mitchiner 1976; Rapson 1975; Raychaudhuri 1972; Senior 2001; Sircar 1980e).

Jiyasa/Jayasa (?). *Vṛishṇi general (?).

Jñāgaṇa. *Vṛishṇi.

Jogelthembhi hoard. This large hoard of around 13,250 silver coins was discovered at the site in the Nasik district of Maharashtra in 1905. It originally comprised a much larger number (up to 14,000 or 15,000) of coins, but many of them were melted down. The hoard contains around 4,000 coins of the *Kshaharāta ruler, *Nahapāna, and about 9,270 coins of that ruler which have been restruck by the Sātavāhana king, Gautamīputra Sātakarṇi. Around 2,000 of the coins in the hoard were found perforated (Jha and Rajgor 1994; Scott 1908; A M Shastri 1995).

Junagarh hoard 1. This hoard of *Kārddamaka silver coins was discovered in the Junagarh district of Gujarat. Although the number of coins in this hoard is given as 32, the breakup of the hoard gives the figure of 68. The rulers represented in this hoard include *Rudradāman I, *Rudrasena I, *Dāmasena, *Dāmajadadaśrī II, *Vīradāman, *Yaśodāman I, *Vijayasena, *Rudrasena II, and *Viśvasiṁha. Five coins are reported as 'imperfect', probably implying that their attribution is not certain (P L Gupta 1969; Jha and Rajgor 1994).

Junagarh hoard 2. Another hoard from the Junagarh district of Gujarat is reported to comprise 335 silver coins (though the breakup of only 332 coins is given), mainly of the *Karddamaka Kshatrapas. The rulers represented in the hoard include *Rudrasiṁha I, *Rudrasena I, *Dāmasena, *Vīradāman, *Vijayasena, *Dāmajadaśrī III, *Rudrasena II, *Viśvasiṁha, *Bhartṛidāman, and *Viśvasena. Besides, the hoard is also said to contain two coins of *Īśvaradatta (P L Gupta 1969; Jha and Rajgor 1994).

Jyeshṭhabhūti. *Kauśāmbī k. He issued copper coins, the obv of which bears a standing male figure to front with the r hand raised, while the left is placed on the hip, and the ld giving the name of the issuer in the genitive. The rev has a *tree-in-railing, and some other symbols which are blurred. K D Bajpai, who published this coin, read the ld as *Jeṭhagata*, and rendered the name of the issuer in Skt as Jyeshṭhagupta. But Bela Lahiri correctly reads *Jeṭhabhata*, and renders the name as Jyeshṭhabhūti. The standing male figure on the rev of his coins connects him with *Jyeshṭhamitra, and some scholars have expressed the possibility of their contemporaneous rule over different parts of Kauśāmbī (K D Bajpai 1960; Bopearachchi and Pieper 1998; Bela Lahiri 1974).

Jyeshṭhadatta. *Ayodhyā k. He is known from the common Ayodhyā type of 'Bull : Combinations of symbols' only; nothing definite can be said about him, although Bela Lahiri places him at the end of the early rulers of Ayodhyā who issued cast coins only. The obv of his coins bears the figure of a *bull before a *dhvajastambha* and the ld *Jeṭhadatasa*, while the rev is blurred, although traces of symbols, like the *tree-in-railing, is visible (Altekar 1946b; Bela Lahiri 1974).

Jyeshṭhagupta (?). *Kauśāmbī k. K D Bajpai, who published this coin, read the ld as *Jeṭhagata*, and rendered the name of the issuer in Skt as Jyeshṭhagupta. But Bela Lahiri correctly reads *Jeṭhabhata*, and renders the name as *Jyeshṭhabhūti (K D Bajpai 1960; Bopearachchi and Pieper 1998; Bela Lahiri 1974).

Jyeshṭhamitra. *Kauśāmbī k. He may be identical with the homonym known from a Kauśāmbī epigraph. He issued copper coins with a *bull on the obv, and a *tree-in-railing and some other symbols, along with the name of the king in the genitive, on the rev. However, some of his coins have the figure of a *horse to the l on the obv, and a standing male figure and the ld *Jeṭhamitasa* on the rev. The symbols on his coins, like the **svastika*, the *Ujjain symbol, and the *taurine symbol, seem to connect him with *Vavaghosha, and he might not have been far removed from the latter in time. The standing male figure on the rev of his coins connects him with *Jyeshṭhabhūti, and some scholars have expressed the possibility of their contemporaneous rule over different parts of Kauśāmbī. The style, execution, and combination of symbols on his coins also connect him with *Praushṭhamitra, *Agnimitra, and *Bahasatimita

II, and some coins of all these four rulers are countermarked with the *nandipada-triśūla* (Altekar 1942b; Bopearachchi and Pieper 1998; Bela Lahiri 1974).

Jyeshṭhapura. City coins. Two round, bronze coins mentioning Jyeshṭhapura in *c* fifth century AD characters, have been noticed by Altekar. One coin bears, on the obv, a *bull, with a crescent above, and the ld *Jaṭhapura*. The obv of the other piece is almost similar, but there is a penon-like object flying above the back of the bull, and the ld reads *Jeshṭhapura*. The rev side of both the pieces is blank. Altekar holds that Jyeshṭhapura might be identical with Pāli Jetuttara, which is mentioned in the *Vessantarajātaka* as the capital of the *Śibis, and he attributes these coins to the Śibi tribe. But the fabric of these two coins differs from that of the usual Śibi *janapada* coins of the third-second centuries BC; there is no evidence to show that the Śibis were flourishing as a tribe as late as the fifth century AD; and numismatic evidence shows that Mādhyamikā was the capital of the Śibis. All these arguments render Altekar's theory untenable. The blank rev sides of these pieces have led K K Dasgupta to suggest that they might be tokens or passports of the city of Jyeshṭhapura, or the impression in bronze, of the seal of that city. Another suggestion is that these pieces might represent the city coins of Jyeshṭhapura (Altekar 1952a; K K Dasgupta 1974; J P Singh 1971).

K

Kācha. *Imperial Gupta k; *c* fourth century AD. He was a ruler of the Imperial Gupta period, known from the Kācha type of coins; the occurrence of the **garuḍadhvaja* on his coins sets at rest all doubts regarding his relations with the Imperial Guptas. There is some controversy among scholars regarding the identity of Kācha, and various scholars regard him as identical with Ghaṭotkacha, the father of *Chandragupta I (with Joe Cribb suggesting that the coins might even have been struck by *Samudragupta in memory of his grandfather); with a son of Ghaṭotkacha, and a younger brother of Chandragupta I; with. *Rāmagupta, the elder brother of *Chandragupta II; with an elder brother of *Samudragupta, who lost his life in the 'war of liberation' fought by Chandragupta I against the *Kushāṇas; and with Samudragupta, himself. But, as Altekar has shown, these arguments put forth in favour of these view are not conclusive. It has been suggested that Kācha might have been a brother of Samudragupta, who usurped the throne immediately after the death of Chandragupta I, or during Samudragupta's absence from northern India while he was engaged in his Dakshiṇāpatha campaigns, or after the death of Samudragupta, the last possibility finding favour with Altekar. The coins of the Kācha type bear, on the obv, the standing figure of the king, dressed in coat and trousers, and holding a *chakradhvaja* in his l hand, while he is sacrificing at an altar with his r hand. There is the vertical ld *Kācha* under the l arm of the king. The circular ld reads *Kācho gāmavajitya divaṁ karmabhiruttamairjayati*. The rev has a standing goddess (*Lakshmī ?), holding a flower in her r hand, and a **cornucopiae* in her l hand. One variety has similar depictions on both the sides of the coin, but

Kācha

there is a **garuḍadhvaja* in front of the king on the obv, and the goddess on the rev holds a *pāśa* in her r hand, in place of the flower (Ashvini Agrawal 1989; Altekar 1957; K D Bajpai 1972; Sibesh Bhattacharya 1992; Chhabra 1986; Cribb 1985a; S R Goyal 2005; P L Gupta 1998; Prashant Srivastava 1996a; Thaplyal, forthcoming).†

Kachchh hoard. This hoard of 142 silver coins of the *Kārddamaka rulers was discovered in the Kachchh district of Gujarat in 1861-1862. The rulers represented in the hoard include *Dāmasena, *Vijayasena, *Dāmajadaśrī III, *Rudrasena II, *Viśvasiṁha, *Bhartṛidāman, son of Rudrasena II (whose name is not clear), *Viśvasena, *Rudrasiṁha II, and Yaśodāman II. One coin has no ld (P L Gupta 1969; Jha and Rajgor 1994).

Kāḍa. Tribe. There are some coins, crude in execution, which bear the ld *Kāḍasa* in *c* second century BC characters. The interpretation of this ld is controversial. Bühler took *Kāḍa* as *Kāla*, which he regarded as the name of a king, while S K Chakrabortty took it as referring to the town of Kāḍasa, the same as Kadrusi, one of the towns established by Alexander near Alexandria under the Caucasus. Cunningham, however, took it as the name of a tribe, which he tentatively identified with Kadrava, the descendants of Kadru. But B R Mani takes *Kāḍa* as the same as Kaṭha, and as derived by affixing *aṇ* to *kaṭha*, which may mean 'the descendants of King Kaṭha', or stand for 'Kaṭhas as a class', or 'the people of Kaṭha country'. The Kaṭhas are identified with Kathoi of the classical writers, who settled between the rivers Ravi and Beas, and bravely fought Alexander. The facts, that one Kāḍa coin has been found with *Kuṇinda coins, and that the British Museum acquired the Kāḍa coins through Rodgers and Whitehead collections, suggest the Punjab region as the habitat of the tribe. The Kāḍa coins are all in copper, and mostly round in shape, though some square coins are also known. Allan has described five varieties of Kāḍa coins. The first variety has the sun on the obv, and a *tree-in-railing and another symbol on the rev. The second variety has an *undulating line and a *taurine symbol on the obv as well as on the rev. The third variety has the undulating line and the taurine symbol on the obv, and a figure holding staff (*Kārttikeya ?), *kalaśa* and **svastika* on the rev. The fourth variety has the undulating line and the taurine symbol on the obv, and an *elephant on the rev;

Kāḍa

the coins of this variety are square in shape. The fifth variety has only the ld on the obv, and a *kalaśa* with flowers on the rev. The ld always occurs on the obv, except for the first variety where it occurs on the rev (Allan 1936; Chakrabortty 1931; Cunningham 1971b; K K Dasgupta 1974; Jayaswal 1988; B R Mani 1978; Marshall 1975; Mitchiner 1975-1976; Smith 1972).

Kaḍare. Guild. *Takshaśilā. Guild coins.

Kahāpaṇa/Kāhāpaṇa. **Kārshāpaṇa*.

Kākaṇī/Kākiṇī. Coin denomination. It was 1/64 of a **kārshāpaṇa*, and is mentioned in the **Ashṭādhyāyī* of Pāṇini and the *Arthaśāstra* of Kauṭilya as a copper coin also known as **pāda-māshaka*. This coin denomination also occurs in the **Aṅgavijjā*, where the context seems to indicate that it was a copper coin, 1.25 *rattīs* in weight. V S Agrawala takes the existence of such minute coins as 'for granted' (V S Agrawala 1953; V S Agrawala 1957; D R Bhandarkar 1984; Chakrabortty 1931; Sircar 1952; Sircar 1968).

Kalanakrama. Title. It is the Pkt rendering of **euergetes*, and used by *Telephos. The Skt equivalent is *kalyāṇakarma* (Cunningham 1970; Gardner 1971; A N Lahiri 1965; Marshall 1975; Narain 1957a; Tarn 1980; Whitehead 1914).

***Kalaśa* type.** Copper. This type of copper coins was struck by *Kumāragupta I among the *Imperial Guptas. The obv bears a *kalaśa* below a crescent. The rev has the figure of a **garuḍa*, with the ld *Kumāra* below it (Allan 1914; Altekar 1957; P L Gupta 1998; Smith 1972).

Kalighat hoard. This hoard, in a brass pot, found in 1783 at Kalighat on the bank of the river Hugli near Calcutta (West Bengal), is the earliest recorded hoard of *Imperial Gupta coins. The finder, Nab Kishore, presented about 200 coins of this hoard to Warren Hastings, the then Governor-General of India, and most of them (172 ?) were sent by the latter to the Directors of the East Indian Company. The Directors, in their turn, distributed these coins among various public and private collections, like the British Museum, London (24 coins), museum of Mr Hunter (24 coins), and the Ashmolean Museum, Oxford; some coins were left with the East Indian Company and were melted down by the Directors. The rulers represented in this hoard include *Chandragupta II, *Narasiṁhagupta, *Kumāragupta II, and *Vishṇugupta (Allan 1914).

Kalliope. *Indo-Greek queen; wife of *Hermaios; first half of the first century BC. Known from the coins she issued conjointly with her husband, *Hermaios, Kalliope seems to be a descendant of *Antimachos, and a daughter of *Hippostratos. It seems that the father of Kalliope had no male heirs, and on his death, his kingdom passed on to her. She ruled over this kingdom conjointly with Hermaios, and issued joint coins with him, during this period of joint rule. These coins, in silver, bear the jugate and diademed bust of Hermaios and Kalliope on the obv, and equestrian king on the rev. The obv Gr ld reads **Basileos *soteros Ermaiou kai Kalliopes*; the rev ld is a literal Pkt rendering of the obv ld. R C Senior has referred to a rare joint issue of Heramios and Kalliope, on which the device of king mounted on a prancing horse occupies the obv, replacing the conjugate busts of the king and the queen (Bopearachchi 1993; Bopearachchi and Pieper 1998; Bopearachchi and Rahman 1995; Cunningham 1970; Gardner 1971; A N Lahiri 1965; Marshall 1975; Narain 1957a; Senior 2001; Sircar 1980a; Prashant Srivastava 1990b; Prashant Srivastava 1996a; Tarn 1980; Whitehead 1914).†

Hermaios and Kalliope

Kāmadatta. *Mathurā k. He issued coins, which show *Lakshmī with lotus in her r hand and some symbols on the obv; and an illegible rev (Allan 1936; Bela Lahiri 1974).

Kanauj. A coin of *Vishṇudeva has been found at Kanauj. Coins of *Brahmamitra and *Sūryamitra, as also *Gomitra (whose coins have been over-struck by another king) have been tentatively ascribed to Kanauj by some scholars on the basis of similarity of types with Vishṇudeva of Kanauj coins, though their coins have not been found at Kanauj. Some scholars do not take Kanauj coins as forming a separate series. The coins referred to above are datable to second-first centuries BC. Śuṅgavarman, a king known from a coin allegedly found at *Kauśāmbī, is also ascribed to Kanauj as his coin shows affinity with the coin of Vishṇudeva. The coins of the kings with

Kanauj

mitra-ending names show on the obv, a *triangle-headed standard, *tree-in-railing, and *Ujjain symbol in different combinations; those of Vishṇudeva and Śuṅgavarman have tree-in-railing, hare-on-moon, and a **caduceus*-like symbol. The rev of the coins of Vishṇudeva and Śuṅgavarman shows a *horse before a *yūpa*. Thus, only tree-in-railing is common to all, and if these coins are ascribed to Kanauj, this may be taken as a typical Kanauj symbol. K D Bajpai is of the view that all those kings, who have been taken by scholars as belonging to Kanauj, were, in fact, rulers of Kauśāmbī. He also considers it possible that Kanauj formed a part of the kingdoms of *Mathurā or *Pañchāla. Bela Lahiri does not consider them as belonging to Kauśāmbī, as they differ typologically and the names of the kings are not met with in the Kauśāmbī series of coins. She prefers to take them as a separate series, though she does not rule out the possibility of their belonging to Mathurā, as kings named *Gomitra, *Brahmamitra, and *Sūryamitra are also known from the Mathurā series; she feels that these three kings might have ruled over some territories between Mathurā and Kanauj. However, the devices on their coins and those on the coins of their homonyms ascribed to Kanauj, show little similarity and much difference (Allan 1936; K D Bajpai 1964; Bela Lahiri 1974; Mitchiner 1975-1976; Smith 1972).

Kandahar hoard. This hoard of over 1,000 coins came to the light in Quetta, and was disposed of from Peshawar, with the best specimens going to Japan. The rulers represented in this hoard include *Orthanges with *Gondopharnes and *Guḍa, Gondopharnes alone, Gondopharnes with *Sasan, *Pakores, and *Sapedana; a number of coins of Pakores seem to have been restruck by *V'ima Takshuma (Senior 2001).

Kanishka I

Kanishka I. *Kushāṇa k; son of *V'ima Kadphises; latter half of the first century AD. Perhaps the greatest, and certainly the most famous, of the Kushāṇa kings, he is known from the combined testimony of the literary, epigraphic, and numismatic sources, to have ruled over an extensive dominion extending from Bihar in the east to Khorasan in the west, and from Khotan in the north to Konkan in the south. The discovery of his coins in Bengal and Orissa should, however, not be taken as indicative of his sway over these territories in the absence of any corroborative evidence. He subjugated the Central Asian provinces of Kashghar, Yarqand, and Khotan, and also dispatched his viceroy, Hsï, at the head of 70,000 horsemen, across the Pamir to give battle to Pan-chao, the general of the Chinese emperor, Ho-ti (89-105 AD). This expedition was, however, unsuccessful. The *Śrīdharmapiṭaka* refers to his expedition against the Parthians. His name is associated with the Fourth Buddhist Council. A vast majority of scholars regards him as the founder of the *Śaka era, beginning 78 AD with his accession. Towards the end of his rule, he seems to have associated one *Vāsishka as his junior co-ruler. He issued coins in gold, silver, and copper. These may be classified according to the metal of the coin and the obv device. Some of his gold coins bear the device of *king sacrificing at an altar, and the Gr ld *Basileus Basileon Kaneshkou*, on the obv, while the rev bears, variously, *Elios* (*Helios), *Ephaistos* (*Hephaistos), **Nanaia*, **Selene*, etc. Some other gold coins bear the same device on the obv, but the ld reads **Shaonanoshao Kaneshki Koshano*. The rev of these coins is occupied variously by **Ardochsho*, **Athsho*, the Buddha, **Lrooaspo*, **Manaobago*, **Mao*, **Mazdooano*, **Miiro*, **Nana*, *Śiva, **Orlagno*, **Pharro*, etc. Still other gold coins bear on the obv a bearded and helmeted bust of the king to the l on clouds, and the figures of *Athsho*, *Mao*, *Nana*, Śiva, both *Nana* and Śiva standing side by side, etc. The silver coins, very few in number, bear the device of king sacrificing at an altar, and the ld *Shaonanoshao Kaneshki Koshano* on the obv, and four-armed, nimbate Śiva on the rev. The obv of the copper coins is mostly occupied by the device of king sacrificing at an altar, and the ld on different coins may be *Basileus Basileon Kaneshkou*, or *Shaonanoshao Kaneshki Koshano*, or simply **Shao Kaneshki*. The rev of these coins has the figure of deities like Helios, **Oado*, the Buddha, *Miiro*, Śiva, *Nana*, etc. One copper type of Kanishka has the figure of enthroned king on the obv, along with a fragmentary ld mentioning Kanishka. The rev has Śiva holding a *triśūla* and *kamaṇḍalu* in his two hands. The name of the deity represented is mentioned in the label inscription on the rev (Cunningham 1971a; Gardner 1971; Marshall 1975; von Mitterwallner 1986; Rosenfield 1967; Sircar 1980c; Whitehead 1914).†

Kanishka I

Kanishka I

Kanishka I

Kanishka III

Kanishka III

Kanishka III. *Kushāṇa k. He was one of the successors of *Vāsudeva I. The ld, distributed on the obv and rev of an interesting copper coin discovered during the excavations at Sonkh near Mathurā, has been read by P L Gupta as *Huvishkasya-putra Kaṇikas[ya]*. If this reading be correct, Kanishka III would appear to be a son of *Huvishka, as suggested by B N Mukherjee. Huvishka could not have been the father of *Kanishka I, who ruled before Huvishka, or of Kanishka II, who is described as the son of Vājeshka (= *Vāsishka) in the Ara inscription of *Śaka year 41. Kanishka III issued two types of gold coins. The obv of both the types bears the device of *king sacrificing at an altar, and the ld **Shaonanoshao Kaneshko Koshano*. The rev of one type has the figure of **Ardochsho*, while that of the other bears the figure of *Śiva. Cunningham and Altekar suggest that the rev device of *Ardochsho* was popular in the eastern provinces of the Kushāṇa empire, while that of Śiva gained popularity in the western provinces. As Kanishka III issued coins bearing both these devices, he appears to have succeeded in retaining hold over the eastern as well as the western provinces. The obv of his coins bears some Br letters in the right, central, and left fields. The letters in the right field are taken by most of the scholars to be abbreviations of the names of provincial governors, showing that during his reign the central authority had weakened and the political influence of the provincial governors had increased to such an extent that their names had to be mentioned on the obv of the gold coins in order to satisfy them (Altekar 1986a; Cunningham 1962; P L Gupta 1973; Gupta and Kulashreshtha 2004; R C Majumdar 1988; Rosenfield 1967).

Kārddamaka. Coins, general features. One of the three branches of the Western Kshatrapas, the Kārddamakas ruled over western parts of India for a period of nearly 300 years. The dynastic name Kārddamaka is mentioned in an inscription of the *amātya* of the daughter of *Rudradāman I from Kanheri. However, in the Gadha inscription of *Rudrasena, the name of the family is given as Bhadramukha. The royal house of the Kārddamaka Kshatrapas was established by *Dāmaghsada I, or by *Chashṭana, who is believed to have started his career as a **kshatrapa* under the *Kushāṇas, but attained the position of a **mahākshatrapa*, although doubts have recently been expressed as to his ever occupying a subordinate position. Chashṭana appointed his son, *Jayadāman, as his *kshatrapa*, but he died during the lifetime of his father, and Chashṭana was followed by his grandson, *Rudradāman I, who was perhaps the greatest, and certainly the most famous, of the Kārddamaka rulers. After the end of the reign of Rudradāman's son, *Dāmajadaśrī I, there seems to have taken place a struggle for succession between his son, *Jīvadāman, and brother, *Rudrasiṁha I. Other rulers of this family include Rudrasena I, *Saṅghadāman, *Dāmasena, *Yaśodāman I, *Vijayasena, *Dāmajadaśrī III, *Rudrasena II, *Viśvasiṁha, *Bhartṛidāman, *Satyadāman, *Pṛithvīsena, *Damajadaśrī II, *Vīradāman, and *Viśvasena. The last-mentioned ruler seems to have been supplanted by *Rudrasiṁha II, who appears to be closely connected with the family of Chashṭana. Next came *Yaśodāman II. Visvasena, Rudrasiṁha II, Yaśodāman II, *Rudrasena III, *Simhasena, *Rudrasena IV, and Satyasiṁha. The last-known Kārddamaka ruler was *Rudrasiṁha III, who was, perhaps, defeated by *Chandragupta II. The Kārddamaka Kshatrapas issued coins in silver, copper, potin, and lead; some coins reveal an admixture of copper and lead. All these rulers struck coins in silver (*Kārddamaka silver type). Copper coins were issued by Chashṭana, Jayadāman, Rudradāman I, and, perhaps, also by Rudrasiṁha I. Potin coins of Jīvadāman and Rudrasiṁha I, and of the period of Rudrasena I and Dāmasena are available. Lead coins were issued during the reigns of Chashṭana and Rudrasena III. The silver and potin coins are round in shape, while the copper and lead coins are square. All these coins have been manufactured by the die-striking method. The obv of the silver coins is occupied by the bust of the king. Coins of the other metals usually have a humped bull, while the copper coins of Chashṭana have a horse. The rev of most of the Kārddamaka coins has a combination of the symbols of *crescent-on-hill, star, crescent, and curved line. The ld, which occurs on the rev, is in Pkt, sometimes influenced by Skt; the script is mostly Br, Kh being used, in addition to Br, on the coins of Chashṭana, *Dāmaghsada I, and Jayadāman only. The silver coins mention the name and titles of the father of the issuer, along with those of the issuer himself, and this helps greatly in determining the genealogy of these rulers. The coins of the baser metals and alloys, when inscribed, do not usually mention the father of the issuer. The obv of most of the coins bears traces of some Greek characters. From the time of Rudrasiṁha I or Jīvadāman onwards, we start getting the date of the issue of the

Jīvadāman

coin, in the *Śaka era, a feature which helps us in determining the chronology of the Kārddamaka Kshatrapas. In various sources, the Kārddamaka coins are perhaps mentioned as **Rudradāmaka* and **Rudradāmakādi* (Jha and Rajgor 1994; Mirashi 1982; Mitchiner 1976; Rapson 1975; Rajgor 1991; Rajgor 1992; Raychaudhuri 1972; Satya Shrava 1981; Senior 2001; Sircar 1980e).†

Kārddamaka silver type. The *Karddamaka rulers issued a very long and uniform series of silver coins. The obv of these coins bears the bust of the king to the r; the date of issue of the coin, if present, is to be seen behind the head of the king, and is in the *Śaka era. The rev has a three-arched hill symbol surmounted by a crescent, another crescent on the left, a star on the right, and an *undulating line below. The circular Br ld on the rev is interesting in that it gives the name and titles of the father of the issuer of the coin, followed by the name and titles of the issuer himself. This is of great help in preparing the genealogy of the Kārddamaka Kshatrapas (Jha and Rajgor 1994; Rapson 1975; Senior 2001).

Kārshāpaṇa. Coin denomination. This term is not known in the saṁhitās, or, with the sole exception of the *Sāmavidhānabrāhmaṇa*, in the brāhmaṇa texts. V S Agrawala regards it as a term of classical Skt, which was coined in the sūtra period. Its earliest mention is to be found in the *Ashṭādhyāyī*. The term *kārshāpaṇa* is also mentioned by Hesychios as *korsipion nomisma*. *Kārshāpaṇa* is generally taken to denote the *punch marked coins. Cunningham feels that the name was derived "from *karsha*, 'a weight,' and *āpaṇa*, 'custom or use,' meaning that they were pieces of one *karsha* weight as established by use or custom". According to Manu, *kārshāpaṇa* is a *paṇa* made of copper, and one *karsha* in weight. Thus, the *kārshāpaṇa* of Manu is a copper coin only. There are other instances also in ancient Indian literature, where the *kārshāpaṇa* appears to be a copper coin. But references to *kārshāpaṇas* of other metals also occur. On the basis of a statement in the *Samantapāsādikā*, Bhandarkar concludes that as late as the fifth century AD, the *kārshāpaṇa* could be of gold, silver, or copper, although Narain says that this also implies that 'the ordinary or the normal (*pakatiko vā*) *kārshāpaṇa* was not in gold or silver'. The *Amarakosha* distinguishes between *kārshāpaṇa* and *paṇa*. Amarasiṁha says that the *paṇa* is *tāmrika*, that is made of copper. His commentators, Kshīrasvāmin and Rāmāśramī, say that the *kārshāpaṇa* should be regarded as a silver coin, perhaps because Amarasiṁha says that the *paṇa* is made of copper, and because he distinguishes between *kārshāpaṇa* and *paṇa*. But Bhandarkar feels that the statement of Amarasiṁha only implies that the *kārshāpaṇa* is not a copper coin, and so, it could be a silver as well as a gold coin. Thus, it is clear that the *kārshāpaṇa* was not only a copper coin as mentioned by Manu, but also denoted silver and gold coin; there is even a mention of *sīsa-kahāpaṇa*, that is a *kārshāpaṇa* of lead, in the Jātaka literature. Bhandarkar concludes that *kārshāpaṇa* was the name given to the standard coin of any town or district, irrespective of its metal. The origin of the term *kārshāpaṇa* is obscure, as no hint of its origin is available in the earlier literary sources. As Sircar observes, no *smṛitikāra*, including Manu and Yājñavalkya, gives the weight of *karsha*, 'from which the name *kārshāpaṇa* was apparently derived'. Amarasiṁha says that the weight of the *kārshāpaṇa* of various metals was one *karsha*, and explains that five *guñjās* (that is *rattīs*) make one *ādyamāsha*, and 16 *ādyamāshas* make one *karsha*. Thus, one *karsha*, according to Amarasiṁha, weighed (16 x 5 =) 80 *rattīs*. Kullūka also gives the weight of a *karsha* as 80 *rattīs*, when he says that a *karsha* was one-fourth of a *pala*, and a *pala* was equal to 320 *kṛishṇalas* (*rattīs*). Regarding gold, Kauṭilya states that five *guñjās* make one *suvarṇamāshaka*, and 16 such *māshakas* make one *suvarṇa* or *karsha*. Hence, the *suvarṇa* of Kauṭilya was of 80 *rattīs*. V S Agrawala suggested that the term *karsha* was taken from the Assyrian *karshu*, and the Greek *kerasos*. Originally, *karshu* meant a fruit of the size of a small *bauṇḍī*. But A K Narain says that the term *karsha* as a unit of weight was well-known in Iran in the Achaemenian period, with the Achaemenian records showing that payments were made in silver bullion, weighed out in *karsha* and *shekels*, one *karsha* being equal to 10 *shekels*, each *shekel* weighing 128.5 grains. He further says that it is 'not unlikely' that the term *karsha* became known in northwestern India, which was under the Achaemenians from the time of Darius I onwards. It came into use in northwestern India during the Achaemenian rule, and became applied to the word *paṇa*, which is used in the brāhmaṇa texts in the sense of 'to barter, purchase, buy'. Not surprising, therefore, that the term *kārshāpaṇa* was used for the first time by Pāṇini, a resident of Salātura in northwestern India. Narain admits that there is much difference in the weights of the Iranian and the Indian *karsha*, the former being much heavier than the latter. Narain feels that the 'tremendous reduction in weight of the Achaemenid *Karsha'* in India, might have been due to some economic exigencies of the sort which forced the Indo-Greeks to issue *tetradrachms* of a much reduced weight in their Indian dominions. S R Goyal seems to support the suggestion of Narain when he expresses the possibility the Indians borrowed just the term *karsha* from Iran, and 'not the weight it signified'. Cunningham says that *karsha* also stands for 'a market', and *kārshāpaṇa* might mean '*kārsha* of commerce', or of 'common use', or the 'current *karsha'*. But his alternative derivation of the term *kārshāpaṇa* seems to be the more appropriate. On the basis of the fact that the 'weights of most of the Hindu coins, as given by Manu…are all raised from the seeds of plants, which still exist for approximate verification', he suggests that the seed of the *Belleric Myrobalan*, "known as *āmalaka* or *Karsha-phala*, that is the '*Karsha* fruit', which reaches up to 140 grains in weight", was the unit on which the *kārshāpaṇa* was based. Interestingly, Monier-Williams explains *karshīphala* as '*Terminalia Bellerica*' or '*Emblica officinalis*', which supports Cunningham. S K Chakrabortty has accepted this view of Cunningham regarding the identification of *karsha*. *Kāhāpaṇa* in the **Aṅgavijjā* is a silver coin, which is said to have substantial value, as against the copper **nāṇaka*, which is said to be of inferior value. The text refers to several types of *kāhāpaṇas*—**ādimūla-kāhāvaṇa*, **bāla-kāhāvaṇa*, **ṇava-kāhāvaṇa*, **uttama-kāhāvaṇa*, **majjhima-kāhāvaṇa*, and **jahaṇṇa-kāhāvaṇa*. This, and the *Samantapāsādikā*, seem to show that *kāhāpaṇa* was a term of 'very wide application', used for all types of old and new silver coins, like **purāṇa*, **khattapaka*, **rudradāmaka*, etc (V S Agrawala 1950; V S Agrawala 1953; V S Agrawala 1956; V S Agrawala 1957; V S Agrawala 1969; Chakrabortty 1931; C D Chatterjee 1931; Cunningham 1971b; Goyal 1995b; Monier-Williams 2005; Narain 1957b; Sircar 1952; Sircar 1968).

Kārttikeya. Divine *generalissimo*. Also known by the names of Skanda, Kumāra, Viśākha, Mahāsena, Guha, Brahmaṇya, Subrahmaṇya, Murugan, etc (the last two names being more common in southern India), he was the divine *generalissimo*. There are indications to show that these various names of the god were originally the names of so many godheads with similar or allied nature and/or functions; some of them were even folk divinities. These various allied godheads were gradually unified into a deity, Kārttikeya. The accounts of his parentage, available from different sources, are very confused, and they variously mention *Śiva and *Pārvatī, or *Agni and *Gaṅgā as his parents. Gaṅgā threw the foetus on the Himavat, where it was nourished by the Kṛittikās; hence the name Kārttikeya, 'the son of Kṛittikā'. Kālidāsa gives a graphic account of the birth of Kārttikeya in the *Kumārasambhavaṁ*. He holds a *śakti* in his hand, and has the *peacock as his 'main cognizance'. The *Vishṇudharmottarapurāṇa* refers to his six heads, and also associates the *cock and the *bull with him. Allan is of the view that Kārttikeya makes his appearance on Class II of the *Ujjayinī coins in his *Catalogue*. He regards the attribute in the r hand of this deity as a spear, and suggests that the three-headed figure on the coins of Class II, Variety l, is actually six-headed, representing *Shaṇmukha* Kārttikeya. But J N Banerjea, on legitimate grounds, identifies these figures on Ujjayinī coins as those of *Śiva. But the anthropomorphic representation of Kārttikeya is quite common on certain classes of *Yaudheya coins. A unique silver coin of this tribal republic bears, on the obv, the figure of hexacephalous Kārttikeya, standing facing. He holds his characteristic attribute, the spear or *śakti* in his r hand, while the l hand rests on his hip. The rev of this coin bears the figure of his consort, Shashṭhī-Devasenā. Similar depiction of Kārttikeya occurs, mostly on the obv but sometimes on the rev, of some copper coins of the Yaudheyas. On most of these coins, the deity holds a spear or *śakti* in his r hand, but on some specimens, the r hand of Kārttikeya is raised towards the spear figuring on his right; on some other specimens, the spear is even shown in the l hand of the deity. The peacock, his 'main object of cognizance', is represented beside him on some of these copper coins. The deity is mostly six-headed, and rarely single-headed. The six heads of Kārttikeya are mentioned in the *Vishṇudharmottarapurāṇa*, while some other texts sanction the depiction of single-headed form also. When Kārttikeya is shown as hexacephalous, his six heads are arranged in two distinct styles on Yaudheya coins. On most of the coins, they are arranged in two rows of three heads each. But on some specimens, one head is in the centre, with the remaining five heads arranged around this central head in a circle. On certain Yaudheya copper coins, the deity is shown standing

Yaudheya

Yaudheya

Huvishka

Huvishka

Kumāragupta I :
Kārttikeya type

on a lotus. As lotus has solar associations, the depiction of Kārttikeya on lotus bloom might hint as the solar basis of this deity. The *śakti* of Kārttikeya is also said to have been fashioned from a portion of the sun god's glory. As noticed above, in the *Vishṇudharmottarapurāṇa*, Kārttikeya is associated with the cock, the harbinger of the rising sun. Interestingly, the legends on the silver coin and on the copper coins bearing the figure of Kārttikeya, mention the name(s) of this deity, together with some titles like *svāmin*, 'lord'. On this basis, J N Banerjea suggests that the Yaudheyas had dedicated their state to their patron deity, and issued these coins in his name. Three aspects of Kārttikeya, namely Skanda-Kumāra, Viśākha, and Mahāsena, appears on the coins of *Huvishka. On some coins, a nimbate and diademed god, described in the label inscription as *Maaseno* (Mahāsena), is shown standing facing, and holding a bird-topped standard in his r hand, and a sword in his left. Another type has two nimbate gods standing side by side. The figure described as *Skando-Komaro* (Skanda-Kumāra) holds a bird-topped standard in his r hand, while the other figure by his side and described as *Bizago* (Viśākha) holds a spear in his l hand. On yet another type, three nimbate male deities with sword tied at waist, stand side by side in a niche on pedestal. They are described as *Skando-Komaro* (Skanda-Kumāra), *Bizago* (Viśākha), and *Maaseno* (Mahāsena), respectively. Bhandarkar suggests that these coins represent that stage of the mythological development of Kārttikeya, when Skanda and Kumāra had come to be identified, but Viśākha and Mahāsena, although they had come to be regarded as allied to the concept of Kārttikeya and shown sharing the pedestal with Skanda-Kumāra, still retained their separate identity. The figure of Kārttikeya as a coin device was adopted by *Kumāragupta I among the *Imperial Guptas. The rev of the *Karttikeya type of his gold coins shows the figure of the deity riding his *vāhana*, the peacock. Kumāragupta I also represented Kārttikeya theriomorphically through the peacock on a number of his gold as well as copper coins. He was also the first Imperial Gupta ruler to issue the **Madhyadeśa* type of silver coins, which bear the figure of a fan-tailed peacock on the rev. This type of silver coins was struck subsequently by *Skandagupta, and *Budhagupta, as well as by the *Hūṇa, *Maukhari, and *Pushpabhūti rulers (R C Agrawala 1967; Allan 1936; Altekar 1957; Banerjea 1951; Banerjea 2002; R G Bhandarkar 1928; Chakrabortty 1931;

Huvishka

Gardner 1971; Handa 2007a; Rao 1985; Rosenfield 1967; Prashant Srivastava 1996a; Prashant Srivastava and Deepak Tiwari 1994; Whitehead 1914; Yaduvanshi 1988).†

Kārttikeya type. Gold. *Kumāragupta I seems to be a worshipper of *Kārttikeya, and he issued this type to honour his patron deity. The obv of this type has the standing figure of nimbate king, offering a bunch of grapes with his r hand to a *peacock standing facing him, while his l hand rests on hip. The circular ld reads *Jayati svaguṇairguṇa...Mahendrakumāraḥ*. The rev bears the nimbate figure of Kārttikeya, riding his *vāhana*, the peacock. He holds a spear in his l hand, while the r hand is scattering something. The peacock is perched on some platform. The rev ld is *Mahendrakumāraḥ*. The type shows two varieties, with the first variety depicting the deity three-fourths to the l, and the second variety depicting him to front. The coins of this type are quite rare (Ashvini Agrawal 1989; Allan 1914; Altekar 1957; R D Banerji 1933; S R Goyal 2005; P L Gupta 1998; Smith 1972; Thaplyal, forthcoming).

Kumāragupta I : Kārttikeya type

Kasarva hoard. This hoard of 17 *Imperial Gupta gold coins was found at Kasarva, in district Ballia (Uttar Pradesh), and acquired by the State Museum, Lucknow. The rulers represented in this hoard are *Samudragupta and *Kācha (Allan 1914).

Kasarwad hoard. This hoard of 130 coins of *Ujjayinī came to the light i 1939-1940 in the course of excavations at Kasarwad in Malwa (Altekar and Diskalkar 1946).

Kashmir (Ambala) hoard. Coins from this hoard from somewhere in Kashmir were disposed of by dealers in Delhi, Srinagar, etc. Besides *punch marked coins, this hoard has coins of rulers, like *Antialkidas, *Antimachos Nikephoros, *Apollodotos, *Artemidoros, *Hermaios, *Hippostratos, *Menander I, *Menander II, *Strato I, *Vonones with *Spalahora, Vonones with *Spalagadama, *Spalirises, Spalirises with *Azes I, *Maues, *Azes I, *Azilises, and *Azes II (Senior 2001).

Kashmir hoard 2. This hoard was discovered somewhere in Kashmir by two brothers, who took the coins to Delhi, where one of the brothers disposed of his share, while the other went back home with his coins. The rulers represented in this hoard include *Hippostratos, *Philoxenos, *Vonones with *Spalahora, Vonones with *Spalagadama, *Spalirises, *Azes I, and *Azilises (Senior 2001).

Katra hoard. This hoard of 86 silver *punch marked coins was discovered at Katra in the Muzaffarpur district of Bihar. Out of these, 80 coins are of the weight of 'double kārshāpaṇa', while six coins weigh less and bear four symbols. P L Gupta has expressed the possibility of their being the issues of the Vajji republic of Vaiśālī on the basis of the provenance of this hoard. But some other scholars are in favour of ascribing these coins to the kingdom of Kāśī or Kosala (B N Mukherjee 1999-2000; P L Gupta 1994).

Kauśāmbī

Kauśāmbī. This ancient capital of the Vatsa *janapada* has been identified with modern Kosam, near Allahabad. The early coins from this site are of four classes, namely uninscribed and inscribed cast coins, die-struck coins of early kings, *Dhanadeva's coins and their degenerate copies, and *Magha coins. The cast coins form the earliest coinage of Kauśāmbī. Barring the city coins of Kauśāmbī, and the coins of kings *Sudeva (?) and Bahasatimita [I] which resemble the uninscribed cast coins, all the coins are uninscribed. Some of these early coins from Kauśāmbī are *ḍamaru-* or drum-shaped. Coins of this shape are so far known only from Kauśāmbī. The second class of coins of Kauśāmbī belongs to the period from the second century BC till the region was conquered by *Kanishka I, whose coins and a seal have been found at Kosam. Coins provide evidence for more than two dozen kings who ruled for about two centuries. Since it gives an average reign of less than eight years, some of these kings would have ruled contemporaneously in different parts of the *janapada*. The kings known from these coins are (alphabetically) *Agrarāja, *Agnimitra, *Aśvaghosha, *Bahasatimita (Bṛihaspatimitra II), *Īśvaramitra, *Jyeshṭhabhūti, *Jyeshṭhamitra, *Parvata, *Prajāpatimitra, *Praushṭhamitra, *Priyamitra, *Rāḍhamitra, *Rājamitra, *Rajanīmitra, *Rāmamitra, *Sarpamitra, *Satyamitra, *Suramitra, *Varuṇamitra, and *Vavaghosha. It has been suggested that the Kauśāmbī rulers, particularly kings with *mitra*-ending names, had blood relationship with the Śuṅgas. If the indigenous coins with names of kings were being manufactured in the first half of the second century BC, then it is difficult to understand as to why Pushyamitra and others of the early Śuṅga rulers did not issue coins in their names. In view of the lack of any other evidence for the chronology of kings, one has to fall back on typology and palaeography of the coin legends. Coins of Vavaghosha, Praushṭhamitra, and Jyeshṭhamitra show, besides *tree-in-railing (which is common on Kauśāmbī coins), the *Ujjain and *taurine symbols, while **svastika* occurs on those of Vavaghosha and Jyeshṭhamitra. Only the coins of Jyeshṭhamitra and Jyeshṭhabhūti bear the device of standing male figure. Some coins of Praushṭhamitra, Jyeshṭhamitra, Agnimitra, and Bṛihaspatimitra II have been countermarked with **nandipada*. Amongst the rulers of Kauśāmbī, Īśvaramitra alone used the title of **rājan* on his coins. *Bull and *tree-in-railing is the most common device on the local Kauśāmbī coins. Other devices include, variously, the *horse (on the coins of Bṛihaspatimitra I), *lion (on the coins of Aśvaghosha), male figure (on the coins of Jyeshṭhamitra and Jyeshṭhabhūti). Ujjain symbol, too, is quite common. Other symbols met with are *nandipada*, **jayadhvaja*, wavy line, etc. There seems to be a break in the issue of the local coins of Kauśāmbī during Kanishka's rule. Shortly thereafter, 'Bull : Tree-in-railing' type of coins of Dhanadeva, and their imitations, were struck. Then follow the coins of *Nava, and those of the *Magha kings (Allan 1936; Altekar 1942a; Altekar 1942b; Altekar 1953; K D Bajpai 1960; Bopearachchi and Pieper 1998; Bela Lahiri 1974; Mitchiner 1975-1976).

Kauśāmbī. City coins. *Kauśāmbī (modern Kosam) was the capital of the kingdom of Vatsa. Coins bearing the name of the city are of three main types. Type 1 bears, on the obv, an *elephant on pedestal, *triangular-headed symbol, six-arched *hill, wavy line, *Ujjain symbol, and the ld *K[o]sa[ṁ]bi* above. On the rev are *tree-in-railing, Ujjain symbol, hill, tank with fishes, and **nandipada*. A variety of this type bears the ld *Kosaṁbi*, with Ujjain symbol on the obv; the rev is blurred. Type 2 is rectangular, and shows the figure of *bull facing a standard on the obv, and a circle in the middle with surrounding ld *Kosaṁbiya* on the rev. Type 3, round in shape, bears the ld *Kasabikanaṁ* on the obv, and a circle with dots surmounted by a crescent on the rev. The ld seems to refer to the people of

Kauśāmbī (Kothari 1991; Bela Lahiri 1974; Bela Lahiri 1976; J P Singh 1971).

Kauśāmbī. Guild coins. Some coins from *Kauśāmbī bear the ld *negama* and *Gadhikana*, respectively. Three *negama* coins are known. They all show the lower portion of a railing, and a three-peaked *hill, and the ld *negama* below, on the obv. On the rev, the first coin, which is rectangular, shows a **svastika*; the second, a round one, shows a seven-spoked wheel inside a circle of dots; and the third, a square one, a **triratna* (or **nandipada*). A round coin bears the ld *Gandhikanaṁ*, in the characters of *c* second century BC, on the obv, and a square with four compartments on the rev, and is taken as a coin of the *gandhikas*, 'dealers in perfume', who formed a guild. The dealers in perfume find reference in epigraphs from Bharhut, Mathurā, Karle, Pitalkhora, and Amaravati (J P Singh 1971; Thaplyal 1996).

Kauśāmbī hoard. This hoard of 2,942 coins of the *Magha rulers was discovered at Kauśāmbī, and published by A M Shastri. It is believed to be the largest hoard of the coins of the Magha dynasty reported so far. The rulers represented in the hoard include King Magha, Vāsishṭhīputra Bhīmasena, Poṭhasiri, Bhadramagha, Śivamagha, Vaiśravaṇa, Bhīmavarman, Styamagha, and Vijayamagha (Bopearachchi and Pieper 1998; Handa 2003-2004; A M Shastri 1979).

Kausia. It was a Greek headdress, which Indo-Greek rulers like *Antimachos I, are found wearing on their coins. Such a headdress is not seen on the coins of the other Greek series, but classical literature does mention this type of cap. It was a Macedonian headdress, and was sometimes worn by Alexander on informal occasions. Trever feels that the *kausia* may be connected with the much later type of Chinese headdress, and she infers on this basis that some regions that Antimachos I ruled might not be very far from the borders of China (A N Lahiri 1965; Narain 1957a).

Kavishiye-nagara-devata. Deity. Occurring on some copper coins of an Indo-Greek king, who is believed to be *Eukratides I, this deity was identified by Cunningham, on the basis of the poor specimens available to him, as enthroned *Zeus, and this identification was accepted for a long time, although some alternative identifications like the 'Elephant god', or Indra the *yaksha* of Indrapura, were also suggested. But Masson, who was the first to discover coins of this type, described the figure as a female deity, and Whitehead correctly identified this figure as that of the city-goddess of Kāpiśī (Cunningham 1970; Gardner 1971; A N Lahiri 1965; Narain 1957a; Rapson 1987; Sircar 1980a; Prashant Srivastava 1996a; Tarn 1980; Whitehead 1914; Whitehead 1947; Whitehead 1950).

Kharaösta. Śaka satrap. He is described on his coins as son of Arṭa. There are also two epigraphic references to him. The Mathurā lion capital inscription of the time of *Rañjuvula and *Śoḍāsha mentions him as *Yuvarāja* Kharaösta, and he was somehow related to Nada Diäka, the chief queen of Rañjuvula (various scholars regard him as either her son or her father). In the reliquary inscriptions of the time of Kharaösta and Indravarman, the former is described as a *yaguraṁña* (perhaps equivalent to *yabgu*, 'chief') and son of a **mahākshatrapa*. His date is not certain, but there is a suggestion that he may be placed in the last two decades of the first century BC. He might have ruled over some territories to the north of Takshaśilā, perhaps in Hazara. Kharaösta issued coins in copper/bronze only, which are all square in shape. The obv of all his types has horseman king, sometimes holding a whip, and the Gr ld on this side of the coin describes him as a satrap and 'son of Arṭa'. The rev devices include *Hermes standing, and *lion. The rev ld in the Kh script also refers to him as a **kshatrapa* and 'son of Arṭa'. Some posthumous Azes coins, too, might have been issued by him (Cunningham 1971a; Gardner 1971; Jenkins and Narain 1957; van Lohuizen de Leeuw 1949; Marshall 1975; B N Mukherjee 1969a; Rapson 1987; Salomon 1996; Senior 2001; Sircar 1980b; Sircar 1986; Prashant Srivastava 2007a; Tarn 1980; Whitehead 1914).

Kharoshṭhī. Script. Written from r to the l, this script was earlier named as Bactrian, Indo-Bactrian, Kabulian, Arianian, Gandhārian, Bactro-Pāli, or Ariano-Pāli. The name, Kharoshṭhī, occurring in some Buddhist and Jaina texts, like the *Lalitavistara* and the *Samavāyāṅgasūtra*, was first used for this script by T de Lacouperie, and was made popular by Bühler. According to the

Chinese encyclopaedia, *Fa-Wan-Shu-Lin*, dated 668 AD, this script was invented by Kia-lu. Kharaoshṭha is generally believed to be the Prakritized form of the Skt *kharaushṭha*, 'ass-lip', and *Fa-Wan-Shu-Lin* takes it to be the personal name of the inventor of the script. Efforts to associate Kh with Kyros, Kuras or Kurish of the cuneiform inscriptions, with the barbarous peoples of the northwest, with the province of Kashghar (which has the Chinese name Kia-lu-shu-tan-le), with Ki-lo-to to the southwest of Kashghar, or with *kharaposta*, 'hide of donkey', on which material the script is believed to have been originally written, are all based on presumptions, and nothing definite can be said about the origin of its name. The close connection between Kh and Aramaic is evident from the direction of writing, the identical forms of some letters like *na*, *ba*, *ra*, and *va*, and 'the employment of one basic form for the initial vowels'. On this basis, it has been suggested that, as the 'peculiarities of the phonology and the grammar of the local languages could not be adequately expressed through Aramaic letters' during Achaemenian rule over northwestern India, Kh originated as a result of the effort to find a system for writing the local languages in a manner 'intelligible to the local people as well as convenient to learn by the administrative staff who were familiar with Aramaic'. The characters of Kh 'were based on Aramaic to the extent the requirements of the Indian alphabet permitted; other letters were created by adding diacritical marks.' Aśokan edicts from Mansehra and Shahbazgarhi are engraved in the Kh script. Thereafter, this script was employed mostly in the epigraphic and numismatic records of the *Indo-Greeks, *Śaka-Pahlavas, and the *Kushāṇas. Its use was mostly confined to northwestern India, with Manikiala in Punjab forming the easternmost limit of its use, Khawat in Afghanistan and Thal valley in Baluchistan forming the westernmost limit, Tirath in the Swat region and Khalaste in Ladakh forming the northernmost limit, and Mohenjodaro in Sind forming the southernmost limit. Of course, a few Kh inscriptions are reported from Kangra and Karnal, and one even from Patna, east of Manikiala; coins with Kh legends have been discovered from Seistan and Khandahar, west of Khawat and Thal valley. Numerous Kh documents and a Pkt *Dhaṁmapada* are available from Chinese Turkestan. In India, Kh was in use from the third century BC to the third-fourth centuries of the Christian era; in Chinese Turkestan, it continued to be in use for some time more. But, despite this history of about six or seven centuries, the characters of this script do not show any signs of evolution. The variations in this otherwise uniform script may be explained as due to the nature of the writing material and the need to the represent new sounds in other languages 'by inventing diacritical strokes' (Bühler 1904; Dani 1997; C C Dasgupta 1958; Diringer 2005; L Gopal 1989; Ojha 1959; R B Pandey 1953).

Khattapaka. Coin denomination. Mentioned in the **Aṅgavijjā*, it denoted the silver coins issued by the *Western Kshatrapa rulers, although it is not certain whether the coins implied here were those of the *Kshaharāta Kshatrapas, or the Kārddamaka Kshatrapas, or of both the families. It may, however, be suggested that, since **rudradāmaka* and **rudradāmakādi* coins probably refer to the Kārddamaka coins, *khattapaka* coins refer to those of the kings of the Kshaharāta family. However, in the inscriptions of the Kshaharāta family, silver coins are mentioned, not as *khattapaka*, but as **kārshāpaṇa* (V S Agrawala 1957; C S Gupta 1982; Sircar 1986).

Khauzikhelai hoard. This hoard of, perhaps, 800 *Indo-Greek coins, was discovered accidentally in 1992, in the village Khauzikhelai in the Swat valley. The rulers represented in this hoard include Antialkidas, Antimachos II, Apollodotos, Lysias, Menander I, Nikias, and Philoxenos (Bopearachchi 1994).

Khiṅgila. *Hūṇa chief. A Hūṇa chief named Khiṅgila is known from a coin of the Sassanian bust type. This coin, bearing the ld *Deva Shāhi Khiṅgila*, was published by Cunningham, who places this ruler around 580 AD. There are also two gold coins of the debased *Kidāra Kushāṇa type, bearing the ld *Kidāra* on the obv, and *Śrī-Narendra* on the rev. Cunningham ascribes these two coins to King Narendrāditya mentioned in the *Rājataraṅgiṇī*. Some copper coins of the period, bearing the ld *Jayatu Śrī-Narendra*, are also known. Kalhaṇa states that Khiṅkhila (= Khiṅgila), one of the successors of *Mihirakula, was the son of Gokarṇa, and was also known by the Hindu title, *Narendrāditya*. But, according to some scholars, this Śrī-Narendra of coins should not be identified with Khiṅkhila Narendrāditya of Kalhaṇa, on numismatic grounds (Altekar 1986b;

Biswas 1973; Cunningham 1962; Cunningham 1967; Upendra Thakur 1967a; Upendra Thakur 1967b).

Kidāra Kushāṇa. Coins, general features. The *Wei-shu* and Matwan-lin inform us that Ki-to-lo, a king of the *Kushāṇa stock, finding himself threatened by some rival tribe (Juan-Juan or Hiung-nu), led his people towards the west, crossed the Hindukush, subjugated Gandhāra, and established his capital at Fu-leu-cha (Peshawar). This Ki-to-lo is identified with *Kidāra Kushāṇa Shāh* of coins found in large numbers from northwestern India. Around the middle of the fourth century AD, Kidāra Kushāṇa was forced to acknowledge the supremacy of the Sassanian ruler, Shapur II, but later, he asserted his independence, founded his line of kings known as the Kidāra Kushāṇas or Kidarites after his name, and issued his own coins. There is a suggestion that, in view of the threats he had to face from the Sassanians and the ruling tribes in Bactria, Kidāra Kushāṇa might have maintained cordial relations with the *Imperial Guptas, and he might be the *Daivaputrashāhi-shāhānushāhi* mentioned in the Allahabad pillar inscription as acknowledging the political supremacy of Samudragupta. Kidāra Kushāṇa was succeeded by Piro and Varahran, who served under the Sassanians. The Kidāra Kushāṇas issued coins in gold, silver, and copper. They show the king standing at an altar on the obv, and seated **Ardochsho* on the rev. The ld on the gold coins is in Kushāṇa script and reads *Bago Kidāra Vuzurko Kushāṇo*, while that on the silver coins is in Br and reads *Kidāra Kushāṇa Shāh*. Some debased gold coins, bearing the device of king standing with spear and the vertical ld *Kida* or *Kidāra* under the king's left arm on the obv, and seated *Ardochsho* on the rev, have been found from the eastern regions like Kanauj, Hardoi, and Kosam. These bear on the rev, names like *Śrī Śīlāditya, Śrī Kṛitavīrya, Śrī Saloṇavīra, Satomala, Sarvayaśa, Prakāśa, Kuśala, Bhāsvan,* etc. These might be Kidāra Kushāṇa rulers, or some Indian rulers 'who adopted the Kidāra pattern' (Altekar 1986a; Craig Alden Burns 1985b; Cunningham 1962; P L Gupta 2004; Gupta and Kulashreshtha 2004; R C Majumdar 1988; Sircar 1980d; Smith 1972).[†]

King sacrificing at an altar. Device. This device, which first appeared on the obv of the coins of the *Kushāṇa ruler, *V'ima

Kadphises, has as its prototype, the similar device on the coins of the Imperial Parthian ruler, Gotarzes II (40/41 AD – 51 AD). On the basis of the *Shāhnāmah* of Firdausi, B N Mukherjee suggests that Kujula Kadphises was killed in battle while fighting Gotarzes II by the side of Vardanes. Later, V'ima Kadphises (whom B N Mukherjee regards as the son and successor of Kujula Kadphises, but who is now known from the Rabatak inscription to be the grandson of Kujula Kadphises and the son and successor of *V'ima Takshuma) avenged this by conquering certain parts of the Parthian empire, perhaps by defeating Gotarzes II, and 'commemorated this victory by copying a type of the latter'. The discovery of some coins of V'ima Kadphises in the Toprak-Kala region to the north of the Oxus would seem to support this (Cunningham 1971a; Gardner 1971; von Mitterwallner 1986; B N Mukherjee 1960; B N Mukherjee 1969a; Whitehead 1914; Wroth 1903).

Kanishka I

Vāsudeva I

King's head type. Copper. This type of copper coins was issued by *Kumāragupta I. The obv bears the uncrowned head of the king to the l, with traces of letters behind it. The rev has the figure of a **garuḍa* above, and the ld *Kumāragupta* below it (Allan 1914; Altekar 1957; P L Gupta 1998; Smith 1972).

King-and-Female type. Gold. *Skandagupta issued a type, on the obv of which, the archer king is shown standing with a female on the right. The female holds a stalked lotus in her l hand, and is offering something to the king with the r hand. The circular ld is uncertain. The rev has *Lakshmī seated on a lotus, with a *pāśa* in her r hand, and a lotus in her l hand. The ld reads *Śrī-Skandaguptaḥ*. Smith identifies the female figure on the obv as the queen, while Allan and Altekar regard her as Lakshmī, and B P Sinha as the mother of Skandagupta (Allan 1914; Altekar 1957; Sinha 1988; Smith 1972).

Skandagupta :
King-and-Female type

King-and-Queen type. Gold. This type was first issued by *Chandragupta I (conjointly with *Kumāradevī), although some scholars ascribe it variously to *Samudragupta, or the Lichchhavis. The obv shows the king, wearing a long coat and trousers (that is the *Kushāṇa type dress) standing left, with a crescent topped standard in his l hand, and offering some object (ring or bangle or *sindūradānī*) to the queen standing to his right. The queen is looking at the object

Chandragupta I and Kumāradevī

Kumāragupta I : King-and-Queen type

being offered to her by the king. Her l hand hangs down; her r hand is on waist. Sometimes, there is a crescent between the heads of the royal couple. The vertical ld below the king's arm reads *Chandra-*, and that outside the standard, *-guptaḥ*. On the left, is the ld *Śrī-Kumāradevī*, or *Kumāradevī-Śrīḥ*. The rev has **Siṁhavāhinī Devī*, with a *pāśa* in her r hand, and a **cornucopiae* in her l hand. The ld reads *Lichchhavayaḥ*. Some scholars believe that this type was issued, by Samudragupta or by the Lichchhavis, to commemorate the marriage of Chandragupta I with Kumāradevī, while others opine that Kumāradevī was not a mere queen-consort, but a queen-regnant, and the type was the result of a rare political situation, when the queen was co-ruling with her husband. Some coins of this type are also available in silver, but as they have not been found in the course of excavations, or in any coin hoard, doubts have been expressed regarding their authenticity, and there is also a suggestion that these silver specimens might be test pieces. The gold type was revived by *Kumāragupta I. The composition is quite similar to the prototype, but as a consequence of the process of Indianization of the coin type, some subtle changes are perceptible on the coins of Kumāragupta I. The king wears a *dhotī* (instead of the *Kushāṇa type dress seen on the prototype), and he offers a bunch of flowers to the queen (instead of a ring or bangle or *sindūradānī*); the goddess on the rev holds a lotus bloom in her r hand (instead of *pāśa*), while her l hand rests on her thigh (instead of holding a *cornucopiae*). The obv ld is indistinct. The rev ld reads *Śrī-Kumāraguptaḥ* (Ashvini Agrawal 1989; Allan 1914; Altekar 1957; R D Banerji 1933; Cribb 1985a; S R Goyal 2005; P L Gupta 1998; Sircar 1976; Smith 1972; Prashant Srivastava 1996a; Thaplyal, forthcoming).

King-and-Queen-on-Couch type. Gold. This type has the king, dressed in coat and trousers, holding a standard in his r hand, and offering incense at an altar on the obv. The circular ld reads **Paramabhāgavata Śrī-Chandraguptaḥ* (?). The rev has the nimbate king and queen sitting on a couch, facing each other, with a crescent between the two. The king is offering something to the queen. The rev ld reads *Śrī-Vikramaḥ*. Allan considers the possibility of this type being an issue of Chandragupta I, who is known to have issued the *King-and-Queen type of coins. But on the basis of the rev ld, Altekar ascribes it to *Chandragupta II, as *Vikrama* or *Vikramāditya* was his *viruda* (Ashvini Agrawal 1989; Allan 1914; Altekar 1957; R D Banerji 1933; S R Goyal 2005; P L Gupta 1998; Smith 1972; Thaplyal, forthcoming).

Kosam hoard. This hoard of 569 coins was found in 1937-1938 at Kauśāmbī in the Allahabad district of Uttar Pradesh. It consists of 93 silver *punch marked coins of the imperial series, 73 copper bent bars, 36 silver plated copper bars, 130 copper punch marked coins and 237 cast and die struck bronze coins. The hoard is presently housed in the Indian Museum, Calcutta (Rajgor 2001).

Kosi Kalan hoard. This hoard of 4,700 silver *punch marked coins of the Śūrasena *janapada* was found around 1985 at Kosi Kalan near Mathurā in Uttar Pradesh (Rajgor 2001).

Kotwa hoard. This hoard of 17 *Imperial Gupta gold coins was found at Kotwa, district Gorakhpur (Uttar Pradesh). The rulers represented in this hoard are *Chandragupta II, and *Kumāragupta I. Allan, however, refers to only 13 coins in this hoard, of which three belong to Chandragupta II, and 10 to Kumāragupta I (Allan 1914; Altekar 1957).

Kṛishṇala. Coin denomination. It is not certain whether the *kṛishṇala* of the *Taittirīyabrāhmaṇa* and the *hiraṇya-kṛishṇala* of the *Kāṭhakasaṁhitā* were coins weighing one *rattī*, or merely lumps of metal, possibly gold in the former case also, of that weight, although D R Bhandarkar is in favour of regarding them as coins. Manu refers to the *kṛishṇala* in connection with the fine to be levied on a hired servant or workman, who fails to perform his work according to the agreement, not because of any illness but out of pride. The *Vishṇusmṛiti* refers to a gold *kṛishṇala* coin, while the **Aṅgavijjā* mentions **suvaṇṇa-guñja*, in all probability a gold coin weighing one *rattī*. The *Bakhshali manuscript refers to the *raktikā* (R C Agrawala 1954b; V S Agrawala 1957; D R Bhandarkar 1984; Chakrabortty 1931).

Kṛita *saṁvat*. *Vikrama *saṁvat*.

Kshaharāta. Coins, general features. One of the three branches of the Western Kshatrapas, the Kshaharātas seem to have started their career as the provincial governors of the Kushāṇas in the southwestern parts of the empire, as shown by the use of the title of **kshatrapa* by *Ābhīraka and *Bhūmaka on their coins, and the titles of *kshatrapa* and **mahākshatrapa* by *Nahapāna in his inscriptions, although doubts have recently been expressed from certain quarters regarding the subordinate status of the Kshaharāta Kshatrapas. Nahapāna, on his coins, uses the title of *rājan*, which shows an increase in the power and prestige of the dynasty during his reign. The rule of the dynasty was brought to an end by the Sātavāhana ruler, Gautamīputra Sātakarṇi. Kshaharāta coins are available in silver, copper, lead, potin, and an alloy of copper and lead. The silver coins seem to be based on *Indo-Greek coins. The device of arrow on left, *thunderbolt on right, and discus in the centre, occurs on the obv of the copper coins and the rev of the silver coins, and there is a suggestion that it might have been the royal insignia of the family. Incidentally, discus, and bow-and-arrow also occur on the coins of the *Śaka-Pahlava rulers, *Spalirises and *Azes II, and the Kshaharāta family might be related to these Śaka-Pahlavas. The legends on the Kshaharāta coins are in Pkt, written in both Br and Kh. Ābhīraka used Greek and Br on his coins. On the silver coins of Nahapāna, the obv ld is written in mixed Greek and Roman characters, which, according to the Rapson, reads *Raño Kshaharātasa Nahapānasa*. In literature, Kshaharāta coins are perhaps referred to as **khattapaka*, although the Nasik inscription of the time of Nahapāna refers to [his] coins as **kārshāpaṇa* (Jha and Rajgor 1994; Mirashi 1982; Mitchiner 1976; Rajgor 1991; Rajgor 1992; Rapson 1975; Raychaudhuri 1972; Senior 2001; Sircar 1980e; Sircar 1986).[†]

Kshatrapa. Title. This title was assumed on their coins by *Hagāmasha, *Hagāna, *Rañjuvula, *Śivadatta, *Śivaghosha, *Śoḍāsha, *Taraṇaḍāsa, and *Zeionises, among the Śakas. It was very popular among the *Western Kshatrapas, and *Ābhīraka, *Bhūmaka, and *Nahapāna in the *Kshaharāta dynasty, and a number of rulers of the *Kārddamaka dynasty assumed this title on their coins. Among the Kārddamaka Kshatrapas, this title is believed to have been assumed by the heir-apparent (Gardner 1971; Jenkins and Narain 1957; Jha and Rajgor 1994; Marshall 1975; Rapson 1975; Senior 2001; Whitehead 1914).

Kshudraka. Tribe. The Kshudrakas are mentioned in the *Gaṇapāṭha* of Pāṇini, and are identified with the Oxydrakai or Hydrakes of the classical writers. According to Megasthenes and Arrian, the Persians hired the Hydrakes as mercenaries. The historians of Alexander inform us that the Oxydrakai were quite powerful, and allied with the Malloi (= *Mālavas) against the Macedonian invader. The confederation of the two tribes is, perhaps, hinted at in the formation *Kshudraka-mālavī-senā* by Pāṇini, and the *Kshatriya-dvandva* in the *Kāśikā* on Pāṇini. The mention of this confederation in Pāṇini seems to suggest that it was a 'permanent arrangement' between the two tribes. The confederate army against Alexander comprised 90,000 infantry, 10,000 cavalry, and 500 chariots. The find of their coins would render untenable the view that they had completely merged with the Mālavas. Smith is of the view that, as the eastern neighbours of the Malloi, the Oxydrakai occupied the Kangra, Gurdaspur, Hoshiarpur, and Amritsar regions. Two coins from Pandusar (Sri Ganganagar district, Rajasthan), round in shape, have been assigned to the Kshudrakas. One coins, weighing 20.3 grains, shows on the obv *tree-in-railing, and the Br ld which has been read as *Khudakāna* (= Skt, *Kshudrakānāṁ*), and on the rev, the ld *jaya*, again in Br. The other, 10.2 grains in weight, shows tree-in-railing on the obv; only *–kana* part of the ld is legible. The rev of this coin is obliterated. Recently, Devendra Handa claims to have read a part of the name of the tribe on a coin in the collection of the Indian Museum, Calcutta, which was published by Smith as an unassigned miscellaneous coin from northern India. The coins have been assigned to the second century BC on palaeographical grounds (Allan 1936; Chakrabortty 1931; Cunningham 1971b; K K Dasgupta 1974; Handa 2007a; Jayaswal 1988; Marshall 1975; Mitchiner 1975-1976; Smith 1972).

Kujula Kadphises. *Kushāṇa k; first century AD. The *Hou Han-shu* informs us that K'ieou-t'sieou-k'io, the chief of Kouei-chouang, one of the five Yueh-chih principalities in Bactria, conquered the other four principalities, and adopted the title of *wang* (king). The Kouei-chouang of this account is identified as Kushāṇa, and K'ieou-

Kujula Kadphises

Kujula Kadphises

t'sieou-k'io as Kujula Kadphises. The same source also reveals that Kujula Kadphises later led an expedition against the Arsakids of Parthia, conquered the Kabul valley, and overran Po-ta near Kabul, as also Ki-pin (Kafiristan and the adjoining areas), before he died at the age of over 80 years. There are some copper coins, which bear the name and/or bust of *Hermaios on the obv, and the name and titles of Kujula Kadphises on the rev. These coins should not be taken to imply that Kujula Kadphises was ever a subordinate ruler or ally of the Indo-Greek king, as suggested by some scholars, as there is a long gap between the end of the reign of Hermaios and the accession of Kujula Kadphises. It seems more likely that these coins are propaganda coins, or imitation coins, issued by Kujula Kadphises. On some coins of this type, the obv has the head of the king, resembling that of a Roman emperor. Other copper coins of Kujula Kadphises bear obv devices like head of the king, and standing *bull; the rev devices include Macedonian soldier, wreath- and palm-bearing *Nike, *Herakles standing, with club and lion's skin, king seated on curule chair, and a two-humped *camel. A rare type from Taxila has the standing figure of *Zeus on the obv, and a seated male figure with the Kh ld mentioning Kujula Kadphises on the rev. The coins have legends in Gr on the obv and Pkt, written in the Kh script, on the rev. Kujula Kadphises uses the title of **yavuga* on his coins. His other title of **dhramaṭhida*, sometimes with *sacha-* prefixed to it, is taken to indicate his inclination towards Buddhism. There is a silver coin from Taxila, bearing the bust of the king and an illegible Gr ld on the obv, and winged *Nike and a fragmentary Kh ld, probably mentioning a Kushāṇa **yavuga* as *maharaja rajatiraja*, on the rev. Some scholars would attribute this coin to Kujula Kadphises (Bopearahchci and Pieper 1998; Cunningham 1971a; Gardner 1971; Marshall 1975; von Mitterwallner 1986; Rosenfield 1967; Senior 2001; Sircar 1980c; Whitehead 1914).†

Kulūta. Tribe. Of the 12 coins, all in copper, of the Kulūta tribe known so far, 11 were found at Taxila in the course of the archaeological excavations conducted by Marshall; the *provenance* of the twelfth coin is not known, but as Cunningham included this among the *Audumbara coins, it probably came from Punjab or Himachal Pradesh. Only the last coin is round in shape; the rest are all square. Earlier, the name of the tribe was wrongly read as *Koputa* by Cunningham, and *Kolūta* by Bergny; it was later corrected as *Kulūta*. The *Ashṭādhyāyī* of Pāṇini has Kulūtara, perhaps a variant of Kulūta. The *Rāmāyaṇa* mentions the Kolūkas or Kaulūtas together with the western tribes. The *Mahābhārata* refers to them as Ulūta and Kaulūta, and mentions them along with such north Indian powers as Kaśmīras, Gandhāras, Bāhlīkas, and Yavanas. At another place, it refers to a country called Kulūta. The tribe is also mentioned in the *Bṛihatsaṁhitā*, Bāṇa's *Kādambarī*, the *Bālabhārata*, and the account of Hiuen-tsang. Kulūna of the *Kāśikā* may also be a variant of Kulūta. Most of the texts place them in northern India, though they might have had offshoots in eastern and southern India also. P L Gupta has suggested that the Kulūtas seem to have formed two distinct groups, one residing in the neighbourhood of the Trigartas, and the other, in that of the Madras. But this should not be taken to imply that they were two different peoples. The Kullu valley is taken, with a great deal of justification, as their original home. The *Mahābhārata* and the *Mudrārākshasa* label the Kulūtas as *mlechchhas*, which term is generally used for the people of foreign origin. Perhaps, they were of foreign (Mongoloid) origin and got Hinduized (the names of their chiefs are purely Indian) and mixed up with the local population. The Kulūta coins are all die-struck, and issued in copper only. They are known in both round and square shapes. The Kulūta coins have been divided into four classes. The coins of Class I have, on the obv, a *wheel surrounded by a circle of dots, **jayadhvaja*, and **nandipada*, and the Br ld mentioning *Vīrayaśas with the title of **rājña* and the tribal name; the rev has a *nandipada* and traces of a Kh ld. This class has a variety on which the Kh ld is given on the obv, and the rev is defaced. Class II shows on the obv, the *hill symbol surmounted by a standard, **svastika*, *jayadhvaja*, and the Br ld mentioning *Vijayamitra with the title of *rājña* and the tribal name; the rev has a shaft surmounted by a *nandipada* within a railing, circle surmounted by four *nandipadas*, conventional lotus, and another symbol, with a Kh ld, *Kulutasa Vijayamitrasa*. Class III and IV bear slightly different legends, very much illegible and according to Allan, mentioning *Satyamitra and *Arya.... Bela Lahiri proposes that Arya[mitra ?], Satyamitra, Vijayamitra, and Vīrayaśas might have ruled in that chronological order. The only coin, the weight of which is recorded, weighs 73.7 grains. The *provenance* of the coins, the use of both Br and

Kh scripts, and the devices, link these coins with the Audumbaras and the *Kuṇindas (second-first centuries BC), but the use of Skt suggests for them a later date of first-second centuries AD, which is supported not only by the palaeography of the coin legends but also by the stratigraphical evidence of Marshall's excavations at Taxila showing that the Kulūta coins were buried in early *Kushāṇa period (Allan 1936; Chakrabortty 1931; Cunningham 1971b; K K Dasgupta 1974; Handa 2007a; Jayaswal 1988; Bela Lahiri 1974; Marshall 1975; Mitchiner 1975-1976; Smith 1972).

Chandragupta I and Kumāradevī

Kumāradevī. *Imperial Gupta queen. This Lichchhavi princess was the chief queen of *Chandragupta I, and appears beside her husband on his *King-and-Queen type of coins. She was the mother of *Samudragupta. The matrimonial alliance between the Imperial Guptas and the Licchchhavis was of significance to the former, more particularly to Samudragupta. Interestingly, Kumāradevī is the first Indian queen, belonging to a dynasty of indigenous origin, whose figure appears on coins (Ashvini Agrawal 1989; Allan 1914; Altekar 1957; R D Banerji 1933; Fleet 1888; S R Goyal 2005; P L Gupta 1998; K P Jayaswal 1933; Smith 1972; Prashant Srivastava 1996a; Thaplyal 1980-1981; Thaplyal, forthcoming).

Kumāragupta I : Horseman type

Kumāragupta I : Lion-slayer type

Kumāragupta I *Mahendrāditya*. *Imperial Gupta k, son of *Chandragupta II; first half of the fifth century AD. We possess no specific information about the military career of Kumāragupta I, but the facts that he issued the **Aśvamedha* type of gold coins and was able to keep the vast empire he inherited from his ancestors intact, testify to his administrative skill and the brilliance of his personality. The scene of the king hunting a rhinoceros on the obv of the *Rhinoceros-slayer type of Kumāragupta I has been taken by some to indicate his conquest of Kāmarūpa (Assam) known for its rhinoceroses. Towards the end of his reign, the royal fortunes of the Imperial Guptas were threatened by an enemy in the form of a tribe named Pushyamitra (though some believe that the correct reading is *yuddhyamitra*, and the term means enemy (or enemies) in general). The *Hūṇa invasion and its being repulsed by *Skandagupta might also have been an event of the last days of Kumāragupta I, though some feel that this event occurred during the reign of Skandagupta himself. The reign of Kumāragupta I witnessed unprecedented numismatic activity, with the king issuing not only new types in gold, but also in silver. Artistically, however, his coins are somewhat inferior to those of *Samudragupta and Chandragupta II. His gold coins were issued in 15 types, some of which were his own innovations, some were continuation of the types of his grandfather and father, while some were produced by combining two types together. The 15 types of gold coins are (i) *Archer type, (ii) *Horseman type, (iii) *Swordsman type, (iv) *Elephant-rider type, (v) *Aśvamedha* type, (vi) **Chhatra* type, (vii) *King-and-Queen type, (viii) *Kārttikeya type, (ix) *Tiger-slayer type, (x) *Lion-slayer type, (xi) *Elephant-rider-lion-slayer type, (xii) *Lyrist type, (xiii) Rhinoceros-slayer type, (xiv) **Apratigha* type, and (xv) **Garuḍa*-with-outstretched-wings type (although some scholars would ascribe this last type, manufactured by the **repoussé* method, to some local ruler of southern Kosala, belonging to the *Nala, the Śūra, or the *Śarabhapurīya dynasty; there is also a suggestion that he may be identified with Mahendrāditya of the *Kathāsaritsāgara*). Apart from issuing silver coins of the *Western India type like those of his father, he also issued the **Madhyadeśa* type of silver coin, on which the bust is slightly different, and the *garuḍa* on the rev is replaced by a fan-tailed *peacock, *mayūra* being the mount of his patron deity, *Kārttikeya. Coins of both these types were also manufactured of copper and plated with silver. His copper coins also reveal an amazing variety : (i) **Chhatra* type, (ii) *Archer type, (iii) *Standing king type, (iv) *Altar or **Garuḍa* type, (v) *King's head type, (vi) **Kalaśa* type, (vii) **Garuḍa*-with-*ku* type, and (viii) *Peacock type. The obv is usually occupied by a **garuḍa*, though a goddess is scene on the Altar or *Garuḍa* type, and a fan-tailed peacock on the Peacock type (Ashvini Agrawal 1989; Nisar Ahmad 1964; Allan 1914; Altekar 1957; R D Banerji 1933; Fleet 1888; S R Goyal 2005; P L Gupta 1998; B C Jain 1960; K P Jayaswal 1933; Smith 1972; Prashant Srivastava 1996a; Thaplyal, forthcoming; T P Verma 1991).†

Kumāragupta I : *Aśvamedha* type

Kumāragupta I : Archer type

Kumāragupta I : Kārttikeya type

Kumāragupta I : *Apratigha* type

Kumāragupta II *Kramāditya*. *Imperial Gupta k. The Sarnath Buddhist image inscription mentions one Kumāragupta, without referring to the name of his father. But he must be different from *Kumāragupta I, as latter's last known date is 455 AD, while Kumāragupta of the Sarnath inscription was ruling in *Gupta era 154

(= 473 AD). The Bhitari and the Nalanda seals of Kumāragupta, and the Nalanda seal of *Vishṇugupta, mention a Kumāragupta as son of *Narasiṁhagupta, besides Kumāragupta [I], the son of successor of *Chandragupta II. Some *Archer type of gold coins were issued by Kumāragupta, who cannot be identified with Kumāragupta I, for the latter bore the epithet *Mahendrāditya*, while the coins in question bear the rev ld *Kramāditya* or *Śrī-Kramādityaḥ*. It is not certain whether all these sources refer to one king of the name of Kumāragupta, or to more that one kings. Here, the numismatic evidence comes to our help. The gold coins of the Archer type mentioned above have been divided into two classes by Altekar. Both the classes bear the ld **Mahārājādhirāja Śrī-Kumāragupta* on the obv, but the rev of Class I has the ld *Kramāditya*, and that of Class II, *Śrī-Karamādityaḥ*. The percentage of pure gold in the coins of Class I is 70-80, which is much higher than that in Class II (about 54 %). The coins of Class II bear single Br letters, like *ru*, *u*, *gre*, *go*, *jo*, and *bhā* on the obv, while such letters are not met with on the coins of Class I. There is also difference in the style, execution, weight, and palaeography of these two classes of coins. Altekar had suggested that both these classes of coins were issued by one and the same ruler, who struck the coins of Class I as a sovereign emperor, and those of Class II as a subordinate ruler under *Budhagupta. But his alternative suggestion that the coins were struck by two different kings—Class I by Kumāragupta II, and Class II by Kumāragupta III, seems to be more convincing. Kumāragupta II has been identified as the Kumāragupta of the Sarnath Buddhist image inscription of Gupta era 154, and regarded as a son of either *Skandagupta or *Pūrugupta. *Kumāragupta III was the son of Narasiṁhagupta, mentioned in the Bhitari and Nalanda seals of Kumāragupta himself, and in the Nalanda seal of Vishṇugupta (Ashvini Agrawal 1989; Allan 1914; Altekar 1957; R D Banerji 1933; Fleet 1888; S R Goyal 2005; P L Gupta 1998; K P Jayaswal 1933; Smith 1972; Thaplyal, forthcoming).

Kumāragupta II : Archer type

Kumāragupta III *Śrī-Kramāditya*. *Imperial Gupta k. There are sufficient grounds to believe that after Kumāragupta I, there were at least two more Imperial Gupta kings named Kumāragupta [*Kumāragupta II]. Kumāragupta III is known from his Bhitari and Nalanda seals, and from the Nalanda seal of *Vishṇugupta, as a son of *Narasiṁhagupta, born of *Mahādevī* Mitradevī. From the findspot of the Bhitari seal, it has been inferred that Kumāragupta III exercised authority on the area around Bhitari. During his reign also, the Parivrājaka *Mahārājas* continued to acknowledge the (nominal ?) suzerainty of the Imperial Guptas. From the inscriptions of Maitraka rulers, issued between 525 and 545 AD, it appears that these kings, too, were ruling under the Imperial Guptas. Some scholars believe that the Gupta king, referred to in the Mandasor inscription as defeated by Yaśodharman, should be identified with Kumāragupta III. There is also a suggestion that it was Kumāragupta III, who received the Chinese embassy, which visited India in 539 AD, and sent Paramārtha to China with the embassy. The reign of Kumāragupta III would have ended some time before 543 AD, which is the known date of his son and successor, Vishṇugupta. Kumāragupta III issued debased gold coins of the *Archer type, mentioning his name on the obv, and bearing the ld *Śrī-Kramādityaḥ* on the rev (Ashvini Agrawal 1989; Allan 1914; Altekar 1957; R D Banerji 1933; Fleet 1888; S R Goyal 2005; P L Gupta 1998; K P Jayaswal 1933; Smith 1972; Thaplyal 1972; Thaplyal, forthcoming).

Kumarkhan hoard. This hoard of nine *Imperial Gupta gold coins was found in 1953 in village Kumarkhan, district Ahmedabad (Gujarat). The rulers represented in this hoard are *Samudragupta, *Kācha, and *Chandragupta II (Altekar 1957).

Kumudasena. *Ayodhyā k. He seems to be among the earliest of the Ayodhyā kings who issued round die-struck coins, as his coins bear a square incuse, and as a symbol on the obv of his coins connects him with the Ayodhyā kings known from the square cast coins. It has been proposed to place him *c* 150 AD. His coins bear the figure of a *bull before a symbol on the obv, and a **nandipada* within a square on the rev. The ld, *Rājña Kumudasenasa*, occurs on the obv. He is the only ruler of Ayodhyā to bear the title of **rājan* on his coins (Bela Lahiri 1974; Smith 1972).

Kuṇinda. Tribe. While the coin ld gives the form Kuṇinda, literature has the forms Kulinda, Kauṇinda, Kaulinda, Kulindrene, etc. The evidence of the *Mahābhārata*, which mentions them as a mountainous people having hundreds of groups (*śata-saṁkulam*), associates them with the Pāṇḍavas and suggests that the tribe was widely diffused.

The *Rāmāyaṇa* also mentions the tribe, as also the *Bṛihatsaṁhitā* which places it in the northwestern division, with the Kaśmīras, *Kulūtas, etc. Ptolemy refers to them as Kulindrene, and places them in the mountainous region. According to the *Mahāmāyūrī*, the worship of Yaksha Ushṭrapāda was popular among the Kuṇindas. Kuṇinda coins have been found at Behat near Saharanpur, Srinagar in Garhwal, and the areas around Jwalamukhi, Karnal, Sunet, Tappa Mewa, and Ropar. According to Cunningham, they inhabited the hill districts on both sides of Sutlej with their capital at Srughna (or Sugh), on the west bank of the Yamuna. Allan considers the strip of land at the foot of the Siwalik hills between the Yamuna and the Sutlej and the territory between the upper courses of the Beas and the Sutlej as their home. To this should be added the Garhwal-Kumaon region, where also their coins have been found. The Kuṇindas, who were *rājaśabdopajīvī* (that is members of the central assembly bore the title of **rājan*), seem to have risen as a political power after the fall of the Mauryas. Tarn suggests that the Kuṇindas, along with some other tribes, were subjugated by *Menander. It appears that during the *Kushāṇa period also, they lost their independence; but later, along with the *Yaudheyas and the *Ārjunāyanas (with whom they might have formed a confederacy), were responsible for the decline of the Kushāṇa power. They do not find mention in the Allahabad pillar inscription of *Samudragupta (*c* 350 AD), which suggests that by that time their power had declined. Some scholars suggest that they were incorporated with the Yaudheyas, whose coins, datable to the second-third centuries AD, show influence of the Kuṇinda coins. Caste names, such as Kanyal, Kanwal, Kanedi, etc, in Garhwal-Kumaon region seem to be survivals of the Kuṇindas. Cunningham connects the Kuṇindas with the Kunets whom he considers the original inhabitants in the long Himalayan belt. The Kuṇinda coins were issued in both silver and copper, and are round in shape. According to Cunningham, they were produced in some mint located at Sugh, while Devendra Handa locates another Kuṇinda mint at Sanghol. The coins have been divided into two series—the *Amoghabhūti series, and the **Chatreśvara* series. The weight of the silver coins of the Amoghabhūti series ranges between 21 and 38 grains, and seems to be based on the *hemidrachms* of later Indo-Greek and *Śaka-Pahlava kings, adopted with a view to competing in the market with the Indo-Greek silver pieces. The copper coins

Kuṇinda : Amoghabhūti series

Kuṇinda : *Chatreśvara* series

of this series weigh between 9.5 and 257 grains, while those of the *Chatreśvara* series weigh between 131 and 291 grains; these seem to be based on the Kushāṇa weight standard. Rapson, Powell-Price, and M P Joshi ascribe the *Almora coins to a branch of the Kuṇinda tribe (Allan 1936; Chakrabortty 1931; Cunningham 1971b; K K Dasgupta 1974; Handa 2007a; Jayaswal 1988; M P Joshi 1989; Marshall 1975; Mitchiner 1975-1976; Powell-Price 1945; Rapson 1987; Smith 1972).

Kurara. City coins. Some coins found from the Hoshangabad district (Madhya Pradesh), from where Bhāgila coins were also discovered, bear the ld *Kurarāya*. Kurara is mentioned as a place name in some Sanchi inscriptions. These coins have been taken to be the city coins of Kurara, the city being situated not far from Sanchi (Bela Lahiri 1974; Bela Lahiri 1976; J P Singh 1971).

V'ima Kadphises

Kanishka I

Kushāṇa. Coins, general features. According to traditional scholarship, about 165 BC, there was much political upheaval in Central Asia, as a result of which the Hiung-nu (Hūṇa) tribe was displaced from its original homeland. This tribe, in its turn, forced the Yueh-chih tribe out of its original habitat in Tocharistan in Central Asia. While one branch, Little Yueh-chih, moved towards Tibet and settled there, the other one, the Greater Yueh-chih, reached northwestern India by way of Seistan and Bactria. Chinese sources inform that in Bactria, the Yueh-chihs had five small principalities, four of which were subjugated by K'ieou-t'sieou-k'io (*Kujula Kadphises), the chief of the fifth one. However, according to some recent writers, the Kushāṇas were a branch of the K'ang-chü race, which was of Skythian descent and originally belonged to the lower Jaxartes region. This branch allied itself with the Yüeh-chih, and settled in Ferghana. The capital of Ferghana was called Erh-shih around 101 BC, but by 36 BC, it was called Kouei-chouan, perhaps after its founder who belonged to Kouei-chouang branch of the K'ang-chü. Kujula Kadphises is known to have ruled up to the age of past eighty, and was succeeded by his son, who was earlier identified as *V'ima Kadphises, but there is epigraphic evidence to show that *V'ima Takshuma was the son and successor of Kujula Kadphises, and that V'ima Kadphises was the son and successor of V'ima Takshuma. The establishment of Kushāṇa power over some

Huvishka

Huvishka

Huvishka

Kanishka I

Vāsudeva I

territories of India proper took place some time during the reign of V'ima Kadphises, or, perhaps, even in the time of V'ima Takshuma. After him came the Kanishka group of kings. *Kanishka I ruled over an extensive dominion extending at least up to Vārāṇasī in the east and Kashghar, Yarqand, and Khotan in the north, and was succeeded by *Vāsishka, *Huvishka, Kanishka II, *Vāsudeva I, etc. The Kushāṇa empire started disintegrating after Vāsudeva I. Numismatic evidence shows that among his successors, *Kanishka III ruled over both the eastern as well as the western provinces of the Kushāṇa empire, but *Vāsudeva II could retain only the western provinces. The Kushāṇas continued as a political power at least up to *circa* 350 AD, when the Allahabad pillar inscription of Samudragupta mentions a *Daivaputrashāhi-shāhānushāhi* as submitting to that *Imperial Gupta ruler. Kushāṇa coins are reported from as remote regions as Ethiopia and Iraq. The Kushāṇas were the first power in India to issue profuse gold coinage. Besides, they also struck abundant copper coins, and rare silver ones. The gold coins of the Kushāṇas were based on the weight standard of the Roman **aurei*, and weighed around 123 grains. The copper coins are available in three weights—260 grains, 130 grains, and 65 grains. The silver coins are so few that nothing definite can be said about their weight standard. It has been suggested that the rarity of the Kushāṇa silver coins might have something to do with the shortage of silver all over the world at that time. 'The line of descent of the new (Kushāṇa gold) issue must be traced...through the Roman *aurei* which were first issued in abundance by Augustus and which at the beginning of the Christian era made their way into India....' The Kushāṇa coins are manufactured by the die-striking method, and are invariably round in shape. The obv of the coins of *Kujula Kadphises bears the bust of the *Indo-Greek ruler, *Hermaios, or his own helmeted head; one type even has the figure of a bull on the obv. But from the time of *V'ima Kadphises onwards, the device of *king sacrificing at an altar becomes common, Huvishka being the only ruler not using it on his coins. Other Ḳushāṇa obv devices include king seated on a throne, or on cushions, or on clouds, or reclining on a couch, or riding an elephant. The bust of the king, sometimes enclosed in a frame, may also be seen on some coins. The rev of the coins of Kujula Kadphises bears, variously, "Macedonian soldier' or camel; V'ima Kadphises depicted *Śiva, anthropomorphically or symbolically. The rev of the coins of Kanishka I and Huvishka are interesting for the great variety of deities appearing on them. These deities belong to a varied pantheon—Indian, Central Asian, West Asian, Zoroastrian, Graeco-Roman. The Zoroastrian deities form the most represented creed on Kushāṇa coins, and we have depictions of **Ardochsho, *Athsho, *Mao, *Miiro, *Lrooaspo, *Oado, *Orlagno, *Oanindo, *Pharro,* etc. The Graeco-Roman pantheon was the least represented, with deities like *Elios* (*Helios), **Selene, *Uron, Ephaistos* (*Hephaistos), *Erakilo* (*Herakles), **Riom*, etc occasionally making their appearance, although usually in Iranian garb. Indian deities include Śiva, *Umā, *Kārttikeya as Skanda-Kumāra, Viśākha, and Mahāsena, and the *Buddha. *Nana-Nanaia-Nanashao* is a very frequently depicted goddess. Such representations, no doubt, reflect the spirit of eclecticism with which the Kushāṇa kings seem to be imbued. The deities depicted on coins also seem to emphasize the 'right and might of the Kushāṇa rule'. The obv ld on the coins of the Kadphises group of kings is in Gr, while the rev ld is in Pkt language and Kh script. These legends give the name and titles of the issuing king. But the rulers of the Kanishka group used only Greek language, written in *Graeco-Kushāṇa script. The obv ld gives the name and titles of the issuing king, while the rev ld gives the name of the deity represented. This label inscription on the rev is very interesting, and helps us in identifying the deity represented when the depiction is indifferent. There are reports of the circulation of Kushāṇa coins in the Punjab region as late as the nineteenth century AD (C J Brown 1999; Cunningham 1971a; Gardner 1971; Jenkins 1977; R C Majumdar 1988; von Mitterwallner 1986; B N Mukherjee 1978; Rosenfield 1967; Senior 2001; Sircar 1980c; Whitehead 1914).

Huvishka

Kanishka III

Kushāṇo-Sassanian. A large number of big sized, cup-shaped *aureii*, 'which mingle in suitable measure elements from imperial Sasanian iconography and from the Kushan numismatic tradition', have been found from Badakshan and the territories north of the Hindukush; some coins of this genre are also known from Seistan, the Kabul valley, and Gandhāra. Ernst Herzfeld dated these coins, called the Kushāṇo-Sassanian coins, to the period from about 230 AD to about 330 AD, and suggested that they were issued by about seven rulers, but scholars like Cunningham, Ghirshman, and Göbl are of the view that the first Kushāṇo-Sassanian coins were struck in the first decade of the fourth century AD. These coins bear only two names of kings—Hormizd and Varahran. The initial coins bearing the name of Hormizd show, on the obv, the nimbate and helmeted king in *Kushāṇa type dress, offering oblations at an altar, the **nandipada* and **svastika* symbols, and the Graeco-Kushāṇa ld mentioning the name and titles of Hormizd. The rev has the bearded and mustachioed figure of *Śiva, wearing tunic and pantaloons, with hair flaming; the bull is seen by his side. This type represents the transition from the Kushāṇa to the Kushāṇo-Sassanian issues. Another type bearing the name of Hormizd has the same devices and ld, but the king wears Sassanian royal dress, and there is a lion head on his helmet. The third type is similar to the second type, but there is the characteristic Sassanian ball like ornament on the shaft of the helmet. The fourth type has the helmeted bust of the king to the r with a Pahlavi ld on the obv, and the conventional Sassanian type fire altar with an attendant on either side on the rev. There are also some copper types associated with this, the rev of which shows the bust of *Ahuramazda emerging from the fire altar, or the figure of Śiva. The gold coins bearing the name Varahran have the helmeted and diademed king standing at an altar and the ld mentioning the name of titles of Varahran. Variety is seen in the crown of the king on these coins. For instance, on some specimens, the royal crown has double ram's horns, seen in Sassanian silver ware. Some of the Varahran coins bear a monogram, which Göbl regards as a combination of the *nandipada*, seen on the Kushāṇa and Kushāṇo-Sassanian coins, and a Hephthalite symbol, and suggests on this basis that at the time of the issue of these coins, the Sassanians held sway over both these peoples (Bivar 1956; Herzfeld 1998; Rosenfield 1967).

Kusumbhi hoard. This hoard of 29 *Imperial Gupta gold coins was found in 1947 at Kusumbhi, district Unnao (Uttar Pradesh). The rulers represented in this hoard are *Samudragupta, *Chandragupta II, and *Kumāragupta I (Altekar 1957).

L

Lae-lih. *Hūṇa chief. Sung-yün, the Chinese ambassador to the Hūṇa court at Gandhāra in 520 AD, states that the Ye-thas had conquered Gandhāra two generations earlier, and Lae-lih was their first ruler. Thus, Lae-lih would have ruled in the latter half of the fifth century AD. But scholars, like Chavannes and Pelliot, believe that what has been read as *Lae-lih* in Sung-yün's account, is actually *Tigin*; coins bearing this name (?) *Tigin are also known. There is also a suggestion that in the account of the Chinese ambassador, the king is mentioned as *Che-le*, which is sought to be associated with **Jaüla*, the title of *Toramāṇa. Some silver coins from the Punjab region bear a ld mentioning one *Udayāditya*, the first part of whose name has been variously read as *Lamata*, *Lakhana*, *Latona*, or *Lanona*. Cunningham ascribes these coins to the lae-lih, whom he regards as the father of Toramāṇa. But if the reading *Lakhana* be correct, they may as well be ascribed to **Lavkhāṇa* (Biswas 1973; Cunningham 1962; Upendra Thakur 1967a; Upendra Thakur 1967b).

Lakshmī. Indian goddess of prosperity. Also known by such names as Śrī, Padmā, and Kamalā, Lakshmī is the goddess of good fortune and luck, bringing to her devotees 'peaceful prosperity and abundance'. She is also looked upon as the goddess of feminine beauty. She was revered in all the religious creeds of India. In the *Ṛigveda*, there is no mention of Lakshmī as such. But in the saṁhitās, the attributes of deities like Purandhī as a goddess of plenty, Rākā as a rich and beautiful goddess, and Sinivālī as the wife of *Vishṇu, are reminiscent of Lakshmī of later texts. However, it cannot be asserted that any one of these vedic goddesses 'could have served

Hagāmasha

Mathurā

Chandragupta II : Archer type

Śaśāṅka

as the sole prototype' of Lakshmī. All this leaves little doubt as to the abstract origin of this goddess. She is most well-known as the consort of Vishṇu, and her worship gained in popularity with the spread of Vaishnavism. In Buddhist literature, Lakshmī in the form of Śrī, is the goddess of beauty, and she is described as a daughter of Śakra (= *Indra). Some texts, like the *Śilparatna* and the *Vishṇudharmottarapurāṇa*, refer to the *abhisheka* of Lakshmī by two elephants [*Gajalakshmī], which in the latter text are described as the two *nidhis* of *śaṅkha* and *padma*. The favourite seat of Lakshmī is the *lotus bloom, although as Rājyalakshmī she may also be shown as enthroned on a lion throne. Sometimes, in literature and art, a *lion may be associated with Lakshmī as her mount (**Siṁhavāhinī Devī*). In the Śrīsūkta of the *Ṛigveda*, Śrī[-Lakshmī] is described as 'a golden coloured antelope decorated with garlands of silver and gold'. Standing Lakshmi, holding her characteristic attribute, the lotus bloom, in one of her raised hands, occurs very commonly on the early coins of *Mathurā, issued by both the Hindu rulers and the Śaka—*Gomitra II, *Brahmamitra, *Dṛiḍhamitra, *Sūryamitra, *Purushadatta, *Uttamadatta, *Balabhūti, *Rāmadatta, *Kāmadatta, *Śivadatta, *Hagāmasha, *Rañjuvula, and *Śoḍāsha. A similar depiction of the goddess may also be seen on some coins of the *Agras, as also on some coins of the *Rājanya *janapada*. The goddess standing facing on a lotus, with a flower in her raised r hand, on the obv of some coins of the *Śaka-Pahlava ruler, *Azes, has been identified as Lakshmī by most of the scholars. However, Gardner expresses the possibility that a lion may be seen lying by the side of the goddess on a specimen, although he admits that what looks like a lion may, in fact, be just a lump of oxide. But on the basis of the supposed depiction of the lion beside the deity on this coin, it has been suggested by J N Banerjea that the deity may be identified as *Durgā, who has the lion as her mount. The obv of a copper type of *Azilises shows Lakshmī seated on an elephant, and flanked by two elephants. The goddess depicted on the rev of the coins of the *Pañchāla ruler, *Bhadraghosha, has been identified as *Bhadrā. Standing Lakshmī may also be seen on the rev of some coins of the *Imperial Guptas. The goddess is mostly shown standing on a lotus, but on certain coins of *Chandragupta II, she has a mat or a pedestal under her feet. She holds a lotus in one of her hands, and a *pāśa* in the other. On the obv of some uninscribed coins from *Ujjayinī, datable to the third-second centuries BC, Lakshmī is shown seated facing on a lotus. Seated figures of Lakshmī quite frequently occur on the rev of the coins of the Imperial Guptas. The goddess is mostly shown seated on a lotus bloom, as, for example on some coins of *Samudragupta, Chandragupta II, and *Kumāragupta I. But on certain issues of Samudragupta and Chandragupta II, she sits on a throne, with her feet resting on a lotus bloom used as a foot stool. Generally, she carries a lotus bloom in one hand, and a *pāśa* in the other. But on some coins of Kumāragupta I, she is shown with a lotus in her l hand, and scattering coins with her r hand; on some other coins of that ruler, she holds a lotus in her r hand, while her l hand is empty and resting on her thigh; on still other coins of Kumāragupta I, she holds a *pāśa* in her raised r hand, while her l hand, which rests on her knee, holds a lotus. A similar depiction may also be seen on some coins of Chandragupta II, *Bhānugupta Prakāśāditya, and *Śaśāṅka. On some coins of Samudragupta, seated Lakshmī holds a **cornucopiae* in one hand and a *pāśa* in the other, while a *cornucopiae* in one hand and a lotus bloom in the other is seen on some coins of Kumāragupta I. On the obv of some *Kuṇinda coins, bearing the name *Amoghabhūti, appears a standing female figure, sometimes on a lotus bloom, holding a flower in her raised r hand. A *deer is seen beside the female figure. On the basis of the association of this figure with the lotus and the deer, to which Śrī is compared in the Śrīsūkta of the *Ṛigveda* (above), the goddess is often identified as Lakshmī. The presence of the **śrīvatsa* among the symbols shown around the goddess on these coins, would seem to support this identification. But some scholars point out that if Lakshmī is depicted on these coins in the anthropomorphic form, her theriomorphic representation as a deer would be an unnecessary duplication. The obv of some *Rājanya coins is occupied by a standing female (?)figure, holding an indistinct object in her r hand. Some scholars feel that the object in the hand of the deity seems to be a lotus bloom, and propose to identify the figure as that of Lakshmī, on this basis, and also on the ground that the figure is similar to that of Lakshmī on the coins from Mathurā. But in view of the uncertainty regarding the gender and the attribute of the deity, this identification cannot be considered as final. Attempts have also been made to identify the female figure standing between a *liṅgam*-like object and a tree on the rev of some *Ārjunāyana coins, as also

Kuṇinda

the six-headed female figure on the *Yaudheya coins bearing the figure of *Kārttikeya on the other side, with Lakshmī. But, at least in the latter case, this identification has been proved to be erroneous, and the hexacephalous female figure on the Yaudheya coins has now been correctly identified as that of *Shashṭhī-Devasenā. The female figure on the rev of some bilingual silver coins of the *Indo-Greek rulers, *Pantaleon and *Agathokles, which was earlier identified as Lakshmī, is now regarded as that of a *yakshiṇī. On some coins, like those of the *Audumbara chiefs, *Mahādeva and *Rudravarman, the lotus on the obv might symbolically indicate the presence of Lakshmī. On a variety of *Agra coins, the goddess seems to be represented symbolically through a *tulasī* plant flanked by two elephants holding inverted pitchers in their trunks (Allan 1936; Altekar 1957; Banerjea 2002; Sukumari Bhattacharji 1970; Chakrabortty 1931; Cunningham 1971a; Cunningham 1971b; K K Dasgupta 1974; Gardner 1971; S R Goyal 1986; Handa 2007a; T R R Iyengar 2003; Bela Lahiri 1974; Macdonell 1897; R B Pande 1988; Rao 1985; Senior 2001; Prashant Srivastava 1996b; Whitehead 1914; Wilkins 2006).[†]

Lakshmī type. Copper. The Lakshmī type of copper coins were issued by *Chandragupta II in the *Imperial Gupta dynasty. The obv shows the crowned head of the king to the l. The rev has *Lakshmī standing facing, with a stalked lotus in her l hand, while her r hand is on her waist; outside the left arm of the deity, written vertically, is the Br ld *Chandra* (Allan 1914; Altekar 1957; P L Gupta 1998; Smith 1972).

Laodike. (Seleukid ?) princess. She was married to *Heliokles, perhaps a Seleukid general or satrap; she was the mother of the *Indo-Greek ruler, *Eukratides I, who commemorated Laodike and his father, Heliokles, on his coins (Bopearachchi 1993; Bopearachchi and Pieper 1998; Bopearachchi and Rahman 1995; Cunningham 1970; Gardner 1971; A N Lahiri 1965; Marshall 1975; Narain 1957a; Rapson 1987; Sircar 1980a; Prashant Srivastava 1996a; Tarn 1980; Whitehead 1914).

Lavkhāṇa. *Hūṇa chief. Some silver coins from the Punjab region bear, on the obv, helmeted head of the king to the r, with the Br ld mentioning one *Udayāditya*, the first part of whose name has been read variously as *Lamata*, *Latona*, *Lanona*, or *Lakhana*. Cunningham ascribes these coins to *Lae-lih, but if the reading *Lakhana* (?) proposed by him be correct, the coins may as well be ascribed to the Lavkhāṇa, a Hūṇa chief mentioned in a Nalanda sealing, which describes him as **mahārāja*. On the basis of the mention of his name in the sealing, it has been suggested that he might have ruled over Nalanda, where the sealing has been found. But sealings can travel to distant places, and the coins of Lakhana/Lavkhāṇa have been found in Punjab and Kashmir, thereby showing that this Hūṇa chief would have ruled over these region, rather than over Nalanda (Biswas 1973; Cunningham 1962; Upendra Thakur 1967a; Upendra Thakur 1967b; Thaplyal 1972).

Lead. Metal for coins. This metal, which was adopted by the Sātavāhanas for the manufacture of coins, was produced in very little quantity indigenously, and the insufficient supply had to be augmented by importing the metal, particularly from Rome. It is interesting to note in this connection, that Pliny states that 'India has neither brass nor lead, but exchanges precious stones and pearls for them'. Walter Elliot opines that lead was imported, mainly for purposes of coinage. Besides the Sātavāhanas, lead coins were also struck by the *Indo-Greek king, *Strato I, the *Śaka-Pahlava ruler, *Azes, and by *Rañjuvula, the Śaka satrap of *Mathurā (Chakrabortty 1931; Cunningham 1970; A N Lahiri 1965; Rapson 1975; Senior 2001).

Liäka Kusulaka. Śaka k. He is mentioned in the Taxila copperplate inscription of year 78 as the *kshatrapa* of Chukhsa (most probably, modern Chach along the river Indus), perhaps serving under *Maues; Marshall would assign to the Liäka Kusulaka a much more extensive satrapy, comprising the Peshawar valley to the west of the river Indus, and a large part of Hazara, Attock, and Mianwali regions to its east. He appears to be the son of *Mahākshatrapa* Patika of the Mathurā lion capital inscription of the time of *Rañjuvula and *Śoḍāsha, and the father of *Mahādānapati* Patika. He issued siver coins, which are imitations of the obols of *Eukratides, and which bear the helmeted head of the king to the r on the obv, and *palms and **pilei* on the rev. The rev Gr ld has been read by Cunningham as *Liako Kozoulo*, although some scholars are not certain about the reading of the first part of the name (Cunningham 1971a; Jenkins and Narain 1957; Marshall 1975; Sircar 1980b; Sircar 1986).

Liṅgaṁ. Symbol. Phallism or Phallicism, the worship of the male reproductive power of nature symbolized by the phallus, is of pre-vedic origin in India. An ithyphallic deity, labelled as the prototype of Śiva-Paśupati by Marshall, is known for the Harappan culture, and there is also some evidence to suggest that the Harappans worshipped the phallus. In the *Ṛigveda*, worshippers of the phallus seem to be alluded to as *śiśnadevas*, in a deprecating manner. But gradually, phallic worship was accorded sanction in orthodox Hindu Brahmanical religion, in association with Rudra-*Śiva. The phallic cult is especially associated with agriculture, the acts of copulation and ploughing being regarded as somewhat analogous, and agricultural deities all over the world, like the Egyptian Osiris, the Assyrian Vul, the Greek Dionysios, the Phoenician Adonis, and the Phrygian Attis, are mostly phallic deities. Coomaraswamy says that among the various symbols that one might expect to find on the punch marked coins, but which fail to make their appearance there, is included the *liṅgam*, and this has been accepted by J N Banerjea. But there is a suggestion that the three cylindrical objects, shown in a line on a pedestal, on some punch marked coins illustrated by Allan, might represent the three forms of the *liṅgams—daivika*, *ārshaka*, and *mānusha*. The central of these three cylindrical objects is higher than the two flanking it, and resembles a similar object on some copper coins from Taxila. A *liṅgam*-like object also appears on a pedestal formed by a wavy line, on the obv of two square copper coins from Taxila. The *liṅgam*, on a square pedestal and beside a tree-in-railing, occurs on the rev of an uninscribed cast copper coin of unknown *provenance*. A similar representation is also seen on an *Ārjunāyana copper coin, but with a female figure (*Lakshmī ?) standing between the two symbols. On the obv of one copper coin from *Ujjayinī, a *liṅgam* is depicted between two trees-in-railing (Allan 1936; Banerjea 2002; Chakrabortty 1931; Mahadev Chakravarti 1994; Bhaskar Chattopadhyay 1977; Cunningham 1971b; Dasgupta 1974; Handa 2007a; Rao 1985).[†]

Lion. Symbol. Although attempts have also been made to associate this animal with the *Buddha (who is known as Śākyasiṁha), or with Mahāvīra (whose cognizance is the lion), the lion, which appears on a number of ancient Indian coins, seems to be associated with Durgā (who has this beast as her *vāhana*), or *Vishṇu (one of whose name is Hari, which also means 'lion', and one of whose incarnations is Nṛisiṁha, 'Man-lion'; in fact, J N Banerjea is of the view that the lion depicted on some seals found at Bhita and Vaishali may have Vaishṇava affiliations. The device of a lion appears on at least two of Allan's classes of the local coins of Taxila, and there is a suggestion that this animal should be regarded as particularly associated with that city. The beast also appears on some *Ujjayinī, *Mālava and *Rājanya coins. On certain *Agra coins, the beast is seen on top of a *hill, and on still other coins of the same tribe, the lion is depicted inside a rayed circle, which seems to hint at the sanctity of the animal. On a coin, doubtfully ascribed to Taxila by Allan, a lion is seen behind the royal hunter mounted on horseback. Maneless lion appears on the coins of the *Indo-Greek rulers, *Pantaleon, *Agathokles, *Menander, and *Artemidoros, and of the *Śaka-Pahlava rulers, *Azes and *Azilises, and some scholars would regard the use of this device as indicative of the sway of these rulers over Takshaśilā. Tarn and A N Lahiri are of the view that the animal on the coins of Pantaleon and Agathokles is a *panther, and as the obv of these coins bears the head of *Dionysos, the animal might be the panther of that deity. The lion may also be seen as the mount of **Nana* on some *Kushāṇa coins, and of the **Siṁhavāhinī Devī* on *Imperial Gupta coins, and as the prey of the king on the *Lion-slayer type of coins of *Chandragupta II and *Kumāragupta I, the *Elephant-rider-lion-slayer type of Kumāragupta I, and the Equestrian-lion-slayer type of *Bhānugupta Prakāśāditya (Allan 1914; Allan 1936; Altekar 1957; Banerjea 2002; Bopearachchi 1993; Bopearachchi and Pieper 1998; Bopearachchi and Rahman 1995; Chakrabortty 1931; Bhaskar Chattopadhyay 1977; K K Dasgupta 1974; Gardner 1971; Handa 2007a; A N Lahiri 1965; Marshall 1975; Narain 1957a; Pathak 1986; Pathak 1988-1989; Senior 2001; Prashant Srivastava 2001; Prashant Srivastava 2004a; Tarn 1980; Whitehead 1914).

Uninscribed cast coin

Agathokles

Azes II

Lion-slayer type. Gold. *Chandragupta II issued the Lion-slayer type of coins, perhaps to commemorate his conquest of the Kathiawar region, known for its *lion population. V S Pathak, however, suggests

Chandragupta II : Lion-slayer type

Kumāragupta I : Lion-slayer type

Kumāragupta I : Lion-slayer type

that it symbolizes the victory of Chandragupta II over the Sassanian ruler, Yazdgird I. The coins have been divided into four classes. The obv of Class I has the king shooting an arrow at a lion. The bow may be seen in either hand of the king. On Class II, the king is also trampling the lion on the belly with one foot, while shooting an arrow at the beast. Class III has the king, often merely looking at the lion, and making no attempt to shoot it with an arrow. On the obv of Class IV, represented by a lone specimen in the State Museum, Lucknow, the king is shown attacking the lion with a sword held in his r hand. The circular ld on the obv is mostly *Narendrachandraḥ prathitaraṇo-raṇe jayatyajeyo bhuvi Siṁhavakramaḥ*, but other varieties like *Devaśrī-mahārājādhirāja Śrī-Chandraguptaḥ*, or *Narendrasiṁhaḥ Chandraguptaḥ pṛithivīṁ jitvā divaṁ jayati*, may be also be seen on different specimens. The rev of all the classes has the **Siṁhavāhinī Devī*, mostly holding a *pāśa* in her r hand, and a **cornucopiae* in her left. The rev ld is *Siṁhavikramaḥ*, sometimes with *śrī*. This type was continued by *Kumāragupta I, but his coins do not compare favourably with the coins of the same type issued by his father. His coins of this type are divided into two classes. Class I coins have, on the obv, the king shooting an arrow at the lion in his front, while on Class II, he is also trampling upon the beast and shooting at it. The circular ld on the various varieties of Class I reads *Kshitipatirajito Mahendraḥ Kumāragupto divaṁ jayati*, or *Kumāragupto vijayī siṁhamahendro divaṁ jayati*, or *Kumāragupto yudhi Siṁhavikramaḥ*. Most of the coins of Class II have the circular ld *Sākshādiva Narasiṁho Siṁhamahendra jayatya niśam*. The rev of these coins has *Siṁhavāhinī Devī*. On some coins of Class I, she holds a stalked lotus in her r hand, while her l hand is on her waist; on other coins of this class, she has a lotus in her l hand, while her r hand is shown scattering coins. The rev ld is *Śrī-Mahendrasiṁhaḥ*. On the coins of Class II, the goddess holds a *pāśa* in her r hand, and a lotus in the left. The rev ld on the coins of this class is *Siṅhamahendraḥ*. P L Gupta has published a gold coin of the Lion-slayer type of Kumāragupta I from the collection of the State Museum, Lucknow, on the obv of which, he sees the king seated on a chair, with the lion shown beside him. But the illustration shows that the king is not seated on a chair, but is standing with both his hands on his waist, akimbo. Thus, it does not seem to be new gold type of Kumāragupta I, as P L Gupta suggests, but a new variety of his Lion-slayer type, in that the king does not appear to be armed (Ashvini Agrawal 1989; Allan 1914; Altekar 1957; R D Banerji 1933; S R Goyal 2005; P L Gupta 1998; P L Gupta 1993; V S Pathak 1988-1989; Smith 1972; Prashant Srivastava 1996a; Prashant Srivastava 2004a; Thaplyal, forthcoming).

Loha-māsaka. Coin denomination. Mentioned by Buddhaghosha in the *Kaṅkhāvataraṇī* commentary on the *Pātimokkha*, it seems to be a copper coin, and identical with the **ṇāṇa-māsaka* of the **Aṅgavijjā* (V S Agrawala 1957).

Lotapur hoard. This hoard was found in 1928 at Lotapur in the Unnao district of Uttar Pradesh. It was reported to have comprised 1,351 silver *punch marked coins, but the State Museum, Lucknow, is said to hold 1,411 coins from this hoard. The coins from this hoard have been ascribed to the Pañchāla *janapada* (Rajgor 2001).

Lotus. Symbol. Owing to its miraculous birth beneath the waters, this flower became 'pre-eminently the symbol of birth'. The flower is also associated with deities like Brahmā and Kālī, and with ideas like *nirvāṇa*. As the lotus blooms at sunrise and withers at sunset, it is sometimes linked to the sun. But gradually, the flower came to be more intimately associated with *Lakshmī, and is often seen in the hand of the goddess, or as her seat or pedestal, on ancient Indian coins. Its occurrence on the obv of the coins of some *Audumbara chiefs, like *Mahādeva and *Rudravarman, might symbolically indicate the presence of that goddess. A lotus in front of a *bull is also seen on the obv of *Vemaki coins. Interestingly, on a recently reported *Yaudheya coin, a goddess (*Shashṭhī) appears with her head represented by a lotus bloom (Allan 1936; Banerjea 2002; Chakrabortty 1931; Mahadev Chakravarti 1994; Bhaskar Chattopadhyay 1977; K K Dasgupta 1974; Handa 2007a; Marshall 1960; Zimmer 1999).†

Chandragupta II : *Chhatra* type

Lrooaspo. Avestan, Luhrasp. The ld *Lrooaspo* on *Kushāṇa coins stands for the Avestan god Luhrasp. Attempts have been made to read the ld as *Drooaspo* and identify the deity with Druvāspa, the guardian of the health of beasts, but without much success. Luhrasp corresponds to the Avestan word *Aurvataspa*, meaning 'swift-horsed'. In the *Avesta*, this is used as an epithet and applied to *Mithra. Interestingly, 'swift-horsed' is also an epithet of the vedic Apāṁ Napāt, whom Darmesteter considers to be the fire-god born from the clouds in the form of lightning. Luhrasp occurs on some gold coins of *Kanishka I on the rev. The deity is bearded and diademed, and holds a diadem or a wreath in his r hand. Beside him is shown a saddled horse, trotting to the r. On a type of *Huvishka, a crude figure of Luhrasp occurs on the rev (Bhaskar Chattopadhyay 1977; Darmesteter 1974; Gardner 1971; Stein 1888).

Samudragupta : Lyrist type

Lyrist type. Gold. The Lyrist type of coins were first issued by *Samudragupta, who is known from his Allahabad pillar inscription to have excelled the divine musicians, Tumburu and Nārada, in musical skill. The obv of this type has the king seated on a couch, with a seven-stringed *vīṇā* in his lap. The circular ld reads **Mahārājādhirāja Śrī-Samudraguptaḥ*. On the rev, *Lakshmī is shown seated on a wicker stool, with a *pāśa* in her r hand, and a **cornucopiae* in her l hand. The ld on the rev is *Samudraguptaḥ*. As this type, like the **Aśvamedha* type of Samudragupta, has the Br letter *si* on the obv, it has been suggested that this type, too, was struck on the occasion of the horse sacrifice, to be given away as *dakshiṇā*. The Lyrist type of Samudragupta has been regarded as 'the highest expression of Gupta numismatic art'. The type was continued by *Kumāragupta I, although there is no corroborative evidence to show that he, too, was skilled in the art of music. The obv has the king seated on a couch, and playing on a four-stringed lute placed in his lap. The circular ld reads *Mahārājādhirāja Śrī-Kumāraguptaḥ*. The rev has the figure of the queen, instead of the goddess seen on the prototype issued by Samudragupta. She is seated on a couch, and holding a stalked flower in her r hand, while her l hand is placed on the couch. The rev ld is *Kumāragupta* (Ashvini Agrawal 1989; Allan 1914; Altekar 1957; R D Banerji 1933; C J Brown 1999; S R Goyal 2005; P L Gupta 1998; Smith 1972; Prashant Srivastava 1996a; Thaplyal, forthcoming).

Samudragupta : Lyrist type

Kumāragupta I : Lyrist type

Lyisas

Lysias. *Indo-Greek k; son of *Zoilos I; *c* last quarter of the second century BC. He seems to have ruled the region to the north of the Hindukush, the Kabul valley, and Ghazni. His coins in the Gandhāra region are relatively few. On the basis of the occurrence of the name of Lysias on one side of some coins and that of *Antialkidas on the other side, it was suggested that the two kings issued joint coins, and Tarn regards this as an evidence of a *rapprochement* between the rival Indo-Greek families of Euthydemos and Eukratides, in view of the *Śaka-Pahlava menace. But Narain regards this piece as a 'mule'. Lysias issued both silver and copper coins. Some silver coins are struck on the Attic standard, while other silver coins, and all the copper coins, are struck on the Indian standard. All the coins are die-struck pieces. The silver coins are all round in shape, while the copper coins are known in both the round and square shapes. The obv of the silver coins mostly has the diademed bust of the king to the r, sometimes in elephant's scalp, or a smooth helmet, or *kausia*. But on two types, the obv is occupied by the diademed and helmeted bust of the king to the l, thrusting javelin. The rev of all the silver types has the figure of naked *Herakles, standing to the front, and holding his club, lion's skin, and palm in his l hand, and crowning himself with his r hand. The obv of the copper coins has the bust of *Herakles to the r, with the club over his shoulder, while the rev has an *elephant to the r. The silver coins, struck on the Attic standard, have the Gr ld, on the rev. But the silver and copper coins, struck on the Indian standard, bear the Gr ld on the obv, and the Pkt ld, written in the Kh script, on the rev. Besides the title of **basileus*, Lysias assumed the epithet **aniketos* on his coins. These are rendered into Pkt as **maharaja* and **apaḍihata*, respectively. The Pkt form of the name of the ruler, as met with on coins, is Lisiä or Lisika (Bopearachchi 1993; Bopearachchi and Pieper 1998; Bopearachchi and Rahman 1995; Cunningham 1970; Gardner 1971; A N Lahiri 1965; Marshall 1975; Narain 1957a; Rapson 1906; Rapson 1987; Senior 2001; Sircar 1980a; Prashant Srivastava 1990c; Prashant Srivastava 1996a; Tarn 1980; Whitehead 1914).[†]

M

Maaseno. Deity. See *Kārttikeya.

Machene. Śaka-Pahlava queen-regent. A silver coin bearing the figure of an enthroned female and the name of Machene in the Gr ld on the obv, and *Zeus Nikephoros and the name of *Maues in the Kh ld on the rev, has come to the light some years back from the *Swat hoard. G le Rider, who first published this coin, regards Machene as the wife of Maues. But it is difficult to explain the occurrence of the name of the queen on the obv, and that of the king on the rev. It seems more likely that Machene was the mother of Maues and took up the reins of administration in her hands during the minority of her son, following the death of her husband. The titles used for her on this coin—**basilissa* and **theotropos*, remind one of *Agathokleia who had to assume regency during the minority of her son, *Strato I, after the death of *Menander. Interestingly, Maues, the minor king, is given full sovereign titles of **rajatiraja mahata* on this coin issued with Machene. Attempts have been made to associate Machene with the Indo-Greeks, particularly *Peukolaos, and to suggest that Maues' mother was of Greek origin, although there are certain problems in accepting this suggestion (B N Mukherjee 1983; Senior 2001; Prashant Srivastava 1996a; Prashant Srivastava 2008b).

Mādhavavarman. *Ayodhyā k. He seems to be among the earliest of the Ayodhyā kings who issued round die-struck coins, as his coins bear a square incuse, and as a symbol on the obv of his coins connects him with the Ayodhyā kings known from the square cast coins. His coins bear the figure of a *bull before a symbol on the obv, and a

**nandipada* within a square on the rev. The coin ld mentions the name of the issuer in the genitive (Bela Lahiri 1974).

***Madhyadeśa* type.** Silver. *Chandragupta II is the first *Imperial Gupta ruler, who is definitely known to have struck silver coins. But all his silver coins are of the *Western Indian type, issued for circulation in the erstwhile *Kārddamaka territories in western India. His son, *Kumāragupta I, issued silver coins for circulation in the Ganga plains or *Madhyadeśa* as well, and these are called the *Madhyadeśa* type of Imperial Gupta silver coins. These are markedly different from the Western Indian type of silver coins. Although the head of the king on the obv, is retained, it does not resemble the Kshatrapa head; the Gr letters are absent; the date of issue is given in front (and not at the back) of the royal head; the **garuḍa* on the rev is replaced by a fan-tailed *peacock; and the prose ld is replaced by a metrical one, reading *Vijitāvaniravanipatiḥ Kumāragupto divaṁ jayati*. On some *Madhyadeśa* type of silver coins of *Skandagupta, the circular ld is *Vijitāvaniravanipatir-jayati divaṁ Skandaguptoyam*, and on some other coins of this type, it is *Vijitāvaniravanipatis-Śrī-Skandagupto divaṁ jayati*. *Budhagupta was the last Imperial Gupta ruler to issue *Madhyadeśa* type of silver coins. These coins bear the ld *Vijitāvaniravanipatiḥ Śrī-Budhagupto divaṁ jayati*. This type of silver coins, with an average weight of around 36 grains, became very popular, and was imitated by the *Hūṇas, *Maukharis, *Pushpabhūtis, and others. These various coins of this type bear the royal head to the r, and the date of issue on the obv; the rev has a fan-tailed peacock, with the Br ld *Vijitāvaniravanipati Śrī*-[name of the issuer] *divaṁ jayati* (Ashvini Agrawal 1989; Allan 1914; Altekar 1957; R D Banerji 1933; S R Goyal 2005; P L Gupta 1998; Smith 1972; Thaplyal, forthcoming).

Kumāragupta I : *Madhyadeśa* type

Kumāragupta I : *Madhyadeśa* type

Mādhyamikā. Town. *Śibi.

Magadha series of punch marked coins. The Magadha series of punch marked coins are divided into a number of types by various scholars. For instance, P L Gupta and Terry Hardaker divide them into six types. Doubts have been expressed regarding the authenticity of the coins placed by them in Type I. Their Types II to IV represent the early local issues of the Magadha *janapada*. These coins are heavier than the coins of the later series, have a big and thin flan, and bear the six-armed symbol almost at the centre of the flan, and the solar symbol; there might be some other symbols, too, but the main types had not yet become fixed. Type V is a transitional series. The weight of the coin was gradually reduced from 'nearly half **śatamāna*' to **kārshāpaṇa*, which weight is adhered to in Type VI; the coins of Type VI, having a small and thick flan, are later issues and ultimately evolved into the imperial series (P L Gupta and Hardaker 1985; Hirano 1999-2000; Rajgor 2001).

Magha. Dynasty. The Maghas, known from coins, seals, and inscriptions ranging from years 51 to 139 (= 128 to 217 AD), are identified by some scholars with the Meghas known from the purāṇas as rulers in Kosala. There is a view that the dynasty should be taken as Māgha, named after its founder, and the name-endings of the kings of this dynasty should also be read as *māgha*. The Magha kings known from coins are King Magha, Vāsishṭhīputra Bhīmasena (also known from inscriptions of year 51 and 52), Poṭhasiri (also known from epigraphs of years 87 and 88), Bhadramagha (also known from inscriptions of years 83, 87, and 88), Śivamagha (also known from a seal and an epigraph), Vaiśravaṇa (also known from inscriptions, one being dated 107), and Bhīmavarman (also known from inscriptions dated years 130 and 139). Kings Satyamagha and Vijayamagha are known from coins alone. There are coins, on which the legends have been tentatively read as *Puramagha* (?), *Yajñamagha* (?), *Śaṅkhamagha* (?), and *Jayamagha* (?). The succession of kings from Bhīmasena to Bhīmavarman can be determined by the dated inscriptions; the other rulers seem to be later than Bhīmavarman. The Maghas appear to have ceased as a political power before *c* 300 AD. The epigraphs of the Maghas have been ascribed to the *Gupta era by Cunningham, Fleet, and Sohoni, the Kalachuri era by K P Jayaswal, and the *Śaka era by Marshall, Sten Konow, and Motichandra. Of these, the Gupta era is ruled out on the grounds that the Guptas could not have allowed members of a feudatory family to issue coins in their own name, and also that the Maghas should have mentioned the Guptas as their overlords in their epigraphs, which is not the case. These inscriptions appear to be dated in the Śaka era. The Magha coins, generally struck in base metal, bear the *tree device, and most of them also show the *bull device. Other symbols like the three-arched *hill, a ladder-like symbol, a **nandipada*, etc, may also be seen on some of these coins. The name of the issuer is given in the obv ld in bold Br characters. A M Shastri has published a hoard of 2,942 Magha coins from Kauśāmbī (Handa 2003-2004; Bopearachchi and Pieper 1998; A M Shastri 1979).

Magha. *Magha k.

Mahābhārata. Text. This epic mentions several coin denominations, like **nishka*, **śatamāna*, **suvarṇa*, **śāṇa*, and **prati*. It may be noted here that these are all indigenous coin denominations, and there is no mention of any foreign coin denomination, which are generally dated to the post-Maurya period. This might throw some light on the controversial issue of the date of this epic (V S Agrawala 1956).

Mahādeva. *Audumbara (?) chief (?). Both copper coins of Class I of *Audumdara coins, and silver coins of Class II of *Audumbara coins, bearing the name of Mahādeva, are available. While some scholars take Mahādeva, occurring on these coins, as the name of the tribal chief, others take it as referring to *Śiva, and suggest that, like the *Kuṇindas, the Audumbaras had dedicated their kingdom to their patron deity. The Śaiva affiliations of this tribe is attested by the names like *Śivadāsa and *Rudradāsa, and devices like *trident, trident-battleaxe, and *bull. There are also some scholars, who believe that the silver coins bearing the name of Mahādeva should not be included in the Audumbara series at all, on the grounds that the tribal name does not occur on these coins; the title **mahadeva* occurring on the other Audumbara coins is missing here; the tree, so characteristic of Audumbara coins, is also not seen on these coins; the title *rajaraja* used on most of these coins, is not a feature of Audumbara coins; these coins resemble the *Vemaki coins to a great extent; etc. But coins, on which the tribal name is conspicuous by its absence, are known in the Kuṇinda and the *Yaudheya series. Mahādeva might have been a powerful chief, who issued coins in his own name, without mentioning the name of the tribe, and assumed the title of *rajaraja*, 'king of kings'. As his own name was Mahādeva, the title *mahadeva* was not used, to avoid repetition. He seems to have ruled towards the end of the first century BC or the beginning of the first century AD. A M Shastri regards *Mahadeva* on these coins as the name of a chief, but is not in favour of associating him with the Audumbara tribe. Devendra Handa, however, regards *mahadeva* on these coins to stand for *māhādeva*, showing the Śaiva leanings of the issuer, as on the coins of other Audumbara chiefs. He suggests that *rajaraña* or *rajaraja* on the coins under discussion is not used as a title of the issuer, but represents his personal name—Rājarājan (Allan 1936; Chakrabortty 1931; Cunningham 1971b; K K Dasgupta 1974; Handa 2007a; Jayaswal 1988; Marshall 1975; Mitchiner 1975-1976; A M Shastri 1972; Smith 1972).

Mahadeva. Title. This title occurs on the *Audumbara coins for all the chiefs, except *Mahādeva. Some scholars believe that the chief of the tribal assembly was called *mahādeva*, in the sense of **mahārāja*, while others take it as referring to *Śiva and suggest that the king is referring to himself as a god. This title is not used for Mahādeva, perhaps to avoid repetition. A M Shastri suggests that *mahadeva* is here used in the sense of *māhādeva*, and denotes the Śaiva affiliations of the Audumbaras. This has the support of Devendra Handa (Allan 1936; Chakrabortty 1931; Cunningham 1971b; K K Dasgupta 1974; Handa 2007a; Jayaswal 1988; A M Shastri 1972; Smith 1972).

Mahākshatrapa. Title. This title was assumed on their coins by *Rañjuvula, *Śoḍāsha, and *Zeionises, among the Śakas. It was very popular among the *Western Kshatrapas, and a number of rulers of the *Kārddamaka dynasty assumed this title on their coins. Among the Kārddamaka Kshatrapas, this title is believed to have been assumed by the sovereign rulers, owing allegiance, perhaps, to no higher authority (Gardner 1971; Jenkins and Narain 1957; Jha and Rajgor 1994; Marshall 1975; Rapson 1975; Senior 2001; Whitehead 1914).

Maharaja. Title. This title, literally meaning 'great king', was first used by the *Indo-Greek rulers, and occurs on the coins of these kings as the Pkt rendering of the Greek title **basileus*, assumed by all of them. Among the Indo-Greeks, it denoted a sovereign, as well as a subordinate, ruler. But by the time of the *Śaka-Pahlavas, it had become the title of a subordinate ruler only, the sovereign rulers assuming the title of **basileos basileon megalos*/**maharaja rajatiraja* (or *rajaraja*) *mahata*. Among the *Kushāṇas, the title of *maharaja* occurs on the coins of *Kujula Kadphises, *V'ima Takshuma, *and *V'ima Kadphises, together with some other titles. Its Skt form is *mahārāja*. By the *Imperial Gupta period, the title of *mahārāja* was assumed by subordinate rulers/feudatories, and even by (hereditary) provincial governors towards the closing years of the rule of the *Imperial Guptas (Altekar 1957; Cunningham 1970; Gardner 1971; A N Lahiri 1965; Marshall 1975; Narain 1957a; Tarn 1980; Whitehead 1914).

Mahārāja. Title. **Maharaja*.

***Maharaja rajatiraja* (or *rajaraja*) *mahata*.** Title. Literally meaning 'great king, king of kings, the great', this was the title assumed by sovereign *Śaka-Pahlava rulers, and was the Pkt rendering of the Greek title **basileos basileon megalos*. The Śaka-Pahlava rulers, who assumed this title on coins are *Azes I, *Azilises, *Azes II, *Guḍa, *Abdagases and *Pakores. On the coins of *Maues, the Greek title is rendered into Pkt as *rajatiraja mahata* (Gardner 1971; Marshall 1975; Rapson 1987; Senior 2001; Tarn 1980; Whitehead 1914).

Mahārājādhirāja. Title. By the time of the *Imperial Guptas, **mahārāja* had become a title of the subordinate rulers/feudatories, and even (hereditary) provincial governors towards the closing years of the Imperial Gupta rule. The sovereign rulers assumed the title of *mahārājādhirāja*, and title is usually found on the coins of most of the Imperial Gupta rulers. Literally, it means 'great king of kings', and might be the Indianized form of **maharaja rajatiraja mahata* (Ashvini Agrawal 1989; Allan 1914; Altekar 1957; Fleet 1888; S R Goyal 2005; P L Gupta 1998; Sircar 1986; Smith 1972; Thaplyal, forthcoming).

***Mahata*.** Title. It is the Pkt rendering of **megas*, and used by *Hippostratos among the *Indo-Greeks, and by *Maues and *Azes I among the *Śaka-Pahlavas. The posthumous *Hermaios coins also bear this title on the rev. The Skt equivalent is *mahataḥ* (Cunningham

1970; Gardner 1971; A N Lahiri 1965; Marshall 1975; Narain 1957a; Tarn 1980; Whitehead 1914).

Mahataka. Title. It is the Pkt rendering of **megas*, and used by *Eukratides I. The Skt equivalent is *mahataka* (Cunningham 1970; Gardner 1971; A N Lahiri 1965; Marshall 1975; Narain 1957a; Tarn 1980; Whitehead 1914).

Māhishmatī. City coins. Māhishmatī was the capital of the southern part of Avantī, and is identified with Mandhata by some scholars, and with Maheshvar by others. Five coins of this city, all rectangular and die-struck, have come to the light. Four specimens have been struck on one side only, and bear a haloed figure (deity ?), a pellet surrounded by four crescents surmounted by a *hill, and the ld below reading *Mahisati*, in second century characters. The fifth is double die-struck, and has, on the obv, a *tree-in-railing, *horse, river with fishes, *Ujjain symbol, and the ld *Mahisati*, and indistinct symbols on the rev. Of these coins, one was found in Navdatoli, one at Ujjain, and one as Maheshvar. The find of one coin each in Maheshvar and Navdatoli (situated on the other side of Narmada opposite Maheshvar), would favour the identification of Māhishmatī with Maheshvar. The *provenance* of the two such coins in the British Museum, London, is not known (Bela Lahiri 1974; Bela Lahiri 1976; J P Singh 1971).

Mahiśvara. Title. Occurring on the coins of the *Kushāṇa ruler, *V'ima Kadphises, this title might be considered as the Pkt rendering of Skt *mahīśvara*, 'lord of the earth'. But, as the Śaiva inclinations of this ruler are quite evident, it seems more appropriate to the regard this title as the Pkt rendering of *māheśvara*, 'devotee of *Śiva' (Cunningham 1971a; Gardner 1971; Rosenfield 1967; Whitehead 1914).

Majjhima-kāhāvaṇa. Coin denomination. Although it is difficult to ascertain as to which coin is implied by *majjhima-kāhāvaṇa* in the **Aṅgavijjā*, it is possible that it refers to the silver (**kārshāpaṇa* ?) coins [**jahaṇṇa-kāhāvaṇa*, **uttama-kāhāvaṇa*] (V S Agrawala 1957).

Makara. Symbol; mount of *Gaṅgā. It is a mythical aquatic creature, represented in art as an elephantine crocodile, that is a crocodile with its snout in the shape of an elephant's trunk. It is conceived as a lusty creature, and adorns the standard of Kāma. It is sometimes represented as the mount of Rati, the consort of Kāma, but the creature is more intimately associated with *Gaṅgā as her mount. The *makara* as the mount of Gaṅgā is seen on the *Tiger-slayer type of *Samudragupta, and the Tiger-slayer and *Rhinoceros-slayer types of *Kumāragupta I. On the last-mentioned type, a stalked lotus is held in the trunk of the *makara* (Allan 1914; Altekar 1957; Banerjea 2002; R B Pande 1988; Rao 1985).†

Kumāragupta I : Tiger-slayer type

Malakand hoard. This hoard consists of 257 debased silver coins in the name of *Azes, *Azes II with *Aśpavarman, *Gondopharnes, and *Abdagases. However, of the coins in the name of Azes, only one coin was issued by him, and the rest are believed to be posthumous coins, mostly issued in his name by the *Apracharajas. This hoard, probably found at Malakand, in the North West Frontier Province of Pakistan, is now in the collection of the Smithsonian Institute, Washington, DC (Bopearachchi 1993; Senior 2001; Prashant Srivastava 2007a).

Mālava. Tribe. According to the *Mahābhārata*, the Mālavas were the descendants of the 100 sons, whom King Aśvapati begat on his queen, Mālavī, as a consequence of the boon Sāvitrī obtained from Yama. This tribe (Malloi) is mentioned by the classical writers as unsuccessfully resisting Alexander by forming an alliance with the Oxydrakai (= *Kshudrakas), in the fourth century BC. The epics, the purāṇas, the *Mahābhāshya*, the *Chāndravyākaraṇa*, and the *Kāśikā* also refer to the Mālavas, often along with the Kshudrakas, and the last two texts mention them as a *saṁgha*, whose members lived by the profession of arms. Hiuen-tsang refers to them as Mo-la-po. References to the Mālavas are also found in the Nasik inscription of Ushavadāta, the Nandsa *yūpa* inscription of (Vikrama) year 283 (= 225 AD), and the Allahabad pillar inscription of *Samudragupta. The classical writers place them in Punjab near the river Ravi. The *Mahābhārata* also mentions them in association with the tribes inhabiting the Punjab region, like the *Trigartas, and Madras, and the *Śibis, thus showing that the Mālavas inhabited the Punjab region.

The *Vishṇupurāṇa* and the evidence of the inscriptions and their earlier coins, however, suggest that they inhabited eastern Rajasthan. *Mālavagaṇa-vishaya* mentioned in the Nandsa inscription is believed by Altekar to comprise the former states of Udaipur, Jaipur, and Tonk, and the district of Ajmer. They appear to have migrated to the Rajasthan from Punjab under the pressure of the Greek invasion; then they moved further south and occupied the region in western Madhya Pradesh, now called Malwa after them. In *c* 350 AD, they submitted to Samudragupta. Perhaps, the Mālavīya brāhmaṇas of Gujarat, Madhya Pradesh, and Uttar Pradesh are the descendants of the Mālavas. Mālava coins are all in copper, and mostly round in shape, although square and rectangular coins are also known. Cunningham places these coins between 250 BC and 250 AD, but most of the scholars prefer the date from the second or first century BC to the fourth century AD, when the Mālavas submitted to Samudragupta; Rapson, however, believes that the upper limit for these coins may be as late as the fifth century AD. The heaviest Mālava coin weighs 43.84 grains, but the smallest coin is only 1.7 grains; most of the other types weigh below 15 grains. The small size of these coins, and their being confined mostly to the area around Nagar, shows that they were meant for local transactions by the self-sufficient agricultural community, and not for external trade. Devendra Handa has recently reported some coins from Sunam (which forms a part of Malwa of Punjab), which he ascribes to the Mālava tribe. If this be correct, then it would follow that the Mālavas had issued coins in the Punjab region also, before they moved to the Rajasthan from where most of their coins are reported. The round coins usually have the Br ld on the obv, which may be *Mālavānāṁ jaya* or its variant; very few coins of this shape have devices like tree, *lion, or female figure on the obv. The rev bears symbols like the sun, **nandipada*, vase, *tree-in-railing, or *undulating line, or devices like *bull, dancing *peacock, human head with curly hair, etc. The square or rectangular coins have been divided into two classes. The coins of Class I have tree-in-railing or solar symbol and the ld *Mālavānāṁ jaya* or its variant on the obv; the rev has devices like vase or bull. The coins of Class II have some enigmatic legends like *Magaja, Mapojaya, Bhapaṁyana, Yama, Pachha, Jāmaka, Paya, Māśapa, Magachha*, etc. But the *provenance*, type, fabric, and the occurrence of the tribal name on one of these coins, leave no doubt about their being Mālava coins. The obv of these coins is usually occupied by the ld; very rarely, we find symbols, like tree-in-railing, on this side of the coins. The rev has devices like lion, elephant, or the *Mālava symbol. In these curious legends, Carllyle recognizes the names of some 40 Mālava chiefs. Smith, considering some as variants of the same name (like *Yama* and *Maya*), thinks that there were about 20 chiefs, and since their names sound non-Indian, he takes them as of foreign origin. But it is difficult to explain the relationship between the indigenous Mālavas and their foreign chiefs, and also the two issuing coins simultaneously. K K Dasgupta takes these as names of indigenous chiefs of non-Aryan stock. Goyal points out that the names of Mālava chiefs, like Jayasena, Śrīsoma (or Nandisoma, as read by some scholars like B Ch Chhabra), etc, occurring in the Nandsa inscription are Sanskritic, and this, together with their performance of vedic sacrifices, as known from that inscription, would rather suggest Aryan origin. According to Bhandarkar, *ma* is the abbreviation of the tribal name *Mālava*, and the remaining letters are contractions of words; thus, *ga* stands for *gaṇa*, and *ja* for *jaya*, and *Magaja* would, thus, stand for *Mālava gaṇasya jaya*. K P Jayaswal tried to explain these legends as personal names with the title *mahārāja*. *Mapaya* and *Magaja*, for example, would stand for *Mahārāja Paya* and *Mahārāja Gaja*, respectively. But Allan objects to this on the grounds that the letters following *ma* do not make intelligible names, and such contractions as *ma* for *mahārāja* are not found in Indian numismatics. He himself regards these legends as 'meaningless attempt to reproduce parts of *Mālavānāṁ jaya*'. According to Sircar, these coins with the curious legends are imitations of Mālava coins, manufactured by incompetent smiths. Nothing definite can be said about the actual significance of these legends (Allan 1936; Chakrabortty 1931; Cunningham 1971b; K K Dasgupta 1974; S R Goyal 1995b; Handa 2007a; Jayaswal 1988; Marshall 1975; Mitchiner 1975-1976; Smith 1972).

Mālava *saṁvat*. *Vikrama *saṁvat*.

Mālava symbol. *Ujjain symbol.

Mamvadi. *Śaka-Pahlava (?) k. He is known from a unique *tetradrachm*, bearing the figure of horseman king holding whip on the obv, and *Zeus Nikephoros on the rev. The obv Gr ld is mutilated and only **basileuontos* can be read; the rev Kh ld, too, is mutilated but the name of the issuer may be read as Mamvadi. He seems to have ruled somewhere in the Gandhāra region after Azes (Senior 2001).

Manā. The *Ṛigveda* has a term, *manā*, which is specifically qualified as *hiraṇyayā*, 'golden'. This *manā* has been taken to mean a gold coin by certain scholars, and, keeping in view India's trade contact with Babylonia, attempts have been made to associate it with *mina* of Babylonia, the heavier variety of which weighed, on an average, 15,606 grains, and the lighter variety, 7,966 grains. But whether *manā* in the *Ṛigveda* was a coin denomination, is uncertain, and Macdonell and Keith take it to mean 'the desirable object' (Macdonell and Keith 1995; Maity 1970b).

Huvishka

Manaobago. Avestan moon god. The ld *Manaobago* on *Kushāṇa coins seems to stand for the Iranian moon god. Attempts have been made to trace in *Manaobago*, the Avestan Amesha Spenta Vohumano, the spirit of wisdom. The component of the ld, *manao*, seems to be derived from the root *mā*, meaning 'to measure'. *Manaobago* is, therefore, the 'god of measure'. In several cultures the world over, time was measured on the basis of the waxing and waning of the moon. Hence, the moon-god may be regarded as the 'god of measure'. On the rev of some gold coins of *Kanishka I, the enthroned moon-god has a crescent behind his shoulders, and is four-armed. He holds sceptre and callipers in two of his hands, the attributes in the other two hands being indistinct, although a **chakra* and a diadem have been suggested. The same deity appears in almost the same posture on the rev of some gold coins of *Huvishka; he is helmeted, and holds sceptre, fire, and wreath in three of his hands, the fourth one being placed on the hip. The callipers in the hand of the deity also indicate his function of a measurer [of time]. Interestingly, what has been identified as a wreath in one of the hands of *Manaobago* on the coins of Huvishka, is regarded as a circle surrounded by 12 dots signifying the 12 months of the year or the 12 signs of the zodiac, by Cunningham. This, too, would favour the identification of *Manaobago* with the moon-god as the measurer of time. The representation of the deity as four-armed has been taken as suggestive of Indian iconographic influence (Bhaskar Chattopadhyay 1977; Cunningham 1971a; Darmesteter 1974; Gardner 1971; Rosenfield 1967; Stein 1888).

Manusmṛiti. Text. This oldest and the most famous of the smṛiti works, which claims for itself divine origin, seems to be based upon a *Mānavadharmasūtra* (now lost). Its date is not known for sure, although it is generally believed that its formulation may be placed some time between 200 BC and 200 AD. In the eighth chapter of the text, a **suvarṇa* of 80 *rattīs* is mentioned as the standard gold coin, a **dharaṇa* or **purāṇa* of 32 *rattīs* as the standard silver coin, and a **kārshāpaṇa* weighing one *karsha* as the standard copper coin; later authorities give 80 *rattīs* as the weight of a *kārshāpaṇa*. The text also refers to gold **māshaka*, **pala*, and *dharaṇa*; and silver *māshaka* (Bühler 2001).

Mao. Avestan moon god. The ld *Mao* on *Kushāṇa coins stands for the Iranian moon god, Māh, venerated in the Māh Yasht of the *Avesta*. *Mao* is derived from the root *mā*, meaning 'to measure', and is the nominative form of the Avestan *mās*. Thus, under the name *Mao* also, the Iranian moon-god is depicted on coins as the measurer of time, like **Manaobago*. On the Kushāṇa coins, *Mao* is generally depicted as a diademed male deity, with a crescent behind his shoulders signifying his lunar character. On the gold coins of *Kanishka I, he holds a sceptre in his l hand, while the right is advanced. The depiction of this deity on the coins of *Huvishka shows variety. On some gold coins, he holds a sceptre in the l hand and callipers in the right. On others, he holds a diadem or a wreath in one hand and a wreath or sword in the other hand. Some gold coins show *Mao* standing face to face with *Mihira. On the rev of some copper coins of Huvishka, the deity labelled as *Mao* is female, and stands with a **cornucopiae* in her hands. While scholars like Whitehead feel that this is a figure of **Ardochsho* wrongly labelled as *Mao*, other see in the representation of *Mao* as a female deity, the impact of western Asia, where the lunar deities are usually female (Bhaskar Chattopadhyay 1977; Cunningham 1971a; Darmesteter 1974; Gardner 1971; Rosenfield 1967; Stein 1888; Whitehead 1914).

Kanishka I

Huvishka

Māsaka-kākaṇī. Coin denomination. Mentioned in the **Aṅgavijjā*, it seems to denote the **kākaṇī* which was one-fourth of a **māshaka* coin. On the basis of a reference in Paṇini, it is believed to be a silver coin, although the possibility of its being a copper coin cannot altogether be ruled out (V S Agrawala 1957).

Māsha. Coin denomination (?). D R Bhandarkar is of the view that, while *māsha* is always a unit of the Indian weight system, its weight depending on the metal, **māshaka*, as a rule, denotes a coin of that metal. However, some *Niya Kh documents refer to *māsha*, and the context seems to suggest that it has been used there as a coin denomination. A document, pertaining to the reign of Hinajhadeva Vijitasiṁha and dated towards the end of the third century AD, refers to the purchase of a camel for 8,000 *māshas* (R C Agrawala 1954a; Burrow 1940; Stein 1929).

Māshaka. Coin denomination. D R Bhandarkar is of the view that, while **māsha* is always a unit of the Indian weight system, its weight depending on the metal, *māshaka*, as a rule, denotes a coin of that metal. A *māshaka* was one-sixteenth of the standard coin, whether **suvarṇa*, **dharaṇa*, or **kārshāpaṇa*. In Manu and Yājñavalkya, a gold *māshaka* weighs 5 *rattīs*, while a silver one, 2 *rattīs*. Sixteen *māshakas* of gold made one **suvarṇa*, and 16 *māshakas* of silver made one silver *dharaṇa*. In the *Arthaśāstra* of Kauṭilya, *māshaka* is the standard copper coin with several submultiples, while **paṇa* is the standard silver coin, of the period. As a coin denomination (form, *māsaka*), it occurs in the *Bakhshali manuscript, and also in the **Aṅgavijjā* where the context seems to indicate that it was a copper coin, 5 *rattīs* is weight [**rayaya-māsaka*, **suvaṇṇa-māsaka*] (R C Agrawala 1954b; V S Agrawala 1957; Altekar 1940; D R Bhandarkar 1984; Bühler 2001; Chakrabortty 1931; Sircar 1952; Sircar 1968).

Maśra. Late *Kushāṇa chief. This chief is known from some gold coins reported by Prem Lata Pokharna, Joe Cribb, and others. The obv of the coins has the device of the *king sacrificing at an altar, and holding a **chakradhvaja* in his l hand as seen on the coins of *Kācha. The obv ld reads *Shaonanoshao Koshan*. The vertical Br ld, *Maśra*, is engraved in the right field, outside the *chakradhvaja*.

The rev has an enthroned female deity, holding a **cornicopiae* and a noose, and labelled as **Ardochsho*. There is a suggestion that this late Kushāṇa type might have served as the prototype for the coins of Kācha (Cribb 1985a).

Mathurā. Situated on the right bank of the river Yamuna, Mathurā was the capital of the Śūrasenas. The early coins of Mathurā may be classified as those of the indigenous rulers and those of the Śaka satraps. In the first group, there are two different families, with *mitra*- and *datta*-ending names, respectively. Of the thirteen early rulers, six have *mitra*-ending names : *Brahmamitra, *Dṛiḍhamitra, *Gomitra, *Satyamitra, *Sūryamitra, and *Vishṇumitra. They all show on the obv *Lakshmī with lotus in the r hand and other symbols, and on the rev usually three *elephants with riders. The kings of Mathurā with *datta*-ending names are *Bhavadatta, *Kāmadatta, *Purushadatta, *Rāmadatta, *Śeshadatta, and *Uttamadatta. Of these, Purushadatta, with the title of **rājan*, is placed as the earliest. After the Datta kings came *Balabhūti, who has a different name-ending. The Datta kings ruled immediately after the Mitra kings, though some scholars hold that Śaka rule intervened and that the Datta kings were vassals of the *Kushāṇas. Goyal points out that the *Ujjain symbol is characteristic of Mitra coins, and the symbol resembling the Br letter *śa*, that of the Datta kings. The latter device also occurs on the coins of *Hagāna, *Hagāmasha, *Śivadatta, and *Śivaghosha, all of whom also ruled over the Mathurā region. The most common symbol met with on Mathurā coins is a tree-like symbol, which occurs on indigenous as well as Śaka coins; Bela Lahiri associates it with Lakshmī. The rule of the Śaka *satrap*, *Rañjuvula, who is placed in the beginning of the first century AD, seems to have followed that of the Mitra and Datta kings. His early coinage shows the impact of *Indo-Greek and *Śaka-Pahlava coinages, but he also issued coins of the indigenous Mathurā type, with Lakshmī and a Br ld on the obv, and *Gajalakshmī on the rev. He was succeeded by his son, *Śoḍāsha, who ruled as both **kshatrapa* and **mahākshatrapa*, and issued coins of the Mathurā type only. Coins of *Taraṇaḍāsa, Ghaṭāka, Hagāna, Hagāmasha, Śivadatta, and Śivaghosha, are also known from Mathurā. The Śakas in Mathurā were replaced by the Kushāṇas; perhaps, *Kanishka I was the first Kushāṇa ruler to occupy that region. The city was an important centre, perhaps the eastern

Mathurā

capital of the Kushāṇas, and remained under their hold at least till the rule of *Vāsudeva I. After *c* 200 AD, it came under the rule of the *Nāgas. In the post-Kushāṇa phase, coins of Śiśuchaṁdāta (or Śaśachaṇḍāta, as Goyal suggests) and Vīrasena are found. The latter is taken as a Nāga ruler, and is identified with the homonym known from an inscription from Jankhat (district Farrukhabad) (Allan 1936; S R Goyal 1995b; Bela Lahiri 1974; Mitchiner 1975-1976).

Maues

Maues

Maues. *Śaka-Pahlava k; one of the earliest known ones; *c* first century BC. He is believed to be among the earliest Śaka-Pahlava rulers to issue coins bearing the king's name. He has been associated with that branch of the Śaka-Pahlavas, which crossed the Pamirs from the Ili valley, and settled in the Swat-Hazara-Kashmir (Chinese Ki-pin) region, some time after 160 BC. On some of his coins, Maues bears the subordinate titles of **basileos* and **maharaja*, while on others, he is **basileos basileon megalos* and **rajatiraja mahata*. This has led to the suggestion that Maues, perhaps, started his career as a subordinate ruler of *Vonones, and asserted independence in northwestern India when *Spalirises overthrew Vonones. But on the coin Maues issued in association with his mother, *Machene, he has the titles of *rajatiraja mahata*, showing his sovereign status even during his minority. He is believed to have advanced west into the Indo-Greek dominions from the Swat-Hazara-Kashmir region. His rule over Gandhāra is vouched for by the Taxila copperplate inscription of [Vikrama *saṁvat*] 78. It appears that when Spalirises, the father of *Azes I, was overthrown in Arachosia, Azes I was forced to come to northwestern India, where he defeated Maues, occupied his throne, and forced him to rule as a subordinate ruler. It was during this period that Maues issued coins with the subordinate titles. He issued coins in both silver and copper, and these are both round and square in shape. His joint type with *Machene seems to be his earliest monetary issue. This is a silver coin, bearing the figure of an enthroned female and the name of Machene in the Gr ld on the obv, and *Zeus Nikephoros and the name of *Maues in the Kh ld on the reverse. He independently struck at least four types of silver coins. One silver type has *Zeus standing with thunderbolt and sceptre on the obv, and wreath- and palm-bearing *Nike on the rev. Another type has *Helios on biga on the obv, and enthroned Zues on the rev. The fourth silver type bears the enthroned figure of a city goddess on the obv, and Zeus Nikephoros on the rev. The obv devices on his copper coins include horseman king, standing king, enthroned city-goddess, *Zeus standing with thunderbolt and sceptre, enthroned Zeus (sometimes holding out Nike), *Helios on biga, *Herakles standing with club and lion's skin, *Artemis standing, *Poseidon trampling on a river god, *Apollo standing, a male deity (*Śiva ?) standing with trident and club, lunar goddess standing, etc. The rev devices on copper coins include enthroned Zeus, Zeus Nikephoros, thundering *Athena, Nike standing with wreath and palm, *Amphitrite between two vines, king seated on cushions, etc. Osmund Bopearachchi has reported a square bronze type of Maues, bearing enthroned Zeus Nikephoros, on the obv, and standing *Herakles crowning himself with his r hand, and holding a club, palm and lion's skin in his l hand, on the rev. One interesting square copper type has an Indian deity walking to the l; according to the R C Senior, he holds a club in his r hand, and a plough over his left shoulder. Senior identifies this deity as 'Bala-Kṛishṇa', by which he, perhaps, means a syncretic deity, *Balarāma-*Vāsudeva-Kṛishṇa. But this identification is, by no means, certain. The rev of this type has a goddess, holding fillet, standing to the r. Animals like *lion, *elephant, *bull, *horse, etc, or simply their head, are seen mostly on the rev, but sometimes on the obv also. Symbols like **aegis*, **tripod lebes*, bow and quiver, and **caduceus*, are also sometimes depicted on the rev. The obv ld is mostly in Gr; the rev Pkt ld is written in the Kh script. Only on one copper coin, there is no ld on the obv, and the Gr ld occupies the rev. Maues uses the title **basileus/*maharaja*, or **basileos basileon megalos/*rajatiraja mahata*. In the Kh ld, the form of his name is Moä (Bopearachchi 2004; Cunningham 1971a; Gardner 1971; Jenkins and Narain 1957; van Lohuizen de Leeuw 1949; Marshall 1975; B N Mukherjee 1969a; Rapson 1987; Senior 2001; Sircar 1980b; Prashant Srivastava 1996a; Prashant Srivastava 2008b; Tarn 1980; Whitehead 1914).†

Maues

Maues

Maukhari. Coins, general features. A number of Maukhari families are known to have ruled in the Gaya region, in Rajasthan, and even in Karnataka in southern India. But the Maukharis of Kanauj played a significant role in the political history of northern India in the sixth-seventh centuries AD. The early kings of this dynasty include Harivarman, Ādityavarman, and Īśvaravarman; all three seem to be subordinate to the *Imperial Guptas. Īśvaravarman's son, *Īśānavarman, was the first independent ruler of the family. He made extensive conquests, assumed the title of *mahārājādhirāja, implying sovereign status, and issued coins. He was followed by *Śarvavarman, *Avantivarman, and Grahavarman, respectively. A Nalanda seal mentions King Su... as the son of Avantivarman; he might have ruled for a short period after the death of Grahavarman at the hands of *Śaśāṅka and Devagupta, before *Harsha took control of Kanauj, or he ascended the throne of Kanauj after Harsha (and probably after Aruṇāśva also). Three Maukhari rulers, Īśānavarman, Śarvavarman, and Avantivarman, are known to have issued coins. Thirty-two such coins, all in silver and with an average weight of 36 grains, are known from the *Bhitaura hoard. They are of the **Madhyadeśa* type of Imperial Gupta silver coins, with the royal head to the r and the date of issue on the obv, and a fan-tailed *peacock with the Br ld reading *Vijitāvaniravanipati Śrī*-[name of the issuer] *divaṁ jayati* on the rev. The reading of the dates on these coins is extremely doubtful, so much so, that N G Majumdar, who examined the coins, reported that the dates have generally totally disappeared and it is not possible to read them. The era used on these coins is also not certain. As some of the dates seem to have two, and some, three digits, the possibility of the use of at least two different eras cannot altogether be ruled out (Richard Burn 1906; D Devahuti 1964; D Devahuti 2001; Pires 1934; Thaplyal 1985).

Megas. Title. Meaning 'great', this title was first adopted in India by *Eukratides I, perhaps in imitation of the Seleukid ruler, Antiochos III, as was also done by the Arsakid rulers, Phriapatios and Phraates I. On some of his coins, he rendered **basileos* and *megalou* separately as *rajasa*, 'king', and **mahatakasa*, 'great', respectively, but on others, we have the combined rendering **maharajasa*, 'great king'. The title was also used by *Hippostratos, and *Apollodotos. The former renders it into Pkt as **mahata* (Cunningham 1970; Gardner 1878; Gardner 1971; A N Lahiri 1965; Marshall 1975; Narain 1957a; Tarn 1980; Whitehead 1914; Wroth 1903).

Menander I. *Indo-Greek k; scion of the family of *Demetrios II; *c* second century BC. It is generally believed that he is identical with King Milinda of the Buddhist text, *Milindapañho*. His wife was *Agathokleia, who might have been a daughter of *Demetrios I. Tarn suggested that he was initially a general of Demetrios I, and assumed kingship on the death of his master, the marriage with Agathokleia being the basis of his claim to the royalty. The find of his coins from Begram and Kabul, and in the Mir Zakah hoard leaves little doubt that he ruled over the Kabul valley. From there, he may have endeavoured to occupy Gandhāra, Arachosia, and Seistan. The discovery of his coins in the excavations at Taxila, in the Sheikhano Dheri hoard near Charsadda, at Charsadda itself, and at places like Rajjar, Mardan, Peshawar, and Rawalpindi, shows that he ruled over Gandhāra, with its two centres of Takshaśilā and Pushkalāvatī. However, no coin of this ruler is reported from Arachosia and Seistan, and hence, there is no definite evidence of his hold over these two regions, although Narain feels that some parts of northern and eastern Arachosia might have been included in his dominions. Menander also conquered Hazara, the Swat valley, and Udyāna, the country between the rivers Suvāstu and Gaurī; the Sind-Sagar *doab*, too, seem to have been under his control. Narain believes that the two sources—Kālidāsa, and the Yugapurāṇa section of the *Gārgīsaṁhitā*, speak of the same Indo-Greek invasion, and as it occurred towards the end of the reign of Pushyamitra Śuṅga around 150 BC, it must have been led by Menander. Numismatic evidence suggests that he left behind a minor son, *Strato I, and his widow looked after the kingdom during the minority of her son. He issued one silver type, struck on the Attic standard. The rest of the silver types, and all the copper types, are struck on the Indian standard. All the coins are die-struck pieces. The silver coins are all round in shape. The copper types are mostly square in shape, but two types are round in shape. The obv of the silver coins mostly bears the royal bust on the obv. On some types, the diademed bust of the king is to the r, sometimes in Medusa helmet, but on others, the royal bust (often helmeted) is to the l, thrusting javelin. The rev of most of the silver coins bears the figure of thundering *Athena, with an **aegis* on her left arm, but one type has an *owl to the r. One silver type has the helemeted bust of Athena to the r on the obv, and an owl to the r on the rev. There is great variety in copper coins, as regards the obv and rev devices. The obv of a number of copper types has the royal bust, sometimes to the r, and at other times to the l and thrusting javelin. The rev of these types has, variously, thundering Athena as on some silver types; or

Menander

Menander

Menander

wreath- and palm-bearing winged *Nike standing to the r; or even lion's skin (of *Herakles) on one type. Another common obv device of the copper types of Menander is the helmeted bust of Athena to the r. The rev device on such coins, variously, is wreath- and palm-bearing winged Nike standing to the r; or thundering Athena to the l, with an *aegis* on her left arm; or buckler with *Gorgon's head; or owl; or prancing horse to the r. One copper type has a young male head, wearing a wreath, to the r on the obv, and a dolphin to the r on the rev. Other copper coins are, variously, of the '*Bull's head: **Tripod lebes*', '*Elephant : *Aṅkuśa*', 'Elephant's head : *Club', 'Bactrian *camel : Bull's head', and '*Boar's head : Palm branch' types. One copper type is very significant, in that its obv has the Buddhist *dharmachakra*, and the rev has the palm branch. This type is taken as indicative of the Buddhist leanings of Menander. Osmund Bopearachchi reports a copper type in the Peshawar Museum, which bears the head of *Poseidon to the r on the obv, and dolphin on the rev. There are some anepigraphous staters, bearing the helmeted bust of Athena to the r on the obv, and a horned owl to the r on the rev. This type is ascribed by some scholars to Menander, but others contest this ascription on the grounds that the owl on these gold coins is not of the Athenian variety as on the coins of Menander, but is of the Indian variety. Further, there is the question as to why Menander should issue his only gold series without inscribing his name on it. These staters, which bear the Gr letter *A* in the left field on the rev, seem to have been rightly attributed to *Agathokleia, the wife of Menander. The silver coins of Menander, struck on the Attic standard, bear the Gr ld on the rev. But the rest of the silver types, and all the copper types, which have been struck on the Indian standard, bear the Gr ld on the obv, and the Pkt ld, written in the Kh script, on the rev. Besides the title of **basileus*, Menander assumed the epithet **soteros* on his coins. These are rendered into Pkt as **maharaja* and **tratara*, respectively. The Pkt form of the name of the ruler, as met with on coins, is Menadra. Posthumous coins in the name of Menander are reported by A D H Bivar (Bivar 1970; Bopearachchi 1993; Bopearachchi and Pieper 1998; Bopearachchi and Rahman 1995; Cunningham 1970; Gardner 1971; A N Lahiri 1965; Marshall 1975; Narain 1957a; Senior 2001; Sircar 1980a; Prashant Srivastava 1996a; Tarn 1980; Whitehead 1914).†

Menander II. *Indo-Greek k; *c* first half of the first century BC. There are some silver and copper coins, all struck on the Indian standard, which bear the name of Menander **Dikaios*. These coins have 'nothing in common' with the coins bearing the name of Menander **Soteros* [*Menander I], and even the canting type (thundering *Athena) of Menander *Soteros* is not known for Menander *Dikaios*. The monograms on the two series are also not common. Hence, Menander *Dikaios* may be regarded as Menander II, different from Menander *Soteros* or Menander I. In view of the use of the rev device of king on prancing horse by both Menander II and *Artemidoros, the two might be regarded as near contemporaries ruling over Taxila, and Menander II might be assigned to the first-second decades of the first century BC, although R C Senior would place him *c* 65 BC. He struck coins in silver and copper, all based on the Indian standard. The silver coins of Menander II are round in shape, while the copper ones are square in shape. They are all die-struck pieces. The obv of all the silver types has the diademed bust of the king to the r, sometimes wearing Medusa helmet. The rev of two silver types has winged *Nike, bearing wreath and palm, 'striding to the r', while that of the third type has the figure of the king on prancing horse to the r. One copper type has Athena standing with spear and shield on the obv, and a *panther to the l on the rev. The other copper type has a helmeted male warrior (king ?) carrying spear and shield on the obv, and panther to the r on the rev. All the types bear the Gr ld on the obv, and the Pkt ld, written in the Kh script, on the rev. Besides the title of **basileus*, Menander II assumed the epithet *dikaios* on his coins. These are rendered into Pkt as **maharaja* and **dhramika*, respectively. The Pkt form of the name of the ruler, as met with on coins, is Menadra (Bopearachchi 1993; Bopearachchi 1994; Bopearachchi and Pieper 1998; Bopearachchi and Rahman 1995; Cunningham 1970; Gardner 1971; A N Lahiri 1965; Marshall 1975; Narain 1957a; Rapson 1987; Senior 2001; Sircar 1980a; Tarn 1980; Whitehead 1914).[†]

Metrago Boudo. *Buddha, Maitreya.

Mian Khan Sanghou hoard. This hoard of 83 silver coins of the *Indo-Greeks was discovered in an earthen pot by a farmer while ploughing a field in Mian Khan Sanghou in district Mardan. The rulers represented in this hoard include *Antmachos II, *Apollodotos, *Menander I, and *Zoilos I (Bopearachchi 1994).

Mihirakula. *Hūṇa chief; son of *Toramāṇa; first half of the sixth century AD. All the sources at our disposal unanimously describe him as a cruel and violent king. From the *Christian Topography* of the Greek navigator, Kosmas, it appears that the kingdom he inherited from his father was confined to the west of the river Indus. Sung-yün, the Chinese ambassador to the Hūṇa court in 520 AD, describes him as the king of Gandhāra; according to Hiuen-tsang, his capital was Sākala (modern Sialkot). Kosmas refers to him as the lord of India; Hiuen-tsang also refers to his subduing the whole of India; Kalhaṇa mentions his conquest of southern India and Srilanka. All these statements seem to be exaggerated. But there is no doubt that he revived the aggressive policy of his father, and occupied a large part of northern India, at least up to Gwalior. However, he had to suffer reverses at the hands of Yaśodharman, the Aulikara king of Mandasor, and of the *Imperial Gupta ruler, *Narasiṁhagupta Bālāditya. Mihirakula died some time after his defeat at the hands of Narasiṁhagupta. Mihirakula issued very few silver coins. They bear on the obv, the bust of the Sassanian type, with an umbrella in front, and *bull, left, and the ld *Jayatu Mihirakula*. The rev has traces of a *fire altar and supporters. A variety of this class of coins has only a bull in front of the Sassanian bust on the obv, sometimes accompanied by a trident, and the ld *Jayatu Vṛishadhvaja*; the rev is the same. These latter coins are relatively smaller in size. The copper coins of Mihirakula are divided into three classes. Class I comprises large sized coins with mounted king and the ld *Mihirakula* on the obv, and the figure of *Lakshmī on the rev. Class II consists of medium sized coins, bearing the figure of the *king sacrificing at an altar and the ld *Shāhi Mihirakula* or simply *Mihirakula* on the obv, and seated Lakshmī with **cornucopiae* on the rev. Class III has small sized coins, with bust of the Sassanian type and the ld *Śrī Mihirakula* on the obv, and a humped bull with the ld *Jayatu Vṛisha* on the rev. These coins with the Śaiva symbols of bull and trident, together with the legends *Jayatu Vṛisha* and *Jayatu Vṛishadhvaja*, indicate the Śaivite inclination of Mihirakula, also hinted at in the Mandasor inscription of Yasodharman (Altekar 1986b; Biswas 1973;

Cunningham 1962; Cunningham 1967; R C Majumdar 1988; Sircar 1986; Upendra Thakur 1967a; Upendra Thakur 1967b).†

Miiro. Avestan sun god. The ld *Miiro*, and its variants like *Mioro*, *Meiro*, and *Miuro*, on *Kushāṇa coins stands for Mihira, which is the corrupt form of the name of the Iranian solar deity, Mihr, invoked in the *Avesta*, especially in the Mihr Yasht. He is closely associated with *Ahuramazda, and is said to preside over and direct the course of the sun. There is a suggestion Mihira is the god of sunlight, 'without being the sun itself'. The name of this Avestan deity, his close association with Ahuramazda, and his functions, connect him with the vedic Mitra so closely associated with Asura *Varuṇa. The figure of Mihira occurs on the coins issued by *Kanishka I and *Huvishka. The radiate and diademed deity is always shown standing, usually with a sword tied at his waist. The attributes in his hands on the Kushāṇa coins, variously, are, sceptre, wreath, callipers, etc. While the sceptre and the wreath might indicate that he bestows royalty and victory, the callipers indicate his role as a measurer of time like **Mao* and **Manaobago*. Interestingly, the chariot and horses, so intimately associated in art with the Greek sun god, *Helios, and the Indian, *Sūrya, are conspicuous by their absence in the representations of Mihira on Kushāṇa coins (Bhaskar Chattopadhyay 1977; Cunningham 1971a; Darmesteter 1974; Gardner 1971; Rosenfield 1967; Stein 1888; Whitehead 1914).

Kanishka I

Huvishka

Huvishka

Mina. It was the weight of 50 *shekels* or **staters*, and is to be distinguished from the weight *mina*, which was used for commodities, and was equal to 60 *shekels*. The *mina* was generally worth 100 **drachms*, the weight standards varying widely with time and place (Hill 1906; Junge 1984).

Mir Zakah hoard 1. This hoard was discovered in May 1947 in the village of Mir Zakah, about 53 km northeast of Gardez in Afghanistan, before the excavation of the site, the results of which were published by Raoul Curiel and Daniel Schlumberger in 1953. The entire composition of the hoard is not certain. This hoard consisted of 5,837 *bent bars and *punch marked coins, five Greek coins, 2,757 *Indo-Greek coins, 4,419 *Śaka-Pahlava coins, and 37 *Kushāṇa coins. The rulers represented in this hoard are almost the same as those in the *Mir Zakah hoard 2 (Bopearachchi 1994; Bopearachchi and Rahman 1995; Senior 2001).

Mir Zakah hoard 2. This large hoard, dubbed the 'mother of all hoards', reported along with over 27 kg of gold jewellery and plate, began to come to the light in 1992; Bopearachchi gives the quantity of gold objects found with this hoard as over 100 kg. According to an estimate, there might have been somewhere between three and four lac coins in this hoard. Some of its contents have reached the markets of Peshawar and the West, while the bulk is reportedly in Switzerland. This hoard covers the period from the Greek and Achaemenian gold and silver coins to the coins of the *Kushāṇa ruler, *Vāsudeva I; some *Hūṇa coins are also reported in the hoard. The hoard contains one autonomous local copper coin. Of the total coins found in this hoard, about 30 to 40% are the posthumous issues of *Hermaios; some 40 to 50% are *Śaka-Pahlava coins. Of the Śaka-Pahlava coins, about 90% are the issues in the name of *Azes. Other rulers represented in this hoard include Andragoras, Alexander (*Poros medals), *Agathokles, *Amyntas, *Antialkidas, *Antimachos I, *Antimachos II, *Apollodotos, *Archebios, *Demetrios I, *Diodotos, *Diomedes, *Eukratides I, *Euthydemos, *Heliokles II, *Hermaios, *Lysias, *Menander I, *Nikias, *Pantaleon, *Philoxenos, *Strato I, *Telephos, *Zoilos I, *Nasthenes, *Vonones, *Maues, *Azilises, Azes II, *Gondopharnes, Gondophanres with *Sasan, *Abdagases, *V'ima Takshuma, *V'ima Kadphises, *Kanishka I, and *Huvishka. The possibility of the hoard containing gold **darics* has also been expressed (Bopearachchi 1994; Bopearachchi and Rahman 1995; Senior 2001).

Miramara. *Parataraja k.

Mirzapur hoard. *Tekri Debra hoard.

Mitathal hoard. This hoard of 86 coins, noticed by R B Whitehead in the *Lahore Museum Report for 1915-1916*, was found at Mitathal, district Hissar (Haryana). Out of these, 33 gold coins belong to *Samudragupta, while 27 are of the later *Kushāṇa type; 26 coins were melted down (Altekar 1957; Vats 1926-1927).

Mitra rulers, so-called. The downfall of the Maurya empire led to the rise of a number of small states in northern India. Curiously, a large number of kings of this period, as is testified by the coins from *Kauśāmbī, *Ayodhyā, *Mathurā, *Pañchāla, etc, bear *mitra*-ending names. Since they mostly belong to the late Śuṅga period and thereafter, and since most of the Śuṅga rulers had *mitra*-ending names, some scholars suggested that they belonged to the Śuṅga family. H C Raychaudhuri thinks it possible that some issuers of coins, who cannot be identified with known Śuṅga kings, might have been members of this dynasty who were originally governors but declared themselves as independent rulers and continued to rule after the Kāṇvas had supplanted the Śuṅgas in the centre. The Śuṅga governors, he opines, enjoyed considerable autonomy, and Agnimitra, the son of Pushyamitra and his governor at Vidiśā, is referred to as **rājan* in the *Mālavikāgnimitram*. However, while the later Śuṅgas had their seat at Vidiśā, 'mitra' coins have been found, not from Vidiśā, but from various other regions, and the palaeography of the coin inscriptions and other pieces of evidence suggest that they are later than the time of the Śuṅga ruler, Agnimitra. The Sātavāhana coins, though obtained from different regions and showing local characteristics, are characterized by certain common devices, such as the *hill symbol and the *Ujjain symbol. In contrast, while the 'mitra' coins of each locality have a lot of uniformity and peculiarity, these coins from different localities do not have any unifying characteristic to the label them as the issues of one dynasty. The Pañchāla coins are characterized by three peculiar symbols, and most of the Kauśāmbī coins, by the device of *bull. On the rev of most of the Ayodhyā coins occur 'cock on post' and palm tree, and on their obv, bull figure. The Mathurā coins are characterized by *Lakshmī on the obv, and elephant with three riders on the rev. The names of *Agnimitra and *Bṛihaspatimitra are known from the coins from Kauśāmbī and Pañchāla, and *Gomitra from coins of *Kanauj and Mathurā. There are some scholars, who express the possibility that identical names known from different local coins of the same age may belong to one and the same king, who ruled over a large dominion. However, the great difference in device and fabric does not favour this view. *Mitra*-ending names are also known to occur on the coins of the republican tribes, like the *Audumbaras and the *Kulūtas, of more or less the same date. Also, all known

Śuṅga kings did not have *mitra*-ending names, and all *mitra*-ending names cannot be labelled as Śuṅga. King Dhanadeva of Ayodhyā, sixth in descent from Pushyamitra, had *deva* name-ending, and the later 'mitra' kings of Ayodhyā, in all probability, had no relation with the Śuṅgas. There is also a suggestion that the practice of naming a prince with *mitra*-ending names in different dynasties, was inspired by the name of Pushyamitra, the performer of *aśvamedha* and the champion of Brahmanical religion. As regards the Audumbaras, there are some round copper coins, belonging variously to Ajamita (Āryamitra), Mahimita (Mahīmitra), Bhānumita (Bhānumitra), and Mahabhutimita (Mahābhūtimitra), which have been included by Cunningham in the Audumbara series on the basis that they were found along with them. But others, like Jagannath, A M Shastri, Nisar Ahmad, and Michael Mitchiner, regard them as later in date and unconnected with the Audumbaras, mainly on the grounds that these coins bearing *mitra*-ending names are different from the Audumbara coins as regards the fabric, shape, devices, legends, etc. The rulers mentioned on these coins have been labelled by scholars, like Nisar Ahmad and Devendra Handa, as 'the Mitras of Punjab' (Nisar Ahmad 1977; Allan 1936; Bopearachchi and Pieper 1998; K K Dasgupta 1974; Handa 2007a; Bela Lahiri 1974; Mitchiner 1975-1976; Raychaudhuri 1972; A M Shastri 1964).

Mohmand hoard. This hoard was found to the north of Shabkadar, about 20 km northwest of Charsadda in Pakistan. The rulers represented in this hoard include *Menander I, *Archebios, posthumous *Hermaios, *Strato I, *Zoilos I, *Azes I, *Azilises, *Azes II, and the Arsakid, Orodes II (Haughton 1943; Jenkins 1955; Senior 2001).

Apollodotos

Monogram. Certain monograms, comprising Greek, and sometimes even Kh, letters, occur on *Indo-Greek and *Śaka-Pahlava coins. The significance of these monograms on coins is a matter of debate among scholars. Bayer suggested that they represent dates. But, as pointed out by Wilson, a single monogram may occur on the coins of several rulers, and, hence, cannot be treated as a date. Dobbins' attempt to associate the different monograms with coin types has also failed to yield concrete results. Cunningham was of the view that they might represent the names of mint cities, although he admitted that all the known monograms, 'or even half' of them, could not be explained in this manner. Moreover, the number of monograms is too large to be the names of mint cities. Gardner also regarded the monograms as representing the names of mints. But Rapson criticized this view on the ground that of the two monograms occurring on the overstruck **Kaviśiye-nagara-devatā* coin, none could be resolved to give the letters which go to make the name Kāpiśī. Recently, Mitchinier put forth the suggestion that the various monograms occurring on these coins may be associated with one of the three regions—(i) north of the Hindukush; (ii) between the Hindukush and the river Indus; and (iii) east of the river Indus. But some of the monograms occur on coins discovered in more than one of these regions, to explain which phenomenon, he has had to take recourse to the theory of 'daughter mints'. Scholars, like Whitehead, Simonetta, and Dani, have sought to associate the monograms with local magistrates or moneyers or assayers. As regards the continued use of a particular monogram over a long period of time, it has been suggested that such monograms were used, not by individual persons, but by their families. Dani would associate the monograms with hereditary assayers or with families of assayers, who might not have been government officials, but who represented the 'market interests', and tested the coins for the purity of the metal. Tarn also thinks on the same lines, but he also finds the theory of McDowell quite 'attractive' that the monograms 'were at the start moneyers' monograms which became stereotyped to mean certain mints'. Bopearachchi seems to be inclined to favour, with certain modifications, the view of Bivar, that the monogram forms, apparently forming a homogenous series, might be linked to particular mints, the difference between the various monograms within each series being due to the various *officinae* attached to the same mint. Bopearachchi proposes 36 such monogram series. *Kushāṇa coins also bear a monogram or symbol on the rev. These symbols are formed by a combination of straight lines, angles, circles and dots; one symbol is similar to a **nandipada*. Dani gives a list of 441 monograms on Indo-Greek coins, but, according to another estimate, over 550 monograms have so far been reported on Indo-Greek coins, although some readings are believed to be incorrect, and, after eliminating these incorrect readings, the total number of monograms on these coins has been reduced to around 250 or 300. R C Senior gives a list of 248 monograms on Śaka-Pahlava coins.

Euthydemos

Lysias

Azes II

Huvishka

Kanishka I

Huvishka

Chandragupta I and Kumāradevī

However, the number of symbols on Kushāṇa coins does not even reach the figure of ten. Also, each symbol on the Kushāṇa coins seems to be peculiar to a particular king, although there are some rare exceptions to this rule. The gold issues of the *Imperial Guptas bear 'a small geometric type of drawing occurring on the rev...and consisting of a circle or parallelogram, usually hanging down from a line with a number of prongs or dots above it.' Smith refers to them as monograms. Very rarely, the Gupta coins bear two symbols on the rev, in which case, the second one is relatively simpler. But the practice of showing a second symbol on the coins was discontinued during or after the reign of *Chandragupta II. On certain coins, the symbol is absent altogether, as in the case of the *Tiger-slayer type of *Samudragupta. The symbols on Imperial Gupta coins have been explained, by various scholars, variously as marks of the mint master, as denoting the mint city, as of religious significance, as auspicious symbols, as denoting the total number of coins of a single type issued in a particular mint operation, or as denoting the date of the issue of a coin. But all these explanations do not appear to be very convincing. Altekar, after examining in detail all these explanations, comes to the conclusion that, most probably, 'early Gupta mint-masters regarded these symbols on their prototype as merely decorative elements which they were free to diversify in any artistic way they liked' (Altekar 1957; Bayer 1738; Bivar 1965; Bopearachchi and Pieper 1998; Cunningham 1970; Dani 1992; Dobbins 1980; Gardner 1971; A N Lahiri 1965; Mitchiner 1975; Rapson 1905; R C Senior 2001; Simonetta 1957; Smith 1972; Tarn 1980; Whitehead 1922; Whitehead 1923; Wilson 1971).

Monometallism. In early stages of the evolution of coinage in India, monometallism must have been in vogue, the coins of standard metal being supplemented with *cowries* or other tokens for smaller transactions. Rapson has pointed out that there is evidence to show that in ancient India, silver and copper coinages were often independent of each other; even when circulating side by side, the copper coinage was not necessarily a mere auxilliary to the silver coinage. But gradually, due to its intrinsic qualities and higher economic development in India, silver began to be favoured for purposes of coinage; copper coins either fell out of use, or were relegated to the subsidiary position of tokens (D R Bhandarkar 1984; Chakrabortty 1931).

Mould. Coin moulds, ranging in date from *c* first century AD to the twelfth century AD, are reported from sites like Atranjikhera, Kodkad, Kondapur, Mathurā, Rajghat, and Sanchi. Coin moulds, datable to *c* first century AD, from Khokhrakot, near Rohtak, provide us with some idea of the progress made in the field of *casting coins in moulds. Some of the moulds could be used more than once. Some moulds from Mathurā bear 'in a single coin-socket designs found on different types of *punch marked coins'; they are usually regarded as cases of forgery (B N Mukherjee and P K D Lee 1988; Birbal Sahni 1945; Thaplyal 1989b).

Mṛigabhūti. *Almora k.

Mudrikā. Coin denomination (?). Mentioned in the *Bakhshali manuscript, it is believed to be the same as the *mudri* of Alberuni (R C Agrawala 1954b).

Mūladeva. *Ayodhyā k. He is regarded as one of the earliest rulers of Ayodhyā, because he issued coins of the 'Bull : Combination of symbols' type alone; *Lakshmī or *Gajalakshmī is never seen on the rev of his coins, like the coins of *Dhanadeva, *Vāyudeva, *Viśākhadeva, and *Śivadatta. The obv ld of his coins gives the name of the issuer in the genitive (Allan 1936; Bela Lahiri 1974).

Muli. Coin denomination (?). This term seems to occur as the name of a class of coins in the *Niya Kh documents from the time of King Pepiye of the Shan Shan kingdom, and by the time of Vashmana, who seems to the third successor of that ruler, it had become the predominant currency in Chinese Turkestan, and might have superseded other coins like the **sadera*/**satera*, **drakhma*/**trakhma*, and, perhaps, also **māsha*. It is not certain whether, as a currency, it was of indigenous or foreign origin. Scholars like H W Bailey, however, express doubts regarding *muli* being at all a coin denomination, and feel that it might have been used in the sense of 'price' or 'value' (Skt, *mūlya*) only (R C Agrawala 1954a; Burrow 1940; Stein 1929).

N

Nāga. Symbol. *Serpent; *Undulating line.

Nāgas. Dynasties. The Nāgas are an ancient people, whose origin is shrouded in mystery. Most of the scholars are of the view that they were originally serpent worshippers, and came to be named after their totem, the nāga. Literary, epigraphic, and numismatic evidence, as also the presence of several localities bearing their name, testify to the wide distribution of their habitation. The existence of several Nāga ruling families is vouched for by the finds of their coins and inscriptions. Puranic evidence shows that the three main centres of their power were Padmāvatī, Kāntipurī, and Mathurā. Of these, Padmāvatī has been identified with Padmapura in Vidarbha, or Narwar near Shivpuri, but its identification with Pawaya, 25 miles to the northeast of Narwar in Madhya Pradesh, suggested by M V Lele, seems to be supported by the discovery of the remains of an ancient city and of a large number of Nāga coins at the site. K P Jayaswal identified Kāntipurī with Kantit between Mirzapur and Vindhyachal, but Wilford and Cunningham seem to be right in identifying it with Kutwal or Kutwar near Moraina, about 20 miles north of Gwalior in Madhya Pradesh. Nāga coins have also been found at Mathurā. K P Jayaswal had suggested that three different lines of Nāga kings ruled from these three centres, and of these, the Bhāraśiva Nāgas of Kāntipurī represented the imperial line, while the ruling families at Padmāvatī and Mathurā were collaterals. But the coins from all these three centres often represent the same kings, and are similar to each other in types. Thus, it is concluded that all the three centres were ruled by the same family of Bhāraśiva Nāgas; Padmāvatī, which has yielded the greatest number of Nāga coins, was, perhaps, the main centre of their power, while Kāntipurī and Mathurā were 'two other important cities of the Nāga kingdom'. From the *provenance* of the Nāga coins, it is concluded that this kingdom comprised the areas of Bharatpur, Dholpur, Gwalior, Bundelkhand, as also some parts of Malwa, and was bounded by Yamuna in the north, Narmada in the south, Chambal in the west, and Ken in the east. Jayaswal had also suggested that the Nāga rulers formed a confederacy against the Kushāṇas, in which the tribal republics, like the *Kuṇindas, the *Mālavas, and the *Yaudheyas, were their subordinate allies. Although there is no evidence to support this, there is no gainsaying that the Nāgas, like all these and other powers, played their part in liberating northern India from the yoke of Kushāṇa supremacy. The coins of the Nāgas are all in copper, and very small in size, resembling in this respect the Mālava coins which are smaller still. They bear some symbol—*bull (the most common symbol), *peacock, *trident, 'sickle-and-arrow', *wheel, etc, on the obv, and mostly a circular ld mentioning the name of the king with the title **mahārāja* or *mahārāja-śrī* covering the whole flan of the rev. The rulers represented by the Nāga coins are (alphabetically) *Bhavanāga, *Bhīmanāga, *Bṛihaspatināga, *Devanāga, *Gaṇapatināga, *Prabhākara, *Ravināga, *Skandanāga, *Vasunāga, *Vibhunāga, *Vṛishanāga, *Vṛishabha, and *Vyāghranāga. The 'Bull' type is used by most of the Nāga rulers; but three other types were issued variously by these kings. The Nāga kings have been divided into three groups on the basis of the use of a particular type by them. Bhīmanāga, Bṛihaspatināga, Skandanāga, and Vasunāga issued 'Peacock' type of coins; Bhavanāga, Bṛihaspatināga, and Devanāga issued 'Trident' type of coins; and Prabhākara (?), Ravināga, and Vibhunāga issued the so-called 'Sickle-and-arrow' type of coins. The 'Wheel' type was not confined to any one group, and was used by Bṛihaspatināga, Devanāga, Gaṇapatināga, Vasunāga, Vibhunāga, and Vyāghranāga. Bhavanāga was a near predecessor of Gaṇapatināga, probably the last Nāga ruler who was exterminated by *Samudragupta. Some of the coins of Bhavanāga are of the 'Trident' type, thus indicating that the rulers, who used the 'Trident' type, were later than the rulers who used the 'Peacock' type (Cunningham 1967; Bela Lahiri 1974; Smith 1972; H V Trivedi 1957).

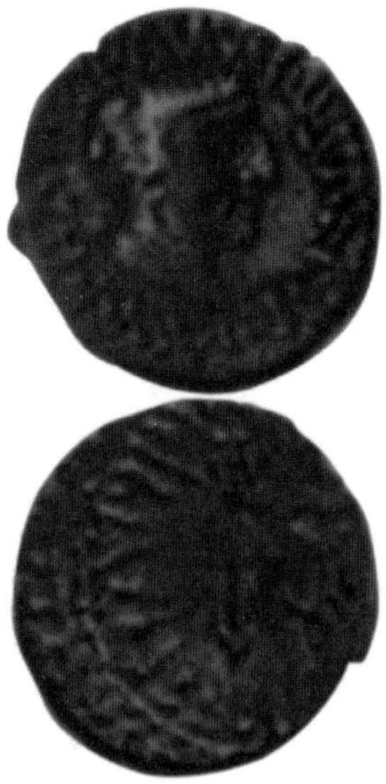

Nahapāna

Nahapāna. *Kshaharāta k; successor of *Bhūmaka; *c* first or second century AD. He seems to have succeeded *Bhūmaka as the **kshatrapa* of the *Kushāṇas. No inscription issued by Nahapāna himself is known so far, but several inscriptions issued in his time by his son-in-law, Ushavadāta (a great donor and the governor of the southern province of the Kshaharāta kingdom), daughter Dakshamitrā, and *Amātya* Aryaman, are known from the Nasik, Karle, and Junnar regions of Maharashtra. These inscriptions bear dates ranging from year 41 to 46. If they are indeed dated in the *Śaka era as has been suggested by a number of scholars, he ruled in the first half of the second century AD. However, some scholars regard these dates to refer to the regnal years of Nahapāna. The external and internal evidence of these inscriptions, as also the findspot of his coins, shows that his rule extended from Ajmer in the north to Nasik-Pune in the south, and from Gujarat and northern Konkan in the west to Malwa in the east. The use of the title **rājan* on his coins, instead of the mere **kshatrapa* met with on the coins of Bhūmaka, shows that he enjoyed a position superior to that of his predecessor. But Nahapāna ultimately had to suffer defeat at the hands of the Sātavāhana ruler, Gautamīputra Sātakarṇi, as attested by epigraphic, numismatic, and perhaps also literary, sources. He issued coins in silver, copper, lead, potin, and an alloy of copper and lead. His silver coins bear on the obv the bust of the king to the r, and mixed Greek and Roman characters, which, according to the Rapson, stand for *Raño Kshaharātasa Nahapānasa*. In fact, on some specimens, the ld has actually been read as *Rannio Saharatas Nahapanas*. The rev has an arrow on the left, a thunderbolt on the right, and a discus in the centre. This side bears legends in both Br and Kh, mentioning the title (*rājan*), family name (Kshaharāta), and the name of the king. The bust of the king on the coins bearing the name of Nahapāna shows great variation, which has been explained by some scholars, like Bhagwanlal Indraji, as due to the representation of the king at different stages of life, during his long reign of around 40 years. But others, like Jouveau-Dubreuil and F W Thomas, have concluded from this, that these coins might have been issued by more than one king bearing the name of Nahapāna; still other scholars, like Scott, suggest that they were issued also by the successors of Nahapāna in his name, but with the bust of the individual issuers. However, the Kshaharāta power seems to have ended with Nahapāna, and A

M Shastri seems to be right when he says that the variety in the depiction of the bust of the king on the coins bearing the name of Nahapāna may be due to the large number of mints employing die cutters with varying degree of artistic skill, over the long reign of Nahapāna. The silver coins are all round in shape, but the coins in the baser metals and alloys may be round or rectangular. The obv of some copper coins, as also that of the coins struck in an alloy of copper and lead, has an arrow on the left, a thunderbolt on the right, and discus in the centre, and a fragmentary Br ld mentioning Nahapāna. The rev has a leafy tree-in-railing. Another type of his copper coins has the same obv, while the rev has the capital of a pillar surmounted by a *lion and a *wheel, as on the rev of the coins of Bhūmaka. Yet another copper type of Nahapāna has the bust of the king to the r on the obv, and an arrow and a thunderbolt on the rev. Some other copper coins have an *elephant (sometimes with upraised trunk), together with an arrow and a thunderbolt on the obv, and a leafy tree-in-railing on the rev. A recently published copper coin has a lion and a hill on the obv, and a thunderbolt on the rev. The lead and potin coins have a lion before a *yūpa* and a three-arched hill on the obv; the rev has a bow, an arrow, a spear (?), and a thunderbolt. Interestingly, the coins in baser metals and alloys refer to the king simply by his name, or with the dynastic name, or with the titles of *raña*, *kshatrapa*, or *mahākshatrapa*. Around 9,270 silver coins of Nahapāna in the Jogelthembi (district Nasik, Maharashtra) coin hoard are found to be restruck by the Sātavāhana ruler, Gautamīputra Sātakarṇi (Jha and Rajgor 1994; Mirashi 1982; Mitchiner 1976; Rapson 1975; Raychaudhuri 1972; Senior 2001; A M Shastri 1995; Sircar 1980e).†

Nala. Dynasty. Known from some inscriptions from Orissa, Amaravati, and Raipur, and from some *repoussé* coins, this dynasty seems to have originally belonged to southern Kosala, and to have extended its sway over parts of Maharashtra for some time at the cost of the Vākāṭakas. Five kings of this dynasty are known—Varāharāja, Bhavadattarāja, Arthapatirāja, Nandanarāja, and Stambharāja. The coins issued by them are in two denominations, with the bigger ones weighing 15 *rattīs*, and the smaller ones, 5 *rattīs*. The bigger coins bear the full name of the issuer, while the smaller ones have only the first part of his name. The obv of these coins is usually divided into two parts by a horizontal line, or two parallel horizontal lines joined at the ends. It bears, in the upper half, a couchant humped *bull with a crescent in front or on its back, while the lower half has the ld consisting of the name of the king with the honorific title *śrī*; the coins of Stambharāja, known only in the smaller denomination, do not have the honorific prefix (Mirashi 1939; L S Nigam 1987; T P Verma 1991).

Kanishka I

Kanishka I

Huvishka

Huvishka

Huvishka

Nana. Oriental goddess. One of the most ancient goddesses of the orient, she was worshipped as Innana-Ishtar by the Assyrians, as Astarte by the Phoenicians, and as Nani by the Syrians. *Nana* seems to be praised in the Ābān Yasht as Ardvi Sūra Anāhita, which, in fact, are three epithets—*ardvi*, 'high sublime', *sūra*, 'strong, excellent', and *anahita*, 'spotless, pure, clean'. She is believed to have bestowed fertility, and to have purified the seed of all males and the womb of all the females. It has, however, been pointed out that while Ardvi Sūra Anāhita is shown carrying a water vessel, a flower or a bird in Sassanian art, *Nana* on *Kushāṇa coins usually has a sword and a sceptre surmounted by the forepart of a horse or a stag as her attributes. Her depiction was very popular on Kushāṇa coins, with her figure appearing on the rev of the coins of *Kanishka I, *Huvishka, and *Vāsudeva I. She is generally shown as nimbate and diademed, often with a crescent on top of her head, and a sword tied at her waist. Her most common attributes are a sceptre surmounted by the forepart of a horse or a stag, and a patera with corn shoots. But on one coin type of Huvishka, she holds a bow in her l hand, and draws an arrow from a quiver at her back with her r hand. This representation reminds one of *Artemis. On some late Kushāṇa coins, she is shown seated on a recumbent *lion, and it is believed that this device served as the prototype for the **Siṁhavāhinī-devī* on *Imperial Gupta coins. On yet another type, that of Huvishka, the king is depicted standing before *Nana*, with his hands joined in supplication before the goddess. The forepart of the horse, which surmounts the sceptre shown in the hand of *Nana* on coins, is reminiscent of the four white horses which draw her chariot and defeat all evils. In the label inscriptions on coins, the goddess is described variously as *Nana*, *Nano*, *Nanashao*, *Nanaia*, etc. Like *Umā, *Nana*, too, is represented on some gold coins of Huvishka as standing beside *Śiva; both the deities are four-armed,

Huvishka

and the goddess holding a branch, and the label inscription reading *Nana-Oesho*. There is a suggestion that the Kushāṇa die-engraver here seems to have identified *Nana* with Umā, the wife of Śiva (Bhaskar Chattopadhyay 1977; Cunningham 1971a; Darmesteter 1974; Gardner 1971; B N Mukherjee 1969b; Rosenfield 1967; Stein 1888; Whitehead 1914).

***Ṇāṇa-māsaka* (= *nāṇaka-māshaka*).** Coin denomination. *Ṇāṇa-māsaka*, mentioned in the **Aṅgavijjā*, seems to be one-sixteenth of a **nāṇaka*, the *Kushāṇa copper coin whose weight ranges from 31 to 270 grains. As the standard weight of the *nāṇaka* is uncertain, the weight of its submultiple, *ṇāṇa-māsaka*, is difficult to determine. It has been regarded as identical with **loha-māsaka* of Buddhaghosha (V S Agrawala 1957; C S Gupta 1982).

***Nanaia*.** Deity. See **Nana*.

***Nāṇaka*.** Coin denomination. This seems to have originally denoted the coins of the *Kushāṇa ruler, *Kanishka I, because of the appearance of the figure of the goddess, **Nana*, on his coins for the first time in India. A commentator on Yājñavalkya explains *nāṇaka* as *Nāṇāṅka ṭaṅka*, that is a coin 'having Nāṇā (*Nana* ?) as... cognisance'. The commentator of the *Mṛichchhakaṭikam* explains it as *Śivāṅka ṭaṅka*, perhaps because of the figure of *Śiva appearing on the coins of this ruler. Most of the scholars hold that *nāṇaka* denoted the Kushāṇa gold coins. But from the **Aṅgavijjā*, which says that a *ṇāṇaka* was much inferior in value to a **kārshāpaṇa*, it appears that *nāṇaka* was a copper coin, and the impression is reinforced by the *Mṛichchhakaṭikam*. Yājñavalkya (*c* 100-300 AD) refers to one who counterfeits coins as *kūṭakṛit-nāṇakasya*, and to coin-examiner as *nāṇaka-parīkshī*. In the *Mṛichchhakaṭikam* occurs the term *nāṇaka-mūśi*, '[one] who robs [people] of *nāṇakas* (= coins or wealth)'. The *Bṛihatkalpasūtrabhāshya* (*c* seventh century AD) refers to coins of gold, silver, and copper as *suvarṇa-nāṇaka*, *rūpamaya-nāṇaka*, and *tāmramaya-nāṇaka*, respectively. From this, it has been inferred that *nāṇaka* seems to have become a generic name for all types of coins [**bhaṁmaka*] (R C Agrawala 1954a; V S Agrawala 1957; C S Gupta 1982; B N Mukherjee 1982b)

Nanashao. Deity. See **Nana*.

Nandanarāja. *Nala k.

Nandgaon hoard. This hoard of over 8,800 silver *punch marked coins, belonging to the Śūrasena *janapada*, was found in 1990-1991 at Nandgaon in the Mathurā district of Uttar Pradesh (Rajgor 2001).

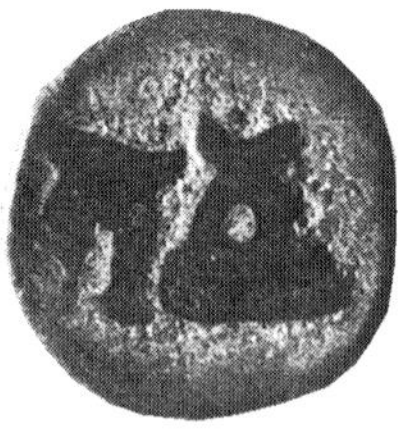

Uninscribed cast coin

Nandipada. Symbol. This symbol, often regarded as having evolved from the *taurine symbol, is very commonly depicted on ancient Indian coins. It may be seen, often in combination with other symbols, on *Ayodhyā, *Audumbara, *Kauśāmbī, *Eran, *Kuṇinda, *Mālava, *Taxila, and *Yaudheya coins. On the coins of the *Kulūta chief, Vīrayaśas, an elaborate *nandipada* occupies the whole rev, while on those of another Kulūta chief, Vijayamitra, as also on the obv of certain *Vṛishṇi coins, the symbol is shown surmounted on top of a standard. A stylized *nandipada* is seen on the 'altar' depicted on the rev of the coins of *Almora. Often on coins, a close association is seen between the *nandipada* and the *bull, the theriomorphic representation of *Śiva. This seems to indicate the Śaivite character of the *nandipada*. Coomaraswamy has shown the association of this symbol with *Lakshmī. The *nandipada* closely resembles the *triratna* symbol representing the Buddha, *dhaṁma*, and *saṁgha* in Buddhist art; in Jaina art, the *triratna* symbol is often seen in the representation of the scene of the nativity of Mahāvīra (Allan 1936; Banerjea 2002; Chakrabortty 1931; Bhaskar Chattopadhyay 1977; Coomaraswamy 1927; Cunningham 1971b; K K Dasgupta 1974; Handa 2007a; Rao 1985; A L Srivastava 1991).

Naradatta. *Ayodhyā k. Although his coins come from Ayodhyā, some scholars regard him as a ruler of *Mathurā. He is known from the common Ayodhyā type of 'Bull : Combinations of symbols' only. Nothing definite can be said about him, although Bela Lahiri places him towards the end of the early rulers of Ayodhyā who issued cast coins only. The obv ld reads *Naradatasa* (Allan 1936; Bela Lahiri 1974).

Narasiṁhagupta *Bālāditya*. *Imperial Gupta k; son of *Pūrugupta (?); *c* sixth century AD. According to Hiuen-tsang, *Mihirakula forced [Narasiṁhagupta] Bālāditya to pay tribute to him. But Bālāditya, while on the run, ambushed him on an island, took him prisoner, and set him free only on the insistence of his (Bālāditya's) mother. Mihirakula died some time later. Thus, Narasiṁhagupta gets the credit for shattering Hūṇa power in India. The seals of Narasiṁhagupta describe him as a **paramabhāgavata*, but there is overwhelming epigraphic evidence to show that he was inclined towards Buddhism. He issued only the *Archer type of gold coins, which have been divided into two classes. The coins of Class I have, on the obv, the vertical ld *Nara* under the king's arm, and the traces of a circular ld; the rev has the ld *Bālādityaḥ*. These coins are of relatively purer metal, and are better executed. The Class II coins are quite similar to the coins of Class I, the difference being that they are of baser metal, are crudely executed, and bear no circular ld on the obv. The percentage of pure gold in the better executed of his coins is around 70, while some crudely executed coins of the same type have about 54 % of pure gold. On this basis, some scholars express the possibility of the existence of two Imperial Gupta rulers named Narasiṁhagupta. But others have rejected this possibility, mainly on the basis of the weight of these coins (Ashvini Agrawal 1989; Allan 1914; Altekar 1957; R D Banerji 1933; Fleet 1888; S R Goyal 2005; P L Gupta 1998; K P Jayaswal 1933; Smith 1972; Thaplyal, forthcoming).†

Narasiṁhagupta : Archer type

Narhan hoard. This hoard of silver *punch marked coins was found by Purushottam Singh in the course of surface exploration at the ancient site of Narhan on the left bank of river Ghaghra in the Gorakhpur district of Uttar Pradesh, in March 1985. The coins were placed in a small earthen pitcher, which itself was secured within two bowls—one Red ware, and the other Black-slipped ware, kept one over the other. According to the discoverer of the hoard, it comprised 51 coins, but P L Gupta was informed of 49 coins, with one reported missing. P L Gupta has divided these coins into five types. Type I is represented by six 'blank pieces', which, according to Gupta, may be placed in the 'pre-coinage period' when metallic pieces of definite weight, made by flattening metal globules, were used in commercial transactions. Type II is represented by 33 coins, ranging in weight between 80.6 and 83.7 grains; some of these coins were made by flattening metal globules and are round in shape, but mostly, they are cut from strips of metal and are square or rectangular in shape. Gupta attributes them to the Malla *janapada* on the bases of the *provenance* of the hoard, in which these coins form the majority, and the fact that such coins are not known from any other source. Types III is represented by a single piece, weighing about 78 grains. It is a 'double observed coin', and has four symbols on either if its sides. Type IV is represented by seven coins, which have been ascribed by Gupta to the Vajji *janapada*, mainly on the basis of the similarity of the bold symbol on these pieces with that occurring on the coins from the *Katra hoard. Most of these coins are rectangular in shape, bear a bold symbol in various forms, together with other smaller symbols, and weigh between 102 and 105 grains. Type V is represented by three coins belonging to the *Magadha series of punch marked coins. They bear the six-armed symbol, besides some other symbols. Purushottam Singh dated the hoard to the sixth-fourth centuries BC. But Gupta, on the basis of the fact that a Red ware bowl, together with a Black-slipped ware bowl, was used to secure this hoard, dates it to the mid-sixth century BC (P L Gupta 1996; B N Mukherjee 1999-2000; Purushottam Singh 1986).

Nastene. K. He is known from a *tetradrachm* bearing the device of the helmeted bust of the king on the obv, and equestrian king on the rev. The ld introduces Nastene as son of Xatran. The coin has been placed in mid-first century AD. It has been suggested that Nastene might have been of *Śaka-Pahlava, *Kushāṇa, or 'mixed parentage', who rose to power, perhaps somewhere to the north of the Hindukush (Bopearachchi 1997; Senior 2001).

Nava. *Kauśāmbī k. His coins are similar to the *Magha coins. Altekar places him later than the Maghas, in the third or fourth century AD, but Bela Lahiri takes him to be earlier than the Maghas, as, in her opinion, the peculiar tree on his coins is similar to that on the coins of *Dhanadeva of Kauśāmbī, rather than that on the coins of the Magha kings. This view is supported by the stratigraphic context of the coins from the Kosam excavations. His copper coins bear the *bull to the r, sometimes with a *wheel above, on the obv; the rev has a *tree-in-railing, spear, and *chāmara*, and the ld *...navasa*

(Allan 1936; Altekar 1942b; Bopearachchi and Pieper 1998; Bela Lahiri 1974).

***Ṇava-kāhāvaṇa*.** Coin denomination. Mentioned in the **Aṅgavijjā*, it seems to be the silver coin of about 20 *rattīs*, issued from the time of *Eukratides I onwards. The prefix, *ṇava*, 'recent', was added to *kāhāvaṇa* to distinguish it from the original **kārshāpaṇa* weighing 32 *rattīs*. These latter now came to be designated **ādimūla-kāhāvaṇa* or **purāṇa* (V S Agrawala 1957).

Nickel. Metal for coins. The *Indo-Greek rulers, *Euthydemos, *Pantaleon, and *Agathokles, get the credit for being the only rulers to issue coins in nickel. However, these coins contain only 20% nickel, the rest being copper. Cunningham is of the view that this metal was used for minting coins also by the Indian tribes of the Oxydrakai (*Kshudrakas), and the Malloi (*Mālavas). D C Sircar does not agree with this (Cunningham 1970; A N Lahiri 1965; Handa 2007a).

***Nikatoros*.** Title. Meaning 'bearer of victory', this title was adopted by *Amyntas, and rendered into Pkt as **jayadhara*. Outside of India, the title was borne by the Seleukid ruler, Demetrios II, and the Arsakid ruler, Artabanos II, who might have borrowed it from the Seleukid ruler (Cunningham 1970; Gardner 1878; Gardner 1971; A N Lahiri 1965; Marshall 1975; Narain 1957a; Tarn 1980; Whitehead 1914; Wroth 1903).

Nike. Greek goddess of victory. She was a daughter of the Titan Pallas and the goddess Styx, and a sister of Zelos, 'zeal', Kratos, 'strength', and Bia, 'force'. That she held a position subordinate to those of *Zeus, *Athena, and *Herakles, is shown by the fact that she is often depicted on coins as standing on the outstretched hand of either of the first two deities, or on the shoulder of the third. The representations of Nike in art are mostly winged. She is usually depicted on *Indo-Greek and *Śaka-Pahlava coins, as a winged figure, standing with her characteristic attributes, the wreath and palm branch. Such a figure of Nike may be seen on the coins of *Antimachos, *Artemidoros, *Menander, *Maues, *Azes I, *Gondopharnes, *Abdagases, and *Pakores, as also on the joint

Antimachos II

coins of *Orthagnes and Gondopharnes. Also quite popular as a coin device was the figure of winged Nike with her characteristic attributes, standing on the outstretched r hand of *Zeus. On some coins of *Antialkidas, Nike is depicted as riding on an elephant, which is walking beside Zeus. The device of Zeus Nikephoros may be seen on the coins of Antialkidas, *Heliokles, Maues, Azes I, *Azilises, Gondopharnes, and Abdagases. The depiction of winged Nike on the outstretched r hand of *Athena is rare, and may be seen on some coins of *Strato I and *Theophilos. On a rare silver type of *Zoilos, Nike is shown standing on the shoulder of *Herakles and crowning him. On the rev of a silver type of the Śaka-Pahlava ruler, *Gondopharnes, wingless Nike is shown standing behind the enthroned king, and crowning him. On the rev of a coin type of the Śaka-Pahlava ruler, *Orthagnes, a female figure is shown standing behind the enthroned king and crowning him. This female figure has been identified as *Tyche, though with doubt. Had the figure been winged, it would definitely have been identified as *Nike. For, there does not appear to be any justification for showing a daughter of Tethys and Okeanos crowning a king. On the type of Gondopharnes, above, it is a wingless Nike who is crowning the king, and it appears that the female figure on the coin of Orthagnes also should be identified as Nike, and not as Tyche. On a copper coin of Antimachos, Nike is represented, with her wreath and palm branch, as standing on the prow of a ship; this device may have something to do with some naval victory achieved by Antimachos. It is generally believed that Nike is not depicted on *Kushāṇa coins, but Cunningham reports that a copper coin of *Kujula Kadphises, lost with the Indus steamer, bore the figure of this goddess. Nike is sometimes also represented symbolically, as, for example, through her wreath and palm branch on the rev of some coins of Antimachos, and through her palm branch alone on some coins of Menander (Bopearachchi 1993; Bopearachchi and Pieper 1998; Bopearachchi and Rahman 1995; Bhaskar Chattopadhyay 1977; Cunningham 1971a; Gardner 1971; Graves 1955; Kerenyi 1951; A N Lahiri 1965; Marshall 1975; Rose 1958; Schoder nd; Prashant Srivastava 2007c; Whitehead 1914).[†]

Antialkidas

Antimachos II

Nikephoros. Title. Meaning 'bearer of victory', this title was used by*Antialkidas, *Antimachos II, *Archebios, and *Epander. It is rendered into Pkt as **jayadhara* (Cunningham 1970; Gardner 1971; A N Lahiri 1965; Marshall 1975; Narain 1957a; Tarn 1980; Whitehead 1914).

Nikias. *Indo-Greek k; son of *Philoxenos; end of the second century BC or early first century BC. He was appointed as a subking by *Apollodotos, perhaps in some parts of western Gandhāra, from where most of his silver coins are reported; his copper ones come from the Jhelum area. It is possible that he might have ruled over the Takshaśilā region for some time before being overthrown by *Telephos; no coin of Nikias was, however, found during the excavations at Taxila. On the basis of the depiction of the figure of *Poseidon on some of his coins, Tarn suggested that he might have achieved some naval victory on the river Jhelum, perhaps against the *Śaka-Pahlavas, but Narain feels that the speed of the currents in this river precludes such a possibility. Nikias issued coins in silver and copper, all struck on the Indian standard. All the coins are die-struck pieces. The silver coins are all round in shape; the copper coins are mostly square, but the round shape in copper is not unknown. The obv of the silver coins is occupied by the diademed bust of the king to the r, sometimes in a smooth helmet. The rev of two types of silver coins has thundering *Athena to the front, with an **aegis* on her left arm, while that of two other types of silver coins has a male figure, perhaps of a warrior, standing to the l, and holding palm in his l hand and an uncertain object in his extended r hand; some scholars are in favour of identifying this warrior as the king. Most of the copper coins have the diademed bust of the king to the r on the obv, and king on a prancing horse to the r on the rev. However, the obv of one type of square copper coins has the head of *Poseidon, with a *trident on his shoulder, while the rev has a 'dolphin twined round anchor'. All the coins have the Gr ld on the obv, and the Pkt ld, written in the Kh script, on the rev. Besides the title of **basileus*, Nikias assumed the epithet **soteros* on his coins. These are rendered into Pkt as **maharaja* and **tratara*, respectively. The Pkt form of the name of the ruler, as met with on coins, is Nikiä (Bopearachchi 1993; Bopearachchi and Pieper 1998; Bopearachchi and Rahman 1995; Cunningham 1970; Gardner 1971; A N Lahiri 1965; Marshall 1975; Narain 1957a; Rapson 1906; Rapson 1987; Senior 2001;

Nikias

Sircar 1980a; Prashant Srivastava and Prachi Srivastava 1993; Tarn 1980; Whitehead 1914).†

Nīla-kāhāpaṇa. Coin denomination. Mentioned in the *Samantapāsādikā*, it appears to be the silver **kārshāpaṇa* of 32 *rattīs*. The prefix *nīla*, 'blue', was added to *kāhāpaṇa*, perhaps due to the deposit of verdigris on the surface of the coin with the passage of time. The *Sāratthadīpanī* commentary on the *Samantapāsādikā* states that a **rudradāmaka* was three-fourth the value of a *nīla-kahāpaṇa* (V S Agrawala 1957; C D Chatterjee 1931; C D Chatterjee 1933).

Nishka. Coin denomination. Max Müller made an attempt to derive *nishka* from *Kanishka, but the occurrence of this term in the *Ṛigveda* would render this suggestion untenable. Eduard Thomas traced *nishka* to the Semitic *miskāl*, 'to be weighed', though the difference in weight between *miskāl* and *nishka* would go against this. D R Bhandarkar derives *nishka* from the root meaning 'to weigh'. He also pleaded strongly for regarding *nishka* of the vedic period as a gold coin, several of which were sometimes strung to make a necklace as the one said to be adorning Rudra in the *Ṛigveda*. But S K Chakrabortty and A S Altekar have argued against this theory on several grounds : no gold coins of an early age are yet available; vedic economy could not have sustained a gold coinage; cow is mentioned even later as the common medium of exchange; there are no references to the *nishka* in the context of commercial transactions, and it is mentioned either as an ornament or as gift or *dakshiṇā* to officiating priests. In the brāhmaṇa period, *nishka* had become a unit of value, and was in the process of superseding cow as a unit, but even then, it could not be said, with certainty, to be a coin. It is only in the *Ashṭādhyāyī* of Pāṇini, where prices of commodities are expressed in *nishka*, and where the wealth of a person is estimated in the same unit, that the *nishka* can definitely be said to be a coin. According to the lawgivers, like Manu and Yājñavalkya, a *nishka* weighed 320 *rattīs*. Four **suvarṇas* of 80 *rattīs* made a *nishka*, and ten such *nishkas* made a gold *dharaṇa*. *Nishka* would have had a value too high for purposes of ordinary exchange, and had the *pāda*, 'quarter', as its submultiple. Another name for *nishka* was **pala* (V S Agrawala 1953; V S Agrawala 1956; D R Bhandarkar 1984;

Bühler 2001; Chakrabortty 1931; Hopkins 1987; Keith 1987; S K Maity 1970b).

Niya Kharoshṭhī documents. These Kh records, about 782 in number, are written in Pkt on small wooden tablets, pieces of leather, fragments of silk, paper, etc, and discovered at Niya by Aurel Stein in the course of his explorations and excavations in Chinese Turkestan. These documents shed light on the political, social, and economic conditions, and everyday life of the people of central Asia in the early centuries of the Christian era. They refer to five rulers of the Shan Shan kingdom, namely Tajaka, Pepiye, Aṁgoka, Mahiri or Mayiri, and Vashmana. They mention some indigenous and foreign coin denominations, like **muli*, *sadera*/**satera*, **drakhma* (sometimes spelt *trakhma*), **māsha*, etc, in the contexts of purchase of slaves, and commodities like wine, textile goods, sugar, animals, and spices, payment of recompense for a slave, and loans. It is interesting to note that there is no mention of any coin in the one document of the reign of Tajaka, the first of these five rulers, when land is purchased in exchange for *agiltsa*, a variety of camel. *Muli* is mentioned for the first time in some documents of the reign of Pepiye, and sometimes, the term is used in the sense of 'price' (Skt, *mūlya*). Gold **staters* (*suvarṇa sadera*) is mentioned in a document pertaining to the twenty-eighth regnal year of Aṁgoka, and there are frequent references to *muli* in the other documents of his period. *Muli*, *suvarṇa sadera*, *trakhma*, and *māsha* are all mentioned in the documents of the reign of Mahiri or Mayiri. While *muli* not only continued to be in use in the time of Vashmana, but also seems to have become the predominant currency of the period, there is nothing to suggest that gold *staters*, *drachms*, and *māshas* were current in that period. This is intriguing, for *māsha* as a coin denomination was in circulation even towards the end of the third century AD, when a document of the time of Hinajhadeva Vijitasiṁha of Khotan refers to the purchase of a camel for 8,000 *māshas* (R C Agrawala 1954a; Burrow 1940; Stein 1929).

Non-metallic materials for coinage. There is some evidence that, in certain primitive societies, token currency continued to be in use even after the regular coinage had come in vogue. *Cowries* served as medium of purchase, even in the *Imperial Gupta period, as per the testimony of the information supplied by the Chinese pilgrim, Fa-hien. Pāṇini refers to *vasana* (cloth piece of definite value) and bovine tail (*go puchchha*) as medium of exchange. Buddhaghosha's commentary on the *Vinayapiṭaka* says that, besides metallic ones, coins could also be of *sāra* wood, bamboo, palm leaf, lac or gum, skin, fruits, and seeds. Some coin devices on clay lumps, may suggest that even clay was used for this purpose (Thaplyal 1971).

Nul Guniar hoard. This hoard might have been discovered at Nul Guniar, Baridkot, or Khawaza Khela, and the coins reached Peshawar with an Afghan dealer. The rulers represented in this hoard include *Hippostratos, *Azes I, and *Azes II (Senior 2001).

O

Oachsho. Deified river, Oxus (?). The rev of some coins of *Huvishka bears the standing figure of a nimbate, diademed, and bearded male divinity, holding a large fish in his l hand, and a staff in his r hand. The ld accompanying the figure describes the deity as *Oachsho*. Although this deity cannot be identified with any certainty, there is a suggestion that he might be associated with the river Oxus (Bailey 1943; Rosenfield 1967; Whitehead 1914).

Oado. Avestan wind god. The ld *Oado* on *Kushāṇa coins seems to be the Greek rendering of Vāta, the name of the Indo-Iranian wind god. The figure of *Oado* occurs on the rev of some copper coins of both *Kanishka I and of *Huvishka. On these coins, the deity is seen running to the l. His loose hair are shown dishevelled. He holds the ends of his garments in his hand, and the garment floats about him, giving the impression of the swift movement of the wind[god]. Interestingly, the depiction of *Oado* on Kushāṇa coins is quite similar to the description of the Indian wind god, Vāyu (Bhaskar Chattopadhyay 1977; Cunningham 1971a; Darmesteter 1974; Gardner 1971; Rosenfield 1967; Stein 1888; Whitehead 1914).

Oanindo. Avestan goddess of victory (?). The ld *Oanindo* in *Kushāṇa coins has been taken by F W Thomas to represent the Iranian god, Anandes, mentioned by Strabo. But mere similarity of names is not sufficient ground to identify the two deities, particularly when *Oanindo* on coins is depicted as a female deity, while Anandes of Strabo was male. Stein seems to be nearer the truth when he identifies *Oanindo* as the Avestan Vanainti Uparatāt, 'victorious superiority', who is often associated with Verethraghna. Hoffman, however, identifies *Oanindo* with Vanaint of the Vanant Yasht, who seems to stand for the star of victory. The winged figure of *Oanindo* appears on the rev of some gold coins of *Huvishka. She holds a wreath in her r hand, and a trophy or a palm in her l hand. The figure closely resembles the representation of *Nike, the Greek goddess of victory, occurring on *Indo-Greek and *Śaka-Pahlava coins (Bhaskar Chattopadhyay 1977; Cunningham 1971a; Darmesteter 1974; Gardner 1971; Rosenfield 1967; Stein 1888).

Obol. Coin denomination. Derived from the Greek, *obelos*, a spit used as currency in pre-coinage times, *obol* was a small silver coin, equal to one-sixth of a **drachm* (Frey 1973; Junge 1984; A N Lahiri 1965).

Obolus. Coin denomination. This is the name given to the cupro-nickel coins issued by the *Indo-Greek rulers, *Euthydemos II, *Pantaloen, and *Agathokles, weighing 134.4 grains. The cupro-nickel coins weighing 67.2 grains have been termed *hemiobolus*. This nomenclature, proposed by Cunningham for the Indo-Greek cupro-nickel pieces, has been accepted by subsequent writers like A N Lahiri. These cupro-nickel coins seem to have replaced the silver **obols*. Interestingly, *obols* of all these three Indo-Greek rulers are extremely rare (Cunningham 1970; A N Lahiri 1965).

Obverse. Technically, it is that side of the coin, which has received its type by the lower die, that is the die embedded in the anvil. However, in practice, it is the more important side of the coin, even if it has received its type by the upper die, that is the die inserted into the lower end of the punch. For the coins bearing the royal figure, obv is the side on which the royal head or figure is depicted, that is 'heads' of 'heads or tails'. The distinction is not so clear when both sides of the coin have devices other than the royal portrait (Hill 1906; Junge 1984).

Kanishka I

Oesho. Deity. The ld *Oesho* on *Kushāṇa coins stands for *Śiva, whose cult seems to be very popular among the ancient Indian rulers of foreign origin also. Various interpretations have been offered for the appellation *Oesho*. While some scholars associate it with Ugra, others take it as representing Bhaveśa, both being names of Śiva. Some connect *Oesho* with *ukshan* or *vṛisha*, the *bull mount of that deity. D R Bhandarkar feels that *Oesho* should be read as *Omsho*, and regarded as the Kushāṇa rendering of Umeśa (Śiva). Attention has also been drawn to a Sogdian god, Wyshprkr (= Wesh-parkar), who has been equated with Śiva in the Sogdian *Vessantarajātaka*, and it has been suggested that *Oesho* might have been derived from the first component of the name of this Sogdian god, *Wesh*-parkar, who has been identified with Śiva. [*Śiva] (Banerjea 2002; Bhaskar Chattopadhyay 1977; Cunningham 1971a; Gardner 1971; Rosenfield 1967; Prashant Srivastava 1998c; M N P Tiwari and Savita Sharma 1983; Whitehead 1914).

Huvishka

Ommo. *Umā.

Onia. Avestan solar (?) god. On some gold coins of *Huvishka occurs the depiction of a radiate and nimbate deity, standing with his right arm extended, and the left one resting on the hilt of the sword tied to his waist. The label inscription beside the figure informs us that the deity is named *Onia*. The depiction closely resembles that of **Ashaeichsho* on the coins of the same ruler, and there is a suggestion that *Onia* may represent some aspect of the solar deity. Like *Ashaeichsho*, *Onia*, too, seems to be an abstract and ethical divinity (Bhaskar Chattopadhyay 1977; Darmesteter 1974; Gardner 1971; Rosenfield 1967; Stein 1888).

Orlagno. Avestan god, Verethraghna. The ld *Orlagno* on *Kushāṇa coins, perhaps, stands for Verethraghna, the old Pahlavi form of whose name, Varahran, is quite similar to *Orlagno*. Verethraghna is praised in the *Bahram Yasht*. Originally, he seems to be identical with the vedic Vṛitrahan Indra, but later on, he came to be looked upon as a 'genius of victory'. *Orlagno* is, thus, the Iranian 'god of victory and royal glory'. The representation of *Orlagno* occurs on the rev of some gold coins of *Kanishka I. The diademed deity, wearing a helmet surmounted by the figure of a bird, stands to the r. He holds a spear in his r hand, and a sword in his left. There is a suggestion that the bird perched on the helmet of the deity should be identified as Vāraghna, mentioned in the *Avesta* as the swiftest of all. It is interesting to note that, although *Orlagno* is a deity associated with victory, he is not shown as winged like *Nike and **Oanindo*; instead, a winged creature, the bird Vāraghna, is depicted as perched on his helmet (Bhaskar Chattopadhyay 1977; Darmesteter 1974; Gardner 1971; Rosenfield 1967; Stein 1888).

Orthagnes. *Śaka-Pahlava k; early first century AD. He was a successor of *Spalirises in Arachosia, or, more probably, the successor of the person who overthrew Spalirises in that region. There are some silver and copper coins bearing the name of Orthagnes with full sovereign titles on the obv, and those of *Gondopharnes and *Guḍa, or that of Guḍa alone, on the rev. All these coins show diademed bust of king on the obv, and wreath- and palm-bearing *Nike on the rev. Scholars like Cunningham, Smith, Whitehead, and Allan regard Orthagnes as a successor of Gondopharnes, while Sten Konow and J E van Lohuizen de Leeuw are of the view that the names Orthagnes and Gondopharnes refer to one and the same person. But Rapson suggests that Orthagnes was the overlord of Gondopharnes and Guḍa, and this is supported by the occurrence of the name of Orthagnes on the obv, and of Gondopharnes and/or Guḍa on the rev of the coins. It appears that, initially, Orthagnes ruled over Arachosia with the help of his subordinates, Gondopharnes and Guḍa. Gondopharnes conquered territories in northwestern India, dissociated himself from the administration of Arachosia, and consequently, Orthagnes nominated Guḍa to succeed Gondopharnes as the viceroy of Arachosia. Later on, perhaps after the death of Orthagnes, that region was reoccupied by Gondopharnes. One silver type, bearing the bust of the king and no ld on the obv, and enthroned king with a female figure crowning him and a ld in which the name of the issuer is not clear on the rev, has been attributed to Orthagnes by some scholars. Interestingly, the device of diademed bust of king appears for the first time on Śaka-Pahlava coinage on the coins of Orthagnes with Gondopharnes and Guḍa. (Cunningham 1971a; Gardner 1971; Jenkins and Narain 1957; van Lohuizen de Leeuw 1949; Marshall 1975; B N Mukherjee 1969a; Rapson 1987; Senior 2001; Sircar 1980b; Prashant Srivastava 1996a; Tarn 1980; Whitehead 1914).

Ouranos. Greek sky god. According to Hesiod, Gaia was born apparently from Chaos, and the earth bore, unaided and as her equal,

Ouranos, the sky. Ouranos covered Gaia, and the couple had a number of off-springs, including the Titans and the Titanesses, the three Kyklopes, the Hekatoncheires, the Erinyes, the Giants, the Meliai, and Aphrodite. Ouranos was later superseded by *Zeus, just as the vedic *Varuṇa was superseded by *Indra. The figure of a bearded and nimbate male deity, standing to the l, appears on the rev of a gold coin type of the *Kushāṇa ruler, *Huvishka. He wears *modius* on his head, and *himation*. His r hand is advanced, and he holds a long sceptre in his l hand. The label inscription accompanying the figure describes it as *Uron*, that is Ouranos (Bhaskar Chattopadhyay 1977; Cunningham 1971a; Gardner 1971; Graves 1955; Kerenyi 1951; Marshall 1975; Rose 1958; Prashant Srivastava 2007b; Prashant Srivastava 2007c; Whitehead 1914).†

Owl. Symbol. Crow was originally the favourite bird of *Athena. But as it was the creature that bore the news of the discovery of the birth of Athena's son, Erichthonios, by two daughters of Kekropes, the first king of the Athenians, it invited the wrath of the goddess. Henceforth, the owl became the favourite bird of Athena. In Indian mythology, the owl, which was originally regarded as the messenger of death in the *Ṛigveda*, later on came to be associated with *Lakshmī as her *vāhana*. The bird is depicted on the coins of the *Indo-Greek rulers, like *Menander, *Agathokleia, and *Archebios. Even when it is of the Indian variety, it seems to be associated with Athena, rather than Lakshmī (Banerjea 2002; Bopearachchi 1993; Bopearachchi and Pieper 1998; Bopearachchi and Rahman 1995; Bhaskar Chattopadhyay 1977; Gardner 1971; Graves 1955; Kerenyi 1951; A N Lahiri 1965; Marshall 1975; Rao 1985; Rose 1958; Whitehead 1914).

Menander

Archebios

'Owls'. Coins of Athens. The coins of Athens (594 BC – 560 BC) bore on the rev, the figure of an *owl to the r, and due to this depiction, these coins themselves were termed 'owls'. These 'owls' of Athens have been found in the northwestern frontier region of India, and appear to have been brought there in the course of the expansion of commerce. It is quite probable that imitations of the Athenian 'owls' were being struck locally in Afghanistan, and, perhaps, the frontier regions of Bactria, even before the arrival of Alexander. Some coins of this type bear the Gr letters *Aig*, which have been taken to stand for the name of the Aigloi, who, according to Herodotos, dwelt to the north of the Bactrians (D R Bhandarkar 1984; Bopearachchi 1993; Bopearachchi and Pieper 1998; Bopearachchi and Rahman 1995; Gardner 1971; Marshall 1975; Narain 1957a).

Encyclopaedia of Indian Coins

(Ancient Coins of Northern India, up to *circa* 650 AD)

Encyclopaedia of Indian Coins

(Ancient Coins of Northern India, up to *circa* 650 AD)

Vol. II

Prashant Srivastava

AGAM KALA PRAKASHAN
DELHI

First Published 2012

ISBN : 978 -81-7320-118-9

Published by:
Dr. Agam Prasad, M.A., Ph.D., Diploma in Museology
For **Agam Kala Prakashan**
34, Central Market, Ashok Vihar
Delhi - 110 052
Tel.: 27212195, 65688806-7 Fax: 91-11-27212195
Email: agambooks@gmail.com, agambook@yahoo.com
www.agamkala.com

Composed by:
Aman Printographics
Mobile: 9891395309

Printed by:
Chawla Offset
Delhi-110 052

Printed in India

Contents

For my wife
Dr Nidhi Srivastava

...pṛithivī tvam
(*Bṛihadāraṇyakopanishad* IV. 4. 20)

Preface

Coins form one of the important sources of the history of ancient India; in fact, for certain periods, like those of the Indo-Greeks, the Śaka-Pahlavas, and the Western Kshatrapas, monetary issues are almost the only source of our information. In the Preface of his *magnum opus*, *The Indo-Greeks* (Oxford, 1957), A K Narain very aptly remarks, 'For certain periods of Indian history the historian has to be a numismatist'.

Several years back, the Numismatic Society of India launched an ambitious scheme of publishing corpuses of Indian coins, from the earliest times to the modern period, in ten volumes, each volume being of between four hundred and five hundred pages, and having illustrations of coins arranged in twenty to twenty-five plates. Unfortunately, only Volume IV, that is A S Altekar's *The Coinage of the Gupta Empire* (Varanasi, 1957), saw the light of day. A N Lahiri, in his individual capacity, published a *Corpus of Indo-Greek Coins* (Calcutta, 1965). Tribal coins were dealt with, first by K K Dasgupta, in his *A Tribal History of Ancient India—A Numismatic Approach* (Calcutta, 1974), and, recently, by Devendra Handa, in *Tribal Coins of Ancient India* (New Delhi, 2007). R C Senior produced the masterly work, *Indo-Scythian Coins and History* (Lancaster, Pennsylvania, London, 2001), in three volumes. However, a concise A-Z encyclopaedia of the coins of ancient India remains a *desideratum*. Hence, the present *Encyclopaedia of India Coins*.

I am well aware that, as early as nineteenth century, while preparing the work, *The Coins of the Mohammadan States of India* (London, 1885), Stanley Lane-Poole had realized, 'To be a general numismatist is beyond the powers of one man'. That is why, for the present work, I have confined myself to the ancient coins of northern India, up to *circa* 650 AD, and further encyclopaediae of the ancient coins of southern India, and the early mediaeval coins of northern India, might be prepared some time in the future.

Even then, in preparing an encyclopaedia of this limited size, I have had to be selective, and, very often, not necessarily out of choice. Still, I am open to charges of ignorance for what I have had to omit. I have also tried to be concise, yet explicit. To avoid repetition, cross referencing has been resorted to, other relevant entries in the *Encyclopaedia* being indicated by means of an asterisk (*). However, I must admit that certain entries (for example, V'ima Takshuma) have exceeded the size limit I had set for each entry, either because some recent material appeared to deserve more detailed handling, or the entries formed some of my favourite subjects; in some cases, for example, those of the Indo-Greek and Śaka-Pahlava rulers, coins form the most important (and, very often, the only) source of our information about them, and, hence, I had, perforce, to give their political history in brief. Also, in a work of this nature, it has not always been possible to avoid repetition altogether.

In the A-Z encyclopaedia, there are some references at the end of each entry. They represent only those books, monographs, and research papers, which had a direct bearing on the subject, and which I have had occasion to consult during the writing of that particular entry. In cases, where more than one publications of a scholar were available on the same subject, I have usually referred to his latest work, and not burdened the reader with the earlier one(s), unless it was otherwise deemed necessary. As a result, the specialist would find many omissions, for which I would crave his indulgence.

An Introduction, in the beginning, deals with such aspects of ancient Indian numismatics, as the origin and antiquity of coinage in India, and the authority to issue coins. This is followed by the A-Z encyclopaedia. In this, the issuers—kings/queens, dynasties, tribes, etc, and the devices—deities, symbols, etc, have been introduced briefly, mostly at the beginning of the respective entry, before dealing with the numismatic aspects. However, it was felt that the introduction of the political background of certain issuers, mostly kings, of the mythological background of certain deities, and the significance of certain symbols, deserves a somewhat fuller treatment, either by virtue of their importance, or their obscurity, even at the cost of some repetition. This has been done, again in an alphabetical order, in the Appendix, 'More About Some Issuers and Devices', which comes after the A-Z Encyclopaedia. All such entries in the body of the A-Z Encyclopaedia, as having a companion entry in the Appendix, have been indicated by means of a cross (†), placed at the end of the entry. A Select Bibliography is given at the end for the benefit of those who wish to pursue further reading.

I am indebted to the University Grant Commission for extending adequate financial assistance for the present work in the form of a major research project grant.

I also wish to thank my first readers, my mentor, Professor Kiran Kumar Thaplyal, and my father, Shri Priyonath Srivastava, who went through the truly rough drafts, and offered some valuable suggestions.

The Indian Institute of Research in Numismatic Studies, Nashik, provided some coin photographs for research purposes. For this, I express my gratitude to Dr Amiteshwar Jha, Shri

Danish Moin, Shri Rehan Ahamad, and other members of the staff at the Institute, and, above all, to Shri (now Dr) K K Maheshwari. I wish to put on record, my thanks to Dr Ram Chandra Tiwari, Dr Rakesh Tewari, Shri I P Pandey, Dr S N Upadhyaya, Dr Anita Chaurasia, and the photographer, Shri Sharada Prasad Tripathi, of the State Museum, Lucknow, for providing some of the photographs illustrating the *Encyclopaedia*.

Professor S P Shukla, formerly of the Kurukshetra University, Dr R S Bisht, former Joint Director-General of the Archaeological Survey of India, and Dr Abhay Kumar Singh, Reader in Ancient History and Culture, M J P Rohilkhand University, Bareilly, provided some study material, for which I am beholden to them.

For providing facilities of study, I wish to thank the librarian and staff of the Tagore Library, University of Lucknow, Lucknow; Central Archaeological Library, New Delhi; National Museum, New Delhi; the Indian Institute of Research in Numismatic Studies, Nashik; American Institute of Indian Studies, Gurgaon; State Museum, Lucknow; State Archaeological Organization, Uttar Pradesh, Lucknow; etc.

As always, my deepest gratitude goes to my parents, Smt Pushplata Srivastava and Shri Priyonath Srivastava, who have been a constant source of inspiration; and to my wife, and my daughters, Pratichi and Purvi, for bearing with me. My sister, Monica, and her family provided me hospitality during my stays at Delhi in connection with this work. My heartfelt thanks to her, to Naveen, and the whole family.

In the end, I thank Dr Agam Prasad of Agam Kala Prakashan, Delhi, and his staff, especially Shri A.K. Pandey, for their cooperation in bringing out this *Encyclopaedia* in its present form.

25 July 2011. **Prashant Srivastava**

Abbreviations

Br	Brāhmī
Gr	Greek
k	king
Kh	Kharoshṭhī
l	left
ld	legend
obv	obverse
Pkt	Prakrit
r	right
rev	reverse
Skt	Sanskrit

P

Pāda-kārshāpaṇa. Coin denomination. It was one-fourth of a **kārshāpaṇa* of silver, and weighed 8 *rattīs* (D R Bhandarkar 1984; Chakrabortty 1931).

Pāda-māshaka. Coin denomination. Mentioned in the *Arthaśāstra* of Kauṭilya, it was a copper coin and a submultiple of the **māshaka*, being one-eighth of it. It was also known as **kākaṇī* (Sircar 1952; Sircar 1968).

Pāda-paṇa. Coin denomination. Mentioned in the *Arthaśāstra* of Kauṭilya, it was a silver coin and a submultiple of the **paṇa*, being one-eighth of it (Sircar 1952; Sircar 1968).

Paḍika. Coin denomination. Mentioned in several cave inscriptions from western India, it is regarded by some scholars as a name of the *Kushāṇa coins. But there is a suggestion that it might also be taken as a form of *pratika*, which is mentioned in Kātyāyana's *vārttika* and the *Mahābhārata*, and is regarded as another name for the **kārshāpaṇa* in the period from at least the fourth century BC to the end of the first century BC; this interpretation of *pratika* as *kārshāpaṇa* is supported by S K Belvalkar (V S Agrawala 1945; V S Agrawala 1956; C S Gupta 1982; Sircar 1986).

Padmāvatī. The coins of Padmāvatī (modern Padam Pawaya) are of two groups. The first group bears the names of kings, Makhadatta (or, Sakhadeva), Mahata, Amitasena, etc, and is datable to the first-second centuries AD. On Makhadatta's coins is seen the Śaiva *triśūla. Some of the coins from Padmāvatī bear *tree-in-railing or *bull. These kings ruled before the *Nāgas. The first group is followed by the second group, which comprises mostly kings with *nāga*-ending names [*Nāga] (Bela Lahiri 1974; H V Trivedi 1957).

Uncertain ascription

Pakhalavadi-devada. The city deity of Pushkalāvatī. There is a gold piece in the collection of the British Museum, London, which bears on the obv, a female figure standing facing front, wearing a mural or turreted crown and *chiton*. She holds a stalked lotus in her 'half raised' r hand, while her l hand rests on her left thigh, although P L Gupta says that she has a mace in the r hand and a spear in the l hand. The Kh ld, arranged on either side of the figure, reads *[Pa]khalavadi-devada* (or *ta*) *Aṁpaë*, 'of Aṁpa, the deity of Pakhalavadi', that is Pushkalāvatī (modern Charsadda). The rev has the figure of a humped *bull to the r, with the Gr ld *Tauros* above the device, and the Kh ld *[U]shabhe* below the device. Thus, this piece, which is regarded by Rapson as reproduction in gold of the devices of two different seals or gems, and by others as a special coin issued by some guild or the local authority, bears the figure of the city goddess of Pushkalāvatī, who is called *Aṁpa*, that is Aṁbā in the third component of the obv Kh ld. Her name, together with the presence of the bull, the theriomorphic representation of *Śiva, and the legends *tauros* (Greek for bull) and [*u*]*shabhe*, the Pkt form of *vṛishabha* (Skt for bull), on the rev, marks her as the consort of Śiva. The association of Śiva, and his bull, with the Gandhāra region is attested by authorities like Hesychios and Hiuen-tsang. Interestingly, a similar goddess also finds representation on some coins of the *Indo-Greek ruler, *Peukolaos (whose very name, according to scholars like Rapson and Tarn, connects him with the city of Pushkalāvatī), and the *Śaka-Pahlava ruler, *Azes. Further, on the coins of Azes, the bull occurs on the rev, as on the gold piece under consideration (Gardner 1971; P L Gupta 1958; B N Mukherjee 1969b; Rapson 1905; Rapson 1987; Tarn 1980).

Pakores. *Śaka-Pahlava k; successor of *Gondopharnes; latter half of the first century AD. On numismatic grounds, he is believed to have ruled after Gondopharnes, although it is not certain whether he immediately followed the latter, or reigned after *Abdagases. It is also quite likely that after the death of Gondopharnes, his vast dominions were divided among Abdagases, Pakores, and *Sasan, all of them ruling simultaneously over different parts of the former empire of Gondopharnes. Numismatic evidence suggests that Pakores ruled over Arachosia, which he might have regained from the *Kushāṇas. Earlier, it was believed that he issued coins in copper/bronze only, but now, his silver coins are also available. The obv of all his coins has the diademed bust of the king, and the Gr ld referring to him as **basileos basileon megas*. The rev usually has *Nike standing, and the Pkt ld, written in the Kh script, giving the titles **maharaja rajatiraja mahata* to Pakores; one silver type, attributed to Seistan, has the figure of the king, enthroned as an archer, on the rev. The form of his name occurring in the Pkt ld is Pakura (Cunningham 1971a; Gardner 1971; Jenkins and Narain 1957; Konow 1929; van Lohuizen de Leeuw 1949; Marshall 1975; B N Mukherjee 1969a; Rapson 1987; Senior 2001; Sircar 1980b; Smith 1972; Prashant Srivastava 1996a; Tarn 1980; Whitehead 1914).

Pala. Coin denomination. **Nishka.*

Palasara. *Parataraja k.

Pallas. Semi-divine being. She was the daughter of the river Triton, the tutor of *Athena according to some versions of the myth. She was the playmate of Athena, and was accidentally killed by the goddess, when they were playing the war game. Athena mourned for her, and from Homer onwards, *Pallas* became a poetical appellation of Athena (Graves 1955; Kerenyi 1951; Rose 1958).

Palm. Symbol. The palm branch, as also palm and wreath, are the symbols of *Nike; besides, palm is also associated with the *Dioskuri. On coins, both Nike and the Dioskuri are shown carrying palm branch in their hand. Palm and wreath as independent device are depicted on some copper coins of the *Indo-Greek ruler, *Antimachos II. When depicted together with the **pilei*, as on the coins of *Eukratides, *Antialkidas, and *Archebios, and on the joint coins of *Lysias with Antialkidas, the palm is to be associated with the Dioskuri. The palm tree may also be seen on some coins of *Ayodhyā and *Taxila (Allan 1936; Bopearachchi 1993; Bopearachchi and Pieper 1998; Bopearachchi and Rahman

1995; Gardner 1971; Graves 1955; Kerenyi 1951; A N Lahiri 1965; Rose 1958; Senior 2001; Whitehead 1914).

Paṁchanekame. Ld. *Takshaśilā. Guild coins.

Paṇa. Coin denomination. It is believed to be the unit of the copper coinage. It is generally assumed on the authority of Manu that the *paṇa* weighed 80 *rattīs*, but the commentary on the *Vinayapiṭaka* and the *Gaṇgamālajātaka* refer to a *paṇa* weighing 20 *māshas* of five *rattīs* each, that is 100 *rattīs*. Vasishṭha, Gautama, and Uśanas are aware of it, as also Nārada. The *Agnipurāṇa* mentions a *paṇa* of 24 *māshas*, that is 120 *rattīs*. However, in the *Arthaśāstra* of Kauṭilya, the *paṇa* is the standard silver coin and has several submultiples like the **ardha-paṇa*, **pāda-paṇa*, and **ashṭabhāga-paṇa*, while the standard copper coin is the **māshaka* [**kārshāpaṇa*] (Altekar 1940; D R Bhandarkar 1984; Chakrabortty 1931; Sircar 1952; Sircar 1968).

Panadatta (Parṇadatta ?). *Almora k.

Pañchāla : Phalgunīmitra

Pañchāla. The *Mahābhārata* associates Pañchāla with the Kurus. The country came to be known as Pañchāla as here, five vedic tribes merged into the predominant Kṛivis. Pañchāla was one of the 16 *janapadas* of northern India in the sixth century BC. The region constituted the area under Bareilly, Badaun, Farrukhabad, and the adjoining districts. It was divided into two parts, with Ahichchhatrā (modern Ramnagar near Aonla) forming the capital of northern Pañchāla, and Kāmpilya (modern Kampil, between Badaun and Farrukhabad), that of southern Pañchāla. Barring a few silver-coated or heavily alloyed ones, all Pañchāla coins are in copper, and round in shape. They 'form one of the largest and most uniform series of ancient Indian coins'. On the obv, most of them bear three constant symbols, with the king's name below, all within an incuse square. On the rev is generally depicted, in anthropomorphic or symbolic form, a deity whose name forms 'a component of the issuer's name'. But at times, symbols like railed platform together with two pillar and crossbars, **chakra*, sun, *Indradhvaja*, *tree-in-railing, triple parasols, *taurine, **vajra*, etc, also occur. The coins of *Varuṇamitra, *Vasusena, *Yugasena, *Anamitra,

*Śivanandiśrī, and *Śrīnandi do not show any deity or his emblem on the rev, which would indicate a late date for them. The kings known from the Pañchāla series are (alphabetically), *Achu[ta], *Agnimitra, Anamitra, *Bahasatimitra (= Bṛihaspatimitra or Bṛihatsvātimitra), *Bhadraghosha, *Bhānumitra, *Bhūmimitra, *Damagupta, *Dhruvamitra, *Indramitra, *Jayagupta, *Jayamitra, *Phalgunīmitra, *Prajāpatimitra, *Rudraghosha, *Rudragupta, Śivanandiśrī, Śrīnandi, *Sūryamitra, *Vaṅgapāla, Varuṇamitra, Vasusena, *Vishṇumitra, *Viśvapāla (?), *Yajñapāla, and *Yugasena. Thus, most of the kings have *mitra*-ending names. The other rulers variously have the following name-endings—*ghosha*, *gupta*, *nandi*, *pāla*, and *sena*. The latter are, however, interconnected by types and symbols with kings having *mitra*-ending names. The rev devices on the Pañchāla coins are of great iconographic interest. In case of the name of the deity depicted forming a component of the name of the issuing king, Allan considers the deity whose figure or attribute occurs on coins as the patron deity of the issuer. But B Bhatt points out that this would mean that kings frequently changed their names in order to suit their new cult allegiance. He himself feels that the figure of the deity is a visual representation of the name of the king, and the illiterate masses could identify the king who issued the coin with the help of the rev device. The figures, however, are so crude that, in most of the cases, their identification, without reference to the king's name, would be very difficult; also, in some cases, scholars have doubted correspondence between the name and the device. *Apollo on the coins of *Apollodotos, and *Kārttikeya (= Kumāra) on the coins of *Kumāragupta I, are cases of names of kings tallying with those of the deities represented on their coins. However, these do not seem to provide examples of changing of name by king according to the deity of his choice, but rather those of selecting a god for representation on the basis of the name of the king who issued the coins. The deities and symbols on Pañchāla coins are all Brahmanical. There is hardly any justification for considering the Pañchāla kings, many of whom bore *mitra*-ending names, as belonging to the Śuṅga dynasty. The names of Agnimitra, Jyeshṭhamitra, and Prajāpatimitra in the Pañchāla series, also occur on *Kauśāmbī coins. However, there is a great difference between their coins in the two series, and they should be taken as issues of different persons. Achyuta and Nandi of coins are identified with the

Pañchāla : Bhūmimitra

homonyms mentioned in the Allahabad pillar inscription, and hence, should be dated to the fourth century AD. The rest of the Pañchāla coins have been dated variously between 200 BC and the end of the first century BC by Allan; between 100 BC and 100 AD by Smith (mainly on palaeographical ground), and between *c* 50 BC and 250 AD by Sircar (Allan 1936; Bela Lahiri 1974; Mitchiner 1975-1976; Sircar 1980d; Smith 1972).

Pandiala hoard. It was reportedly discovered at Pandiala Daneshkur. The rulers represented in this hoard include *Archebios, *Telephos, and *Maues (Senior 2001).

Paṇṇika. Coin denomination. This is mentioned in a Jaina work, the *Vyavahārabhāshya*, datable to *c* seventh century AD. According to V S Agrawala, Parṇī was the name of the tribe to which the Sassanian king, Arsakes, belonged, and the coins issued by the Sassanian kings of the Parṇī tribe were called *parṇika* or *paṇṇika* in India. Some other scholars, however, read it as *paṇṇaga*, and identify it as a *paṇa*. There is a also a suggestion that *paṇṇika* was not a metallic piece, but a leaf-coin, and might have had some connection with the *panika-seni* or guild of merchants dealing in (betel ?) leaves (V S Agrawala 1950; J C Jain 1984; S R Goyal 1994; Jai Prakash Singh 1971; U P Shah 1952).

Pantaleon. *Indo-Greek k; son of *Demetrios I; first half of the second century BC. It is suggested that after his conquest of Arachosia and Drangiana, Demetrios I left behind his two sons, Pantaleon and *Agathokles, as joint subkings of those provinces, and the two ruled jointly after the death of Demetrios I in Bactria. Narain is of the view that, taking advantage of the conflict between *Eukratides and *Demetrios II, the two brothers occupied the Kabul valley. They then proceeded to conquer western Gandhāra in the east, but Pantaloen died before Takshaśilā could be occupied. He issued silver, cupro-nickel, and copper coins. All the silver and cupro-nickel coins, and one type of copper coins, are struck on the Attic standard, while one type of copper coins is based on the Indian standard. All the coins are die-struck pieces. All the coins struck on the Attic standard are round in shape, while the copper type struck on the Indian standard is square in shape. The obv of the silver coins has the diademed bust of the king to the r, while the rev has the figure of enthroned *Zeus, holding a sceptre in the l hand, and *Hekate on his extended r hand. The cupro-nickel type, as also the copper type struck on the Attic standard, have the bust of *Dionysos to the r on the obv, and *panther to the r on the rev. The obv of the copper coins struck on the Indian standard has the panther to the r on the obv, and *Yakshiṇī Aśvamukhī on the rev. The coins based on the Attic standard have the Gr ld, on the rev. But the copper type with the yakshiṇī on the rev has the Gr ld on the obv, and the Pkt ld, written in the Br script, on the rev. Pantaleon assumed the title of *basileus* on his coins, which is rendered into Pkt in the Br ld on the rev of the copper type struck on the Indian standard, as *rajane*. The Pkt form of the name of the ruler, as met with on the square copper coins, is Pataleva (Bopearachchi 1993; Bopearachchi and Pieper 1998; Bopearachchi and Rahman 1995; Cunningham 1970; Gardner 1971; A N Lahiri 1965; Marshall 1975; Narain 1957a; Rapson 1987; Sircar 1980a; Prashant Srivastava 1996a; Tarn 1980; Whitehead 1914).†

Pantaleon

Panther. *Lion.

Paramabhāgavata. Title. This title was assumed by a number of *Imperial Gupta rulers on their coins, as well as inscriptions, and shows their Vaishṇava inclination (Ashvini Agrawal 1989; Allan 1914; Altekar 1957; Fleet 1888; S R Goyal 2005; P L Gupta 1998; Sircar 1986; Smith 1972; Thaplyal, forthcoming).

Paratarajas. Dynasty (?). Rulers of this dynasty are known from a very rare coin series, which has been placed to northwestern India or its borderland to the south of the Hindukush. There is a view tracing the series to the laoralai in the Quetta district of Pakistan, between Quetta to Multan. According to B N Mukherjee, the *Paratarajas* started issuing coins some time in the first century AD, and their coins from the Jhelum region may be dated as late as the second half of the third century AD, or even later. R C Senior would, however, place the early *Parataraja* coins in the latter half of the first century BC. There is a suggestion to identify the *Paratarajas* with the Pāradas, mentioned as a people in early Indian literary texts, like the *Mahābhārata*, the *Harivaṁśa*, the *Manusmṛiti*, and the *Bṛihatsaṁhitā*, and the Paraitakenoi of the Greek sources. The coins of the *Paratarajas* are both in silver and copper, and have been divided into three groups by B N Mukherjee. Most of the coins bear, on the obv, the bust of the king to the r. But there are some specimens, which have the standing figure of the king on this side of the coin. The rev of the coins of the first group of B N Mukherjee has the mounted king on the rev, being crowned by flying *Nike from behind. The ld on the obv of the coins of this group is in Kh, and that on the rev, in Gr. The rev of the remaining coins has a **svastika* in the centre, surrounded by a ld, in Kh on the coins of the second group, and in Br on the coins of the third group. In most of the legends, the dynastic name, *Parataraja*, may be read. The names of the issuer on most of the coins is not clear, and have been read variously as *Puḍena*, *Puḍhana*, *Puḍhena*, *Hvavamira*, *Miramara*, *Palasara*, *Ajuna*, *Spajhana*, *Spajhama* (?), *Bhimajhunasa*, etc. Interestingly, the coin legends also give the name of the father of the issuer, which has been taken to associate this series with the *Kārddamaka series (B N Mukherjee 1972; Senior 2001).

Parvata. *Kauśāmbī k. Allan places him in the second century BC, but Bela Lahiri, on the basis of the facts that he issued both round and square copper coins, and that his square coins are of comparatively thin fabric, connects him with *Aśvaghosha, who ruled in the beginning of the first century AD. His coins bear the figure of a *bull to the r on the obv; the rev has a *hill symbol, *tree-in-railing, and *undulating line, and the ld *Pavatasa* (Allan 1936; Bopearachchi and Pieper 1998; Bela Lahiri 1974).

Pārvatī. Indian goddess. *Umā immolated herself in the sacrificial fire of Daksha, and was reborn as Pārvatī, a daughter of Himavat. In this later birth, she obtained *Śiva as her husband by severe austerities. She is the mother of *Kārttikeya and Gaṇeśa. She is usually described as engaged in love, or, occasionally, in philosophical discussions, with Śiva on Kailāsa, independent achievements ascribed to her being very rare. In the *Ardhanārīśvara form, she form the left half of the body, while the right half represents Śiva. It has recently been reported by Devendra Handa that the obv of a *Yaudheya coin bears the figure of a goddess seated in *lalitāsana*. Her r hand is raised up, while the left one is placed on her left knee. Handa proposes to identify this goddess with Pārvatī, whose divine spouse, Śiva, appears on the rev of this coin. On the solitary specimen of the gold coinage of *Harsha, her nimbate figure appears on the rev as seated with Śiva on Nandin. The god is embracing the goddess with his lower l hand. Her left leg is placed on her right thigh. Her l hand is outstretched, and the right one is placed on the left thigh of Śiva. She is lovingly looking at her husband. The device bears a striking similarity to the depiction of Śiva and Pārvatī on Nandin on a stone panel from Kanauj, datable to the seventh century AD. This similarity has led to the suggestion that the same artist might have been responsible for the execution of the stone sculpture and the die of the gold coin of Harsha (K D Bajpai 1976; K D Bajpai 1991; Banerjea 2002; Sukumari Bhattacharji 1970; S R Goyal 1986; Handa 2007a; T R R Iyengar 2003; Prashant Srivastava 2004a; Wilkins 2006).[†]

Paurava. Tribe. According to the *Mahābhārata*, this tribe was founded by Pūru, the son of Yayāti and Śarmishṭhā. In the *Ṛigveda*, the powerful Pūru ruler, Sudāsa, won a spectacular victory in the Dāśarājña battle fought on the banks of the river Parushṇī (modern Ravi). In the *Rāmāyaṇa*, it is told that Purūravas, the great-grandfather of Pūru, was the son of a ruler who had migrated from Bāhli in central Asia. The *Ṛigveda* locates the Pūrus somewhere in the vicinity of the river Sarasvatī. The *Mahābhārata* refers to a city protected by the Pauravas, which was located somewhere near Kashmir. At the time of the invasion of India by Alexander, the land between the rivers Jhelum and Chenab was ruled by Poros, which seems to be the Greek form of Pūru or Paurava. The *Bṛihatsaṁhitā* also refers to the Pauravas with such northern tribes as the Madrakas, the *Mālavas, and the *Trigartas. There are some seven copper or billon coins in the collection of the British Museum, London, which seem to have been issued by the Pauravas. The coins weigh between 23.8 and 62.5 grains. The obv of these coins bears the figure of a *lion to the r and a curved line below. The rev has a *tree-in-railing, with some symbols, like the **jayadhvaja*, flanking it. Mitchiner read the names of two chiefs—Datamita and Vijayanaya, along with the title *rājña* and the tribal name, in the coin ld on some of these coins. P L Gupta agrees that these coins reveal the names of two rulers, but is not satisfied with the reading of their names. Devendra Handa suggests that the name, which has been read as *Datamita* by Mitchiner, should be read as *Iṁdrotamita*. He also proposes to read *Vijayayayī* in place of *Vijayanaya* of Mitchiner. He identifies a third Paurava ruler, named Mahādeva, on a coin in the collection of the British Museum, London, published by Allan, and he places Mahādeva before Iṁdrotamita and Vijayayayī. The Paurava coins have been placed in the first century BC or first century AD, on palaeographical grounds (Allan 1936; P L Gupta 1988; Handa 2007a; Mitchiner 1975-1976; Mitchiner 1978).

Kumāragupta I : Kārttikeya type

Kumāragupta I : *Madhyadeśa* type

Peacock. Symbol. The Dravidians and the Kolerians worship the peacock as the earth goddess, and this is taken to indicate the association of this bird with the female principle since primitive times. But the bird came to be more closely associated with *Kārttikeya as his mount. The peacock makes its appearance on the *punch marked coins, where it is sometimes shown perched on top of a *hill. The bird may also be seen depicted on the rev of some *Mālava coins. *Kumāragupta I gave a pride of place to the peacock on his coins, most probably because of its association with Kārttikeya, his patron deity. On the *Kārttikeya type of his gold coins, the peacock appears on the obv as being fed grapes by the king, and on the rev, as the mount of Kārttikeya. On the rev of a class of the *Horseman type of his gold coins, and the rev of the *Tiger-slayer type of his gold coins, the goddess is shown feeding a peacock. The bird again appears beside the goddess on the rev of the *Elephant-rider-lion-slayer type of his gold coins. When Kumāragupta I issued the **Madhyadeśa* type of silver coins, he replaced the **garuḍa* on the rev of the *Western Indian type of silver coins, with a fan-tailed peacock, and this was continued by a number of subsequent powers, who imitated the *Madhyadeśa* type of *Imperial Gupta silver coins (Allan 1914; Altekar 1957; Banerjea 2002; Bhaskar Chattopadhyay 1977; Handa 2007a; Hopkins 1902; Hopkins 1915; Rao 1985).†

Peacock type. Copper. The Peacock type of copper coins was struck by the *Imperial Gupta ruler, *Kumāragupta I. The obv bears the crowned head of the king to the r. The rev has the figure of a fan-tailed *peacock, with the metrical circular ld *Vijitāvaniravanipatiḥ Kumāragupto divaṁ jayati* (Allan 1914; Altekar 1957; P L Gupta 1998; Smith 1972).

Petluripalem hoard. This hoard of over 230 silver coins (235 according to H V Trivedi; 238 according to D C Sircar) was discovered in the Guntur district of Andhra Pradesh in 1959. Besides some coins which could not be ascribed with any certainty, and a coin of *Īśvaradatta, the hoard contains coins of the *Kārddamaka Kshatrapas—*Vīradāman, *Vijayasena, *Dāmajadaśrī III, *Dāmasena's son (whose name is not clear), *Rudrasena II, *Viśvasiṁha, *Bhartṛidāman, son of Rudrasena II (whose name is not clear), *Viśvasena, *Rudrasiṁha II, *Yaśodāman II (Jha and Rajgor 1994; Sircar 1968; H V Trivedi 1964).

Peukolaos. *Indo-Greek k; early first century BC. He is believed to be a subking of *Apollodotos, who later asserted independence for a short while. Tarn associates him with the Pushakalāvatī region, but according to Narain, he seems to have ruled over the Kabul region also. He issued silver and copper coins, all based on the Indian standard. All the coins are die-struck pieces. The silver coins are round in shape, while the copper ones are square in shape. The obv of the silver coins has the diademed bust of the king to the r, while the rev has *Zeus standing to the l, holding a long sceptre in his l hand, and an uncertain object (callipers ?) in his r hand. The copper coins have, on the obv, *Artemis standing to the front, and drawing an arrow from the quiver at her back; the rev has a crowned city deity standing to the l, with a *lotus in her r hand, and *palm in her l hand. All the coins have the Gr ld on the obv, and the Pkt ld, written in the Kh script, on the rev. Besides the title of **basileus*, Peukolaos assumed the epithets **dikaios* and **soteros* on his coins. These are rendered into Pkt as **maharaja*, **dhramika*, and **tratara*, respectively. The Pkt form of the name of the ruler, as met with on coins, is Peükulaä (Bopearachchi 1993; Bopearachchi and Pieper 1998; Bopearachchi and Rahman 1995; Cunningham 1970; Gardner 1971; A N Lahiri 1965; Marshall 1975; Narain 1957a; Rapson 1987; Senior 2001; Sircar 1980a; Tarn 1980; Whitehead 1914).[†]

Phalgunī. Constellation as deity. The rev of the coins of the *Pañchāla ruler, *Phalgunīmitra, bears the figure of a female divinity, standing on a lotus bloom. In her raised r hand, she holds an uncertain object, which has doubtfully been identified as 'a tree branch with three leaves attached to it', while the l hand rests on her hip. There is a suggestion that the deity on the coins of Phalgunīmitra be identified as Agni. The basis for this suggestion is, probably, the fact that the hair of this deity is represented by five flames. But as regards the identification of this deity as Agni, it must be pointed out that one would expect Agni to be represented as a male, while the deity on the rev of the coins of Phalgunīmitra is female. Cunningham and Allan regard this figure as the personification of the constellation Phalgunī, solely on the basis of the peculiar numismatic tradition of representing, on the rev of the Pañchāla coins, a deity, anthropomorphically or symbolically, whose name generally forms a component of the name of the issuer. It has, however, been pointed out that the representation of the deity visible on these Pañchāla coins does not conform to the description of either Pūrvaphalgunī or Uttaraphalgunī, given in iconographic texts. For, according to Hemādri, while Pūrvaphalgunī is elephant-faced, holding a parrot in her two hands, and seated upon a wheel, Uttaraphalgunī is tiger-faced, holding the sun, the moon, a rosary, and a *khaṭvāṅga* in her four hands, and riding a cow (Allan 1936; Banerjea 2002; Cunningham 1971b; Prashant Srivastava 1993b; S K Srivastava 1989).

Pañchāla : Phalgunīmitra

Phalgunīmitra. *Pañchāla k. The appearance of the rev symbol of *Vaṅgapāla on the coins of Bhadraghosha and Phalgunīmitra is taken to indicate that they ruled after Vaṅgapāla. Bela Lahiri places Phalgunīmitra in the sixth chronological position among the Pañchāla kings known from coins. The female deity represented on the rev of his coins is recognized as *Phalgunī (Allan 1936; Bela Lahiri 1974).

Kanishka I

Pharro. Avestan god of 'kingly glory'. On some *Kushāṇa coins issued by *Kanishka I, and also by *Huvishka, there occurs the figure of a male deity, usually diademed and nimbate, the attributes in his hands varying on various coins; the inscription beside the figure of the deity labels him *Pharro*. On some gold coins of Kanishka I, this deity stands to the r, and hold fire (?) in his r hand, and a spear in his l hand. On some gold coins of Huvishka, he holds fire (?) in his r hand as on the coins of Kanishka I above, but his l hand rests on the hilt of the sword tied at his waist; sometimes, flames may be seen arising from his shoulders. On other coins of Huvishka occurs a similar figure, but the deity holds a sceptre in his l hand instead of the sword. On still other coins of this ruler, *Pharro* may be seen holding a purse in one hand, and a sceptre or a **caduceus* in the other. The figure of *Pharro*, holding a sceptre and an elephant goad, is also known on Kushāṇa coins. Cunningham is of the view that what has been identified as fire in the hand of *Pharro* on some coins by Gardner, is actually the depiction of 'some sprouts of corn', and he suggests that the deity should be identified as Parjanya, 'the begettor of corns'. But the name of the deity, that is *Pharro*, seems to be derived from the Old Persian *farr*, which probably signifies fire, and, according to Gardner and a number of other scholars, *Pharro* is seen on coins as holding out fire, and with flames issuing from his shoulders. Hoffmann identifies *Pharro* with the Avestan Kavaem Khvareno, 'mighty kingly glory', a creation of *Ahuramazda, and invoked in the *Zāmyad Yasht*. The royalty and prosperity of the deity is emphasized by depicting sceptre and purse in his hands on Kushāṇa coins. The Iranians were fire worshippers, and it is not surprising that fire has come to be associated with kingly glory in Zoroastrian tradition. On the rev of a gold coin of Kanishka I, reported by Craig Alden Burns, there occurs a four-legged *Pharro*. The four legs of the deity are rather difficult to explain. But it may be pointed out that in vedic hymns, Agni is described as possessing three feet. The association of *Pharro* with fire seems to be certain. Could there have been some tradition, both in India and Iran, of showing fire god with more than the normal two feet ? Interestingly, in India, we have some images of Sadāśiva from Khajuraho, which show that deity with four feet (Craig Alden Burns 1990; Bhaskar Chattopadhyay 1977; Cunningham 1971a; Darmesteter 1974; Gardner 1971; Rosenfield 1967; Prashant Srivastava 1997; Stein 1888; Whitehead 1914).

Huvishka

Huvishka

Huvishka

Philopator. Title. Meaning 'beloved of [his] father', this title was adopted by *Apollodotos and *Strato II. Outside of India, it was used by the Seleukid ruler, Antiochos IX, and his successors, and the Arsakid ruler, Sinatrokes, who might have adopted it from the Seleukids. On the joint coins of *Strato I with Strato II, the title is rendered into Pkt as **priyapita* (Cunningham 1970; Gardner 1878; Gardner 1971; A N Lahiri 1965; Marshall 1975; Narain 1957a; Tarn 1980; Whitehead 1914; Wroth 1903).

Philoxenos

Philoxenos. *Indo-Greek k; son of *Antimachos II; last quarter of the second century BC. From the evidence of the Mir Zakah hoard, he seems to have succeeded *Archebios in northern Arachosia. The *provenance* of his coins shows that he, at times, ruled over parts of the Kabul valley, western Gandhāra, and Takshaśilā. R C Senior regards him as, perhaps, the last Indo-Greek ruler 'to control a unified kingdom south of the Hindu Kush'. He issued silver and copper coins. One silver type is struck on the Attic standard, while the rest of the silver types, and all the copper ones, are struck on the Indian standard. All the coins are die-struck pieces. The silver type based on the Attic standard is round in shape; some of the silver types struck on the Indian standard are round in shape, while the rest are square in shape. The copper coins are all square in shape. The obv of all the silver types has the diademed, and often helmeted, bust of the king. On most of the coins, the royal bust is to the r, but when the king is shown thrusting javelin, the royal bust is to the l. The rev of all the silver coins has the figure of the helmeted king on a prancing horse to the r. The copper coins usually have the standing figure of *Demeter, bearing **cornucopiae*, on the obv, and a humped *bull to the r on the rev. But the obv of one copper type has *Helios, radiate and bearing a long sceptre, while the rev has the winged *Nike, bearing wreath and palm. The silver coins struck on the Attic standard have the Gr ld on the rev. But the coins struck on the Indian standard have the Gr ld on the obv, and the Pkt ld, written in the Kh script, on the rev. Besides the title of **basileus*, Philoxenos assumed the epithet **aniketos* on his coins. These are rendered into Pkt as **maharaja* and **apaḍihata*, respectively. The Pkt form of the name of the ruler, as met with on coins, is Philasina (Bopearachchi 1993; Bopearachchi and Pieper 1998; Bopearachchi and Rahman 1995; Cunningham 1970; Gardner 1971; A N Lahiri 1965; Marshall 1975; Narain 1957a; Rapson 1987; Senior 2001; Sircar 1980a; Tarn 1980; Whitehead 1914).†

Phseigacharis

Phseigacharis. *Kushāṇa (?) k. He is believed to belong to the period when the Kushāṇa power was on the rise. His coins, in silver, are known from Bactria, and bear the diademed bust of the king on the obv; the rev has standing *Herakles with club in the r hand and lion's skin in the left. The ld, on the rev, reads *Phseigacharis*

(Cunningham 1971a; Gardner 1971; Rosenfield 1967; Senior 2001; Tarn 1980; Whitehead 1914).

Pilei. Symbol. These two egg-shaped caps symbolize the presence of the *Dioskuri. The *Indo-Greek ruler, *Eukratides I, and a number of princes of his family used the device of the figures of the Dioskuri on their coins. The *pilei* (singular *pilos*) of the Dioskuri, together with palm, appear on the rev of the coins of Eukratides, *Antialkidas, and *Archebios, on the joint coins of *Lysias with Antialkidas, and on some coins of the Śaka ruler, *Liäka Kusulaka. It has been suggested that *pilei* on the rev became the local type of the mint at *Taxila under the Indo-Greeks, and later, was copied by the Liäka Kusulaka. But Allan is of the view that 'the original of Liäka Kusulaka's coinage belongs not to Taxila but to Arachosia, Gedrosia, and Paropamisadae'. Moreover, A K Narain seems to be correct in his assumption that the type was not as common at Takshaśilā as one would expect a local type to be (Bopearachchi 1993; Bopearachchi and Pieper 1998; Bopearachchi and Rahman 1995; Gardner 1971; Graves 1955; Kerenyi 1951; A N Lahiri 1965; Marshall 1975; Narain 1957a; Rapson 1987; Rose 1958; Senior 2001; Whitehead 1914).

Eukratides

Antialkidas

Eukratides

PL. Abbreviation. This is the symbol for *plumbum*, the Latin for lead, and is commonly used as the abbreviation for lead coinage.

Plated hoard. This hoard forms a group of coins, which are all silver plated, and resemble a larger hoard donated to the British Museum, London. The rulers represented in this hoard include *Gondopharnes, Gondopharnes with *Aśpavarman, Gondopharnes with *Sasan, *Abdagases, and some ruler of the family of *Kharaösta (Senior 2001).

Plato. *Indo-Greek k; son of *Eukratides I; mid-second century BC. He was appointed as joint king by his father, Eukratides I, and left behind in Bactria when his father embarked upon his ambitious campaign to conquer the Kabul valley, Arachosia and Drangiana. Justin informs us that when Eukratides was returning in triumph to Bactria, his son got him killed, 'drove his chariot through his blood', and had the corpse cast away without a funeral. The name

Plato

of this parricide is not mentioned by Justin. Narain proposes that this parricide son of Eukratides I be identified with Plato. The parricide himself was done away by *Heliokles I, who, perhaps, called himself 'just' after punishing the killer of his father. Plato's brief reign is suggested by the rarity of his coins. He issued only silver coins, and they are all struck on the Attic standard. All the coins are die-struck pieces, and round in shape. The obv of all the coins bears the diademed bust of the king to the r, wearing a smooth helmet on one type. The rev has the figure of *Helios on a quadriga, to the r. The deity is shown holding a sceptre in his r hand on one type, and a sceptre in his l hand and an uncertain object (callipers ?) in his extended r hand, on another type. The possible depiction of the callipers as one of the attributes in the hands of the deity has led to the identification of the divine figure as that of Helios-Mithra. The coins of Plato have the Gr ld on the rev, in which he uses the titles of **basileus* and **epiphanes* (Bopearachchi 1993; Bopearachchi and Pieper 1998; Bopearachchi and Rahman 1995; Cunningham 1970; Gardner 1971; A N Lahiri 1965; Marshall 1975; Narain 1957a; Rapson 1987; Sircar 1980a; Prashant Srivastava 1996a; Tarn 1980; Whitehead 1914).[†]

Polyxenos. *Indo-Greek k; latter half of the second century BC. He is believed to be a subking of *Menander I, and to have governed some territory to the west of the river Indus. His coins, which are very rare, are reported from the Mir Zakah hoard, and from Peshawar and Utmanzai, but none from Taxila. He issued silver and copper coins, all based on the Indian standard. All the coins are die-struck pieces. The silver coins are round in shape, while the copper ones are square in shape. The obv of the silver coins has the diademed bust of the king to the r, while the rev has thundering *Athena with **aegis* on her left arm. The copper coins have the helmeted bust of Athena to the r on the obv, and *aegis* on the rev. The coins bear the Gr ld on the obv, and the Pkt ld, written in the Kh script, on the rev. Besides the title of **basileus*, Polyxenos assumed the epithets **epiphanes* and **soteros* on his coins. In the rev ld on the silver coins, the *epiphanes* is not rendered into Pkt, while **maharaja* and **tratara* occur as the Pkt equivalents of *basileus* and *soteros*, respectively. **Prachachha* as the Pkt equivalent of *epiphanes* is found only in the rev ld on the copper coins. The Pkt form of the name of the ruler, as met with on coins, is Palisina (Bopearachchi 1993; Bopearachchi and Pieper 1998; Bopearachchi and Rahman 1995; Cunningham 1970; Gardner 1971; A N Lahiri 1965; Marshall 1975; Narain 1957a; Rapson 1987; Senior 2001; Sircar 1980a; Tarn 1980; Whitehead 1914).[†]

'Poros' Medal. There are seven quite interesting *decadrachms*, one from Khullum in Bokhara, the second, perhaps from Babylon, three from a hoard unearthed in Babylonia in 1974, and two published in an auction catalogue issued by a Zurich bank. The first specimen, which was discovered by A W Franks, bears on the obv, the figure of a horseman wearing conical helmet and cuirass, behind two warriors 'retreating on an elephant'. One of the elephant riders seems to be attacking the horseman with a lance held in one of his hands, although according to Macdonald, it is the horseman who is 'overtaking and attacking two warriors retreating on an elephant'. The rev has a male figure, wearing cuirass, cloak, and sword, standing with thunderbolt in his r hand, and spear in his l hand. In the left field is a monogram. The second specimen, from Babylon (?), shows some variety, in that on the obv, there are two lances, of which one is in hand of one of the elephant riders, and the other, in the hand of the horseman; on the rev, Nike is shown 'flying to crown the standing figure'. The three specimens from the Babylonia hoard of 1974, as also the sixth specimen, published by P L Gupta from an *Auction Catalogue* issued by the Bank Leu AG, Zurich, for an auction held on 30 April 1975, are of the same variety. The seventh specimen, published by P L Gupta from the same *Auction Catalogue*, is unique, in that it shows the scene of the pursuit of two riders on an elephant by a horseman on the rev (as shown on the obv of the other six *decadrachms*), while the obv has an archer riding a quadriga, thus presenting a third variety of these *decadrachms*. According to Gardner, the scene of the pursuit of the two elephant riders by the horseman on these *decadrachms* represents some victory of a Graeco-Bactrian king, like Eukratides or Heliokles, over the Yueh-chihs, some time before 125 BC. Deena Bandhu Pandey sees something Persian about the dress of the human figures depicted on these coins, and suggests that the composition commemorates the victory of Alexander over Darius III Kodomannos in the Battle of Gaugamela. But Head, 'after a careful study of the fabric' of these coins, comes to the conclusion that they belong 'to Alexander's own time', and record

Fig. 3: 'Poros' Medal

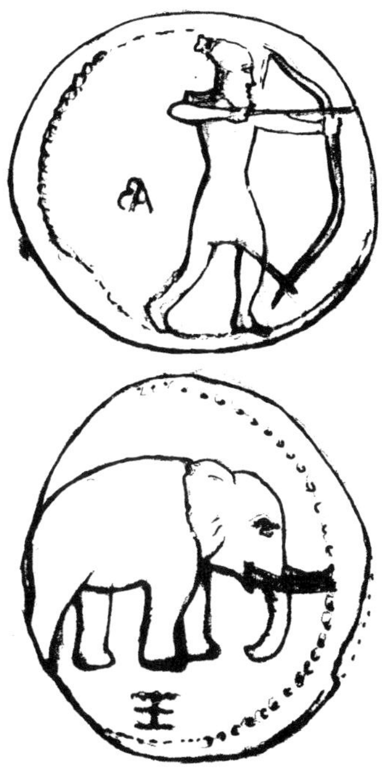

Fig. 4: 'Poros' Medal

'the historical event of his invasion of the Punjab in 326 BC'. He is of the view that the composition, showing the pursuit of the elephant riders by the horseman, of these coins represents a stage in the Battle of Jhelum, when, towards the end of the battle, the wounded and exhausted Poros had left the battle field, and Taxiles was sent after him with Alexander's message of peace. Head also reads the name of Alexander, with the royal epithet, that is *Basileos Alexandrou*, in the monogram seen on the rev of the 'Poros' medal, and this is supported by Macdonald. Gardner admits that one who looks at the medal for the first time "will be tempted to exclaim 'Alexander and Porus'." Head is further inclined to see Alexander represented as Zeus on the rev of first six specimens of these coins. Durr is of the view that the issue of these coins was decreed by Alexander himself, perhaps in the course of the festivities at Susa in 325 BC. He also publishes some *tetradrachms* from the Babylonia hoard of 1974, bearing the figure of an archer to the r on the obv, and an elephant to the r on the rev. On the basis of the occurrence of the same monogram on the obv of these *tetradrachms*, and on the *decadrachms*, as also the supposition that the dies for both the *tetradrachms* and the *decadrachms* were engraved by the same artist, Durr proposes to identify the archer on the obv of the *tetradrachms* as Poros, and to take the elephant on the rev as alluding to his famous elephant unit. Incidentally, P L Gupta tentatively identifies the chariot-borne archer on the obv of the seventh *decadrachm* as Poros, and feels that the standing archer on the obv of the *tetradrachms* reminds one of this chariot-borne archer (J N Banerjea 1950; Bhandare 2007; Durr 1978; Gardner 1887; P L Gupta 1978; Head 1906; Head 1911; Head 1932; Macdonald 1987a; Macdonald 1987b; McCrindle 1896; Deena Bandhu Pandey 1971; Prashant Srivastava 1996a; Prashant Srivastava 2009; Tarn 1948).

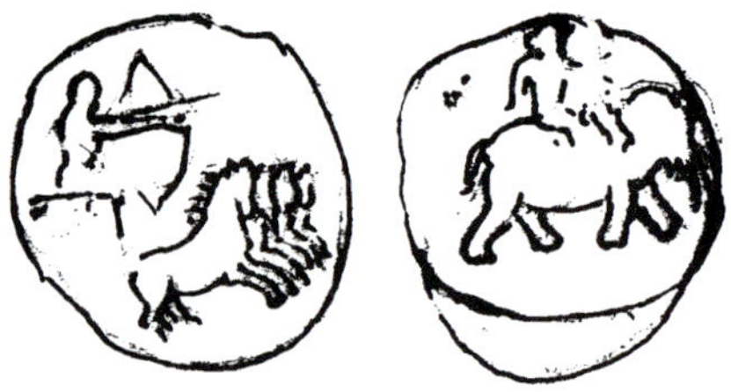

Fig. 5: 'Poros' Medal

Poseidon. Greek sea god. Originally the master of the entire earth, by the time of Homer, Poseidon had become pre-eminently a sea god. He was the son of Kronos and Rhea, and a brother of Hades, *Zeus, Hestia, *Demeter, and Hera. Among his several divine and human consorts, mention may be made of Gaia, Medousa, and Theophane. His most famous marriage was with *Amphitrite, who bore him a son, *Triton, and a daughter, Rhodos. The *trident of Poseidon, which was to be the emblem of his power, is said to have

Antimachos

been fashioned by the Telchines. *Hippios*, 'the lord of the horses', as one of his surnames, hints at his association with the horse. The bearded head of the deity, to the r, and with a trident resting over the shoulder, may be seen on the obv of some copper coins of the *Indo-Greek ruler, *Nikias. The figure of the bearded and diademed deity, wearing *himation* and standing facing to front, occurs on the rev of some silver coins of *Antimachos. He holds a long trident in his r hand, and a palm bound with fillet is seen under his left arm. Of the *Śaka-Pahlava rulers, *Maues and *Azes I depicted Poseidon on their coins. On one type of Maues, the figure of Poseidon, standing facing front and clad in *himation*, occupies the obv. He holds a long trident in his l hand, while the r hand rests on hip akimbo on some coins of this type, or rests on his knee on some others, or is outstretched on yet other coins of this type. On this type, the deity is trampling on a 'river god' with his r foot. On the second type of Maues depicting Poseidon, the sea god stands facing front, with his trident in the l hand, while with his r hand, he hurls a thunderbolt at a small figure to the r. His r foot rests on a small, radiate river god. The small figure, at which Poseidon is hurling the thunderbolt, clings to the aplustre or poop ornament of a boat. On the third type of Maues showing Poseidon, the sea god is striding to the l, hurling thunderbolt with his r hand at a river god, who is shown leaping up and clinging to an object (which is either aplustre or palm branch) held in Poseidon's l hand. The trident is here conspicuous by its absence. On one type of Azes, Poseidon is seen on the obv, walking to the r, with a long trident in his l hand, while the r hand is advanced. On the second type of Azes depicting Poseidon, the sea god is standing to front with his face turned to the l. He is clad in *himation*. His l hand holds the conventional trident. The right one is on hip akimbo. The r foot of Poseidon rests on a river god, as seen on some coins of Maues, above. On the rev of a large sized copper coin of *Demetrios, Poseidon is believed by some scholars to be represented symbolically through his characteristic attribute, the trident (Bopearachchi 1993; Bopearachchi and Pieper 1998; Bopearachchi and Rahman 1995; Bhaskar Chattopadhyay 1977; Cunningham 1971a; Gardner 1971; Graves 1955; Kerenyi 1951; A N Lahiri 1965; Marshall 1975; Narain 1957a; Rose 1958; Prashant Srivastava 2007c; Tarn 1980; Whitehead 1914).†

Maues

Azes I

Poṭhasiri. *Magha k.

Potin. Metal (alloy) for coins. Some amount of alloy was required to impart the necessary hardness to the metal used for the manufacture of coins; some amount might have remained due to the difficulty in separating the metals. But the deliberate use of mixed metals, like potin, *billon, and *brass, for coinage was, perhaps, 'the result of conscious attempt at depreciation promoted by avarice or due to financial stress'. Potin is an alloy 'composed of yellow and red copper, lead, tin and some dross'. Its use in coinage is seen among the Sātavāhanas and the *Kārddamaka Kshatrapas (Rapson 1975; Senior 2001).

Prabhākara. *Nāga k. Although his name on coins is not a *nāga*-ending one, he is regarded as a Nāga ruler on the basis of the similarity of his coins with the coins of the other Nāga rulers in *provenance*, fabric, type, size, shape, ld, etc. He is associated with *Ravināga and *Vibhunāga by the use of the 'Sickle-and-arrow' type. They are among the late Nāga rulers, and not much is known about them. He also issued the 'Bull' type of coins. He assumed the title of **mahārāja-śrī* on coins (Bela Lahiri 1974; H V Trivedi 1957).

Prabhākaravardhana. *Pushpabhūti k; end of the sixth century AD to the early years of the seventh century AD. He was the first ruler of his dynasty to be designated **mahārājādhirāja*, thereby showing his sovereign status. The *Harshacharita* of Bāṇa speaks of his [successful] conflicts with, or his posing a threat to, the *Hūṇas, Gurjaras, Lāṭas, Mālavas, and the rulers of Sindhu and Gandhāra. From his wife, Yaśomatīdevī, he had three issues, namely Rājyavardhana II, *Harsha, and Rājyaśrī. Towards the end of his reign, the Pushpabhūti kingdom was troubled by the Hūṇas, while *Śaśāṅka, and the Mālava ruler, Devagupta, attacked the Maukhari kingdom, killed Prabhākaravardhana's son-in-law, Grahavarman, and imprisoned Rājyaśrī. Prabhākaravardhana was succeeded by his elder son, Rājyavardhana II, who had a very short reign. Nine silver coins of the **Madhyadeśa* type of the *Imperial Guptas were found in the *Bhitaura hoard. These bear the bust of the king to the r and the date of issue (year 11) on the obv. The rev has a fan-tailed *peacock, and the Br ld *Vijitāvaniravanipati Śrī-Pratāpaśīla divaṁ jayati*. Hoernle would ascribe them to Pratāpaśīla Śīlāditya of Kashmir. However, as Pratāpaśīla is mentioned in the *Harshacharita* as another name of Prabhākaravardhana, Richard Burn and D Devahuti regard these coins as issued by this Pushpabhūti ruler (Richard Burn 1906; D Devahuti 1964; D Devahuti 2001; Pires 1934; Thaplyal 1985).†

Prachachha. Title. It is the Pkt rendering of **epiphanes*, and used by *Polyxenos and *Strato I. The Skt equivalent is *pratyaksha*, meaning '[God-] manifest' (Cunningham 1970; Gardner 1971; A N Lahiri 1965; Marshall 1975; Narain 1957a; Tarn 1980; Whitehead 1914).

Prajāpati Akhya. *Kuṇinda chief (?). There are certain 'copper, brass and steel coins', reportedly from the Ambala district, which have the same obv as the silver coins of the *Amoghabhūti series of the Kuṇindas, but the rev has the ld *Raña Kunidasa Prajapati Akhyasa Maharajasa*. It apparently seems that they are joint issues of Amoghabhūti and Prajāpati Akhya. But scholars like Devendra Handa regard these coins as modern forgeries (L C Gupta 1983; Handa 2007a; Prashant Srivastava 1996a).

Prajāpatimitra. *Kauśāmbī k. The arrangement of the ld along the margin on his round coins seems to connect him with *Rājamitra and *Rajanīmitra, and he seems to have ruled between their respective reigns. There is no definite ground to connect him with the homonym known from the *Pañchāla series. The coins bear, on the obv, the figure of a *bull to the r before a *dhvajastambha*, while the rev has a *tree-in-railing, flanked by the *Ujjain symbol and another uncertain symbol, and the ld *Pajāpatimitasa* (Altekar 1942a; Altekar 1942b; Bopearachchi and Pieper 1998; Bela Lahiri 1974).

Prajāpatimitra. *Pañchāla k. He seems to be near in time to *Indramitra and *Jayagupta, because all the three of them show the divinity on the rev of their coins as standing within a domed shrine. Bela Lahiri places Prajāpatimitra in the sixteenth chronological position among the Pañchāla rulers known from coins. The deity on the coins of Prajāpatimitra is indistinct, and his identification with

Prajāpati is based on the analogy of the name of the issuer (V S Agrawala 1941; Bela Lahiri 1974).

Prasannamātra. *Śarabhapurīya k.

Praushṭhadeva. *Ayodhyā k. He issued copper coins, bearing on the obv, the figure of an *elephant, and never the *bull common to the cast coins of Ayodhyā, and on this basis, he is placed before *Mūladeva who seems to have introduced the practice of depicting the bull on the obv of the coins. The rev of his coins shows a *tree-in-railing, curved line, and another uncertain symbol. The ld *Poṭhadevasa* occurs on the obv (Allan 1936; Bela Lahiri 1974).

Praushṭhamitra. *Kauśāmbī k. The style, execution, and combination of symbols on his coins connect him with *Jyeshṭhamitra, *Agnimitra, and *Bahasatimita II, and some coins of all these four rulers are countermarked with the *nandipada-triśūla*. The obv of his coins bears the figure of a *bull to the l, the *hill symbols, and a **nandipada* (?), while the rev has a *tree-in-railing, a *taurine symbol to the l, and an *undulating line, and the ld *Poṭhamitasa* (Altekar 1942b; Bopearachchi and Pieper 1998; Bela Lahiri 1974).

Pṛithvīsena. *Kārddamaka k. He was the son of *Rudrasena I, and ruled as **kshatrapa* only. His coins bear the date of *Śaka year 144. On the basis of a coin, the date on which bears the date of year 146, it has been suggested that Pṛithvīsena also ruled as **mahākshatrapa*, at least in the year 146. But Amitshwar Jha and Dilip Rajgor doubt the authenticity of this coin. As the reign of Rudrasena I as *mahākshatrapa* ended in Śaka year 145, and as the date of year 144 was read on a coin issued by *Saṅghadāman as *mahākshatrapa*, it was surmised that Pṛithvīsena could have served under either of these two. But it is more likely that he served as *kshatrapa* under Rudrasena I, and never attained to the office of *mahākshatrapa*. He issued coins of the *Kārddamaka silver type (Jha and Rajgor 1994; Mirashi 1982; Mitchiner 1976; Rapson 1975; Raychaudhuri 1972; Senior 2001; Sircar 1980e).

Priyamitra. *Kauśāmbī k. He issued square copper coins of comparatively thin fabric, and the square shape and thin fabric of his coins connect him with *Aśvaghosha, *Parvata, *Rāḍhamitra, and *Īśvaramitra. This may be taken as a ground to place him, in time, near Aśvaghosha, who, perhaps, ruled towards the beginning of the first century AD. The obv of his coins has the Br ld *Prayamitasa*, while the rev has a *tree-in-railing (K D Bajpai 1960; Bopearachchi and Pieper 1998; Bela Lahiri 1974).

Priyapita. Title. It is the Pkt rendering of **philopator*, and used for *Strato II on the joint coins of *Strato I with Strato II. The Skt equivalent is *priyapitṛika* (Cunningham 1970; Gardner 1971; A N Lahiri 1965; Marshall 1975; Narain 1957a; Tarn 1980; Whitehead 1914).

Puḍena. *Parataraja k.

Puḍhana. *Parataraja k.

Puḍhena. *Parataraja k.

Punch. It is a bar of some hard metal, which is used to hold a *blank in place at the time of the manufacture of *punch marked coins and die-struck coins. In the *punch marking method, the lower end of the punch had the symbol, in the negative and generally in relief, which was to be impressed on the blank. In the *die-striking method, for double die-struck coins, the upper *die was inserted into the lower end of the punch. The impression was obtained by striking the upper end of the punch with a hammer.

Punch marked coins. This name, first used by James Prinsep in 1835, is merely a descriptive appellation derived from the system of manufacture peculiar to these coins, the coins being made by the *punching technique. With the advent of these coins, believed by a vast majority of scholars to be the earliest available coins of India, 'we see money in the very infancy of the numismatic art'. Some scholars believe that the punch marked coins are of foreign origin, but their indigenous origin has been conclusively proved by Cunningham and others [See Introduction, under Origin]. According to a vast majority of scholars, the earliest punch marked coins were issued by the silversmiths or bankers, but later on, the state took

Punch marked coin

Punch marked coin

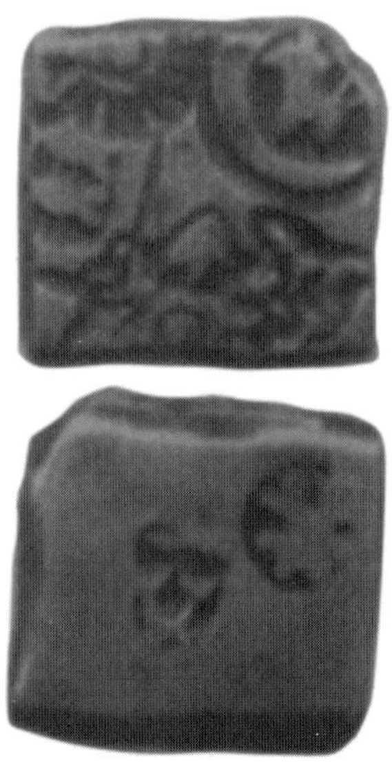

Punch marked coin

over the responsibility for issuing coins, and made it its prerogative. Punch marked coins are available in silver and copper, the silver ones being more numerous than the copper ones; a few gold punch marked coins have been reported, but some scholars have doubts as to whether they are genuine or not. The silver punch marked coins were called **dharaṇa*, and the standard silver coin weighed 32 **rattīs*, that is about 56 grains. Kauṭilya speaks of silver *dharaṇa* of almost 80 *rattīs*, but no such actual specimen is known so far. The copper punch marked coins were denoted by the term **kārshāpaṇa*, and the standard copper coin weighed 80 *rattīs* or about 144 grains. In practice, there were some other additional denominations also. Cunningham had in his collection, punch marked coins varying in weight from 250 grains to 9 grains, that is from 1-3/4 *kārshāpaṇa* to 1/16 *kārshāpaṇa* or a **māshaka*. Punch marked coins can be, and have been, classified variously, but Smith's classification, based on the metal (silver or copper), shape (ingots, bent bars, rectangular, square, oval, or circular), and the number of symbols on the rev (none, one, two, three, or more), proposed for the punch marked coins in the collection of the Indian Museum, Calcutta, seems to be by far the most scientific. On the basis of their area of circulation, the punch marked coins have been divided into two classes—(i) those confined to some area, that is the punch marked coins of the local series, and (ii) those that circulated almost throughout the country, that is the universal or imperial series. According to P L Gupta, the punch marked coins of the local series were issued variously by the Śūrasena (Mathurā region), Uttara Pañchāla (Rohilkhand), Dakshiṇa Pañchāla (doab region), Vatsa (capital at Kauśāmbī), Kuṇāla (Gonda-Bahraich districts), Kosala (Avadh), Kāśī (Varanasi region), Malla (area around Deoria), Magadha (south Bihar), Vaṅga (Bengal), Kaliṅga (Orissa), Andhra (Godavari-Krishna region), Aśmaka (area south of Godavari), Mūlaka (area west of Hyderabad), Saurāshṭra (Kathiawar), and Gandhāra (Takshaśilā-Pushkalāvatī region). The coins from these regions differ from one another in fabric, weight, quality of metal, and devices. The coins of Śūrasena, Uttara Pañchāla, Dakshiṇa Pañchāla, and Saurāshṭra use the same symbols, but there is difference in form and execution. *Bent bar coins are peculiar to the Gandhāra region. The coins from Bengal bear three symbols, while some *janapadas* issued coins with four symbols. The coins of Kāśī, Magadha, Vatsa, and Saurāshṭra have thin fabric, while those of Malla, thick. Some Kāśī (?) coins are *cup-shaped. The universal series has five symbols, the sun and *shaḍarachakra* being constant, and three others, variable. In almost all hoards of the punch marked coins of the local series, coins of the universal series are absent, and *vice versa*; in very rare cases are the two series of punch marked coins found together. From this, it is inferred that when Magadha became a pan-Indian empire, the local type of punch marked coins of the kingdom of Magadha became the universal series. While Pāṇini in the fifth century BC refers to **nishka*, **śatamāna*, *viṁśatika*, *triṁśatika*, etc, besides *paṇa*, Kauṭilya in the fourth century BC refers only to *paṇa* with its fractions. This has been taken to show that by the time of the *Arthaśāstra*, *paṇa* currency had superseded other types of currencies. Michael Mitchiner, too, classifies the punch marked coins into the local series and the universal series (which he calls the 'Magadha-Maurya' series), but he further classifies these coins into four sub-classes : (i) heavy weight-standard with multiple-punch type, in middle Ganga valley west of Varanasi, that is the Kosala region; (ii) heavy weight-standard with single-punch type, in Gandhāra; (iii) light weight-standard with single-punch type, in Avanti and Konkan; and (iv) light weight-standard with multiple-punch type—the Magadha-Maurya series, which had a wide area of circulation. The symbols on the punch marked coins were impressed by separate punches at various points on the surface of the coin. They often overlap, and on certain coins, where the symbols are numerous, this overlapping results in 'a confused jumble'. Some scholars are of the view that the different symbols were impressed at different times; others are of the opinion that all the symbols were impressed at the same time, but using different punches, when the blank was hot. The symbols on the obv are larger in size, and usually different, from the symbols on the rev. Coins of the universal series bear, on the obv, five symbols on an average; the rev is either blank, or occupied by two symbols on an average. Rarely are both the surfaces of the coin equally crowded with symbols, whose number on one side is known to go up to even 10 or 12. It has been noticed that often a symbol is confined to the coins of one area, or a particular type or variety, or a particular period. These symbols are regarded as the official guarantee of the validity of the coin, and are considered, variously, as of religious or mythological in nature, or as official marks or

Punch marked coin

Punch marked coin

Punch marked coin

Punch marked coin

Punch marked coin

Punch marked coin

Punch marked coin

symbols of the ruling dynasty or king, or as marks of bankers. Theobald's classification of the symbols on the punch marked coins, proposed nearly a century ago when only about 400 of them were known, is no longer acceptable. A new classification has been proposed, in which these symbols are divided into five classes : (i) natural symbols, including quadrupeds, birds, aquatic creatures, reptiles, insects, human figures, trees and plants, and heavenly bodies; (ii) geographical symbols, of which the hill and the river are the most common; (iii) geometrical symbols, like the straight line, curved line, circle, dotted circle, square, divided square, rectangle, etc; (iv) weapons and structures, like bow-and-arrow, spear, *trident, **stūpa* (?), *chaitya* (?), etc; and (v) miscellaneous symbols, like the **nandipada*, triskeles, **svastika*, *taurine symbol, etc. The human figure, sometimes armed, on punch marked coins, is usually shown singly or in groups of three. Quite interesting is the appearance of an ithyphallic man on a punch marked coin reported from the collection of Jan Lingen of the Netherlands. This might very well be the first representation of this kind in ancient Indian coinage. According to Cunningham, punch marked coins were in circulation in India as early as 1000 BC. But the antiquity of coinage in India cannot be taken much before the sixth century BC [See Introduction, under Antiquity]. Loventhal says that in southern India, punch marked coins circulated up to 300 AD, while in northern India, they went out of circulation three or four centuries before their use was discontinued in the south. The belief that punch marked coins circulated in southern India for three or four centuries longer than in northern India, seems to be based on the find of some punch marked coins with the *denarius* of Augustus, as also the fact that certain later coinages of southern India, like the *padmaṭaṅkas*, might be the 'immediate successors' of punch marked coins, having apparently evolved from them. But in certain archaeological excavations, punch marked coins were found in levels datable from the sixth century BC to the early centuries of the Christian era. Three punch marked coins were unearthed by Cunningham from under the foot of the *vajrāsana* of the Buddha at the Mahabodhi temple at Bodhgaya, the deposit being made in the time of the Kushāṇa ruler, *Huvishka (second century AD). The *purāṇas* in a Mathurā inscription of Huvishka may refer to silver punch marked coins. At Sisupalgarh, moulds for manufacturing punch marked coins were found in the stratum datable to *c* 300 AD. Buddhaghosha, in the Gupta period, refers to the prevalence of the old **nīla-kārshāpaṇa* side by side with the silver coins of the Śakas. The view of S R Goyal, however, that the find of punch marked coins along with those of King Hoshangshah of Malwa, who ruled in the first half of the fifteenth century AD, shows that they continued in circulation as late as that period, does not seem to be convincing (Allan 1936; Pratipal Bhatia 1989; C J Brown 1999; Cribb 2005; S R Goyal 1995b; Gupta and Hardaker 1985; Kosambi 1992; Mitchiner 1973; Murphy 2003-2004; Rajgor 2001; Upadhyaya and Chaturvedi 1972).

Punch marked coin

Punching method. *Technique of manufacture of coins. The method has been very succinctly described by Pratipal Bhatia thus : 'The metal was melted in crucibles and purified with alkalis; the metal was first beaten into sheets on the anvil with a hammer and then cut into pieces with clippers. An adjustment of the weight was made by cutting small bits of one or more corners of the heavier pieces and this led to a deviation from their rectangular shape. Finally these pieces were stamped with punches either on one or both of their faces. After final verification by money-testers these coins were put into circulation' (Pratipal Bhatia 1989; Chakrabortty 1931; B N Mukherjee and P K D Lee 1988).

Puramagha (?). *Magha k.

Purāṇa. Coin denomination. The same as **ādimūla-kāhāvaṇa* or the original **kārshāpaṇa*, it was the standard coin circulating in India from *c* sixth century BC to *c* sixth century AD. Manu refers to it as **rājata-purāṇa*, and gives its weight as 16 *raupya-māshakas* (= 32 *rattīs*) (V S Agrawala 1957; D R Bhandarkar 1984; Chakrabortty 1931).

Pūrugupta. *Imperial Gupta k; son of *Kumāragupta I; latter half of the fifth century AD. It is not certain whether he ruled before his brother, *Skandagupta, or some time after him, but most of the scholars are inclined to place him after Skandagupta. There is also the suggestion that Pūrugupta contested the succession of Skandagupta. Earlier, some gold coins of the *Archer type, bearing the epithet *Vikrama*, were ascribed to Pūrugupta by scholars, like Allan, but S K

Saraswati, and following him, A S Altekar, have expressed the view that the name under the king's left arm on the obv of these coins is not *Pūru* as read by Allan, but *Budha*, and they have ascribed these coins to *Budhagupta (Ashvini Agrawal 1989; Allan 1914; Altekar 1957; R D Banerji 1933; Fleet 1888; S R Goyal 2005; P L Gupta 1998; K P Jayaswal 1933; Smith 1972; Thaplyal, forthcoming).†

Purushadatta. *Mathurā k. He is regarded as the earliest of the Datta kings of Mathurā. He issued coins, which show *Lakshmī with lotus in her r hand and some symbols on the obv; and three *elephants with riders on the rev. The rev device is degenerate (Allan 1936; Bela Lahiri 1974).

Pushkalāvatī hoard. This hoard of about 20 kg of base silver *Śaka-Pahlava coins was found in February 1994, in an earthen pot in the ancient city of Pushkalāvatī. The whole hoard was found tightly clumped together. It has been acquired by Aman ur Rahman (Bopearachchi 1994).

Pushpabhūti. Coins, general features. The Pushpabhūtis, who played an important role in the political history of northern India in the sixth-seventh centuries AD, are believed to be of vaiśya origin. In the *Harshacharita*, Bāṇa refers to Pushpabhūti as the first ruler of this dynasty, but the genealogy, found in the epigraphs, is Naravardhana, Rājyavardhana [I], Ādityavardhana, *Prabhākaravardhana, and his two sons, Rājyavardhana II and *Harsha. While the first three are called **mahārāja*, denoting their feudatory status, the last three are called **mahārājādhirāja*, showing that they were sovereign rulers. The predecessors of Harsha are generally placed in the period *c* 500-606 AD. The rule of the Pushpabhūtis came to an end with Harsha in 647 AD. Two kings of this dynasty, namely Prabhākaravardhana and Harsha, are known from the *Bhitaura hoard to have issued coins; Rājyavardhana had an exceptionally short reign and could not strike his money. Prabhākaravardhana issued silver coins of the **Madhyadeśa* type of the *Imperial Guptas, and he is called *Śrī-Pratāpaśīla* on these coins. Harsha issued silver coins of the same type, on which he is called *Śrī-Śīlāditya*. Besides, a single gold coin of Harsha is also available, which bears a Br ld mentioning Harsha on the obv, and *Śiva and *Pārvatī on Nandin on the rev.

The Pushpabhūti silver coins have an average weight of around 36 grains. The lone gold coin weighs 113.5 grains. All these coins are die-struck and round in shape (K D Bajpai 1976; Richard Burn 1906; Devahuti 1964; D Devahuti 2001; Pires 1934; Thaplyal 1985).

Q

Qunduz hoard. This important hoard of *Indo-Greek coins was reportedly discovered in 1948, 'at a spot approximately half-way between the towns of Qunduz and Khanabad, in the Afghan province of Kataghan'. Some coins from the hoard might have been disposed off, before 610 coins from the hoard could be recovered by the Kabul Museum. The kings represented in this hoard include Alexander, Antiochos Hierax, Alexander I Balas, *Agathokles, *Amyntas, *Antialkidas, *Antimachos I, *Archebios, *Demetrios I, *Diodotos I, *Eukratides I, *Eukratides II, *Euthydemos I, *Euthydemos II, *Heliokles, *Hermaios, *Lysias, *Philoxenos, *Plato, and *Theophilos. Heliokles and Eukratides I are the most abundantly represented rulers in this hoard. It brings to the light Attic tetradrachms of several later Indo-Greek rulers, indicating the hold of the Indo-Greeks over these regions as late as their times. The double-*decadrachms* of Amyntas were found in this hoard (Bivar 1955).

R

Rāḍhamitra. *Kauśāmbī k. He issued square copper coins of comparatively thin fabric, and the square shape and thin fabric of his coins connect him with *Aśvaghosha, *Parvata, *Priyamitra, and *Īśvaramitra. This may be taken as a ground to place him, in time, near Aśvaghosha, who, perhaps, ruled towards the beginning of the first century AD. The obv of his coins bear the figure of a *bull to the r before a *dhvajastambha*, while the rev has a *lion, and the ld *Rādhamitasa* (Altekar 1942a; Altekar 1942b; Bopearachchi and Pieper 1998; Bela Lahiri 1974).

Rājādhirāja. Title. This title, meaning 'king of kings', occurs on the coins of some *Imperial Gupta rulers, like *Kumāragupta I [**rajatiraja*] (Altekar 1957).

***Rājalīlā* type.** Gold. Issued by *Samāchāradeva, this coin has the king seated on couch in *rājalīlā* pose, with a queen or female attendant on either side, and the vertical ld *Samāchā[ra]*, on the obv. The rev has nimbate *Sarasvatī on a lotus bed, both her hands engaged with stalked lotus blooms, a **haṁsa* beside her, and the ld *Narendravinīta* (Altekar 1957).

Rājamitra. *Kauśāmbī k. The arrangement of the ld along the margin on his round coins seems to connect him with *Prajāpatimitra and *Rajanīmitra. But, as some of his coins also have the ld in a straight line in accordance with the earlier tradition, he seems to be the earliest of the three. The obv of his coins bears a *bull to the r before a *dhvajastambha* (?), while the rev has a *tree-in-railing, flanked by two blurred symbols, and the ld *Rājamitasa* (Altekar 1942a; Bopearachchi and Pieper 1998; Bela Lahiri 1974).

Rajanīmitra. *Kauśāmbī k. He may be identical with the homonym known from the Allahabad Municipal Museum inscription of [regnal] year 28. Allan places him in the second century AD. The arrangement of the ld along the margin on his round coins seems to connect him with *Rājamita and *Prajāpatimitra. But he seems to be the latest of the three, as the peculiar tree on his coins closely resembles that on the coins of *Dhanadeva and *Nava. The obv of his coins has a *bull to the r, while the rev has a *tree-in-railing, and the ld *Rajanimitasa* (Altekar 1942a; Bopearachchi and Pieper 1998; Bela Lahiri 1974).

Rājanya

Rājanya. Tribe. First discovered by James Prinsep, the coins issued by this tribe were earlier ascribed to the Mahārāja *janapada* due to the faulty reading of the ld on these coins, and Jayaswal postulated the existence of a state of that name and tried to trace its antiquity to Pāṇini. Later, the ld was correctly read by V A Smith as *Rajaña janapadasa*, and thereafter, the theory that the coins belong to a Mahārāja *janapada* has passed into the limbo. Rājanya in the Purushasūkta of the *Ṛigveda* and the epics stands for the kshatriyas. It has been variously suggested that the Rājanyas might be the Kshatriyas mentioned in the *Arthaśāstra* along with the Kambojas and the Surāshṭras as subsisting by arms, and the Kshatriyas (Khatiyas) whose pride Gautamīputra Sātakarṇi subdued, and the Kathaoi and Xathroi of the classical writers, and also that the ld means '[coin] of the Kshatriya *janapada* (country)'. But Rājanya as people are known in the *Gaṇapāṭha* of Pāṇini, the *Mahābhārata, Mahābhāshya, Chāndravyākaraṇa, Kāśikā, Sarasvatīkaṇṭhābharaṇa*, etc. The *Mārkaṇḍeyapurāṇa* locates them in the northeast. But the *Mahābhārata* groups them with such north Indian tribes as the *Śibis, *Yaudheyas, Madras, etc, and this is supported by the *Bṛihatsaṁhitā*, which refers to the Rājanyas as a people of the north. The Rājanyas of coins should be identified with them. Of about 26 coins of the tribe, some were found from regions around Mathurā, but most of them come from the Hoshiarpur district of Punjab. The *provenance* and the use of the Kh script suggest that the Rājanyas inhabited eastern Punjab, and later migrated to Mathurā and eastern Rajasthan. The coins, which weigh between 15 and 121 grains, are either of copper or brass, either die-struck or cast, and, with the single exception of a squarish coin, round in shape. They are datable, on palaeographical grounds, to second-first centuries BC; Allan places the coins with the Kh ld in the second century BC, and those with the Br ld, in the first century BC. The coins have been divided into two classes. Most of the coins have, on the obv, a female figure standing and holding lotus (?) in the raised r hand, but some coins of Class II have a human figure sitting under a canopy. The female figure has generally been identified with *Lakshmī, but Devendra Handa proposes to identify her with Rājinīdevī, who might have been the tutelary goddess of the Rājanyas, and to whom was dedicated a temple located on a mound in the village of Rajini, about 10 km south of Hoshiarpur in the Rājanya territory. Handa says that the attribute in the hand of the goddess on the coins is not clearly visible, and it might not be a lotus, but a ball, the intention being to show the goddess as a '*Kundakī*, lady playing with a ball'. I am not at all sure if a goddess would be shown in such a playful mood in Indian iconography. The ld on the obv is *Rajaña janapadasa* in Kh on the coins of Class I, and in Br on the coins of Class II. The rev of most of the coins has a bull in a rayed circle, with some coins of Class I having a crescent over the head of the bull and a **vajra* like symbol over its back. The depiction of the bull within a rayed circle might hint at its sanctity and some scholars propose to identify it with Nandin (Allan 1936; Chakrabortty 1931; Cunningham 1971b; K K Dasgupta 1974; Handa 2007a; Jayaswal 1988; Marshall 1975; Mitchiner 1975-1976; Smith 1972).

Rajaraja. Title. It is the Pkt rendering of **basileus basileon*, and used regularly by the *Śaka-Pahlavas, and the early *Kushāṇa kings. It occurs on the posthumous *Hermaios coins as well. The Skt equivalent is *rājarāja* (Cunningham 1970; Gardner 1971; A N Lahiri 1965; Marshall 1975; Narain 1957a; Tarn 1980; Whitehead 1914).

Rajasthan, early local coins. Six coins—two rectangular, three square, and one round, and all bearing the *Ujjain symbol and the ld *Senāpatisa Vachhaghosha*, were found in the excavations at Rairh. K N Puri, the excavator, considers *senāpati* as the title of Pushyamitra Śuṅga. Altekar ascribes it to the chief of the *Yaudheyas or the *Ārjunāyanas, and R C Agrawala, to the chief of the *Mālavas. K K Dasgupta suggests that *Vachhaghosha* is a place name, and the coins were probably issued by Pushyamitra's provincial governor. However, a place of that name is not known, and one would expect that a coin issued by a provincial governor would bear the name of Pushyamitra, the overlord. Rairh yielded 14 'mitra' coins, belonging to Sūryamitra, Brahmamitra, and Dhruvamitra. Kings of identical names are known from *Kanauj, *Mathurā, etc. However, it is difficult to say if the homonyms known from these series are identical. There is one coin, with the legends *Udehaki* and *Suyamitasa*, together with the Ujjain symbol on the obv, and an *elephant and *bull on the rev. Five coins from this place bear *Sudavapa* in place of *Udehaki*, and five other coins, the legends *Sudavapa* and *Dhruvamitra* [*Uddehikas] (Allan 1936; Altekar 1986a; Altekar 1986b; Bopearachchi and Pieper 1998; K K Dasgupta 1974; Handa 2007a; Mitchiner 1975-1976).

Rājata-purāṇa. **Purāṇa*.

Rajatiraja. Title. It is the Pkt rendering of **basileus basileon*, and used regularly by the *Śaka-Pahlava rulers, and the early *Kushāṇa kings. Interestingly, it occurs for the first time on some copper coins of *Eukratides I, where its Greek equivalent is not found on the obv. On some coins, *rajatiraja* is spelt *rajadiraja*. The Skt equivalent is *rājātirāja* (Cunningham 1970; Gardner 1971; A N Lahiri 1965; Marshall 1975; Narain 1957a; Tarn 1980; Whitehead 1914).

***Rālimata/Tālimata* (?)**. Guild. *Takshaśilā. Guild coins.

Rāmadatta. *Mathurā k. He issued coins, which show *Lakshmī with lotus in her r hand and some symbols on the obv; and three *elephants with riders on the rev. The rev device is degenerate. On some of his coins, he uses the title **rājan*, while on others, this title is absent. On this basis, Allan considers the possibility of two kings of this name. But it would appear more probable that he issued coins, first without, and then with, the title of *rājan* (Allan 1936; Bela Lahiri 1974).

Rāmagupta. *Imperial Gupta k; son of *Samudragupta; latter half of the fourth century AD. This son of *Samudragupta was earlier regarded as a figment of some historians' imagination, but now, there is sufficient literary, epigraphic, and numismatic evidence to vouch for his historicity. The occurrence of the **garuḍa* and the **garuḍadhvaja* on some of the copper coins bearing the name of Rāmagupta provide irrefutable evidence to associate Rāmagupta with the Imperial Guptas. It appears that Samudragupta selected his abler son, *Chandragupta II, as his heir, and appointed Rāmagupta, his eldest son, as the governor of Malwa. When, perhaps on the death of Samudragupta, the Imperial Gupta throne at Pāṭaliputra was usurped by *Kācha, Rāmagupta declared himself an independent ruler in Malwa. He tried to enter into a disgraceful treaty with the Śaka invader, and was killed by his younger brother, who seized his kingdom and wife. Rāmagupta is believed to be the first Imperial Gupta ruler to issue coins in copper. On some coins, the obv has the ld *Rāma* in the centre, with a crescent at the top, while the rev has a lion. Although such coins were found during the course of D R Bhandarkar's excavations at Besnagar, neither the device could be identified, nor the ld could be deciphered. On other coins, the obv is occupied by the ld *Rāmagupta*, with crescent and circle on top and clustre of dots below, while the rev has a *garuḍa* with outstretched wings. Some other coins have, on the obv, a *garuḍadhvaja* in the centre, with *Ra-* to the l and *-ma* to the r of it; the rev has *garuḍa* in human form. Yet another type has *garuḍa* and the ld *Śrī Rāmagupta* on the obv, and *garuḍa* with outstretched wings on the rev (Ashvini Agrawal 1989; Altekar 1957; K D Bajpai 1972; S R Goyal 2005; P L Gupta 1998; Prashant Srivastava 1996a; Thaplyal, forthcoming).†

Rāmamitra. *Kauśāmbī k. He issued square copper coins, bearing a *tree-in-railing 'with prominent leaves', a **nandipada*, and the ld *Rāmamitasa*, on the obv, while the rev is blank. He is assigned to the first century BC or the first century AD, on palaeographical grounds (K D Bajpai 1960; Bopearachchi and Pieper 1998; Bela Lahiri 1974).

Rāmānīla/Ramanila. *Hūṇa chief. This Hūṇa chief of Zabula is known from some coins, which have been studied by Roman Ghirshman. His identity with *Toramāṇa has been suggested by that scholar, though apparently on insufficient grounds (Biswas 1973; Upendra Thakur 1967a).

Ranjangaon hoard. This hoard of 1,519 silver coins was discovered at the site in the Pune district of Maharashtra, in 1974. The rulers represented in the hoard include the *Kārddamaka Kshatrapas, *Rudrasiṁha I, *Rudrasena I, *Pṛithvīsena, *Dāmasena, *Dāmajadaśrī II, *Vīradāman, *Yaśodāman I, *Vijayasena, *Dāmajadaśrī III, *Rudrasena II, *Viśvasiṁha, *Bhartṛidāman, *Viśvasena, *Rudrasiṁha II, and *Yaśodāman II. Nine coins belong to *Īśvaradatta; seven coins are uncertain. The hoard also contains a copper coin, which is an issue of Rudrasena II (Shobhana Gokhale 1976; Jha and Rajgor 1994).

Rañjuvula

Rañjuvula. Śaka satrap; late first century BC or early first century AD. He was the first known Śaka **kshatrapa* of *Mathurā. His coins show that he first ruled as a *kshatrapa*, the coins referring to him as such being rather rare, and later attained the position of a **mahākshatrapa*. His coins testify to his hold over Takshaśilā, or territories to its northeast, Hazara to Akhnoor-Jammu, the Punjab and western Uttar Pradesh, particularly Mathurā, which he seems to have occupied quite 'late in life'. The fact that he uses the titles of **basileos basileon *soteros*, and **apratihatachakra* on his coins seems to suggest that, for all practical purposes, he was ruling as an independent king. He issued coins in silver, copper, and potin. All his coins are round in shape. One type of his silver coins has the bust of the king on the obv, and *Athena thundering on the rev. The other type has horseman king holding whip on the obv, and *Zeus Nikephoros on the rev. The copper types have the bust of the king on the obv, or show horseman king. The rev is occupied by Athena thundering as on the silver coins, or by *Zeus Nikephoros. One potin type has *Lakshmī standing on the obv, and *Gajalakshmī on the rev. Other potin types have variants of the devices of *lion on the obv, and *Herakles standing with club and lion's skin on the rev. The obv ld is always in Gr. The rev ld is in Pkt, written in Br and/or Kh. The Gr ld of his coins refers to him as **basileos basileon *soteros*, probably meaning 'king of kings, the saviour', while the Kh ld gives him the title of *kshatrapa* or *mahākshatrapa*, often with the additional title, **apratihatachakra* (Allan 1936; Cunningham

1971a; Gardner 1971; Jenkins and Narain 1957; Konow 1929; Marshall 1975; B N Mukherjee 1969a; Rapson 1987; Senior 2001; Sircar 1980b; Sircar 1986; Tarn 1980; Whitehead 1914).†

Raupya-dīnāra. Coin denomination. There are literary references to the *raupya-dīnāra*, as well as *suvarṇa-dīnāra*, as coin denominations. The original *Pañchatantra*, as reconstructed by Edgerton, also refers to this coin denomination. Although it is not certain as to which coin is meant by *raupya-dīnāra*, there is a suggestion that it might denote the silver **drachm* [**denarius*, **dīnāra*] (V S Agrawala 1957).

Rāvaṇa. This name (?) occurs on the obv of Class VIII of the *Yaudheya coins (Allan 1936; K K Dasgupta 1974; Handa 2007a).

Ravināga. *Nāga k. He is associated with *Vibhunāga and *Prabhākara by the use of the 'Sickle-and-arrow' type. They are among the late Nāga rulers, and not much is known about them. He also issued the 'Bull' type of coins. He assumed the title of **mahārāja-śrī* on coins (Bela Lahiri 1974; H V Trivedi 1957).

***Rayaya-māsaka* (= *rajata-māshaka*).** Coin denomination. The *rayaya-māsaka* of the **Aṅgavijjā* seems to be the silver **māshaka* coin mentioned by Manu as *raupya-māshaka*, weighing 2 *rattīs*. This coin is identified with the silver *punch marked coins of the *māshaka* variety (V S Agrawala 1957).

***Repoussé* method.** Technique of manufacture of coins. This technique of manufacture of coins was used very rarely in ancient India, and coins fabricated by this method are extremely rare; it was used more for the manufacture of medals. Earlier, a number of scholars were hesitant in recognizing the pieces manufactured by this technique as coins, and were more in favour of regarding them as medals or seals. The use of this technique for the manufacture of coins seems to be confined to the southern Kosala region, that is the Bastar-Chhattisgarh territory; some coins are also reported from the adjoining areas of Orissa and the Vidarbh region of Maharashtra, but it is believed that they must have originated in the southern Kosala region and reached Orissa and Vidarbha by way of trade. In this technique, a thin sheet of metal, cut according to the desired weight and size, was placed on an anvil, on which were engraved the device and ld in positive and in relief. The sheet was then struck lightly with a wooden hammer several times, so that the device and ld engraved on the anvil were marked on this piece, in positive and in relief on one side, while the same may be seen in the negative and in intaglio on the other side. B N Mukherjee states that the device and ld on the anvil may also be 'in a sunken state', in which case the positive impression on the piece of metal would be in intaglio on one side, while the same may be seen in the negative and in relief on the other side. Besides the coins of the *Nala dynasty of southern Kosala, there are some coins bearing the figure of a *garuḍa*-with-outstretched-wings and the ld variously as *Śri-Prasannamātra*, *Śrī-Mahendrāditya*, *Śrī-Kramāditya*, or their abbreviated forms. The coins bearing the names of Śrī-Mahendrāditya and Śrī-Kramāditya have been attributed by some scholars to the *Imperial Gupta rulers, *Kumāragupta I and *Skandagupta, respectively, and by others to some local rulers (the Nalas, the Śūras, or the *Śarabhapurīyas) of southern Kosala; Nisar Ahmad proposes to identify Śrī-Mahendrāditya with Mahendrāditya of the *Kathāsaritsāgara*, and regards Śrī-Kramāditya as his predecessor (Nisar Ahmad 1964; C S Gupta 1993; B C Jain 1960; Mirashi 1939; B N Mukherjee and P K D Lee 1988; L S Nigam 1987; L S Nigam 1988; T P Verma 1991).

Reverse. Technically, it is that side of the coin, which has received its type by the upper die, that is the die inserted into the lower end of the punch. However, in practice, it is the less important side of the coin, even if it has received its type by the lower die, that is the die embedded in the anvil. It is 'tails' in 'heads or tails'.

Rhinoceros. *Rhinoceros-slayer type.

Kumāragupta I : Rhinoceros-slayer type

Rhinoceros-slayer type. Gold. The Rhinoceros-slayer type is a new type introduced by *Kumāragupta I, perhaps to commemorate his conquest of Kāmarūpa (Assam), known for its rhinoceros population. On the obv, the equestrian king leans forwards to attack a rhinoceros with a sword held in his r hand. The circular ld reads *[Bhartā ?]-khaḍgatrātā Kumāragupto jayatya niśaṁ*. The rev has *Gaṅgā standing on **makara*, with a female umbrella bearer behind her. The forefinger of her extended r hand is pointing at some object, not visible on the coin. A stalked lotus is seen in the trunk of the *makara*. The rev ld is *Śrī-Mahendrakhaḍga* (Ashvini Agrawal 1989; Allan 1914; Altekar 1957; R D Banerji 1933; S R Goyal 2005; P L Gupta 1998; Smith 1972; Prashant Srivastava 1996a; Thaplyal, forthcoming).

River. Symbol. *Undulating line.

Roma. City goddess of Rome. The *Kushāṇa ruler, *Huvishka, on the rev of some of his gold coins, depicted the figure of a helmeted female divinity, standing to the r. She wears a long *chiton*, and carries spear and shield. Cunningham read the label inscription accompanying the figure as *Ride*, and proposed to identify the figure as that of Riddhi, the consort of Kubera. But Gardner read it as *Riom*, and identified the deity as Roma, which seem to be preferable to Cunningham's reading and identification. Roma is believed to be the presiding deity of the city of Rome, and the adoption of her figure as a coin device by the Kushāṇas may have something to do with the brisk Indo-Roman trade during that period. Initially, her worship does not seem to have been very popular, as there was no temple in Rome dedicated to her prior to the time of Augustus, but afterwards a number of her temples were erected, not only in Rome, but all over the Roman empire. Gardner alternatively proposes to identify the deity depicted on these coins of Huvishka as Pallas[-Athena]. It is to be remarked that the depiction of *Athena on coins was quite popular on the *Indo-Greek and *Śaka-Pahlava coins, but the deity is conspicuous by her absence on Kushāṇa coins. There is a suggestion that this absence is probably due to the replacement of Athena by Roma on Kushāṇa coins. On one specimen, the ld accompanying the female figure appears to the read *Rishno* or *Rishmo*, but it is difficult to identify the deity with the Avestan Rashnu, on the ground that the deity on the coin is female, while Rashnu is a male attendant of Mithra (Bhaskar Chattopadhyay 1977; Cunningham 1971a; Gardner 1971; Rosenfield 1967; Stein 1888).

Royal hunter. Device. The hunt was a favourite pastime of royalty, and the scene of a royal hunt was sometimes used as a device on ancient Indian coins. The earliest appearance of this device in India is met with on a round copper coin, doubtfully ascribed to *Taxila

Chandragupta II : Lion-slayer type

Bhānugupta :
Horseman-lion-slayer type

by Allan. On the obv of this coin, the equestrian king is shown to the r, and a slain beast is depicted below. A *lion is shown behind the king. Afterwards, the *Imperial Guptas used the device of the royal hunt on some of their coins, with the various types showing the *tiger, *lion, or *rhinoceros, as the prey. [*Tiger-slayer type, *Lion-slayer type, *Elephant-rider-lion-slayer type, *Rhinoceros-slayer type, *Horse-rider-lion-slayer type] (Allan 1914; Altekar 1957; Pathak 1986; Pathak 1988-1989; Prashant Srivastava 2001; Prashant Srivastava 2004a).

Rudradāmaka. Coin denomination. This denomination is mentioned in the *Săratthadīpanī*, the commentary on the *Samantapāsādikā* of Buddhaghosha by Śāriputra. According to C D Chatterjee, it implied the silver coins struck by *Rudradāman [I] (*Rudradāmena uppādito*). D C Sircar, however, regards the *rudradāmaka* as the silver coins issued by the *Western Kshatrapas in general, and named after Rudradāman I, 'the greatest and most famous of the Śaka rulers of Western India'. According to this commentary, it was three-fourth the value of a **nīla-kahāpaṇa*, the standard silver **kārshāpaṇa* of 32 *rattīs*. From this, it has been inferred that the *rudradāmaka* weighed 24 *rattīs* (or, more probably, 20 *rattīs*). However, in the inscriptions, Western Kshatrapa silver coins are often mentioned as **kārshāpaṇa* (V S Agrawala 1957; C D Chatterjee 1931; C S Gupta 1982; Sircar 1968; Sircar 1986).

Rudradāmakādi. Coin denomination. This denomination occurs in the *Samantapāsādikā* of Buddhaghosha, and the *Vinayatthamañjūshā*, the commentary on the *Kaṅkhāvitaraṇī* of Buddhaghosha by Buddhanāga. C D Chatterjee interprets it as silver coins which have been modelled after the **rudradāmaka*, and issued by the successors of Rudradāman I. D C Sircar, however, objects to this on the ground that all the *Western Kshatrapa coins are based on the same weight standard, and it would not have been possible for the common man of the time to distinguish between the coins of the *Kārddamaka Kshatrapas from those of the other Śaka rulers of western India. He, himself, regards *rudradāmakādi* as denoting the whole class of silver coins, issued on the weight standard of 36 grains, issued by the *Western Kshatrapas, as well as the 'non-Śaka silver coins of about the same weight standard such as those of the Sātavāhanas and the

Guptas'. However, in inscriptions, Western Kshatrapa silver coins are mentioned as **kārshāpaṇa* (V S Agrawala 1957; C D Chatterjee 1931; C S Gupta 1982; Sircar 1968; Sircar 1986).

Rudradāman I. *Kārddamaka k; son of *Jayadāman; second century AD. He succeeded his father, Jayadāman, as heir-apparent of his grandfather, **Mahākshatrapa* *Chashṭana, when Jayadāman appears to have died during the reign of Chashṭana, and later succeeded his grandfather as *mahākshatrapa*. The Junagarh inscription informs us that Rudradāman I twice defeated the Sātavāhana ruler, and the *Yaudheyas, who inhabited southern Punjab and its adjoining areas. The Junagarh inscription gives a list of the provinces under his rule, which shows that his authority extended from Multan in the north to Nasik and Sopara in the south. He issued *Kārddamaka silver type of coins. The Br ld on the rev of these coins reads *Rājño kshatrapasa Jayadāmaputrasa rājño mahākshatrapasa Rudradāmasa*. But one coin refers to him only as *rājan*, which reminds one of the use of this title for him in the Andhau inscription of year 52, and in the Khavada inscription of year 5[3] where he is called *rājan* and *svāmin*. Rudradāman I also issued some coins in copper, which are very few in numbers and are known in three types. The obv of the first type has a crescent and a star, and the Br ld *Rājño mahākshatrapasa Rudradāmasa* on the obv, and *crescent-on-hill on the rev. A specimen of this type from Prakash is reported to have an admixture of lead with copper. The second type of copper coins has a *bull and the Br ld *Svāmi Rudradāmasya* on the obv, and the hill symbol on the rev. The third type has an *elephant on the obv, and the crescent-on-hill symbol on the rev. The Br ld on this type reads *Rājño mahākshatrapasa Rudradāmasa*, sometimes with *svāmi* added before the name of the issuer. All the silver coins, as also the copper coins of the first type, are round in shape; the other two types of copper coins are rectangular (Jha and Rajgor 1994; Mirashi 1982; Mitchiner 1976; Rapson 1975; Raychaudhuri 1972; Senior 2001; Sircar 1980e).†

Rudradāsa. *Audumbara chief. He issued copper coins of Class I of *Audumbara coins. On these coins, he uses the titles of **raña* and **mahadeva*. On palaeographical grounds, these coins are dated to the second or first century BC (Allan 1936; Chakrabortty 1931;

Cunningham 1971b; K K Dasgupta 1974; Handa 2007a; Jayaswal 1988; Marshall 1975; Smith 1972).

Rudraghosha. *Pañchāla k. Nothing much is known about him, except that he is to be placed among the early Pañchāla kings on palaeographical grounds, and might have preceded *Bhadraghosha. The rev of his coins is not clear (K D Bajpai 1962; Bela Lahiri 1974).

Rudragupta. *Pañchāla k. He is placed among the later rulers of Pañchāla known from coins, on palaeographical grounds. His coins are associated with those of *Dhruvamitra at Rohtayya and Ramnagar; the rev device on the coins of these two rulers is the same—a *trident or trident-battleaxe on a pedestal between two pillars. This seems to be the symbolic representation of *Śiva, who is also known as Rudra and Dhruva, the names these two rulers bore, respectively (Allan 1936; Bela Lahiri 1974).

Rudrasena I. *Kārddamaka k. He was the son of *Rudrasiṁha I, and began is career as a **kshatrapa*, perhaps serving under *Jīvadāman, from *Śaka year 121 to 122 (?). After Jīvadāman, he attained to the position of **mahākshatrapa*, and issued coins as such from Śaka year 122 to 145. He is also known from the Mulwasar inscription of year 122, and the Gadha inscription of year 127. He married his sister, *Mahādevī* Prabhudamā, to a Lichchhavi chief of Vaiśālī, as per the testimony of a sealing from Basarh. Towards the end of his reign, he appointed his son, *Pṛithvīsena, as his *kshatrapa*. His coins are of the *Kārddamaka silver type. There are some potin coins which bear on the obv, the figure of an *elephant to the r, with a star above to the l, and a crescent to the r. The rev has a *crescent-on-hill, star, and crescent. There is no ld on these coins, but the date of issue of the coins is engraved on the rev. As both the dates—Śaka year 131 and 133, occurring on these coins fall within the reign of Rudrasena I, these coins seem to have been issued during his reign, for circulation in the Malwa region (Jha and Rajgor 1994; Mirashi 1982; Mitchiner 1976; Rapson 1975; Raychaudhuri 1972; Senior 2001; Sircar 1980e).

Rudrasena II. *Kārddamaka k. He was the son of *Vīradāman, and ruled as **mahākshatrapa* from *Śaka year 177 to 200. He seems to have succeeded his uncle, *Dāmajadaśrī III, to that position. In the year 197, towards the end of his reign, he appointed his son, *Viśvasiṁha, as **kshatrapa*. Another son of his, named *Bhartṛidāman, started issuing coins as *kshatrapa* in the year 200; he, too, might initially have served under Rudrasena II. He issued coins of the *Kārddamaka silver type (Jha and Rajgor 1994; Mirashi 1982; Mitchiner 1976; Rapson 1975; Raychaudhuri 1972; Senior 2001; Sircar 1980e).

Rudrasena III. *Kārddamaka k. He was the son of Rudradāman II, and ruled as **mahākshatrapa* from *Śaka year 270 to 300. The coins of his father are not available, but Rudrasena III refers to him as *mahākshatrapa* in his own coin ld. There is a suggestion that Rudradāman II might have ruled in the 16 year interval following the end of the reign of *Yaśodāman II, for which no Kārddamaka coins are available. But Amiteshwar Jha and Dilip Rajgor find this 'difficult to justify'. Some scholars identify Rudrasena III with Rudradeva, described in the Allahabad pillar inscription as a north Indian ruler defeated by *Samdragupta. There is also a suggestion that during his reign, the Kārddamakas had to face the invasion of the Sassanian ruler, Shapur II, of Iran. Trouble might also have been made for him by Śarvva Bhaṭṭāraka, or the Ābhīras, or the Traikūṭakas. Rudrasena III issued coins of the *Kārddamaka silver type. Besides, there are some lead coins, which bear the figure of a humped *bull to the r on the obv, and a *crescent-on-hill, star, crescent, and curved line on the rev. These coins do not bear any ld, but the dates on the rev on the various coins range from Śaka year 280 to 294. All these dates fall within the reign period of Rudrasena III; the rev of these lead coins resembles the rev of the silver and potin coins of the *Kārddamaka Kshatrapas. On this basis, it is assumed that these lead coins might have been issued during the reign of Rudrasena III. Interestingly, the lead coins are square in shape, as against the round shape of the majority of the Kārddamaka coins (Jha and Rajgor 1994; Mirashi 1982; Mitchiner 1976; Rapson 1975; Raychaudhuri 1972; Senior 2001; Sircar 1980e).

Rudrasena IV. *Kārddamaka k. He was the son of *Siṁhasena, and ruled as **mahākshatrapa*. But the dates of issue of his coins have not been read with any certainty. He issued coins of the *Kārddamaka silver type (Jha and Rajgor 1994; Mirashi 1982; Mitchiner 1976; Rapson 1975; Raychaudhuri 1972; Senior 2001; Sircar 1980e).

Rudrasiṁha I. *Kārddamaka k. He was the son of *Rudradāman I and the younger brother of *Dāmajadaśrī I (and also of *Dāmaghsada II, if he is regarded as different from Dāmajadaśrī I). According to the Rapson, he contested the succession of *Jīvadāman after the death of Dāmajadaśrī I, but was initially not successful, and had to serve Jīvadāman as a **kshatrapa*. But from Śaka year 103-110, and from Śaka year 113-118, he ruled as **mahākshatrapa*, on the basis of which Rapson postulated that after the initial success, Jīvadāman was removed from the position of *mahākshatrapa* by his uncle. This view is based on Rapson's reading of the date of year 1[00] on a silver coin of Jīvadāman as *mahākshatrapa*. However, Amiteshwar Jha and Dilip Rajgor doubt this reading and suggest that there is no evidence of a struggle between Rudrasiṁha I and Jīvadāman. They are of the view that Rudrasiṁha I initially served as a *kshatrapa* under his brother, Dāmaghsada II, and had a 'smooth elevation' to the office of *mahākshatrapa*. They also read the dates of years 100 to 102 on a number of coins mentioning Rudrasiṁha I as *mahākshatrapa*. But the evidence of the Gunda inscription of year 103, which refers to Rudrasiṁha I as *kshatrapa* only, would seem to go against this theory. However, Jha and Rajgor give preference to the numismatic evidence over epigraphic evidence. Between Śaka year 110 and 112, Rudrasiṁha I issued coins as *kshatrapa* only, either because Jīvadāman had again occupied the position of *mahākshatrapa*, or because of the rise of the power of the Ābhīra (?) chief, *Īśvaradatta, or because Yajña Sātakarṇi had eclipsed the power of the Kārddamaka Kshatrapas during this period. By Śaka year 119, Rudrasiṁha I had been succeeded as *mahākshatrapa* by Jīvadāman. If this internal feud did, indeed, take place, it is suggested that the Sātavāhanas seem to have taken advantage of the situation and occupied some of the southern territories of the Kārddamaka Kshatrapas towards the end of the second century AD. But, ultimately, there seems to have been a *rapprochement* between the two rival claimants to the position of *mahākshatrapa*, for *Rudrasena I, the son of Rudrasiṁha

I, apparently served as a *kshatrapa* under Jīvadāman during the second reign of the latter as *mahākshatrapa*. Rudrasiṁha I issued *Kārddamaka silver type of coins, as well as potin coins. The latter bear the figure of a humped *bull to the r, and some Greek characters on the obv; the rev has a *crescent-on-hill, star, crescent, and curved line, and a Br ld mentioning only his name and titles and not those of his father. A copper type bears a bull on the obv, and a *hill on the rev, but the last part of the name of the issuer in the obv Br ld is obliterated. It has been tentatively ascribed to the Rudrasiṁha I by some scholars (Jha and Rajgor 1994; Mirashi 1982; Mitchiner 1976; Rapson 1975; Raychaudhuri 1972; Senior 2001; Sircar 1980e).

Rudrasiṁha II. *Kārddamaka k. He seems to have supplanted *Viśvasena of the main line of *Chashṭana among the *Kārddamaka Kshatrapas. On his coins, he refers to himself as the son of Svāmi Jīvadāman; the absence of any royal title for the latter seems to indicate that he was not a king, but was, perhaps, a member of some collateral branch of the Kārddamaka dynasty, as proposed by scholars like Bhagwanlal Indraji. Rudrasiṁha II ruled only as a **kshatrapa*, and his coins, which are all of the *Kārddamaka silver type, bear the dates of *Śaka year 226-238 (Jha and Rajgor 1994; Mirashi 1982; Mitchiner 1976; Rapson 1975; Raychaudhuri 1972; Senior 2001; Sircar 1980e).

Rudrasiṁha III. *Kārddamaka k. He was the son of Satyasiṁha. The coins of the latter are not available, but he is referred to as a **mahākshatrapa* on the coins of his son. Rudrasiṁha III issued coins as a *mahākshatrapa*, and these silver coins, which are of the *Kārddamaka silver type, bear dates from *Śaka year 307 to 337. He is the last known Kārddamaka ruler, and has been identified as the king of Kathiawar who was defeated by *Chandragupta II. There is, however, evidence to show that a brother and another relative of Rudrasiṁha III also issued coins, although their names have so far baffled all attempts at decipherment (Jha and Rajgor 1994; Mirashi 1982; Mitchiner 1976; Rapson 1975; Raychaudhuri 1972; Senior 2001; Sircar 1980e).

Rudravarman. *Vemaki chief.

Rūpaka. Coin denomination. It was the name used for the silver coin of about 20 *rattīs*, at least from the time of the *Imperial Guptas. According to A M Shastri, the first definite reference to the term in that sense occurs in the **Bṛihatsaṁhitā* of Varāhamihira. However, it is believed that in inscriptions, this denomination occurs for the first time in the Baigram copperplate inscription of Gupta year 128 (= 447 AD). The Siyadoni inscription of 712 AD mentions 10 **viṁśopakas* as making half a **dramma*, while the charter of Vishṇusheṇa of 592 AD makes five *viṁśopakas* as equal to a quarter of a *rūpaka*. This seems to show that *rūpaka* and *dramma* denote the same silver coin. The *Bṛihatsaṁhitā* also seems to indicate that *rūpaka* and **kārshāpaṇa* denote the same coin (A M Shastri 1967; Sircar 1964; Sircar 1986).

S

Sadera. **Satera.*

Śaka-Pahlava. Coins, general features. The origin of the Śaka-Pahlavas is a much debated subject among scholars, and various theories have been proposed, of which the most reasonable one seems to be that of R C Senior, which is mainly based on the account of the Śakas as given by Laszlo Torday. The Śakas were confederations of a number of apparently racially and linguistically homogenous tribes or clans, originally from central Asia, although sometimes they may have also assimilated other ethnic nomadic tribes. These people referred to themselves as Śaka. The Chinese called them Sai. The Greeks called these people Skythians, from their supposed founder, Skulatai, which name was corrupted by the Greeks into Skolotai, Skules, Skylas, or Skythes. According to Herodotos, he was a descendant, either of Targitaus, a son of Zeus, or of Herakles, another son of that deity. The name Skythes may mean 'shooter or archer', which suits the Śakas well. It may also be connected to Sogdia (Transoxiana)—Skytha becoming Skuda<Suguda<Sogdia. The Skythians had been migrating from their original homeland towards the west since the beginning of the first millennium BC. Arsakes I, the founder of the Parthians dynasty, belonged to the Aparni tribe, which was a part of the Dahae confederation of Chorasmia, the Dahae themselves being a part of the Śaka confederation. This, incidentally, shows a close connection between the Skythians and the Parthians, and, hence, the use of the term Śaka-Pahlava throughout this work. In the latter half of the third century BC, the Hiung-nu tribe inhabited some region to the north

Spalyris and Spalagadama

Azes II

Azes II

Azes II and Aśpavarman

of the Mangolian plateau, while the Yüeh-chih tribe occupied Kansu to the west of the Ordos plateau which lay outside the Great Wall of China, but within a loop formed by the river Hwang-ho. The two tribes often fought with each over the possession of Orodes. Some time before 221 BC, the Yüeh-chih defeated the Hiung-nu *Shan-yü* (king) T'ou-man, and took his son, Mao-tun as hostage. In 221 BC, the Chinese emperor, Cheng, forced the Hiung-nu to the retreat towards the north, but on his death in 210 BC, they returned and attacked the Yüeh-chih, and Mao-tun escaped. He became the king, occupied Ordos, and defeated a number of nomadic tribes, forcing them to join his confederation. Around this time (208-206 BC), intense volcanic activity seems to have led to a decline in world temperatures, and a number of peoples migrated south from Siberia towards the river Oxus. In 200 BC, the first Han emperor, Kao-tsu, attacked the Hiung-nu, but was besieged and forced to sign a treaty in 198 BC. In 177 BC, during the reign of the next emperor, Wen-ti, the Hiung-nu crossed the Hwang-ho, and breached the Great Wall. According to the *Shih Chi*, Mao-tun sent a letter to Wen-ti, claiming that he had punished his commander, 'Right Wise King', for this breach of the treaty, and sent him west to give fight to the Yüeh-chih, whom he had succeeded in wiping out. He also claims that he had defeated the Wu-sun, Hu-chieh, and 26 states, and that 'all the people who live by drawing the bow are now united into one family'. The Yüeh-chih, however, did not join this confederation. Some scholars believe that the Yüeh-chih migration from their original homeland began after this battle in *c* 177-176 BC. But it was Left Wise King (called Old Shan-yü by the Chinese), the son and successor of Mao-tun, who finally defeated the Yüeh-chih sometime before 159 BC, killed their ruler, and forced them to migrate. Most of the Yüeh-chih, called Ta Yüeh-chih by the Chinese, migrated westwards from Kansu, and then north to Etsin Gol, to the Turfan basin, crossed the Tien Shan mountains, and settled in the Ili valley, the homeland of the Śakas; in 128 BC, Chang Ch'ien, the emissary of the Chinese emperor, Wu-ti, found the Ta Yüeh-chih in K'ang-chü along the north bank of the river Jaxartes. Some Yüeh-chih remained in Kansu and Etsin Gol, at least up to 121 BC, and they are called Hsiao Yüeh-chih by the Chinese. Under the pressure of the Ta Yüeh-chih, the Śakas fled their homeland in the Ili valley, and moving towards the south, occupied Chi-pin (Kashmir). The tribe spilt repeatedly, and established several states, like the Hsui-hsn and Chan-tu to the northwest of Shu-lo (Kashgar). According to the Chinese accounts, the Śakas invaded India only from the north, which is not entirely correct. However, some Śakas from the Ili valley did cross the Pamirs, and entered India, settling in the Hazara-Kashmir region. *Maues belonged to this branch of the Śakas, who colonized the Hazara and Kashmir regions, and he later advanced west into the Indo-Greek territories. This is suggested by the high quality of his silver coins in the Hazara-Kahsmir region, as also by several of his coin types being imitated from Indo-Greek coinage. A western branch of the Śakas was pushed by the Yüeh-chih across the Jaxartes and the Oxus. Another branch was already moving from Sogdia. They first occupied Merv and northern Bactria, and then crossed the Hindukush into India, occupying Kapiśā, the Kabul valley, and western Gandhāra, that is they advanced east into the Indo-Greek territories. *Vonones and the related rulers, *Spalahora, *Spalagadama, *Spalirises, *Azes I, *Azilises, and *Azes II, belonged to this branch of the Śakas. This branch began the posthumous *Hermaios coinage, which developed into the initial coinage of the family of Vonones in the Gandhāra region, there being strong monogram links between the posthumous Hermaios coinage and the initial coinage of the family of Vonones. The two branches of Maues and Vonones were mainly responsible for the end of Indo-Greek rule, and were finally united by Azes. The Parthian emperor, Phraates II, hired Śaka mercenaries, perhaps from Margiane, Traxiane, and Aria, for his campaign against Antiochos VII. But after the campaign, he had a dispute with the Śakas, and he, as also his uncle and successor, Artabanos I, lost their lives at the hands of these Śaka mercenaries. The next ruler, Mithridates II, initially fought with these Śakas. But later, he reversed his policy *vis-à-vis* the Śakas, and settled them in Drangiana, which henceforth became known as Sakastene (Seistan). *Orthagnes, *Gondopharnes, *Guḍa, *Abdagases, and perhaps, also *Pakores, probably belonged to this branch of the Śakas from Seistan. Gondopharnes was the last great Śaka-Pahlava ruler; after him, the empire disintegrated, and, finally, the *Kushāṇas occupied most of the Śaka-Pahlava territories. There are also certain satrapal families, like those of *Rañjuvula and *Śoḍāsha; of *Hagāna and *Hagāmasha; of *Kharaosta and *Hajatriā; of Liāka Kusulaka; of *Zeionises; and of the *Apracharajas.

Azilises

Sanabares

Maues

Azes II

The Śaka-Pahlava rulers do not appear to have any numismatic tradition of their own, and, for the greater part, their coins are but crude imitations of the *Indo-Greek coins, with certain features of the Arsakid coins of Parthian. They issued coins in silver, copper, bronze, and billon, their weight standard being based on that of the Indo-Greek coins of these metals. The coins of the Śaka-Pahlavas are both round and square in shape, though later, there is a greater preponderance of round coins than the square ones; the billon coins are always round. All the Śaka-Pahlava coins appear to have been manufactured by the die-striking method. By the time the Śaka-Pahlavas reached the Kabul valley, they had established their characteristic type of 'Mounted king : Deity'. The equestrian king is usually shown holding a spear or a whip, or, rarely, both the weapons. On a type of Spalirises with Azes I, the king holds a whip over his shoulder, and an *aṅkuśa* in hand. *Aṅkuśa* is also seen in the hand of Azes riding a camel. On some types, the king is being crowned by some deity, usually *Nike. Some rulers, like Orthagnes, Gondopharnes, and the Śaka Kshatrapas of Mathurā, issued coins showing the bust of the king on the obv. Some coins of rulers, like Maues, depict the king on the obv, while those of others, like Azes, bear armed king, seated crosslegged on a cushion. Enthroned king may also sometimes be seen, as, for instance, on some coins of Gondopharnes. The rev of Śaka-Pahlava coins is usually occupied by the figure of some deity, but sometimes, a divine figure may be seen on the obv as well. These deities are from both the Greek and Indian pantheons; city deities are also often depicted. The deities depicted of these coins include *Apollo, *Artemis, *Athena, *Demeter, the *Dioskuri, *Helios, *Hephaistos, *Herakles, *Hermes, *Indra, *Lakshmī, Nike, *Poseidon, *Selene, *Śiva, *Tyche, and *Zeus. In certain cases, the deities may be represented by their emblems, like the **aegis* of Athena, the **tripod lebes* of Apollo, the bow-and-arrow of Artemis, the *thunderbolt of Zeus. Among the animals that appear on Śaka-Pahlava coins, the *horse is the most common, being represented as the mount of the king on the obv, though there are instances of the horse appearing as an independent device also. Other animals include maneless *lion, humped *bull, and *elephant. Sometimes only the head of the animal may be depicted. Birds are, however, not seen on Śaka-Pahlava coins. Śaka-Pahlava coins bear legends, usually on both the sides, but sometimes only on one side. The language of the obv ld is Greek, while that of the rev ld is Pkt, written in the Kh script. Sovereign Śaka-Pahlava rulers use the title **basileos basileon megalos*/**majaraja rajaraja* (or *rajatiraja*) *mahata*; while subordinate rulers use **basileus*/**maharaja*. Besides, on various coins, we come across additional epithets like *adelphou tou basileos*/*maharajabhrata*, 'brother of the king', or **basileuontos basileon*, **dikaios*/**dhramika*, **soteros*/**tratara*, **autokratoros*, **epiphanes*, **theos*, *satrapei*, **devavrata*, **apratihata*, *apratihatachakra*, *stratega*, etc (Bopearachchi 1993; Bopearachchi and Pieper 1998; Bopearachchi and Rahman 1995; Sudhakar Chattopadhyaya 1955; Cunningham 1971a; Gardner 1971; Marshall 1975; Senior 2001; Sircar 1980b; Prashant Srivastava 1996a; Torday 1997; Whitehead 1914).

Zeionises

Śaka *saṁvat*. This era, beginning in 78 AD, though not uncommon in western India, and parts of eastern and central India, has been more predominant in southern India, and continues to be in use to the present day. A tradition, as recorded by authorities like Brahmagupta and Alberuni, that the founding of this era marked the second expulsion of the Śakas by Vikramāditya, seems to have no historical basis. The same may be said of the traditions, which associate the era with King Śālivāhana. The identity of the founder of this era has been a subject of debate among scholars for long, though most of the modern writers on the subject ascribe it to *Kanishka I. An Andhau inscription of *Chashṭana is dated in the year 11, and some scholars express the possibility that the year might be referred to the Śaka *saṁvat*, and Chashṭana may be regarded as the founder of that era. The maga-brāhmaṇas preferred the Śaka *saṁvat* to other reckonings. The earliest 'authentic' inscription to refer to the era by the name, Śaka, is believed to be the Vāla inscription of Suketuvarman, which is dated Śaka year 322 (= 400 AD). The era seems to have been ousted by the *Gupta *saṁvat* in the greater part of northern India. The years, when cited in the Śaka *saṁvat*, are generally counted as expired, though there are some rare instances of the year being counted as current. The year begins in the month of Chaitra. The months are generally *amānta*, though *pūrṇimānta* months are also known in some instances from northern India. The dates on the coins of the *Kārddamaka rulers are in the Śaka *saṁvat* (Salomon 1998; Sircar 1965).

Sakayamo Boddo. *Buddha, Śākyamuni.

Sakori hoard. This hoard of 24 *Imperial Gupta gold coins was found in 1914 at Sakori, district Damoh (Madhya Pradesh). The rulers represented in this hoard are *Samudragupta, *Kācha, *Chandragupta II, and *Skandagupta. These coins are housed in the Central Museum, Nagpur (Altekar 1957).

Samāchāradeva *Narendravinīta.* K. This ruler was earlier known only from coins in the collection of the Indian Museum, Calcutta. But now, there is a seal from Nalanda, and the Ghugrahatti (District Faridpur, Bangladesh) copperplate, which refer to him. The title of the king, on the coins of both the types, was read as *Narendrāditya* by Allan, N K Bhattasali, and R D Banerji. But later, Banerji read it as *Narendravinīta*, and this has been accepted by Altekar. On the basis of the reading *Narendrāditya*, Allan was 'half inclined' to identify Samāchāradeva with *Śaśāṅka, who had *Narendrāditya* as his title. But Bhattasali regarded Samāchāradeva as the father of Śaśāṅka, while Hoernle identified him with Narasiṁhagupta II. Altekar argues that the vertical ld on the obv, in the *Imperial Gupta numismatic tradition, indicated the personal name of the issuer, and as on both types of coins, the vertical ld reads *Samāchāra*, they could not be regarded as the issues of either Śaśāṅka or Narasiṁhagupta II. The script of the coins, as also of the Ghugrahatti plates, is of the sixth century AD; Ghugrahatti, the place from which the copperplate of Samāchāradeva has been found, is just 30 miles from the findspot of the *Jessore hoard, which contains one coin each of both Samāchāradeva and Śaśāṅka; bull standard appears on one of the coins of Samāchāradeva, and *Śiva and Nandin are seen on the coins of Śaśāṅka, thereby showing the Śaiva leanings of both these rulers. On these bases, Altekar suggests that both Samāchāradeva and Śaśāṅka belonged to the same dynasty, and the former was a predecessor of Śaśāṅka, and ruled after Gopachandra and Dharmāditya. Samāchāradeva is known to have issued two types of gold coins, weighing 148.2 grains and 149 grains, respectively : (i) *Archer type, and (ii) **Rājalīlā* type (Ashvini Agrawal 1989; Allan 1914; Altekar 1957; R D Banerji 1933; N K Bhattasali 1923; S R Goyal 2005; P L Gupta 1998; Smith 1972; Thaplyal, forthcoming).

Samudragupta *Parākramāditya.* *Imperial Gupta k; son of *Chandragupta I; fourth century AD. He was born of the Lichchhavi princess, *Kumāradevī. From the Allahabad pillar inscription, we come to know that he had an eventful career, in the course of which he brought several lands under various degrees of subjection. In the Āryāvartta, he defeated at least nine rulers, and annexed their kingdoms to the Imperial Gupta dominions. A number of frontier kingdoms and tribal states, as also the Śaka-Kushāṇa rulers of western Punjab and Afghanistan, and even Siṁhala and other islands of south-east Asia, are said to have accepted his political influence. He also brought all the forest kingdoms (*āṭavika rājyas*) under his influence. In southern India, he defeated at least 12 kings, who were captured, but later set free, and, perhaps, allowed to the rule over their kingdoms as vassals of the Gupta emperor. As a fitting *finale* to his victorious career, Samudragupta performed the *aśvamedha*, perhaps towards the end of his rule. Samudragupta is known to have issued at least six types of coins in gold : (i) *Standard type, (ii) *Archer type, (iii) *Battle-axe type, (iv) *Tiger-slayer type, (v) **Aśvamedha* type, and (vi) *Lyrist type. Some scholars have also ascribed the *King-and-Queen type bearing the names of Chandragupta I and Kumāradevī, and the *Kācha type, to Samudragupta, but this has not found universal acceptance. The early monetary issues of this ruler bear a discernable impact of the Kushāṇa prototype, but gradual Indianization of the coins in respect of the king's dress, his attributes, rev depiction, may be seen in later types. Himself a poet of repute, he seems to have introduced metrical legends on coins (Ashvini Agrawal 1989; Allan 1914; Altekar 1957; R D Banerji 1933; Fleet 1888; S R Goyal 2005; P L Gupta 1998; K P Jayaswal 1933; Smith 1972; Prashant Srivastava 1996a; Thaplyal, forthcoming).†

Samudragupta : Standard type

Samudragupta : Battle-axe type

Samudragupta : Archer type

Samudragupta : *Aśvamedha* type

Samudragupta II (?). A gold coin of the *Archer type, bearing the name of Samudragupta on the obv, and the ld *Parākrama(ḥ)* on the rev, and weighing 136 grains, was published by P L Gupta. The weight of the coin seems to conform to the standard of the traditional Indian **suvarṇa* of around 144 grains, which was first adopted for *Imperial Gupta gold coinage during the reign of *Skandagupta. On this basis, P L Gupta placed this coin some time after Skandagupta, and ascribed it to a second Imperial Gupta ruler named Samudragupta, who was different from the famous *Samudragupta, the son of *Chandragupta I. However, there is no other evidence to corroborate the existence of a Samudragupta II, and scholars are generally in favour of regarding this coin as a forged one (Ashwini Agrawal 1989; Altekar 1957; P L Gupta 1954).

Śāṇa. Coin denomination. It was a [metal ?] coin, weighing 12.5 *rattīs* (about 22.5 grains). It was one-eighth of a **śatamāna*. V S Agrawala derives its weight as 1205 *rattīs* or 22.5 grains. From the **Ashṭādhyāyī*, it appears to be quite popular at the time of Pāṇini (R C Agrawala 1953a, and Altekar's editorial note on it; V S Agrawala 1952; V S Agrawala 1953).

Sanabares

Sanabares. Śaka-Pahlava k; related to *Gondopharnes (?); mid-first century AD. Numismatic evidence suggests that he exercised authority over Arachosia and Seistan. The occurrence of an Arsakid symbol on a number of his coins shows some connection with the Parthian empire also. Gardner feels that the conspicuous absence of any Indian script on his coins suggests that he ruled 'exclusively or principally to the north of the Indian Caucasus'. Sanabares issued coins in silver and copper/bronze. The obv of most of his coins shows the bust of the king in Parthian tiara; only on one bronze type, we find the diademed head of the king. The rev usually has the figure of the king enthroned or seated as an archer, although some silver and bronze types have the figure of *Nike or *Apollo on the rev. The silver types have a Pahlavik ld on the obv mentioning the name of the king or its abbreviated form, while the rev has a Gr ld. The copper/bronze coins have Gr ld only. In the Gr ld on the silver coins, the king uses the titles **basileus* **megas*, but on the copper/bronze coins, he has dropped the additional title, *megas* (Cunningham 1971a; Gardner 1971; Jenkins and Narain 1957; Marshall 1975; B N Mukherjee 1969a; Rapson 1987; Senior 2001; Sircar 1980b; Tarn 1980; Whitehead 1914).

Sanadiya hoard. This hoard of 125 silver coins of the *Kārddamaka Kshatrapas was discovered at Sanadiya in the Junagarh district of Gujarat. The rulers represented in the hoard include *Dāmajadaśrī I, *Rudrasiṁha I, *Rudrasena I, *Dāmasena, *Dāmajadaśrī II, *Vīradāman, Yaśodāman I, *Vijayasena, *Dāmajadaśrī III,

*Viśvasiṁha, *Bhartṛidāman, *Viśvasena, and *Rudrasena III (Jha and Rajgor 1994).

Sanchi hoard. This hoard of 41 silver coins was discovered at Sanchi in the Raisen district of Madhya Pradesh in 1916-1917. Most of the coins in the hoard belong to the *Kārddamaka Kshatrapas, like *Rudrasena I, *Rudrasena II, *Viśvasiṁha, *Bhartṛidāman, *Viśvasena, *Rudrasiṁha II, and *Rudrasena III; nine coins are uncertain (Hamid *et al* 1922; Jha and Rajgor 1994).

Saṅghadāman. *Kārddamaka k. He was the son of *Rudrasiṁha I and seems to have ruled as **mahākshatrapa* after his brother, *Rudrasena I. Rapson read the date of year 144 on his coin issued as *mahākshatrapa*, and suggested that he ruled between *Rudrasena I and *Dāmasena. But Amiteshwar Jha and Dilip Rajgor regard 144 as a 'misreading' of the date, and say that only year 149 is certain for Saṅghadāman as *mahākshatrapa*; this is supported by R C Senior. The fact, that the year 149, when Saṅghadāman was ruling as *mahākshatrapa*, falls within the reign of Dāmasena as *mahākshatrapa* (years 145-158), has led Jha and Rajgor to the regard Saṅghadāman as a rebel against his brother. He issued coins of the *Kārddamaka silver type (Jha and Rajgor 1994; Mirashi 1982; Mitchiner 1976; Rajgor 1991; Rapson 1975; Raychaudhuri 1972; Senior 2001; Sircar 1980e).

Saṅghamitra. *Ayodhyā k. A seal from Rajghat mentions one Saṅghamitra as the son of Vishṇumitra and grandson of Bhavasena. This Saṅghamitra of the seal might be identical with the homonym of Ayodhyā coins. He, along with *Vijayamitra, is connected with *Kumudasena, *Ajavarman, and *Mādhavavarman by the use of the rev device of a **nandipada* within a square, and seems to be earlier than the other Ayodhyā rulers with *mitra*-ending names, who issued round die-struck coins. As Saṅghamitra used the rev device of *nandipada* within a square alone, while Vijayamitra used the device of a *cock on a post and *tree-in-railing on some of his coins, Saṅghamitra has been regarded as a predecessor of Vijayamitra. The obv of the coins of Saṅghamitra bear the device of a *bull to the l, and the ld mentioning the name of the king in the genitive (Allan 1936; Bela Lahiri 1974).

Śaṅkhamagha (?). *Magha k.

Sanund hoard. This hoard of 1,395 silver coins was discovered at Sanund in the Ahmedabad district of Gujarat. Of these, 1,103 coins belong to the *Imperial Guptas, 283 to Śarvva of Valabhī, and nine to a *Kārddamaka Kshatrapa, who might be *Rudrasiṁha II or *Rudrasena III (P L Gupta 1969; Jha and Rajgor 1994).

Sapadbizes (?). *Kushāṇa (?) k. There is no unanimity among scholars regarding the name of this ruler, and an alternative Sapaleizes has also been suggested. His silver coins bear the helmeted bust of the king and the ld *Sapadbizes* on the obv, and a *lion to the r and the ld *Nanaia* on the rev. The rev inscription, perhaps referring to the goddess, *Nana*, seems to place Sapadbizes among the Kushāṇa rulers who mostly mention the name of the deity depicted in the rev label inscription. Although *Nana* is not depicted on the coin of Sapadbizes in her anthropomorphic form, the rev device of lion reminds one of the lion-mount of *Nana* seen on some Kushāṇa coins (Gardner 1971; Senior 2001; Whitehead 1914).

Sapedana. *Apracha (?) k. Some good quality silver coins from Taxila bear on the obv, diademed bust of the king, *Gondopharnes symbol, and a Gr ld referring to the king, usually as **basileos basileon megas*, but sometimes as **basileuontos basileon megalos*. The rev has *Nike standing with wreath and palm, and the Kh ld **Rajarajasa* **tratarasa* **dhramiäsa Sapedanasa*. There are also some similar bronze coins, but the incomplete Gr ld on the obv mentions Sorpedonos (= Sapedana). Rapson believed that the portrait on the obv of these coins is that of *Gondopharnes, and suggested that Sapedana issued these coins as a subordinate of Gondopharnes. But the use of the title, 'king of kings', by him shows that he acknowledged the suzerainty of Gondopharnes only nominally. However, Marshall and Whitehead regard the portrait on these coins as that of Sapedana himself, and if this be accepted, there is no definite evidence to show that he ruled as a subordinate under Gondopharnes. The occurrence of the Gondopharnes symbol on his coins, however, shows some connection with the *Śaka-Pahlava ruler. Marshall suggests that Sapedana was a successor of

*Sasan, and if we accept this suggestion, Gondopharnes could not possibly have been his overlord. His coins suggest that he ruled over Arachosia and the lower Indus regions (Cunningham 1971a; Gardner 1971; Jenkins and Narain 1957; Marshall 1975; B N Mukherjee 1969a; Rapson 1987; Senior 2001; Sircar 1980b; Prashant Srivastava 1996a; Prashant Srivastava 2007a; Tarn 1980; Whitehead 1914).

Śarabhapurīya. Dynasty. The actual name of this dynasty is not known, and it is named as such on the basis of the fact that the records of the kings were initially found from a place called Śarabhapura, which seems to be their capital and which might have been founded by Śarabharāja mentioned in the Eran pillar inscription of the time of Bhānugupta (510 AD) as the maternal grandfather of Goparāja. Inscriptions have revealed the names of Nandana, Prasannamātra, Jayarāja, Durgarāja Mānamātra, Sudevarāja, and Pravararāja. Of these kings, the coins of only Prasannamātra are known, in three metals—gold, silver, and copper. Besides, there are some gold coins, which bear the legends variously as *Śrī-Mahendrāditya* and *Śrī-Kramāditya*. Over one hundred coins each of Prasannamātra and Śrī-Mahendrāditya are reported so far, while only three coins of Śrī-Kramāditya are known. All these coins, manufactured by the **repoussé* method, are in two denominations, with the bigger ones weighing 15 *rattīs*, and the smaller ones, 5 *rattīs*. The bigger coins bear the full name of the issuer, while the smaller ones have only the first part of his name. The obv of these coins is usually divided into two parts by a horizontal line, or two parallel horizontal lines joined at the ends. It bears, in the upper half, a **garuḍa* with outstretched wings, with a crescent and a **chakra* to the l and a *chakra* and a *śaṅkha* to the r; the lower half has the ld consisting of the name of the king with the honorific title *śrī*. One piece ascribed to Prasannamātra bears the device of a *chakra*. There is some controversy regarding the identification of Śrī-Mahendrāditya and Śrī-Kramāditya. Some scholars, like Prayag Dayal and B C Jain, identify the Śrī-Mahendrāditya with the *Imperial Gupta ruler, Kumāragupta I, who assumed the title of Mahendrāditya, and Śrī-Kramāditya with Skandagupta, who assumed the title of Kramāditya. Ajit Ghose objects to this on the ground that these two Imperial Gupta rulers belonged to the fifth century AD, while these coins have to be places in the sixth-seventh centuries AD on the basis of their script. Several scholars are in favour of identifying Śrī-Mahendrāditya and Śrī-Kramāditya as some local rulers of southern Kosala, and there are suggestions that they might have belonged to the *Nala, or the Śūra, or the Śarabhapurīya dynasty (Altekar 1957; B C Jain 1960; Mirashi 1939; L S Nigam 1987; L S Nigam 1988; T P Verma 1991).

Śāradā script. Believed by certain scholars to be a descendant of the western type of Br script of the *Imperial Gupta period, it originated in the eighth century AD, although a proto-Śāradā script had emerged around the beginning of the seventh century AD. The Śāradā script is employed, mainly by the Hindus, for writing the Kashmiri language; the Muslims, as also the Hindus who have had Muslim education, generally employ 'a variety of Persian-Arabic alphabet' to write Kashmiri. Skt inscriptions in the Śāradā script are also known from Afghanistan. The script 'corresponds letter for letter' with the Devanāgarī, but the shapes of the characters are quite different. Stiffness and thickness of strokes marks the Śāradā script. Later on, when long top strokes came to be employed, the heads of several letters became closed. Each letter in the Śāradā script has a separate name (Diringer 2005; Salomon 1998).

Sarai Denguri hoard. This hoard of 333 silver *punch marked coins, was found in an earthen pot in July 1997, at the village Sarai Denguri near Varanasi. These coins belong to five series, and represent as many as 76 varieties. The hoard is presently with the Bharat Kala Bhavan, Hindu University, Varanasi, since 1998 (Savita Sharma 2007).

Sarai Saleh (Haripur) hoard. This hoard, perhaps consisting of around 2,000 *Indo-Greek and *Śaka-Pahlava coins, from Sarai Saleh between Haripur and Bagra, about 30 km to the northeast of Taxila, began to come to the light early in 1994. The true composition of the hoard is not known. The Indo-Greek rulers represented in this hoard include *Agathokleia with *Strato I, *Amyntas, *Antialkidas, *Apollodotos, *Archebios, *Artemidoros, *Diomedes, *Epander, *Heliokles II, *Hermaios, Hermaios with *Kalliope, *Hippostratos, *Lysias, *Manander I, *Menander II, *Philoxenos, *Polyxenos, Strato I alone, and, possibly also *Hippostratos, *Peukolaos, and *Telephos. The Śaka-Pahlava rulers represented in this hoard include

*Vonones with *Spalahora, Vonones with *Spalagadama, *Spalirises with *Azes I, *Maues, Azes I alone, and *Azes II (Bopearachchi 1994; Bopearachchi and Rahman 1995; Senior 2001).

Sarapis. Graeco-Egyptian deity. Alternatively known as Serapis, he is actually the compound name given by the Greeks to Osiris-Apis, the dual god resulting from the death of the sacred bull, Apis (an incarnation of Osiris), and his soul consequently becoming joined with that of Osiris; the Egyptians actually pronounced the compound name as Asar-Hapi. He was the supreme deity of the Alexandrian pantheon, and as he was identified with *Zeus, Hades, Ammon, *Helios, and *Poseidon, he was regarded as the lord of the sky, sea, land, and the underworld. The *Kushāṇa ruler, *Huvishka, on the rev of some of his gold coins, depicted a diademed deity, dressed in *himation*, standing to the l. His r hand is advanced, while he holds a sceptre in his l hand. The label inscription, accompanying the figure, describes it as *Sarapo* (= Sarapis). The rev of some other coins of the same ruler portrays this deity as enthroned, and with *modius* on head. He carries a noose in his r hand, and a sceptre in his l hand. The adoption of Sarapis as a coin device by the Kushāṇas may have something to do with the brisk Indo-Roman trade during that period (Banerjea 2002; Bhaskar Chattopadhyay 1977; Cunningham 1971a; Gardner 1971; Rosenfield 1967; Lewis Spence 1949).†

Huvishka

Sarapo. *Sarapis.

Sarasvatī. Deity. Like *Lakshmī, Sarasvatī, too, has come to be revered in all the religious creeds of India. The vedic river Sarasvatī and several folk elements played a significant role in giving her a concrete form. The manuscript and the *vīṇā*, as her attributes, indicate her association with speech, learning, and music. She is variously described as the daughter and *śakti* of Brahman; as Pushṭi, she is also the *śakti* of *Vishṇu. The **haṁsa* is her mount. The depiction of Sarasvatī on the coins of ancient India is extremely rare. She is seen on the rev of the **Rājalīlā* type of coins of *Samāchāradeva. The representation is beautiful, with the goddess standing in *tribhaṅga* posture on a lotus bed, her l hand resting on a stalked *lotus, and the r hand drawing up another stalked lotus in front of her face. Below her r hand is a stalk with lotus bud, and underneath it is her mount, the *haṁsa*, with its neck craning up (Altekar 1957; Banerjea 2002; Sukumari Bhattacharji 1970; R B Pande 1988; Rao 1985).†

Sargodha hoard. This hoard of 38 gold coins of the later Kushāṇa type, was discovered at Sargodha in Punjab, around 1970, and is housed in the Lahore Museum. All the coins have *king sacrificing at an altar on the obv, and **Ardochsho* on the rev. This hoard comprisies coins of the *Shāka and *Shilāda tribes (von Mitterwallner 1994).

Sarpamitra. *Kauśāmbī k. He may be assigned to the first century BC or the first century AD. Nothing definite can be said about him, as his coins are not very well-preserved. He might have ruled contemporaneously with the *Aśvaghosha group of kings in some part of Kauśāmbī. The obv of his coins bears the figure of a *bull to the r, while the rev has a *tree-in-railing, a *Ujjain symbol, and the ld *Sapamitasa* (Altekar 1942b; Bopearachchi and Pieper 1998; Bela Lahiri 1974).

Sarvaloga iśvara. Title. This title, meaning 'lord of all the world', was assumed on his coins by the *Kushāṇa king, *V'ima Kadphises (Cunningham 1971a; Gardner 1971; Rosenfield 1967; Whitehead 1914).

Sarvania hoard. This large hoard of 2,393 silver coins was discovered at Sarvania in the Banswara district of Rajasthan in 1911. Besides six coins of *Iśvaradatta, and 13 uncertain coins, the hoard has coins belonging to the *Kārdamaka rulers, like *Rudrasiṁha I, *Rudrasena I, *Saṅghadāman, *Dāmasena, *Dāmajadaśrī II, *Vīradāman, *Yaśodāman I, *Vijayasena, *Dāmajadaśrī III, *Rudrasena II, *Viśvasiṁha, *Bhartṛidāman, *Viśvasena, *Rudrasiṁha II, *Yaśodāman II, *Rudrasena III, son of Rudrasiṁha I (whose name is not clear), son of Dāmasena (whose name is not clear), son of Rudrasena II (whose name is not clear) (D R Bhandarkar 1913-1914; Jha and Rajgor 1994).

Śarvavarman. *Maukhari k. He was the son and successor of *Īśānavarman. From his grant of land in different regions, it appears that during his rule, Maukhari supremacy had been established over the great part of Magadha, and also over Bundelkhand. The Maukhari victory over the *Hūṇas might have taken place during his rule, and he might have also occupied the Kangra region in the course of this campaign. Śarvavarman issued silver coins of the **Madhyadeśa* type of the Imperial Guptas, with the royal head to the r and the date of issue on the obv, and a fan-tailed *peacock with the Br ld reading *Vijitāvaniravanipati Śrī-Śarvavarman divaṁ jayati* on the rev. Their average weight is around 36 grains. They have been found in the *Bhitaura hoard. The dates on these coins have been read as 58 by Smith, 254 by Brown, and 258, 259, etc by Dikshit. N G Majumdar is of the view that the dates on these coins have generally totally disappeared and it is not possible to the read them (Richard Burn 1906; D Devahuti 1964; Pires 1934; Thaplyal 1985).

Sasan. *Apracha k. He started his career as a subordinate ruler of *Gondopharnes, with whom he issued at least four types of joint coins three in copper, and one in bronze or billon. All these types have horseman king and a corrupt Gr ld on the obv. The rev of the first type in copper has *Zeus standing, and a Kh ld mentioning both Gondopharnes and Sasan, in that order. The bronze or billon type has *Zeus Nikephoros and the Kh ld mentions both Gondopharnes and Sasan as on the rev of the copper type above. The second copper type has Zeus standing with sceptre, and the Kh ld mentions Sasan only, with the titles **rayaraya* **apratihatachakra* **devavrata*. Here, Sasan seems to have become bolder, and has removed the name of Gondopharnes from the rev ld. But the third type in copper is even more interesting. Here, the obv ld seems to mention Sasan only. The rev has Zeus Nikephoros, and the Kh ld mentions both Gondopharnes and Sasan. The last two types hint at the increasing power of Sasan. Most of these coins bear the peculiar Gondopharnes symbol. Later on, perhaps after the death of Gondopharnes, Sasan assumed sovereignty, and issued his independent silver coinage, bearing the bust of the king in Parthian tiara and a corrupt Gr ld on the obv, and *Nike and a Kh ld mentioning Sasan only on the rev. Interestingly, this rev ld refers to Sasan as *Aśpabhataputra*, 'brother's son of *Aśpa[varman]', thereby showing that he was a nephew of Aśpavarman; the name of the father of Sasan is not known. Numismatic evidence suggests that he ruled over Takshaśilā, Seistan, Arachosia, and the lower Indus regions. His authority over Pushkalāvatī-Gandhāra region is not proved by the available sources;

Sasan

perhaps it was occupied by Phraotes and/or the *Kushāṇas after Gondopharnes (Cunningham 1971a; Gardner 1971; Jenkins and Narain 1957; Marshall 1975; B N Mukherjee 1969a; Rapson 1987; Senior 2001; Sircar 1980b; Prashant Srivastava 1996a; Prashant Srivastava 2007a; Tarn 1980; Whitehead 1914).

Śaśāṅka. Gauḍa k; first half of the seventh century AD. His antecedents are not known for certain. He seems to have begun his career as a feudatory, although some scholars would place his stint as a feudatory after his defeat at the hands of *Harsha. Literary and epigraphic sources show his hold over Karṇasuvarṇa, Tāmralipti, and Kaliṅga; he also led a successful expedition against Kāmarūpa. Around 606 AD, Śaśāṅka entered into an alliance with Devagupta of Malwa, attacked the *Maukhari kingdom of Kanauj, and killed Grahavarman. Bāṇa and Hiuen-tsang inform us that *Prabhākaravardhana's son and successor, Rājyavardhana II, was treacherously murdered by Śaśāṅka, an act which overshadows all his brilliant achievements. Harsha had vowed to avenge these acts of Śaśāṅka, but there is no definite evidence to show that the two ever met each other in the battlefield. The suggestion that Harsha and Bhāskaravarman conjointly defeated Śaśāṅka, and shared his territories on either side of the river Ganga, seems untenable in view of the fact that the supremacy of the Gauḍa king was being acknowledged by the Śailodbhava rulers, at least up to 619 AD. Śaśaṅka issued gold coins on the traditional Indian **suvarṇa* standard of 80 *rattīs*. The obv of these coins has the figure of nimbate *Śiva, with a crescent on the forehead and an uncertain object in the uplifted l hand, reclining to the l on a *bull (Nandin) to the l. The ld reads *Śrī-Śa-* (on right); *jaya* (below). The rev bears the nimbate figure of *Gajalakshmī, seated on lotus, holding a lotus in her l hand, while the r hand is empty. The rev ld reads *Śrī-Śaśāṅkaḥ*. Two silver coins of Śaśāṅka, along with two of his gold coins, were found in the course of explorations of the 24 Parganas region of West Bengal; both these silver coins are roughly executed. The obv and rev are similar to those of the gold coins. The ld on the obv is illegible. The rev ld, written vertically below the elephant, reads *Śrī-Śaśāṅka*. It has been remarked that, although D C Sircar says that Gajalakshmī does not occur on coins after the first century AD, the coins of Śaśāṅka show the motif in the seventh century AD (Allan

Śaśāṅka

1914; P K Bhattacharyya 1979; D Devahuti 2001; Pires 1934; Sircar 1970; B N Srivastava 1962; Thaplyal 1985).†

Śatamāna. Coin denomination. It is mentioned at several places in vedic literature, as in the *Taittirīyasaṁhitā*, *Śatapathabrāhmaṇa*, *Taittirīyabrāhmaṇa*, etc, but it is not certain whether it denoted a coin at that time. The term suggests that it was evidently 100 times (*śata*) the unit of measurement (*māna*). D R Bhandarkar, Keith, and others identify this unit as the *rattī*, with an average weight of 1.8 grains, and this would make the *śatamāna* about 180 grains in weight. V S Agrawala identifies the standard *bent bar pieces, which have weights ranging from 165.8 to 174.1 grains, with the *śatamāna*. However, Pāṇini, Manu, Yājñavalkya, and Kātyāyana, all refer to it as a gold coin, 320 *rattīs* in weight, and there is a suggestion that the *māna* was the *mañjāḍi*, the seed of the *Adenanthera pavonina*, quite common in India, which, according to Elliot, was the earliest to be used as a measure of weight, and weighed 3.2 *rattīs*. This would make the *śatamāna* (100 x 3.2 =) 320 *rattīs* in weight. This is also the weight of the **nishka*. There is evidence from the *Maitrāyaṇīsaṁhitā*, the *Śatapathabrāhmaṇa*, and the *Kātyāyanaśrautasūtra* to show that silver *śatamāna* existed side by side with a gold one. The traditional Indian standard gold coin, the **suvarṇa*, would be one-fourth of a gold *śatamāna*, and the traditional Indian standard silver coin, the **dharaṇa*, would be one-tenth of a silver *śatamāna* (V S Agrawala 1956; D R Bhandarkar 1984; Chakrabortty 1931).

Satavastra. *Apracha (?) k. Some good quality silver coins from Takshaśilā bear on the obv the bust of the king in Parthian tiara, Gondopharnes symbol, and a corrupt Gr ld. The rev has *Nike standing with wreath and palm, and an incomplete Kh ld *...rasa Satavastrasa *maharajasa*. Rapson believed that the portrait on these coins is that of Gondopharnes, and that Satavastra ruled as a subordinate of that *Śaka-Pahlava ruler. But both Marshall and Whitehead regard the portrait on these coins as that of Satavastra himself, and if this be accepted, there is no definite evidence to show that Satavastra served as a subordinate ruler under Gondopharnes. However, the occurrence of the Gondopharnes symbol on the obv of these coins shows some connection of Satavastra with Gondopharnes. Marshall suggests that Satavastra, like *Sapedana, was a successor of *Sasan, and if we accept this suggestion, Gondopharnes could not possibly have been his overlord. His coins suggest that he ruled over the lower Indus region, and possibly also Arachosia (Cunningham 1971a; Gardner 1971; Jenkins and Narain 1957; Marshall 1975; B N Mukherjee 1969a; Rapson 1987; Senior 2001; Sircar 1980b; Prashant Srivastava 1996a; Prashant Srivastava 2007a; Tarn 1980; Whitehead 1914).

Satera. Coin denomination. According to the *Sphuṭārtha* commentary on the *Abhidharmakosha* of Vasubandhu, two **dīnāras* were equal to one *satera*. Although it is not certain as to which *dīnāra* is meant here, there is a suggestion that it might refer to the silver **drachm*, which was half the weight of a gold **stater* and which might have been designated **raupya-dīnāra* mentioned in literary sources (R C Agrawala 1953b; R C Agrawala 1954a; R C Agrawala 1954b; V S Agrawala 1957).

Sateraka. Coin denomination. Mentioned in the **Aṅgavijjā*, it is derived from the Greek standard gold coin denomination, **stater*. Although this term occurs in the text compiled towards the close of the *Kushāṇa period, it was not a new coin minted in the Kushāṇa period, but the *Indo-Greek gold *stater*, 'which continued to be in free circulation for several hundred years after the end of that dynasty'. Some variant forms of *sateraka*, like **satera* and *sadera*, are known from some central Asian Kh documents (V S Agrawala 1957).

Sattragupta. *Vṛishṇi general (?).

Satyadāman. *Kārddamaka k. He was the son of *Dāmajadaśrī I. He issued coins as **kshatrapa* only, and never seems to have attained the position of a **mahākshatrapa*. His coins are of the *Kārddamaka silver type. The rarity of his coins might hint at his short reign, his only known date being the year 124 (Jha and Rajgor 1994; Mirashi 1982; Mitchiner 1976; Rapson 1975; Raychaudhuri 1972; Senior 2001; Sircar 1980e).

Satyamagha. *Magha k.

Satyamitra. *Ayodhyā k. He is placed after *Saṅghamitra, *Vijayamitra, and *Devamitra, and before *Āyumitra by Bela Lahiri on the basis of a comparative study of the letter *ma* occurring in the coin legends. He issued copper coins, bearing the figure of a *bull to the l before a standard, and the ld *Satyamitasa* on the obv, while the rev has a *cock on a post to the r, and a palm tree on the right (Allan 1936; Bela Lahiri 1974; Smith 1972).

Satyamitra. *Kauśāmbī k. He may be assigned to the first century BC or the first century AD. Nothing definite can be said about him, as his coins are not very well-preserved. He might have ruled contemporaneously with the *Aśvaghosha group of kings in some part of Kauśāmbī. He seems to be different from, and much earlier in date than, *Satyamitra of *Ayodhyā. The obv of his coins has the figure of a *bull to the r, while the rev has a *tree-in-railing, a *Ujjain symbol, and the ld *[Sa]tamitasa* (Altekar 1942b; Bopearachchi and Pieper 1998; Bela Lahiri 1974).

Satyamitra. *Kulūta chief. He ruled in the first-second centuries AD, and issued the Class III of *Kulūta coins, on which the ld is hardly legible, but the name of Satyamitra has been read by Allan (Allan 1936; Chakrabortty 1931; Cunningham 1971b; K K Dasgupta 1974; Handa 2007a; Jayaswal 1988; Marshall 1975; Smith 1972).

Satyamitra. *Mathurā k. He issued coins, which show *Lakshmī with lotus in her r hand and some symbols on the obv; and three *elephants with riders on the rev (Allan 1936; Bela Lahiri 1974).

Saucer-shaped coins. *Cup-shaped coins.

Sāvitriputra. Tribe. Among the Rajanya coins, Allan published a die-struck square copper coin, resembling the coin of the *Trigarta *janapada*. This coin had an indistinct obv device, which was regarded as, perhaps, a standing human figure. The obv Kh ld was read by Allan as *Khatapasa janapadasa* in the Catalogue part, but in the Introduction part, which seems to have been finalized after the coin had been cleaned, he felt that the first letter might be *sa* or *ga*, and the second letter, *vi*. The rev has a *horse to the l. Michael Mitchiner identified the standing figure on the obv as that of *Śiva, and read the obv ld as *Śivachatrapura janapadasa*, suggesting that the Śivachatrapura *janapada* flourished somewhere in north India in the late second century BC. But Devendra Handa, after examining the coin in the collection of the British Museum, London, concludes that the obv device consists of 'an elaborate stylized multi-branched tree'. He restores the obv ld as *Sāvitriputra janapadasa*, which restoration, he says, is supported by another coin acquired by the British Museum in 1986. A tribe named Sāvitriputraka is mentioned by Pāṇini among the Dāmnyādi group of *āyudhajīvi saṁghas*. It is also mentioned in the *Mahābhārata*, amongst the people who fought by the side of the Kurus. The tribe seems to have traced its origin from the 100 sons the Śālva prince, Satyavān, and his wife, the Madra princess Sāvirtī, obtained as a boon from Yama. Pāṇini also mentions the Sālveyas and Sālvāvayavas as independent tribes. V S Agrawala regards Sālveyas as a branch of the Śālvas, and identifies them with the Śālvaputras. Devendra Handa feels that the Śālvaputras were identical with the Sāvitriputras. V S Agrawala places the Sālveyas in the region around Alwar in northern Rajasthan. However, on the basis of the use of only the Kh script on these coins, Handa locates the Sāvitriputras in the region to the north of the river Sarasvatī (V S Agrawala 1969; Allan 1936; Handa 2007a; Mitchiner 1975-1976).

Selene. Greek lunar goddess. This Greek lunar goddess was a daughter of the Titan, Hyperion, and the Titaness, Theia, and a sister of *Helios and Eos. But in some accounts, her father is Pallas. Although sometimes described as a winged goddess, she is never shown as such on coins. Later, Selene seems to have come to be identified with *Artemis. The representation of Selene is not found on *Indo-Greek coins, but the *Śaka-Pahlava ruler, *Maues, and the *Kushāṇa ruler, *Kanishka I, depicted her on their coins. On the obv of some coins of Maues, the lunar goddess stands to front between two 'star-like' objects, and holds a long sceptre in her hand. But on the rev of some gold coins of Kanishka I, the deity, labelled as *Selene* in the accompanying inscription, is male. He is diademed, has a crescent behind his shoulders, and stands dressed in *chiton* and *himation*, with a sword at waist. His r hand is extended, while the l hand holds a long filleted sceptre. This representation is very unlike that of the Greek lunar goddess met with in art and on the coins of Maues, and resembles to a great extent the figure of the Zoroastrian moon god, **Mao*, on Kushāṇa coins (Bhaskar Chattopadhyay 1977; Cunningham 1971a; Gardner 1971; Graves 1955; Kerenyi 1951; Marshall 1975; Rose 1958; Rosenfield 1967; Prashant Srivastava 2007c; Stein 1888; Whitehead 1914).†

Serpent. Symbol. The serpent, which occupies 'a prominent place in ancient Indian legends and folklore', is considered as a common representative of the deities of procreation. In Indian mythology, it is associated with both *Śiva and *Vishṇu. The connection between water and the snake seems to be 'the vital factor in the Nāga-worship'. As a water spirit, the snake, on being duly propitiated, granted ample and timely rains for irrigation. [*Undulating line] (Sircar 1971; Vögel 1926).†

Śeshadatta. *Mathurā k. He issued coins, which show *Lakshmī with lotus in her r hand and some symbols on the obv; and three *elephants with riders on the rev. The rev device is degenerate (Allan 1936; Bela Lahiri 1974).

'Shafqat' hoard. This hoard of 27 coins was discovered probably in the Charsadda region. The rulers represented in this hoard are *Azes I, *Azilises, and *Azes II (Senior 2001).

Shāka. Tribe. Taking advantage of the weakening authority of the *Kushāṇas, the Shāka tribe seems to have asserted its independence, and issued coins of its own around the fourth century AD. They appear to be of some foreign stock, like the Kushāṇas. Their coins, in gold and found from the Punjab and its adjoining regions, reveal the names of chiefs like Saya, Śayatha, Sita, and Sena, (or Seṇa), along with the name of the tribe. Some scholars, however, regard Shāka as the name of some chief. These coins bear the device of *king sacrificing at an altar on the obv, and the figure of seated **Ardochsho* on the rev. The rev also has the symbol of *Vāsudeva I in a slightly modified form (Altekar 1986a; Craig Alden Burns 1985b; Cunningham 1962; R C Majumdar 1988; von Mitterwallner 1994; Sircar 1980d; Smith 1972; Prashant Srivastava 1996a).

Shāka (Saya)

Shao. *Kushāṇa title. This title, meaning 'king', was adopted on coins by all the Kushāṇa kings from the time of *Kanishka I.

However, in the Rabatak inscription, the title has been used for the three predecessors of Kanishka I, as well. In Kushāṇa epigraphic records, it is rendered as *shāhi*. The Chinese sources inform us that the Tuholo or Tochari kings adopted the title of *shao-wu* (Cunningham 1962; Nicholas Sims-Williams and Joe Cribb 1995-1996).

Shaonanoshao. *Kushāṇa title. This title, meaning 'king of kings', was adopted by all the Kushāṇa kings from the time of *Kanishka I, mostly in association with **shao*. In the Allahabad pillar inscription of *Samudragupta, it is rendered into Skt as *shāhānushāhi* (Cunningham 1971a; Gardner 1971; Rosenfield 1967; Whitehead 1914).

Huvishka

Huvishka

Shaoreoro. Avestan deity of metals. Some gold coins of the *Kushāṇa ruler, *Huvishka, bear on the rev the figure of a helmeted and armoured god standing to the r. He holds a spear in one hand, and a shield in the other. The label inscription beside the figure describes the deity as *Shaoreoro*. Gardner regarded the first part of the inscription, that is **shao*, to mean king, while the remaining part, according to him, stands for Ares, the Greek god of war. It is true that the armoured figure holding spear and shield, is a very apt representation of a war god. But most of the scholars are inclined to identify *Shaoreoro* with the Amesha Spenta Khshathra Vairya, 'perfect rule', whose name was later rendered into Pahlavi as Shahrevar. In Zoroastrian mythology, he is the presiding deity of metals and bestows wealth. According to Cunningham, this Iranian deity may be compared to the Indian Airavara or Kubera. As the Avestan name of the deity, that is Khshathra Vairya, means 'perfect rule', *Shaoreoro* may also be associated with royalty, and on the coins of Huvishka, he is represented as a royal warrior (Bhaskar Chattopadhyay 1977; Cunningham 1971a; Darmesteter 1974; Gardner 1971; Rosenfield 1967; Stein 1888; Whitehead 1914).

Shashṭhī-Devasenā. Deity. On the rev of the unique *Yaudheya silver coin, as also on some Yaudheya copper coins, bearing the figure of *Kārttikeya, occurs the representation of a six-headed goddess, standing facing on a lotus bloom. Her r hand is usually raised, while her l hand rests on her hip. On the copper coins, where the figure of Kārttikeya occupies the obv, the six-headed goddess appears on the rev. Allan identified the goddess as *Lakshmī, and this was accepted by scholars like J N Banerjea. Deena Bandhu Pandey proposed to identify the six-headed goddess with Kṛittikā, a combined form of the six Kṛittikās, the foster mothers of Kārttikeya. But R C Agrawala does not find this identification as quite convincing, on the ground that nowhere is there 'any reference to one Kṛittikā alone and that too with all the six heads together meant for Skanda Kumāra'. V S Agrawala, however, was inclined to identify this female divinity as Shahshṭhī-Devasenā, on the basis of the Bālagrahachikitsā chapter of the *Kāśyapasaṁhitā*. This Shashṭhī or Devasenā is mentioned in the *Mahābhārata* as the consort of Skanda-Kārttikeya. That Shashṭhī is identical with Devasenā is pointed out by the epithets *Shashṭhīpriyaḥ* and *Devasenāpriyaḥ* of Kārttikeya. She is associated with child birth, and is worshipped on the sixth day of the birth of a child. On a recently reported Yaudheya coin, the head of Shashṭhī on the rev is represented by a *lotus, a flower associated with, besides other things, fecundity. This seems to associate her with Lajjāgaurī, who, too, is sometimes shown with a lotus for her face, and who, too, presides over fertility and child birth. Interestingly, in some sculptural representations of the third-fourth centuries AD, Lajjāgaurī is shown together with *Kārttikeya. There is both literary and sculptural evidence for a six-headed Shashṭhī-Devasenā (R C Agrawala 1967; V S Agrawala 1943b; V S Agrawala 1970; Allan 1936; Banerjea 2002; Chakrabortty 1931; Dasgupta 1974; Handa 2007a; Deena Bandhu Pandey 1957; Prashant Srivastava 1996a).

Yaudheya

Yaudheya

Sherdi hoard. This hoard of over 400 silver *punch marked coins of the Saurāshṭra janapada was discovered in 1964 at Sherdi in the Junagarh district of Gujarat (Rajgor 2001).

Shilāda. Tribe. Taking advantage of the weakening authority of the *Kushāṇas, the Shilāda tribe seems to have asserted its independence, and issued coins of its own around the fourth century AD. They appear to be of some foreign stock, like the Kushāṇas. Their coins, in gold and found from the Punjab and its adjoining regions, reveal the names of chiefs like Bhadra, Bacharṇa, and Pāshaṇa, along with the name of the tribe. Some scholars, however, regard Shilāda as the name of a chief, and also propose to the read it as Kshiṇatha. These coins bear the device of *king sacrificing at an altar on the obv, and the figure of seated **Ardochsho* on the rev. The rev also has the symbol of *Vāsudeva I in a slightly modified form (Altekar 1986a; Craig Alden Burns 1985b; Cunningham 1962; R C Majumdar 1988; von Mitterwallner 1994; Sircar 1980d; Smith 1972; Prashant Srivastava 1996a).

Shingavaram hoard. This hoard, which is originally believed to have contained over 60,000 *punch marked coins, was found in 1934, at Shingavarman in the Krishna District of Andhra Pradesh. Unfortunately, most of the coins were melted down, and only 25 cup-shaped coins could be examined, of which, 22 are presently in the State Museum, Lucknow, and one specimen in the British Museum, London (Rajgor 2001).

Shinkiari hoard 1. This hoard of 45 coins, in excellent condition, was discovered at Shinkiari, in Hazara, about 15 km north of Mansehra. The rulers represented in this hoard include *Azes I and Azes II (Senior 2001).

Shinkiari hoard 2. This hoard of 28 coins, in excellent condition, was discovered at Shinkiari, in Hazara, about 15 km north of Mansehra. The rulers represented in this hoard include *Azes I and Azes II (Senior 2001).

Śibi. Tribe. The *Ṛigveda* mentions Śivas as one of the tribes defeated by Sudāsa in the Battle of Ten Kings. The *Aitareyabrāhmaṇa* has a tribal name Śivi (= Śibi). The *Mahābhārata*, at one place, groups the Śibis with the *Rājanyas, *Yaudheyas, *Trigartas, Madras, and Kekayas, and places them in the Punjab, while at another place, it refers to the Śibis along with the Trigartas and the *Mālavas in the context of Nakula's western expedition. In this epic, Sunandā, the mother of Śāntanu, is described as a Śibi princess, while Yudhishṭhira marries a daughter of the Śibi king, Govāsana. Classical writers, like Diodoros, Strabo, and Curtius, refer to a Punjab tribe as Siboi or Sibae (= Śibi), who wore skin and had the club as weapon, and lived in the area between the rivers Beas and Chandrabhāgā. The Śibis are also mentioned in the Jātaka tales, which refer to Ariṭṭhapura and Jetuttara as two of their cities. The *Mahābhāshya* shows the existence of a tribe Śibi and refers to their town, Śivapura, as *udīchyagrāma*, 'northern village'. Śivapura also finds mention in the *Mahāmāyūrī*, which text also refers to *Śiva as the tutelary deity of that town. A fifth century inscription from Shorkot in the Jhang district, between the Ravi and Chenab, mentions Śibipura, and Vögel considers the mound of Shorkot as representing the city of the Śibis. Though Śibi coins have been reported from Punjab, their association with that region may be accepted. The Sibia Jats of Haryana and Rajasthan might be the descendants of the Śibis. King Śibi Uśīnara, who is referred to in the *Mahābhārata*, the Jātaka tales, and the purāṇas, seems to have been the ancestor of the Śibis. The find of Śibi coins in and around Nagari in Rajasthan shows their migration to that area from Punjab region before the second century BC, to which period the coins are datable; Devendra Handa, however, feels that these coins should be dated from the latter half of the second century BC to mid-first century BC. The absence of any reference to them in the Allahabad pillar inscription of *Samudragupta shows that they had ceased to exist as a political power by that time. Śibi coins are all of copper, and round in shape, their weight ranging between 18 and 100 grains. Devendra Handa suggests that they might have been struck on the **paṇa* weight standard, and represent 1/8, 1/4, 3/8, 1/2, 5/8, and 3/4 *paṇa*. Of the main coin types of the tribe, some coins have on the obv, a tree and the Br letter *ta*, and the ld *Śibijanapadasa*, while the rev has the *hill symbol and 'river'. Other coins show a *tree-in-railing the same ld on the obv, while the rev has a hybrid animal before *yūpa*, and the ld *rājño*. Still other coins have a **svastika* with taurine at the four ends and a tree on the obv, and the ld *Majhamikāya Śibijanapadasa*; the rev has a **nandipada*, a hill symbol, and a river. The first part of the ld *Majhamikāya Śibijanapadasa* may stand for *Mādhyamikāyāḥ* (for, or on Mādhyamikā), or *Mādhyamikāyāṁ* (in Mādhyamikā). Mādhyamikā is known as a city from literary and epigraphic evidence. The *Mahābhāshya* refers to the Yavana siege of Mādhyamikā. The *Mahābhārata* mentions Mādhyamikās along with Daśārṇa, and the *Bṛihatsaṁhitā* places them with the *Yaudheyas and *Ārjunāyanas and in the central division of India. The Barli and Chittorgarh inscriptions also refer to Mādhyamikā. It was, in all probability, the capital of the Śibi *janapada* and is identical with Nagari near Chittor. D C Sircar and K K Dasgupta interpret the ld *Majhamikāya Śibijanapadasa* as meaning '[this is the coin] of the Śibi *janapada* from [ie struck at] Mādhyamikā'; this has the support of Devendra Handa. There is a suggestion that the Mādhyamikās were neighbouring allies of the Śibis, who, like them, originally inhabited the Punjab region. Both tribes migrated to the Rajasthan due to political and/or economic pressures; the Mādhyamikās probably came early and founded the city of Mādhyamikā and the Śibis came after the siege of this city was a thing of the past. The name Śibi and the hill symbol—a Śaiva device, would suggest that the tribe was follower of the Śaiva religion. Altekar has attributed to the Śibis two coins showing, on the obv, standing bull and the Br ld *Jeshṭhapura* in *c* fifth century characters; the rev is blank. He identifies Jeshṭhapura (= Skt, Jyeshṭhapura) with Jetuttara of *Vessantarajātaka*, which is referred to as the capital of the Śibis [*Jyeshṭhapura] (Nisar Ahmad 1996; Allan 1936; Altekar 1952a; Chakrabortty 1931; Cunningham 1971b; K K Dasgupta 1974; Handa 2007a; Jayaswal 1988; Marshall 1975; Mitchiner 1975-1976; Sircar 1980d; Smith 1972).

Siglos. Coin denomination. It was the silver coin of ancient Iran, struck from the fifth century BC till the defeat of Darius III Kodomannos at the hands of Alexander, *c* 330 BC. The weight of a *siglos* was about 86.45 grains. It resembled the **daric* in type. According to Xenophon, in the Achaemenian empire, 20 *sigloi* were equal to one gold *daric* in value (Altekar 1940; Junge 1984).

Silver. Metal for coins. Cunningham asserts that India 'produced little or no silver'. The quantity produced indigenously was, indeed, small, and had to be supplemented by import, mostly from western Asia; some silver also flowed in from the Roman empire in the form of coins and bullion. S K Chakrabortty is of the opinion that, in view of the facts that one system of weight was adopted for gold and copper, and another for silver; that silver had to be imported from other countries; that several ancient Indian states retained copper coins only, even when silver coins were circulating in neighbouring states; and that the early Buddhist literature of the sixth century BC does not speak of a silver currency (**dharaṇa* or **purāṇa*), it should be inferred that silver was used for minting coins in India, later than copper. It was used to mint coins, both by the indigenous and foreign rulers of ancient India (Altekar 1940; D R Bhandarkar 1984; Chakrabortty 1931; Cunningham 1970; A N Lahiri 1965; Senior 2001).

Siṁhasena. *Kārddamaka k. He was the sister's son of *Rudrasena III, and succeeded the latter as **mahākshatrapa*, in which capacity he ruled from *Śaka year 304 to 306 (?), although on one type, R C Senior has tentatively read the date as the year 300. He issued coins of the *Kārddamaka silver type only. On these coins, he does not mention the name of his father, but refers to himself as the 'sister's son of Rudrasena' (Jha and Rajgor 1994; Mirashi 1982; Mitchiner 1976; Rapson 1975; Raychaudhuri 1972; Senior 2001; Sircar 1980e).

Siṁhavāhinī Devī. Deity. The rev of some *Imperial Gupta coin types bears the figure of a goddess seated on a couchant lion. She makes her first appearance on the *King-and-Queen type of *Chandragupta I and *Kumāradevī. There, she holds a *pāśa* in her r hand and a **cornucopiae* in her l hand. The goddess on lion, seen on the coins of *Azes I, *Huvishka, and *Kanishka III, seems to have served as the prototype for this device. Some elements have also been borrowed from **Ardochsho* appearing on *Kushāṇa coins. The identification of the *Siṁhavāhinī Devī* on Imperial Gupta coins poses a difficult problem. Scholars like Smith do not attempt to identify her. On the basis of the *pāśa* and the lion mount, some scholars tend to identify her with Durgā. Some other scholars suggest that this deity should be identified as Sarvamaṅgalā, who is described in the *Vishṇudharmottarapurāṇa* as riding a lion. But this text gives the attributes of Sarvamaṅgalā as *akshamālā*, *padma*, *śūla*, and *kamaṇḍalu*, while the goddess on the Imperial Gupta coins holds a *pāśa* and a *cornucopiae* in her two hands. The *cornucopiae* in the hand of the *Siṁhavāhinī Devī* seems to indicate the identity of this goddess with *Lakshmī, for the *cornucopiae* in Greek mythology is the 'horn of plenty', and the symbol of prosperity. In the Indian context, this attribute seems to fit in better with Lakshmī, the goddess of prosperity. There is a reference to *Siṁhavāhinī Lakshmī* by Hemādri. We also have two sculptural representations of *Siṁhavāhinī* Gajalakshmī, and a third one depicting Lakshmī seated in the lap of *Vishṇu, with her l foot resting on a lion. However, these representations, which come from Khajuraho, belong to a period later than these coins. In the *Devyatharvaśīrsha*, the noose is mentioned as an attribute of Ādyāśakti Mahālakshmī, and in the

Chandragupta I and Kumāradevī

Chandragupta II : Lion-slayer type

Kumāragupta I : Lion-slayer type

Toramāṇa

Atharvaṇarahasya, Vaishṇavī Mahālakshmī is described as holding a lotus bloom and riding a lion. The *Siṁhavāhinī Devī* appears again on the rev of the *Lion-slayer type of *Chandragupta II. But there, with the exception of a few specimens of Class II of this type, the goddess is shown holding a *lotus bloom in her l hand, while the r hand still holds the *pāśa*. The *Siṁhavāhinī Devī* on the rev of the Lion-slayer type of *Kumāragupta I also holds a stalked lotus in one of her hands. These depictions agree fully with the above textual description of Vaishṇavī Mahālakshmī. The Imperial Guptas were **paramabhāgavatas*, that is devout worshippers of Vishṇu, and this seems to the render the identification of the *Siṁhavāhinī Devī* on their coins, as Lakshmī, the consort of Vishṇu, more likely. Interestingly, S V Sohoni takes the couchant lion as a lion-throne (*siṁhāsana*), and recongizes the deity as Rājyalakshmī. *Siṁhavāhinī Devī* also occurs on the rev of some copper coins of *Toramāṇa (For references, see Prashant Srivastava 1996a).

Siranwali hoard 1. This hoard of 400 *Indo-Greek coins was discovered in 1990 from a field in the village of Siranwali, about 3 km from Daska, midway between Gujranwala and Sialkot. The rulers represented in the hoard include *Amyntas, *Antimachos II, *Apollodotos, and *Menander I (Bopearachchi and Pieper 1998).

Siranwali hoard 2. This hoard of 300 *if coins was discovered in 1993, while digging the earth in the village of Siranwali. The rulers represented in the hoard include *Amyntas, *Antimachos II, *Apollodotos, *Lysias, *Menander I, and *Philoxenos (Bopearachchi and Pieper 1998).

Sīsa-kahāpaṇa. Coin denomination. It is believed to be a **kārshāpaṇa* of lead, and finds mention in the *Jātaka* literature (C D Chatterjee 1931).

Śiva. Deity. The history of the worship of Śiva, in one form or the other, goes back to very early times, and it is not unlikely that he was revered even in pre-vedic times. The character of Śiva was apparently formed by the assimilation of the attributes of many deities, the earliest among them being the Harappan 'proto Śiva-Paśupati' of the Mohenjodaro seal, and the vedic Rudra. He was but a minor deity in vedic times, and is represented 'as a malevolent deity causing death and disease among men and cattle and is therefore prayed to by the hymnists for allaying his wrath towards them, sparing them, their families and cattle, and attacking and damaging their enemies and their belongings'. Initially, he was not accorded a share of the sacrifice, and it was only by the entreaties of *Umā that 'Śiva established for the first time in the *yāga* of Daksha his right to the receive oblations'. Gradually, the awesome vedic Rudra was transformed with the evolution of Śaivism into an 'Infinite Intelligence...Creator of the World...Redeemer of Mankind'. In the Hindu triad of Brahmā, Vishṇu, and Śiva, the last deity was regarded as 'the destroyer of the universe when it requires to be created anew'. The **triśūla* and *sarpa* is his characteristic attributes, and Mount Kailāsa, his abode. A white *bull is his *vāhana*. Śiva, in his anthropomorphic form, appears for the first time, perhaps, on some coins from *Ujjayinī. The identity of the male deity depicted on Allan's Class II of Ujjayinī coins, is a matter of controversy among scholars. On most of these coins, the deity is monocephalous, and holds a staff in the r hand, and a *kamaṇḍalu* in the left. The obv of Variety l of Class II shows the deity as three-headed, and holding the same attributes. Allan regards the attribute in the r hand of this deity as a spear, and identifies him as *Kārttikeya. He further suggests that the deity on Class II, Variety l, is actually six-headed, with the three front heads being visible, and the three behind, being 'naturally not represented because they cannot be seen'. He refers to this deity as *Shaṇmukha* Kārttikeya, though he admits the possibility of the deity being Śiva. He, however, adds that the absence of the *triśūla* with the figure, goes against this latter possibility. J N Banerjea is of the view that both the monocephalous and the tricephalous figures on these Ujjayinī coins are representations of Śiva. On some coins, a bull is shown by the side of the single-headed deity, looking up at him. According to the *Matsyapurāṇa*, the bull-*vāhana* should be shown by the side of Śiva in the attitude of looking at the god (*devavīkshaṇatatparaḥ*). Banerjea further compares the three-headed figure on these coins, with the representation of three-headed Śiva [**Oesho*] on *Kushāṇa coins. He says that the attribute in the r hand of the deity on the Ujjayinī coins is definitely a staff, and not a spear as suggested by Allan. Staff in the hand of Śiva is seen on some Kushāṇa coins. In this connection, it has been pointed out, that

Ujjayinī

V'ima Kadphises

Huvishka

Kanishka I

Vāsudeva I

the deity on the Ujjayinī coins, whether single-headed or three-headed, is shown as holding in his l hand, a *kamaṇḍalu*, which is an attribute characteristic of Śiva. What is even more significant is that on an Ujjayinī coin from Kamrej, the deity is shown holding an object, which has been identified by A S Gadre as a 'crescent-topped staff'. But it seems more like a *triśūla*, the two outer prongs of which are visible, giving the impression of a crescent. The appearance of a *triśūla-paraśu* on the obv of another Ujjayinī coin from Kamrej, would seem to support this. Thus, the association of the *vṛishabha*, the *kamaṇḍalu*, and the *triśūla* with the deity on these Ujjayinī coins would seem to dispel all doubts regarding the identification of this divinity with Śiva. Also, the absence here of the *peacock, which is often seen associated with Kārttikeya on *Yaudheya and *Imperial Gupta coins, would seem to support this identification. The standing figure of Śiva, holding a *triśūla-paraśu* in his r hand, while the l hand is placed on hip, appears on the obv of the *Chatreśvara series of coins of the *Kuṇinda tribe. Some recently reported coins of this series, however, bear the figure of three-headed Śiva, seated on the *apasmāra purusha*, and holding a *triśūla* in his r hand, while the l hand rests on his knee. The deity appearing on the obv of the silver coins of the *Audumbara chief, *Dharaghosha, who was earlier identified as Śiva by some scholars, is now correctly identified as *Viśvāmitra. Śiva also appears on some coins of the Yaudheyas. The figure of Śiva does not seem to occur on the *Indo-Greek coins known so far. But a number of *Śaka-Pahlava rulers, like *Maues, *Azilises, and *Gondopharnes, depicted this deity on their coins, though much diversity is not seen in the representation of Śiva on their coins. He is generally two-armed, and his bull-*vāhana* is never present beside him. On some coins of Maues, Śiva is shown walking to the l. He is dressed in flowing draperies, and holds a club in his r hand and a long spear (or sceptre) in his l hand. Whitehead does not name this deity, but even though the *triśūla* is not shown with the god, it seems to be quite likely that Śiva is intended, for the club is mentioned in the purāṇas as an attribute of Śiva. As regards the spear in the hand of the deity, it has been pointed out that in a specimen of this type of Maues in the British Museum collection, Śiva is shown holding a *triśūla* in place of a spear, and the 'spear found on the Punjab Museum specimen actually represents a trident'. In their work on the coin types of the Śaka-Pahlava kings of India, Jenkins and Narain have described a similar deity on a coin type of *Azes I. But Marshall, to whose work these two scholars have referred for this type, ascribes these coins to Maues, and not to Azes I. A deity holding a club in his l hand, and carrying *Nike on his r hand, appears on the obv of some coins of Azilises, and on the rev of some other coins of this ruler. Neither Cunningham, nor Marshall, identifies this deity with Śiva. But Jenkins and Narain suggest this tentative identification; the club in the hand of the deity would seem to support it. Some variety is seen in the representation of Śiva on the coins of Gondopharnes. On one type of his coins, he is shown as standing facing front, and holding a *triśūla* in the l hand, while the r hand is extended. A British Museum specimen of Gondopharnes depicts Śiva as holding a *triśūla-paraśu* in his r hand, while a skin is seen hanging down from his left arm. On yet another type, Śiva stands facing front. He has a *triśūla* in his r hand, and a palm in his l hand. It is interesting to note that on most of his coins, Gondopharnes takes the epithet of *devavrata*. This *deva*, to whom Gondopharnes declares his devotion, appears to be Śiva, for in the *Matsyapurāṇa*, Śiva is mentioned as such. The *Kushāṇa rulers, *V'ima Kadphises, *Kanishka I, *Vāsishka, *Huvishka, *Vāsudeva I, *Kanishka III, and *Vāsudeva II, depicted the figure of Śiva on some of their coins, the deity being called **Oesho* on the coins of all these Kushāṇa rulers, except for V'ima Kadphises. The depiction of Śiva on Kushāṇa coins is interesting for the multiplicity of heads and arms of the deity, and for the variety in the attributes he is shown holding in his hands. The figures of Śiva on the coins of *V'ima Kadphises are among the earliest anthropomorphic representations of this deity. Śiva is always two-armed, has matted hair, and holds the **triśūla* or *triśūla-paraśu* in one hand, and a *kamaṇḍalu* in the other. His bull mount, Nandin, is usually seen beside him. New elements are seen in the representation of Śiva on the coins of *Kanishka I and *Huvishka. For one thing, the deity is always described as *Oesho* in the label inscription, and for another, the bull is always absent. Śiva may be one-headed or three-headed, and two-armed or four-armed. His attributes include the *triśūla* or *triśūla-paraśu*, *kamaṇḍalu*, *pāśa*, *aṅkuśa*, spear or staff, *gadā*, *vajra*, deer, etc. On a gold coin of Huvishka, described by Gardner, Śiva holds a **chakra* in one of his hands, and this has been regarded as the beginning of the *saṁhāramūrtis* and *Hariharamūrtis* of Śiva. Interestingly, on this

Vāsudeva I

coin of Huvishka, as also on a gold coin of Kanishka I published recently by Paul Murphy, Śiva is ithyphallic. This feature is seen for the first time in the images of the deity in the post-Kushāṇa period, and its occurrence on these Kushāṇa coins is remarkable. It may, however, be mentioned here that a *punch marked coin in the collection of Jan Lingen of the Netherlands, reportedly bears the figure of an ithyphallic male on the rev, which might be the first representation of this kind in ancient Indian coinage. On some copper coins of Huvishka, the deity depicted is described in the Br label inscription as *Gaṇeśo*, but the iconographic features do not support his identification with Gaṇapati. There is a suggestion that the figure should be identified as that of Śiva, who bears the name Gaṇeśa in the *Rāmāyaṇa*. The figure holds a bow in his hand, and this reminds one of the Tripurāntaka form of Śiva. On some coins, Śiva is depicted standing face to face with *Umā, and the label inscription reads *Ommo-Oesho*; while on some other coins, he is depicted beside **Nana*, and the label inscription reads *Nana-Oesho*. Not much variety is seen in the depiction of Śiva on the coins of *Vāsudeva I. The deity may be one-headed or three-headed, but mostly two-armed; the bull is usually present. On one coin published by Cunningham, Śiva is three-headed, and holds the *triśūla*, *pāśa*, *kamaṇḍalu*, and lion's skin in his four hands; a bell is tied round the neck of Nandin. During the reign of the later Kushāṇa rulers, coins with the figure of Śiva became very popular in the western provinces of the empire. Attempts to identify the divine figure on a coin of *Kanishka III as Śiva-*Ardhanārīśvara, have not met with much success. On the obv of the gold and silver coins of *Śaśāṅka, Śiva is shown reclining to the l, on his *vāhana*, Nandin, standing to the l. He holds an indistinct object in his raised l hand. Above, on the left, is the moon, *śaśāṅka*, in allusion to the name of the issuer. On ancient Indian coins, Śiva is also represented theriomorphically through the *bull, and symbolically through the **liṅgaṁ*, **triśūla*, and *crescent-in-hill (Allan 1914; Altekar 1957; Banerjea 2002; R G Bhandarkar 1928; Sukumari Bhattacharji 1970; Chakrabortty 1931; Bhaskar Chattopadhyay 1977; A S Gadre 1939; S R Goyal 1986; Handa 2007a; T R R Iyengar 2003; Jenkins and Narain 1957; Macdonell 1897; Murphy 2003-2004; R B Pande 1988; Rao 1985; A M Shastri 1984; O P Singh 1968; Prashant Srivastava 1996a; Prashant

Srivastava 1996b; Prashant Srivastava and Deepak Tiwari 1994; Tiwari and Sharma 1983; Wilkins 2006; Yaduvanshi 1988).†

Śivadāsa. *Audumbara chief. He issued copper coins of Class I of *Audumbara coins. On these coins, he uses the titles of **rañа* and **mahadeva*. On palaeographical grounds, these coins are dated to the second or first century BC (Allan 1936; Chakrabortty 1931; Cunningham 1971b; K K Dasgupta 1974; Handa 2007a; Jayaswal 1988; Marshall 1975; Smith 1972).

Śivadatta. *Almora k. He is known from one base silver coin, bearing on the obv, a symbol comprising a curved line ending a circle to its right, in the centre, and a *bull before a *tree-in-railing. The rev has an elaborate symbol, regarded by some scholars as an altar bearing a conventional **nandipada* on its façade, and surmounted by a *triangular-headed symbol, while others associate it with some Greek tradition. The Pkt ld on the obv has the name of the issuer in the genitive (Allan 1936; Handa 2007a; M P Joshi 1989; Bela Lahiri 1974).

Śivadatta. *Ayodhyā k. Although known from the coins of Ayodhyā, some scholars regard him as a ruler of *Mathurā. He is believed to be the earliest of the Ayodhyā kings with *datta*-ending names, as he is connected with *Dhanadeva and *Viśākhadeva by the style and fabric of his coins, and also by his use of the rev device of *Gajalakshmī. Great variety is seen in his monetary issues, which are all in copper. Some of his coins have an *elephant to the l and the ld *Sivadatasa* on the obv, and Gajalakshmī on the rev; others have a **vajra*-like symbol between two uncertain symbols on the rev, in place of Gajalakshmī, while still others have a combination of symbols including the *tree-in-railing and the *Ujjain symbol. One variety has the figure of a *bull to the l on the obv, and a combination of symbols on the rev (Allan 1936; Bela Lahiri 1974; Smith 1972).

Śivadatta. Śaka satrap. He was probably a Hinduized Śaka, who is known to have ruled over the *Mathurā region from his only available copper coin, presently in the British Museum collection. It bears the figure of *Lakshmī standing facing, flanked by symbols, and the ld *Khatapasa Śivadatasa* on the obv. The rev has a *horse facing left (Allan 1936; Senior 2001; Sircar 1980b).

Śivaghosha. Śaka satrap. He was probably a Hinduized Śaka, who is known to have ruled over the *Mathurā region from a single known copper coin in the Richard Burn collection. It bears the figure of *Lakshmī standing facing, flanked by symbols, and the ld *Khatapasa Śivaghoshasa* on the obv. The rev has a *horse facing left (Allan 1936; Senior 2001; Sircar 1980b).

Śivaghosha. *Vemaki chief.

Śivamagha. *Magha k.

Śivanandiśrī. *Pañchāla k. The rev of the coins of Śivanandiśrī, *Anamitra, *Śrīnandi, *Varuṇamitra, *Vasusena, and *Yugasena does not bear the anthropomorphic or symbolic representation of any divinity, as is the usual case with the Pañchāla series, and, on this basis, it has been suggested that they might have ruled at a later period, when the practice of representing a deity alluding to the name of the issuing king on the rev of the coin had become lax. The use of *śri* associates Śivanandiśrī with Śrīnandi, and the use of the rev device of a *tree-in-railing seems to connect him with *Yugasena. The coins of Śivanandiśrī are so different from the usual Pañchāla series, that some scholars suggest that he might not at all have ruled over Ahichchhatrā, but over some other region of Pañchāla, like Kāmpilya (K D Bajpai 1953; Bela Lahiri 1974).

Śivapālita. *Almora k. He is known from a single base silver coin in the British Museum collection. The obv of this coin shows a crude human figure in the centre, and a *bull before a *tree-in-railing. The rev has an elaborate symbol, regarded by some scholars as an altar bearing a conventional **nandipada* on its façade, and surmounted by a *triangular-headed symbol, while others associate it with some Greek tradition. The Pkt ld on the obv has the name of the issuer in the genitive (Allan 1936; Handa 2007a; M P Joshi 1989; Bela Lahiri 1974).

Śivarakshita. *Almora k.

Six-armed symbol. It appears on the local *punch marked coins of Magadha, and the so-called 'Magadha-Maurya' or the imperial series of silver punch marked coins. It is often referred to as *shaḍarachakra* . D R Bhandarkar regards it as one of the seven jewels, symbolic of permanent sovereignty (Allan 1936; D R Bhandarkar 1984; Chakrabortty 1931; Cunningham 1971b; S R Goyal 1995b; Rajgor 2001).

Siyr. Coin denomination. **Stater*.

Skandagupta *Kramāditya*. *Imperial Gupta k; son of *Kumāragupta I; latter half of the fifth century AD. There are indications that he had to face the opposition of other aspirants to the Imperial Gupta throne. A statement in the Junagarh rock inscription is taken as referring to Skandagupta's victory over the *Nāgas, perhaps in the context of this struggle for succession. While a prince, Skandagupta had proved his calibre by defeating the Pushyamitras [*Kumāragupta I]. His most notable achievement seems to be his victory over the *Hūṇa invaders. The Buddhist text, *Chandragarbhaparipṛichchhā*, would suggest that this event, too, took place during the reign of his father, But the Junagarh rock inscription and the Bhitari pillar inscription, while describing this victory, make no mention of Kumāragupta I in this context. It has been remarked that the 'crave for numismatic variety...comes to an end with the accession of Skandagupta', perhaps because the king was busy defending his empire from the Hūṇas. Perhaps, he issued only four types of coins in gold : (i) *Archer type, (ii) **Chhatra* type, (iii) *Horseman type, and (iv) *King-and-female type. Some **repoussé* gold coins of the **garuḍa*-with-outstretched-wings types, bearing the ld *Śrī-Kramāditya*, are known from the southern Kosala region, which have been ascribed to Skandagupta by some scholars like B C Jain, but most of the scholars are in favour of identifying this Śrī-Kramāditya as some local (*Nala, Śūra, or *Śarabhapurīya ?) ruler of southern Kosala; there is also a suggestion that he may be identified as a predecessor of Mahendrāditya of the *Kathāsaritsāgara*. As regards his silver coinage, he is believed to be the last Imperial Gupta ruler to issue both the *western Indian and the **Madhyadeśa* types of coins (Ashvini Agrawal 1989; Nisar Ahmad 1964; Allan 1914; Altekar

Skandagupta :
King-and-Female type

Skandagupta :
Archer type

1957; R D Banerji 1933; Fleet 1888; S R Goyal 2005; P L Gupta 1998; B C Jain 1960; K P Jayaswal 1933; Sinha 1988; Sircar 1986; Smith 1972; Prashant Srivastava 2004b; Thaplyal, forthcoming; T P Verma 1991).†

Skandanāga. *Nāga k. He is associated with *Bhīmanāga, *Vasunāga, and *Brīhaspatināga by the use of the 'Peacock' type. He seems to be later than Bhīmanāga and Vasunāga, as he also issued the 'Bull' type of coins. He assumed the title of **mahārāja* on coins (Cunningham 1967; Bela Lahiri 1974; H V Trivedi 1957).

Skando-Komaro. Deity. See *Kārttikeya.

Śoḍāsha

Śoḍāsha. *Śaka-Pahlava k. He was the Śaka **Kshatrapa* of Mathurā, and the son and successor of *Rañjuvula. His known date is 15 AD. The Mathurā lion capital inscription of the time of Rañjuvula and Śoḍāsha refers to the former as **mahākshatrapa*, and to the latter as *kshatrapa*. On his earlier coins also, Śoḍāsha refers to himself as a *kshatrapa* and 'son of Rañjuvula' or 'son of *mahākshatrapa*'. But later, he issued coins as a *mahākshatrapa*, and, interestingly, dropped the patronymic in the coin ld. The paucity of his *mahākshatrapa* coins indicates his short reign. Śoḍāsha issued coins in potin and copper. The obv of all his coins shows *Lakshmī standing, while the rev always bears the device of *Gajalakshmī. But one type, from the Jammu region, has a *horse to the r on the obv, and *Herakles standing with club and lion's skin on the rev. The ld is in Pkt, written in the Br script, and always on the obv of the coin (Allan 1936; Cunningham 1971a; Gardner 1971; Jenkins and Narain 1957; Marshall 1975; B N Mukherjee 1969a; Rapson 1987; Senior 2001; Sircar 1980b; Sircar 1986; Tarn 1980; Whitehead 1914).

Solidus. Coin denomination. It was first struck at Trier *c* 309 AD by the Roman emperor, Constantine the Great, and was being manufactured at the other mints also over the next fifteen years. It continued to be struck till the later Byzantine times. It was known for its full weight and value (Junge 1984).

Sonepur hoard. This hoard of 162 silver *punch marked coins was discovered some time before 1951 at Sonepur in the Balagir district of Orissa. All the coins are of one type, bearing four symbols-- *elephant, *bull, a pair of bullocks yoked to a plough, and another symbol made of a pellet surrounded by a circle of dots. It is presently housed in the Orissa Museum, Bhubaneshwar (Rajgor 2001).

Sonpur hoard. This hoard of 670 silver coins was discovered in 1925, at Sonpur in the Chhindwara district of Madhya Pradesh. Of these coins, 37 were melted down by the discoverer of the hoard, while 50 are uncertain. The rulers represented in the hoard include *Rudrasena I, *Dāmasena, *Dāmajadeśrī II, *Vīradāman, *Yaśodāman I, *Vijayasena, *Dāmajadaśrī III, *Rudrasena II, *Viśvasiṁha, *Bhartṛidāman, *Viśvasena, *Rudrasiṁha II, *Yaśodāman II, *Rudrasena III, and *Īśvaradatta (Jha and Rajgor 1994).

Sophytes. K. Cunningham, who published the first known coin in the name of this ruler, identified him with the Indian prince, Sopeithes, mentioned in classical sources as a contemporary of Alexander, and, this identification was accepted by most of the writers on the subject. Consequently, Sophytes was regarded as a ruler of the Salt Range in the Punjab. However, Whitehead, who had earlier himself regarded Sophytes as a satrap in the Punjab region, later, on the basis of the *provenance* of his coins, placed him in the Oxus region, and this has now been accepted by all the subsequent writers on the subject; Bopearachchi is of the view that this is supported by the recent discoveries of coins and coin hoards in Afghanistan. Cunningham proposes 316-306 BC as the date for Sophytes. Rapson regarded the coins of Sophytes as older than those of Seleukos I and contemporaneous with Alexander, and Whitehead also places them as early as 320 BC. Narain regards Sophytes as 'an eastern satrap under Achaemenid rule, a Greek with the semblance of an Iranian name', and is of the view that these coins were struck prior to the invasion of Indian by Alexander. But one type of Sophytes, showing the head of *Zeus on the obv, though similar to the coins issued by Philip and Alexander in Macedonia, is nearer to the coins of Seleukos I minted in Bactria, a fact also remarked by scholars like Gardner, Smith, and B V Head, and this has led to the suggestion that he was ruling, not only at the time of the invasion of India by Alexander, but also during the eastern expedition of Seleukos I. On this basis, von Sallet suggested 306 BC as the date for the Sophytes coins, while Smith placed them in 305 BC. The coins of Sophytes are linked, geographically and chronologically, to the 'owls' and 'eagles' by *provenance*, stylistic features, symbols, attributes, and die-adjustment. Besides, a type of Sophytes, bearing the bust of *Athena, wearing the Corinthian helmet, to the r, on the obv, is derived from the gold coins of Alexander. A similar coin for Egypt (?) bears the Egyptian hieroglyph *uah* in the place where the name of Sophytes occurs on his coins, and E T Newell says that this coin from Egypt is copied from the gold *staters* of Alexander or his immediate successors. Hence, according to Bopearachchi, Sophytes cannot be placed before Alexander's invasion, as suggested by Narain. Bopearachchi is of the view that as the coins of Sophytes are copied from those of Seleukos I struck after his eastern expedition c 305 BC, these coins should be dated towards the close of the fourth century BC. Sophytes is known to have issued two types of coins. The first types has, on the obv, the head of the king, wearing 'an Attic helmet ornamented with a laurel wreath, and a cheek-piece with a bird's wing' to the r; the rev has a cock to the r, and the ld *Sophytou*. The second type has the head of Athena, wearing a Corinthian helmet, to the r, on the obv, while the rev is similar to that of the first type. Both the types have the symbol, **caduceus*, on the rev (Bopearachchi 1993; Bopearachchi and Pieper 1998; Bopearachchi and Rahman 1995; Cunningham 1970; Gardner 1971; Head 1906; Rapson 1904; Rapson 1914; von Sallet 1883; Smith 1972; Narain 1957a; Newell 1938; Whitehead 1914; Whitehead 1943).

Sophytes

Soter Megas. *Kushāṇa k. *V'ima Takshuma.

Soter megas. Title. This title, meaning 'saviour, the great' or 'the great saviour', appears on the coins of the *Kushāṇa rulers, *V'ima Takshuma and *V'ima Kadphises (Cunningham 1971a; Gardner 1971; Rosenfield 1967; Whitehead 1914).

Soteros. Title. Meaning 'saviour', this popular Greek title was used by *Apollodotos, *Apollophanes, *Diomedes, *Dionysios, *Eukratides, *Hermaios, *Hippostratos, *Menander, *Nikias, *Peukolaos, *Polyxenos, *Strato I, and *Zoilos II, among the *Indo-Greeks. Commemorative coins show that the title was used for

*Diodotos I, perhaps after his death. Among the Śakas, *Rañjuvula appears to be the only ruler to assume this title on his coins. Its Pkt rendering is **tratara*, sometimes spelt *tradara* (Cunningham 1970; Gardner 1971; A N Lahiri 1965; Marshall 1975; Narain 1957a; Tarn 1980; Whitehead 1914).

Spajhama (?). *Parataraja k.

Spajhana. *Parataraja k.

Spalagadama. *Śaka-Pahlava k. He was the son of *Spalahora and served under his uncle, *Vonones. There are some silver and copper coins, which bear the name of Vonones on the obv, and that of Spalagadama on the rev. The rev ld describes Spalagadama as the 'son of Spalahora'; instead of any royal title, Spalagadama is given the title of **dhramika*. The silver coins have horseman king on the obv, and standing *Zeus with thunderbolt and sceptre on the rev. The copper coins have standing *Herakles crowning himself on the obv, and *Athena holding spear and shield on the rev. Spalagadama also issued copper coins with his father, whose name is mentioned on the obv as *Spalyris (Cunningham 1971a; Gardner 1971; Jenkins and Narain 1957; Marshall 1975; B N Mukherjee 1969a; Rapson 1987; Senior 2001; Sircar 1980b; Prashant Srivastava 1996a; Tarn 1980; Whitehead 1914).

Spalyris and Spalagadama

Spalahora. *Śaka-Pahlava k. On some coins bearing the name of *Vonones on the obv, the rev ld mentions Spalahora as 'brother of the king' without according him any royal title. While Tarn regards 'king's brother' as a title of honour, most of the scholars believe that Spalahora was, indeed, a brother of Vonones, the 'king' mentioned on the obv of these coins. Most of the scholars believe that the coins of Vonones with Spalahora belong to Arachosia, showing that the former served under Vonones in that region. R C Senior, however, places the circulation of these coins in 'the greater Gandhāra region, west of Taxila'. The coins mentioning Spalahora on the rev are both in silver and copper. The silver coins have horseman king on the obv, and standing *Zeus on the rev, while the copper coins have standing *Herakles crowning himself on the obv and *Athena holding spear and shield on the rev. The rev ld has the additional title of

Vonones and Spalahora

Spalyris and Spalagadama

dhramika for Spalahora. He also issued copper coins with his son *Spalagadama, which bear mounted king and the name of *Spalyris (= Spalahora; Osmund Bopearachchi would, however, identify him with *Spalirises) on the obv; the rev has Herakles seated on rock with a club in his hand, and the name of Spalagadama. The obv Gr ld again refers to Spalahora as 'brother of the king'. Neither he, nor his son, uses any royal title, showing that they issued these coins as subordinate rulers, serving under Vonones. These joint issues of Vonones with Spalahora (or Spalagadama), and of Spalahora with Spalagadama, were restruck by *Spalirises. This seems to suggest that when Spalirises usurped the throne from Vonones, he removed Spalahora, along with his son, from power, perhaps because of their loyalty towards Vonones (Bopearachchi 1993; Bopearachchi and Pieper 1998; Cunningham 1971a; Gardner 1971; Jenkins and Narain 1957; Marshall 1975; B N Mukherjee 1969a; Rapson 1987; Senior 2001; Sircar 1980b; Prashant Srivastava 1996a; Tarn 1980; Whitehead 1914).

Spalirises

Spalirises. *Śaka-Pahlava k. He was a brother of *Vonones, and seems to have begun his career as a subordinate ruler of the latter. There are certain satrapal coins, which mention Spalirises as 'brother of the king', and do not use any royal title for him. The coins bear horseman king on the obv, and standing *Zeus holding thunderbolt and sceptre on the rev. Although the name of the 'king' is not mentioned on these coin, most of the scholars identify him with Vonones; the suggestion, that he might be *Maues, is not acceptable. The publication of a silver coin bearing the figure of horseman king and the ld *Basileos basileon megalou Ononou* on the obv, and standing *Zeus with the ld *Maharajabhrata dhramiäsa Spalirishasa* on the rev, would seem to set the controversy at rest. Spalirises also issued coins with his son, *Azes I. Such silver coins have horseman king and the name of Spalirises on the obv, and standing Zeus with thunderbolt and sceptre and the name of Azes [I] on the rev. The copper coins have a similar obv, but bow and arrow on the rev. Both Spalirises and Azes I are called 'great king'. Most of the scholars believe that these coins were issued during the reign of Vonones, with both Spalirises and Azes I serving as his subordinate rulers. But Marshall feels that by assuming the title of 'great king', they are announcing the end of Vonones' overlordship.

Spalirises also issued copper coins on which he assumed the sovereign titles of **basileos basileon megalos*. These coins bear king walking with battle-axe and bow on the obv, and enthroned Zeus holding sceptre on the rev. He also restruck the joint coins of Vonones with *Spalahora (or *Spalagadama), and of Spalahora with Spalagadama. This seems to show that Spalirises overthrew Vonones in Arachosia, and also removed Spalahora and his son from power. Most of the scholars believe that the coins of Spalirises come from Arachosia (although R C Senior would place their circulation in 'the greater Gandhāra region, west of Taxila'). But his son, Azes I, ruled only in northwestern India. This shows that Spalirises was himself overthrown by some one, perhaps some direct descendant of Vonones, and Azes I had to move to northwestern India (Cunningham 1971a; Gardner 1971; Jenkins and Narain 1957; Marshall 1975; B N Mukherjee 1969a; Rapson 1987; Senior 2001; Sircar 1980b; Prashant Srivastava 1996a; Tarn 1980; Whitehead 1914).

Spalirises

Spalyris. *Spalahora.

Śrīnandi. *Pañchāla k. The rev of the coins of Śrīnandi, *Anamitra, *Śivanandiśrī, *Varuṇamitra, *Vasusena, and *Yugasena does not bear the anthropomorphic or symbolic representation of any divinity, as is the usual case with the Pañchāla series, and, on this basis, it has been suggested that they might have ruled at a later period, when the practice of representing a deity alluding to the name of the issuing king on the rev of the coin had become lax. The use of *śri* associates Śrīnandi with Śivanandiśrī. Śrīnandi has been identified with Nandin, who is mentioned in the Allahabad pillar inscription of *Samudragupta as one of the rulers of northern India defeated by that *Imperial Gupta emperor. The coins of Śrīnandi are so different from the usual Pañchāla series, that some scholars suggest that he might not at all have ruled over Ahichchhatrā, but over some other region of Pañchāla, like Kāmpilya. Besides, if Achyu[ta] of the Pañchāla series is to be identified as the ruler defeated by Samudragupta, and Śrīnandi with Nandin, who, too, was vanquished by the Imperial Gupta ruler, both of them could not very well have ruled over the same region. The rev of the coins of Śrīnandi bears the first Pañchāla symbol (Bela Lahiri 1974; R R Tripathi 1962).

Śrīvatsa. Symbol. Some scholars believe that the earliest representation of this symbol occurs outside India, on a Hittite inscription from Boghazkoi, datable to *c* fourteenth century BC. *Śrīvatsa*, as an auspicious symbol, was adopted by almost all the major Indian religious creeds. The symbol occurs on a number of ancient Indian coins, like the *punch marked coins, tribal coins like those of the *Audumbaras, *Kuṇindas *Kulūtas, and the *Yaudheyas, and the local series like those of *Kauśāmbī, *Mathurā, *Pañchāla, *Ayodhyā, etc. Its occurrence is also reported on some coins from *Taxila (Allan 1936; Chakrabortty 1931; Bhaskar Chattopadhyay 1977; K K Dasgupta 1974; Handa 2007a; Bela Lahiri 1974; Rajgor 2001; Savita Sharma 1990).[†]

Stambharāja. *Nala k.

Standard. It is 'a system of weights according to which the various denominations of a coinage are fixed' (Hill 1906).

Samudragupta : Standard type

Standard type. Gold. This was the most popular type of *Samudragupta. The obv composition is a close imitation of the *Kushāṇa prototype, but with a few differences pointing at the process of Indianization of the coin type. The king wears a close fitting headdress (instead of the Kushāṇa peaked cap); the trident in front of the king is replaced by the **garuḍadhvaja*; the corrupt and meaningless Gr ld is replaced by a metrical Skt ld; the rev ld gives the *viruda* of this king (instead of the name of deity depicted). The obv has the king, dressed in coat and trousers, holding a standard in his l hand, and offering oblations at an altar with the right. The vertical ld beneath the king's left arm reads *Samudra-*, and that outside the standard, *-gupta*. The circular ld is *Samara-śata-vitata vijayojita ripurajito divaṁ jayati*. The rev has the nimbate goddess, enthroned, with a *pāśa* in her r hand, and a **cornucopiae* in the left. The rev ld reads *Parākramaḥ*. The king as his own standard bearer does not go well with Indian etiquette, and the *Imperial Gupta moneyers replaced the standard in the hand of the king with a bow [*Archer type] or a battle-axe [*Battle-axe type]. There is a coin of the Standard type, which has the obv quite similar to the Standard type of Samudragupta, but the vertical ld below the king's left arm reads *Chandragu[pta]*, and the circular ld is *Vasudhāṁ* *vijitya jayatitridivaṁ pṛithivīśvaraḥ* (*puṇyaiḥ*). The rev is similar to the rev of the Standard type of Samudragupta, but the ld reads **Paramabhāgavata*. Chhabra ascribes this type to *Chandragupta I, and suggests that it was issued by him after the death of *Kumāradevī. But P L Gupta and Altekar attribute it to *Chandragupta II, who is shown holding a standard on the obv of his *King-and-Queen-on-Couch type as well (Ashvini Agrawal 1989; Allan 1914; Altekar 1957; R D Banerji 1933; B Ch Chhabra 1949; S R Goyal 2005; P L Gupta 1998; Smith 1972; Prashant Srivastava 1996a; Thaplyal, forthcoming).

Standing king type. Copper. This type was first issued in copper by *Chandragupta II in the *Imperial Gupta dynasty. The obv has the standing figure of the king, as on the **Chhatra* type (copper), but there is no attendant accompanying him. The rev bears the figure of a **garuḍa* in totally bird form, and the Br ld *Śrī-Chandraguptaḥ*. *Kumāragupta I continued this type of copper coins. On the obv, the standing king wears a waist cloth, and is probably offering incense at an altar with his r hand. The rev is similar to the prototype issued by his father, but the ld below the *garuḍa* reads *Kumāragupta* (Allan 1914; Altekar 1957; P L Gupta 1998; Smith 1972).

Stater. Coin denomination. It is a Greek word of varied meaning. Although attempts have been made to establish that it was not a coin denomination at all, there is a suggestion that *stater* denoted the 'principal currency unit of any particular city', varying in value, and perhaps even metal, according the wealth and importance of the city. It most usually referred to the standard denomination of gold coins among the Greeks, and weighed 134.4 grains on the Attic standard. According to Yaśomitra, the commentator of *Sphuṭārthā-bhidharmakosha*, the ratio of the value of *stater* to **dīnāra* was 1 : 2. The denomination was Indianized as *sadera*, **satera*, **sateraka*, **stir*, and **siyr*, in various Kh inscriptions and literary texts. Among the *Indo-Greeks, *Diodotos I, *Diodotos II, *Eutheydemos I, and *Eukratides I issued *staters*. Some anepigraphous *staters*, bearing the Greek character *alpha*, have been ascribed to *Menander I, but were more probably issued by *Agathokleia. Eukratides I issued a twenty-*stater* piece (weight, 2593.5 grains), which is believed to be the largest available gold coin issued by a ruler of Greek origin anywhere in the world. Electrum coins were also known as *staters*. R C Agrawala, on the authority of Grünwedel, refers to a silver *stater* (R C Agrawala 1952; R C Agrawala 1953b; R C Agrawala 1954a; Frey 1973; Junge 1984; A N Lahiri 1965).

Steelyard. Symbol. This symbol occurs on the coins of *Ayodhyā and *Taxila (Allan 1936).

Stir. Coin denomination. **Stater*.

Stratega. Title. This is the Pkt rendering of the Greek title, *strategos*, and occurs for *Aśpavarman on his coins with *Azes I, and with *Gondopharnes. Under the Seleukids of Syria, *strategos* was equivalent to the **kshatrapa* (provincial governor). But Marshall observes that no such evidence is available for India, where satrap was called *kshatrapa*. He says that under the *Śaka-Pahlavas, *strategos* was commander-in-chief of the imperial forces, was directly responsible to the emperor for the safety of the realm, and had authority over satraps and local chiefs. Rapson also translates *strategos* as *senāpati*, and suggests that Aśpavarman belonged to some powerful family of military chiefs. The appearance of the name of Aśpavarman on coins seems to indicate that although he was a *strategos*, his functions and authority were not confined to military matters alone; he seems to be associated with civil administration as well. He might have discharged the combined duties of a commander-in-chief and a provincial governor. There is also a suggestion that, in practice, particularly in the outlying provinces, the offices of *strategos* and *kshatrapa* were often combined in one person. Marshall believed that Aśpavarman is the only Scytho-Parthian *strategos* known so far. But later discoveries of inscriptions have revealed the names of at least three more *strategoi*—Viśpavarman (= Vishṇuvarman), and his sons, Indravarman and Vaga (Gardner 1971; Marshall 1975; Rapson 1987; Senior 2001; Prashant Srivastava 2007a; Tarn 1980; Whitehead 1914).

Strategos. **Stratega*.

Strato I. *Indo-Greek k; son of *Menander I; latter half of the second century BC. He was a minor when his father died in camp, and for some time, his mother, *Agathokleia, administered the kingdom as regent. During this period, he issued joint coins with his mother [for these coins, see *Agathokleia]. Later on, Strato I assumed independent charge of his kingdom. He is depicted on his various coins in different stages of life, from a young boy in his teens, to an old man 'with toothless jaws and sunken cheeks', and on this basis it was suggested by scholars, like Rapson, that he had a long reign of around 70 years. But there is no portrait, which might link his middle-aged portrait on the coins bearing the title of **epiphanes*, with those, which show him as an old man of around 70 years of age. On this ground, Narain suggests that after he had ruled for about 35 years, Strato I was superseded by other kings for about 15 years, till he could regain authority. His coins, though relatively few in number keeping in view his long reign, are very widely distributed, being found in western Gandhāra and Takshaśilā, Ghazni, and the Jammu-Sialkot region, thereby showing that, at least in the first phase of his reign, he retained authority over the larger part of the territories he inherited from Menander. Strato I issued coins in silver, lead, billon, and copper. All the coins are struck on the Indian standard. All the coins are die-struck pieces. All the silver, billon, and lead coins are round in shape. The copper coins are mostly square in shape, but the round shape for them is not unknown. All the silver coins have the royal bust, often wearing a helmet, on the obv; on some of the types, the diademed bust of the king is to the r, while on others, the bust of the king is to the l and thrusting javelin. The rev of most of the silver types has thundering *Athena, with an **aegis* on her left arm; but one type has Athena standing to the l, and holding out *Nike on her r hand. The billon type has a crude diademed bust of the king to the r on the obv, and thundering Athena, with *aegis* on her left arm, on the rev. The obv of the lead type has *Apollo standing with an arrow in both his hands, and the rev has the **tripod lebes*. There is variety in the obv and rev devices on the copper coins of Strato I. Some copper coins have the bust of *Herakles to the r on the obv, and wreath- and palm-bearing winged Nike on the rev. One type has the bust of Apollo to the r on the obv, and wreath- and palm-bearing Nike on the rev, while another type, round in shape, has a similar bust of Apollo on the obv, but bow and quiver on the rev. The obv of yet another copper type has Apollo standing with bow and arrow, while the rev has the *tripod lebes*. The coins of Strato I bear the Gr

Agathokleia and Strato I

ld on the obv, and the Pkt ld, written in the Kh script, on the rev. Besides the title of *basileus*, Strato I assumed the epithets **soteros*, **dikaios*, and *epiphanes* on his coins; on some types, only *soteros* has been used in addition to *basileus*, on others, *soteros* and *dikaios*, and on still others, *soteros* and *epiphanes*, have been used together in addition to *basileus* in the obv ld, and their Pkt equivalents in the Kh ld. *Basileus* is rendered into Pkt as **maharaja*, *soteros* as **tratara*, *dikaios* as **dhramika*, and *epiphanes* as **prachachha*, in the rev ld. The Pkt form of the name of the ruler, as met with on coins, is Strata. Towards the end of his career, he associated his grandson, *Strato II, in administration, and issued joint coins with him. Such silver joint coins bear the bust of the king on the obv, and thundering *Athena on the rev. The obv Gr ld has been read by Rapson as *Basileos soteros Straons [kai philo-] Stratons*. The rev Kh ld on some coins he reads as *Maharajasa tratarasa Stratasa potrasa cha sa *priyapita Stratasa*; on other coins occurs the same ld, but the first word is *Maharajanaṁ* instead of *Maharajasa*. The lead coins have, on the obv, *Apollo with arrows in both hands, and traces of a Gr ld. The rev has **tripod lebes*, and the Kh ld *Maharajasa tratarasa Stratasa potrasa cha sa priyapita Stratasa*. But Strato II apparently predeceased him, leaving him alone to the rule for some time more (Bopearachchi 1993; Bopearachchi and Pieper 1998; Bopearachchi and Rahman 1995; Cunningham 1970; Gardner 1971; A N Lahiri 1965; Marshall 1975; Narain 1957a; Rapson 1906; Rapson 1987; Senior 2001; Sircar 1980a; Prashant Srivastava 1996a; Tarn 1980; Whitehead 1914).†

Strato I

Strato II. *Indo-Greek k. He is known from the coins he issued conjointly with his grandfather, *Strato I, who, in his old age, appointed him as his subking. There is a suggestion that there was a break in the rule of Strato I, and Strato II might have assisted him in re-establishing his power. The grandfather-grandson duo struck joint coins in both silver and lead [for these coins, see *Strato I]. The bust on the obv of the silver coins is that of an old man, and seems to be that of the elder Strato. But on a coin issued by Strato I alone, housed in the British Museum, London, Rapson sees an even older Strato, leading to the suggestion that Strato II might have predeceased his grandfather. A N Lahiri and some other scholars have expressed the possibility of the existence of three kings named

Strato, and they regard Strato *Soteros* of these joint coins as Strato II, and Strato *Philopator* as Strato III. But others do not agree with this, on valid grounds (Bopearachchi 1993; Bopearachchi and Pieper 1998; Bopearachchi and Rahman 1995; Cunningham 1970; Gardner 1971; A N Lahiri 1965; Marshall 1975; Narain 1957a; Rapson 1906; Rapson 1987; Sircar 1980a; Prashant Srivastava 1996a; Tarn 1980; Whitehead 1914).

Stūpa. Symbol. The *stūpa*, which, more commonly, symbolizes the *mahāparinirvāṇa* of the *Buddha, was used as a coin device by the *Audumbara and *Rājanya tribes, and by some rulers of *Ayodhyā, showing the Buddhist leanings of the issuers. It also appears on the some coins of the *Indo-Greek ruler, *Agathokles, and it is believed that he used this device to win over the Buddhists elements to his side, in his struggle against the Eukratids (Allan 1936; Chakrabortty 1931; Bhaskar Chattopadhyay 1977; Cunningham 1971b; K K Dasgupta 1974; Handa 2007a; Handa 2007b; A N Lahiri 1965; Bela Lahiri 1974; Narain 1957a; Tarn 1980).

Sudavapa. See *Uddehika.

Sudeva. *Kauśāmbī k. He is placed in the second century BC. He issued cast copper coins, which bear an *elephant to the l, and the name of the king in the genitive on the obv, while the rev has a *tree-in-railing on the right, and some other uncertain symbols on the left. He is placed earlier than *Bahasatimita I, on the grounds that, while his coins bear the figure of elephant alone, the coins of the latter have, in addition to the elephant on the rev, the figure of *horse on the obv. Recently, however, it has been suggested that what has been read on coin by Cunningham as *Sudevasa*, is actually the depiction of some symbols above the elephant (Allan 1936; Bopearachchi and Pieper 1998; Bela Lahiri 1974; Sharad Sharma 1981).

Sultanpur hoard. This hoard of over 120 silver *punch marked coins, tentatively attributed to the Kuntala *janapada*, was discovered in 1991 at Sultanpur, near Wai, in the Satara district of Maharashtra (Rajgor 2001).

Śuṅgavarman. *Kanauj k. He is known from a coin type from *Kauśāmbī, but this type shows affinity with the coin of the Kanauj king, *Vishṇudeva. Śuṅgavarman is placed earlier than him on palaeographical grounds, and Bela Lahiri proposes that he might have been the founder of the local dynasty at Kanauj, to which Vishṇudeva also belonged; she assigned Śuṅgavarman to the latter half of the second century BC. The coin of Śuṅgavarman has *tree-in-railing, hare-on-moon and a **caduceus*-like symbol on the obv, and a *horse before *yūpa* on the rev. K D Bajpai is of the view that the coin type was issued by Pushyamitra Śuṅga, the performer of two horse sacrifices, or some other ruler of his dynasty. However, the name is *varman*-ending (and not *mitra*-ending) (K D Bajpai 1965; Bela Lahiri 1974).

Suramitra. *Kauśāmbī k. He may be assigned to the first century BC or the first century AD. Nothing definite can be said about him, as his coins are not very well-preserved. He might have ruled contemporaneously with the *Aśvaghosha group of kings in some part of Kauśāmbī. The obv of his coins has the figure of a *bull to the r and another symbol which is blurred; the rev has a *tree-in-railing, *Ujjain symbol, *undulating line, and another blurred symbol, and the ld *Suramitasa* (Altekar 1942a; Bopearachchi and Pieper 1998; Bela Lahiri 1974).

Punch marked coin

Punch marked coin

Sūrya. Deity. Worshipped for 'progeny, protection, health, light and joy', Sūrya is 'the most concrete of the solar deities', as he represents 'primarily the orb of the physical sun itself'. As the son of Aditi, he is Āditya, *par excellence*. In various sources, his father is Dyaus, or Vṛitra, or he arose from the eye of Purusha. In the *Rāmāyaṇa*, his wife is Suvarchalā. He is likened to a bird travelling across the sky, to an *eagle (sometimes a golden one), to a *bull, to a white *horse, to a gem, to a brilliant car, and to a *wheel. His car is pulled by one horse, or by seven horses, or by an indefinite number of horses, or by seven mares. Anthropomorphic representation of Sūrya is not met with on ancient Indian coins, although the figures of the Greek sun god, *Helios, and the Zoroastrian sun god, Mithra (**Miiro*), are found on *Indo-Greek and *Kushāṇa coins. However, symbolic representations of Sūrya are quite common on ancient Indian coins. The **chakra* on the punch marked coins, and on local and tribal coinages, like those of *Kāḍa, *Taxila, *Ujjayinī, etc, symbolically denotes the presence of Sūrya. On the rev of the coins of the *Pañchāla ruler, *Sūryamitra, occurs 'a ball from which rays radiate; below it is a symbol, and the whole is placed on a platform...between two pillars with cross-bars'. Similarly, on the rev of the coinage of another Pañchāla ruler, *Bhānumitra, 'a radiate globe placed immediately on a railed platform between two pillars' may be seen. In view of the Pañchāla tradition, that mostly the name of the deity, anthropomorphically or symbolically represented on the rev of the coin, forms a component of the name of the issuer, it is certain that the 'ball' and the 'globe' depicted on these coins symbolize Sūrya/Bhānu. Also, according to the *Śatapathabrāhmaṇa*, at the time of the piling of the sacrificial altar, a gold disc represents the sun. The *lotus and the *triskeles also have solar associations, and some of the lotus blooms and the triskeles appearing on ancient Indian coins may be taken to the represent Sūrya, as also some of the *horse figures appearing on certain local and tribal series (Banerjea 2002; R G Bhandarkar 1928; Sukumari Bhattacharji 1970; Bhaskar Chattopadhyay 1977; K K Dasgupta 1974; S R Goyal 1986; Handa 2007a; T R R Iyengar 2003; Macdonell 1897; R B Pande 1988; Rao 1985; Wilkins 2006).†

Punch marked coin

Sūryamitra. *Kanauj k. His coins are not known from Kanauj, and he has been regarded as a ruler of Kanauj only on the basis of the general similarity of his coins with that of *Vishṇudeva, in that they all bear three symbols on the obv. However, only the *tree-in-railing on the obv is common with the coin of Vishṇudeva; the other two symbols on the coins of Sūryamitra are the *Ujjain symbol, and the *triangular-headed symbol. The rev of the coins of Sūryamitra is not very clear. K D Bajpai regards him as a ruler of *Kauśāmbī, but this is not likely as his coins are quite different from the Kauśāmbī series. Bela Lahiri proposes to identify him with *Sūryamitra of *Mathurā, whose coins, too, bear the Ujjain symbol. She feels that Sūryamitra of Mathurā might have extended his sway towards Kanauj. Bela Lahiri assigned him to the first century BC (Allan 1936; K D Bajpai 1964; Bela Lahiri 1974).

Sūryamitra. *Mathurā k. He issued coins, which show *Lakshmī with lotus in her r hand and some symbols on the obv; and three *elephants with riders on the rev. He is also known from an inscription, datable to the end of the second century BC. Some scholars take him as identical with the homonym known from *Kanauj coins (Allan 1936; Bela Lahiri 1974).

Sūryamitra. *Pañchāla k. He seems to be associated with *Bhadraghosha and *Bhānumitra, because on some coins of all these three kings, the second Pañchāla symbol is counterstruck by the third one. Bela Lahiri places him in the tenth chronological position among the Pañchāla kings known from coins. The rev of his coins bears the solar disc over a 'triangle-headed object' between two pillars (Allan 1936; Bela Lahiri 1974).

Sūryamitra. *Uddehika chief. Belonging, perhaps, to the second-first centuries BC, he issued two classes of copper coins. One class has on the obv, the *tree-in-railing and two fish within a square, and the legends *Udehaki* and *Suyamitasa*; the rev has *elephant, *bull, and another symbol countermarked on them. The other class has the *Ujjain symbol, bull, **jayadhvaja*, and **śrīvatsa*, and the legends *Sudavapa* and *Suyamitasa* on the obv, and a river with fish, sun, six-arched hill, and **triśūla* on the rev. Devendra Handa, however, does not regard this second class of coins as the issues of the Uddehikas. The metrology and devices go against the identification of this Sūryamitra with the homonymous king known from the *Pañchāla and *Mathurā series of coins, and, according to some scholars, seem to favour his identification with the king of that name known from the *Kanauj coins (Allan 1936; Chakrabortty 1931; Cunningham 1971b; K K Dasgupta 1974; Handa 2007a; Jayaswal 1988; Bela Lahiri 1974; Marshall 1975; Smith 1972).

Suvaṇṇa-guñja. Coin denomination. This term in the **Aṅgavijjā* means a *guñjā* or *rattī* of gold, and seems to the refer to a gold coin of one *rattī* weight. The *Vishṇusmṛiti* also refers to a gold **kṛishṇala* coin (V S Agrawala 1957).

Suvaṇṇa-kākaṇī. Coin denomination. It is mentioned in the **Aṅgavijjā*. We know from the *Arthaśāstra* of Kauṭilya that a **māshaka* was one-sixteenth of the standard coin, and **kākaṇī* was one-fourth of a *māshaka*. As the traditional Indian gold coin, *suvarṇa*, weighed 80 *rattīs*, the *māshaka* would weigh 5 *rattīs*, and the *suvaṇṇa-kākaṇī*, 1.25 *rattīs*. However, no actual specimen of such minute gold coins is available for the period of the *Aṅgavijjā* (V S Agrawala 1957).

***Suvaṇṇa-māsaka* (= *suvarṇa-māshaka*).** Coin denomination. Mentioned in the Jātaka literature and the **Aṅgavijjā*, it seems to the refer to one-sixteenth (**māshaka*) of the standard gold coin, **suvarṇa*. As the weight of a *suvarṇa* is given as 80 *rattīs*, the *suvaṇṇa-māsaka* would weigh 5 *rattīs*. Kauṭilya refers to *suvarṇa-māshaka* weight of 5 *guñjās* (= *rattīs*). The references to the coin denomination, *suvaṇṇa-māsaka*, are taken to indicate that, besides the standard gold coin *suvarṇa*, its submultiples were also minted. However, no actual specimen of a *suvaṇṇa-māsaka* has yet been found (V S Agrawala 1957; D R Bhandarkar 1984; Sircar 1952; Sircar 1968).

***Suvarṇa*.** Coin denomination. It is referred to in the **Ashṭādhyāyī* of Pāṇini; in the Arthaś*āstra* of Kauṭilya it forms a part of the weight system, which comprises one *suvarṇa*, two *suvarṇas*, four *suvarṇas*, eight *suvarṇas*, ten *suvarṇas*, twenty *suvarṇas*, thirty *suvarṇas*, forty *suvarṇas*, and one hundred *suvarṇas*. But it does not seem to state that the *suvarṇa* was a coin current in that period. The *suvarṇa*, as the Indian standard gold coin weighing 80 *rattīs*, is mentioned in literature, but actual specimens make their first appearance only in the time of *Skandagupta, when the weight of the *Imperial Gupta gold coin was raised from 132 grains to 144 grains, so as to conform to the weight of the *suvarṇa*, the increase in the weight of the gold coins being counterbalanced by the heavy admixture of alloy. There is a suggestion that the *suvarṇa* might be equivalent, in gold, to the value of a full-grown cow, just like the Greek **stater* and the Achaemenian *daric* (R C Agrawala 1954b; V S Agrawala 1953; V S Agrawala 1956; Altekar 1940; D R Bhandarkar 1984; C J Brown 1999; Chakrabortty 1931; Maity 1970b; Sircar 1952; Sircar 1968).

Skandagupta : King-and-Female type

***Svastika*.** Symbol. The name *svastika* seems to be derived from *svasti*, which means welfare, happiness, good luck, etc. In India, it has been a popular auspicious symbol, since prehistoric times, in rock art, pottery, sculpture, painting, terracotta art, ivory art, architecture, and numismatic and glyptic art. In various contexts, it represents the four directions, Gaṇapati, *Lakshmī, *nāda-sṛishṭi*, creation and birth, religious harmony, cycle of seasons, etc, but, primarily, it symbolizes the sun, or, more particularly, the movement of that heavenly body. The representation of the varied forms this symbol—without arms, with arms, etc—was very common on ancient Indian coins, like the *punch marked coins, cast coins, local and tribal coins, etc. On punch marked coins, the symbol may sometimes be seen within a frame, as on some coins from Taxila. On the cast coins of *Kauśāmbī, this symbol may occur on the obv with the *bull device, as also on the rev. Armless *svastika* may be seen on some coins of Tripuri, which have been dated to the third century BC. The obv of some coins of *Ayodhyā bears this symbol, sometimes within the orbs of the *Ujjain symbol. On some coins from Mathurā, *svastika* is reported occurring with Lakshmī, as on some copper coins from Karur in Tamilnadu. *Svastika*, sometimes alternating with **nandipada*, may be seen occurring in the orb of the Ujjain symbol on some coins from *Ujjayinī. A copper coin from the same site, now in the collection of the State Museum, Lucknow, has the symbol accompanying *Śiva with bull. Armed *svastika*, with a *nandipada* or *taurine attached to the end of each arm, may be seen on some *Śibi coins discovered by Sankalia during archaeological explorations in Rajasthan, as also on certain coins from *Ujjayinī. *Svastika* above *elephant on the obv of two silver coins of the *Audumbaras in the collection of Jan Lingen, is worth notice. The symbol also occurs on the rev of some *Kuṇinda coins, as also on some silver and copper coins of the *Kulūtas, and the copper coins of the *Yaudheyas (Allan 1936; Chakrabortty 1931; Bhaskar Chattopadhyay 1977; K K Dasgupta 1974; Handa 2007a; Rajgor 2001; Savita Sharma 1990; A L Srivastava 2004-2005).[†]

Swabi hoard. This hoard of, perhaps, 75 coins of *Menander I, was found in 1993 (Bopearachchi 1994).

Swat hoard 1. This hoard of 29 *tetradrachms* was published by G le Rider in 1967. The rulers represented in this hoard are *Vonones with *Spalahora, *Machene with *Maues, and Maues alone (G le Rider 1967; Senior 2001).

Swat hoard 2. This hoard of around 400 *Indo-Greek coins was accidentally discovered in a broken vase near Saidu Sharif, in the bed of the river Swat. The rulers represented in this hoard include *Antimachos II, *Apollodotos, *Lysias, *Menander I, and *Nikias (Bopearachchi and Rahman 1995).

Swat hoard 3. This hoard of over 600 coins was discovered somewhere in the Swat region. The rulers represented in this hoard include *Antialkidas, *Apollodotos, *Lysias, *Menander I, and *Maues (Senior 2001).

Swordsman type. Gold. This type, introduced by *Kumāragupta I, is actually a modification of the *Standard type of *Samudragupta, with the standard in the hand of the king being replaced by a sword, on which the l hand of the king rests. The obv has the nimbate king, standing facing right, offering oblations at an altar with the r hand, while his l hand rests on the hilt of the sword hanging below the waist. There is the Br letter *Ku* under a crescent beside the sword. The circular ld reads *Gāmavajitya sucharitaiḥ Kumāragupto divaṁ jayati*. The rev bears the figure of *Lakshmī seated on a lotus, with a *pāśa* in her r hand, and a stalked lotus in the left. The rev ld is *Śrī-Kumāraguptaḥ* (Ashvini Agrawal 1989; Allan 1914; Altekar 1957; R D Banerji 1933; S R Goyal 2005; P L Gupta 1998; Smith 1972; Thaplyal, forthcoming).

Kumāragupta I : Swordsman type

Symbol. It is a 'subsidiary *type'. It might be an attribute of the chief type, like the *eagle of *Zeus, or the *bull of *Śiva. Alternatively, it might be independent of the chief type, and serve to identify the issuer, mint, etc (Hill 1909).

T

Tagara. City coins. C S Gupta reads the ld on a coin, which was attributed to the *Rājanyas by earlier scholars, as *Tagara*. He takes it as a coin of the city, Tagara, modern Ter in Osmanabad district (C S Gupta 1971; Bela Lahiri 1974; Bela Lahiri 1976; J P Singh 1971).

Takshaśilā

Takshaśilā. City coins. A large number of uninscribed coins are reported from Takshaśilā, and these have been divided by Allan into seven classes. Class I consists of square coins, bearing stamp on one side only. The *crescent-on-hill symbol is common to all the coins of this class, sometimes accompanied by other symbols, like *tree-in-railing, *undulating line, *svastika*, taurine symbol, etc. One variety of this class has a human figure, perhaps female, in a worshipful attitude. The coins of Class II are similar in fabric to those of Class I, and have been further divided into two groups, each with several varieties. The first group has an *elephant, usually with a crescent-on-hill, on one side, and a *lion, usually with a crescent-on-hill and *svastika*, on the other. The second group is similar to the first, but a *horse replaces the lion. One variety of Class III consists of square cast coins, with a device, identified as 'a flowering plant in railing', with a crescent-on-hill on either side of it, on the obv, and a crescent-on-hill and a hollow cross on the rev. The rest of the varieties in this class are die-struck. The second variety has a grotesque head, called rākshasa by Cunningham, and a 'fish standard' in railing, on the obv, and a 'flowering plant in railing' on the rev. The other varieties have various symbols, like the crescent-on-hill, hollow cross, *svastika*, etc, on one side, or both the sides. Class IV comprises a large number of coins, exhibiting great variety, bearing various symbols, of which the crescent-on-hill, and *svastika* are common to all. On the obv of one variety found at Sirkap, an elephant with symbols is seen on the obv. The coins of Class V are connected to those of Class IV by the crescent-on-hill and the hollow cross. The obv of the various varieties has an elephant, lion, or bull, often accompanied by symbols. Some varieties have a bull on the obv, and a lion on the rev. Class VI consists of some rare coins. One variety is represented by a single gold coin, found by Cunningham at Taxila. It has a bull on the obv, and an elaborate symbol on the rev. Another variety, represented by a copper coin, has a tree-in-railing, *svastika*, and taurine symbol on the obv, and a symbol, comprising of a pellet surrounded by four crescents, on the rev. The obv of Class VII has a 'realistic' tree-in-railing, with a crescent-on-hill on the left and a *svastika* on the right; the rev is blank. All these uninscribed coins from Takshaśilā have been regarded as city coin by some scholars. Inscribed coins from Takshaśilā are believed to be guild coins [*Takshaśilā. Guild coins] (Allan 1936; Bopearachchi and Pieper 1998; Cunningham 1971b; Bela Lahiri 1974; Mitchiner 1975-1976).

Takshaśilā. Guild coins. *Takshaśilā, the capital of eastern Gandhāra, is represented by modern Shahji ki Dheri near Rawalpindi, with its three mounds—Bhir, Sirkap, and Sirsukh, representing three different cities in that sequence. Of the large variety of coins found there, some are guild (*negama*) coins. They are of three classes—(i) the *negama*, (ii) the *paṁchanekame*, and (iii) the *hirañasame* coins. The *negama* coins, belonging to Class I, are datable to the second century BC. They are oblong, die-struck pieces, having incuse, and are of five varieties : (a) Br ld *neġama* on the obv, and *Rā*(*Tā*)*limata* on the rev; (b) *Negama* in Br on the obv, *Dojaka*, either in Br or Kh on the rev; with the Kh ld a steelyard; (c) Ld *negama* on the obv, and *Atakatakā* on the rev, both in Br; (d) Ld *negama* and a steelyard on the obv, the rev ld being illegible, with only ...*ra-ma* clearly visible; and (e) Ld *Kaḍare-nekame* in Kh on the obv, female (deity) on the rev. The coins of Class II are cast, square in shape, and show on the obv, a sixteen-spoked wheel, with a *'hill' symbol above, and on the rev, a *svastika* between two *nandipadas*, and the Kh ld *Paṁchanekame*, that is joint issue of five *negamas*, may be the five ones referred to under Class I; alternatively, the ld might refer to a *nigama* called *paṁchanigama*. Class III coins are square and die-struck, and bear

Takshaśilā :
Paṁchanekame coin

on the obv, *elephant, palm tree, and hill symbol surmounted by a crescent, above a hollow cross, and a *horse; the rev bears the Kh ld *Hirañasame*, or *Dotana*, or *Dośanasa*, or *Dosadasa*. A subvariety of this type shows a plant, and the ld *hirañasame* on the obv, and a star over a 'hill' on the rev (which type, with slight modification, was copied by the *Indo-Greek ruler, *Agathokles). The *negama* coins do not show uniformity in fabric, devices, and legends. Jai Prakash is of the view that the *negama* coins are quite few, and the devices on them are not in conformity with those met with on the uninscribed coins from the site, and, therefore, they cannot be taken as regular coins, and should be considered as some sort of identity tokens. The *negama* (= Skt, *naigamaḥ*) coins were issued by trade guilds. Allan thought that *Rālimata*, *Dojaka*, *Atakatakā*, were names of the districts, whose local authorities issued coins with coordination from the central authority. These have been taken as names of 'mofussil town as distinguished from the capital city' by some. But Cunningham, Bühler, and many others take them to be the issues of guilds (without any control of the state authority). Rapson takes them as issues of the heads of guilds (Bopearachchi and Pieper 1998; J P Singh 1971; Thaplyal 1996).

Talent. It was the heaviest of all ancient weight systems. In the Babylonian and Greek systems, it was equivalent to 60 **minae* or 3,000 **staters*. A *talent* of gold was generally equivalent to 6,000 *drachms*, the weight standards varying widely with time and place (Hill 1906; Junge 1984).

***Tālimata/Rālimata* (?)**. Guild. *Takshaśilā. Guild coins.

Tanda hoard. This hoard of 25 *Imperial Gupta gold coins was found in 1885 in Tanda, district Faizabad (Uttar Pradesh). The contents of this hoard have not been carefully recorded. The rulers represented in this hoard are *Chandragupta I, *Samudragupta, and *Kācha (Allan 1914; Altekar 1957).

Taraṇaḍāsa. Śaka satrap. Kown only from a single coin in the Richard Burn collection on which he is described as a **kshatrapa* and son of a **mahākshatrapa*, he appears to belong to the family of *Rañjuvula, and may have been a son of *Śoḍāsha. He ruled from *Mathurā. The obv of the coin has the figure of *Lakshmī standing holding a lotus, a tree beside her, and the Br ld. The rev has the device of *Gajalakshmī. According to some scholars, the name of the *kshatrapa* on the coin may even be Bharaṇaḍāsa, but Allan prefers the reading *Toraṇaḍāsa* (Allan 1936; Sircar 1980b).

Taurine. Symbol. Formed by a circle surmounted by a crescent, some scholars regard it as a combined symbol of the sun and the moon, while others see in it the head of a bull represented by the circle, topped by the horns in the shape of a crescent; in fact, it gets its name from *tauros*, the Greek for bull. There is a suggestion that this symbol was also associated with the fertility cult, the suggestion being reinforced by the occurrence of a taurine in front of a female figure, identified as a goddess, on at least three of Allan's classes of the coins of *Ujjayinī. On certain coins from Ujjayinī, as also on some *Śibi coins, the taurine is seen attached to the end of each arm of a **svastika*. The taurine symbol was quite commonly used on ancient Indian coins, often in combination with other symbols. It may be seen on the silver *punch marked coins, the uninscribed cast copper coins, on the coins of *Eran, *Kauśāmbī, *Kāḍa, *Mathurā, *Taxila, and Ujjayinī, and also on the coins of *Bhānumitra of *Pañchāla (Allan 1936; Chakrabortty 1931; Bhaskar Chattopadhyay 1977; Cunningham 1971b; K K Dasgupta 1974; Handa 2007a; Bela Lahiri 1974; Rajgor 2001; Savita Sharma 1990).

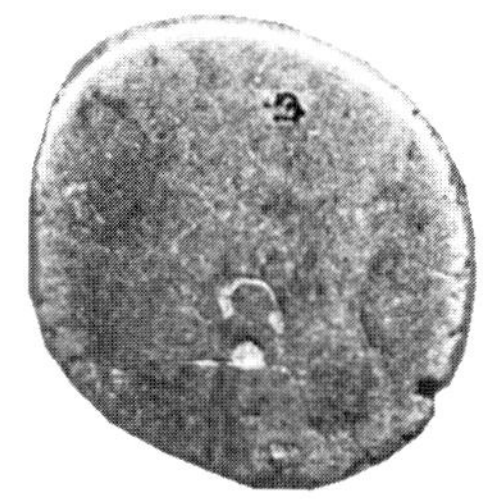

Punch marked coin

Punch marked coin

Taxila. *Takshaśilā.

Tekri Debra hoard. This hoard of 40 *Imperial Gupta gold coins was found in 1912 at Tekri Debra, district Mirzapur (Uttar Pradesh). It is also known as the Mirzapur hoard. The rulers represented in this hoard are *Samudragupta, *Chandragupta II, and *Kumāragupta I (Altekar 1957).

Telephos. *Indo-Greek k; son of *Antialkidas; first half of the first century BC. He is believed to have ruled over Gandhāra and Takshaśilā in the period between the end of the reign of *Apollodotos, and its occupation by *Maues; one coin even comes from the Hazara region. Tarn regards him as a usurper and even doubts if he was at all a Greek. There is no evidence to support Tarn's claim that he ruled

Telephos

over Kapiśā or the Kabul valley. Telephos issued both silver and copper coins, all struck on the Indian standard. All the coins are die-struck pieces. The silver coins are round in shape, while the copper ones are square in shape. The obv of the silver type has a snake-legged *yaksha standing to the front, while the rev has *Helios (?), bearing a long sceptre in his r hand, standing beside a female figure 'wrapped in mantle', identified as *Selene by Osmund Bopearachchi. The obv of all the copper coins has the figure of enthroned *Zeus, bearing a long sceptre in his l hand, while the r hand is extended. The rev of one type has a naked male figure squatting to the r, perhaps on a *lotus, while that of the other has a berobed and armed male figure walking to the r, with a 'tiny mountain' shown beside him. All the coins of Telephos bear the Gr ld on the obv, and the Pkt ld, written in the Kh script, on the rev. Besides the title of **basileus*, Telephos assumed the epithet **euergetes* on his coins. These are rendered into Pkt as **maharaja* and **kalanakrama*, respectively. The Pkt form of the name of the ruler, as met with on coins, is Teliphasa (Bopearachchi 1993; Bopearachchi and Pieper 1998; Bopearachchi and Rahman 1995; Cunningham 1970; Gardner 1971; A N Lahiri 1965; Marshall 1975; Narain 1957a; Rapson 1987; Senior 2001; Sircar 1980a; Tarn 1980; Whitehead 1914).†

Temple. Symbol. 'Roman art is more at home in depicting architectural objects…' and the 'justifiable pride of the Romans in their buildings is displayed in numerous types of coins'. Among the prominent Roman structures making their appearance on coins, the Capitol and the Temple of Vesta may be seen on the coins of Vespasian; the Forum appears on the coins of Trajan; the Circus Maximus on the coins of Nero; and the famous Coliseum on the coins of Titus. But the depiction of buildings never seems to have become very popular on ancient Indian coins. On the rev of the *Audumbara square copper coins bearing the names of *Śivadāsa, *Rudradāsa, *Dharaghosha, and *Mahādeva, there occurs a two or three storeyed structure, which has been identified as a **stūpa* by Allan, and a 'mote hall or some other public building' by K P Jayaswal. Cunningham regards it as a 'pyramidal temple', and this is supported by scholars like Coomaraswamy and S V Sohoni, the latter also proposing to identify the structure as a Śaiva shrine due to the presence of the *triśūla-paraśu* beside it. This structure is regarded as one of the earliest representations of a Hindu shrine on coins. When various deities are represented on their anthropomorphic form on the coins of the *Pañchāla series, the divine figure is usually shown standing on a low pedestal surrounded by a railing. On the coins of the *Kushāṇa ruler, *Huvishka, representations of the various manifestations of *Kārttikeya are shown within simple architectural structures formed of a canopy supported on two upright columns. Recently, Devendra Handa has tried to identify various symbols and structures on *Ujjayinī, *Trigarta, and *Yaudheya coins, as temples dedicated to various deities, whose identity he has sought to determine on the basis of the accompanying symbols (Allan 1936; Banerjea 2002; Chakrabortty 1931; C C Chamberlain 1960; Coomaraswamy 1927; Cunningham 1971a; Cunningham 1971b; K K Dasgupta 1974; Gardner 1971; Handa 2007a; Handa 2007b; S V Sohoni 1942; Whitehead 1914).

Audumbara : Dharaghosha

Tewar hoard. This hoard of over 200 silver coins of the *Kārddamaka Kshatrapas was discovered in 1989-1990, at Tewar in the Jabalpur district of Madhya Pradesh. The rulers represented in the hoard include *Rudrasena I, *Dāmasena, *Yaśodāman I, *Vijayasena, *Dāmajadaśrī III, *Rudrasena II, *Viśvasiṁha, *Bhartṛidāman, *Viśvasena, *Rudrasiṁha II, *Yaśodāman II, *Rudrasena III, and Siṁhasena (Jha and Rajgor 1994).

Theophilos. *Indo-Greek k; scion of the family of *Euthydemos I, and son of *Lysias (?); latter half of the second century BC or early first century BC. Although some of his coins are reported from Rawalpindi and Sialkot, the *provenance* of most of his coins is difficult to establish. Narain suggests that he did not immediately succeed his father, but rebelled and set up an independent kingdom in some regions north of the Hindukush. Shortly afterwards, he seems to have been overthrown by *Amyntas. Theophilos issued coins in silver and copper. One silver type is struck on the Attic standard, while the rest of the silver types, and all the copper types, are struck on the Indian standard. All the coins are die-struck pieces. The silver coins are round in shape, while the copper ones are square in shape. The obv of all the silver coins has the diademed bust of the king to the r. The rev of the silver coins struck on the Attic standard has helmeted *Athena, seated and holding spear and shield in her l hand, and *Nike on her extended r hand. The silver coins struck on the Indian standard bear the figure of standing Herakles, holding his club and lion's skin; on one type, he is shown crowning himself with his r hand. The obv of the copper coins bears the bust of Herakles, sometimes draped in lion's skin, to the r. The rev of one copper type has a **cornucopiae*, while that of the other type has the *club, the thick end of which is shown up. The silver coins based on the Attic standard have the Gr ld, on the rev. But all the coins struck on the Indian standard have the Gr ld on the obv, and the Pkt ld, written in the Kh script, on the rev. Besides the title of **basileus*, Theophilos assumed the epithet *autokratoros* on his coins struck on the Attic standard, and **dikaios* on his coins struck on the Indian standard. On the coins struck on the Indian standard, *basileus* and *dikaios* are rendered into Pkt as **maharaja* and **dhramika*, respectively. The Pkt from of the name of the ruler, as met with on coins, is Theüphila (Bopearachchi 1993; Bopearachchi and Pieper 1998; Bopearachchi and Rahman 1995; Cunningham 1970; Gardner 1971; A N Lahiri 1965; Marshall 1975; Narain 1957a; Rapson 1987; Senior 2001; Sircar 1980a; Tarn 1980; Whitehead 1914).†

Theos. Title. Meaning 'god', this title was adopted by *Antimachos I. *Euthydemos I was given this title on the commemorative coins issued by Antimachos I and *Agathokles, apparently after his death. Among the *Śaka-Pahlavas, this title was used on some of his coins by *Gondopharnes. Outside of India, the title was adopted by the Seleukid ruler, Antiochos IV, and by Arsakes of Parthia (Cunningham 1970; Gardner 1878; Gardner 1971; A N Lahiri 1965; Marshall 1975; Narain 1957a; Senior 2001; Tarn 1980; Whitehead 1914; Wroth 1903).

Theotropos. Title. This title was first adopted by the *Indo-Greek queen-regent, *Agathokleia, and later, by the *Śaka-Pahlava queen-regent, *Machene. The real significance of the epithet has not yet been satisfactorily explained. In the context of Agathokleia, Prinsep took it to mean 'god-nourisher' in allusion to her royal offspring, evidently confusing *tropos* for *trophos*. Wilson translated it as 'servant of god'. Lassen, on the authority of Heliodoros, gave its meaning as 'god-like, divine', and this has been accepted by most of the later scholars. Rapson sees in this title a probable reference to her position as queen-regent. The use of this title by another queen-regent, Machene, seems to support Rapson (Cunningham 1970; Gardner 1971; A N Lahiri 1965; Marshall 1975; Narain 1957a; Prinsep 1858; Rapson 1906; Prashant Srivastava 1996a; Whitehead 1950; Wilson 1971).

Thrason. *Indo-Greek k. He is known from a single coin in a hoard of the coins of *Menander I. The portrait on this coin shows the king as 'a young boy'. The coin bears a strong resemblance to the issues of Menander. On this basis, R C Senior regards him as another son of Menander, besides *Strato I and *Apollodotos, and places him *c* 130 BC (Senior 2001; Senior and MacDonald 1998).

Ṭhujana. *Hūṇa chief. He is known from a coin, and is sought to be identified with Tuñjina II mentioned by Kalhaṇa, who says that he also had two other names—Śreshṭhasena and Pravarasena. There is also a suggestion that he may be identical with *Tigin (Biswas 1973).

Thunderbolt. Symbol. In Greek mythology, it is the attribute of *Zeus, and helped the gods in attaining a decisive victory over the Titans. It was given to Zeus by the Kyklopes, the three sons of *Ouranos. Besides being shown in the hands of deities like Zeus and *Athena, the thunderbolt also occurs on coins as an independent device. On the coins of the *Indo-Greek rulers, *Demetrios I and *Antimachos I, the winged thunderbolt seems to be associated with Zeus. The same cannot be said when the weapon, together with the discus and arrow, makes it appearance on the obv of the coins of the *Kshaharāta *Kshatrapa*, *Bhūmaka, and the rev of the coins of *Nahapāna. A *vajra* like symbol is seen over the back of the *bull on the rev of some *Rājanya coins. In Indian mythology, this weapon, *vajra*, is associated with *Indra, and it played a decisive role in the conflict between the devas and the asuras. It is believed to have been fashioned by Uśanas or Tvashṭṛi (Banerjea 2002; Bopearachchi 1993; Bopearachchi and Pieper 1998; Bopearachchi and Rahman 1995; Cunningham 1970; Cunningham 1971a; K K Dasgupta 1974; Gardner 1971; Graves 1955; Jenkins and Narain 1957; Kerenyi 1951; A N Lahiri 1965; Marshall 1975; Macdonell 1897; Rao 1985;

Diodotos

Nahapāna

Rapson 1975; Rose 1958; Senior 2001; Prashant Srivastava 2007f; Whitehead 1914).

Tiger. Symbol. Carnivoros beasts have been associated with the female procreative principle since primitive times; the association of the tiger with the mother goddess seems to be hinted at on an Harappan seal, where the posterior part of a female figure is shown attached to the body of a tiger. Thus, it is quite likely that when the tiger appears on the *punch marked coins, it theriomorphically represents the mother goddess. But on the *Tiger-slayer type of coins of the *Imperial Guptas, the tiger may be seen as the prey of the imperial hunter (Allan 1914; Allan 1936; Altekar 1957; Bhaskar Chattopadhyay 1977; Neumann 1955; Pathak 1986; Pathak 1988-1989; Prashant Srivastava 2001; Prashant Srivastava 2004a).†

Samudragupta : Tiger-slayer type

Kumāragupta I : Tiger-slayer type

Tiger-slayer type. Gold. First introduced by *Samudragupta, perhaps to commemorate his victory of the Ganga valley, the Tiger-slayer type has the king shooting at a tiger with a bow, and, at the same time, trampling upon the beast, on the obv. Behind the tiger is a crescent standard. The circular ld reads *Vyāghraparākramaḥ*. The rev has the goddess, *Gaṅgā, standing on a **makara*, with a lotus bloom in her l hand; her r hand is outstretched and empty. On the left is a filleted crescent standard. The ld on the rev is *Vyāghraparākramaḥ* on some specimens, and *Rājā Samudraguptaḥ* on others. V S Pathak is, however, of the view that this type of Samudragupta symbolizes the taming of the later Kushāṇas, who are mentioned in the Allahabad pillar inscription as the *daivaputrashāhishāhānushāhi*. This type was continued by *Kumāragupta I, and his coins of this type are quite well executed. The obv is similar to that of the same type of Samudragupta. On some specimens, there is the Br letter *Ku* in the field. The circular ld reads *Śrīmāṁ-vyāghrabalaparākramaḥ*. The rev has the figure of Gaṅgā, standing on a *makara*, and feeding a *peacock by her r hand. Her l hand holds a stalked lotus. The rev ld is *Kumāragupto'dhirājā* (Ashvini Agrawal 1989; Allan 1914; Altekar 1957; R D Banerji 1933; S R Goyal 2005; P L Gupta 1998; V S Pathak 1988-1989; Smith 1972; Prashant Srivastava 1996a; Prashant Srivastava 2004a; Thaplyal, forthcoming).

Tigin. *Hūṇa chief. He ruled over the Khurasan region, and issued coins mentioning Zābulistān (the land of the Zābulas or Hūṇas). These coins have, on the obv, the head of the king wearing a tiara surmounted by a tiger's head and two tridents, and on the rev, a figure with a 'fire-nimbus'. This rev figure is variously identified as representing the Sun god of Multan, or the *Bodhisattva* Maitreya, or Khurāsān Zarrah (the Glory of Khurāsān), and is believed to have been borrowed from the later Sassanian coins. These coins of Tigin bear, on the obv, a long circular ld in the Śāradā script, probably reading *Śrī Hitavīra Khurāsān Parameśvara Śrī Shāhi Tiginadeva kāritam*, and meaning '[the coin was] struck by Śrī Shāhi Tiginadeva, the lord of Khurāsān, who is called Hitavīra, (and) whose valour lies in doing good to others'. Attempts have been made to identify Tigin with *Lae-lih. Originally, *tigin* was a Turkish title used by provincial governors. But the coin ld above leaves little doubt that it is here used as a proper name (Biswas 1973; Cunningham 1962; P L Gupta 2004).

Tirthahalli hoard. This hoard of 61 silver coins was discovered from the site in the Shimoga district of Karnataka in 1949-1950. Besides two coins of *Īśvaradatta, and two coins which are uncertain, all the coins in the hoard belong to the *Kārddamaka Kshatrapas, like *Dāmasena, *Vīradāman, *Vijayasena, son of Dāmasena (whose name is not clear), *Rudrasena II, *Viśvasiṁha, *Bhartṛidāman, son of *Rudrasena II (whose name is not clear), *Viśvasena, *Rudrasiṁha II, and *Yaśodāman II (P L Gupta 1980; Jha and Rajgor 1994).

Topi hoard. This hoard of 21 *Kushāṇa gold coins was found in 1987, in the village Topi, 8 km west of the Tarbella dam on the river Indus, and 40 km northwest of Taxila. The rulers represented in the hoard include *Huvishka and *Vāsudeva I (Craig A Burns and Shafqat Mirza 1990).

Toramāṇa. *Hūṇa (?) chief; early sixth century AD. He seems to have advanced from his base, probably in Gandhāra, and overran a large part of western and northern India. The *provenance* of his coins testifies to his rule over parts of Uttar Pradesh, Rajasthan, Punjab, Kashmir, and as far south as Eran (Madhya Pradesh). According to the Kura inscription, he took the title of *Shāhi Jaūvla*. The Jaina text,

Toramāṇa

Kuvalayamālā (778 AD) informs us that he adopted Jainism, and lived at Pavvaiyā on the banks of the river Chandrabhāgā (Chenab) in Punjab. But, after the initial successes, he seems to have been defeated by the Aulikara chief, Prakāśadharman, as per the evidence of the Risthal inscription, and also apparently by *Bhānugupta, and forced to fall back to the west of the river Indus. A S Altekar suggests that Toramāṇa imitated the Sassanian type of coinage in Afghanistan, *Kushāṇa type in Kashmir, and the *Imperial Gupta type in the rest of his Indian territories. His silver coins fall into three classes. Class I has a horseman to the r, with **chakra* and **śaṅkha* or vase in field, and the Br ld *Sāhi Jabula* or *Shāhi Janabula* on the obv; the rev bears a *fire altar with supporters. Class II has the bust of the Sassanian type, with a club in front, and the ld *Śāhi Jabūvlaḥ* or *Jabula* on the obv; the rev is the same as that of Class I. Class III has the king's head to the l on the obv; the rev bears a fan-tailed *peacock, and the ld *Vijitāvaniravanipati Śrī-Toramāṇa*. Some coins of Class III also bear the date of issue, ascribable perhaps to a White Hūṇa era. The copper coins of Toramāṇa, struck in Kashsmir, are similar to the *Kidāra Kushāṇa coins of that region. The obv bears the figure of the standing king, with the Br ld *Śrī-Toramāṇa*. The rev has a crude figure of **Ardochsho* holding *lotus, and the vertical ld *Kidāra*. For the Punjab region and the territory between the Satluj and the Yamuna, Toramāṇa imitated the Sassanian bust type of copper coins. The obv has the bust of the modified Sassanian type to the r, and the latter *bu* (?) in front of the face. The rev bears a *chakra* in the upper field, and the ld *Tora*. Smaller coins of this variety seem to have been issued for eastern Punjab and Rajasthan. But on these coins, sometimes the ld *Zoboä* or *Jabula* replaces *Tora* on the rev. The presence of the (solar ?) wheel on these coins has been taken by some scholars to indicate that Toramāṇa was a sun worshipper (Altekar 1986b; Biswas 1973; Cunningham 1962; Cunningham 1967; R C Majumdar 1988; Sircar 1986; Upendra Thakur 1967a; Upendra Thakur 1967b).[†]

Trakhma. Coin denomination. **Drakhma*, **drachma*, **dramma*.

***Tratara*.** Title. It is the Pkt rendering of **soteros*, and used by *Apollodotos, *Apollophanes, *Diomedes, *Dionysios, *Hermaios, *Hippostratos, *Menander, *Nikias, *Peukolaos, *Polyxenos,

*Strato I, and *Zoilos II. Among the *Śaka-Pahlavas, it was assumed by *Abdagases, and *Gondopharnes. On some coins, *tratara* is spelt *tradara*. Heliodoros, the Greek ambassador sent by *Antialkidas to the court of the King Bhāgabhadra, uses this epithet for the Indian king. It is also used for Jñagaṇa on the *Vṛishṇi coin. The Skt equivalent is *trātā* (Allan 1936; Cunningham 1970; Gardner 1971; A N Lahiri 1965; Marshall 1975; Narain 1957a; Rapson 1987; Sircar 1986; Tarn 1980; Whitehead 1914).

Tree-in-railing. Symbol. The tree, shown within a railing to emphasize its sacred character, as seen on Harappan seals, was a very common ancient Indian coin device. Tree worship in India has a hoary antiquity. The tree is also associated with knowledge. According to Spooner, the tree-in-railing might represent the *bodhi* tree, or the *haoma* tree of the Zoroastrians. But J N Banerjea regards it as the representation of the *sthalavṛiksha* or *chaityavṛiksha* mentioned in the purāṇas and the epics, as abodes of devas, *yakshas, *nāgas, apsarases, bhūtas, etc. It appears on the *punch marked coins, the uninscribed cast coins, as also on the *Audumbara, *Ayodhyā, *Eran, *Kāḍa, *Kanauj, *Kauśāmbī, *Mathurā, *Rājanya, *Taxila, *Ujjayinī, *Uddehika, and other coins. Sometimes a tree may be seen depicted on top of a *hill. It may be mentioned here that in most of the cases of the representation of a tree on ancient Indian coins, it is generally not easy to identify the species, except for the *pipal* tree, which can be identified on the basis of the peculiar shape of its leaves; it has been suggested that the tree on the Audumbara coins may be *udumbara*, only on the basis of the name of the tribe. A symbol appearing on some *Kuṇinda and *Yaudheya coins is regarded as a conventional tree-in-railing by some scholars, but others, like J N Banerjea, V S Agrawala, and K K Dasgupta, identify as *indradhvajasaṁpat* (V S Agrawala 1970; Allan 1936; Banerjea 2002; Chakrabortty 1931; Bhaskar Chattopadhyay 1977; Cunningham 1971b; K K Dasgupta 1974; Handa 2007a; Handa 2007b; Bela Lahiri 1974; Rajgor 2001; Savita Sharma 1990).

Uninscribed cast coin

Uninscribed cast coin

Kuṇinda

Kauśāmbī

Triangular-headed symbol. The exact significance of this symbol is not known; it has been referred to as 'life symbol', while Prinsep labels it as *jayadhvaja*. It appears, often in combination with other symbols, on the silver *punch marked coins, the uninscribed cast

Uninscribed cast coin

copper coins, and *Kauśāmbī, *Eran, *Almora, *Ayodhyā, *Kanauj, *Taxila, *Ujjayinī, *Kulūta, *Audumbara, *Kuṇinda, and *Pañchāla coins (Allan 1936; Chakrabortty 1931; Cunningham 1971b; K K Dasgupta 1974; Handa 2007a; Bela Lahiri 1974; Rajgor 2001).

Trident. Symbol. **Triśūla*.

Trigarta. Tribe. The Trigartas are referred to as an *āyudhajīvī saṁgha* in the *Ashṭādhyāyī* of Pāṇini, which text also associates the Bhārgāyaṇa *gotra* with this tribe. In the *Gaṇapāṭha*, they are referred to, along with the *Yaudheyas and other tribes, and in the *Mahābhārata*, with the Yaudheyas, *Śibis, *Rājanyas, etc. *Trigarta-shashṭha* in Pāṇini is explained by *Kāśikā* as a confederacy of six members—(i) Kauṇoparatha, (ii) Dāṇḍaki, (iii) Kraushṭaki, (iv) Jālamāni, (v) Brāhmagupta, and (vi) Jānaki. V S Agrawala identifies Brāhmagupta with Bharmor (Chamba), and points out that, in the *Mahābhārata*, members of Jānaki confederacy are mentioned as helpmates of Trigarta king, Suśarman. The *Bṛihatsaṁhitā* locates the Trigartas, along with the *Kulūtas and the Chīnas, in the northern region, and a puranic text, in the Himalayan region. The tribe also finds mention in various purāṇas, like the *Vishṇupurāṇa*, *Matsyapurāṇa*, *Vāyupurāṇa*, *Vāmanapurāṇa*, etc, as also in such texts as the *Chāndravyākaraṇa*, the *Daśakumāracharita* of Daṇḍin, the *Rājataraṅgiṇī* of Kalhaṇa, the *Sarasvatīkaṇṭhābharaṇa*, and the *Gaṇaratnamahodadhi*. A Trigarta king is mentioned in the Chamba copperplate inscription of 1050 AD. The word *trigarta* means 'three pits', and it has been suggested that the tribe occupied three valleys—those of the rivers Ravi, Beas, and Sutlej. Hiuen-tsang, and the *Vaijayantī* and the *Abhidhānachintāmaṇi*, take Trigarta as corresponding to Jālandhara, and Cunningham places the Trigarta region between Kangra and Jalandhar, to the south of Chamba. A square copper coin, weighing 43 grains, shows a four-tiered structure and traces of a Kh ld on the obv, and the branch of a tree, a **nandipada*, and another symbol on the rev with the Br ld *Trakata-janapadasa* (= Skt, *Trigarta-janapadasya*, ie 'of the territory of the Trigartas') in second or first century BC characters. The four-tiered structure on the obv of the coin is described by Allan as a '*stūpa*'. But P L Gupta feels that it might even be a secular building, 'a multi-storeyed residence or a palace'. Devendra Handa, after an examination of the coin in the collection of the British Museum, London, suggests that the structure is three-tiered and has a pillared post in front, surmounted by a bird, probably a cock. As the cock is one of the birds associated with *Kārttikeya, he proposes to identify the structure as a Brahmanical temple dedicated to that deity, who might have been the patron deity of the warlike Trigartas (V S Agrawala 1969; Allan 1936; Chakrabortty 1931; Cunningham 1971b; K K Dasgupta 1974; P L Gupta 1988; Handa 2007a; Jayaswal 1988; Marshall 1975; Mitchiner 1975-1976; Smith 1972).

Triṁśatika. Coin denomination. The **Ashṭādhyāyī* refers to this coin, which is believed to be a silver coin weighing 30 *māshas*. This coin denomination is known only from this text (V S Agrawala 1953).

Tripod lebes. Symbol. It was the seat, from which Pythia proclaimed oracles. Once *Herakles stole the tripod. This led to a dispute between him and *Apollo, which was settled by their father, *Zeus, and Herakles returned the *tripod* to Apollo. This symbol of Apollo, as an independent device, appears, usually on the rev, of the coins of several *Indo-Greek rulers, like *Euthydemos II, *Apollodotos, *Menander, *Strato I, *Hippostratos, *Zoilos, and others. Of these, Apollodotos, Hippostratos, and Strato I depicted on their coins, a peculiar type of *tripod lebes*, with pronounced foot. And it was this type of *tripod lebes* that was adopted on some of his coins by the *Śaka-Pahlava ruler, *Maues (Bopearachchi 1993; Bopearachchi and Pieper 1998; Bopearachchi and Rahman 1995; Cunningham 1970; Cunningham 1971a; Gardner 1971; Graves 1955; Jenkins and Narain 1957; Kerenyi 1951; A N Lahiri 1965; Marshall 1975; Rose 1958; Senior 2001; Whitehead 1914).†

Apollodotos

Zoilos II

Tripurī. City coins. A few coins from Tripurī (Tewar, near Jabalpur, Madhya Pradesh) bear, on the obv, a hollow cross above a crescent-topped *hill, and the ld *Tipuri*, written from the bottom upwards, in the third or second century BC Br characters. One coin is reported to have been found in the deposit, which has been assigned to the third century BC (Bela Lahiri 1974; Bela Lahiri 1976; A M Shastri 1971; J P Singh 1971).

Triratna. Symbol. **Nandipada.*

Triskeles. Symbol. It is believed to be a solar symbol, and to represent the motion of the sun, like the **svastika* and the cross. The symbol makes its appearance on the *punch marked coins and some uninscribed cast copper coins (Allan 1936; Chakrabortty 1931; Rajgor 2001; Savita Sharma 1990).

Triśūla. Symbol. This characteristic attribute of *Śiva was quite commonly depicted on ancient Indian coins. It is seen represented on some *punch marked coins. The device on the rev of a copper coin, doubtfully ascribed to Taxila, has been described by Allan as a tree flanked by a standing figure on either side. But J N Banerjea sees here a *triśūla* with a worshipper on either side. A *triśūla* within railing seems to occur on the rev of some uninscribed cast copper coins. *Triśūla*, sometimes with a *paraśu*, appears along with other symbols, on the rev of the *Audumbara coins bearing the names of *Śivadāsa, *Rudradāsa, *Mahādeva, *Dharaghosha, and *Rudravarman. The weapon may also be seen on the rev of certain *Mālava and *Vemaki coins. A *triśūla* with a *bull, appears on the obv of the coins of *Dhanadeva and *Jeṭhamitra of *Kauśāmbī. On the rev of the coins of the *Pañchāla ruler, Rudragupta, may be seen a *triśūla* flanked by two pillars. A 'double-trident' is seen on some other specimens of this ruler. A *triśūla* within railing appears on the rev of the coins of another Pañchāla ruler, Dhruvamitra. According to Cunningham, this *triśūla*, too, is associated with Śiva, who has Dhruva as one of his names. But Allan regards it as an emblem of the pole star (Dhruva). The *Kushāṇa ruler, *V'ima Kadphises, is known to be a devotee of Śiva, and it is not surprising that the *triśūla-paraśu* of that deity appears on the rev of some of his coins. A *triśūla* over the altar may also be seen on some coins of *Vāsudeva I. A trident also finds representation on the rev of some copper coins of the *Indo-Greek ruler, *Demetrios, but it is difficult to regard it as a Śaiva emblem there; on these coins, it is most probably depicted as an attribute of *Poseidon. Often on coins, the trident is seen in the hand of the anthropomorphic figure of both Śiva and Poseidon (Allan 1936; Banerjea 2002; Chakrabortty 1931; Bhaskar Chattopadhyay 1977; Cunningham 1971b; K K Dasgupta

1974; Graves 1955; Handa 2007a; Kerenyi 1951; Rose 1958; Nidhi Srivastava 1994; Rao 1985).

Triton. Minor Greek sea god. He was a son of *Poseidon and *Amphitrite, and a brother of Rhodos. He might have been adopted in Greek mythology from Minoan or Anatolian belief. He is a merman, human from the waist up, and fish-shaped from the waist down. Triton is described as very dangerous under provocation. In art, he is often shown as blowing a conch shell. Depictions of Triton are quite rare on ancient Indian coins. On the obv of a square copper type of *Hippostratos, Triton is shown standing and holding a dolphin and rudder. On the rev of some coins issued by *Maues, Amphitrite's r hand is extended towards a small figure whose posterior half resembles that of a fish, and this figure might be identified as Triton, the son of Amphitrite and Poseidon appearing, respectively, on the rev and obv of these coins (Bopearachchi 1993; Bopearachchi and Pieper 1998; Bopearachchi and Rahman 1995; Bhaskar Chattopadhyay 1977; Cunningham 1971a; Gardner 1971; Graves 1955; Kerenyi 1951; Marshall 1975; Rose 1958; Prashant Srivastava 2007c; Whitehead 1914).[†]

Tulasī-vṛindāvana. Symbol. The *Imperial Guptas borrowed the device of *king sacrificing at an altar from *Kushāṇa coins, but gradual attempt at Indianization of the device is seen in that the oblations being offiered by the king on the obv of some coins of *Samudragupta clearly resemble the traditional Indian rounded sacrificial offering, the *puroḍāśa*. Similarly, the altar sometimes looks like 'a flower pot with a plant'; and in view of the Vaishṇava leanings of the Imperial Guptas, it has been suggested that it might represent a *tulasī-vṛindāvana*, *tulasī* being a plant sacred to the worshippers of *Vishṇu. Such a depiction is seen, not only on the gold coins, like the *Standard type of Samudragupta, but also on some silver coins of *Skandagupta (Altekar 1957).

Skandagupta : *Madhyadeśa* type

Tyche. Greek goddess of 'fortune'. She was one of the 41 daughters that Tethys bore to Okeanos, of whom Styx was the mightiest. The name Tyche means 'what may hap', or 'chance'. Tyche has the power to decide the fortune of men, but is 'altogether irresponsible in her awards'. On the rev of a coin type of the *Śaka-Pahlava ruler, *Orthagnes, a female figure is shown standing behind the enthroned king and crowning him. This female figure has been identified as Tyche, though with doubt. Had the figure been winged, it would definitely have been identied as *Nike. For, there does not appear to be any justification for showing a daughter of Tethys and Okeanos crowning a king. It may be pointed out that on a coin of *Gondopharnes, Nike is shown crowning the enthroned king from behind the throne. There, too, the goddess is wingless, and it appears that the female figure on the coin of Orthagnes also should be identified as Nike, and not as Tyche. Tyche, however, appears on two types of *Maues. On the rev of one type, she stands facing front. She is diademed, wears a turreted crown, and holds a patera containing offerings in her r hand, while her l hand rests on a wheel. On the rev of the other type, she is again shown standing facing front, and wearing a turreted crown. But here, she holds a long sceptre in her l hand, while with her r hand she holds out her veil (Cunningham 1971a; Gardner 1971; Graves 1955; Kerenyi 1951; Rose 1958; Prashant Srivastava 2007c; Whitehead 1914).[†]

Type. In the narrower sense, it is 'the essential portion of the design (as distinct from adjunct, inscription, border, etc), which is the distinguishing mark of the issuing authority', and guarantees the quantity and quality of the metal content of the coin. However, in the course of time, it has come to 'imply a distinguishing device more or less artistic in character' (C J Brown 1999; Hill 1909).

Tyrannountos. Title. This title, assumed by *Heraos among the *Kushāṇa rulers, is believed to mean 'tyrant' or 'under the rule of' (Cunningham 1971a; Gardner 1971; Rosenfield 1967; Whitehead 1914).

U

Uddehika. Tribe. The *Bṛihatsaṁhitā* locates the Uddehikas in northern India, and mentions them along with such other tribes as the Gaurgrīvas, Aśvatthas, Pāṇḍus, Guḍas, and the Pañchālas. Of these, the Pāṇḍus, who were, perhaps, identical with the Pandae of Ptolemy, may be located in Thaneshwar, while the Pañchālas occupied the Rohilkhand region. The Uddehikas, hence, might have lived in some region, 'not far from these tribes'. They are mentioned, together with the Pāṇḍus, Guḍas and the Madhyamikās, in the *Samāsasaṁhitā*. Alberuni places them near Bazana, which is identified variously with Narayanpur (former Alwar state), Naraina, and Bayana (Bharatpur district). Bela Lahiri regards the *madhyadeśa* as their area. Some others consider Bari Udai in the Gangasagar *tehsil* (old Jaipur state) as the old capital of the Uddehikas. Their territory would have comprised Rairh (Jaipur district, where their coins have been found), together with Bari Udai and the adjoining regions. Besides Uddehika coins, Rairh has yielded coins bearing the ld *Sudavapa*, which can be equated with Udvapa of *Kāśikā* as a place name, though some take it as a family name. There is similarity of fabric and palaeography between Uddehika and *Sudavapa* coins, and the name *Sūryamitra is common to both. K K Dasgupta takes *Sudavapa* as a city of the Uddehikas. The *Sudavapa* coins have been included in the Uddehika series by most of the scholars, although Devendra Handa does not accept this attribution. The Uddehika coins are in copper, and manufactured by the die-striking method. Palaeographically, they can be ascribed to the second or first century BC, though Rapson placed them in the third century BC. The weight of these coins ranges between 35.5 and 80 grains. The names of the chiefs—Sūryamitra and *Dhruvamitra—are mentioned without any titles. The Uddehika coins are divided into three classes. Class I has, on the obv, the *Ujjain symbol, two fish within square, *tree-in-railing, and the Br ld *Udehaki*; the rev has tree-in-railing and *bull. The coins of Class II have on the obv, the tree-in-railing and two fish within a square, and the legends *Udehaki* and *Suyamitasa*; the rev has *elephant, bull, and another symbol countermarked on them. Class III is subdivided onto two varieties : the coins of the first variety have the Ujjain symbol, bull, **jayadhvaja*, and **śrīvatsa*, and the legends *Sudavapa* and *Suyamitasa* on the obv, and a river with fish, sun, six-arched hill, and **triśūla* on the rev; the second variety has a *svastika* and Ujjain symbol and the legends *Sudavapa* and *Dhruvamitasa* on the obv, and indistinct symbols on the rev (Allan 1936; Chakrabortty 1931; Cunningham 1971b; K K Dasgupta 1974; Handa 2007a; Jayaswal 1988; Bela Lahiri 1974; Marshall 1975; Mitchiner 1975-1976; Sachau 1887; Smith 1972).

Ujjayinī

Ujjain symbol. Also known as the Mālava symbol, it has the form of a cross with small spheres attached to the ends of the four arms of the cross. It is believed to make its first appearance on the uninscribed cast copper coins, and is commonly used on the local and tribal coins of ancient India, usually in combination with other symbols. It may be seen on the *Ayodhyā, *Eran, *Kanauj, *Kauśāmbī, *Mathurā, *Uddehika, *Yaudheya, and *Karddamaka coins; it occurs invariably on the coins of *Ujjayinī, which fact accounts for the name of this symbol. On the coins of Ujjayinī, the Ujjain symbol often occurs in combination with the anthropomorphic or theriomorphic representation of *Śiva, or with the phallic emblem of that deity in front of a *tree-in-railing. On the basis of this interrelationship, it has been suggested that the Ujjain symbol might have Śaiva affiliations (Allan 1936; Bopearachchi and Pieper 1998; Chakrabortty 1931; Bhaskar Chattopadhyay 1977; K K Dasgupta 1974; Handa 2007a; Bela Lahiri 1974; Rajgor 2001; Rapson 1975; Savita Sharma 1990).

Ujjayinī. City coins. Ujjayinī (modern Ujjain, Madhya Pradesh) was the capital of the *janapada* of Avanti, in the sixth-fifth centuries BC, and a great centre of trade and culture. Of a large number of coins obtained from the city, a couple refer to the city. On the obv occurs an *elephant, and on the rev, and an eight-armed symbol and a hand; above, occurs the ld *Ujeni*, in second century Br letters (Allan 1936; Bela Lahiri 1974; Bela Lahiri 1976; J P Singh 1971).

Ujjayinī. Local coins. This capital of Avanti was ruled over by Chaṇḍa Pradyota in the sixth century BC; Aśoka served here as viceroy in the third century BC. The *Periplus* refers to it as the capital of Tiastanes [*Chashṭana]. Cunningham grouped the Ujjayinī and *Eran coins under Avanti coins, but, as Allan points out, they are 'of very distinct fabric', with separate identity. Allan classifies the uninscribed coins of Ujjayinī into six classes. The punch marked coins have generally five symbols on the obv in different combinations, and a single symbol on the rev. Coins of all these classes, except one, bear the *Ujjain symbol. According to a recent suggestion, these coins may be divided into as many as 13 classes. Some Ujjayinī coins bear the figure of *Śiva. Some others have a seated female figure, identified as *Lakshmı by some scholars. Animals like *bull, *elephant, *lion, *horse, tortoise, etc, also appear on the various coins of Ujjayinī. Of the inscribed coins, some bear the ld *Ujeni*; on the obv of these coins occurs an elephant, and on the rev, an eight-armed symbol and a hand, together with the ld in second century BC Br characters. Some coins, variously bearing the names Hanugama, Valākadāsa, and Manu, in first century BC characters, on one side, and some symbols on the other, are ascribed to the Śakas, and taken to be corroborative evidence for the Śaka invasion of Ujjain in the first century BC. Of the same age are the coins of a king (*raño*), the first part of whose *datta*-ending name is lost (Allan 1936; Bopearachchi and Pieper 1998; Bela Lahiri 1974; Prashant Srivastava and Deepak Tiwari 1994).

Ujjayinī

Ujjayinī

Umā. Deity. She is usually described as the consort of *Śiva, although some upanishads mention her as his sister. She sometimes has the epithet *Haimavatī*, 'daughter of Himavat', but she is mostly described as the daughter of Daksha. Feeling slighted when Daksha did not invite Śiva to his sacrifice, she entered the sacrificial fire, and immolated herself, to be born again, as *Pārvatī. In the *Kenopanishad*, Umā reveals the identity and nature of *brahman* to Indra, and on this basis, some scholars associated her with divine knowledge. The ld *Ommo* on *Kushāṇa coins stands for Umā.

Independent representations of Umā on coins are not met with, but her figure appears along with that of Śiva on some gold coins of *Huvishka. On one coin in the Cunningham collection of the British Museum, London, the goddess stands beside her husband, and holds a flower in one of her hands. Cunningham had read the ld describing the goddess on this coin as *Nana*, but Rapson corrected it to *Ommo*. A gold coin in the Punjab Museum, Lahore, collection has a similar depiction, but the goddess her holds a **cornucopiae* in her hand. The ld describing the goddess on this coin has also been read as *Ommo*, and the goddess shown standing beside Śiva has been identified as Umā. R Göbl proposes to the read *Oemo* in place of *Ommo*, and suggests that on these Kushāṇa coins, Huvishka seems to be commemorating *V'ima Kadphises, and it is the latter who is shown worshipping Śiva on the rev. But Rosenfield does not agree with this, on valid grounds (Banerjea 2002; Sukumari Bhattacharji 1970; Bhaskar Chattopadhyay 1977; Cunningham 1971a; Rosenfield 1967; Whitehead 1914).†

Ayodhyā

Undulating line. Symbol. Representations of the undulating line, in combination with other symbols, may be seen on some silver *punch marked coins, and on the *Ayodhyā, *Kauśāmbī, *Kuṇinda, *Śibi, and *Yaudheya coins. In *Mathurā, this symbol may be seen on the coins of the indigenous rulers, like Rāmadatta and Śivadatta, as also on the coins of the Śaka ruler, *Śoḍāsha. This symbol, when it appears on ancient Indian coins, leads to the confusion as to whether it represents a serpent or a river. On the coins of some rulers of Ayodhyā, like, *Mūladeva, *Vāyudeva, *Viśākhadeva, and *Dhanadeva, the left end of the undulating line is thick, giving the impression of a serpent's head, and this may be regarded as the representation of a serpent. S K Chakrabortty is of the opinion that when the undulating line accompanies a *hill symbol, it may represent a river. Indians have believed in the ceremonial significance of water since prehistoric times, and various water bodies, like rivers and ponds, are held sacred to this day. On the *Kārddamaka Kshatrapa coins, an undulating line is seen below the *crescent-on-hill symbol on the rev. On some coins of the *Audumbaras, the undulating line has been regarded as a river, and tentatively identified as Udumbarāvatī, mentioned in the *Mahābhāshya* of Patañjali and the *Harivaṁśa* (Allan 1936; Chakrabortty 1931; Cunningham 1971b;

Jīvadāman

K K Dasgupta 1974; Handa 2007a; Bela Lahiri 1974; Rajgor 2001; Rapson 1975; Sircar 1971; Vögel 1926).

Uoromozdo. *Ahuramazda.

Uparkot hoard. This hoard of around 1,200 silver coins was found at Uparkot in the Junagarh district of Gujarat. The rulers represented in the hoard include *Rudrasena I, *Dāmasena, *Vīradāman, *Vijayasena, *Dāmajadaśrī III, *Rudrasena II, *Viśvasemha, *Bhartṛidāman, *Viśvasena, *Rudrasimha II, *Yaśodāman II, *Rudrasena III, and *Īśvaradatta. Nothing can be said with certainty about the attribution of around 226 coins (Jha and Rajgor 1994; Scott 1898-1901).

Uttamadatta. *Mathurā k. He issued coins, which show *Lakshmī with lotus in her r hand and some symbols on the obv; and three *elephants with riders on the rev. The rev device is degenerate. On some of his coins, he uses the title **rājan*, while on others, this title is absent. On this basis, Allan considers the possibility of two kings of this name. But it would appear more probable that he issued coins, first without, and then with, the title of *rājan* (Allan 1936; Bela Lahiri 1974).

Uttama-kāhāvaṇa. Coin denomination. It is difficult to ascertain as to which coin is implied by this denomination in the **Aṅgavijjā*. But the *Kāśikā* commentary mentions gold **kārshāpaṇa*, which might be the same as the **suvarṇa* or **dīnāra*, and this gold *kārshāpaṇa* might be the *uttama-kāhāvaṇa* of the *Aṅgavijjā* [**jahaṇṇa-kāhāvaṇa*, **majjhima-kāhāvaṇa*] (V S Agrawala 1957).

Uziaraghat hoard. This hoard of 256 local punch marked coins was discovered at Uziaraghat, between Ghazipur in Uttar Pradesh and Baxar in Bihar, in 2002. of the coins found in this hoard, 188 are reported to be the local punch marked coins of the Magadha *janapada*, while the remaining 68 remind one of the coins found in the Narhan hoard (Sharad Sharma 2003-2004).

V

Vainyagupta *Dvādaśāditya*. *Imperial Gupta k; son of Pūrugupta (?); early sixth century AD. He is known from three sources—the Gunaighar (District Comilla) copperplate grant of *Gupta era 188 (= 507 AD), the Nalanda seal, and gold coins. No inscription, coin, or seal of Vainyagupta has been found from the western provinces of the Imperial Guptas, thereby indicating that his authority was confined to the eastern provinces. According to the *Āryamañjuśrīmūlakalpa*, Dvādaśa (Vainyagupta *Dvādaśāditya*) ruled for a few months only, before he was murdered. He issued gold coins of the *Archer type only. The vertical ld under the king's arm on the obv of these coins was read by Rapson as *Chandra*, and these coins were ascribed to *Chandragupta III, as the title on the rev of these coins, *viz Dvādaśāditya*, was different from *Vikramāditya*, the title of *Chandragupta II. But the reading of the vertical ld on these coins was later on corrected as *Vainya*, and the coins, along with the title *Dvādaśāditya*, were ascribed to Vainyagupta. The percentage of pure gold in some of these coins is as low as 70, suggesting troubled times (Ashvini Agrawal 1989; Allan 1914; Altekar 1957; R D Banerji 1933; Fleet 1888; S R Goyal 2005; P L Gupta 1998; K P Jayaswal 1933; Smith 1972; Thaplyal, forthcoming).[†]

Vaiśravaṇa. *Magha k.

***Vajra*.** Symbol. *Thunderbolt.

Valabhī *saṁvat*. *Gupta *saṁvat*.

Vaṅgapāla. *Pañchāla k. He is, perhaps, identical with the homonym of the Pabhosa inscription, mentioned therein as the father of Bhāgavata, and the grandfather of Āshāḍhasena. He seems to be one of the earliest rulers known from Pañchāla coins. There is a restruck coin involving Vaṅgapāla and Damagupta. Some scholars are of the view that the coin was originally struck by the former, and restruck by the latter. But Bela Lahiri states that the devices of Vaṅgapāla on both the obv and the rev are more prominent than those of Damagupta, and the coin should be regarded as the issue of Damagupta restruck by Vaṅgapāla, which would place Vaṅgapāla later than Damagupta. The rev of some coins of Vaṅgapāla bears a **chakra*; other coins have a peculiar symbol, also seen on the rev of some coins of *Bhadraghosha and *Phalgunīmitra (Altekar 1942c; K D Bajpai 1962; Dar 1940; Bela Lahiri 1974; Sircar 1986; Prashant Srivastava 1989; Prashant Srivastava 1996a).

Varāharāja. *Nala k.

Vārāṇasī. City coins. Kāśī was one of the 16 *mahājanapadas* in the sixth century BC. Vārāṇasī, its capital, has yielded two coins, both rectangular, and with identical devices, *viz* a *horse on the obv, and *Ujjain symbol and the ld *Bārānasī* in first century BC Br characters on the rev. One of the coins bears, above the obv ld, another ld, of which ...*trasa* alone could be read, and the complete ld may have been the name of the official responsible for its issue (Bela Lahiri 1974; Bela Lahiri 1976; J P Singh 1971).

Varuṇa. Deity. He is the king of the gods, and called *samrāj*, 'emperor'. The epithet, *asura*, is more closely associated with him than with any other deity. The power of Varuṇa rests on his supernatural knowledge, his omniscience. Due to this supernatural power of knowledge, he becomes the upholder of *ṛita*. But Varuṇa's personality seems to undergo transformation with time. From the judge, the upolder of *ṛita*, he becomes the punisher of those who transgress *ṛita* or *dharma*. Reverence for Varuṇa yields place to dread, and he is found being superseded by the warrior god, *Indra. And ultimately, because the deity had exhausted his mythological potentiality, Varuṇa is 'pensioned off' as a *dikpāla*, the guardian of the western quarter in epic and puranic mythology. One would have expected to find the anthropomorphic or symbol representation of Varuṇa, at least on the coins of the *Pañchāla ruler, *Varuṇamitra. But the rev of the coins of this ruler bears the figures of 'two trees side by side'. As, in later Hindu mythology, Varuṇa is associated with 'the water of atmosphere and on the earth', he might have some connection with vegetation, which is sustained by these waters, and the two trees appearing on these Pañchāla coins may be said to the represent him symbolically. It is *Ouranos, the Greek counterpart of Varuṇa, who makes his appears on some *Kushāṇa coins (Sukumari Bhattacharji 1970; Eliade 1958; Eliade 1961; Hillebrandt 1999; Bela Lahiri 1974; Macdonell 1897; Radin 1955; Prashant Srivastava 2007b; Prashant Srivastava 2007d; Wilkins 2006).[†]

Varuṇamitra. *Kauśāmbī k. He may be identical with the homonym, Gauptīputra Varuṇamitra, known from an inscription of his son, Kohaḍiputra…, dated to *c* first century BC. The obv of his coins has the figure of a *bull to the r, while the rev has a *tree-in-railing, an *undulating line, and the ld *Varuṇamitasa* (Altekar 1942a; Altekar 1942b; Bopearachchi and Pieper 1998; Bela Lahiri 1974).

Varuṇamitra. *Pañchāla k. The rev of the coins of Varuṇamitra, *Anamitra, *Śivanandiśrī, *Śrīnandi, *Vasusena, and *Yugasena does not bear the anthropomorphic or symbolic representation of any divinity, as is the usual case with the Pañchāla series, and, on this basis, it has been suggested that they might have ruled at a later period, when the practice of representing a deity alluding to the name of the issuing king on the rev of the coin had become lax. However, Varuṇamitra uses the three Pañchāla symbols on the obv, and this seems to place him before Anamitra, Śivanandiśrī, and Śrīnandi. The rev of his coins shows 'two trees side by side' (A Ghosh 1943; Bela Lahiri 1974).

Vase type. Copper. Among the *Imperial Guptas, the Vase type was issued in copper by *Chandragupta II. The obv depicts a crescent on top, and the ld *Chandra* below it. The rev has a vase with foliage within a dotted circle. These coins are very small in size, one of them weighing as little as 3.3 grains (Allan 1914; Altekar 1957; P L Gupta 1998; Smith 1972).

Vāsishka. *Kushāṇa k. He is generally believed to be a co-ruler, associated in administration by *Kanishka I towards the end of his own reign. He seems to have succeeded Kanishka I as an independent ruler, and appointed *Huvishka as his junior co-ruler. Some scholars would, however, place him after *Vāsudeva I. He appears to be an ephemeral ruler. He is mentioned in two inscriptions from Sanchi, dated years 22 and 28, respectively, and in a *yūpa* pillar inscription from Isapur near Mathurā, dated year 24. The Ara inscription of the year 41 mentions him as the father of Kanishka II. He has been identified with Jushka of Kalhaṇa. Earlier, it was believed that he did not issue any coins. But some time back, two types of gold coins bearing the name of Vāsishka have been published by R Göbl. The obv of both the types bears the figure of *king sacrificing at an altar, and the ld *Shaonanoshao Bazeshko Koshano*. The rev of one type has the figure of enthroned **Ardochsho* holding lotus in one hand. The other type has the figure of *Śiva holding diadem in his r hand and a *triśūla* in the left; behind the deity is his mount, the *bull. The rev legends on the two types mention the respective deities depicted. A number of scholars, like Craig Alden Burns, Gritli von Mitterwallner, B N Mukherjee, and Sarojini Kulashreshtha, however, place these Vāsishka coins in the period following the death of Vāsudeva I, and regard the Vāsishka of these coins as a successor of that king. It is interesting to note that, initially, R Göbl also ascribed these coins to Vāsishka II (Craig Alden Burns 1984; Sarojini Kulashreshtha 1986; Marshall 1975; von Mitterwallner 1986; Rosenfield 1967; Sircar 1980c).

Vāsishṭhīputra Bhīmasena. *Magha k.

Vasoj hoard. This hoard of 591 silver coins was discovered at Vasoj in the Junagarh district of Gujarat. Besides the nine coins which are uncertain, all the coins in the hoard belong to the *Kārddamaka Kshatrapas, like *Rudrasiṁha I, *Rudrasena I, *Dāmasena, *Dāmajadaśrī II, Vīradāman, *Vijayasena, *Dāmajadaśrī III, *Rudrasena II, *Viśvasiṁha, *Bhartṛidāman, *Viśvasena, *Rudrasiṁha II, *Yaśodāman II, and *Rudrasena III (Jha and Rajgor 1994).

Vāsudeva I

Vāsudeva I. *Kushāṇa k. The last great Kushāṇa ruler, he was reigning about a hundred years after *Kanishka I. His dated inscriptions from Mathurā attest to a reign of over 20 years. There is evidence of disturbances in northwestern India, Afghanistan, and Russian central Asia during or after his reign. This was, perhaps, the consequence of the Sassanian onslaught, against which power he seems to have sought Chinese help and formed an alliance with the Armenians. He issued coins, mostly in gold and rarely in silver. The obv of all his coins bears the figure of *king sacrificing at an altar, and the ld **Shaonanoshao Bazo* (sometimes, *Bazodeo*) *Koshano*. The rev of one of his gold types shows **Nana* holding sceptre and patera; there is a crescent on top of her head. One gold type has **Mao* on the rev, and a unique gold coin is believed to bear a four-armed deity on the rev, who is labelled *Bazodeo* and identified as *Vāsudeva-Kṛishṇa. But mostly, the rev of his types is occupied with the figure of *Śiva, usually three-headed but sometimes monocephalous, and having four or two arms. The attributes of Śiva include *triśūla*, *pāśa*, *ḍamaru*, etc. Often, the *bull mount of the deity is shown behind him. The rev of the silver type also has three-headed and two-armed Śiva standing with Nandin. The rev legends of the various types mention the name of the deity depicted (Basham 1957; Craig Alden Burns 1985a; Cunningham 1971a; Gardner 1971; Marshall 1975; von Mitterwallner 1986; Rosenfield 1967; Sircar 1980c; Whitehead 1914).

Vāsudeva I

Vāsudeva II. *Kushāṇa k. He was among the last rulers of the Kushāṇa dynasty. He issued gold coins, which are rather crudely minted, and this distinguishes them from the monetary issues of *Vāsudeva I. All his coins have the device of *king sacrificing at an altar and the ld mentioning Vāsudeva [II] on the obv; the rev has the figure of *Śiva, which device was popular in the western provinces of the Kushāṇa empire. As he did not issue coins with **Ardochsho* rev, it has been suggested that he had lost the eastern provinces where coins with *Ardochsho* rev were popular. Like the coins of *Kanishka III, the obv of the coins of Vāsudeva II also bears Br letters in the right, central, and left fields, the letters in the right field perhaps denoting the abbreviated forms of the names of the provincial governors. This is taken to show the weakening of the central authority, and the rising political influence and ambitions

Vāsudeva II

of the provincial governors towards the end of the Kushāṇa rule (Altekar 1986a; Cunningham 1962; Rosenfield 1967).

Vāsudeva-Kṛishṇa. Deity. This eighth incarnation of *Vishṇu—a total incarnation (*pūrṇāvatāra*), as against the others who are only partial incarnations (*aṁśāvatāras*), is worshipped as the central cult figure in Bhāgavatism. It is generally believed that Vāsudeva-Kṛishṇa, the son of Vasudeva and Devakī, was the hero of the Yādava-Sātvata-Vṛishṇis, who was deified by his tribe, and his cult gradually became popular. He occupies the most important position in the *chaturvyūha* doctrine in the Bhāgavata sect. Several elements are found amalgamated together in the personality of Vāsudeva-Kṛishṇa, and we see him as 'a warrior, a preacher, a child-god of some pastoral tribe and a love-god of the popular lore, all blended into one'. The epics and the purāṇas give stories of his killing the demons; he humbled the pride of *Indra, and assisted and guided the Pāṇḍava brothers in the Bhārata war. According to the *Mahābhārata*, he preached the *Gītā* to Arjuna before the commencement of this war. Six coins issued by the *Indo-Greek ruler, *Agathokles, were discovered in the course of excavations at Ai Khanum, on the border of Afghanistan and the former USSR, by Paul Bernard. These coins bear on the obv, the figure of *Balarāma. The rev has the figure of a helmeted male deity, dressed in *dhotī* and *uttarīya*, and wearing 'strange half-boots having curved sole-ends'. According to Bernard, he holds a *kamaṇḍalu* in his r hand, while in his l hand, he holds a **chakra*. A sword in a sheathe hangs on a cross belt at his left. Bernard proposes to identify this figure, either as that of the king represented as a *chakravartin*—although he is not very keen about this identification—or of Vishṇu. But A K Narain suggests that this figure should be identified as that of Vāsudeva-Kṛishṇa, instead of that of Vishṇu. A unique gold coin of *Vāsudeva I bears, on the rev, a four-armed deity, holding a *gadā* in his lower r hand, a *śaṅkha* in his lower l hand, a *chakra* in his upper l hand, and an uncertain object in his upper r hand. The label inscription describes him as *Bazodeo*, and he has been identified by Joe Cribb as Vāsudeva-Kṛishṇa. On the obv of a square copper type of the *Śaka-Pahlava ruler, *Maues, there occurs the figure of an Indian deity walking to the l, who, according to the R C Senior, holds a club in his r hand, and a 'plough' over his left shoulder. Senior identifies this deity as 'Bala-

Fig.6: Vāsudeva-Kṛishṇa

Fig.7: Vāsudeva-Kṛishṇa

Fig.8: 'Bala-Kṛishṇa'?

Kṛishṇa', by which he seems to mean a syncretic deity, Balarāma-Vāsudeva-Kṛishṇa. This representation would be interesting, if the identification proposed by Senior is correct, as such a syncretic form of Balarāma and Vāsudeva-Kṛishṇa is, perhaps, not known from any other source. Although there seems to be no doubt that the object in the upraised r hand of the deity on the coin is a club, the presence of the plough on the left shoulder of the deity, as suggested by Senior, is open to doubt. On the rev of the coins of Agathokles (above), the plough in the upraised l hand of Balarāma is quite clear, the deity holding it by its pole. However, on the obv of the type of Maues, the l hand of the deity depicted hangs down and appears to touch the thigh; it does not seem to be holding any object. From the illustration produced by Senior, the curved object over the left shoulder of the deity seems to be surmounted by something, which would be difficult to explain if the curved object is taken to be a plough. A similar curved object, though somewhat smaller in size, is also seen over the right shoulder. The pole of the 'plough' is also not visible on the coin. On the whole, nothing definite can be said about the object over the left shoulder of the deity, or about the identity of the deity himself. Senior reports the occurrence of a similar deity holding a female divinity in one hand on some types of Azilises (Sukumari Bhattacharji 1970; Craig Alden Burns 1985a; Gonda 1993; S R Goyal 1986; Suvira Jaiswal 1981; von Mitterwallner 1986; Narain 1973; Senior 2001; Sircar 1971; Wilkins 2006).†

Vasunāga. *Nāga k. He is associated with *Bhīmanāga, *Skandanāga, and *Brīhaspatināga by the use of the 'Peacock' type. He seems to be later than Bhīmanāga, as the ld on his coins is engraved in the circular fashion. He is among the few Nāga rulers who did not issue the 'Bull' type of coins. However, his 'Wheel' type of coins are known. He assumed the title of **mahārāja* on coins (Bela Lahiri 1974; H V Trivedi 1957).

Vasusena. *Pañchāla k. The rev of the coins of Vasusena, *Anamitra, *Śivanandiśrī, *Śrīnandi, *Varuṇamitra, and *Yugasena does not bear the anthropomorphic or symbolic representation of any divinity, as is the usual case with the Pañchāla series, and, on this basis, it has been suggested that they might have ruled at a later period, when the practice of representing a deity alluding to the name of the issuing king on the rev of the coiṇ had become lax. However, Vasusena uses the three Pañchāla symbols on the obv, and this seems to place him before Anamitra, Śivanandiśrī, and Śrīnandi. The rev of the coins of Vasusena shows a *horse (Dar 1940; Bela Lahiri 1974).

Vasusena. *Vṛishṇi general (?).

Vāyudeva. *Ayodhyā k. He is connected with *Dhanadeva on the basis of their use of the standing figure of *Lakshmī (?) between two symbols on the rev of their coins, and might not have been far separated from him in time. His copper coins are of two varieties. The first variety has an *elephant to the l on the obv, and a combination of symbols on the rev. The second variety has a *bull to the r on the obv, and Lakshmī (?) on the rev. The ld, *Vāyudevasa*, occurs on the obv of both the varieties (Allan 1936; Bela Lahiri 1974).

Vavaghosha. *Kauśambī k. Some scholars render his name as Varaghosha, others as Suvaghosha, and still others as Śivaghosha. As his coins bear the square incuse, which is characteristic of the early die-struck coins, he is placed about the beginning of the first century BC. The obv of his coins has the figure of a *bull, a *taurine symbol, and a *tree-in-railing; the rev has a **svastika*, *Ujjain symbol, and an uncertain symbol within an incuse square, and the ld *Vavaghosha* (Altekar 1942a; Bopearachchi and Pieper 1998; Bela Lahiri 1974).

Vemaki

Vemaki. Tribe. *Vemaka* in Skt means 'weaver'. In the *Harivaṁśa* and the *Brahmapurāṇa*, as pointed out by D C Sircar, it is the name of a sage, perhaps the patron saint of the tribe. The Vaiyāmakas of the *Mahābhārata*, are referred to along with the *Audumbaras, and their inhabiting territories close to each other is corroborated by the find of Vemaki and Audumbara coins together. Some editions of the *Mahābhārata*, as also the *Mahāmāyūrī*, have the form Vairāmaka, which tribe has to be identified with the Vemakis. Bhaṭṭa Utpala, the commentator on the *Bṛihatsaṁhitā*, mentions a tribe named Vaimaka in the northern region. Earlier, only two Vemaki coins were known—one of silver, round in shape, and found at Jwalamukhi along with *Kuṇinda coins; and another of copper, square in shape, probably from Hoshiarpur. The silver coin bears a *bull and a *lotus and the Kh ld *Raña Vemakisa Rudravarmasa vijayata* (or, *-ya*, or

Vemaki

even, *-ka*) on the obv, and an *elephant and a *trident with axe and the Br ld *Rājño Vemakisa Rudravarmasa vijayaka* on the rev. Devendra Handa reports another silver coin of Rudravarman, quite similar to the one described above, but struck from a different die, in the collection of Jan Lingen. He also publishes a third Vemaki silver coin, which is quite similar to the above two coins in all respects, except that the issuer's name in the ld on both the sides of this coin is Bhavavarman instead of Rudravarman. Handa suggests that Bhavavarman might have ruled after Rudravarman, as his coins shows some advancement in the art of die-cutting. The copper coin bears an *elephant and a **nandipada* with a Br ld on the obv, and a bull, a *nandipada*, and a **svastika* on the rev. The Br ld on the obv is usually read as *Vemaka janapadasa*. But Mitchiner reads it as *Rājña Vemakisa...*, while Devendra Handa, after an examination of the coin in the British Museum, London, deciphers the complete ld as *Rājño Vemakisa Śivaghoshasa*, perhaps with some word, like *vijayaka*, out of flan. He, thus, expresses the possibility of the existence of a third Vemaki chief—Śivaghosha. He also reports another Vemaki copper coin from some private collection, which is quite similar to the coin in the collection of the British Msueum, London, but the Br ld on its obv reads *Vemakisa Śivaghoshasa*. The copper coins with the Br ld alone do not bear any foreign influence, and hence, are earlier than the Rudravarman silver coins bearing foreign influence in their shape, fabric, metal, weight, device, and the use of the Kh script. Some scholars, on the basis of the identity of *provenance* and similarity of the device—bull and elephant, have bracketed these coins along with those of the Audumbaras. But in the coin legends, Rudravarman, Bhavavarman, and Śivaghosha are referred to as Vemaki, ie a member of the Vemaki tribe. Some scholars attribute the coins bearing the name of *Mahādeva to the Vemakis on the basis of common motifs like lotus, elephant, bull, trident, etc. The Vemaki coins may be assigned to the second-first centuries BC (Nisar Ahmad 1972; Allan 1936; Chakrabortty 1931; Cunningham 1971b; K K Dasgupta 1974; P L Gupta 1988; Handa 2007a; Jayaswal 1988; Bela Lahiri 1974; Marshall 1975; Mitchiner 1975-1976; Smith 1972).

Vesha (?).*Vṛishṇi general (?).

Vibhunāga. *Nāga k. He is associated with *Ravināga and *Prabhākara by the use of the 'Sickle-and-arrow' type. They are among the late Nāga rulers, and not much is known about them. Vibhunāga also seems to be connected by the 'Crescent' type with *Bhavanāga. He also issued the 'Bull' and 'Wheel' types of coins. He assumed the title of **mahārāja-śrī* on coins (Bela Lahiri 1974; H V Trivedi 1957).

Vidiśā. City coins. Twenty-one coins obtained by a dealer from Vidiśā, the ancient capital of eastern Mālavā, bear on the obv, a wheel, and on the rev, the ld *Vedisa* or *Veddasa*, in early second century BC Br characters. The coins are taken as issues of the city of Vidiśā, which was quite an important city during the Śuṅga rule. Located on the important trade route, it was a centre of Bhāgavatism, and, as per the testimony of a Sanchi inscription, was known for its ivory carving (Bela Lahiri 1974; Bela Lahiri 1976; J P Singh 1971).

Vijayabhūti. *Almora k.

Vijayamagha. *Magha k.

Vijayamitra. *Ayodhyā k. One Vijayamitra is also known from a Rajghat seal, and he might be identical with the homonym of Ayodhyā coins. He, along with *Saṅghamitra, is connected with *Kumudasena, *Ajavarman, and *Mādhavavarman, by the use of the rev device of a **nandipada* within a square, and seems to be earlier than the other Ayodhyā rulers with *mitra*-ending names who issued round die-struck coins. As Saṅghamitra used the rev device of *nandipada* within a square alone, while Vijayamitra used the device of a *cock on a post and *tree-in-railing also on some of his other coins, Vijayamitra has been regarded as a successor of Saṅghamitra. His coins, all in copper, show great variety. Some of them have the figure of a *bull to the l before a standard on the obv, and a cock on a post and a tree-in-railing on the rev. Others have a bull to the l on a pedestal on the obv, and an uncertain type for the rev. Still others have an uncertain type for the obv, and a *stūpa* on the rev. The fourth variety has a bull on a pedestal on the obv, and a *nandipada* on the rev. The ld *Vijayamitasa* occurs on the obv of all the varieties (Allan 1936; Bela Lahiri 1974; Smith 1972).

Vijayamitra. *Kulūta chief. He ruled in the first-second centuries AD, and issued the Class II of *Kulūta coins, on which he assumes the title of **rājña*, and also uses the tribal name. This chief is identified by some scholars with **Apracharaja* Vijayamitra of the Shinkot-Bajaur relic casket inscription and the father of *Indravasu known from coins. But *Apracharaja* Vijayamitra is earlier in date, and the Kulūta coins are different in all respects from *Śaka-Pahlava coins (Allan 1936; Chakrabortty 1931; Cunningham 1971b; K K Dasgupta 1974; Handa 2007a; Jayaswal 1988; Marshall 1975; Sircar 1986; Smith 1972).

Vijayasena. *Kārddamaka k. He was the son of *Dāmasena, and was serving as a **kshatrapa* in the *Śaka year 160, perhaps under his brother, *Yaśodāman I. But in the Śaka year 161, he had succeeded Yaśodāman I as **mahākshatrapa*, and continued to the rule in that capacity till Śaka year 172. His available coins are of the *Kārddamaka silver type (Jha and Rajgor 1994; Mirashi 1982; Mitchiner 1976; Rapson 1975; Raychaudhuri 1972; Senior 2001; Sircar 1980e).

Vikrama *saṁvat*. This era, beginning in 57 BC, is one of the most popular ones in ancient India, and continues to be in use to the present day. It has been more predominant in northern and western India. Earlier known variously as the Kṛita and Mālava *saṁvat*, it was only from the eighth-ninth centuries AD onwards that it came to be designated the Vikrama *saṁvat*. According to tradition, the founding of the era commemorates the expulsion of the Śakas from Ujjain by the legendary king, Vikramāditya, who, later on, came to be identified with *Chandragupta II Vikramāditya. Sircar expresses the possibility that the founder of the era might have been *Vonones. But the recent discovery of some inscriptions seems to associate this era with *Azes I with some amount of certainty, and this has been accepted by a majority of modern writers on the subject. The years, when cited in the Vikrama *saṁvat*, are generally counted as expired, though there are some rare instances of the year being counted as current. The 'northern' Vikrama year begins in the month of Chaitra, while the 'southern' year begins in the month of Kārttika. The months in the 'northern' calendrical system are *pūrṇimānta*, and those in the 'southern', *amānta* (Salomon 1982; Salomon 1998; Sircar 1965; Sircar 1969).

V'ima Kadphises. *Kushāṇa k. He was earlier identified as Yen-kao-tchien the son of Kujula Kadphises, mentioned in the Chinese annals. But now, with the discovery of the Rabatak inscription which mentions V'ima Takshuma as the son and successor of Kujula Kadphises, this identification has to be discarded; the inscription refers to V'ima Kadphises as the son and successor of V'ima Takshuma. V'ima Kadphises occupies an important place in Kushāṇa numismatics as he was perhaps the first ruler of his dynasty to issue profusely in gold. His gold coins are based on the weight standard of the Roman *dinarius aureus*, and weigh around 123 grains. The obv is occupied by the figure of the king—seated cross-legged on clouds, or enthroned, or riding a biga, or mounted on an elephant. Somctimes only the helmeted bust of the king, within a square frame or without it, may be seen depicted. The obv of the silver (very few) and copper coins has the figure of the king sacrificing at an altar, a device which seems to be imitated from the Arsakid coins of Parthia. The rev always bears the representation of *Śiva, usually with his mount, the *bull. In most cases, the god is shown in human form, holding a **triśūla* or *triśūla-paraśu*, but on some coins with the bust of the king within a square frame, the presence of Śiva is shown symbolically through the *triśūla-paraśu* only. The obv Gr ld uses the titles of *basileos basileon soter megas* for V'ima Kadphises. The rev Pkt ld, written in the Kh script, refers to V'ima Kadphises as *maharaja rajatiraja *sarvaloga iśvara *mahiśvara* and *trata*. The appearance of Śiva or Śaiva symbol on the rev of all his coins, together with the use of the title *mahiśvara* (= *māheśvara*, great devotee of Śiva), shows that V'ima Kadphises had adopted Śaivism (Cunningham 1971a; Gardner 1971; Marshall 1975; von Mitterwallner 1986; Rosenfield 1967; Sircar 1980c; Whitehead 1914).

V'ima Kadphises

V'ima Kadphises

V'ima Takshuma. *Kushāṇa k. Earlier, it was believed that among the Kushāṇas, there was only one ruler with V'ima as his forename, namely *V'ima Kadphises, and he was regarded as the son and successor of *Kujula Kadphises. However, in recent years, epigraphic and numismatic evidence has been forthcoming to the reveal the

V'ima Takshuma

existence of a Kushāṇa ruler with V'ima as his forename, the last component of the name being read variously as *Takpio*, *Takta*, *Taktoo*, *Takkashama*, *Takshomo*, or *Takshuma*. Of the epigraphic sources, the first inscription is engraved between the feet of a seated royal statue discovered in the Kushāṇa *devakula* at Mat near Mathurā. The inscription refers to V[e]ma Ta[kshu]ma, who is called *mahārāja rājātirāja devaputra Kushāṇaputra shāhi*. Five inscriptions, two in Graeco-Bactrian, two in Kh, and one in 'an unknown script (and language ?)', were discovered on a peak of Mount Qarabayu to the west of Dasht-i-Nawur in Afghanistan. The Graeco-Bactrian inscription refers to *Ooemo Tak[..]o*, while a Kh inscription refers to the reign of Vhama Kuśa. B N Mukherjee feels that it is 'impossible to be sure of any reading' of the second part of the name in the Graeco-Bactrian version 'beyond *Tak*', but he had earlier restored it as *Takshomo*. The recently discovered Rabatak (Baghlan) inscription from northern Afghanistan refers to the construction of certain divine images for the *devakula*, for the merit of four generations of Kushāṇa kings—*Kanishka [I], and his father, grandfather, and great-grandfather, who are all mentioned by name, followed by the title of *shao* in each case. The names of Kanishka [I] (*Kaneshko*), his father V'ima Kadphises (*Ooemo Kadphiso*), and great-grandfather Kujula Kadphises (*Kozoulo Kadphiso*), are quite clear. But the left side of the rock, on which the inscription is engraved, is badly damaged, and, consequently, the name of Kanishka's grandfather in line 13 is not fully legible. The first part of the name can be restored on the basis of the Graeco-Bactrian version of the Dasht-i-Nawur inscription, where the forename seems to be *Ooemo*. As regards the last name of the grandfather of Kanishka I in the Rabatak inscription, Sims-Williams restores it as *Taktoo*. Senior proposes *Takkashama* as an alternative reading. But Mitchiner reads the name of Kanishka's grandfather in the Rabatak inscription as *Ooemo Takzoo*, which he finds 'compatible' with the Kh form *Takshuma* met with in the coin legends, and the Br form *Tākshuma* met with in the Mat inscription. There are certain coins known from the region extending from Mathurā to Peshawar and into the Russian Turkestan; some coins are reported from as far east as Varanasi and Ghazipur in eastern Uttar Pradesh. These coins bear only the epithets *Soter Megas*, and no personal name. These anonymous coins are struck in both base silver or billon and copper. The obv of the base silver or billon coins

V'ima Takshuma

V'ima Takshuma

has the equestrian king to the r, holding an *aṅkuśa* in his raised r hand, and the Gr ld *Basoleos basileon soter megas*; the rev has *Zeus standing to the r, holding a sceptre in his l hand, and the Kh ld *Maharajasa rajatirajasa mahatasa tratarasa*. These coins have been associated with western Gandhāra. The obv of the copper coins, which have been associated with Mathurā and southeastern Punjab, bears the diademed bust of the king to the r, while the rev has Zeus standing to the l, holding a long sceptre in his l hand, and a thunderbolt over an altar in his r hand; the rev has the Gr ld *Basoleos basileon soter megas*. Then there are some rare copper coins, which have been associated with the Kapiśā or Bactria region. These bear, on the obv, the helmeted bust of the king, holding a spear, to the l; the rev has the equestrian king to the r, holding an *aṅkuśa*, and the Gr ld *Basoleos basileon soter megas*. A large number of copper coins have the diademed and radiate bust of the king to the r, holding a long sceptre, on the obv, and equestrian king to the r, holding an *aṅkuśa*, and the Gr ld *Basoleos basileon soter megas*, on the rev, and this type is termed as the 'general coinage' of the issuer of these anonymous coins. As to the identity of this issuer, some scholars proposed to regard him as a viceroy of V'ima Kadphises, but the extensive distribution of this anonymous coinage is 'fatal' to this theory. This same argument rules out the acceptance of the suggestion that *Soter Megas* was the title of the military governor of Takshaśilā, and that the *Soter Megas* coins were issued anonymously by successive *strategoi*. Oikonomides takes *Soter* as a personal name on the analogy of the occurrence of *Soter* as a common name in the 'Hellenistic and Roman Near-East and Egypt', and regards him as 'the last of the Indo-Greek kings'. Interpreting **sterossu* occurring in the ld *Basileos sterosssu Hermaios* on some coins, believed to be posthumous issued in the name of *Hermaios, as 'Soter Co-(regent) of', he proposes that King Soter first served as the 'co-regent' of Hermaios, and then accepted Kujula Kadphises, and finally V'ima Kadphises, as his sovereign. But this suggestion of Oikonomides is no longer acceptable in the light of the fact that the personal name of *Soter Megas* is now known to be Vi'ma Takshuma. M E Masson pointed out some similarities between the anonymous coinage and the coinage of Kujula Kadphises, and suggested that the coins with the 'non-personal inscriptions' might have been struck by Kujula Kadphises. But this suggestion has been rightly rejected by D W

V'ima Takshuma

MacDowall. MacDowall points out the 'noticeable absence of any clear link in denomination or coin types' between the anonymous series and the coinage of Kujula Kadphises, and on this basis, he postulates a chronological break, in which he places the dynasty of *Gondopharnes. According to him, this is supported by the excavations at Taxila, which reveal that after Kujula Kadphises, there ruled the dynasty of Gondopharnes, which was overthrown by the issuer of the anonymous coinage. He places Kujula Kadphises in the earlier decades of the first century AD, Gondopharnes in the middle of that century, and the issuer of the coins with the non-personal inscriptions' somewhat later. The anonymous coinage has Kushāṇa features, which proves that its issuer was a Kushāṇa ruler. MacDowall, however, feels that the Bactrian links of the issuer of this anonymous coinage 'reveal a very different origin from Kujula Kadphises'. He, thus, regards the issuer of these coins as 'the founder of a new empire and a new dynasty', and responsible for 'the reconquest and consolidation of the Kushāṇa empire' in northwestern India. But this theory, too, is not acceptable in view of what follows. Cunningham pointed out several similarities between this anonymous coinage and the coins of V'ima Kadphises—both bear the titles *Basileos basileon soter megas*; both use the same peculiar form of the Kh letter *ja*; on some anonymous coins, the king holds a sceptre upright in front of his face, just as V'ima Kadphises is shown holding a club on some of his coins. Yet, the issuer of the anonymous coins should not be identified with V'ima Kadphises, because, despite of the similarities between the anonymous coinage and the coinage of V'ima Kadphises, there are some significant differences between the two. V'ima Kadphises issued a copper coinage, which was 'remarkably uniform throughout all his territories'; on the contrary, besides the 'general coinage', several types of the anonymous coins had 'a local circulation in different areas'. V'ima Kadphises struck all his coins on the Attic standard; most of the coins of the anonymous series are struck on the same standard, but the base silver/billon *tetradrachms* are struck on the Indian standard. Besides, V'ima Kadphises issued gold coins, but there are no gold coins in the anonymous series. No wonder, even after pointing out some similarities between the anonymous coinage and the coins of V'ima Kadphises, Cunningham was still inclined to the regard the issuer of the anonymous coinage and V'ima Kadphises as 'two princes', distinct from each other. As will be seen below, the coins of Classes I and II apparently form a link between this anonymous coinage, and the coins of Class III which clearly bear the name of V'ima Takshuma. This seems to show that the bulk of the coinage minted by the so-called 'nameless king *Soter Megas*', was issued by V'ima Takshuma. It must be noted that Cunningham, with his admirable and almost unerring foresight, included some coins with the Kh letter *vi* in the field, in the anonymous series. Apart from these coins, there are three classes of coins, which may be ascribed to V'ima Takshuma. The coins of Class I have the Kh character *vi* occupying a prominent place in the coins field, and are divided into three groups. The first group, linked with Bactria on the bases of the 'Attic' coin devices and the *provenance* of the coins, has the helmeted bust of the king and the character *vi* in the field on the obv, and a horseman and the Gr ld *Basileos Basileon Soter Megas* on the rev. The second group, linked with northwestern India on the bases of the devices and the *provenance* of the coins, has the horseman and the Gr ld *Basileos Basileon Soter Megas* on the obv, and sceptre-bearing Zeus with the character *vi* and a flower vase in the field on the rev. The third groups, linked with northwestern India and the previous groups on the bases of the flower vase and the *provenance* of the coins, has a standing male figure bearing a trident or sceptre and lion's skin and the character *vi* in the field on the obv, and a standing goddess bearing **cornucopiae* with a flower vase and a **nandipada* in the field on the rev; the ld is conspicuous by its absence. It has been suggested that the Kh character *vi* on these coins cannot be regarded as mint control mark, as they come from a wide geographical area spreading over Bactria and northwestern India, it should be taken as the abbreviated form of the personal name of the issuer, that is V'ima. Class II consists of two coins, similar to the second group of Class I, with the difference that the Kh ld on these two coins is slightly longer with some extra characters at the end. On one of these coins, Cribb has read the Kh ld as *Vemasa*, and this has been accepted by Mitchiner. Class III consists of copper coins, which circulated in the foothill regions of Swat, Hazara, and Kashmir. These coins have the figure of a humped bull standing to the r and a corrupt Gr ld on the obv, and a two-humped Bactrian camel standing to the r and a Kh ld on the rev. These coins are in two sizes : the small-sized ones weigh, on an average, 60 grains, and the large-sized ones weigh, on an average,

165 grains. The Gr ld on the obv of these coins is not fully legible. But on one coin bearing Greek characters on both the sides, Cribb reads *Ooemo Takta*. However, B N Mukherjee is of the view that what has been read as a *tau* by Cribb is actually 'an ill-formed Doric *san* with its semicircle at the top not fully closed', with a trace of an *omikron* after it. On this basis, he reads this part of the coin ld as *Ooemo Taksho*. Cribb reads the Kh ld on the rev of the small sized coins as *Maharayasa rajatirajasa devaputrasa Vema Takho*, while Senior reads it as *Maharajasa rajatirajasa devaputrasa Vema Takha-(?)*. But in the rev ld on one coin procured by Mitchiner from Mapusa (Goa), the last component of the surname of the issuer is a compound character, of which the top portion is off the flan, while the bottom portion is definitely a *sha* with the *u*-medial quite clear. On this basis, Mitchiner reconstructs the Kh ld on the small-sized coins as *Maharajasa rajatirajasa devaputrasa Vema Takshuma*. According to Cribb, the large-sized coins generally bear, on the rev, the Kh ld *Maharayasa rayatirayasa devaputrasa Vema Tak[ta] maha*. But there is debate regarding the reading of the last component of the surname of V'ima. This component is a compound character, which has been read as *Taktu* by Senior, and *Takshuma* by B N Mukherjee. Mitchiner puts forth some arguments in support of Mukherjee's reading. He says that the Kh character *ta* should project only to the l side of the vertical stroke, but a careful observation of the compound character shows there is 'an arcuate, umbrella-like, cross-stroke' passing completely across the vertical stroke. This indicates that this part of the compound character is to be read as *sha*. Also, the *u*-medial is clear in the character, thus indicating that the compound character should be read as *kshu*. On this basis, Mitchiner suggests that what has been read as *Tak[ta] maha* on these large-sized coins, should better be read as *Takshumasa*. According to Mitchiner, one coin has a slightly longer Kh ld, which ends in *Vema Takshumahatasa*; he believes that *Takshumahatasa* is to be understood as the contraction of *Takshuma mahatasa*, with the character *ma* not duplicated. On this basis, he reads the longer ld as *Maharayasa rayatirayasa devaputrasa Vema Takshumahatasa* (= *Vema Takshuma mahatasa*). B N Mukherjee, too, is in the favour of reading the surname of the issuer as *Takshuma* in the Kh ld on several of these coins. Before the discovery of the Rabatak inscription, most of the scholars favoured the identification of *V[e]ma Takshuma* of the Mat inscription and

Ooemo Tak[shomo] of the Dasht-i-Nawur inscription, as V'ima Kadphises. However, the Rabatak inscription shows that *Ooemo Takzoo* (V'ima Takshuma) was the son of Kujula Kadphises, while V'ima Kadphises was the grandson of Kujula Kadphises. This seems to clearly establish the separate identity of V'ima Takshuma and V'ima Kadphises. Also, if V'ima Takshuma was identical with V'ima Kadphises, it is hard to explain away the non-occurrence of the two epithets, *Kadphises* and *Takshuma*, together with each other, in any inscription or coin ld, especially when we see a number of epithets being used for the king named Vema in the Mat inscription and in the ld on the coins of Class III. As noticed earlier, V'ima Kadphises issued coins in gold, but there are no gold coins either in the anonymous series which has been ascribed to V'ima Takshuma or in the series of coins bearing the whole or part (*Vi*, *Vema*) of the name of V'ima Takshuma. Therefore, the alleged identification of V'ima Takshuma with V'ima Kadphises does not hold ground. V'ima Takshuma, the son of Kujula Kadphises, was the father of V'ima Kadphises, and intervened between Kujula Kadphises and V'ima Kadphises. The vast number of the coins of V'ima Takshuma, and the extensive area from which they are reported, 'testify to a long and powerful reign'. But a very long independent reign for V'ima Takshuma is apparently precluded by the fact that his father, Kujula Kadphises, is known from the *Hou Han-shu* to have ruled till (at least) the age of 80. There is a suggestion that V'ima Takshuma served as the governor of his father in the northern provinces of the Kushāṇa empire for a long time before his accession to the throne, which is hardly surprising in view of the above. V'ima Takshuma, during this period, very probably had his seat at Balkh or Bactria. In the northern provinces of Bactria and Sogdia, the Kushāṇas seem to have had a tradition of issuing coins bearing 'non-personal inscriptions', that is the coin legends mentioned the title(s) of the issuer, and not his personal name. Following this tradition, V'ima Takshuma issued the anonymous coinage with the ld *Basileos Basileon soter megas*, while he served his father as governor in the northern provinces. MacDowall observes that the issuer of the coins with anonymous series, 'being the founder of a new empire and a new dynasty', was to be known by his grandiloquent titles *Basileos basileon soter megas* only, just as the first Roman emperor Octavian ceased using his personal name, and came to be known by the titles

Cæsar Augustus Imperator, after the Battle of Actium. But the explanation of Mitchiner for the 'non-personal inscriptions' on these coins is more acceptable than that of MacDowall, because the issuer of this series (V'ima Takshuma) was the son and successor of Kujula Kadphises as per the evidence of the Rabatak inscription (above), and not 'the founder of a new empire and a new dynasty' as MacDowall believed. Perhaps, V'ima Takshuma's being a governor under Kujula Kadphises would explain the fact, observed by M E Masson, that the 'palaeography on coins of *Soter Megas* (that is, V'ima Takshuma) shows the same wide range of letter forms that we find on the various coinages of Kujula Kadphises'. According to the *Hou Han-shu*, Kujula Kadphises was succeeded by his son, Yen-kao-chen, who conquered India and appointed military commanders as governors there. This Yen-kao-chen should now be identified with V'ima Takshuma. He would have immediately succeeded his father, and there could not possibly have been scope for any chronological break between Kujula Kadphises and V'ima Takshuma, in which to place the dynasty of Gondopharnes as proposed by MacDowall. V'ima Takshuma might have carried on the tradition of issuing coins with 'non-personal inscriptions' even after ascending the throne. As the issuer of the anonymous coinage, V'ima Takshuma has been given the credit for several innovations in the Kushāṇa coinage. The coinage of Kujula Kadphises was local in character, that is he 'almost always follows the pattern of the denominations that he found in each of his provinces'. V'ima Takshuma initially seems to have had followed a similar pattern, but later on he inaugurated a 'general coinage' for circulation throughout his empire, and this system of uniform coinage was adopted and elaborated upon by his son, V'ima Kadphises. The coinage of Kujula Kadphises does not in general have his personal symbol or *tamga*, although some of his coins do have a peculiar symbol made of a circle and three prongs. V'ima Takshuma started the practice of placing his personal symbol invariably on all his coins, and this practice—the origin of which has been traced back to the Gondopharnes symbol—was followed by his successors like V'ima Kadphises, Kanishka I, and others. V'ima Takshuma could be said to have had a 'long' reign, if this is taken to include the period he served as the governor of his father in the northern provinces of the Kushāṇa empire, together with his independent rule. Incidentally, the *Hou Han-shu* refers to the son and successor of Kujula Kadphises as Yen-kao-chen. Now that we know, from epigraphic and numismatic sources, that the Graeco-Bactrian form of the name of the son and successor of Kujula Kadphises was *Ooemo Takzoo/Ooemo Tak[shomo]*, and the Kh-Br form was *V'ima Takshuma/V'ima Tākshuma*, it becomes difficult to understand their correlation with Yen-kao-chen. It has been suggested that the Chinese chronicler was either using an alternative form of the name of the son and successor of Kujula Kadphises, or *Yen-kao-chen* was the title of that ruler (C J Brown 1999; Cunningham 1971a; Davary and Humbach 1976; Fussman 1974; Gardner 1971; Ghirshman 1948; Lüders 1961; MacDowall 1968; MacDowall 2002; Mitchiner 2001-2002; von Mitterwallner 1986; B N Mukherjee 1995; B N Mukherjee 1997-1998; Oikonomides 1973; Rosenfield 1967; Salomon 1986; Senior 2001; Sircar 1980c; Sims-Williams and Cribb 1995-1996).

Viṁśatika. Coin denomination. The **Ashṭādhyāyī* refers to this coin, which is believed to be a silver coin weighing 20 *māshas* (V S Agrawala 1953).

Viṁśopaka. Coin denomination. Known from several inscriptions, it seems to be derived from the Pkt *vīsovaga* (= Skt, *viṁśopaga*), 'belonging to twenty', and was 1/20 of the standard silver coin in value. Epigraphic evidence shows that 20 *viṁśopakas* made one silver **dramma* or **rūpaka*. The weight of the *dramma* or *rūpaka* was around 20 *rattīs*, thus making a *viṁśopaka* equal to about one *rattī* in weight. From this, it is inferred that *viṁśopaka* was a copper coin, equal to a twentieth of a *dramma* or *rūpaka in value. Pāvīsā* of late mediaeval Rajasthan seems to be derived from Skt *pāda-viṁśopaka*, and was a quarter of a *viṁśopaka*. There is a suggestion that the later day *paisā* might be a modified form of *pāvīsā* (Sircar 1964).

Vīradāman. *Kārddamaka k. He was the son of *Dāmasena, and started his career as a **kshatrapa* under his father in *Śaka year 156, and continued in that capacity up to Śaka year 160. He issued coins of the *Kārddamaka silver type only (Jha and Rajgor 1994; Mirashi 1982; Mitchiner 1976; Rapson 1975; Raychaudhuri 1972; Senior 2001; Sircar 1980e).

Vīrayaśas. *Kulūta chief. He ruled in the first-second centuries AD, and issued the Class I of *Kulūta coins, on which he assumes the title of **rājña*, and also uses the tribal name (Allan 1936; Chakrabortty 1931; Cunningham 1971b; K K Dasgupta 1974; Handa 2007a; Jayaswal 1988; Marshall 1975; Smith 1972).

Viśākhadeva. *Ayodhyā k. He is connected with both *Dhanadeva and *Śivadatta by his type. Like Dhanadeva, he depicted standing figure of *Lakshmī, but instead of being flanked by two symbols as on the coins of Dhanadeva, the deity is flanked by two elephants [*Gajalakshmī] on the coins of Viśākhadeva. Śivadatta also depicted Gajalakshmī on his coins, but there, the goddess is seated, and not standing as on the coins of Viśākhadeva. On this basis, Viśākhadeva is placed between Dhanadeva and Śivadatta in time. His coins bear the device of standing Gajalakshmī and the ld *Viśākhadevasa* on the obv, and a combination of symbols on the rev. Some of the coins of the common 'Bull : Combination of symbols' type of Ayodhyā, issued by this ruler, are also available (Allan 1936; Bela Lahiri 1974; Smith 1972).

Vishṇu. Deity. He was not very important in the Rigvedic period; in the vedic period, his most frequently mentioned achievements are his three steps, and the assistance he provided his friend, *Indra, in slaying Vṛitra. His weapon *par excellence* is the **chakra* (wheel), which represents the sun. His vehicle is the **garuḍa*. In the brāhmaṇa texts, he is constantly identified with sacrifice. In the post-vedic period, he gained in importance, got identified with the cosmic god, Nārāyaṇa, and the Vṛishṇi hero, *Vāsudeva-Kṛishṇa, and eventually had a cult of his own, named variously as Bhāgavatism or Vaishṇavism. He is the second god in the puranic triad of Brahmā, Vishṇu, and *Śiva, who are believed to create, preserve, and destroy the universe, respectively. The worship of the various incarnations of Vishṇu gained popularity, mostly in the Gupta period, although a germ of the idea of incarnations existed even in the vedic period. In the early mediaeval and mediaeval periods, there are instances of the worship of the *Ardhanārī* forms of Vishṇu. In view of the popularity of the worship of Vishṇu, even among the ancient Indian rulers of foreign origin, one would have expected the depiction of this deity to be quite common on ancient Indian coins, particularly of Mathurā, the city intimately associated with *Vāsudeva-Kṛishṇa. But the coins issued by the early Hindu and Śaka rulers of Mathurā do not bear the figure of Vishṇu. It is true that, initially, the standing figure seen on these coins of Mathurā was identified as that of Vishṇu, but this identification has long since been given up, and the figure is now correctly identified as that of *Gajalakshmī. On the rev of the coins of the *Pañchāla ruler, *Vishṇumitra, however, occurs the figure of a male deity, who has been identified as Vishṇu, mainly on the basis of the Pañchāla tradition of anthropomorphically or symbolically depicting that deity on the rev of the coin, whose name generally forms a component of the name of the issuer. Allan is of the view that Vishṇu on the coins of Vishṇumitra is two-armed. But Cunningham, Coomaraswamy, and Banerjea regard the figure as four-armed. As regards the attributes in the hands of this deity, only the *chakra* in the upper l hand is certain. Allan feels that he holds a trident in his r hand, but this object is not very distinct. Smith read the ld accompanying the figure of a male four-armed deity on the rev of a copper coin of the *Kushāṇa ruler, *Huvishka, as *Oosno*, and, perhaps, on this basis, D C Sircar identified the divine figure on this coin as that of Vishṇu. But the reading of the ld is doubtful, and the attributes in the hands of the deity—*triśūla*, *vajra*, antelope, etc—would favour his identification with *Śiva, instead of Vishṇu. The *Imperial Guptas, who proudly refer to themselves as **paramabhāgavata*, that is 'devout worshipper of Vishṇu', do not represent Vishṇu on their coins in his anthropomorphic form, although *Chakrapurusha, the *chakra* of Vishṇu personified, makes his appearance on the **Chakravikrama* type of *Chandragupta II. But *garuḍa* and **garuḍadhvaja* theriomorphically represent Vishṇu on Imperial Gupta coins. The *lion appearing on some ancient Indian coins may also represent Vishṇu theriomorphically, for this deity is also known as Hari, which also means 'lion', and Nṛisiṁha, 'Man-lion', is one of the incarnations of Vishṇu. In fact, J N Banerjea is of the view that the lion depicted on some seals from Bhita and Vaishali, might have Vaishnavite affiliations. The *chakra* on some ancient Indian coins, like those of the *Vṛishṇi tribe, the *Kulūta Vīrayaśas, and the Pañchāla (?) ruler, Achu[ta], seems to be the *sudarśanachakra* of Vishṇu, and represents him symbolically (Allan 1936; Banerjea 2002; R G Bhandarkar 1928; Sukumari

Bhattacharji 1970; Bhaskar Chattopadhyay 1977; Coomaraswamy 1928-1929; Cunningham 1971b; Hillebrandt 1999; Hopkins 1915; Suvira Jaiswal 1981; Bela Lahiri 1974; Macdonell 1897; Rao 1985; Sircar 1971; Sircar 1980f; Wilkins 2006).†

Vishṇudeva. *Kanauj k. His coin, reported from Kanauj, is different from those of *Gomitra, *Brahmamitra, and *Sūryamitra, leading to the suggestion that he might not be connected with the rulers having *mitra*-ending names. However, his type—*tree-in-railing, hare-on-moon, and a **caduceus*-like symbol on the obv, and a *horse before *yūpa* on the rev—associates him with *Śuṅgavarman. Vishṇudeva has been placed after Śuṅgavarman on palaeographical grounds, and is assigned to the first century BC (Allan 1936; K D Bajpai 1964; Bela Lahiri 1974).

Vishṇugupta *Chandrāditya*. *Imperial Gupta k; son of *Kumāragupta III; mid-sixth century AD. He is mentioned in his Nalanda seal, and in his Damodarpur copperplate inscription dated *Gupta era 225 (= 543 AD). It is evident from the seal and the inscription that Vishṇugupta had parts of Bengal and Magadha under his rule. No Imperial Gupta ruler is known after Vishṇugupta. He issued gold coins of the *Archer type only, which bear the vertical ld *Vishṇu* under the king's arm on the obv; the rev has the ld *Śrī-Chandrāditya*. The weight of these coins ranges from 147.4 to 152 grains, and their gold content is as low as 43%. Allan dates the coins of Vishṇugupta between *c* 540 and 560 AD on numismatic grounds (Ashvini Agrawal 1989; Allan 1914; Altekar 1957; S R Goyal 2005; P L Gupta 1998; K P Jayaswal 1933; Smith 1972; Thaplyal, forthcoming).†

Vishṇumitra. *Mathurā k. He issued coins, which show *Lakshmī with lotus in her r hand and some symbols on the obv; and three *elephants with riders on the rev. He is also known from an inscription, datable to the first century BC (Allan 1936; Bela Lahiri 1974).

Vishṇumitra. *Pañchāla k. He seems to be near in time to *Indramitra, because both of them show the divinity on the rev of some of their coins as standing on a pedestal, and on other coins as standing within a domed shrine. Bela Lahiri places Vishṇumitra immediately after Indramitra. According to Cunningham, Coomaraswamy, and J N Banerjea, the deity, *Vishṇu, represented on the coins of Vishṇumitra, is four-armed, although earlier, Allan had described him as two-armed (Allan 1936; Bela Lahiri 1974).

Viśvāmitra. Sage. The figure of Viśvāmitra, standing, facing, with the r hand raised, and an animal skin draped over the left arm, occurs on the obv of the silver coins of the *Audumbara chief, *Dharaghosha. The obv ld specifically refers to the figure as *Viśpamitra* (= Skt, Viśvāmitra). Earlier scholars identified the figure with *Śiva, one of whose names is Viśvāmitra. But K K Dasgupta has pointed out that in the *Kālikāpurāṇa*, it is told that Sage Viśvāmitra's mother embraced an *udumbara* tree while longing for a child, and this shows the connection of Viśvāmitra with that tree, and hence, also with the Audumbaras who might have had the tree as their totem. Viśvāmitra was the son of Kuśika, and the Audumbaras are said to be of the Kauśika *gotra*. Bela Lahiri has pointed out that according to the *Harivaṁśa*, certain descendants of Viśvāmitra are called Audumbaras (Allan 1936; Chakrabortty 1931; Cunningham 1971b; K K Dasgupta 1974; Handa 2007a; Jayaswal 1988; Marshall 1975; Smith 1972).

Audumbara : Dharaghosha

Viśvapāla (?). *Pañchāla k. The ld on the obv of a coin in the British Museum, London, has been tentatively read by Allan as *[Viśva ?]pāla*. K D Bajpai ascribes this coin to *Vaṅgapāla. But Bela Lahiri feels that the ld 'seems to be neither Viśvapāla nor Vaṅgapāla, but something else'. The rev of this coin is blurred (Allan 1936; K D Bajpai 1962; Bela Lahiri 1974).

Viśvasena. *Kārddamaka k. He was the son of *Bhartṛidāman, and the last ruler of the family of *Chashṭana in the *Kārddamaka dynasty. He started his career as a **kshatrapa* in *Śaka year 214, under his father. He never seems to have attained the position of a **mahākshatrapa*, although he issued coins up to Śaka year 226. After him, the main line of Chashṭana seems to have been supplanted by *Rudrasiṁha II. Viśvasena issued coins of the *Kārddamaka silver type (Jha and Rajgor 1994; Mirashi 1982; Mitchiner 1976; Rapson 1975; Raychaudhuri 1972; Senior 2001; Sircar 1980e).

Viśvasiṁha. *Kārddamaka k. He was the son of *Rudrasena II, and started his career as a **kshatrapa* in *Śaka year 197. The coins he issued in this capacity bear dates up to the Śaka year 202. He is also known to have issued coins as **mahākshatrapa*, but the dates on these coins are not certain, although Amiteshwar Jha and Dilip Rajgor propose to place his reign as *mahākshatrapa* from the year 202 or 203 to year 204. His coins are all of the *Kārddamaka silver type (Jha and Rajgor 1994; Mirashi 1982; Mitchiner 1976; Rapson 1975; Raychaudhuri 1972; Senior 2001; Sircar 1980e).

Vonones and Spalahora

Vonones. *Śaka-Pahlava k; earliest known Śaka-Pahlava ruler; first half of the first century BC. Cunningham regards him as originally a lieutenant of *Maues, left behind in Seistan to govern the region when Maues himself pushed forward into India. Later, Vonones was either installed as the king of Seistan by Maues himself, or he rebelled against Maues and declared himself the supreme sovereign in Seistan. But Tarn regards Vonones as originally serving under the Arsakid emperor, Orodes II, as his vassal, and later asserting his independence. It is generally believed, by scholars like Alexander Cunningham, J H Marshall, and G K Jenkins, that the 'chief centre of rule' of the family of Vonones was Arachosia. But R C Senior is of the view that a western branch of the Śaka-Pahlavas was pushed by the Yueh-chihs across the rivers Jaxartes and Oxus, while another branch of these peoples was already moving from Sogdiana. They first occupied Merv and northern Bactria, and then crossed the Hindukush into India, occupying Kapiśā, the Kabul valley, and western Gandhāra, that is they advanced east into the *Indo-Greek territories. In the Kabul valley, they imitated the coins of *Hermaios. Senior associates Vonones with this branch of the Śaka-Pahlavas, and regards the coins issued by him and his associates as 'successors of the imitation Hermaios coinage'. On the evidence of the *provenance* of coins, Senior places the circulation of the coins of the family of Vonones mainly in 'the great Gandhāra region, west of Taxila'. No coin bearing the name of Vonones alone is known so far. However, his name occupies the place of honour on the obv on the coins of *Spalahora and *Spalagadama, who seem to have ruled as his viceroys. Of these, the former styles himself 'brother of the king', while the latter is introduced as 'son of Spalahora'.

The coins mentioning Vonones on the obv and Spalahora on the rev are both in silver and copper. The silver coins have horseman king on the obv, and standing *Zeus on the rev, while the copper coins have standing *Herakles crowning himself on the obv and *Athena holding spear and shield on the rev. There are some silver and copper coins, which bear the name of Vonones on the obv, and that of Spalagadama on the rev. The silver coins have horseman king on the obv, and standing *Zeus with thunderbolt and sceptre on the rev. The copper coins have standing *Herakles crowning himself on the obv, and *Athena holding spear and shield on the rev. Another brother of Vonones was *Spalirises, who issued satrapal coins on which he refers to himself as 'brother of the king'. The name of the 'king' is not mentioned on these coin; however, most of the scholars identify him with Vonones, and the suggestion, that he might be *Maues, is not acceptable. The publication of a silver coin bearing the figure of horseman king and the ld *Basileos basileon megalou Ononou* on the obv, and standing *Zeus with the ld *Maharajabhrata dhramiäsa Spalirishasa* on the rev, would seem to set the controversy at rest. Some scholars have doubted that Vonones, Spalahora and Spalirises were brothers, without valid grounds. A joint coin type of Spalirises with Azes I, on which both call themselves 'great king', is believed to have been issued when both of them were serving as subordinate rulers under Vonones. Spalirises later on issued independent coins and also restruck the joint coins of Vonones with Spalahora (or Spalagadama) and also the joint coins of Spalahora with Spalagadama. From this, it has been inferred that Vonones was overthrown by Spalirises, who also removed from power Spalahora and Spalagadama, perhaps because they remained loyal to Vonones even after the usurpation of the throne by Spalirises (Cunningham 1971a; Gardner 1971; Jenkins and Narain 1957; Marshall 1975; B N Mukherjee 1969a; Rapson 1987; Senior 2001; Sircar 1980b; Prashant Srivastava 1996a; Tarn 1980; Whitehead 1914).

Vṛishabha. *Nāga k. He seems to be the first Nāga king known from coins. He issued round coins of the 'Bull' type. H V Trivedi reads his name as Vṛishabhava, and suggests that he might be a successor of Vṛisha or *Vṛishanāga. Bela Lahiri seems to consider the possibility of the identity of Vṛishabha and Vṛishanāga (Bela Lahiri 1974; H V Trivedi 1957).

Vṛishanāga. *Nāga k. H V Trivedi has read the name Vṛishanāga on some rectangular copper coins from Padmāvatī, bearing the device of humped *bull on both the sides. The ld, however, on the obv all the coins published by him is incomplete, and hence, it is difficult to be certain about the reading of the name of the issuing king. But this issuer seems to be an early Nāga ruler. Bela Lahiri considers the possibility of his identity with *Vṛishabha (Bela Lahiri 1974; H V Trivedi 1957).

Vṛishṇi. Tribe. The *Ashṭādhyāyī* of Pāṇini speaks of the Andhaka-Vṛishṇi *saṁgha*; the *Mahābhārata* includes some other tribes also in this confederation, and refers to Vāsudeva as its leader. The purāṇas and the *Arthaśāstra* also mention the tribe. In the epic-puranic tradition, they are associated with the Mathurā region, but the evidence of the *Śatapathabrāhmaṇa* seems to suggest that in the later vedic period, they inhabited some area in Haryana or Punjab. The *Harivaṁśa* informs that, when attacked, they left Mathurā under the leadership of Kṛishṇa, and settled in Dvārakā. Only one coin of this tribe, of silver, round in shape, and of unknown *provenance* but procured by Cunningham along with the *Audumbara coins, is known for certain. It weighs 32 grains, and bears, on the obv, a symbol, a **nandipada* standard in railing, with an animal which is half-lion-half-elephant, and the ld *Vṛishṇi rājajñāgaṇasya tratarasya*; the rev has a *wheel and the Kh ld *Vṛishṇi rājaṇṇa[ga]..tra*.... In the context of the Vṛishṇis, the wheel should be taken as *sudarśanachakra* of *Vāsudeva-Kṛishṇa, and not the Buddhist *dharmachakra* as suggested by some scholars. The ld has been interpreted variously as 'of the protector of the tribe Vṛishṇirājanya', ie 'of the protector of the Rājanya (or warrior) tribe of the Vṛishṇis'; or 'of a family whose name (?) is Vṛishṇirāja' or 'whose royal name (?) is Vṛishṇi'; or '[the coin] of him whose family are Vṛishṇi kshatriyas'; or '[coin] of the saviour of the host of Vṛishṇi kings', etc. P L Gupta regards this coin as a joint issue of a confederation of the Vṛishṇis and the Rājanyas. Some even take Jñāgaṇa as a personal name, and translate the ld as '[This is the coin] of Jñāgaṇa, King of the Vṛishṇis, the Saviour'. On the basis of the mention of *Vṛishṇi-rājanya-gaṇa* at the beginning of the ld on two sealings from Sunet, Devendra Handa proposes to the read the ld on the coin as *Vṛishṇi-rājanya-*

gaṇasya trātārasya, and suggests that the coin was issued in the name of Vāsudeva-Kṛishṇa, who is mentioned in the *Mahābhārata* as the saviour (*trātā*) of the Vṛishṇis, and whose emblem, the wheel, occurs on the rev of this coin. He further suggests that, the Vṛishṇis might have dedicated their state to Vāsudeva-Kṛishṇa, and issued the coin in his name. This reminds one of the *Kuṇindas, who seem to have dedicated their state to *Śiva, and of the *Yaudheyas, who apparently dedicated their state to *Kārttikeya. Devendra Handa has published certain copper coins, mostly from Sunet, which bear, on the obv, a Br ld, variously mentioning such names as Yajñasoma, Vyāghrasoma, Vyāghrasattra, Jayasa/Jiyasa, Vasusena, Jayasoma/Āryyasoma, Yajñadeva, Sattragupta, Balavighna/Balavāhana, Vesha (?), etc. The rev of these coins has a wheel, which, according to Handa, associates these coins with the silver coin of the Vṛishṇis. He regards the persons mentioned on these copper coins as Vṛishṇi generals (like the *mahāsenāptis* mentioned on the sealings from Sunet), who seem to have been elected by the *gaṇa* as their rulers, and were vested with the right to issue coins in their own names. Handa places these copper coins bearing names of issuers, after the silver coin, which, he says, were issued in the name of Vāsudeva-Kṛishṇa. Though the literary evidence places the Vṛishṇis in Mathurā, the likely *provenance* of the coin (Punjab), the *chakra* which also occurs on *Kulūta coins, the epithet **tratara* which is a translation of the Greek **soter*, and the use of the Kh script, point out that at the time of the issue of the coin, Punjab was the homeland of the Vṛishṇis. Either these Vṛishṇis were different from those of Mathurā, or else originally the Vṛishṇis belonged to Mathurā, from where they migrated to Dvārakā, and after the destruction of that city, some migrated thence to Punjab. The *Vishṇupurāṇa* states that after the destruction of Dvārakā, Arjuna settled the Vṛishṇis in the Pañchanada country (Punjab), and 20 seals of the Vṛishṇis have been reported from Sunet. Interestingly, the Vārshaṇeyas of today, who are considered as the descendants of the Vṛishṇis, claim Agroha in Hissar district as their original home. This would suggest that the Vṛishṇis, at some point of time, inhabited the area between the upper courses of the Ravi and Beas (Allan 1936; Chakrabortty 1931; Cunningham 1971b; K K Dasgupta 1974; P L Gupta 1988; Handa 2007a; Jayaswal 1988; Bela Lahiri 1974; Marshall 1975; Mitchiner 1975-1976; Omanand Saraswati VS2031; Smith 1972).

Vyāghranāga. *Nāga k. He is known from a unique coin bearing the device of a *wheel on the obv, and the ld on the rev. The rectangular shape of this coin seems to indicate his affinity with *Vṛishanāga, who is also known to have issued rectangular coins, and on this basis, Vyāghranāga is believed to be among the early Nāga rulers. He is among the few Nāga rulers who did not issue 'Bull' type of coins. He assumed the title of **mahārāja* on coins (Cunningham 1967; Bela Lahiri 1974; H V Trivedi 1957).

Vyāghrasattra. *Vṛishṇi general (?).

Vyāghrasoma. *Vṛishṇi general (?).

W

Wesa hoard. This hoard of around 1,220 *Indo-Greek coins was found in January 1994, in the village of Wesa in the Chach region of Pakistan. The rulers represented in this hoard include *Antialkidas, *Antimachos II, *Apollodotos, *Heliokles, *Lysias, and Menander I (Bopearachchi 1994; Bopearachchi and Rahman 1995).

Western Indian type. Silver. *Chandragupta II, after conquering and annexing the *Kārddamaka territories in Kathiawar, was obliged to issue silver currency for the convenience of his new subjects, who were accustomed to the use of silver. He, thus, became the first *Imperial Gupta ruler to definitely strike money in silver (if the silver coins of the *King-and-Queen type of *Chandragupta I and *Kumāradevī are regarded as forged, as they most probably should be). Chandragupta II tried to make his silver monetary issues, to a great extent, similar to the *Western Kshatrapa coins. These coins of Chandragupta II, weighing, on an average, about 36 grains, show the bust of the king on the obv, together with traces of the Gr ld and the date of issue of the coin, in the *Gupta era, behind the head of the king. On the rev, the *hill symbol of the Kārddamaka silver issues, was replaced by the figure of the **garuḍa*. The rev circular ld gives the name and titles of the king. The earliest silver coins of Chandragupta II seem to be dated in Gupta era 90, that 409 AD. The circular ld on some coins of Chandragupta II is **Paramabhāgavata-mahārājādhirāja Śrī-Chandragupta-Vikramāditya*, and on other coins, it is *Śrī-Guptakulasya-mahārājādhirāja Śrī-Chandragupta-Vikramāṅkasya*. These coins, issued for circulation mainly in the

Chandragupta II : Western Indian type

Chandragupta II : Western Indian type

Kumāragupta I : Western Indian type

Skandagupta : Western Indian type

western provinces, are called the Western Indian type of *Imperial Gupta silver coins. This type of silver coinage was continued by *Kumāragupta I, and his coins of this type was divided into four classes, on the basis of the rev circular ld or the fabric of the coins. Class I coins have the ld *Paramabhāgavata-mahārājādhirāja Śrī-Kumāragupta Mahendrādityaḥ*. The circular ld on some coins of Class II is *Paramabhāgavata-*rājādhirāja Śrī-Kumāragupta-Mahendrāditya*, and on other coins of this class, it is *Bhāgavata-rājādhirāja-Śrī-Kumāragupta Mahendrāditya*. The coins of Class III are similar to those of Class I, but they are smaller and thicker in fabric, and the rev ld sometimes has *rājādhirāja* in place of *mahārājādhirāja*. Class IV is extremely rare. Its rev seems to bear a trident in place of the usual *garuḍa*, and the ld reads *Paramabhāgavata-[rājādhirāja ?] Śrī-Kumāragupta Mahendrasya*. *Skandagupta seems to be the last Imperial Gupta ruler to issue Western Indian type of silver coins. They are divided into three classes. Class I is the regular type, with the ld *Paramabhāgavata-mahārājādhirāja Śrī-Skandagupta Kramādityaḥ*. Class II has a *bull recumbent to the r on the rev, in place of the *garuḍa*. Class III coins have an altar in the centre on the rev, and the circular ld, on various coins of this class, is *Paramabhāgavata Śrī-Vikramāditya Skandaguptaḥ*, or *Paramabhāgavata Śrī-Skandaguptaḥ Kramādityaḥ*. Some scholars regard the altar on this type as **tulasī-vṛindāvana* (Ashvini Agrawal 1989; Allan 1914; Altekar 1957; R D Banerji 1933; S R Goyal 2005; P L Gupta 1998; Smith 1972; Prashant Srivastava 1996a; Prashant Srivastava 2004b; Thaplyal, forthcoming).

Western Kshatrapas. These rulers of Śaka origin held sway over the western parts of India, particularly in Gujarat, Maharashtra, Rajasthan, and Malwa, and most of them assumed the title of **kshatrapa* or **mahākshatrapa*. As such, they have become famous in Indian history as Western Kshatrapas. Three branches of these Western Kshatrapas—*Kshaharāta dynasty, *Kārddamaka dynasty, and the Kshatrapas of Vidarbha, are known so far. The Western Kshatrapas ruled for over 300 years, and the rulers of the first two branches issued coins in silver, copper, potin, lead, and an alloy of copper with lead. Their coins influenced the issues of the subsequent Indian rulers for several centuries (Jha and Rajgor 1994; Mirashi

1982; Rapson 1975; Raychaudhuri 1972; Senior 2001; Sircar 1980e).

Wheel. Symbol. *_Chakra_.

Wheel marked coins. See *Bent bars.

Y

Yajñadeva. *Vṛishṇi general (?).

Yajñamagha (?). *Magha k.

Yajñapāla. *Pañchāla k. There is a suggestion that he is to be connected with *Dhruvamitra and *Rudragupta on the basis of the rev device, and if this be accepted, Yajñapāla may be placed near them in time. The device on the rev of the coins of Yajñapāla shows a sacrificial altar, flame, sacrificer, and *yūpa*, all connected with *yajña* (Altekar 1942c; Bela Lahiri 1974).

Yajñasoma. *Vṛishṇi general (?).

Yaksha. Semi-divine being. The term *yaksha* occurs for the first time in the *Jaiminīyabrāhmaṇa*, but simply in the sense of 'a wondrous thing'; as a genius, it appears only in the gṛihyasūtras. The yakshas are believed to be non-Aryan-pre-Aryan deities or 'beneficent powers of wealth and fertility'. It is only in the later period that they were degraded, and often confused with the rākshasas with whom they seem to share a common origin. Their chief is Kubera. They are sometimes grouped with the nāgas and gandharvas. In some works, they are associated with disease. But one of the chief characteristics of yakshas is their role as guardians and supporters. J N Banerjea is of the opinion that, though they occur rather rarely, the yakshas and yakshiṇīs do not altogether fail to make their appearance on early Indian indigenous coins. On three coins of *Ujjayinī in the British Museum collection, Allan sees 'two draped female figures

Telephos

standing facing', with the one on the left holding an uncertain object in her raised r hand. There is a river with fishes below. J N Banerjea, who published a coin with similar device from Ujjayinī or Avantī, is of the view that the figures are not both female, but that one is male and the other female. He proposes to identify the figures as a yaksha and a yakshiṇī, respectively, on the basis of their dress and attitude, which is not unlike that of the yaksha and yakshiṇī images from Bhilsa. This identification is also supported by the fact that on the coins from Ujjayinī, river and fishes are associated with these figures, and, according to Coomaraswamy, fishes are the *vāhanas* of yakshas and yakshiṇīs. But it has been pointed out that in the textual descriptions of yakshas, they are usually pot bellied, and holds *nidhis* in their hands. The male figure on the coins above, identified as yaksha by Banerjea, does not show either of these two features, and on this ground, the identification has been doubted. On the obv of some silver coins of the *Indo-Greek ruler, *Telephos, appears a figure, the body of which ends in serpents. According to Gardner, the figure holds hammers in both hands, and on this basis, he identifies it as the giant, Skythes, of Greek mythology. It is true that, as indicated by Whitehead, Telephos was the patron hero of Pergamon in Asia Minor, and in the Pergamene frieze (dated *c* 180 BC), there is a depiction of the contest between the gods and snake-legged giants. But Marshall points out that the figure does not hold hammers, but in each of the two hands is shown a lotus stalk, which develops from the serpent-like legs. He identifies the figure as that of a yaksha, and this identification has been accepted by scholars like Whitehead (who regards it as a 'lotus yaksha') and A N Lahiri. Images of yakshas, with lotus plants issuing from their mouths, navels, etc are not unknown. Recently, R C Senior has tentatively proposed to identify this deity with Echidna, or some river deity, or even *Lakshmī on the basis of the lotus stalks in her hands (Bhaskar Chattopadhyay 1977; Coomaraswamy 2001; Gardner 1971; Pulak Kundu 1982; A N Lahiri 1965; Marshall 1975; R N Misra 1981; Senior 2003; Whitehead 1975).†

Yakshī/Yakshiṇī. Semi-divine being. She is the female counterpart of *yaksha, and associated with wealth, marriage, and fertility. There is a suggestion that the Saptamātṛikās, Śītalā, the Ḍākinīs and the Yoginīs, village divinities, Mīnākshī the consort of *Śiva to

Pantaleon

whom the famous temple at Madurai is dedicated, and even Durgā, might originally have been yakshiṇīs. Yakshiṇīs are associated with marriage in the *Maṇichūḍāvadāna*. Yakshiṇīs are often associated with trees, and even regarded as born in trees (*vṛikshajā*). According to J N Banerjea, a yakshiṇī appears standing by the side of a yaksha on three coins from *Ujjayinī, and on a fourth coin from Ujjayinī or Avantī, but this has been doubted by some scholars (*yaksha). On the rev of some square copper coins issued by the *Indo-Greek rulers, *Agathokles and *Pantaleon, there occurs a female figure, dressed in 'oriental drapery with trousers' standing to the l, 'with long pendants from her ears'. She holds a flower in her r hand. This figure has been identified as *Lakshmī on the basis of the flower in her hand, and as a 'dancing girl'. Attempts have been made to identify her as Ekānaṁśā or Subhadrā, the sister of *Vāsudeva-Kṛishṇa and *Balarāma. But J N Banerjea regards this figure as that of a yakshiṇī, and on the basis of the long 'non-human head', calls her 'Yakshiṇī Aśvamukhi' (Allan 1936; Banerjea 1938; Banerjea 2002; Bopearachchi 1993; Bopearachchi and Rahman 1995; Bhaskar Chattopadhyay 1977; Coomaraswamy 2001; Cowell 2005; Pulak Kundu 1982; A N Lahiri 1965; R N Misra 1981).†

Yaśodāman I. *Kārddamaka k. He was the son of *Dāmasena, and started his career as a *kshatrapa* in *Śaka year 160. But the next year, or, perhaps, even in the same year, he is found issuing coins as **mahākshatrapa*, though his career as a *mahākshatrapa* was very short, ending some time around the middle of the year 161. He issued coins of the *Kārddamaka silver type (Jha and Rajgor 1994; Mirashi 1982; Mitchiner 1976; Rapson 1975; Raychaudhuri 1972; Senior 2001; Sircar 1980e).

Yaśodāman II. *Kārddamaka k. He was the son of *Rudrasiṁha II, and ruled as **kshatrapa* from *Śaka year 239 to 254, although R C Senior places his initial issues in the year 237. He never seems to have attained the position of a **mahākshatrapa*. The end of his reign is followed by a period of 16 years, when we do not hear of any Kārddamaka *kshatrapa* or *mahākshatrapa*. His coins are of the *Kārddamaka silver type (Jha and Rajgor 1994; Mirashi 1982; Mitchiner 1976; Rapson 1975; Raychaudhuri 1972; Senior 2001; Sircar 1980e).

Yaudheya

Yaudheya. Tribe. The *Ashṭādhyāyī* of Pāṇini mentions the Yaudheyas as an *āyudhajīvī saṁgha*, but, recently, attempts have been made to trace the antiquity of this tribe up to the later vedic period on the basis of the occurrence of *Yaudheya* in the pre-Pāṇini *Śākaṭāyanavyākaraṇa* and the *Jaiminīyabrāhmaṇa*. The tribe also finds mentions in the *Mahābhāshya*, the purāṇas, the *Bṛihatsaṁhitā*, the *Chāndravyākaraṇa*, and *Kāśikā*. The *Mahābhārata* refers to Yaudheya as a son of Yudhishṭhira and his wife, Devikā or Devakī, but, according to the *Vishṇupurāṇa*, Yudhishṭhira won the hand of the Princess Yaudheyī in a *svayaṁvara*. The name of the princess (Yaudheyī) seems to show that she belonged to the Yaudheya tribe; if this be correct, the Yaudheyas must have existed before Yudhishṭhira, and the tribe could not have descended from Yudhishṭhira's son. The *Yaśastilaka* of Somadevasūri (tenth century AD) refers to the Rājapura city (identified with Rajapur in former Patiala state) of the Yaudheyas. Still later, the tribe is mentioned in the *Sarasvatīkaṇṭhābharaṇa* and the *Vaijayantī*. The *Harivaṁśa* and some purāṇas consider the Yaudheyas as descendants of Nṛiga, the son of Uśīnara. The Junagarh inscription of *Rudradāman I, the Bijayagadh inscription and the Allahabad pillar inscription of *Samudragupta also refer to this tribe. The first of these inscriptions refers to the defeat of the Yaudheyas at the hands Rudradāman I. The Bijayagadh inscription of the third century AD, mentions their elected leader, a **mahārāja* and *mahāsenāpati*. A sealing from Agroha refers to *mahārāja*, *mahākshatrapa*, and *mahāsenāpati* as titles of Indramitra or Rājyamitra, who, as per the testimony of the sealing, had been selected as such by the Yaudheya *gaṇa*. Curiously, the classical writers make no mention of this tribe, although Arrian's description of a people beyond the Hyphasis as good agriculturists and gallant fighters and having a constitutional government, is taken by some scholars, like K P Jayaswal, to the refer to the Yaudheyas. Cunningham considers the Johiya Rajputs as the descendants of the Yaudheyas. Yaudheya coins have been found in various parts of Punjab, Haryana, Himachal Pradesh, Delhi, Rajasthan, and Uttar Pradesh; or, in other words, from western Uttar Pradesh in the east to eastern Rajasthan in the west, and from Kangra in the north to Sambhar in the south. Their coin moulds have been found at Sunet near Ludhiana (over 30,000), at Khokra Kot near Rotak (around

Yaudheya

1,000), and at Naurangabad near Bhiwani (about 8,500); these appear to be the great mint sites of the Yaudheyas. A Yaudheya terracotta seal with the ld, *Yaudheya janapada*, is known from Naurangabad. According to A M Shastri, this seal refers to the town of Prakṛitānākanagara of the Yaudheya *janapada* of Rohīta (that is Rohtak). Devendra Handa suggests that the old Yaudheya capital, Rohītaka, might have been destroyed in the course of some *Indo-Greek invasion, that Prakṛitānākanagara might have been the new capital of the tribe. Naurangabad has also yielded four clay sealings, one copper seal, one lead seal, and one lead sealing, all associated with the Yaudheyas. Rohītaka is mentioned in the *Mahābhārata* as abounding in cattle and crops, a favourite abode of *Karttikeya, and inhabited by the Mattamayūrakas. These Mattamayūrakas are identified with the Yaudheyas, the devotees of Kārttikeya whose *vāhana* is **mayūra*. It has been suggested that the territory of the Yaudheyas extended 'from Ludhiana to Saharanpur and beyond in Garhwal in one direction and from there to Bahawalpur in another', with Rohtak and its environs as its core. Richard Mann, however, is of the view that at the time of the issue of their early coinage, the tribe inhabited the Rohtak-Naurangabad region. But it was forced to move towards the foothills of the Himalayas as a result of the invasion of *V'ima Takshuma. According to him, there are no Yaudheya coins for the period when *Kanisha I and *Huvishka were ruling, and the Yaudheyas seem to have started issuing their coinage again only towards the end of the reign of *Vāsudeva I. In this period, the tribe sems to have, once again, occupied the Rohtak-Naurangabad region, expanded its territories, at least up to Hissar in the west, and the river Yamuna in the east, and established Sunet as one of its centres. The Yaudheya coins are in silver, copper, potin, and brass. The silver coin weighs about 26 grains; the weight-range of the copper coins is 9.5-200 grains, of potin coins 14.5-77 grains, and of brass coins 35.8-42 grains, the heavier weight coins being more common. These coins have been placed between the second century BC and mid-fourth century AD (when the tribe submitted to Samudragupta, as per the evidence of the Allahabad pillar inscription). The Yaudheya coins have been divided into eight classes. Class I has a *tree-in-railing, with or without *Ujjain symbol, on the obv, and the rev is plain; only on one specimen the ld, *Mahārājasya*, occurs on the rev. Although K D Bajpai takes these coins as issued from

Kauśāmbī, they have been ascribed to the Yaudheyas as they resemble the coins of this tribe in their metal, fabric, and *provenance*; this has the support of scholars like Osmund Bopearachchi and Wilfried Pieper. Devendra Handa, however, regards them as the local coins of Behat. Class II has either a *bull or a *horse before *yūpa*, and the ld *Yaudheyānāṁ bahudhāñake* on the obv, and an *elephant and **nandipada* on the rev. One variety of this Class, represented by a specimen in the Jhajjar Gurukula, is reported to bear a *chakradhvaja* on the rev. Michael Mitchiner has published a variety of this Class, which has only the Br ld on the obv, arranged in two lines. *Bahudhāñake* of the coins is identified by the Bahudhānyaka country (originally comprising present day Jhunjhunu, Gurgaon, Rohtak, Naurangabad-Bamla, Meerut, and Saharanpur regions) mentioned in the *Mahābhārata* and the *Mahāmāyūrī*. The silver coin of Class III has the standing figure of six-headed *Kārttikeya, holding spear in the r hand, and the ld, *Bhagavata svāmino Brahmaṇya Yaudheya*, on the obv, and six-headed *Shashṭhī and some symbols on the rev. P L Gupta has doubted the existence of *Yaudheya* as the last component of the ld on the silver coin. But Devendra Handa, after an examination of the coin in the collection of the British Museum, London, is convinced of its occurrence in the coin ld. The copper coins of this class have similar devices, but the ld on the rev reads *Bhagavata svāmino Brahmaṇyadevasya Kumārasya*. The view of Nisar Ahmad, supported by P L Gupta, that these copper coins, bearing *Kumāra* as part of the ld, were the issues of the tribe, Kumāra, known from the purāṇas and the *Mahābhārata*, is not acceptable, as *Kumāra* in the coin ld is in the singular and the coins are typologically similar to the Yaudheya coins. It has been suggested that the name Kumāra occurs together with Brahmaṇyadeva on the copper coins because, although Brahmaṇyadeva was one of the names of Kārttikeya, it was also used for *Vishṇu, Mahāpurusha, Durgā/*Umā (who are called Brahmaṇyā), and *Śiva. The engraver seems to have added *Kumāra* at the end of the ld on the copper coins to make it clear that on the coins, *Brahmaṇyadeva* is being used for Kārttikeya. On one copper coin, reported by Devendra Handa, the head of Shashṭhī is represented by a *lotus. Handa also draws attention towards a copper coin published by Cunningham, the obv of which shows a *cock perched on the shoulder of six-headed Kārttiekeya. On some copper coins, the figure of a *deer replaces the goddess on the rev. One coin of this variety is reported to bear a ld, read as *Bhadrapuru[shasya]*, which has been compared with Bhadra-śākha, a name or epithet of Kārttikeya. Some copper coins of this class have the figure of three-headed Śiva and some symbols on the rev. One copper coin of this variety reportedly bears the figure of a goddess, who has been identified as *Pārvatī, on the obv, and Śiva on the rev. On the basis of the occurrence of the figure of Kārttikeya on most of the coins of this class and on the coins of other types of the Yaudheyas, as also of the coin legends of this class mentioning the god, it has been suggested that the Yaudheyas might have dedicated their state to their patron deity, and administered their territories in his name (as the *Kuṇindas did in the name of **Chatreśvara* Śiva). Class IV has the figure of Kārttikeya with spear and traces of a ld on the obv, and symbols, like *deer, *hill, *tree-in-railing, **svastika*, **śrīvatsa*, etc, on the rev. One variety of this class has the figure of Śiva with trident on the obv. Class V has a hill symbol and *svastika* and a Br ld mentioning *Bhānuva*, sometimes with the title **rājña*, on the obv; the rev of various coins of this class have a standard and trident, or some deity, or six-headed Kārttikeya. K K Maheshwari has read the names, *Bhānugh[osha] and *Jayava[rmā], on some copper coins from a hoard, perhaps the *Chakkar hoard from the Mandi district of Himachal Pradesh. He feels that they might have been Yaudheya chiefs. But P L Gupta attributes these coins to the family of Varsha *gaṇa*. Scholars like Devendra Handa, too, are not in favour of attributing these coins to the Yaudheyas. Class VI has a *bull and the Br ld *Yaudheyānāṁ* on the obv, while the rev is obliterated. Class VII coins have six-headed Kārttikeya with spear, a *peacock, and the ld *Yaudheyagaṇasya jaya* on the obv; the rev has a female deity walking. In one variety of this class, the ld *dvi*, and in another variety, *tri* has been added. The significance of these additional legends is not certain. Various scholars have suggested that they denote the second and third divisions of the Yaudheya tribe, or the second and third republics of the Yaudheyas, or the second and third components of the federation the Yaudheyas had formed with the Kuṇindas and the *Ārjunāyanas. Bela Lahiri suggests that the *Mahābhārata* refers to Rohītaka (Rohtak), Marubhūmi (Bikaner and Bahawalpur), and Śirīshika (Sunet) as three centres of the Yaudheyas, and *dvi* and *tri* may refer to the second and third of these centres. Devendra Handa proposes that *dvi* and *tri* on these coins might denote 'the politico-administrative units of the Yaudheyas with headquarters at Sunet, Naurangabad and Agroha'. It has even been suggested that *dvi* and *tri* on these coins refer, respectively, to the second and third Yaudheya mints, or to the second and third victory of the Yaudheyas over the Kushāṇas. Class VIII consists of coins with the figure of a goddess or a symbol and the ld *Rāvaṇa* or *Rāvaṇasya* on the obv, and a male figure or trident, alone or with other symbols, on the rev. These coins have been attributed to the Yaudheyas only on stylistic and typological grounds. Some 12 coins of Shashṭhī type with the ld *Brahmaṇya-devasya Dvimātteya* (or, *Darmattaya*), from Tehri Garhwal, are also known. Devendra Handa informs us that a coin dealer reported having obtained a gold coin bearing the figure and name of Kārttikeya on the obv, and the figure of Shashṭhī on the rev. But, as he had not seen the coin or even its photograph, he could not vouch for its existence or authenticity. Devendra Handa is of the view that the **Chateśvara* series, generally ascribed to the Kuṇindas, was issued by the Yaudheyas, after they had wrested the Garhwal region from the Kuṇindas (Allan 1936; K D Bajpai 1973; Bopearachchi and Pieper 1998; Chakrabortty 1931; Cunningham 1971b; K K Dasgupta 1974; P L Gupta 1987; P L Gupta 1988; Handa 2007a; Jayaswal 1988; Bela Lahiri 1974; K K Maheshwari 1978; Mann 2007; Marshall 1975; Mitchiner 1975-1976; Smith 1972).

Yavuga. *Kushāṇa title. This title appears in the Kh ld on the coins of *Kujula Kadphises, and is believed to the Pkt rendering of **zaoos* (Cunningham 1971a; Gardner 1971; Rosenfield 1967; Whitehead 1914).

Yerrinemmapadu hoard. This hoard of 24 silver coins of the *Kārddamaka Kshatrapas was discovered in the Krishna district of Andhra Pradesh. The rulers represented include *Vijayasena, *Rudrasena II, *Viśvasiṁha, Bhartṛidāman, and *Viśvasena (Jha and Rajgor 1994).

Yugasena. *Pañchāla k. The rev of the coins of Yugasena, *Anamitra, *Śivanandiśrī, *Śrīnandi, *Varuṇamitra, and *Vasusena does not bear the anthropomorphic or symbolic representation of any divinity, as is the usual case with the Pañchāla series, and, on this basis, it has been suggested that they might have ruled at a later period, when the practice of representing a deity alluding to the name of the issuing king on the rev of the coin had become lax. However, Yugasena uses the three Pañchāla symbols on the obv, and this seems to place him before Anamitra, Śivanandiśrī, and Śrīnandi. The rev of his coins bears the figure of a *tree-in-railing (Allan 1936; Bela Lahiri 1974).

Z

Zaoos. *Kushāṇa title. Appearing on the coins of *Kujula Kadphises, the title seems to be the Greek rendering of *shao-wu*, which title, according to the Chinese, was adopted by the kings of the Tuholo or Tochari with whom the Kushāṇas are identified. In Kh ld, *zaoou* is rendered as **yavuga* or *yaüa* (Cunningham 1962; Cunningham 1971a; Gardner 1971; Rosenfield 1967; Whitehead 1914).

Zeionises. Śaka satrap. On numismatic grounds, he seems to be associated with western Punjab and eastern parts of Hazara-Kashmir, and to be a contemporary of *Azes II. His coins describe him as a **kshatrapa* and a son of **Kshatrapa* Maṇigula. A Taxila inscription of [Vikrama *saṁvat*] 191 (= 134 AD) refers to one Jihoṇika as a *kshatrapa* of Chukhsa (modern Chach, northwest of Taxila, although Pushkalāvatī, or some region in Kashmir, have also been proposed as possible identifications). The inscription also refers to him as *maharajabhrata*, but the identity of this *maharaja* is not clear. Jihoṇika seems to be a Pkt rendering of Zeionises, and Zeionises of the Taxila inscription seems to be a grandson of Zeionises, son of Maṇigula, known from coins. R C Senior regards him as a successor of *Azilises in the Hazara-Kashmir region. Zeionises issued coins in both silver and copper/bronze. The silver coins are all round in shape, while the copper coins are mostly round; square shape, though is seen in some copper issues, is rather rare. The obv of his silver coins has horseman king, and a Gr ld referring to his father Maṇigula, and to his own title of *satrap*. The rev has the king being crowned, by two figures on one type, by *Nike holding palm on another type, and by the city-goddess holding **cornucopiae* on the

Zeionises

Zeionises

third type; the rev ld in Kh refers to Zeionises himself as *kshatrapa*, and as the son of *Kshatrapa* Maṇigula, but one silver type refers to him as **mahākshatrapa*, and a son of Maṇigula. The obv devices of his copper/bronze types include *bull and *elephant, while the rev devices include *lion and bull. The obv ld is the same as that on the silver types, or its variant. The rev ld mentions Zeionises as a *kshatrapa* and son of Maṇigula, but there is no title used for the latter. The form of the name of Zeionises in the Kh ld is Jihuniä (Gardner 1971; Jenkins and Narain 1957; Marshall 1975; B N Mukherjee 1969a; Senior 2001; Sircar 1980b; Tarn 1980; Whitehead 1914).

Zero. Avestan goddess, Zahr. The rev of some gold coins of *Huvishka bears the figure of a goddess standing to the r. She holds a bow in her l hand, and is shown drawing an arrow from a quiver, with her r hand. The suggestion of von Sallet to read the label inscription beside the deity as *Meiro* is not accepted by other scholars. Stein read it as *Teiro*, and identified the deity as the Iranian Tishtrya, the star Sirius known as Tir in Pahlavi and invoked in the Tir Yasht as the god who fertilizes the earth by swiftly causing rains. But the deity on the *Kushāṇa coins is female, while Tishtrya is male. Besides, her figure closely resembles that of *Artemis on *Indo-Greek and *Śaka-Pahlava coins, in that both are represented as wielding the bow and arrow. As such, Cunningham and F W Thomas seem to be correct in reading the label inscription as *Zero*, and identifying the deity depicted with the Iranian Zahr who corresponds to the Greek Artemis and the Roman Venus (Bhaskar Chattopadhyay 1977; Cunningham 1971a; Darmesteter 1974; Gardner 1971; Rosenfield 1967; Stein 1888).

Antialkidas

Zeus. Greek supreme god. This foremost among the Greek gods and dweller of the Olympus, was the son of Kronos and Rhea, and brother of Hestia, Hera, *Demeter, *Poseidon, and Hades. He was originally conceived of as a sky god, and corresponds to Dyaus, the Indian sky god. He later led his siblings against the Titans, defeated them, and imprisoned them in Tartaros. The *thunderbolt and lightning of Zeus were fashioned by the Kyklopes, and are the emblem of his power. Zeus is closely associated with the *eagle. He had a number of immortal and mortal lovers, like Hera, Themis, Aphrodite, Metis, Maia, Semele, Eurynome, Mnemosyne, *Demeter, and Europa, and fathered several children. Zeus was a very popular coin device among the *Indo-Greeks and the *Śaka-Pahlavas; the figure of the deity also occurs on the coins of the early *Kushāṇa rulers. The laureate head of Zeus appears on the obv of some coins of the Indo-Greek rulers, *Diodotos I and *Euthydemos I, while the diademed head of this deity appears on some coins of *Archebios. On the obv of some coins of *Antialkidas is depicted the bust of Zeus hurling his thunderbolt. On the rev of some coins of Diodotos I, *Demetrios, *Agathokles, and *Antimachos Theos, appears the figure of Zeus hurling his thunderbolt. He holds an **aegis* on his left arm, and sometimes an eagle is seen in front of him. The deity, standing with a thunderbolt in his r hand and a long sceptre in his l hand, occurs on some coins of *Heliokles and Archebios among the Indo-Greeks, and on some joint coins of *Vonones with *Spalahora, of Vonones with *Spalagadama, of *Spalirises, of Spalirises with Azes I, and of Azes I alone among the Śaka-Pahlavas. The figure of standing Zeus, holding a long transverse sceptre in his l hand, and an uncertain 'two horned object' in his outstretched r hand, may be seen on some silver coins of *Peukolaos. On some coins of *Maues, Azes, *Gondopharnes, and *Abdagases occurs the figure of standing laureate Zeus, holding a long sceptre in his l hand, while the r hand is extended. Among the Kushāṇas, *Kujula Kadphises issued some coins bearing a similar device. A similar representation of the deity may be seen also on the coins of **Soter Megas* (= *V'ima Takshuma); but on some of his coins, the god is shown bearing a thunderbolt in his r hand. On one type of Azilises, diademed Zeus is depicted as standing facing to the r. In his l hand, he holds a sceptre, resting on his shoulder. An uncertain, ring-like object—perhaps a wreath—is held in his r hand, which is advanced. On some coins, Zeus may be seen associated with some goddesses, like *Nike or *Hekate. On some silver coins of Antialkidas, Zeus, holding a sceptre, is seen walking by the side of Nike being borne on an *elephant. The device of standing Zeus, holding a sceptre in his l hand, and wreath and palm bearing Nike on his outstretched r hand, may be seen on some coins of Maues, Azes, Azilises with Azes II, Abdagases, Gondopharnes with *Sasan, Arsakes, and *Rañjuvula. The figure of standing Zeus, holding a sceptre in his l hand, and three-headed Hekate on his outstretched r hand, occurs on some coins of Agathokles. The rev of a coin type of Azilises bears an interesting composition. Here, a

Diodotos

Heliokles

Abdagases

Azes II

Hermaios

Antialkidas

Antialkidas

male and a female figure stand side by side facing to front. The male figure carries a long sceptre in his l hand, and can be identified as Zeus. He points with his advanced r hand towards the female figure, which holds a diadem in her r hand along with a mural crown, and a **cornucopiae* on her left arm. This female figure has been identified as the city goddess of Pushkalāvatī. Enthroned Zeus, holding a long sceptre and an eagle in his hands, is depicted on some coins of Agathokles; on some coins of *Telephos, Maues, and Spalirises, the r hand of the enthroned god is outstretched. Enthroned Zeus Nikephoros also seems to have been a quite popular coin device. On some coins of Indo-Greek rulers, like Heliokles and Antialkidas, and of the Śaka-Pahlava ruler, Maues, Zeus is enthroned; he holds a long sceptre in his l hand, and holds Nike bearing wreath and palm on his r hand; sometimes the forepart of an elephant is seen in the field. On some other coins of Antialkidas, the presence of Nike on the r hand of Zeus is shown symbolically through her wreath and palm. *Amyntas represented on some of his coins, the figure of enthroned Zeus, holding sceptre and palm branch in his l hand, while on his r hand, he holds a goddess bearing shield, who is identified by some scholars as 'Athena-Nike'. On some coins of *Pantaleon occurs the figure of seated Zeus, holding a long sceptre in his l hand, and three-headed Hekate on his extended r hand. On one type of Maues, radiate Zeus is seen enthroned to the l. In his l hand is held the usual long sceptre. But his r hand is extended towards a small winged female figure. This female figure is identified as the 'embodiment of the thunderbolt' by Gardner. The rev of some coins of *Hermaios bears the figure of enthroned and radiate 'Zeus-Mithra', bearing a long sceptre in his l hand, and callipers in his r hand. On some coins of Demetrios and Antimachos Theos, instead of the anthropomorphic representation of Zeus, the god has been represented symbolically through his characteristic attribute, the thunderbolt (Bopearachchi 1993; Bopearachchi and Pieper 1998; Bopearachchi and Rahman 1995; Bhaskar Chattopadhyay 1977; Cunningham 1971a; Foss 1995; Gardner 1971; Graves 1955; Kerenyi 1951; A N Lahiri 1965; A N Lahiri 1995; Marshall 1975; Pinsent 1969; Rose 1958; Prashant Srivastava 2007b; Prashant Srivastava 2007c; Whitehead 1914).†

Zoilos I. *Indo-Greek k; latter half of the second century BC. Some coins bearing the name of Zoilos use the title **dikaios*, while others use the title **soter*. On the basis of the *provenance* of these coins, the coins of Zoilos *Dikaios* have been placed to the west of the river Indus, and those of Zoilos *Soteros*, to the east of that river. Scholars like Alexander Cunningham did not distinguish between Zoilos *Dikaios* and Zoilos *Soteros*, but the remarkable difference in style of the two series has been taken as evidence of the existence of two Indo-Greek kings bearing the name of Zoilos, the one using the title of *dikaios* being Zoilos I, and the other with the title of *soteros* being Zoilos II. He might have been a subking of *Menander I, and was appointed in the Swat valley by *Agathokleia when she transferred *Antimachos II from there to northern Arachosia. The rarity of his coins shows his brief reign. He issued silver and copper coins, all struck on the Indian standard. All the coins are die-struck pieces. The silver coins are round in shape, while the copper ones are square in shape. The obv of the silver coins bears the diademed bust of the king to the r. The rev of these coins has Herakles, standing and holding a wreath in his outstretched r hand, and club and lion's skin in his l hand; but while on one type, Herakles is shown wearing an ivy wreath, on the other type, there is a tiny figure of *Nike standing on the left shoulder of Herakles, crowning him. The obv of the copper coins have the head of bearded Herakles, draped in lion's skin, to the r, while the rev has a bow-case and *club. All the coins bear the Gr ld on the obv, and the Pkt ld, written in the Kh script, on the rev. Besides the title of **basileus*, Zoilos I assumed the epithet *dikaios* on his coins (above). These are rendered into Pkt as **maharaja* and **dhramika*, respectively. The Pkt form of the name of the ruler, as met with on coins, is Jhoïla (Bopearachchi 1993; Bopearachchi and Pieper 1998; Bopearachchi and Rahman 1995; Cunningham 1970; Gardner 1971; A N Lahiri 1965; Marshall 1975; Narain 1957a; Rapson 1987; Sircar 1980a; Tarn 1980; Whitehead 1914).†

Zoilos I

Zoilos II. *Indo-Greek k; early first century BC. His coins seem to associate him with *Apollodotos, and he appears to have ruled over the Jammu-Sialkot region in the interval between the two phases of the reign of *Strato I, perhaps immediately after Apollodotos whose coins he restruck. Zoilos II issued only one type of silver coins, and several types of copper coins, all of which are struck on the Indian standard. All the coins are die-struck pieces. The silver coins are all round in shape; the copper coins are mostly round in shape, but one

Zoilos II

Zoilos II

type is rectangular. The obv of the silver type has the diademed bust of the king to the r, while the rev has thundering *Athena, holding an **aegis* on her left arm. Some variety is seen in the obv and rev devices on copper coins. The obv of at least three copper types has the figure of *Apollo standing to the r and holding an arrow in both his hands on the obv; the rev of two of these types has **tripos lebes*, while one has an *elephant to the r. The obv of two other copper types has an elephant to the r on the obv; the rev of one such type has the *tripod lebes*, while that of the other has a 'standing male figure'. The rectangular copper type has a male figure standing to the r on the obv, and an elephant to the r on the rev. Apart from the last three copper types above, which have no Gr ld, all the remaining types of Zoilos II have the Gr ld on the obv, and the Pkt ld, written in the Kh script, on the rev. In the Gr ld, Zoilos II uses the titles of **basileus* and **soteros*. The Kh ld has **maharaja* and **tratara* as their Pkt equivalents, respectively. The three types having no Gr ld on the obv, have only the Pkt ld, on the rev. The Pkt form of the name of the ruler, as met with on coins, is Jhoïla (Bopearachchi 1993; Bopearachchi and Pieper 1998; Bopearachchi and Rahman 1995; Cunningham 1970; Gardner 1971; A N Lahiri 1965; Marshall 1975; Narain 1957a; Rapson 1987; Sircar 1980a; Tarn 1980; Whitehead 1914).

Appendix

More About Some Issuers and Devices

A

Abdagases. *Śaka-Pahlava k. He was the nephew of *Gondopharnes, and refers to himself as such in the obv and rev legends of some of his coins. He seems to have started his career as a subordinate of Gondopharnes, perhaps in western Gandhāra, and assumed subordinate titles of **basileus* and **maharaja* on some of his coins. But later on, perhaps after the death of his uncle, he seems to have assumed sovereignty on some territories of the empire formerly ruled by Gondopharnes, and there are coins referring to Abdagases as **basileuontos basileon*, and even **basileos basileon megalos*. Numismatic evidence shows that he exercised sway over Arachosia, Seistan, and Takshaśilā (Cunningham 1971a; Gardner 1971; Jenkins and Narain 1957; Marshall 1975; B N Mukherjee 1969a; Rapson 1987; Senior 2001; Sircar 1980b; Tarn 1980; Whitehead 1914).

Agathokleia. *Indo-Greek queen-regent. She is believed to belong to the family of *Euthydemos on the basis of the presence of seated *Herakles on her coins, and most of the scholars regard her as the daughter of *Demetrios and sister of *Agathokles. She struck joint coins with *Strato I. Earlier scholars, like Cunningham and Gardner, described her as the wife of Strato I, but Prinsep, and following him, Rapson, Smith, Brown, Tarn, Narain, A N Lahiri, B N Mukherjee, and others regard her as the mother of Strato I. For, on the coins showing their conjugate busts, Agathokleia is a mature woman, while Strato I looks in his teens. Also, if they were man and wife, it would become very difficult to explain as to how the queen had come to occupy the more important position on the obv, while the king had been relegated to the rev of some of their joint coins. On the basis of the close resemblance between the bust of *Athena on the coins of *Menander and that of Agathokleia on her own coins, Rapson suggests the possibility of Agathokleia's being the wife of Menander. According to Plutarch, Menander died in camp. Perhaps his son, Strato I, was a minor at that time, and Agathokleia assumed the regency of the kingdom during the minority of her son. Her tenure as regent has been placed between *c* 130 BC and 123 BC (Bopearachchi 1993; Bopearachchi and Pieper 1998; Bopearachchi and Rahman 1995; Cunningham 1970; Gardner 1971; A N Lahiri 1965; Marshall 1975; Narain 1957a; Rapson 1906; Rapson 1987; Senior 2001; Prashant Srivastava 1996a; Tarn 1980; Whitehead 1914).

Agathokles. *Indo-Greek k. He is believed to be a son of *Demetrios I, and a younger brother of *Pantaleon. There is a possibility that when Demetrios I died, these two sons of his were ruling conjointly over Arachosia and Drangiana. From Arachosia, they together expanded their sway by conquering Kabul and western Gandhāra. But Pantaleon predeceased Agathokles, and the latter alone established his authority over Takshaśilā, where he issued the *hirañasame* and the '*stūpa* and tree-in-railing' types of coins. Narain is of the view that the two brothers might have ruled from *c* 185 BC to 165 BC (Bopearachchi 1993; Bopearachchi and Pieper 1998; Bopearachchi and Rahman 1995; Cunningham 1970; Gardner 1971; A N Lahiri 1965; Marshall 1975; Narain 1957a; Rapson 1987; Senior 2001; Sircar 1980a; Prashant Srivastava 1996a; Tarn 1980; Whitehead 1914).

Agni. Deity. Chief among the terrestrial deities in the vedic period, being celebrated in as many as 200 hymns of the *Ṛigveda*, Agni the fire god was the most closely associated with human life than any other god, and consequently, he alone of all the deities is frequently given the epithet *gṛihapati*, 'lord of the house'. He alone is called *atithi*, 'guest', indeed the first guest of settlers. He is described variously as the son of Asura, or of Dyaus (and Pṛithivī), or of Tvashṭṛi (and Āpaḥ). The two *araṇīs* or fire sticks are also described as his parents or two mothers. He was born in the highest heaven, but was brought from thence by Mātariśvan, and established on earth in the form of sacrificial fire by the Atharvan priests. As Agni is also the designation of fire, his anthropomorphism did not find much scope for development. There are references to his three or seven tongues, which represent the flames of fire; his sharp and shining teeth are also mentioned. He devours all, but *ghee* and wood are his favourite food, and melted butter his favourite beverage. He is *dhūmaketu*, 'the smoke-bannered'. Great emphasis is placed on his brightness. He burns and dispels 'evil spirits and hostile magic'. He is the intermediary between the worshipper and the worshipped, and acts as a *dūta*, 'messenger', between the two. But his most important function is that of a *purohita*, 'domestic priest'. His association with knowledge is clear from his epithets, like *viśvavid*, 'all knowing'; *viśvavedas*, 'possessed of all knowledge'; *kavi*, 'seer'; *kavikratu*, 'possessing the intelligence of a seer'; etc. He also plays the role of the 'intercessor and judge'. He is associated with several gods, like *Indra, *Varuṇa, Mitra, Savitṛi, and others. As *somagopā*, he is 'the guardian of Soma'. He is likened to several animals, such as the *bull, calf, *horse, and serpent. His 'course is a flight', and consequently, he is often compared to birds, like the *eagle and the **haṁsa* (Banerjea 2002; R G Bhandarkar 1928; Sukumari Bhattacharji 1970; Bhaskar Chattopadhyay 1977; Darmesteter 1974;

Griswold 1999; Hillebrandt 1999; Hopkins 1915; Macdonell 1897; Rao 1985; Prashant Srivastava 1993b; Wilkins 2006).

Ahuramazda. Deity. He is the supreme godhead in the religion of Zoroaster. His name literally means 'the Lord of high Knowledge' or 'the Wise Lord'. It is quite clear from the *Avesta* that he is the 'Heaven God'. 'He is white, bright, seen afar, and his body is the greatest and fairest of all bodies; he has the sun for his eye...the fire of lightning for his son; he wears the heaven as a star-spangled garment, he puts on the hard stone of heaven, he is hardest of all gods.' Ahuramazda is the creator-god, and at many places in the Fargard, Zoroaster calls him 'O Maker of the material world'. In the Sirozah, there is a long list of the things in the world created by Ahuramazda. But the attribute most closely associated with him is *asha*, that is morality, which is the Avestan equivalent of *ṛita*. Thus, Ahuramazda is the supreme guardian of moral law. His bodily nature is the *varana*, the all-embracing sky. Avestan Ahura is believed by some scholars to be the same as the vedic Asura. Ahuramazda seems to correspond to the vedic Asura-*Varuṇa and the Greek *Ouranos (Barton 1990; Sukumari Bhattacharji 1970; Darmesteter 1974; Noss 1949; Prashant Srivastava 2007d).

Amphitrite. Deity. According to Hesiod, she was one of the 50 Nereides or daughters of Nereos. Homer expressly refers to her as '*the* mistress and proprietress of the sea, to whom belong all foaming waves and sea-monsters'. *Poseidon saw her on the island of Naxos while she was dancing with her sisters, and ravished her. The dolphins persuaded her to marry Poseidon, and it was this marriage that established Poseidon as the ruler of the sea. She bore to Poseidon a son, *Triton, and a daughter, Rhodos (Graves 1955; Kerenyi 1951; Rose 1958; Prashant Srivastava 1993a; Prashant Srivastava 2007c).

Amyntas. *Indo-Greek k. He is believed to be a son of *Antialkidas, although he did not immediately succeed his father. After the death of Antialkidas, the territories to the north of the Hindukush were occupied by *Theophilos, the Pushkalāvatī region and the Kabul valley by *Peukolaos, and western Gandhāra by *Diomedes, while *Apollodotos ruled over the remainder of the kingdom of Antialkidas. But some time after the death of Apollodotos, Amyntas regained the territories his father had lost to Apollodotos, and also overthrew Theophilos and Peukolaos in the region to the north of the Hindukush and in the Pushkalāvatī region and the Kabul valley, respectively. Coins of Amyntas from western Gandhāra show that he superseded Diomedes in that region. Narain suggests that he might have issued the two types of his double-*decadrachms* and assumed the title of **nikatoros* to commemorate the re-establishment of his authority. On the basis of the appearance of *Athena-Pallas, a type usually associated with *Menander and his successors, on some coins of Amyntas, it has been suggested that the descendants of *Eukratides I and those of Menander, might have formed an alliance in view of the Śaka-Pahlava and Yueh-chih menace. The marriage of his son, *Hermaios, with *Kalliope of the family of Menander might have been the result of this alliance. Coin portraits reveal that Amyntas was able to establish himself as a king in his middle age around 85 BC, although R C Senior would date his accession about a decade later, and Osmund Boearachchi places it between 95 BC and 90 BC, and seems to have ruled for about 10 years (Bopearachchi 1993; Bopearachchi and Pieper 1998; Bopearachchi and Rahman 1995; Cunningham 1970; Gardner 1971; A N Lahiri 1965; Marshall 1975; Narain 1957a; Rapson 1987; Senior 2001; Sircar 1980a; Prashant Srivastava 1996a; Tarn 1980; Whitehead 1914).

Antialkidas. *Indo-Greek k. He is believed to be a son of *Heliokles II, who retrieved the fallen fortunes of his family some time around 115 BC, and the *provenance* of his coins shows that he established his sway over the Kabul valley, western Gandhāra, and Takshaśilā. There are certain coins bearing the name of *Lysias on one side, and that of Antialkidas on the other, which are regarded by some scholars as joint issues of the two kings, while others regard such pieces as 'mules'. Antialkidas also restruck a coin of Lysias. He is mentioned in the Besnagar **garuḍa* pillar inscription of the time of King Bhāgabhadra, and the language of the inscription gives the indication that the seat of his power was Takshaśilā. He sent an envoy, Heliodoros, to the court of that Indian ruler, and in the inscription the envoy uses the title of *trātāra* (Pkt equivalent of the Greek title **soteros*) for Bhāgabhadra, leading to the inference that the Indian king might have saved Antialkidas from some enemy. Narain, however, believes that towards the close of his reign, the authority of Antialkidas was confined to the Takshaśilā region alone, with *Apollodotos occupying almost all his territories to the west of the river Indus, and *Strato I ruling over the Jammu-Sialkot region to the east of the river Jhelum. Beleaguered by these problems, Antialkidas might have sought the help of Bhāgabhadra, but to no avail. He ruled up to *c* 100 BC, when he was, perhaps, overthrown by Apollodotos. Senior, however, places his reign from *c* 127 BC to 120 BC (Bopearachchi 1993; Bopearachchi and Pieper 1998; Bopearachchi and Rahman 1995; Cunningham 1970; Gardner 1971; A N Lahiri 1965; Marshall 1975; Narain 1957a; Rapson 1987; Senior 2001; Sircar 1980a; Prashant Srivastava 1990c; Tarn 1980; Whitehead 1914).

Antimachos I. *Indo-Greek k. A 'myterious king', he was earlier regarded as one of the three original founders of the Indo-Greek kingdom. But there can be no doubt that he was one of the early Indo-Greek kings of Bactria. He has been variously described as a son or close relative of *Diodotos II, a son of *Euthydemos I, a Sogdian with a Greek name, etc. He is believed to have ruled after Euthydemos I, and there is a suggestion that he might have risen to power around 190 BC by 'eliminating' *Euthydemos II. From eastern Bactria, he moved on to the Kabul valley and the Upper Indus valley, and occupied parts of Paropamisadae. Whitehead and Allan even postulate his temporary occupation of Takshaśilā on the basis of his unique square coin of Taxila type. He is not known to have struck bilingual coins; had his occupation of the Takshaśilā region been permanent, he would have started the practice of issuing bilingual coins. After the death of *Demetrios I, he seems to have annexed the whole of Bactria, and even conquered Margiana. The appearance of the Greek sea-god, *Poseidon, on his coins has led to the suggestion that he might have gained some naval victory on the river Oxus, but some scholars associate the depiction of this god on his coins with his hold over some territories where the 'heavenly horses' of the Chinese sources were bred. However, the suggestion of a naval victory seems to gain ground in view of the fact that he issued a round copper type, the rev of which is occupied by the figure of *Nike standing on the prow of a ship. Antimachos I assumed the title of **theos* on coins, perhaps under the influence of some local tradition. He seems to have started ruling late in his life, his career coming to an end around 180 BC (Bopearachchi 1993; Bopearachchi and Pieper 1998; Bopearachchi and Rahman 1995; Cunningham 1970; Gardner 1971; A N Lahiri 1965; Marshall 1975; Narain 1957a; Rapson 1987; Senior 2001; Sircar 1980a; Tarn 1980; Prashant Srivastava 1996a; Whitehead 1914).

Antimachos II. *Indo-Greek k. He is believed to be a subking and general of *Menander, and to have belonged to family of *Antimachos I and *Demetrios II with whom he shares several coin types; Osmund Bopearachchi, however, suggests that Menander I succeeded Antimachos II. Narain regards him as a grandson of Antimachos I, and a brother of Menander. Tarn regards him as a subking of Gandhāra. But no coin of Antimachos II has been found in the excavations at Taxila, while they are reported in the *Bajaur hoards and the *Mir Zakah hoard, from which Narain infers that he first governed the Swat valley and was later transferred to northern Arachosia by *Agathokleia during her regency. The large number of his coins shows that he might not have submitted to the regency of Agathokleia, and set himself up as an independent king in northern Arachosia some time after the death of Menander, perhaps from *c* 130 BC to 125 BC. There is, however, a view suggesting the overlapping of the reigns of Antimachos I and Antimachos II. The discovery of his coins from Charsadda shows the extension of his authority in western Gandhāra. R C Senior, however, suggests that he might have succeeded *Apollodotos in the territories to the south of the Hindukush. Bopearachchi suggests his hold over Paropamisadae as well (Bopearachchi 1993; Bopearachchi and Pieper 1998; Bopearachchi and Rahman 1995; Cunningham 1970; Gardner 1971; A N Lahiri 1965; Marshall 1975; Narain 1957a; Rapson 1987; Senior 2001; Sircar 1980a; Tarn 1980; Whitehead 1914).

Apollo. Deity. This son of Leto by *Zeus, and the twin of *Artemis, was the third greatest deity, besides Zeus and Athena, in the Greek pantheon. He was conceived at Didyma near Miletos. All the goddesses, with the exception of Hera, Zeus' wife, were present at the time of his birth on the island of Delos. Immediately after his birth, he had to fight and vanquish several enemies. These included the giant Tityos, the son of Zeus and Elara; Pythos, the son of Gaia; the gragoness Delphyne; Phegyas; and the Kyklopes. *Herakles stole the **tripod lebes* from Apollo's temple at Delphi, which led to a fight between the two, but the dispute was settled by their father, Zeus. Among the prominent lovers of Apollo were the maidens Daphne, Dryope, and Kyrene, and the boys Adonis, Hyakinthos, and Kyparissos. But most of these love-stories 'ended tragically'. From his oracular shrine at Delphi, Apollo proclaimed the will of his father, while seated on the *tripod lebes*. In the assembly of gods on Mount Olympus, Apollo played on his lyre and sang in the midst of the Muses. As Paieon, he was the divine physician. Although the usual attribute of Apollo is the lyre, sometimes in art he is shown holding a bow in his l hand and a cup (of offering to Athena ?) in his r hand. Apollo was later recognized as the sun god, *Helios, probably because his arrows are believed to be intended to dispel darkness (Graves 1955; Kerenyi 1951; Rose 1958; Prashant Srivastava 2006b; Prashant Srivastava 2007c).

Apollodotos. *Indo-Greek k. On the basis of the amendation in a statement of Justin suggested by Bayer, a number of scholars express the possibility of the existence of two Indo-Greek kings named Apollodotos, but Narain feels that the numismatic evidence does not support such a hypothesis. Subsequent writers on the subject, however, still believe in the existence of two Apollodoti. Apollodotos is believed to be a son of *Menander I, and a younger brother of *Strato I, who began his career as a subking or joint king of Strato I around 115 BC, initially ruling over the Swat valley. He seems to have proved to be a very effective joint ruler, and to have helped Strato I in recovering most of the western regions he had earlier lost to other kings. He reoccupied western Gandhāra, the Kabul valley, and the Ghazni area. Around 100 BC, he seems to have overthrown Antialkidas in Takshaśilā, and perhaps this encouraged him to declare his independence; he might even have replaced Strato I. The *provenance* of his coins shows that, for some time at least, he ruled over almost the whole of the kingdom of his father. However, taking advantage of his engagements in Gandhāra, Kabul, and Ghazni regions, *Maues might have occupied some territories in the Swat valley and the Hazara region, and perhaps also Takshaśilā. The fact that Apollodotos restruck a copper coin of Maues seems to show that the former tried to the recover the territories he had lost to the *Śaka-Pahlava ruler, although the recovery proved to be of a short duration. His reign ended *c* 95 BC. R C Senior, however, regards him as a contemporary and rival of *Antimachos I, and the first Indo-Greek ruler to conquer territories to the south of the Hindukush and issue square silver coins based on the Indian weight standard. But Osmund Bopearachchi regards Apollodotos as the immediate successor of *Pantaleon, *Agathokles, and Antimachos I, and a predecessor of Menander I (Bivar 1970; Bopearachchi 1993; Bopearachchi and Pieper 1998; Bopearachchi and Rahman 1995; Cunningham 1970; Gardner 1971; Jenkins 1959; A N Lahiri 1965; Marshall 1975; Narain 1957a; Rapson 1987; Sircar 1980a; Tarn 1980; Whitehead 1914).

Apollophanes. *Indo-Greek k. His coins seem to associate him with *Apollodotos, and he appears to have ruled over the Jammu-Sialkot region in the interval between the two phases of the reign of *Strato I, perhaps towards its end after *Zoilos II and *Dinysios; Osmund Bopearachchi associates him with western Punjab. Strato I seems to have regained his authority by overthrowing him around 80 BC, possibly with the help of *Strato II and *Maues (Bopearachchi 1993; Bopearachchi and Pieper 1998; Bopearachchi and Rahman 1995; Cunningham 1970; Gardner 1971; A N Lahiri 1965; Marshall 1975; Narain 1957a; Rapson 1906; Rapson 1987; Sircar 1980a; Tarn 1980; Whitehead 1914).

Archebios. *Indo-Greek k. He is believed to be a son and immediate successor of *Eukratides II. Rapson, Tarn, and Marshall regard the type **pilei* of the *Dioskuri as associated with Takshaśilā, and as Archebios issued this type of coins, it was suggested that he ruled over that region, which, after him, passed into the hands of the *Śaka-Pahlavas; Osmund Bopearachchi is also in favour of associating Archebios with Takshaśilā. But Narain feels that the association of this type with the Takshaśilā region is by no means certain, and that there is no definite evidence to suggest Archebios' hold over Takshaśilā. He, however, occupied the territories of Kabul and Ghazni to the south of the Hindukush by taking advantage of the death of *Menander, and also parts of western Gandhāra. He ruled for about seven or eight years from *c* 140 BC, and was succeeded by his uncle, *Heliokles II; R C Senior, however, places him between *c* 95 BC and 80 BC (Bopearachchi 1993; Bopearachchi and Pieper 1998; Bopearachchi and Rahman 1995; Cunningham 1970; Gardner 1971; A N Lahiri 1965; Marshall 1975; Narain 1957a; Rapson 1987; Senior 2001; Sircar 1980a; Tarn 1980; Whitehead 1914).

Ardochsho. Deity. The ld *Ardochsho* on *Kushāṇa coins seems to represent the Avestan female divinity ('angel') Ashi Vanguhi, later known as Ashishang, 'good truth'. She is described as a daughter of *Ahuramazda and a sister of the Amesha Spentas, 'good spirits'. She is associated with prosperity and wisdom, and is praised in the *Ashi Yasht*. She granted wealth, victory, and progeny to her worshippers like Zoroaster and Kava Vishtaspa, and reminds one of Śrī of the *Śatapathabrāhmaṇa*, who granted wealth, universal sovereignty, holy lustre, etc to *Agni, Soma, *Indra, and others. She may be compared to the Greek *Demeter, and the Roman Fortuna. Some scholars relate her to Ardvi Sūra Anāhita, and regard her as a local goddess of water and moisture in eastern Iran. There is also a suggestion that the Greek *Tyche is the prototype of the Kushāṇa *Ardochsho*. In numismatic art, she is generally shown holding the **cornucopiae*, the horn of plenty (Bhaskar Chattopadhyay 1967; Bhaskar Chattopadhyay 1977; Darmesteter 1974; Stein 1888).

Artemidoros. *Indo-Greek k. He is believed to be a subking of *Apollodotos, who might have later asserted his independence for a short while. Tarn associates him with the Pushkalāvatī region, but Narain feels that his authority was confined to the Peshawar area. Tarn's suggestion that in the Peshawar region, Artemidoros was succeeded by *Maues, according to Narain, is not based on sufficient grounds. R C Senior has read a Gr ld meaning 'Artemidoros, son of the king of kings, Maues' on a coin, and, on this basis, as also on the basis of the similarity of devices, suggested that Artemidoros was a son of Maues. Osmund Bopearachchi associates him with the Takshaśilā region. His reign may be placed some time in the period *c* 95-85 BC, although Senior would place his reign between *c* 65 BC and 60 BC, and Osmund Bopearachchi, in the second decade of the first century BC. He is known to have restruck the joint coins of *Hermaios with *Kalliope (Bopearachchi 1993; Bopearachchi 1994; Bopearachchi and Pieper 1998; Bopearachchi and Rahman 1995; Cunningham 1970; Gardner 1971; A N Lahiri 1965; Marshall 1975; Narain 1957a; Rapson 1987; Senior 2001; Sircar 1980a; Tarn 1980; Whitehead 1914).

Artemis. Deity. She was the daughter of Leto by *Zeus, and a twin of *Apollo, though she was born first. Her birth place was Ortygia. Like Apollo, she is an archer, though the bow has come to be associated more closely with Artemis. The Greeks assimilated her to a 'pre-Greek mistress of wild beasts'. Although Great Artemis was one of the names of the mother goddess in Asia Minor, Artemis of the Greek pantheon is 'the everlastingly virginal,...a sister figure', and is called *Parthenos*, 'unmarried woman'. She is famous as a virgin huntress, and a bringer of sudden death. She is also the 'goddess of plant life' and 'the physician goddess of animals'. She is often associated with nymphs, like Kallisto and Britomartis. Her lunar character is indicated by her surnames like *Hegemone* and *Keladeine*, her radiate head, and the torch in her hand. Artemis was identified with the Bactrian Anahid by the *Indo-Greeks, and she is believed to have been 'the immediate predecessor' of goddess **Nana* found with lion on *Kushāṇa coins and later on identified with *Umā (Durgā) the consort of *Śiva (Graves 1955; Kerenyi 1951; Rose 1958; Prashant Srivastava 2007c).

Arthaśāstra. Text. The most famous work on statecraft, divided into 18 *adhikaraṇas* and 180 *prakaraṇas*, is traditionally ascribed to Kauṭilya Vishṇugupta Chāṇakya, the minister of Chandragupta Maurya. This would date the work to the fourth century BC. But some scholars place it as late as the time of the *Imperial Guptas. The text seems to have undergone several revisions (Kangle 2000).

Ashṭādhyāyī. Text. This work on Skt grammar by Pāṇini has been dated variously from the seventh-sixth to fourth centuries BC. As ten of the *janapadas* mentioned by Pāṇini belong to the list of the *śoḍasha mahājanapadas*, some scholars place him as early as 'the early phase of the age of the sixteen *mahājanapadas*, ie 7th-6th century BC', although the generally accepted date for him is the fifth century BC (V S Agrawala 1953).

Athena. Deity. This most important Greek deity after *Zeus, has as her mother Metis, 'wise counsel', daughter of Okeanos and Tethys. But actually, Athena was the Father's daughter, as she was born from the head of her father, Zeus, who had devoured her mother. *Hephaistos or Prometheos assisted in her birth by smoting Zeus' skull with an axe or hammer, and out sprang Athena, bearing in her hands the **aegis* and her sharp javelin. Some versions give Pallas as the name of her father. As she was born on the bank of the river Triton, she was called *Tritogeneia*. In various sources, Triton or the Kyklopes are referred to as her tutors. All the sources refer to Athena as *Parthenos*, 'virgin', but she is also invoked as *Meter*, 'mother', and she seems to be a manifestation of a pre-Greek mother goddess. Although a virgin, she had a son, Erichthonios, by Hephaistos, and he was put in a chest and entrusted to the care of the three daughters of Kekropes, the first king of the Athenians. She was regarded as 'the patron and model worker of all those arts of life which demand ingenuity and dexterity'. But the most notable aspect of her character was that of a victorious war goddess, as reflected in her epithets like *Promachos*, 'one who fights in the foremost rank', and *Alalkomene*, 'the parrier'. Sometimes, she is shown with a *thunderbolt, which not only indicates her original role as a goddess of storm and lightning, but also that the functions of Zeus, whose attribute the thunderbolt was, might have been discharged to a certain extent by Athena. Her traditional dress is the *peplos*, and her traditional attribute is the spear. *Owl is her favourite bird. Certain ancient scholars, including Aristotle, hold that 'disguised beneath the name of Athena was, in fact, the moon'. Athena is sometimes portrayed as winged. There is a story that Pallas, who is sometimes described as the father of Athena, sought to do violence to her, but was overcome by the daughter who took his skin and donned it. As Pallas the father was winged, so was Athena in her early representations. **Pallas* was also one of the epithets of Athena (Graves 1955; Kerenyi 1951; Rose 1958; Prashant Srivastava 2007c).

Avantivarman. *Maukhari k. He was the son and successor of *Śarvavarman; he is referred to as **parameśvara* in one inscription, but a Nalanda seal accords him full imperial titles. He held sway over Magadha in the early part of his reign. Some scholars believe that the Later Gupta king, Mahāsenagupta, and *Śaśāṅka of Gauḍa served him as his feudatories. His reign ended some time before 606 AD, the year when his son, Grahavarman, was killed by Devagupta of Malwa, who had invaded the Maukhari kingdom jointly with Śaśāṅka (Richard Burn 1906; D Devahuti 1964; Pires 1934; Thaplyal 1985).

Azes I. *Śaka-Pahlava k. Azes I started his career as a junior subordinate ruler of *Vonones, while his father, *Spalirises, was the senior subordinate ruler; he issued some silver coins bearing the name of Spalirises on the obverse and that of Azes [I] on the rev. On these coins, neither Spalirises nor Azes I uses the sovereign title of 'king of kings', showing that these were issued at a time when both of them were subordinate to Vonones. But Marshall suggests that the use of the title of 'great king' by both of them almost announces the end of the overlordship of Vonones. Numismatic evidence shows that later on, Azes I succeeded, not his father Spalirises in Arachosia, but *Maues in India. Sircar suggests the possibility that Azes I might have been the son-in-law of Maues, and succeeded to the territories of Maues peacefully. But it is more likely that Spalirises was overthrown in Arachosia, and Azes I had perforce to go to northwestern India, where he defeated Maues, and occupied his territories; he even seems to have forced Maues to serve under him, and during this period, Maues issued coins with subordinate titles. Azes I extended Śaka-Pahlava sway towards eastern Punjab, where he seems to have defeated Indo-Greek kings of the family of *Euthydemos. He not only imitated the *Athena Promachos type of *Menander and his successors, but also restruck the coins of *Apollodotos and *Hippostratos of the Euthydemid family. Some of the monograms of these two princes appear on the coins of Azes I also. He is regarded as one of the great rulers of ancient India, who unified a great part of northwestern India. His 'huge output of coinage' testifies to the prosperity of his kingdom. He seems to have founded an era, perhaps at the time of his accession, which came to be known as *Vikrama *saṁvat*. Towards the end of his rule, he associated his son, *Azilises, in government, as shown by their joint coins (Cunningham 1971a; Gardner 1971; Jenkins and Narain 1957; Marshall 1975; B N Mukherjee 1969; Senior 2001; Senior 2003; Sircar 1980b; Prashant Srivastava 1996a; Tarn 1980; Whitehead 1914).

Azes II. *Śaka-Pahlava k. He started his career as a junior co-ruler of his father, *Azilises, and issued at least three types of joint coins with him. Ultimately, Azes II succeeded his father to the throne and issued his independent coinage. He also struck joint coins with *Indravasu, and with *Aśpavarman. Aśpavarman is known to have served under both Azes II and *Gondopharnes in the capacity of **strategos*. There is a possibility that when Gondopharnes invaded the kingdom of Azes II, Aśpavarman switched over his loyalty to the invader and helped him in defeating Azes II. The victorious invader permitted Aśpavarman to continue as *strategos* as a reward for the help received from him. Scholars like Rapson and Sten Konow, however, believe that Gondopharnes succeeded Azes II peacefully (Bopearachchi and Rahman 1995; Cunningham 1971a; Gardner 1971; Jenkins and Narain 1957; Marshall 1975; B N Mukherjee 1969a; Rapson 1987; Raychaudhuri 1982; Senior 2001; Sircar 1980b; Prashant Srivastava 1996a; Tarn 1980; Whitehead 1914).

Azilises. *Śaka-Pahlava k. He seems to have started his career as a junior co-ruler of his father, *Azes I, with whom he issued joint coins, and whom he ultimately succeeded. On succeeding his father, he ruled over the extensive territories, which had earlier been under the authority of *Maues and Azes I, his coins showing his hold over the Hazara-Kashmir region, and parts of western Gandhāra. His silver coins bearing the device of *Gajalakshmī on the rev remind one of the coins of *Mathurā depicting a similar device, and might be indicative of the extension of his sway up to Mathurā in the east. The *Herakles seated type of his coins might be indicative of his hold over parts of southern Afghanistan. Some numismatists suggest that there might be two Śaka-Pahlava rulers named Azilises. But the extensive coinage bearing the name of Azilises does not show any great difference in style and execution to support this suggestion. Towards the end of his reign, Azilises seems to have associated his son, *Azes II, in government as a junior co-ruler, and issued at least three types of joint coins with him. R C Senior, however, regards these joint issues as 'mules'. He tentatively proposes new interrelationships between the Śaka-Pahlava rulers. He is of the view that Azilises was the '*sole* successor' of Maues in Hazara, and might have been his son, although he also expresses the possibility of Azilises being a son of *Spalirises. On the basis of the close proximity of some types of Azilises and those of 'Azes', he regards the two as 'closely related', perhaps as brothers or as father and son. According to him, hoard evidence seems to show that Azilises' coins from Hazara predate some coins of 'Azes', and that if the two were father and son, Azilises would have been the father of 'Azes'. He does not accept the suggestion of scholars like Ernst Herzfeld and J E van Lohuizen de Leeuw that Azes and Azilises might be two forms of the same name, on the grounds that the two forms sometimes occur on the same coin, and that coins of Azilises overstruck on coins on Azes are known. All these difficulties in the chronology of the Śaka-Pahlava rulers seem to arise out of the fact that Senior believes in the existence of only one Śaka-Pahlava king named Azes [*Azes] (Cunningham 1971a; Gardner 1971; Herzfeld 1932; Jenkins and Narain 1957; van Lohuizen de Leeuw 1949; Marshall 1975; B N Mukherjee 1969a; Senior 2001; Sircar 1980b; Prashant Srivastava 1996a; Prashant Srivastava 2007a; Tarn 1980; Whitehead 1914).

B

Balarāma. Deity. This son of Vasudeva and Rohiṇī, and the elder brother of *Vāsudeva-Kṛishṇa, is one of the five deified heroes of the Yādava-Sātvata-Vṛishṇi clan, one of the four *vyūhas* worshipped by the followers of Bhāgavata sect, and is sometimes regarded as one of the incarnations of *Vishṇu; according to one view, while Vāsudeva-Kṛishṇa was a full manifestation of Vishṇu, Balarāma was a partial *avatāra* of that deity. Balarāma had Revatī as his only consort, and from her, he had two sons, Niśatha and Ulmuka. He is first mentioned (as Saṁkarshaṇa) in the *Arthaśāstra* of Kauṭilya. Some inscriptions, like the Ghosundi inscription of the time of King Sarvatāta, the Naneghat inscription of Nāganikā, and the Nasik inscription of year 19 of Vāsishṭhīputra Pulumāvi, refer to him. On the basis of the fact that Balarāma is regarded as an incarnation of Ananta, the serpent which serves as the couch of Vishṇu; the mention in the *Mahābhārata* of a serpent named Baladevan; and the legend that a snake came out of the mouth of Balarāma when he died under a banyan tree on the outskirts of Dvārakā, it has been suggested that Balarāma is closely associated with serpent worship, and Vögel is of the view that the worship of Balarāma in Bhāgavatism is the result of the assimilation of a nāga deity in that cult. He shares two of his epithets, namely *Halāyudha* and *Mūśalin*, with *Śiva, and this has led to an occasional identification of Balarāma with Śiva. Balarāma is also known by the name of Saṅkarshaṇa, which literally means the act of furrowing, and he has the plough (*hala*) as his attribute. This seems to hint at his association with agriculture. In the *Vishṇudharmottarapurāṇa*, he is equated with knowledge. Two very important traits of his character are his violent temper, and his love for wine. He has a fan-palm for his banner, and is called *Tāladhvaja*. Several of his exploits, like his slaying of the demons Dhenuka, Pralamba, and Dvivida, his support to Vāsudeva-Kṛishṇa in his struggle with Kaṁsa, and his securing the release of Sāmba, the son of Vāsudeva-Kṛishṇa, from the Kauravas, are described in detail in the purāṇas and the *Mahābhārata*. In the Bhārata war, he refused to side with either the Pāṇḍavas or the Kauravas. He is represented in art as of fair complexion, dressed in red or blue garments, and bearing a club, a plough, and a pestle (Banerjea 2002; Sukumari Bhattacharji 1970; S R Goyal 1986; T R R Iyengar 2003; Sircar 1971; Sircar 1986; Wilkins 2006).

Bhānugupta *Prakāśāditya*. *Imperial Gupta k. Bhānugupta is known from the Eran pillar inscription of *Gupta era 191 (= 510 AD). The name of his father is not known, although some scholars would regard him as a son of *Pūrugupta. The inscription records that Goparāja, an ally of Bhānugupta, died fighting, most probably the Hūṇas, and his wife committed *satī*. The result of this battle is not known from this inscription. The Eran pillar inscription of the Gupta era 165 (= 484 AD) shows that this area was under *Budhagupta; another inscription from the same site testifies to the hold of *Toramāṇa over this area some time after Budhagupta. The erection of the inscribed pillar recording Bhānugupta's struggle with the Hūṇas at Eran would suggest that Bhānugupta succeeded in worsting his adversaries. The inscription refers to Bhānugupta as **rājā mahān*, instead of **mahārājādhirāja*, but this should not be taken to mean that he was not a sovereign ruler. In view of the facts that the known dates of Bhānugupta, *Vainyagupta, and *Narasiṁhagupta are quite near to each other, and that the only inscription mentioning Bhānugupta comes from Malwa, and that mentioning Vainyagupta, from Bengal, R C Majumdar suggested the possibility of the division of the Gupta empire among these three rulers, with Bhānugupta ruling over of the western provinces, Vainyagupta over the eastern provinces, and Narasiṁhagupta over the rest of the territories. His alternative suggestion is that Vainyagupta, Bhānugupta, and Narasiṁhagupta might have ruled one after the other, in that order (Ashvini Agrawal 1989; Allan 1914; Altekar 1957; R D Banerji 1933; Fleet 1888; S R Goyal 2005; P L Gupta 1998; K P Jayaswal 1933; R C Majumdar 1988; K S Shukla 1980; Smith 1972; Prashant Srivastava 1996a; Thaplyal, forthcoming).

Bhūmaka. *Kshaharāta k. He is one of the earliest known **kshatrapas*, who was appointed by the Kushāṇa ruler to administer the southwestern parts of the empire, although doubts have recently been expressed from certain quarters regarding his subordinate status. The find of his coins from the coastal regions of Gujarat, parts of Malwa, and the Ajmer region of Rajasthan give us an idea of the territories under his rule. The use of both Br and Kh scripts on his coins shows that he also ruled over the western Rajasthan and Sind regions, where Kh was prevalent, although there is a view that the ancestors of the Kshaharāta rulers might have brought this script to the Deccan from the 'North-west'. Sylvain Lévi's view, that Bhūmaka should be identified with Ysāmotika, the father of *Chashṭana, as *ysama* is the Śaka word for the earth (Skt, *bhūmi*), does not seem to be convincing. No inscription of this ruler is known so far (Jha and Rajgor 1994; Mirashi 1982; Mitchiner 1976; Rapson 1975; Raychaudhuri 1972; Senior 2001; A M Shastri 1995; Sircar 1980e).

Buddha, Śākyamuni. Deified human being. The Buddha, born Siddhārtha, was the son of the Śākya Śuddhodana and his Koliya wife Māyādevī. Soon after his birth at Lumbini, it was predicted that he would become, either a *rājachakravartin* or a *dharmachakravartin*. Although he was brought up in all luxury, at the age of 29, he renounced the world, and after an effort of six years, attained *saṁbodhi*, thus becoming the Buddha, 'the enlightened one'. He delivered his first sermon at Sarnath near Vārāṇasī, and in Buddhist literature, this act is euphemistically termed *dharmachakrapravarttana*, 'the setting into motion the wheel of law'. He spent the next 45 years of his life in preaching his doctrine, mainly in eastern Uttar Pradesh and Bihar. He taught the Four Great Truths (*chatvāri ārya satyāni*)—sorrow (*duḥkha*), the cause of sorrow (*duḥkhasamudaya*), the elimination of sorrow (*duḥkhanirodha*), and the path leading to the elimination of sorrow (*duḥkhanirodhagāmī pratipadā*). This path was the middle path (*majjhimapratipadā*), which comprised the right kind of view (*dṛishṭi*), resolve (*saṁkalpa*), speech (*vāk*), conduct (*karma*), livelihood (*ājīva*), effort (*vyāyāma*), recollection (*smṛiti*), and meditation (*samādhi*). In Buddhist philosophy, 'everything is in a flux, nothing is permanent and one should aim at and strive for *nirvāṇa* which would make one free from the chain of life and death'. The number of the Buddha's followers soon swelled up. He entered the *parinirvāṇa* at Kuśīnārā *c* 483 BC, at the age of 80 years. Although the Buddha forbade his worship before his death, his followers, overwhelmed as they were by his personality, deified him, and installed his images on the altars of the various temples and pagodas throughout India and central and southeast Asia, where 'he sits enveloped in clouds of incense amid a buzz of prayers' (K D Bajpai 1989; Coomaraswamy 2003; Foucher 2003).

Budhagupta *Vikramāditya*. *Imperial Gupta k. He is known from his Nalanda sealing to be a son of Pūrugupta, born of *Mahādevī* Chandradevī. His earliest known date is *Gupta era 157 (= 476 AD), known from his Sarnath inscription. He would have ascended the throne some time after 473 AD, the date of the Sarnath inscription of *Kumāragupta II. The evidence of Hiuen-tsang has been taken to suggest that Budhagupta occupied the throne by force. His last known date seems to be Gupta era 176 (= 495 AD) on his silver coin, though some scholars have also read Gupta era 180 (= 499 AD) on another silver coin of this ruler. Therefore, his reign would have ended some time between 495 AD and 507 AD, which is the only known date of Vainyagupta. The find of his inscriptions and seals from such far flung places as Sarnath and Rajghat (District Varanasi), Paharpur (District Rajshahi), Damodarpur (District Dinajpur), Eran (District Sagar), Nandanpur (District Monghyr), and Nalanda would suggest that his empire extended from the Himalayas in the north to at least eastern Malwa in the south, and from eastern Punjab in the west to Bengal in the east. The non-mention of the name of Budhagupta in the inscriptions issued during his reign by his erstwhile feudatories, like the Parivrājaka *Mahārājas* and their neighbours the Uchchakalpa rulers, as well as by *Mahārāja* Subandhu of Māhishmatī, together with the assumption of the hereditary title of **mahārāja* by his governors of Bengal, Malwa, and Saurashtra, suggest that towards the end of his reign, there was a decline in the power and prestige of the Imperial Guptas. In Malwa, the provincial governor, Suśarman, uses the *Mālava era instead of the Gupta era, and refers to the Vākāṭaka ruler, Narendrasena, in place of the Gupta emperor, leading to the inference that Malwa, too, was lost to the Guptas. According to the Eran inscription of *Toramāṇa, Dhanyavishṇu was serving under this Hūṇa chief, while his elder brother, Mātṛivishṇu, had served in the same area under Budhagupta. On this ground, it has been concluded that the Eran region had been conquered by the Hūṇas, some time after Budhagupta. Some scholars identify Budhagupta with Deva or Devarāja of the *Āryamañjuśrīmūlakalpa*, whose last days, according to this text, were full of troubles and who was killed by his enemies. Budhagupta was the last Imperial Gupta emperor to the rule over extensive territories (Ashvini Agrawal 1989; Allan 1914; Altekar 1957; R D Banerji 1933; Fleet 1888; S R Goyal 2005; P L Gupta 1998; K P Jayaswal 1933; Smith 1972; Thaplyal 1972; Thaplyal, forthcoming).

Bull. The earliest evidence for the bull in India goes back to *c* 3,500 BC in the Quetta valley and the Zhob region of Baluchistan. It is generally believed that the bull was originally worshipped independently, 'without any human or divine master to the ride him', since the neolithic period in (southern) India; the bull was sometimes associated with the mother goddess as her consort. But later this cult was absorbed by Śaivism, and *Śiva 'displaced the Primeval Bull who was the fecundative power of the archetypal feminine deity'. Even in the *Ṛigveda*, Rudra is compared to a white bull to describe his complexion and power. Gradually, the bull not only became the **vāhana* of *Śiva, but the deity also came to be represented theriomorphically by that animal. In later literature, Śiva has epithets like *Mahāvṛisha*, *Vṛishadhvaja*, and *Vṛishavāhana*. The association of the bull with Śiva is also indicated by the accounts of such classical writers as Hesychios and Stobaios (Badam 1989; Banerjea 1968; Banerjea 2002; R G Bhandarkar 1928; Sukumari Bhattacharji 1970; Mahadev Chakravarti 1994; Bhaskar Chattopadhyay 1977; Kosambi 1965; Macdonell 1897; O'Flaherty 1975; R B Pande 1988; Rao 1985; Prashant Srivastava 2004b; Prashant Srivastava and Deepak Tiwari 1994).

C

Chandragupta I. *Imperial Gupta k. The Imperial Guptas rose to prominence during the reign of Chandragupta I, as revealed by the fact that, in the epigraphs and seals detailing the genealogy of the Imperial Guptas, he is given the title of **mahārājādhirāja*, while his grandfather Gupta and father Ghaṭotkacha are simply **mahārāja*. On his gold coins, the figure and name of his Lichchhavi queen, *Kumāradevī, occur by the side of his own figure and name. Their son, *Samudragupta, is invariably referred to as *Lichchhavidauhitra*, 'daughter's son of the Lichchhavis', in the genealogical portions of Imperial Gupta inscriptions and seals. The importance attached to the Lichchhavi relations has led V A Smith to suggest that Chandragupta I must have gained politically from this matrimonial alliance. The view of Allan, that the 'pride of the Guptas in their Licchavi blood... was probably due rather to the ancient lineage of the Licchavis than to any material advantages gained by this alliance', seems to be rendered untenable by the fact that *Manusaṁhitā* refers to the Lichchhavis as vrātya kshatriyas. It appears that, at the time of Chandragupta I, the Guptas and the Lichchhavis ruled over adjoining principalities, and the marriage led to an amalgamation of the two states, which was later inherited by Samudragupta. On the basis of a puranic passage, it is believed that Chandragupta I ruled over nearly the whole of Bihar and parts of Uttar Pradesh and Bengal. The *Gupta era is generally assumed to have commenced in 319 AD with his accession or coronation, although some scholars suggest the possibility of its commemorating the coronation of Samudragupta. There is nothing to support the view of R D Banerji that Chandragupta I successfully fought a 'war of liberation' with the Scythians. K P Jayaswal's reconstruction of the early history of the Imperial Guptas on the basis of the drama, *Kaumudīmahotsava* of Vijjakā, too, has not been accepted by a vast majority of scholars (Ashvini Agrawal 1989; Allan 1914; Altekar 1957; R D Banerji 1933; Fleet 1888; S R Goyal 2005; P L Gupta 1998; K P Jayaswal 1933; Prashant Srivastava 1996a; Thaplyal, forthcoming).

Chandragupta II *Vikramāditya*. *Imperial Gupta k. He was the son and successor of Samudragupta, and was born of *Mahādevī* Dattadevī. There is literary, epigraphic, and numismatic evidence to show that he killed his elder brother, *Rāmagupta, captured his throne, and married his widow. He completed the work of conquest begun by his father. He is known to have defeated *Rudrasiṁha III, the *Kārddamaka ruler of Gujarat-Kathiawar. In his endeavour, he seems to have been assisted by his ministers and feudatories, like Vīrasena Śāba, Sanakānīka Mahārāja, and Āmrakārddava. Some time in the last decade of the fourth century AD and the first decade of the fifth century AD, Chandragupta II annexed the Kārddamaka kingdom to his empire, and issued silver coins in imitation of the *Western Kshatrapa silver money. His *Lion-slayer type is believed to commemorate his victory of Kathiawar. It is known from the Udaigiri inscription of Vīrasena Śāba that Chandragupta II had set out 'to conquer the whole world', and his general, Āmrakārddava, claims in his Sanchi inscription to have won many battles. But, apart from his victory over the Kārddamaka Kshatrapas, we have no definite information about any of the military achievements of Chandragupta II. However, if King Chandra of the Mehrauli iron pillar inscription has rightly been identified with Chandragupta II, it may be said that in the east, Chandra/Chandragupta II 'defeated a confederacy of hostile chiefs in Vaṅga', that is eastern Bengal, while in the west, 'having crossed in warfare the seven mouths of the river Sindhu, conquered the Vāhlīkas', that is Bactria (Balkh). A recently reported copper type, bearing the figure of a horse, perhaps from Bangladesh and ascribed to Chandragupta II, seems to indicate his hold over the Bengal region. Chandragupta II's presence in Balkh seems to be vouched for by the inscriptions at Hunza. Eastern Bengal and Balkh were both under the political influence of Samudragupta, and Chandragupta II might have led arms against these two countries, either to quell some rebellion, or to bring them under the direct control of the Imperial Guptas. As early as 1927, a fragmentary inscription, on a stone figure of a horse from the village Nigawa near Varanasi, was read as *Chandramgu*, and the horse was regarded as representing the sacrificial animal of some *aśvamedha* performed by Chandragupta II. Most of the scholars had reservations about it. But the discovery of these coins, bearing the figure of a horse, if genuine, might indicate, in a more tangible manner, the performance of the horse sacrifice by Chandragupta II. Besides Dhruvadevī, the widow of Rāmagupta whom he had slain, Chandragupta II married Kuberanāgā, a *Nāga princess, and his daughter born of her, *viz.* Prabhāvatīguptā, was married to the Vākāṭaka king, Rudrasena II. It is also likely that his son, *Kumāragupta I, had married a daughter of the Kadamba ruler, Kākutsthavarman (Ashvini Agrawal 1989; Allan 1914; Altekar 1957; R D Banerji 1933; Fleet 1888; S R Goyal 2005; P L Gupta 1998; K P Jayaswal 1933; Rhodes and Saha 2006; Prashant Srivastava 1996a; Thaplyal, forthcoming).

Chashṭana. *Kārddamaka k. He was the son of Ysā(Ghsā)motika, and, perhaps, the first known ruler of his family. The discovery of his statue from the *Kushāṇa *devakula* at Mat near Mathurā seems to indicate some relation with the Kushāṇas. He is believed to have started his career as a governor of the southwestern provinces of the Kushāṇa empire, especially entrusted with the task of recovering the territories lost to the Sātavāhanas as a result of the defeat of *Nahapāna at the hands of Gautamīputra Sātakarṇi, which task, as per the numismatic evidence, he succeeded in accomplishing to a certain extent. Scholars like Oldenberg and Jouveau-Dubreuil expressed the possibility of his being initially a governor of the Sātavāhana ruler, Gautamīputra Sātakarṇi.

But, recently, doubts have been expressed as to his ever occupying a subordinate position under any political power. On his early coins, he uses the title of **kshatrapa*, but on later coins, he calls himself **mahākshatrapa*. V V Mirashi has read the name of this ruler and the date of year 6 in an inscription from Daulatpur. A recently discovered Andhau inscription of year 11 also seems to mention him, although, according to the R C Senior, the name is not clear in the inscription, and has been proposed as Chashṭana only because the ruler is mentioned as *Ghsāmotikaputra*. However, with the discovery of *Dāmaghsada I as another son of Ghsāmotika, this identification can no longer be regarded as certain. Another Andhau inscription, this one dated Śaka year 52 (130 AD), refers to him as **rājan*. He seems to have appointed his son, *Jayadāman, as *kshatrapa* on his own elevation to the position of *mahākshatrapa*. But Jaydāman predeceased Chashṭana, and the former's son, *Rudradāman I, was appointed as heir-apparent. This seems to be indicated by the Andhau inscription of year 52, which refers to both Chashṭana and Rudradāman I as *rājan*. From Ptolemy, who apparently refers to Chashṭana as Tiastenes, it is known that Ujjayinī (Ozene) had become the headquarters of the Kārddamaka Kshatrapas as early as the time of Chashṭana himself. But the use of the Kh script on his coins shows his hold over some Kh areas like Sind also. On epigraphic grounds, he is assigned the dates 84-130 AD, but Jaina sources would show that he was ruling even in 78 AD. Senior regards him as the younger brother of Dāmaghsada I, and places him after the latter. Incidentally, this would make Dāmaghsada I the first ruler of the Kārddamaka dynasty. But at another place in the same work, he states that he would 'opt for the later date for Dāmaghsada', and places him after Chashṭana (Jha and Rajgor 1994; Mirashi 1982; Mitchiner 1976; Rajgor 1991; Rapson 1975; Raychaudhuri 1972; Senior 2001; Sircar 1980e).

Cornucopiae. In Greek mythology, the *cornucopiae* is generally associated with *Zeus, the foremost among the Greek gods. It is said that his father, Kronos, was afraid that he would be replaced by his son, and according to one version of the tale, he flung his son Hades into Tartaros and Poseidon into the sea; according to another version, he devoured his children as soon as they were born. To save Zeus the same fate, his mother Rhea gave the child upon birth to her own mother Gaia, and handed over a stone wrapped in cloth to Kronos, who swallowed it at once. Zeus was brought up in Krete, where he was reared by the nine Telchines. In various versions, a number of wet-nurses of the infant Zeus are mentioned, like Adrasteia and Ide. But most of the accounts name Amaltheia as the wet nurse. She is sometimes said to be herself a goat who suckled Zeus. Later, Zeus took the horn of the goat, filled it with fruits, flowers, etc, and placed it, along with the goat, among the stars. But some authorities inform us that Amaltheia was not herself a goat, but rather the owner of the goat the horn of which was used to feed Zeus. According to Ovidius and Apollodoros, Amaltheia had a bull's horn, which could fill itself with any sort of meat and drink desired by its owner. This horn became the *cornucopiae*, 'the horn of plenty', and was commonly depicted in Greek art as a symbol of prosperity. On the basis of the shape of the *cornucopiae* as seen in art, it has been suggested that it was the prototype of the vessel called *rhyton* used for drinking. According to another version, *Herakles desired Deianeira, the daughter of Oinaios of Kalydon, and, for her, he had to struggle with the river god, Achelöos, the son of Tethys and Okeanos. This river god, like *Triton, was a man from the waist up, a serpent-fish from the waist down, and had bull's horns on his head. He could assume various shapes like that of a bull or a serpent. Herakles wrestled with him, and broke off one of his horns. Blood dripped from the wound, and from it, the Sirens were born. The broken horn of Achelöos was picked up by the Naiads, who filled it with fruits and flowers, and it was this horn which became the *cornucopiae*. There is, again, a third version, which seems to combine the earlier two versions in an attempt to the reconcile them. It tells us that Herakles returned the horn he had broken off the head of Achelöos to him, and, in return, received from him the horn of Amaltheia (Kerenyi 1951; Rose 1958; Prashant Srivastava 2007e).

D

Demeter. Deity. This Greek goddess of agriculture and especially associated with corn, was the daughter of the Titan Kronos and the Titaness Rhea, and a sister of *Zeus, Hades, *Poseidon, Hestia, and Hera. Her name Demeter (= *Da-mater*, that is Da-mother) probably signifies her quality as the Earth-mother, Da being the 'primitively ancient name' for the Greek earth goddess, Gaia. According to some accounts, Zeus took her as his wife, and begat on her a daughter, Persephone, whom he gave in marriage to his brother Hades, the ruler of the underworld. But in most of the accounts, Demeter is the wife of Poseidon. She recovered her daughter from the underworld, and pleased at this, she 'despatched Triptolemos (a culture hero) to teach men agriculture'. As the goddess of agriculture and as the deity associated with bestowing prosperity upon mankind, she has the **cornucopiae* as her characteristic attribute. In these aspects, she corresponds to the Roman deity Ceres, the Iranian **Ardochsho*, and the India *Lakshmī (Bhaskar Chattopadhyay 1977; Graves 1955; Kerenyi 1951; Rose 1958; Prashant Srivastava 2007c).

Demetrios I. *Indo-Greek k. He was the son of *Euthydemos I, and had shown such promise even as a young prince, that the Seleukid, Antiochos III, decided to give him one of his own daughters in marriage. He succeeded his father, and scholars have attributed him wide-ranging conquests. According to Tarn, he annexed Aria, Arachosia, and Seistan to his kingdom. But Aria was already a part of the Indo-Greek kingdom during the reign of Euthydemos I, who met Antiochos III on the river Arius. The suggestion of the conquest of Seistan by Demetrios is based on the evidence of the find of a few of his coins in that region, and Justin's reference to the conflict of the 'Drangians' with the Bactrians. The conquest of Arachosia by Demetrios is proved by the reference to a city named Demetrias in Arachosia, by Isidore of Charax. He could also have occupied the eastern parts of Gedrosia. The conquests of Sogdiana, and perhaps Ferghana, also seem to have been achieved by *Euthydemos II, during his reign. It was earlier almost universally believed that Demetrios crossed the Hindukush, and occupied the Kabul and the Indus valleys, on the basis of two bilingual types, one each in silver and copper, bearing the name of Demetrios, believed to be the son of Euthydemos I by scholars like Cunningham and Whitehead. It was argued that after his conquest of the Indian territories, Demetrios was obliged to introduce the Kh ld for the benefit of his Indian subjects. But the bust of the king on the obv of the silver type is shown in a flat *kausia*, while that on the copper one is clumsily depicted wearing an elephant's scalp, and these are unlike the depiction of the king on the other coins of Demetrios I. Besides, on the bilingual coins, there occurs the additional epithet, **aniketos* (Kh, **aparajita*), which is not found on the other coins of Demetrios. On these grounds, scholars like Macdonald and Narain ascribe these bilingual coins to *Demetrios II, although A N Lahiri includes these two types among the issues of Demetrios I. The other reasons for suggesting the conquest of some Indian territories by Demetrios I are that Justin calls him 'king of the Indians'; that Apollodoros' statement referred to by Strabo is interpreted to mean that Menander and Demetrios, between them, conquered Patalene, Saraostus, Segerdis, and regions as far as Seres and Phryni; that there is a mention of Demetrios as a *yavanādhipa*, and of a town Dattāmitrī in the *Mahābhārata*; that there is mention of Demetrios as Ḍimita in the Hathigumpha inscription of Khāravela; etc. But Narain has shown that Demetrios is called 'king of the Indians' in a very vague sense; Apollodoros, whom Strabo finds not always reliable, seems to have confused Demetrios the son of Euthydemos I, with Demetrios who subdued the Indians; Dattāmitra of the *Mahābhārata* was the epithet of Sumitra, a king of Sauvīra, and the name of the *yavanādhipa* was Vittala, and hence, the association of Dattāmitrī with Demetrios has no solid basis; even the reading of the name Ḍimita in the Hathigumpha inscription is not certain, much less the identification with Demetrios. Tarn says that 'it is just possible that Paropamisadae were his already; anyhow he took Gandhāra, crossed the Indus, and occupied Taxila'. But, according to Narain, no coins of Demetrios, the son of Euthydemos I, have been found in the Kabul valley, or at Taxila, and there is no impact of the local coinage of Taxila on the coins of Demetrios; *lion, the only 'Taxila animal' to occur on Indo-Greek coins, is seen on the coins, not of Demetrios but of *Agathokles. Thus, there is no evidence to support the theory of the extensive conquests of Demetrios in India, and there is nothing to prove Tarn's contention that Demetrios eyed the throne of Aśoka because he regarded himself as an heir to the Mauryas through alleged matrimonial relations of both his family and that of the Mauryas with the Seleukids, and that he succeeded in this endeavour through the help of his able generals and sons. Demetrios had to face danger of the nomads from the north, and the Imperial Parthians from the west, besides restive elements in Sogdiana, Aria, Drangiana, and India. He, therefore, very wisely desisted from disturbing the powers on the other side of the Hindukush, and, rather, utilized his energies in consolidating the territories he had already conquered. But the subsequent discoveries of his coins from several places in the North West Frontier Province, and the use of the elephant's scalp as his headdress on coins, have led Osmund Bopearachchi to suggest that Demetrios I might have attempted conquests to the south of the Hindukush (Bopearachchi 1993; Bopearachchi 1994; Bopearachchi and Pieper 1998; Bopearachchi and Rahman 1995; Cunningham 1970; Gardner 1971; A N Lahiri 1965; Macdonald 1987; Marshall 1975; Narain 1957a; Rapson 1987; Senior 2001; Sircar 1980a; Prashant Srivastava 1996a; Tarn 1980; Whitehead 1914).

Demetrios II. *Indo-Greek k. Coins reveal the existence of two Indo-Greek kings bearing the name of Demetrios—Demetrios the son of *Euthydemos I (that is *Demetrios I), and Demetrios **Aniketos* (that is Demetrios II). On the basis of the rules of nomenclature, Demetrios II might be regarded as a younger son or a grandson of Demetrios I, but Narain has shown very convincingly that Demetrios II was related to *Antimachos I, and was perhaps the son and successor of the latter. He is believed by some scholars to be the first Indo-Greek king to issue bilingual coins, the Kh ld on the rev being meant for his Indian subjects. This has led to the inference that Demetrios II was perhaps the first Indo-Greek king to cross the Hindukush, and occupy the Kabul valley. He seems to have assumed the title of **aniketos* after this achievement. He might also have conquered Gandhāra and some of its western territories. One of his coins has been found during the excavations at Taxila, but it would not be fair to assume his occupation of that city on the basis of the discovery of a solitary piece alone. But when he was busy in these southern ventures, *Eukratides I occupied Bactria. Demetrios II rushed to Bactria, and besieged Eukratides I with a large army. But Justin informs us that, in spite of having only 300 soldiers with him, Eukratides was able to defeat Demetrios II, who might even have been killed in this encounter. If Demetrios II succeeded Antimachos I around 180 BC, he might have ruled up to *c* 165 BC (Bopearachchi 1993; Bopearachchi and Pieper 1998; Bopearachchi and Rahman 1995; Cunningham 1970; Gardner 1971; A N Lahiri 1965; Macdonald 1987; Marshall 1975; Narain 1957a; Rapson 1987; Sircar 1980a; Tarn 1980; Whitehead 1914).

Diodotos I. *Indo-Greek k. Originally a satrap of the Seleukids in Bactria, he rebelled in 256 BC, during the reign of Antiochos II. The rebellion is mentioned by Justin, Trogus, and Strabo. On the basis of the monograms occurring on the coins bearing the name of Diodotos, Macdonald and Tarn suggested that the revolt of Diodotos was not sudden; rather, Diodotos rose gradually to power. But Narain has rejected the idea, and believes that the 'breakaway was abrupt'. Not much is known about the subsequent career of Diodotos I, except that, besides Bactria, he also ruled over Margiana and Sogdiana. The Parthians seem to have held him in awe, and Arsakes was forced to keep a large army battle-ready for fear of an attack by Diodotos I. On the commemorative coins issued by *Demetrios I and *Agathokles in honour of Diodotos I, he is given the title of **soteros*, but it is not known if this title was used by Diodotos I himself in his lifetime (Bopearachchi 1993; Bopearachchi and Pieper 1998; Bopearachchi and Rahman 1995; Cunningham 1970; Gardner 1971; Kovalenko 1995-1996; A N Lahiri 1965; Marshall 1975; Narain 1957a; Newell 1938; Rapson 1987; Sircar 1980a; Prashant Srivastava 1996a; Tarn 1980; Whitehead 1914).

Diodotos II. Indo-Greek k. According to Justin, he was the son and successor of *Diodotos I. The Parthians maintained friendly relations with him, for mutual security, as also to foil any attempts on the part of the Seleukids to the re-establish their authority over the two breakaway satrapies of Bactria and Parthia. He was able to the retain hold over Bactria and Sogdiana On the basis of the portraits of Diodotos II appearing on his coins, it has been suggested that his rule ended *c* 235 BC.

Polybios seems to suggest that Diodotos II lost his life at the hands of *Euthydemos I (Bopearachchi 1993; Bopearachchi and Pieper 1998; Bopearachchi and Rahman 1995; Cunningham 1970; Gardner 1971; Kovalenko 1995-1996; A N Lahiri 1965; Marshall 1975; Narain 1957a; Newell 1938; Rapson 1987; Sircar 1980a; Prashant Srivastava 1996a; Tarn 1980; Whitehead 1914).

Diomedes. *Indo-Greek k. On the basis of his use of the mounted *Dioskuri type which is generally associated with the family of *Eukratrides, it was suggested by Cunningham that he might have been a son of Eukratides. But his use of monograms associated with later kings shows that he was, perhaps, a son of *Antialkidas, who managed to establish himself in parts of western Gandhāra, apparently after the death of *Apollodotos, *c* 95 BC, and ruled for about 10 years, when he was supplanted by *Amyntas in that region. R C Senior, however, places him between *c* 100 BC and 90 BC, and regards him as a contemporary, and, perhaps, also an assistant, of *Philoxenos (Bopearachchi 1993; Bopearachchi and Pieper 1998; Bopearachchi and Rahman 1995; Cunningham 1970; Gardner 1971; A N Lahiri 1965; Marshall 1975; Narain 1957a; Rapson 1987; Senior 2001; Sircar 1980a; Tarn 1980; Whitehead 1914).

Dionysios. *Indo-Greek k. His coins seem to associate him with *Apollodotos, and he appears to have ruled over the Jammu-Sialkot region in the interval between the two phases of the reign of *Strato I, perhaps succeeding *Zoilos II, and preceding *Apollophanes. His reign may be placed in the second decade of the first century BC (Bopearachchi 1993; Bopearachchi and Pieper 1998; Bopearachchi and Rahman 1995; Cunningham 1970; Gardner 1971; A N Lahiri 1965; Marshall 1975; Narain 1957a; Rapson 1906; Rapson 1987; Sircar 1980a; Tarn 1980; Whitehead 1914).

Dionysos. Deity. An outsider from Thrace and Phrygia, he was accepted in the Greek pantheon as the youngest immortal son of *Zeus. According to some sources, he was born of Persephone, the queen of the underworld, and, as such, had the surname Chthonios, 'the subterranean'. Other accounts have it that he was the son of Zeus, born of a mortal, Semele the daughter of King Kadmos. The name of his mother, Semele, seems to be derived from Zemelo, the Phrygian earth goddess, and this connects Dionysos with the earth. Semele, instigated by Hera, asked Zeus to come to her in all his divine glory, but she could not bear the flashes of his lightning, and was burnt to ashes. Zeus plucked Dionysos from the womb of Semele, and put him in his thigh, from which he was later born. He was nursed by Ino, sister of Semele, and later, by the nymphs of the rain and the mountain on Mount Nysa, where he was disguised as a girl to keep him safe from the evil designs of Hera. On his way to Naxos, he discovered the grape vine, and invented wine. He persecuted those who doubted his divinity, like Pentheus, the successor of Kadmos; the daughters of Proitos; and the three daughters of Minyas of Orchomenos. He granted the golden touch to King Midas of Phrygia. He is credited with exploits in Egypt, Libya, Syria, and even India. The Maenads, Satyrs, and nymphs were his constant companions. After he was introduced into the Olympian pantheon by Zeus, he succeeded in making his mother a minor goddess. Although Dionysos was always accompanied and worshipped by women, only Ariadne is ever mentioned as his wife. He appears, sometimes as a bull, sometimes as a goat, and often as a serpent. His association with intoxicating drinks and his wild followers remind one of the Indian *Śiva (Bhaskar Chattopadhyay 1977; Graves 1955; Kerenyi 1951; Rose 1958; Prashant Srivastava 2007c).

Dioskuri, The. Deities. The twins, Kastor and Pollox (or Polydeukos) were the sons of Leda by *Zeus, and perhaps the brothers of Helena and Klytemnestra. Of the twins, Kastor was mortal, while Pollox was immortal. The Dioskuri, or *Dios kouroi*, 'sons of Zeus', are believed to be originally the daemons of the morning and evening twilight. They are the tutelary deities of the sailors, inventors of war dance, patrons of games and poetry, and revered as heroes. There is a tradition that Zeus placed them as stars in the constellation Gemini. In art, they are mostly represented as two handsome youths, mounted on horses and carrying spears. The special egg-shaped cap, the **pilos*, is associated with them, and often represents them in a symbolic form. The Dioskuri seem to correspond to the Aśvinikumāras of Indian mythology, and certain scholars believe that they might have been 'originally adaptation of the Indian twin deities' (Bhaskar Chattopadhyay 1977; Graves 1955; Kerenyi 1951; Rose 1958; Prashant Srivastava 2007c).

E

Eagle. This bird is closely associated with *Zeus. It is told that a boy, Aetos, 'eagle', was a playmate of Zeus, and he was turned into a bird by the jealous Hera, who suspected that her husband, Zeus, loved him. According to another account, Zeus once himself took the form of an eagle to pursue Asteria. In Indian mythology, *Agni and *Sūrya are compared with the eagle [**Garuḍa*, **Garuḍadhvaja*] (Graves 1955; Kerenyi 1951; Rose 1958).

Elephant. It is generally believed that the earliest evidence for the domestication of elephant in India dates back to the Harappan period. This animal is associated with a number of deities—as Airāvata, it is the mount of *Indra; it gladdens *Lakshmī by bathing her in her *Gajalakshmī aspect. It also seems to be associated with fertility, as in the Buddhist art at Bharhut, lotus stalks are seen issuing from the mouth of elephants. In Hellenistic art, the beast is sometimes associated with *Zeus (Badam 1989; Banerjea 2002; Bhaskar Chattopadhyay 1977; Graves 1955; Handa 2007a; Kerenyi 1951; Rao 1985; Rose 1958).

Epander. *Indo-Greek k. He is believed to be a subking of *Menander. His rare coinage does not help us in identifying the province governed by him, but Cunningham places him in the upper Kabul valley. He seems to have ruled very briefly sometime in the seventh decade of the second century BC, although R C Senior places him *c* 80 BC. His relationship with other Indo-Greek kings in not known (Bopearachchi 1993; Bopearachchi and Pieper 1998; Bopearachchi and Rahman 1995; Cunningham 1970; Gardner 1971; A N Lahiri 1965; Marshall 1975; Narain 1957a; Rapson 1987; Senior 2001; Sircar 1980a; Tarn 1980; Whitehead 1914).

Eukratides I. *Indo-Greek k. According to Justin, he started his career simultaneously with the Arsakid, Mithridates I of Parthia. As the Arsakid ruler is believed to have ascended the throne *c* 171 BC, Eukratides I would have started ruling around that date. On some of his coins, he commemorated his parents, Heliokles and *Laodike. The obv of these silver coins, struck on the Attic standard, bears the helmeted bust of the king, to the r on one variety, and to the l with the king thrusting a javelin on the other variety, the ld mentioning the name and titles of Eukratides I. The rev has the conjugate busts of Heliokles and Laodike to the r, with the ld mentioning their names. As on these coins, Laodike is shown with a diadem, the mark of royalty, while Heliokles is bareheaded, scholars like Tarn believe that Laodike was a Seleukid princess, a daughter of Seleukos II, and Heliokles was, perhaps, a governor under Antiochos III. Tarn further suggested that Eukratides was sent by his cousin, Antiochos IV, to stir a revolt against Demetrios in Bactria, in which endavour he was successful. But Narain feels that Antiochos IV had 'neither the statesmanship to envisage nor the resources to carry out' such a plan. He regards Eukratides as an upstart, who was born of a princess, perhaps a daughter of *Diodotos II or *Euthydemos I. Recently, R C Senior has suggested that Laodike was a daughter of the Seleukid ruler, Antiochos III. Justin informs us that when *Demetrios [II] was busy in his southern campaigns, *Eukratides I occupied Bactria. Demetrios II rushed to Bactria, and besieged Eukratides I with a large army. But Justin states that, in spite of having only 300 soldiers with him, Eukratides was able to defeat Demetrios II, who might even have been killed in this encounter. Justin also refers to his wars in Sogdiana, Aria, Arachosia, Drangiana, and India. From Justin's account, it appears that after consolidating his position in Bactria, Eukratides I embarked upon an ambitious campaign. Aria and Margiana would have been inherited by Demetrios II from Antimachos I, and the victory of Eukratides over Demetrios II must have resulted in these territories also passing into the hands of the victor. He would also have occupied the Kabul valley before he proceeded towards Arachosia and Drangiana, and assumed the title of **megas*, 'the great', perhaps to commemorate this achievement. The discovery of his coins in Arachosia and Seistan, and in the *Mir Zakah hoard near Ghazni, has led to the inference that from the Paropamisadae, he advanced to Arachaosia and Seistan *via* Ghazni, and occupied a considerable part of these provinces. He also advanced towards Gandhāra, but the rarity of his coins in that region shows that he was not very successful in this direction, and could not cross the river Indus. Justin informs us that when he was returning in triumph to Bactria, his son, whom he had left behind in Bactria as his joint king, killed him, 'drove his chariot through his blood', and cast away his corpse. Justin does not name this parricide. One of the sons of Eukratides was *Heliokles I, but as he assumed the title of **dikaios*, some scholars hesitate in identifying him as the parricide. Narain regards *Plato as the eldest son of Eukratides I, who killed him, perhaps on being instigated by the Arsakids. The possibility of the parricide being *Eukratides II, has also been expressed. Senior, on the basis of a statement of Justin, that the Bactrians lost their territories, and even their liberty, as a result of their defeats at the hands of Mithridates, suggests that Eukratides I was responsible for the 'final decline' of the Greek power in Bactria, and that due to this, he was killed by one of his sons. But it must be remembered that, according to Justin, Eukratides I was returning to Bactria from a *victorious* campaign, when he was killed. Tarn, however, believes that Eukratides I was killed, not by his own son, but by the son of Demetrios, and that this information of Justin is erroneous. Eukratides I ruled from *c* 171 to 155 BC, although Senior would take his reign up to 145 BC (Bopearachchi 1993; Bopearachchi and Pieper 1998; Bopearachchi and Rahman 1995;

Cunningham 1970; Gardner 1971; A N Lahiri 1965; Marshall 1975; Narain 1957a; Rapson 1987; Senior 2001; Sircar 1980a; Prashant Srivastava 1996a; Tarn 1980; Whitehead 1914).

Eukratides II. *Indo-Greek k. Scholars expressed the possibility of the existence of two Indo-Greek kings named Eukratides as early as 1738, but other scholars like Cunningham and Trever opposed this view, while some others like Whitehead refused to commit themselves. However, with the discovery of more coins bearing the name of Eukratides and the title **soter*, the possibility of a second Eukratides has increased, with most of the modern writers on the subject accepting the existense of Eukratides II. Tarn regarded him as a son or brother of *Heliokles I, appointed as the governor of the territories to the north of the Hindukush. But as his coins are nearer to those of Heliokles I than to those of *Eukratides I, Narain prefers to take him as a son of Heliokles I. He seems to have ruled over Bactria and Badakshan. The possibility of his rule over regions to the south of the Hindukush is precluded by the presence of *Menander in those regions. There is a suggestion that during his reign, the *Śaka-Pahlavas of the Jaxartes-Oxus area crossed the river Oxus, and occupied Bactria, which would make Eukratides II the last Indo-Greek king to the rule over Bactria proper. Henceforth, the authority of the Indo-Greeks to the north of the Hindukush remained confined mainly to Badakshan. Eukratides II seems to have ruled from *c* 140 BC to 130 BC (Bopearachchi 1993; Bopearachchi and Pieper 1998; Bopearachchi and Rahman 1995; Cunningham 1970; Gardner 1971; A N Lahiri 1965; Marshall 1975; Narain 1957a; Rapson 1987; Sircar 1980a; Prashant Srivastava 1996a; Tarn 1980; Whitehead 1914).

Euthydemos I. *Indo-Greek k. According to Polybios, he belonged to city of Magnesia, but it is not certain whether he meant the Ionian city of that name, or the Lydian. He might have been a high-ranking military official or a satrap (of Sogdiana or of Aria and Margiana) under *Diodotos II. Polybios' account suggests that Euthydemos attained kingship of Bactria by 'destroying' the descendants of the original rebels. From this, it has been surmised that he killed Diodotos II and occupied his throne, *c* 235 BC, about the same time as the death of Aśoka. It has been suggested that Diodotos II might have formed an alliance with the Parthians against the Seleukids, and this might have provided Euthydemos with an excuse to 'destroy' the family of Diodotos. He appears from his coin portraits to have been young at the time of his accession to the throne, and to have had a long reign of around 30 years. Very little is known of the career of Euthydemos, till the eastern expedition of Antiochos III, around 208 BC, to the reassert Seleukid authority over Parthia and Bactria. Euthydemos met the Syrian invader on the river Arius (modern Hari-rud), was worsted, and had to withdraw to his capital, Bactra, which Antiochos besieged for two years. Euthydemos made overtures for peace, emphasizing its need in view of the danger from the nomads from the north. Incidentally, this has been taken to indicate that the Śaka-Pahlavas, from the north of the river Jaxartes and from Sogdia, had begun their migration towards the south by this time. A treaty was agreed upon, after which Antiochos retired to Syria. It is not known whether Euthydemos acknowledged the suzerainty of Antiochos III; even if he did, 'it soon became a dead letter'. Euthydemos exercised control over Bactria, Sogdiana, Kabul, Kandahar, Seistan, southern Afghanistan, and adjoining parts of Iran. He, however, took care to extend his sway in such directions as would not invite a fresh Seleukid attack. The end of his reign is generally placed about 190 BC, though scholars like Narain and R C Senior would date it about ten years earlier (Bopearachchi 1993; Bopearachchi and Pieper 1998; Bopearachchi and Rahman 1995; Cunningham 1970; Gardner 1971; A N Lahiri 1965; Marshall 1975; Narain 1957a; Rapson 1987; Senior 2001; Sircar 1980a; Prashant Srivastava 1996a; Tarn 1980; Whitehead 1914; Wilson 1971).

Euthydemos II. *Indo-Greek k. There are some silver coins bearing the name of Euthydemos, with a 'youthful bust with draped shoulders' on the obv, and *Herakles standing with a wreath in his extended r hand on the rev. These coins were earlier attributed to *Euthydemos I, but scholars like von Sallet, Gardner, and Macdonald regard these coins as the issues of a second ruler of that name, on the grounds that the youthful portrait of the king on these coins varies from those on the coins of Euthydemos I, and Herakles on these coins is standing 'in a singular way which is not typically Greek', while this deity is shown as seated on the coins of Euthydemos I. Some scholars regard Euthydemos II as a son of *Demetrios, but he is generally believed to be a younger brother of the latter. There is a suggestion that he was dispatched by Euthydemos I to conquer territories in the north, and he finally succeeded in occupying the regions as far as Sogdiana, and even Ferghana in its north and north-east, possibly after the death of his father, when Demetrios had ascended the throne. It was this conquest which enabled him to strike in nickel, Euthydemos II being the first Indo-Greek ruler to issue nickel coins. He seems to have ruled as a joint-king or sub-king of Demetrios, and predeceased him, *c* 190 BC (Bopearachchi 1993; Bopearachchi and Pieper 1998; Bopearachchi and Rahman 1995; Cunningham 1970; Gardner 1971; A N Lahiri 1965; Marshall 1975; Narain 1957a; Rapson 1987; Sircar 1980a; Prashant Srivastava 1996a; Tarn 1980; Whitehead 1914).

F

Fire altar. Fire worship has occupied an important place in the religious life of the Indians since pre-historic times. Recent evidence from sites like Lothal, Kalibangan and Banawali seems to suggest the prevalence of fire worship even among the Harappans. Fire altars were especially constructed for various vedic sacrifices. The Zoroastrians in Iran also accorded a prominent place to the fire altar (Darmesteter 1974; B B Lal 1997; Macdonell 1897).

G

Gaṅgā. Deified river. Much sanctity is attached to the waters in India since times immemorial. The Great Bath at Mohenjodaro, according to some scholars, shows that the Harappans believed in the ceremonial importance of water. The vedic people worshipped the waters as the goddess Āpaḥ. Among the rivers, Gaṅgā occupied a very important place in India. In the *Gītā*, Kṛishṇa states that he is Gaṅgā among the rivers. It was believed that the river originally flowed in heaven, and when she descended on the earth, *Śiva received her in his matted locks. Since then, Gaṅgā became the second wife of Śiva, the first one being *Umā. The **makara* is associated with Gaṅgā as her mount. Depiction of Gaṅgā, along with Yamunā, became very popular in Gupta art, the river goddesses, with their respective mounts, the *makara* and the *kūrma*, occupying the door jambs of the temples of that period. Gaṅgā is usually shown in art as an 'exceedingly beautiful' woman of a 'voluptuous type', standing gracefully on the back of the *makara* (Banerjea 2002; R B Pande 1988; Rao 1985).

Garuḍa. The earliest reference to *garuḍa* is to be found in the *Ṛigveda*, where the sun is likened to a golden-winged *garuḍa* (*suparṇo garutmān*). But in later literature, as also in art, he came to be more closely associated with *Vishṇu as his *vāhana*. The sun has to journey across the sky every day, and therefore, requires a powerful and fast mount. And Vishṇu is a solar deity. The *garuḍa* as the mount of Vishṇu is the result of this imagery. The *garuḍa* is an imaginary creature, with the head, beak, and wings of a bird, while the rest of his body is usually human. In epic and puranic mythology, he is the son of Kaśyapa and Vinatā. His mother was on inimical terms with her co-wife, Kadrū, the mother of the serpents, and this accounts for the traditional rivalry between the *garuḍa* and the *nāgas*. Unnati or Vināyakā was the wife of *garuḍa*, and Sampāti was his son. Aruṇa, the charioteer of *Sūrya, was his elder brother. *Garuḍa* is once said to have had a struggle with *Indra over *amṛita*, in which the **vajra* of Indra got damaged. According to the iconographical texts, the head of *garuḍa* should be white, the body golden or emerald, and the wings red or lustrous golden. He is pot-bellied, and two-, four-, or six-armed. A pot of *amṛita* is his most common attribute. When shown with Vishṇu, the god is riding astride on the shoulders of *garuḍa*, who supports the feet of the god with two of his hands [**Garuḍadhvaja*, *eagle] (Banerjea 2002; Feller 2004; R B Pande 1988; Rao 1985).

Garuḍadhvaja. This is a banner or standard surmounted by the figure of a **garuḍa*, and has Vaishṇava affiliations. According to a story in the *Mahābhārata*, *garuḍa's* mother, Vinatā, had been enslaved by the serpents, who were the sons of her co-wife, Kadrū. These serpents promised to set her free if *garuḍa* could bring them *amṛita* from the celestial world. *Garuḍa* went to the capital of *Indra, and was able to wrest the pot of ambrosia from its guards. When he was returning with it, he met *Vishṇu, and promised to act as his mount and as the device on his standard, which henceforth came to be called the *garuḍadhvaja* because of the device of the *garuḍa* on it. Interestingly, *Garuḍadhvaja* is also one of the name of Vishṇu. To end the story, *garuḍa* brought the pot of *amṛita* to the serpents, who set Vinatā free. But before they could partake of ambrosia, Indra came and took away the pot, and the serpents had to satisfy themselves by licking the *kuśa* grass on which the pot has been placed by *garuḍa*. The *Imperial Guptas had adopted the *garuḍa* as their royal insignia, and the appearance of the *garuḍadhvaja* on their coins need not occasion any surprise. The Besnagar pillar inscription of the time of King Bhāgabhadra shows that the *garuḍadhvaja* was a common motif with the devotees of Vishṇu [*Eagle] (Banerjea 2002; Feller 2004; R B Pande 1988; Rao 1985).

Ghaṭotkachagupta *Kramāditya.* *Imperial Gupta k. An *Archer type of gold coin, bearing the ld *Ghaṭo* under the king's arm on the obv, and the epithet *Kramādityaḥ* on the rev, has been ascribed by scholars variously to Ghaṭotkacha, the father of *Chandragupta I, to Ghaṭotkacha of the Tumain record, to Ghaṭotkacha of a Vaiśālī seal, or to a hitherto unknown ruler of that name. Altekar feels that the Ghaṭotkacha of this coin might be identical with Ghaṭotkachagupta of the Tumain inscription, who was the governor of Malwa during the reign of his father, *Kumāragupta I, and who asserted his independence for a short period of time during the initial troubled years of the reign of *Skandagupta. But the newly discovered Ramtek inscription shows that Ghaṭotkachagupta was not the son, but the brother, of Kumāragupta I. This inscription eulogizes *Chandragupta II and Ghaṭotkachagupta, but makes no mention of Kumāragupta I. This omission, if deliberate, has been taken as an evidence of strained relationship between Ghaṭotkachagupta and Kumāragupta I. This inscription also shows that Ghaṭotkachagupta married the daughter of his sister, the Vākāṭaka queen, Prabhāvatīguptā. It has been suggested that, perhaps with Vākāṭaka help, Ghaṭotkachagupta revolted against Kumāragupta I in Malwa, and set himself up as an independent king for some time. As Ghaṭotkachagupta was serving as governor in 435 AD, as per the evidence of the Tumain inscription, he would have been too old in 455 AD to make a bid for the throne after the death of Kumāragupta I. Hence, his rebellion has to be placed during the reign of Kumāragupta I itself. But the rebellion was soon crushed by his brother, and he lost his life (Ashvini Agrawal 1989; Allan 1914; Altekar 1957; R D Banerji 1933; Fleet 1888; S R Goyal 2005; P L Gupta 1998; K P Jayaswal 1933; Smith 1972; Thaplyal, forthcoming).

Gondopharnes. *Śaka-Pahlava k. He seems to have started his career in Arachosia as a subordinate ruler under *Orthagnes, with whom he issued some joint coins. On these coins, also associated with the administration of Arachosia, is one *Guḍa, a brother of Gondopharnes. Gondopharnes seems to have been sent by his overlord to northwestern India, where he appears to have defeated *Azes II. *Aśpavarman, the **strategos* of Azes II, later served under Gondopharnes in the same capacity. He appears to have switched over his loyalty to the invader, and the victorious invader permitted him to continue as *strategos* as a reward for the help rendered. Some scholars, like Rapson and Sten Konow, however, believe that Gondopharnes succeeded Azes II peacefully. Gondopharnes, after his successes in northwestern India, seems to have dissociated himself from the administration of Arachosia, and declared himself independent. Orthagnes nominated Guḍa as the viceroy of Arachosia, and issued joint coins with him alone. Later, however, Gondopharnes issued Arachosia type of coins, on the rev of which occurs the name of Guḍa. This shows that, perhaps after the death of Orthagnes, Gondopharnes occupied Arachosia and Guḍa continued to serve there as his viceroy. The distinctive Gondopharnes symbol is found countermarked on some coins of the Arsakid rulers, Orodes I and Artabanos III, which has been taken to indicate the conquest of certain parts of the Parthian empire by Gondopharnes. His hold over the Kabul valley is attested by Philostratos and Fan-ye. The Takht-i-Bahi inscription shows that the Gandhāra region formed a part of his empire. Interestingly, this inscription dated in [*Vikrama *saṁvat*] 103 (= 46 AD), refers to [regnal] year 26 of Gondopharnes, showing that he ruled from *c* 19 AD to 46+ AD, although attempts have been made to place him in the latter half of the first century BC. He is identified with Gūdnaphar or Goundaphoros, 'the king of India', who received Apostle Thomas about the middle of the first century AD, and this Christian tradition also supports the date *c* 19 AD to 46+ AD for Gondopharnes. The date of Gondophanres is a contentious issue, and may be discussed in some detail here, as it has a bearing on the history and coinage of the Śaka-Pahlava rulers. Initially, when the coins of Gondopharnes were discovered, they were dated to the first century BC. But this date did not find favour in the light of the evidence provided by the Christian legend and the Takht-i-Bahi inscription (above). However, attempts were made, by scholars like J E van Lohuizen de Leeuw, to place Gondopharnes in the first century BC, by rejecting the legend of St Thomas' visit to India and regarding the year 103 of the Takht-i-Bahi inscription as referring to some earlier Śaka-Pahlava era commencing 129-128 BC. Recently, R C Senior has once again argued for placing Gondopharnes known from coins in the second half of the first century BC. His main arguments, together with comments, may briefly be dealt with as follows : The head of the king on the Seistan silver coinage of Gondopharnes resembles that on the silver *drachms* of Gotarzes I and Phraates III, to a great extent, both these the Imperial Parthians (Arsakids) ruling in the first century BC. The Arsakid coins struck before the accession of Phraatekes in 2 BC are very artistic with 'plastic and raised style', while the Arsakid coins struck from 2 BC onwards are 'flat and stylized'. The coins of Gondopharnes fall in the first category. Certain epithets used by Gondopharnes on his coins have also been taken to indicate a first century BC date for him. For instance, the title of *autokratoros* was first assumed by the founder of the Imperial Parthian dynasty,

Arsakes I, or by Mithridates I, and by Orodes I and Tiridates II, both ruling in the first century BC. Incidentally, the Indo-Greek ruler, Theophilos, who assumed this title, too, belonged to the beginning of the first century BC. Another title of Gondopharnes was *nikephoros*. Besides the Imperial Parthian rulers, Arsakes II and Gotarzes I, this title was assumed by a number of Indo-Greek rulers, like Antimachos, Antialkidas, Amyntas, Archebios, Artemidoros, Epander, Lysias, and Philoxenos. It is true that all of them ruled before 50 BC as pointed out by Senior, but then, Indo-Greek rule seems to have ended *c* 55 BC. Besides, the dates of the Indo-Greek rulers, named above, range between the third century BC and mid-first century BC. The appearance of the title of *nikephoros* on the coins of these rulers just shows the popularity of this title among kings. The rev device of some coins of Gondopharnes is enthroned king with Nike standing or flying behind him and placing a wreath on his head. Senior compares this device to a silver coin of Phraates III, where Tyche is shown standing behind the enthroned king. But on this Imperial Parthian coin, the deity standing behind enthroned king is Tyche, and not Nike as shown on the coins of Gondopharnes. Some features, like the use of the titles *autokratoros* and *nikephoros*, the style of the ld 'who is called Sae', the device of Nike flying behind enthroned king, the peculiar Gondopharnes symbol, of the coins of Gondopharnes seem to be adopted from the Arsakid coins of the first century BC. But this just shows that Gondopharnes flourished after the issuers of those coins; it need not necessarily place Gondopharnes in the first century BC with them. Senior argues that the copper coins of Gondopharnes from the Pathankot area were copied from the crude copper issues of Rañjuvula in that region, showing that Gondopharnes conquered that region from Rañjuvula. Śoḍāsha, the son of Rañjuvula, succeeded his father as *mahākshatrapa*. But the similarity between the coins of Gondopharnes from the Pathankot area and those of Rañjuvula may only show that Gondopharnes came in possession of this area after Rañjuvula. It is not necessary for him to have succeeded Rañjuvula immediately in the Jammu-Pathankot areas by way of conquest. Besides, it may also be pointed out that D C Sircar is of the view that Rañjuvula ruled from *c* 1 AD to 15 AD, and Śoḍāsha, up to *c* 25 AD. Thus, we see that there is no solid ground for placing Gondopharnes in the latter half of the first century BC as proposed by Senior. On the contrary, there are reasons to accept *c* 19 AD to 46+ AD as the reign period of Gondopharnes. According to Rapson, the peculiar Gondopharnes symbol is found struck on some coins of Orodes II (57-37/36 BC). The same mark was found by Alexander Cunningham on some coins of Artabanos III who ruled from 11/12 AD to *c* 38 or 40 AD. Rapson, however, doubted this, and suggested that Cunningham might have meant 'Orodes'. But there is a coin type of Artabanos III, the rev of which shows the king mounted on horse, left, and being offered a palm-branch by Tyche standing before him. This type was issued *c* 27/28 AD. This coin type of Artabanos III seems to have served as the prototype for the obv device of a bronze type of Gondopharnes, which has king on horseback, left, and being received by a female figure, identified as Nike by Gardner, though some doubts have been expressed regarding this identification. If this suggestion regarding the inspiration for the coin device of Gondopharnes be correct, Gondopharnes must have ruled in the first century AD to copy this Arsakid device on the type issued *c* 27/28 AD. He was served, not only by Aśpavarman, but also by the latter's nephew, *Sasan, with whom he issued joint coins, and his own nephew, *Abdagases. He was the last great Śaka-Pahlava ruler, and after him, Abdagases, *Pakores, and Sasan are known to have ruled as independent kings, though their order of succession is not certain. His empire disintegrated soon after, paving the way for the establishment of Kushāṇa supremacy in northwestern India (Bopearachchi and Rahman 1995; Cunningham 1971a; Gardner 1971; Huxley 1983; Jenkins and Narain 1957; van Lohuizen de Leeuw 1949; Marshall 1975; B N Mukherjee 1969a; Rapson 1987; Senior 2001; Sircar 1980b; Sircar 1986; Prashant Srivastava 1996a; Prashant Srivastava 2005c; Prashant Srivastava 2007a; Tarn 1980; Whitehead 1914;).

Gorgons. The Gorgons were the three daughters of Phorkys, named Stheno, Euryale, and Medousa. Of these, the last one was a mortal creature, and she was also taken as a wife by *Poseidon. The Gorgons had golden wings, but heads of brass, and boar's tusks. Their heads and bodies were 'girdled with serpents', and anyone who stared at the face of the Gorgons was rendered breathless and turned into stone immediately. How Gorgon's head came to be associated with *Athena is told in the story of Perseus, who was instructed by Athena not to look at the head of Medousa directly, but in his polished shield. In this manner, Perseus was able to confront Medousa without directly seeing her terrible face, and to cut off her head with a sickle. He presented this head to Athena, and from that time, the Gorgon's head was worn by her, sometimes as a sign on her shield, and sometimes attached to her breast-plate, the **aegis* (Graves 1955; Kerenyi 1951; Rose 1958).

H

Harsha. *Pushpabhūti k. This younger son of *Prabhākaravardhana ascended the throne of Thaneshwar on the death of his elder brother, Rājyavardhana II. We get a fairly detailed account of his early life and reign from the *Harshacharita* of Bāṇa and the narrative of the Chinese pilgrim, Hiuen-tsang, besides other sources. Immediately before his accession, *Śaśāṅka and Devagupta of Malwa had invaded the *Maukhari kingdom of Grahavarman, to whom Harsha's sister, Rājyaśrī was married. Grahavarman had lost his life in the struggle, and the invaders had occupied his capital Kanauj, and imprisoned Rājyaśrī. Rājyavardhana had succeeded in worsting Devagupta, but had himself been killed by Śaśāṅka. On becoming king, Harsha marched towards Kanauj to free his sister, but she had somehow escaped from prison and Harsha met her in the Vindhya forest. According to Hiuen-tsang, the vacant throne of Kanauj was offered to Harsha, and he later transferred his capital from Thaneshwar to Kanauj. Harsha, on his accession, had vowed to the rid the earth of the Gauḍas, but there is no clear evidence to suggest that he defeated Śaśāṅka, or even that the two ever came face to face with each other in battle. Śaśāṅka continued to the rule at least till 619 AD. Harsha was 'king of Magadha' in 641 AD, and he had conquered Utkal and Ganjam regions of Orissa by 643 AD. A Gurjara record shows that Harsha had defeated a Maitraka ruler of Valabhī, probably Dhruvasena II, but he was later restored to the throne, and Harsha married his daughter to him. His conquests of Sindh and Nepal (allegedly hinted at in the *Harshacharita*), and of Kashmir and southern India, are doubtful. Harsha invaded the territories of the Chālukya ruler, Pulakeśin II, but was defeated in a battle, perhaps fought on the river Narmada, sometime between 630 and 634 AD. Harsha sent three embassies to China, and the Chinese emperor sent an equal number of embassies, of which the third reached India one year after the death of Harsha, which occurred in 647 AD. Harsha is said to have founded the Harsha era, commencing 606 AD, with his accession. Initially a Śaiva, he was later attracted towards Buddhism. He is credited with the authorship of works like *Ratnāvalī*, *Priyadarśikā*, and *Nāgānanda* (Richard Burn 1906; D Devahuti 1964; D Devahuti 2001; Pires 1934; Thaplyal 1985).

Hekate. Deity. She was the daughter of the star goddess Asteria and of Perses the son of Eurybia. Her mother was a sister of Leto, which makes Hekate a cousin of *Apollo and *Artemis. The name Hekate, perhaps, means 'the distant one', although the goddess is close to men. She was allowed by *Zeus to continue to enjoy the threefold honour she earlier enjoyed under the Titans. She had a daughter, Skylla, by Phorkys. Her lovers include several sea gods, particularly *Triton. Hekate is a goddess of fertility, and helped women at childbirth. She is a grim goddess, associated with the underworld as queen of the ghosts, and in this capacity, she is also the goddess of magic, and of the cross-roads where three paths meet. This explains why her images are often triple, or why she is sometimes represented as three-headed (Bhaskar Chattopadhyay 1977; Graves 1955; Kerenyi 1951; Rose 1958; Prashant Srivastava 2007c).

Heliokles I. *Indo-Greek k. A son of *Eukratides I, he ascended the throne of Bactria, perhaps after removing his brother, the parricide (?) *Plato. Besides Bactria, his authority extended over the territories of Badakshan and Sogdiana. During his reign, the Arsakids wrested the outlying Indo-Greek provinces, and Mithridates I seems to have conquered territories as far east as Aria. The coins of Heliokles come mostly from the regions to the north of the Hindukush; the regions to the south were under *Menander. Heliokles was believed to be the last Indo-Greek king to the rule over Bactria, but, according to some scholars, with the discovery of the Attic *tetradrachms* of later Indo-Greek kings, like *Eukratides II, *Archebios, and others, in the *Qunduz hoard, this view can no longer be entertained. He seems to have ruled from *c* 155 BC to 140 BC, although Osmund Bopearachchi would place the end of his reign *c* 130-129 BC. Some scholars like Cunningham and Marshall believed in the existence of only one Indo-Greek king named Heliokles. However, Gardner expressed the possibility of the existence of two Indo-Greek kings bearing that name on the basis of the marked contrast between the portraits of Heliokles appearing on the monolingual coins bearing the name of Heliokles on the one hand, and that on the bilingual coins on the other. This suggestion of Gardner has been supported by Tarn, Whitehead, Narain, and others, with the monolingual coins being attributed to Heliokles I, and the bilingual ones, to Heliokles II (Bopearachchi 1993; Bopearachchi and Pieper 1998; Bopearachchi and Rahman 1995; Cunningham 1970; Gardner 1971; A N Lahiri 1965; MacDowall 2003-2004; Marshall 1975; Narain 1957a; Rapson 1987; Senior 2001; Sircar 1980a; Prashant Srivastava 1996a; Tarn 1980; Whitehead 1914).

Heliokles II. *Indo-Greek k. On the basis of the marked contrast between the portrait of Heliokles on the monolingual coins, and that on the bilingual coins, Gardner has expressed the possibility of the existence of two Indo-Greek kings named Heliokles, and this is supported by a number of scholars, with the monolingual coins being attributed to *Heliokles I and the bilingual ones to Heliokles II. Narain regards Heliokles II as a son of *Heliokles I, and a brother of *Eukratides II. He seems to have come to power after his nephew, *Archebios. He ruled over the Kabul and Ghazni regions, and parts of western Gandhāra where his coins are quite numerous. He is identified with that Heliokles who restruck the joint coins of *Agathokleia and *Strato I, as the restruck pieces are also bilingual. It is generally believed that he expanded his dominions at the expense of Strato I, then a minor. Almost all his coins show him as 'a man well advanced in middle age', and seems to have had a brief reign from *c* 120 BC to 115 BC, although R C Senior places his reign between *c* 85 BC and 75 BC, and Osmund Bopearachchi, between *c* 110 BC and 100 BC (Bopearachchi 1993; Bopearachchi and Pieper 1998; Bopearachchi and Rahman 1995; Cunningham 1970; Gardner 1971; A N Lahiri 1965; Marshall 1975; Narain 1957a; Rapson 1987; Senior 2001; Sircar 1980a; Tarn 1980; Whitehead 1914).

Helios. Deity. *Apollo was a Greek solar deity, but Helios was the sun god himself. Helios, a Titan, was the son of the Titan Hyperion and the Titaness Theia, and he had two sisters, *Selene and Eos, 'dawn'. His wife is variously called Perse, Persies, and Neaira. From Neaira, he had two daughters— Lampetia and Phaethousa, and two sons—Aiestes and Phaethon; later, the number of his daughters was raised to three, or even seven. The Greeks saw in the sun, a ball of fire, an eye, a spoked wheel, but 'the most commanding and persistent likeness which they saw was that of a chariot and horses'. Homer describes Helios as wearing a helmet of gold, but the god is usually portrayed in art as wearing a crown of rays, and not a helmet. Interestingly, Homer does not refer to the chariot of the sun god. Helios is seen in art as a handsome youth, mounted on a chariot drawn by winged horses, sometimes accompanied by his two sisters, Selene and Eos. The identification of Helios has been suggested with the vedic *Sūrya. Interestingly, in the *Bhavishyapurāṇa*, the sun god is called Heli, and his world as Heliloka (Bhaskar Chattopadhyay 1977; Graves 1955; Kerenyi 1951; Rose 1958; Prashant Srivastava 2007c; Stein 1888).

Hephaistos. Deity. He was, according to Homer, the son of *Zeus and Hera, but according to Hesiod, he was especially Hera's son. He was thrown down from heaven by Hera herself to conceal his birth, or by Zeus when Hephaistos sought to aid Hera against the king of gods. The fall made him a lame. He fell on Lemnos, where the Sintians took care of him, and henceforth, Lemnos became the seat of his cult. The name, Hephaistos, means 'quivering flame', or simply 'fire', and Hephaistos was the 'god of subterranean fire'. He was a master-craftsman, and an incomparable worker in metals. By his humorous nature, he acted as peacemaker among the immortals. He had for his wife Aglaia, 'the glorious'. Aphrodite, too, was his consort, and when she fell in love with Ares, the brother of Hephaistos and the Greek god of war, Hephaistos bound Ares and Aphrodite together in bed, and released them only upon *Poseidon's intervention. Hephaistos assisted Zeus at the time of the birth of *Athena, and is said to have demanded her as his wife in return. Interestingly, Hephaistos, the Greek god of fire, cannot be compared to the vedic fire god, *Agni, as their functions differ. He might, however, be likened to Viśvakarman, the Brahmanical divine architect and workman (Bhaskar Chattopadhyay 1977; Graves 1955; Kerenyi 1951; Rose 1958; Prashant Srivastava 2007c).

Herakles. Deified hero. He was the son of Amphitryon and Alkmene, though Homer describes *Zeus as his father. His very name, which means 'Hera's glory', suggests his close association with Hera. He was born in Thebes. Though originally purely human, he was eventually admitted to Olympus, and became 'the object of cult, though only rarely as a god, mostly as a kind of very superior hero'. As a 'subduer of monsters', he slew the Nemean lion, the giant Porphyrion, the Lernaean hydra, and Skylla the wild bitch. He also had conflicts with deities like *Apollo and *Triton. His twelve labours for King Eurystheos of Tiryns won him great fame. He was a mortal, and 'recognizing and consenting to his fate, immolated himself on Mount Oeta'. From the pyre, he rose and ascended to Olympus in the form of an eagle, and received Hebe, daughter of Zeus and Hera, to wife. Although he was received at Olympus as a divinity, he was never given divine honours on earth. Arrian refers to the reverence paid to Herakles by the Sourasenoi (= Śūrasenas), while Curtius states that an image of Herakles was carried in front of the army of Paurava. This Indian Herakles has been identified variously with *Śiva, a *yaksha, or *Vāsudeva-Kṛishṇa, though the last identification seems to be the most probable, not only in view of the close association of *Vāsudeva-Kṛishṇa with the Śūrasenas, but also because the exploits of Vāsudeva-Kṛishṇa might have reminded the Greeks of the labours of Herakles. Herakles is usually armed with a bow and arrow in art, but on coins, a club is his invariable attribute (R G Bhandarkar 1928; Bhaskar Chattopadhyay 1977; S R Goyal 1986; Graves 1955; Kerenyi 1951; McCrindle 1896; McCrindle 1901; Pinsent 1969; Rose 1958; Prashant Srivastava 2007c).

Hermaios. *Indo-Greek k. There are some coins on which the name and/or portrait of Hermaios is associated with the *Kushāṇa ruler, *Kujula Kadphises. The suggestion of scholars like Percy Gardner, V A Smith, R B Whitehead, and Alberto M Simonetta, that Kujula Kadphises began his career as a subordinate ally of the *Indo-Greek ruler and later displaced him, as also that of other scholars like, Cunningham, Whitehead, Smith, and initially also Rapson, that in view of the *Śaka-Pahlava menace, Hermaios formed an alliance with the Kushāṇa ruler and they issued these coins conjointly, and then Kujula Kadphises immediately succeeded Hermaios, on the basis of these coins, can no longer be entertained in view of the strong evidence indicating an interval of at least 70 years between the end of the reign of Hermaios and the accession of Kujula Kadphises. A long gap between the end of the reign of Hermaios and the accession of Kujula Kadphises, as suggested by F W Thomas, is supported by the result of the excavations at Taxila. The *Hou Han-shu* also informs us that the Yueh-chihs conquered the Kabul valley from the Śaka-Pahlavas [not from the Indo-Greeks]. Tarn suggested that these coins were issued by Kujula Kadphises who desired to legitimize his hold over the Kabul valley by proclaiming his relationship with Hermaios, a princess of whose family was married to *Heraos, a predecessor of Kujula Kadphises. But Bachhofer proposed that when Kujula Kadphises occupied the Kabul valley, he imitated the type of Hermaios which was popular in that region. The *provenance* of the coins of Hermaios shows his hold over an extensive dominion, comprising the Paropamisadae, some regions to the north of the Hindukush, upper Arachosia, and perhaps even eastern Gandhāra and Takshaśilā. There seems to have been an alliance between the descendants of *Eukratides and those of *Menander against the Śaka-Pahlavas and the Yueh-chihs, during the reign of Amyntas, and perhaps as a result of this alliance, *Kalliope, a princess of the family of Menander and a daughter of *Hippostratos, was married to Hermaios. The joint coins of Hermaios and Kalliope seem to show that Kalliope was a 'queen regnant', and there is a possibility that, following the death of Hippostratos, Hermaios and Kalliope might have jointly ruled over some territories previously ruled by Hippostratos. But towards the end of his reign, Hermaios lost most of his provinces to *Azes I. Narain suggests that the Śaka-Pahlava ruler first occupied upper Arachosia, and then Gandhāra and the Paropamisadae. Hermaios also lost the regions to the north of the Hindukush to the Yueh-chihs. The reign of Hermaios seems to have come to an end *c* 55 BC, although some scholars, like Osmund Bopearachchi and R C Senior, would place the end of his reign around 70 BC, and with this seems to have ended the rule of the Indo-Greeks (Bopearachchi 1993; Bopearachchi 1994; Bopearachchi and Pieper 1998; Bopearachchi and Rahman 1995; Cribb 1982; Cunningham 1970; Dobbins 1970; Gardner 1971; A N Lahiri 1965; Macdonald 1987b; Marshall 1975; Narain 1957a; Rapson 1987; Senior 1995; Senior 2001; Simonetta 1958; Sircar 1980a; Smith 1972; Prashant Srivastava 1990b; Prashant Srivastava 1996a; Tarn 1980; Whitehead 1914).

Hermes. Deity. Born of a nymph named Maia, Hermes was one of the youngest sons of *Zeus. He was born in a cave on Mount Kyllene in Arkadia. Immediately after his birth, he made a lyre from out of a tortoise shell, and stole 50 cows of *Apollo from Peiria. This led to a conflict between them, and their father reconciled them by making Hermes return the cows to Apollo and present the lyre to him. Apollo, in his turn, sent him to be tutored in the art of divination by his own teachers, and made him the master of the beasts. Hermes is a master-thief, and the god of all forms of magic and trickery. As a traveller, he was the spirit of the *herms*, the piles of stones, which, in ancient Greece, marked paths, boundaries, and also holy places. He was the Psychopompos, 'the conductor of souls', and sometimes acted as the messenger of gods, a role usually performed by Iris. Some of his characteristics remind one of the Indian Rudra-*Śiva. His most distinguishing attribute is the **caduceus*. As a traveller, he is shown wearing winged boots in art. According to some accounts, his wife was *Hekate, and their daughters were the three Charites or Graces. He was the lover of Herse and Brimo. He also played a role, along with Zeus and *Poseidon, in the birth of Orion. He helped *Demeter in bringing back her daughter, Persephone, from Hades, and planted 'lies, flatteries, and treachery' in the heart of the first woman, Pandora (Graves 1955; Kerenyi 1951; Rose 1958; Prashant Srivastava 2006a; Prashant Srivastava 2007c).

Hippostratos. *Indo-Greek k. Tarn regarded him as the father of *Nikias, but Narain seems to be right in suggesting that he was actually the son of the latter; Nikias depicted *Poseidon on his coins, while his son Hippostratos depicted Poseidon's son, *Triton, on his coins. Hippostratos seems to have succeeded Nikias in western Gandhāra. Whitehead has placed him in the Peshawar and Hazara regions, but, according to Narain, this seems doubtful in view of the scarcity of his coins at Takshaśilā. He, however, might have controlled some territories to the east of the river Indus. Osmund Bopearachchi regards him as the last Indo-Greek king to the rule over western Punjab, including Takshaśilā and Pushkalāvatī. He started ruling *c* 85 BC, and was, perhaps, overthrown by *Azes I around 70 BC, and this marked the end of the rule of the Indo-Greeks in the regions to the east of the Kabul valley; R C Senior, however, places his reign between *c* 60 BC and 50 BC (Bopearachchi 1993; Bopearachchi and Pieper 1998; Bopearachchi and Rahman 1995; Cunningham 1970; Gardner 1971; A N Lahiri 1965; Marshall 1975; Narain 1957a; Rapson 1987; Senior 2001; Sircar 1980a; Prashant Srivastava and Prachi Srivastava 1993; Tarn 1980; Whitehead 1914).

Horse. In India, Bagor gives the earliest evidence for the domestication of horse, which dates back to *c* 4,500 BC. This animal is the symbol of speed and strength, especially military strength of kings and warriors in general; it is also sometimes associated with the mother goddess as her consort. It is associated with a number of deities, like Kubera, Revanta, and Kalkin, as their *vāhana*, but more particularly with *Indra and *Sūrya. Horse seems to be very important to the vedic Indians. The head of the horse signifies knowledge. In Buddhism, the horse denotes the renunciation of the *Buddha. It is one of the seven treasures of a *chakravartin*. In Greek mythology, the horse is associated with *Poseidon, who has the epithet *hippios*. In the *Avesta*, the horse is associated with *Ahuramazda (Badam 1989; Banerjea 2002; R G Bhandarkar 1928; Sukumari Bhattacharji 1970; Bhaskar Chattopadhyay 1977; Darmesteter 1974; Kerenyi 1951; Macdonell 1897; R B Pande 1988; Rao 1985; Rapson 1975; Rose 1958).

Hūṇa. Tribe/Dynasty. The Hūṇas were a nomadic tribe, inhabiting the northern shores of the Caspian Sea, from where they spread over Asia and Europe. They were skilled horse riders and warriors. 'They engaged all the civilized peoples of the world in fearful cataclysmic wars; and, wherever they could, they killed, destroyed, burnt and devastated with demoniac ruthlessness.' The branch of the Hūṇas, which occupied the valley of the river Oxus, is known as Ye-tha, Ephthalites, or Hephthalites. At one time, they were under the authority of the Juan-Juan tribe. Around the middle of the fifth century AD, they threw off the yoke of that tribe, advanced towards both Iran and India, and, crossing the Hindukush, occupied Gandhāra. But their efforts to enter further into India were rendered unsuccessful by *Skandagupta. The Hūṇas brought about the downfall of the Iranian empire, and, after destroying the later *Kushāṇa rulers of northwestern India, they again invaded India. In the first half of the sixth century AD, a Hūṇa (?) chief, *Toramāṇa, had overrun northern India up to Eran (Madhya Pradesh), and, after some reverses, perhaps at the hands of the Aulikara Prakāśadharman, as per the evidence of the Risthal inscription, his son, *Mihirakula, occupied a vast part of northern India from Punjab in the west to at least Gwalior in the east. But Mihirakila was defeated by both Yaśodharman of Mandasor and [Narasiṁhagupta] Bālāditya. The latter defeat crushed the power of the Hūṇas in India. The *Maukharis and the *Pushpabhūtis also claim to have worsted the Hūṇas. But the final death blow to the Hūṇa power in India was dealt by the combined forces of the Turks and the Iranians, who defeated the Hūṇas some time between 563 and 567 AD. Coins reveal the names of about a dozen rulers of Hūṇa origin, who ruled over parts of Punjab, Kashmir, and Afghanistan. These include, besides Toramāṇa and Mihirakula, chiefs like *Lae-lih, *Rāmānīla/Ramanila, and *Khiṅgila (Altekar 1986b; Biswas 1973; Cunningham 1962; Cunningham 1967; R C Majumdar 1988; Upendra Thakur 1967a; Upendra Thakur 1967b;).

I

Indra. Deity. Invoked in as many as 250 hymns of the *Ṛigveda*, and worshipped along with other deities in at least 50 more, he is believed to be the greatest of the vedic gods. He is one of the 11 atmospheric deities, the god of 'power and valour', and 'the lord of all that moves and breathes'. 'As his name does not designate any phenomenon of nature, he has become more anthropomorphic and more invested with mythological imagery than any other member of the pantheon'. According to the *Śatapathabrāhmaṇa*, the name Indra is derived from *indha*, 'the kindler'. He is the wielder of the **vajra*, fashioned by Tvashṭṛi or Uśanas from the bones of Dadhyañch. This *vajra*, Indra used to kill the demon Vṛitra. The *Ṛigveda* also describes him as holding a bow and arrow, or an *aṅkuśa*. In that text, he rides a chariot driven by two, a hundred, a thousand, or even eleven hundred horses. But in later mythology, his mount is the elephant Airāvata, which came out of the churning of the Ocean of Milk. Later, with the rise in the popularity and prominence of the puranic triad of Brahmā, *Vishṇu, and *Śiva, Indra, one of the supreme deities of the vedic pantheon, was reduced to the position of the 'chief of the minor gods', and, finally, was transformed into one of the eight *dikpālas* or guardian deities of the eight quarters of the universe. Indra is identified with Verethraghna of Avestan mythology, and with the Greek god *Zeus whose attribute, like that of Indra, is the thunderbolt. Texts like the āgamas, the *Bṛihatsaṁhitā*, and the *Vishṇudharmottarapurāṇa*, describe Indra as two-armed, possessed of handsome features, adorned with ornaments, and seated or standing upon a lotus seat, or seated on an *elephant. His attributes include the *vajra*, *śakti*, *aṅkuśa*, *padma*, and *nīlotpala*-bloom. Airāvata, his mount, should have four tusks, two on either side (Banerjea 2002; Sukumari Bhattacharji 1970; Hillebrandt 1999; Macdonell 1897; R B Pande 1988; Rao 1985; Prashant Srivastava 1996b; Prashant Srivastava 2007b; Wilkins 2006).

Īśānavarman. *Maukhari k. This ruler, whose only known date is Vikrama *saṁvat* 611 (= 554 AD), was the son and successor of Īśvaravarman and his wife, Upaguptādevī. The main source of information regarding his reign is his Haraha inscription, which records his victory over the Andhras (Vishṇukuṇḍins), Śūlikas (Chālukyas ?), and Gauḍas, before ascending the throne. Emboldened by these conquests, he asserted independence from the *Imperial Guptas, and assumed the title of **mahārājādhirāja*. He might have also defeated the *Hūṇas. But the Later Gupta king, Kumāragupta, is known to have defeated him, and probably extended the boundaries of his principality up to Prayāga. Some scholars identify the Maukhari ruler defeated by the Later Gupta king, Dāmodaragupta, also with Īśānavarman. The Haraha inscription mentions Sūryavarman as the son of Īśānavarman, but the Maukhari genealogy, given in the seal inscriptions, refers to Śarvavarman as the son and successor of Īśānavarman (Richard Burn 1906; D Devahuti 1964; Pires 1934; Thaplyal 1985).

Īśvaradatta. Ābhīra (?) k. The coins of one **Mahākshatrapa* Īśvaradatta, have been found in several hoards of *Kārddamaka coins, and these bear a close affinity to the coins of the Kārddama Kshatrapas. However, he cannot be regarded as a Kārddamaka ruler, mainly on the bases of the facts that his name does not appear to fit in with those of the Kārddamaka rulers, and that he dates his coins in his regnal years while the Kārddamaka Kshatrapas date their issues in the *Śaka era. On this basis, it has been proposed that he was an interloper, who either usurped the Kārddamaka throne, or ruled simultaneously with some Kārddamaka ruler after wresting some of his territories from him. Although his coins make no mention of his antecedents, Bhagwanlal Indraji regarded him as associated with the Ābhīras mentioned in a Nasik inscription. Various dates have been proposed for his reign. Bhagwanlal Indraji places him between the years 171 and 176; Rapson, on the basis of the greater similarity of his coins with those of *Vīradāman, *Yaśodāman I, and *Vijayasena, dates his coins between the years 158 and 161; Bhandarkar indentifies him as the intruder who forced *Rudrasiṁha I to the revert to the position of a **kshatrapa* between the years 110 and 112; P L Gupta earlier dated his reign between the years 273 and 284, but later placed it between the years 254 and 270. On the basis of a coin, on which Shobhana Gokhale has read the date of year 154 in numerals on the obv, and identifying Īśvaradatta with Īśvarasena of a Nasik record which is dated in the ninth regnal year of that ruler, she places the rule of Īśvaradatta between the years 151 and 162. Mirashi is of the view that Īśvaradatta ruled over northern Maharashtra, and wrested some parts of Malwa and Saurashtra from the Kārddamaka Kshatrapas. B N Mukherjee suggested that he might have occupied some Kārddamaka territories, and ruled simultaneously and independently for some time with some Kārddamaka ruler. Similar is the view of P L Gupta, who regards central Gujarat and western Malwa as having comprised the dominions of Īśvaradatta. But Amiteshwar Jha and Dilip Rajgor read the date on the coin published by Shobhana Gokhale as year 164, and suggest that Īśvaradatta ruled simultaneously with Vijayasena (For references, see Jha and Rajgor 1994).

K

Kācha. *Imperial Gupta k. Kācha is a ruler of the Imperial Gupta period, known from the Kācha type of coins, and the occurrence of the **garuḍadhvaja* on his coins sets at rest all doubts regarding his relations with the Imperial Guptas. There is some controversy among scholars regarding the identity of Kācha, and the main views may be cited here. Some scholars regard him as identical with Ghaṭotkacha, the father of *Chandragupta I; Joe Cribb suggests that the coins might even have been struck by *Samudragupta in memory of his grandfather, Ghaṭotkacha. But the name on the coins is always Kācha, and not Kacha, and this view cannot be entertained. B Ch Chhabra regards Kācha as a son of Ghaṭotkacha, and a younger brother of Chandragupta I. D R Bhandarkar suggested that Kācha was identical with *Rāmagupta, the elder brother of *Chandragupta II, mentioned in literary works, like the *Devīchandraguptam*, where the name *Kācha* was written as *Rāma*(*gupta*) due to the fault of the scribe. But now that we have coins and inscriptions already bearing the name of Rāmagupta, the view has to be rejected. R D Banerji expressed the view that the Kācha type was issued by Samudragupta in memory of his elder brother, who lost his life in the 'war of liberation' fought by Chandragupta I against the *Kushāṇas. But there is no evidence of any such struggle. There is also a suggestion identifying Kācha with Samudragupta on the basis of similar weight standard of coins (that is 116 grains); similarity in the meanings of the circular ld of the Kācha type and the *Archer type of Samudragupta; similarity in the rev device of the Kācha type and the *Tiger-slayer and **Aśvamedha* types of Samudragupta; and the rev ld *Sarvvarājochchettā* of the Kācha type being an epithet of Samudragupta. But, as Altekar has shown, these arguments are not conclusive. Besides, the position of the ld *Kācha* under the king's left arm on the obv of the Kācha type, a place reserved for the personal name of the issuer on the Imperial Gupta coins, shows that Kācha was not another name of Samudragupta, but the personal name of the issuing king. The *chakradhvaja* is peculiar to the Kācha type alone, and it does not appear on any type of Samudragupta. There is literary and epigraphic evidence to show that brothers of Samudragupta disputed his succession. The *Āryamañjuśrīmūlakalpa* speaks of a brother of Samudragupta named Bhasma, which means 'alkaline ashes', the same as Kācha. On this basis, it has been suggested that Kācha might have been a brother of Samudragupta, who usurped the throne immediately after the death of Chandragupta I, or during Samudragupta's absence from northern India while he was engaged in his Dakshiṇāpatha campaigns, or after the death of Samudragupta, the last possibility finding favour with Altekar (Ashvini Agrawal 1989; Altekar 1957; K D Bajpai 1972; Sibesh Bhattacharya 1992; Chhabra 1986; Cribb 1985a; S R Goyal 2005; P L Gupta 1998; Prashant Srivastava 1996a; Thaplyal, forthcoming).

Kalliope. *Indo-Greek queen. Known from the coins she issued conjointly with her husband *Hermaios, Kalliope seems to be a descendant of *Antimachos because her joint coins bear on the rev the device of equestrian king, popular in the family of Antimachos; it has been suggested that she might be a daughter of *Hippostratos. As Hermaios belonged to the family of *Eukratides, Cunningham believes that these joint coins 'refer to a royal alliance' between the families of Antimachos and Eukratides. It seems that the father of Kalliope had no male heirs, and on his death, his kingdom passed on to her. From the fact that the device of equestrian king was adopted by Hermaios for the joint coins, as also for the obv of some of his other coins, it has been inferred that the family of Kalliope might have been more powerful than that of Hermaios. She ruled over this kingdom conjointly with Hermaios, and issued joint coins with him (Bopearachchi 1993; Bopearachchi and Pieper 1998; Bopearachchi and Rahman 1995; Cunningham 1970; Gardner 1971; A N Lahiri 1965; Marshall 1975; Narain 1957a; Senior 2001; Sircar 1980a; Prashant Srivastava 1990b; Prashant Srivastava 1996a; Tarn 1980; Whitehead 1914).

Kanishka I. *Kushāṇa k. Perhaps the greatest, and certainly the most famous, of the Kushāṇa kings, he is known from the combined testimony of the literary, epigraphic, and numismatic sources, to have ruled over an extensive dominion extending from Bihar in the east to Khorasan in the west, and from Khotan in the north to Konkan in the south. The discovery of his coins in Bengal and Orissa should, however, not be taken as indicative of his sway over these territories in the absence of any corroborative evidence. He also subjugated the Central Asian provinces of Kashghar, Yarqand, and Khotan, and also dispatched his viceroy, Hsï, at the head of 70,000 horsemen across the Pamir to give battle to Pan-chao, the general of the Chinese emperor, Ho-ti (89-105 AD). This expedition was, however, unsuccessful, and, according to a legend, Kanishka lamented this failure about the time of his death. The *Śrīdharmapiṭaka* refers to his expedition against the Parthians. His name is associated with the Fourth Buddhist Council, which he is said to have convoked on the advice of Pārśva. There is no unanimity among scholars regarding the date of his accession. The inscriptions issued by him and his successors show that he founded an era which, however, is not named in these epigraphs. Consequently, the name of Kanishka I is associated with the various eras—*Vikrama, Traikūṭaka-Kalachuri-Chedi, etc. But a vast majority of scholars regards him as the founder of the *Śaka era, beginning 78 AD with his accession. Towards the end of his rule, he seems to have associated one *Vāsishka as his junior co-ruler. Although Kanishka is generally regarded as a Buddhist, the deities from varied pantheons appearing on the rev of his coins seem to show 'a sort of religious eclecticism' (Cunningham 1971a; Gardner 1971; Marshall 1975; von Mitterwallner 1986; Rosenfield 1967; Sircar 1980c; Whitehead 1914).

Kārddamaka. Dynasty. One of the three branches of the Western Kshatrapas, the Kārddamakas ruled over western parts of India for a period of nearly 300 years. The dynastic name Kārddamaka is mentioned in an inscription of the *amātya* of the daughter of *Rudradāman I from Kanheri, and some scholars relate it with the river Kardama in Bactria. Satya Shrava, however, feels that it is associated with Kardama, a territory identified with modern Sidhpur in Gujarat, and proposes that the branch might have originally hailed from that region. However, in the Gadha inscription of *Rudrasena, the name of the family is given as Bhadramukha. The royal house of the Kārddamaka Kshatrapas was established by *Chashṭana, who is believed to have started his career as a **kshatrapa* under the *Kushāṇas, but attained the position of a **mahākshatrapa*, although doubts have recently been expressed as to his ever occupying a subordinate position. R C Senior, however, regards *Dāmaghsada I as the elder brother of Chashṭana, and, perhaps, 'the first Satrap of the dynasty'. Chashṭana was followed by his grandson, *Rudradāman I, who was perhaps the greatest, and certainly the most famous, of the Kārddamaka rulers. After the end of the reign of Rudradāman's son, *Dāmajadaśrī I, there seems to have taken place a struggle for succession between his son, *Jīvadāman, and brother, *Rudrasiṁha I. Other rulers of this family include Rudrasena I, *Saṅghadāman, *Dāmasena, *Yaśodāman I, *Vijayasena, *Dāmajadaśrī III, *Rudrasena II, *Viśvasiṁha, and *Bhartṛidāman. There were also some members of this family, who served only as *kshatrapa*, and could never attain the position of a *mahākshatrapa*, like *Jayadāman, *Satyadāman, *Pṛithvīsena, *Damajadaśrī II, *Vīradāman, and *Viśvasena. The last-mentioned ruler seems to have been supplanted by *Rudrasiṁha II, who appears to be closely connected with the family of Chashṭana but whose father, Jīvadāman, is not given any royal title in the ld of the coins of Rudrasiṁha II. Next came *Yaśodāman II. Visvasena, Rudrasiṁha II, and Yaśodāman II ruled as *kshatrapa* only, indicating a temporary eclipse of the power of the Kārddamaka rulers. The end of the reign of Yaśodāman II is followed by an interval of 16 years, when we do not hear of any Kārddamaka *kshatrapa* or *mahākshatrapa*. But when in *Śaka year 270, *Rudrasena III issued coins as a *mahākshatrapa*, he refers to his father, Rudradāman II, also as a *mahākshatrapa*, although the coins of the latter are not known. Rudrasena III was succeeded by his sister's son, *Simhasena, and the latter, by *Rudrasena IV and Satyasiṁha, respectively. The last-known Kārddamaka ruler was *Rudrasiṁha III, who was, perhaps, defeated by *Chandragupta II (Jha and Rajgor 1994; Mirashi 1982; Mitchiner 1976; Rapson 1975; Rajgor 1991; Rajgor 1992; Raychaudhuri 1972; Satya Shrava 1981; Senior 2001; Sircar 1980e).

Kārttikeya. Deity. Also known by the names of Skanda, Kumāra, Viśākha, Mahāsena, Guha, Brahmaṇya, Subrahmaṇya, Murugan, etc (the last two names being more common in southern India), he was the divine *generalissimo*. There are indications to show that these various names of the god were originally the names of so many godheads with similar or allied nature and/or functions; some of them were even folk divinities. These various allied godheads were gradually unified into a deity, Kārttikeya. The accounts of his parentage, available from different sources, are very confused. The Liṅgāyat traditions regard him as a son of *Śiva and Pārvatī, and this has the support of the purāṇas. But the *Rāmāyaṇa* describes him as a son of *Agni from *Gaṅgā. Gaṅgā threw the foetus on the Himavat, where it was nourished by the Kṛittikās; hence the name Kārttikeya, 'the son of Kṛittikā'. The *Mahābhārata*, at one place, describes him as the son of Agni and his consort Svāhā. But at another place in the same epic, it is told that he was the son of Śiva and Pārvatī, who had taken the form of Agni and Svāhā. The confusion seems to have its origin in the epithet Rudra, which was used for both Śiva and Agni. Kālidāsa gives a graphic account of the birth of Kārttikeya in the *Kumārasambhavaṁ*. When identified with Sanatkumāra, Kārttikeya becomes the son of Brahman. The iconographic texts describe him as boyish in appearance, holding a *śakti* in his hand, and with the *peacock as his 'main cognizance'. The *Vishṇudharmottarapurāṇa* refers to his six heads, and also associates the *cock and the *bull with him. The cock as the harbinger of the rising sun seems to hint at the solar connection of Kārttikeya. The āgama texts refer to a number of varieties of the images of this deity as Śaktidhara, Skanda, Senāpati, Subrahmaṇya, Gajavāhana, Śaravaṇabhava, Kārttikeya, Kumāra, Shaṇmukha, Tārakāri, Senānī, Śikhivāhana, etc. Although Kārttikeya is worshipped independently and with great devotion in southern India, his worship in northern India got completely merged in that of Śiva; temples dedicated to Kārttikeya are not commonly to be found, his images mostly appearing among those of the subsidiary deities in Śaiva shrines. *Shashṭhī-Devasenā is sometimes described as the wife of Kārttikeya (Banerjea 2002; R G Bhandarkar 1928; Rao 1985; Prashant Srivastava 1996a; Prashant Srivastava and Deepak Tiwari 1994; Yaduvanshi 1988).

Kidāra Kushāṇa. Tribe. The *Wei-shu* and Ma-twan-lin inform us that Ki-to-lo, a king of the *Kushāṇa stock, finding himself threatened by some rival tribe (Juan-Juan or Hiung-nu), led his people towards the west, crossed the Hindukush, subjugated Gandhāra, and established his capital at Fu-leu-cha (Peshawar). This Ki-to-lo is identified with *Kidāra Kushāṇa Shāh* of coins found in large numbers from northwestern India. Around the middle of the fourth century AD, Kidāra Kushāṇa was forced to acknowledge the supremacy of the Sassanian ruler, Shapur II, but later, he asserted his independence, founded his line of kings known as the Kidāra Kushāṇas or Kidarites after his name, and issued his own coins. From the account of the Armenian historian, Faustos of Byzantium, he even appears to have inflicted at least two defeats on the Sassanians in 367-368 AD. There is a suggestion that, in view of the threats he had to face from the Sassanians and the ruling tribes in Bactria, Kidāra Kushāṇa might have maintained cordial relations with the *Imperial Guptas, and he might be the *Daivaputrashāhi-shāhānushāhi* mentioned in the Allahabad pillar inscription as acknowledging the political supremacy of Samudragupta. Kidāra Kushāṇa was succeeded by his son, Piro, who was forced by Shapur III to acknowledge Sassanian sovereignty. Piro's successor, Varahran, too, served under the Sassanians. There is also a suggestion that the Kidāra Kushāṇas may be identical with the *mlechchhas* defeated by Skandagupta, as per the testimony of the Junagarh rock inscription, although most of the scholars tend to regard these *mlechchhas* as Hūṇas (Altekar 1986a; Craig Alden Burns 1985b; Cunningham 1962; P L Gupta 2004; Gupta and Kulashreshtha 2004; R C Majumdar 1988; Sircar 1980d; Smith 1972).

Kshaharāta. Dynasty. One of the three branches of the Western Kshatrapas, the Kshaharātas seem to have started their career as the provincial governors of the Kushāṇas in the southwestern parts of the empire, as shown by the use of the title of **kshatrapa* by *Ābhīraka and *Bhūmaka on their coins, and the titles of *kshatrapa* and **mahākshatrapa* by *Nahapāna in his inscriptions, although doubts have recently been expressed from certain quarters regarding the subordinate status of the Kshaharāta Kshatrapas. But Nahapāna, on his coins, uses the title of **rājan*, which shows an increase in the power and prestige of the dynasty during his reign. The rule of the dynasty was brought to an end by the Sātavāhana ruler, Gautamīputra Sātakarṇi. Various interpretations of the family name, Kshaharāta, have been suggested. According to H C Raychaudhuri, it may be identical with Karatai, a branch of the Śakas mentioned by Ptolemy. Michael Mitchiner has tried to associate the Kshaharāta Kshatrapas with Ladhanes, a nephew of *Gondopharnes, mainly on the basis of certain coins on which he reads the name *Chaharata*, together with Ladhanaputra. But what he has read as *Chaharata*, is regarded as *Parama* or *Parata* (= Pārada) by other scholars. The Taxila copper-plate inscription of Patika refers to his father, Liäka Kusulaka, as *Kshahara Chukhsasa cha kshatrapa*, *kshatrapa* of Chhahara and Chukhsa (?), Chhahara being a place name in the vicinity of Taxila. There is a suggestion that the Kshaharāta branch might have derived its name from this place, which might have been its original home. If this Chhahara has anything to do with Kshaharāta, this Western Kshatrapa branch might have been related to the family of Liäka Kusulaka and Patika also (Jha and Rajgor 1994; Mirashi 1982; Mitchiner 1976; Rajgor 1991; Rajgor 1992; Rapson 1975; Raychaudhuri 1972; Senior 2001; Sircar 1980e; Sircar 1986).

Kujula Kadphises. *Kushāṇa k. The *Hou Han-shu* informs us that K'ieou-tsieou-k'io, the chief of Kouei-chouang, one of the five Yueh-chih principalities in Bactria, conquered the other four principalities, and adopted the title of *wang* (king). The Kouei-chouang of this account is identified as Kushāṇa, and K'ieou-tsieou-k'io as Kujula Kadphises. The same source also reveals that Kujula Kadphises later led an expedition against the Arsakids of Parthia, conquered the Kabul valley, and overran Po-ta near Kabul, as also Ki-pin (Kafiristan and the adjoining areas), before he died at the age of over 80 years. The date of Kujula Kadphises is not certain, although attempts have been made to place him between *c* 25 BC and 25 AD; Osmund Bopearachchi dates his reign from *c* 30 AD to 80 AD, which would seem difficult if *Kanishka I ascended the throne in 78 AD, and founded the *Śaka era. There are some copper coins, which bear the name and/or bust of *Hermaios on the obv, and the name and titles of Kujula Kadphises on the rev. The suggestions, on the basis of these coins, that Kujula Kadphises was a subordinate ruler or ally of the Indo-Greek king, are hardly tenable, as there is a long gap between the end of the reign of Hermaios and the accession of Kujula Kadphises. These coins might have been issued by Kujula Kadphises, either as propaganda coins, or as imitation coins (Bopearahchci and Pieper 1998; Cunningham 1971a; Gardner 1971; Marshall 1975; von Mitterwallner 1986; Rosenfield 1967; Senior 2001; Sircar 1980c; Whitehead 1914).

Kumāragupta I *Mahendrāditya.* *Imperial Gupta k. He was the son and successor of *Chandragupta II, born of *Mahādevī* Dhruvadevī. His first and last known dates, respectively, are 415 AD and 455 AD. We possess no specific information of the military career of Kumāragupta I, but the facts that he issued the **Aśvamedha* type of gold coins and was able to keep the vast empire he inherited from his ancestors intact, testify to his administrative skill and the brilliance of his personality. The scene of the king hunting a rhinoceros on the obv of the *Rhinoceros-slayer type of Kumāragupta I has been taken by some to indicate his conquest of Kāmarūpa (Assam) known for its rhinoceroses. This region was within the sphere of influence of *Samudragupta, as per the evidence of the Allahabad pillar inscription. Kumāragupta I might have led an expedition against Kāmarūpa to bring it under the direct control of the Imperial Guptas and performed his *aśvamedha* to commemorate this achievement. Towards the end of his reign, the royal fortunes of the Imperial Guptas were threatened by an enemy in the form of a tribe named Pushyamitra (though some believe that the correct reading is *yuddhyamitra*, and the term means enemy (or enemies) in general). In his Bhitari pillar inscription, his son, *Skandagupta, claims to have defeated this enemy and restored the 'fallen fortunes' of his family. The *Hūṇa invasion and its being repulsed by Skandagupta might also have been an event of the last days of Kumāragupta I, though some feel that this event occurred during the reign of Skandagupta himself. The last known date of Kumāragupta I is believed to be *Gupta era 136 read by Smith on a silver coin, or Gupta era 135 read again by Smith on another silver coin, but there are some scholars who doubt these readings (Ashvini Agrawal 1989; Nisar Ahmad 1964; Allan 1914; Altekar 1957; R D Banerji 1933; Fleet 1888; S R Goyal 2005; P L Gupta 1998; B C Jain 1960; K P Jayaswal 1933; Smith 1972; Prashant Srivastava 1996a; Thaplyal, forthcoming; T P Verma 1991).

L

Lakshmī. Deity. Also known by such names as Śrī, Padmā, and Kamalā, Lakshmī is the goddess of good fortune and luck, bringing to her devotees 'peaceful prosperity and abundance'. She is also looked upon as the goddess of feminine beauty. She was revered in all the religious creeds of India. In the *Ṛigveda*, there is no mention of Lakshmī as such. But in the saṁhitās, the attributes of deities like Purandhī as a goddess of plenty, Rākā as a rich and beautiful goddess, and Sinivālī as the wife of *Vishṇu, are reminiscent of Lakshmī of later texts. However, it cannot be asserted that any one of these vedic goddesses 'could have served as the sole prototype' of Lakshmī. All this leaves little doubt as to the abstract origin of this goddess. Lakshmī is credited with multiple origins in literature. According to the *Śatapathabrāhmaṇa*, when Prajāpati became tired of creating beings, Śrī emanated from him. The epic and puranic accounts tell us that Lakshmī came out of the churning of the Ocean of Milk, and she fell to the share of Vishṇu, who took her as his consort. According to a still later tradition, Lakshmī came out of the *lotus that grew out of the forehead of Vishṇu. Sometimes, this goddess is also associated with Āditya, and with Kubera. However, she is most well-known as the consort of Vishṇu, and her worship gained in popularity with the spread of Vaishnavism. In Buddhist literature, Lakshmī in the form of Śrī, is the goddess of beauty, and she is described as a daughter of Śakra (= *Indra). Lakshmī is often equated mythologically with the Greek goddess *Demeter, Roman goddess Fortune, and the Iranian goddess **Ardochsho*. In the form of Rājyalakshmī or the goddess of royal fortune, she might be taken to correspond to the Greek deity *Nike. Lakshmī is also sometimes identified with *Athena-Pallas; the account of the birth of Lakshmī from the tired body of Prajāpati is quite similar to the birth of Athena-Pallas out of the aching head of *Zeus. The iconographic texts lay down that the image of Lakshmī should be like a maiden of very beautiful appearance, and richly adorned with ornaments. When shown by the side of Vishṇu, she should be two-armed, but when alone, she may be four-armed or even sixteen-armed. Her most common attributes are the lotus bloom and the *bilva* fruit. Other attributes include the *amṛitaghaṭa*, and the citron. Some texts, like the *Śilparatna* and the *Vishṇudharmottarapurāṇa*, refer to the *abhisheka* of Lakshmī by two elephants [*Gajalakshmī], which in the latter text are described as the two *nidhis* of *śaṅkha* and *padma*. The favourite seat of Lakshmī is the lotus bloom, although as Rājyalakshmī she may also be shown as enthroned on a lion throne. Sometimes, in literature and art, a *lion may be associated with Lakshmī as her mount (**Siṁhavāhinī Devī*). In the Śrīsūkta of the *Ṛigveda*, Lakshmī is described as 'a golden coloured antelope decorated with garlands of silver and gold'. As such, the antelope may be regarded as the theriomorphic representation of Lakshmī (Banerjea 2002; Sukumari Bhattacharji 1970; S R Goyal 1986; T R R Iyengar 2003; Macdonell 1897; R B Pande 1988; Rao 1985; Prashant Srivastava 1996b; Wilkins 2006).

Liṅgaṁ. Phallism or Phallicism, the worship of the male reproductive power of nature symbolized by the phallus, is of pre-vedic origin in India. An ithyphallic deity, labelled as the prototype of Śiva-Paśupati by Marshall, is known for the Harappan culture, and there is also some evidence to suggest that the Harappans worshipped the phallus. In the *Ṛigveda*, worshippers of the phallus seem to be alluded to as *śiśnadevas*, in a deprecating manner. But gradually, phallic worship was accorded sanction in orthodox Hindu Brahmanical religion, in association with Rudra-Śiva. The phallic cult is especially associated with agriculture, the acts of copulation and ploughing being regarded as somewhat analogous, and agricultural deities all over the world, like the Egyptian Osiris, the Assyrian Vul, the Greek Dionysios, the Phoenician Adonis, and the Phrygian Attis, are mostly phallic deities. In Indian mythology, Śiva, who is looked upon as the father god and is the lord of both the plant and the animal kingdoms as *Pādapeśvara* and *Paśupati*, respectively, is associated with procreation as well as cultivation. The worship of Śiva in his *liṅgaṁ* form gradually became so popular that in Śaiva shrines, it is usually the Śivaliṅgaṁ that is installed in the *sanctum sanctorum*, while anthropomorphic icons of the deity may be seen as accessory figures (Banerjea 2002; Mahadev Chakravarti 1994; Bhaskar Chattopadhyay 1977; Rao 1985).

Lotus. Owing to its miraculous birth beneath the waters, this flower became 'pre-eminently the symbol of birth'. The lotus flower, which rises from the depths of water, 'is the most beautiful evidence offered to the eye of the self-engendering fertility of the bottom', making it 'peculiarly suitable as a symbol of the androgynous creative god'. In the *Śatapathabrāhmaṇa*, it represents the womb. The flower is also associated with deities like Brahmā and Kālī, and with ideas like *nirvāṇa*. As the lotus blooms at sunrise and withers at sunset, it is sometimes linked to the sun. But gradually, the lotus bloom came to be more intimately associated with *Lakshmī (Banerjea 2002; Mahadev Chakravarti 1994; Bhaskar Chattopadhyay 1977; Zimmer 1999).

Lysias. *Indo-Greek k. He is believed to have belonged the family of *Euthydemos I, and to be a grandson of *Demetrios I and a son of *Zoilos I. He seems to have ruled the region to the north of the Hindukush, the Kabul valley, and Ghazni. His coins in the Gandhāra region are relatively few. On the basis of the facts that *Heliokles II restruck the coins of *Philoxenos, and *Antialkidas, those of Lysias, Narain suggests that Philoxenos and Lysias 'were in league against the family of *Eukratides'. On the basis of the occurrence of the name of Lysias on the obv and that of Antialkidas on the rev of one bronze coin, and that Antialkidas on the obv, and that of Lysias on the rev, of another bronze piece in the American Numismatic Society, it was suggested that that the two kings issued joint coins, and Tarn regards it as an evidence of a *rapprochement* between the rival Indo-Greek families of Euthydemos and Eukratides, in view of the *Śaka-Pahlava menace. But Narain regards this piece as a 'mule'. Lysias seems to have ruled from *c* 120 BC to 110 BC, although R C Senior would place his reign from *c* 130 BC to 125 BC (Bopearachchi 1993; Bopearachchi and Pieper 1998; Bopearachchi and Rahman 1995; Cunningham 1970; Gardner 1971; A N Lahiri 1965; Marshall 1975; Narain 1957a; Rapson 1906; Rapson 1987; Senior 2001; Sircar 1980a; Prashant Srivastava 1990c; Prashant Srivastava 1996a; Tarn 1980; Whitehead 1914).

M

Makara. It is a mythical aquatic creature, represented in art as an elephantine crocodile, that is a crocodile with its snout in the shape of an elephant's trunk. It is mentioned in the *Yajurveda* among the sacrificial animals on the occasion of the horse sacrifice. It is conceived as a lusty creature, and adorns the standard of Kāma; hence, this Indian god of love has *Makaradhvaja* as one of his names. It is sometimes represented as the mount of Rati, the consort of Kāma. But the creature is more intimately associated with *Gaṅgā as her mount. The door jambs of the Gupta temples bear figures of Gaṅgā and Yamunā on their respective mounts, the *makara* and the *kūrma* (Banerjea 2002; R B Pande 1988; Rao 1985).

Maues. Śaka-Pahlava k. He is believed to be among the earliest Śaka-Pahlava rulers to issue coins bearing the king's name. He has been associated with that branch of the Śaka-Pahlavas, which crossed the Pamirs from the Ili valley, and settled in the Swat-Hazara-Kashmir (Chinese Ki-pin) region, some time after 160 BC. On some of his coins, Maues bears the subordinate titles of **basileos* and **maharaja*, while on others, he is **basileos basileon megalos* and **rajatiraja mahata*. This has led to the suggestion that Maues, perhaps, started his career as a subordinate ruler of *Vonones, and asserted independence in northwestern India when *Spalirises overthrew Vonones. But on the coin Maues issued in association with his mother, *Machene, he has the titles of *rajatiraja mahata*, showing his sovereign status even during his minority. This indicates that if his family ever served under the family of Vonones, it must have thrown off the yoke of vassalage some time before the accession of Maues. Attempts have been made to associate him with the *Indo-Greek ruler, *Peukolaos, through Machene, although there are certain difficulties in accepting this suggestion. He seems to have ruled in the first century BC; his dates are not certain, although R C Senior is in favour of placing him between *c* 95/85 BC and 60/57 BC. Maues imitated the coin types of the Euthydemid and Eukratid families of *Indo-Greek rulers, like *Demetrios I, *Antimachos, *Menander, *Antialkidas, *Strato I, Peukolaos, *Theophilos, *Heliokles II, and *Polyxenos, showing that he must have ruled over territories wrested from both of the families. He is believed to have advanced west into the Indo-Greek dominions from the

Swat-Hazara-Kashmir region. However, the scarcity of his 'westernmost coinage' has been taken to suggest that this advance was not 'too successful or of long duration'. His rule over Gandhāra is vouched for by the Taxila copperplate inscription of [Vikrama *saṁvat*] 78, and there is a suggestion that the year might belong to some era founded by Maues, *c* 95 BC. He, however, seems to have lost Takshaśilā, perhaps to the Indo-Greeks, towards the end of his reign. His name might be mentioned in the Mathurā lion capital inscription of the time of *Rañjuvula and *Śoḍāsha, as also in some inscriptions from Chilas. Numismatic evidence suggests that Maues was succeeded by *Azes I. Some scholars believe that Maues might have married his daughter to Azes I, and the succession from Maues to Azes I might have been peaceful. But it seems to be more likely that when Spalirises, the father of Azes I, was overthrown in Arachosia, Azes I was forced to come to northwestern India, where he defeated Maues, occupied his throne, and forced him to the rule as a subordinate ruler. It was during this period that Maues issued coins with the subordinate titles (Bopearachchi 2004; Cunningham 1971a; Gardner 1971; Jenkins and Narain 1957; van Lohuizen de Leeuw 1949; Marshall 1975; B N Mukherjee 1969a; Rapson 1987; Senior 2001; Sircar 1980b; Prashant Srivastava 1996a; Prashant Srivastava 2008b; Tarn 1980; Whitehead 1914).

Menander I. *Indo-Greek k. It is generally believed that he is identical with King Milinda of the Buddhist text, *Milindapañho*. Therein, it is related that he was born in a village called Kālasī near Alasanda (Alexandria of the Caucasus), and he belonged to a royal family. He seems to be a scion of the family of *Demetrios II, as *Pallas is the commonest device on the coins of both these rulers. His wife was *Agathokleia, who might have been a daughter of *Demetrios I. Tarn suggested that he was initially a general of Demetrios I, and assumed kingship on the death of his master, the marriage with Agathokleia being the basis of his claim to the royalty. If this be accepted, it stands to the reason that Menander would have been a mature person when he ascended the throne, but it has been pointed out that he appears as a very young man on his earliest coins. Narain suggests that he started his career immediately after the end of the reign of *Eukratides I, *c* 155 BC; R C Senior, however, places the end of the reign of Eukratides I *c* 145 BC, and says that the reign of Menander overlaps that of Eukratides I. Osmund Bopearachchi expresses the possibility that Menander might have started ruling as early as 165 BC, and regards him as a close contemporary of Eukratides I. Although Tarn felt that there is not enough evidence of his rule over the Paropamisadae, the find of his coins from Begram and Kabul, and in the Mir Zakah hoard leaves little doubt that he ruled over the Kabul valley. From there, he may have endeavoured to occupy Gandhāra, Arachosia, and Seistan. The discovery of his coins in the excavations at Taxila, in the Sheikhano Dheri hoard near Charsadda, at Charsadda itself, and at places like Rajjar, Mardan, Peshawar, and Rawalpindi, shows that he ruled over Gandhāra, with its two centres of Takshaśilā and Pushkalāvatī. However, no coin of this ruler is reported from Arachosia and Seistan, and hence, there is no evidence of his hold over these two regions; they seem to have been occupied by the Arsakids after Eukratides I. Narain feels that some parts of northern and eastern Arachosia might have been included in his dominions. Menander also conquered Hazara and the Swat valley, as is evident from the discovery of his coins in the two Bajaur hoards, and also of his mention in the Shinkot-Bajaur relic-casket inscription of the time of Viyakamitra who seems to have served under him as his governor in the Swat valley. Udyāna, the country between the rivers Suvāstu and Gaurī, and the Sind-Sagar *doab*, too, seem to have been under his control. There is nothing definite to testify to his conquest of the Jhelum-Chenab *doab*, or the Kashmir valley. The classical accounts give Menander the credit for conquests in India, and Strabo, quoting Apollodoros, says that he crossed the Beas, and also, perhaps, the Yamuna. Kālidāsa refers to an Indo-Greek invasion of India towards the end of the reign of Pushyamitra Śuṅga. The Yugapurāṇa section of the *Gārgīsaṁhitā* states that the Indo-Greeks, together with the Pāñchālas and the Māthuras, attacked Sāketa and Pāṭaliputra and destroyed the city, but retired due to internal dissensions. Narain believes that the two sources speak of the same Indo-Greek invasion, and as it occurred towards the end of the reign of Pushyamitra Śuṅga around 150 BC, it must have been led by Menander. Menander's coins are generally not found to the east of the river Ravi; such coins as have been reported from places like Saharanpur, Sonipat, Bundelkhand, Kangra, and Hoshiarpur, seem to be the result of the popularity of his coins in those regions, and not of the extension of his rule over those territories. Tarn's view that his kingdom included the territories of the *Audumbaras, *Kuṇindas, *Yaudheyas, and the *Ārjunāyanas, as also the Broach region in Gujarat, does not seem to rest on solid grounds. The suggestion that Menander ruled over Mathurā, also seems to be unwarranted; had Indo-Greek rule intervened between the rule of the local kings of Mathurā and that of the Śaka Kshatrapas, the latter would have copied Indo-Greek coin types, and not the local types of Mathurā as done by *Rañjuvula and *Śoḍāsha. Scholars generally believe that beyond the Ravi and the Beas, the incursions of Menander in the Yamuna valley were more in the nature of raids, rather than regular conquests. Plutarch and Strabo refer to Menander as a Bactrian king, on which basis scholars like Cunningham and Narain suggest that encouraged by his military successes in India and regions to the south of the Hindukush, Menander might have made a bid for Bactria, but died in the course of this expedition; Plutarch refers to his death in camp, although the Buddhist tradition says that he retired from the world after handing over his realm to his son. His reign seems to have ended around 130 BC. Numismatic evidence suggests that he left behind a minor son, *Strato I, and his widow looked after the kingdom during the minority of her son. Another son was *Apollodotos, who was younger than Strato I, and began his career as a subking or joint king of the latter. Recently, the possibility of the existence of yet another son, *Thrason, has been expressed, on numismatic grounds. The coins bearing the name of Menander use the titles of **soteros* and **dikaios* for him. Narain ascribes the coins with both these titles to one king only, and feels that as the coins with the title of *dikaios* are rarer than those with the title of *soter*, and as the king on the former coins is depicted as older than that on the latter coins, Menander would have issued the coins with the title of *dikaios* towards the end of his reign. But a number of scholars, on the basis of the use of two different epithets, as also on some other grounds, postulate the existence of two Indo-Greek kings named Menander [*Menander II]. Menander seems to have appointed several subkings, like *Antimachos II, *Polyxenos, and *Epander, to help him in the administration of his vast kingdom (Bopearachchi 1993; Bopearachchi and Pieper 1998; Bopearachchi and Rahman 1995; Cunningham 1970; Gardner 1971; A N Lahiri 1965; Marshall 1975; Narain 1957a; Senior 2001; Sircar 1980a; Prashant Srivastava 1996a; Tarn 1980; Whitehead 1914).

Menander II. *Indo-Greek k. There are some silver and copper coins, all struck on the Indian standard, which bear the name of Menander **Dikaios*. These coins have 'nothing in common' with the coins bearing the name of Menander **Soteros* [*Menander I], and even the canting type (thundering *Athena) of Menander *Soteros* is not known for Menander *Dikaios*. The monograms on the two series are also not common. The *omicron* on the coins of the Menander *Soteros* series is normal, while that on the coins of the Menander *Dikaios* series takes the form of a dot, suggesting a late date for the latter series. In view of the use of the rev device of king on prancing horse by both Menander II and *Artemidoros, the two might be regarded as near contemporaries ruling over Taxila, and Menander II might be assigned to the first-second decades of the first century BC, although R C Senior would place him *c* 65 BC. On these grounds, some scholars regard Menander *Soteros* as Menander I, and Menander *Dikaios* as Menander II, who is believed to have had a 'short and comparatively insignificant reign' (Bopearachchi 1993; Bopearachchi 1994; Bopearachchi and Pieper 1998; Bopearachchi and Rahman 1995; Cunningham 1970; Gardner 1971; A N Lahiri 1965; Marshall 1975; Narain 1957a; Rapson 1987; Senior 2001; Sircar 1980a; Tarn 1980; Whitehead 1914).

Mihirakula. *Hūṇa chief. He seems to have succeeded his father, *Toramāṇa, *c* 515 AD. All the sources at our disposal unanimously describe him as a cruel and violent king. From the *Christian Topography* of Kosmas, it appears that the kingdom he inherited from his father was confined to the west of the river Indus. Sung-yün, the Chinese ambassador to the Hūṇa court in 520 AD, describes him as the king of Gandhāra; according to Hiuen-tsang, his capital was Sākala (modern Sialkot). Sung-yün refers to his 700 war elephants, while according to Kosmas, he possessed no less than 2,000 elephants and a large cavalry. This Greek navigator refers to him as the lord of India; Hiuen-tsang also refers to his subduing the whole of India; Kalhaṇa mentions his conquest of southern India and Srilanka. All these statements seem to be exaggerated. But there is no doubt that he revived the aggressive policy of his father, and occupied a large part of northern India, at least up to Gwalior. But he had to suffer reverses at the hands of Yaśodharman, the Aulikara king of Mandasor, and of the *Imperial Gupta ruler, *Narasiṁhagupta Bālāditya. The former, in his inscription, claims that respect was paid to his feet by Mihirakula. But this defeat does not seem to have destroyed the power of the Hūṇa chief, and he became active again after some time. According to Hiuen-tsang, Mihirakula forced [Narasiṁhagupta] Bālāditya to pay tribute to him, but Bālāditya ambushed him on an island, took him prisoner, but set him free on the insistence of his (Bālāditya's) mother. Mihirakula died some time later (Altekar 1986b; Biswas 1973; Cunningham 1962; Cunningham 1967; R C Majumdar 1988; Sircar 1986; Upendra Thakur 1967a; Upendra Thakur 1967b).

N

Nahapāna. *Kshaharāta k. He seems to have succeeded *Bhūmaka as the **kshatrapa* of the *Kushāṇas, but the relation between these two Kshaharāta rulers is not known for certain. He has been identified with Nambanus of the *Periplus*, and with Naravāhana or Navavāhana of certain Jaina texts, like the *Harivaṁśa*. No inscription issued by Nahapāna himself is known so far, but several inscriptions issued in his time by his son-in-law, Ushavadāta (a great donor and the governor of the southern province of the Kshaharāta kingdom), daughter Dakshamitrā, and *Amātya* Aryaman, are known from the Nasik, Karle, and Junnar regions of Maharashtra. These inscriptions bear dates ranging from year 41 to 46. If they are indeed dated in the *Śaka era as has been suggested by a number of scholars, he ruled in the first half of the second century AD. However, scholars like A S Altekar, Karl Khandalavala, Amiteshwar Jha and Dilip Rajgor, A M Shastri, and R C Senior, have pointed out certain difficulties, mainly chronological, in referring the dates mentioned in these inscriptions to the Śaka era. They regard these dates to refer to the regnal years of Nahapāna, but have proposed different dates for this ruler—Altekar places him between 55 and 105 AD; Khandalavala opines that he began his rule some time between 55 and 64 AD, and it came to an end between 101 and 111 AD; Jha and Rajgor feel that his reign may be placed between 48 and 94 AD or 52 and 98 AD; Senior regards the second last decade of the first century BC as representing the middle of Nahapāna's reign. The external and internal evidence of these inscriptions, as also the findspot of his coins, shows that his rule extended from Ajmer in the north to Nasik-Pune in the south, and from Gujarat and northern Konkan in the west to Malwa in the east. The use of the title **rājan* on his coins, instead of the mere **kshatrapa* met with on the coins of Bhūmaka, shows that he enjoyed a position superior to that of his predecessor. His overlord is not mentioned in any source. One of the Nasik inscriptions of his son-in-law informs us that Ushavadāta defeated the Mālayas (Mālavas settled in Rajasthan) at the command of the *Bhaṭṭāraka*. But Nahapāna ultimately had to suffer defeat at the hands of the Sātavāhana ruler, Gautamīputra Sātakarṇi, as attested by epigraphic, numismatic, and perhaps also literary, sources. A Sātavāhana epigraph claims that Gautamīputra Sātakarṇi totally uprooted the Kshaharāta dynasty (Jha and Rajgor 1994;

Mirashi 1982; Mitchiner 1976; Rapson 1975; Raychaudhuri 1972; Senior 2001; A M Shastri 1995; Sircar 1980e).

Narasiṁhagupta *Bālāditya*. *Imperial Gupta k. Narasiṁhagupta is known from his own Nalanda seals, the Bhitari and Nalanda seals of *Kumāragupta III, and the Nalanda seal of *Vishṇugupta. Hiuen-tsang refers to him as Bālāditya. Gold coins of this ruler are also known. The percentage of pure gold in the better executed of these coins is around 70, while some crudely executed coins of the same type have about 54 % of pure gold. On this basis, some scholars express the possibility of the existence of two Imperial Gupta rulers named Narasiṁhagupta. But others have rejected this possibility, mainly on the basis of the weight of these coins. It appears from the Nalanda seal of Vishṇugupta that Narasiṁhagupta was a son of *Pūrugupta. According to Hiuen-tsang, *Mihirakula forced [Narasiṁhagupta] Bālāditya to pay tribute to him. But Bālāditya, while on the run, ambushed him on an island, took him prisoner, and set him free only on the insistence of his (Bālāditya's) mother. Mihirakula died some time later. Thus, Narasiṁhagupta gets the credit for shattering Hūṇa power in India. If Narasiṁhagupta reigned after Bhānugupta, he would have ascended the throne some time after 510 AD, the only known date of Bhānugupta. The seals of Narasiṁhagupta describe him as a **paramabhāgavata*, but there is overwhelming epigraphic evidence to show that he was inclined towards Buddhism. According to Hiuen-tsang, Bālāditya renounced the world, and took the Buddhist order. The *Āryamañjuśrīmūlakalpa* also seems to hint at this. The reign of Narasiṁhagupta would have ended some time around 530 AD (Ashvini Agrawal 1989; Allan 1914; Altekar 1957; R D Banerji 1933; Fleet 1888; S R Goyal 2005; P L Gupta 1998; K P Jayaswal 1933; Smith 1972; Thaplyal, forthcoming).

Nike. Deity. This Greek goddess of victory was a daughter of the Titan Pallas and the goddess Styx, and a sister of Zelos, 'zeal', Kratos, 'strength', and Bia, 'force'. In Greek mythology, Nike is closely associated with *Athena as her companion, and, interestingly, *Nike* is one of the surnames of Athena. That she held a position subordinate to those of *Zeus, Athena, and *Herakles, is shown by the fact that she is often depicted on coins as standing on the outstretched hand of either of the first two deities, or on the shoulder of the third. Nike appears to correspond to the Roman Victoria, and also to the Indian *Lakshmī, who is believed to have bestowed not only prosperity and royalty upon her worshippers, but also victory. The representations of Nike in art are mostly winged. The most famous sculpture of this goddess is the Nike of Samothrace, sculpted sometime between 250 BC and 180 BC, presently housed in the Louvre, Paris (Bhaskar Chattopadhyay 1977; Graves 1955; Kerenyi 1951; Rose 1958; Schoder nd; Prashant Srivastava 2007c).

Nikias. *Indo-Greek k. He is believed to be a son of *Philoxenos, and was appointed as a subking by *Apollodotos, perhaps in some parts of western Gandhāra, from where most of his silver coins are reported; his copper ones come from the Jhelum area. It is possible that he might have ruled over the Takshaśilā region for some time before being overthrown by *Telephos; no coin of Nikias was, however, found during the excavations at Taxila. On the basis of the depiction of the figure of *Poseidon on some of his coins, Tarn suggested that he might have achieved some naval victory on the river Jhelum, perhaps against the *Śaka-Pahlavas, but Narain feels that the speed of the currents in this river preclude such a possibility, and agrees with Tarn's alternative suggestion that Nikias might only be imitating the Poseidon type of one of his ancestors, *Antimachos I. The small number of his coins shows that he had a short reign, from *c* 95 BC to 85 BC, although R C Senior has placed him between *c* 120 BC and 115 BC (Bopearachchi 1993; Bopearachchi and Pieper 1998; Bopearachchi and Rahman 1995; Cunningham 1970; Gardner 1971; A N Lahiri 1965; Marshall 1975; Narain 1957a; Rapson 1906; Rapson 1987; Senior 2001; Sircar 1980a; Prashant Srivastava and Prachi Srivastava 1993; Tarn 1980; Whitehead 1914).

O

Ouranos. Deity. According to Hesiod, Gaia was born apparently from Chaos, and the earth bore, unaided and as her equal, Ouranos, the sky. Ouranos covered Gaia, and the couple had a number of off-springs. These include the Titans—Okeanos, Koios, Krios, Hyperion, Iapetos, and Kronos, and the Titanesses—Theia, Rhea, Themis, Mnemosyne, Phoibe, and Tethys. Gaia also bore to Ouranos, the three Kyklopes, namely Steropes, Brontes, and Arges; also the Hekatoncheires, namely Kottos, Briareos, and Gyes. Ouranos hated his children, and hid them in the body of their mother. Gaia appealed for help to her children, and Kronos castrated his father with a sickle provided by Gaia, and threw the male member away into the sea. Gaia received some drops of blood from it, and produced the Erinyes, the Giants, and the Meliai, who were the nymphs of the ash trees. From the foam that gathered around the severed member, while it floated in the sea, arose the goddess Aphrodite. Several peoples conceived of the sky and the earth as the original begettors, the former as the father, and the latter as the mother. Ouranos, the Greek sky god, may be compared with the vedic *Varuṇa. He was later superseded by *Zeus, just as the vedic Varuṇa was superseded by *Indra (Bhaskar Chattopadhyay 1977; Graves 1955; Kerenyi 1951; Rose 1958; Prashant Srivastava 2007b; Prashant Srivastava 2007c).

P

Pantaleon. *Indo-Greek k. He is believed to be a son of *Demetrios I, and the elder brother of *Agathokles. It is suggested that after his conquest of Arachosia and Drangiana, Demetrios I left behind his two sons, Pantaleon and Agathokles, as joint subkings of those provinces, and the two ruled jointly after the death of Demetrios I in Bactria. Tarn proposed that after some time, *Antimachos I occupied these regions. But Narain regards the find of only a few coins of Antimachos I in Arachosia and Seistan as not sufficient grounds to prove the hold of that king over those regions. Narain is of the view that, taking advantage of the conflict between *Eukratides and *Demetrios II, the two brothers occupied the Kabul valley and struck the coins bearing the figure of Dionysos, the mythical conqueror of the Kabul valley before Alexander. They then proceeded to conquer western Gandhāra in the east, but Pantaloen died before Takshaśilā could be occupied. Pantaloen would have ruled roughly from 185 BC to 175 BC (Bopearachchi 1993; Bopearachchi and Pieper 1998; Bopearachchi and Rahman 1995; Cunningham 1970; Gardner 1971; A N Lahiri 1965; Marshall 1975; Narain 1957a; Rapson 1987; Sircar 1980a; Prashant Srivastava 1996a; Tarn 1980; Whitehead 1914).

Pārvatī. Deity. According to the *Brahmavaivartapurāṇa*, *Umā immolated herself in the sacrificial fire of Daksha, and when *Śiva was mad with grief, she appeared before him and promised to be reborn as Pārvatī, a daughter of Himavat. According to the *Varāhapurāṇa*, she was born along with *Sarasvatī and *Lakshmī from the refulgence of Brahmā, *Vishṇu and Śiva, to slay the demon, Andhaka. In this later birth, she obtained Śiva as her husband by severe austerities. She is the mother of *Kārttikeya and *Gaṇeśa. She is usually described as engaged in love, or, occasionally, in philosophical discussions, with Śiva on Kailāsa, independent achievements ascribed to her being very rare. She had a dark complexion, for which she was once teased by Śiva. Annoyed at this, she pleased Brahmā through austerities, and received from him golden complexion as a boon, thereby becoming Gaurī. In art, she is represented as a fair damsel, usually with two arms. In one of her hands, she holds a *lotus, or this hand is in the *kaṭaka* pose; the other hand hangs down by her side. Rarely, she may be four-armed, holding a *pāśa* and *aṅkuśa* in her two upper hands, while the two lower ones are in the *abhaya* and *varada* poses. In the *Ardhanārīśvara form, she form the left half of the body, while the right half represents Śiva (Banerjea 2002; Sukumari Bhattacharji 1970; S R Goyal 1986; T R R Iyengar 2003; Prashant Srivastava 2004a; Wilkins 2006).

Peacock. The Dravidians and the Kolerians worship the peacock as the earth goddess, and this is taken to indicate the association of this bird with the female principle since primitive times. This association was continued in historical times, and in the purāṇas, Kumārī is described as riding a peacock. But the bird came to be more closely associated with *Kārttikeya as his mount. In the epics, this bird is described as a devourer of snakes (Banerjea 2002; Bhaskar Chattopadhyay 1977; Hopkins 1902; Hopkins 1915; Rao 1985).

Peukolaos. *Indo-Greek k. He is believed to be a subking of *Apollodotos, who later asserted independence for a short while. Tarn associates him with the Pushakalāvatī region, but according to Narain, he seems to be ruled over the Kabul region also. His coins are, however, not reported from Takshaśilā and Ghazni. His reign may be placed some time during the period *c* 95-85 BC. Recently, attempts have been made to associate him with *Maues, through *Machene (Bopearachchi 1993; Bopearachchi and Pieper 1998; Bopearachchi and Rahman 1995; Cunningham 1970; Gardner 1971; A N Lahiri 1965; Marshall 1975; Narain 1957a; Rapson 1987; Senior 2001; Sircar 1980a; Tarn 1980; Whitehead 1914).

Philoxenos. *Indo-Greek k. He is believed to be a son of *Antimachos II, with whom he shares the type of 'equestrian king', and also the use of some common monograms. From the evidence of the Mir Zakah hoard, he seems to have succeeded *Archebios in northern Arachosia. The *provenance* of his coins shows that he, at times, ruled over parts of the Kabul valley, western Gandhāra, and Takshaśilā. He started his career *c* 125 BC, and seems to have been replaced by *Heliokles II around 115 BC. R C Senior, however, dates Philoxenos between *c* 110 BC and 95 BC, and regards him as, perhaps, the last Indo-Greek ruler 'to control a unified kingdom south of the Hindu Kush' (Bopearachchi 1993; Bopearachchi and Pieper 1998; Bopearachchi and Rahman 1995; Cunningham 1970; Gardner 1971; A N Lahiri 1965; Marshall 1975; Narain 1957a; Rapson 1987; Senior 2001; Sircar 1980a; Tarn 1980; Whitehead 1914).

Plato. *Indo-Greek k. He is believed to be the eldest son of *Eukratides I, who was appointed as joint king and left behind in Bactria when his father embarked upon his ambitious campaign to conquer the Kabul valley, Arachosia and Drangiana. Justin informs us that when Eukratides was returning in triumph to Bactria, his son got him killed, 'drove his chariot through his blood', and had the corpse cast away without a funeral. The name of this parricide is not mentioned by Justin, but scholars hesitate to identify him with *Heliokles I because he assumed the title of **dikaios*. Narain proposes that this parricide son of Eukratides I be identified with Plato, on the grounds that the head of Plato on his coins closely resembles that of Eukratides I, and that Plato is the only Indo-Greek king to issue coins with the device of *Helios on quadriga, which device, according to Narain, might have something to do with the parricide son of Eukratides I driving his chariot through the blood of his father. He feels that no other Indo-Greek king used this device because it had come to be associated with the parricidal act of Plato. Justin says that the Arsakids were interested in Tapuria and Traxiana, the two satrapies of the kingdom of Eukrarides, and Mithridates I seems to have occupied them soon after. On this basis, Narain suggests that Plato might have been instigated to kill his father by the Arsakids. But he himself was done away by Heliokles I, who perhaps called himself 'just' after punishing the killer of his father. He seems to have ruled for a short time from *c* 155 BC, his brief reign being suggested by the rarity of his coins (Bopearachchi 1993; Bopearachchi and Pieper 1998; Bopearachchi and Rahman 1995; Cunningham 1970; Gardner 1971; A N Lahiri 1965; Marshall 1975; Narain 1957a; Rapson 1987; Sircar 1980a; Prashant Srivastava 1996a; Tarn 1980; Whitehead 1914).

Polyxenos. *Indo-Greek k. He is believed to be a subking of *Menander I, and to have governed some territory to the west of the river Indus. His coins, which are very rare, are reported from the Mir Zakah hoard, and from Peshawar and Utmanzai, but none from Taxila. Although he assumed the high-sounding titles of **epiphanes* and **soter*, he seems to have had a very short reign, sometime around 130 BC, although R C Senior places his reign between *c* 110 BC and 105 BC. His relationship with other Indo-Greek kings is not known (Bopearachchi 1993; Bopearachchi and Pieper 1998; Bopearachchi and Rahman 1995; Cunningham 1970; Gardner 1971; A N Lahiri 1965; Marshall 1975; Narain 1957a; Rapson 1987; Senior 2001; Sircar 1980a; Tarn 1980; Whitehead 1914).

Poseidon. Deity. Originally the master of the entire earth, by the time of Homer, Poseidon had become pre-eminently a sea god. He was the son of Kronos and Rhea, and a brother of Hade, *Zeus, Hestia, *Demeter, and Hera. He was brought up by the Telchines, the skilled craftsmen of the island of Rhodos. It is these people, who are said to have fashioned the *trident of Poseidon, which was to be the emblem of his power. Among his several divine and human consorts, mention may be made of Gaia, who begat Charybdis; Aithra, the priestess of *Athena; Medousa, the Gorgon; Theophane, the daughter of King Bisaltes of Makedonia. He coupled with Demeter in the form of a stallion, and sired an unnamable daughter, and a son, Arion. His most famous marriage was with *Amphitrite, who bore him a son, *Triton, and a daughter, Rhodos. Poseidon is said to have played a role in the birth of Orion. He caused the first horse to spring from the earth, when he was competing with Athena for the mastery of Attika. From this time, horse became an animal sacred to Poseidon, and *Hippios*, 'the lord of the horses', is one of his surnames. Onchestos was his sacred grove (Bhaskar Chattopadhyay 1977; Graves 1955; Kerenyi 1951; Rose 1958; Prashant Srivastava 2007c).

Prabhākaravardhana. *Pushpabhūti k. He was the first ruler of his dynasty to be designated **mahārājādhirāja*, thereby showing his sovereign status. His name occurs not only in the Pushpabhūti epigraphs detailing genealogy, but also in the *Harshacharita* of Bāṇa. The latter source speaks of his [successful] conflicts with, or his posing a threat to, the *Hūṇas, Gurjaras, Lāṭas, Mālavas, and the rulers of Sindhu and Gandhāra. He had three issues from his wife, Yaśomatīdevī, namely Rājyavardhana II, *Harsha, and Rājyaśrī; the daughter was married to the *Maukhari, Grahavarman. Towards the end of his reign (*c* 580-606 AD), the Pushpabhūti kingdom was troubled by the Hūṇas, while *Śaśāṅka and the Mālava ruler, Devagupta, attacked the Maukhari kingdom, killed Grahavarman, and imprisoned Rājyaśrī. Prabhākaravardhana was succeeded by his elder son, Rājyavardhana, who had a very short reign (Richard Burn 1906; D Devahuti 1964; D Devahuti 2001; Pires 1934; Thaplyal 1985).

Pūrugupta. *Imperial Gupta k. Some Imperial Gupta seals, detailing their genealogy, mention Pūrugupta as the son and successor of *Kumāragupta I, born of *Mahādevī* Anantadevī. It is not certain whether he ruled before his brother, *Skandagupta, or some time after him. But the date of *Gupta era 136 is read on a silver coin of Kumāragupta I, and the same year is mentioned in the Junagarh rock inscription of Skandagupta. Hence, if Pūrugupta succeeded to the throne immediately after his father, he could have ruled for only a few months in Gupta era 136 (= 455 AD) itself. As such, most of the scholars are inclined to place him after Skandagupta. There is also the suggestion that Pūrugupta contested the succession of Skandagupta, and in this context, he was helped by his maternal uncles, the *Nāgas, but Skandagupta worsted him and Pūrugupta could ascend the Imperial Gupta throne only after the death of his brother. Some scholars read the name of Pūrugupta in the Bihar pillar inscription, although others read Skandagupta in its place. Pūrugupta is sometimes identified with Vikramāditya, mentioned as the king of Ayodhyā in the *Life of Vasubandhu* by Paramārtha. Attempts have also been made to identify Pūrugupta with Prakāśāditya of coins, but this is not acceptable (Ashvini Agrawal 1989; Allan 1914; Altekar 1957; R D Banerji 1933; Fleet 1888; S R Goyal 2005; P L Gupta 1998; K P Jayaswal 1933; Smith 1972; Thaplyal, forthcoming).

R

Rāmagupta. *Imperial Gupta k. This son of *Samudragupta is known from the *Devīchandraguptam* of Viśākhadatta. According to this drama, now lost, but passages from which are quoted in other works, and other sources, Samudragupta was succeeded by his son, Rāmagupta. He was besieged by a Śaka king, and agreed to surrender his queen, Dhruvadevī, to the invader in order to save his people. His younger brother, *Chandragupta [II], protested against this, went to the enemy camp in the guise of Dhruvadevī, and killed the Śaka king. Then, he somehow killed Rāmagupta, seized his kingdom, and married his widow. This story is corroborated by literary and epigraphic evidence, directly or indirectly. Among the literary works, mention may be made of the *Harshacharita* of Bāṇabhaṭṭa, the *Kāvyamīmāṁsā* of Rājaśekhara, and the *Mujmal-ut-Tawarikh* of 'Abu Hasan Ali. Epigraphic evidence is provided by the Sanjan copperplate inscription of the Rāshṭrakūṭa, Amoghavarsha I (ninth century AD), and the Cambey (930 AD) and Sanjan (933 AD) copperplate inscriptions of the Rāshṭrakūṭa, Govinda IV. Three Jaina image inscriptions from Durjanpur, datable to the last quarter of the fourth century AD on palaeographical grounds, refer to a **Mahārājādhirāja* Rāmagupta. Copper coins bearing the name of Rāmagupta are known from the Mālwa region. These resemble *Nāga coins from this region in fabric and shape, as also in the occurrence of the figure of a *lion on some coins and the use of the honorific prefix *śrī* for Rāmagupta. Earlier, it was suggested that the Rāmagupta of these coins was some local ruler of Malwa. But no local ruler of this name is known to have ruled over Malwa about this period (last quarter of the fourth century AD). The Jaina image inscriptions from Durjanpur refer to the Rāmagupta as *mahārājādhirāja*, showing that he was no local ruler. Besides, the occurrence of the **garuḍa* and the **garuḍadhvaja* on some of these copper coins bearing the name of Rāmagupta provide irrefutable evidence to associate Rāmagupta with the Imperial Guptas. It appears that Samudragupta selected his abler son, Chandragupta II, as his heir, and appointed Rāmagupta, his eldest son, as the governor of Malwa. When, perhaps on the death of Samudragupta, the Imperial Gupta throne at Pāṭaliputra was usurped by *Kācha, Rāmagupta declared himself an independent ruler in Malwa. He tried to enter into a disgraceful treaty with the Śaka invader, and was killed by his younger brother, who seized his kingdom and wife. As the Imperial Gupta genealogies mention only father-to-son succession (and no son of Rāmagupta succeeded to the throne), his name is not mentioned in the genealogical portions. Besides, he had also brought infamy to the family by agreeing to surrender his wife to the Śaka ruler. He could not issue gold coins because, as suggested by K D Bajpai, during the early period of Imperial Gupta rule, the only gold mint of the dynasty was located at Pāṭaliputra, which was under the control of Kācha. Later, Chandragupta II seems to have dethroned Kācha, and occupied the capital (Ashvini Agrawal 1989; Altekar 1957; K D Bajpai 1972; S R Goyal 2005; P L Gupta 1998; Prashant Srivastava 1996a; Thaplyal, forthcoming).

Rañjuvula. Śaka satrap. He was the first known Śaka **kshatrapa* of *Mathurā. As his son and successor, *Śoḍāsha, was ruling in 15 AD, he may be placed in the beginning of the first century AD. R C Senior, however, places him between *c* 25 BC and 5 AD. His coins show that he first ruled as a *kshatrapa*, the coins referring to him as such being rather rare, and later attained the position of a **mahākshatrapa*. His coins testify to his hold over Takshaśilā, or territories to its northeast, Hazara to Akhnoor-Jammu, the Punjab and western Uttar Pradesh, particularly Mathurā. It has been pointed out that his earlier coins bear legends in both Br and Kh, while the later ones have legends in Br only. Also, his commonest type is copied from *Indo-Greek coins (particularly those of *Strato I), while his rarest coins are modelled after the local issues of Mathurā. These facts seem to suggest that he occupied Mathurā 'late in life', but made it the centre of power of his family towards the end of his rule. The Mathurā lion capital inscription of the time of Rañjuvula and *Śoḍāsha refers to the consecration of Buddhist relics by Nada Diäka, the chief queen of Rañjuvula, who, according to different interpretations, was either the daughter or the mother of *Kharaoasta. Rañjuvula, in his records, does not refer to his overlord. The Gr ld of his coins refers to him as **basileos basileon* **soteros*, probably meaning 'king of kings, the saviour', while the Kh ld gives him the title of *kshatrapa* or *mahākshatrapa*, often with the additional title, **apratihatachakra*. All this seems to suggest that, for all practical purposes, he was ruling as an independent king (Allan 1936; Cunningham 1971a; Gardner 1971; Jenkins and Narain 1957; Konow 1929; Marshall 1975; B N Mukherjee 1969a; Rapson 1987; Senior 2001; Sircar 1980b; Sircar 1986; Tarn 1980; Whitehead 1914).

Rudradāman I. *Kārddamaka k. He succeeded his father, *Jayadāman, as heir-apparent of his grandfather, **Mahākshatrapa* *Chashṭana, when Jayadāman appears to have died during the reign of Chashṭana. The Andhau inscription of Śaka year 52 (130 AD) refers to both Chashṭana and Rudradāman [I] as **rājan*. Some time after the date of this inscription, Rudradāman I succeeded his grandfather as *mahākshatrapa*. The Khavada inscription, which refers to him independently for the first time, is believed to be dated in the year 5[3]. If this reading of the date be correct, he would have succeeded Chashṭana before a year had elapsed since the issue of the Andhau inscription of year 52. But according to the Junagarh rock inscription of Śaka year 72 (150 AD), a very important source of information about the reign of this ruler, Rudradāman I himself attained the designation of *mahākshatrapa*. The absence of any reference to the Kushāṇas in his records seems to indicate that he ruled as a sovereign king for all practical purposes. The Junagarh inscription informs us that Rudradāman I twice defeated the Sātavāhana ruler, and recovered most of the territories the *Kshaharāta Kshatrapas had lost to the Sātavāhanas. The defeated Sātavāhana ruler is identified variously as Gautamīputra Sātakarṇi, Vāsishṭhīputra Puãumāvi, Yajña Sātakarṇi, etc. He also claims to have defeated the *Yaudheyas, who inhabited southern Punjab and its adjoining areas. The Junagarh inscription gives a list of the provinces under his rule, which shows that his authority extended from Multan in the north to Nasik and Sopara in the south. The Suivihar inscription of *Kanishka I shows his hold over the lower Indus region. In his Junagarh inscription, Rudradāman I mentions the Sindhu-Sauvīra region as a forming part of his dominions, and he would have wrested these territories from some successor of Kanishka I. Rudradāman I was a great conqueror, an able administrator, a person well-versed in grammar, polity, music, and logic, and an accomplished composer of Skt verse and prose. He won the hands of a number of princesses in several *svayaṁvaras* (Jha and Rajgor 1994; Mirashi 1982; Mitchiner 1976; Rapson 1975; Raychaudhuri 1972; Senior 2001; Sircar 1980e).

S

Samudragupta *Parākramāditya.* *Imperial Gupta k. This son and successor of *Chandragupta I was born of the Lichchhavi princess, *Kumāradevī. His career and personality are detailed in the Allahabad pillar inscription. His selection as heir apparent by his father seems to have caused discontent among the other aspirants to the throne, and he might have had to face their rebellion; *Kācha seems to be one such brother of Samudragupta. Samudragupta had an eventful career, in the course of which he brought several lands under various degrees of subjection. In the Āryāvartta, he defeated at least nine rulers, namely Nāgasena, Gaṇapatināga, Achyuta, Chandravarman, Rudradeva, Matila, Nāgadatta, Nandin, and Balavarman, and annexed their kingdoms to the Imperial Gupta dominions. Frontier kingdoms, like Samataṭa, Ḍavāka, Kāmarūpa, Nepāla, and Kartṛipura, and tribal states, like *Mālava, *Ārjunāyana, *Yaudheya, Mādraka, Sanakānīka, Ābhīra, Prārjuna, Kāka, and Kharaparika, are said to have 'paid taxes, obeyed orders and rendered obeisance in person' to Samudragupta. He also brought all the forest kingdoms (*āṭavika rājyas*) under his influence. The Śaka-Kushāṇa rulers of western Punjab and Afghanistan, and even Siṁhala and other islands of south-east Asia, 'sought to win the favour of the great emperor by personal attendance in his court, offering daughters in marriage, and asking permission for the use of imperial coins or soliciting imperial charters confirming them in the enjoyment of their territories'. In southern India, he defeated kings Mahendra of Kosala, Vyāghrarāja of Mahākāntāra, Mahendragiri of Pishṭapura, Hastivarman of Veṅgi, Ugrasena of Pālakka, Vishṇugopa of Kañchī, Damana of Eraṇḍapalla, Kuvera of Devarāshṭra, Maṇṭarāja of Kaurāla, Svāmidatta of Koṭṭūra, Nīlarāja of Avamukta, and Dhanañjaya of Kusthalapura. Fleet identified Eraṇḍapalla with Erandol in Khandesh, and Devarāshṭra with Maharashtra, and came forth with the suggestion that, after his successful campaign on the eastern coast, Samudragupta passed through western Deccan. But other scholars have located Eraṇḍapalla in the Ganjam, and Devarāshṭra in the Vishakhapatnam districts, both on the eastern coast itself. Besides, there is no evidence of Samudragupta ever coming into conflict with the Vākāṭakas, who were ruling over the western Deccan at the time. These defeated kings of southern India were captured, but later set free, and, perhaps, allowed to the rule over their kingdoms as vassals of the Gupta emperor. As a fitting *finale* to his victorious career,

Samudragupta performed the *aśvamedha*, perhaps towards the end of his rule (Ashvini Agrawal 1989; Allan 1914; Altekar 1957; R D Banerji 1933; Fleet 1888; S R Goyal 2005; P L Gupta 1998; K P Jayaswal 1933; Smith 1972; Prashant Srivastava 1996a; Thaplyal, forthcoming).

Sarapis. Deity. Sarapis, alternatively known as Serapis, is actually the compound name given by the Greeks to Osiris-Apis, the dual god resulting from the death of the sacred bull, Apis (an incarnation of Osiris), and his soul consequently becoming joined with that of Osiris; the Egyptians actually pronounced the compound name as Asar-Hapi. Since Osiris was 'the great god of the underworld', the Greeks identified Sarapis with Hades, the Greek god of the underworld. According to tradition, this identification took place during the reign of Ptolemy Soter, who is said to have had a statue of Sarapis brought from Sinope to Alexandria, in response to a dream he had. Thus, the worship of Sarapis seems to have been introduced among the Greeks at a time when the Ptolemies were ruling over Egypt, penetrated into Italy by way of Sicily and the southern part of the peninsula, and reached as far north as Britain. He was the supreme deity of the Alexandrian pantheon, and as he was identified with *Zeus, Hades, Ammon, *Helios, and *Poseidon, he was regarded as the lord of the sky, sea, land, and the underworld. Both the Egyptians and the Greeks regarded Sarapis as 'the male counterpart' of Isis. As Sarapis is believed to preside over the 'invisible world', he reminds one of the Indian Yama. Interestingly, on the Kushāṇa coins, Sarapis carries the noose, which is also the characteristic attribute of Yama (Bhaskar Chattopadhyay 1977; Lewis Spence 1949).

Sarasvatī. Deity. Like *Lakshmī, Sarasvatī, too, has come to be revered in all the religious creeds of India. The vedic river Sarasvatī and several folk elements played a significant role in giving her a concrete form. She is the goddess of speech, learning, and music. She is variously described as the daughter and *śakti* of Brahman; as Pushṭi, she is also the *śakti* of *Vishṇu. The iconographic texts describe her as four-armed, fair complexioned, dressed in white, and decked with ornaments. Her attributes include manuscript, white lotus, rosary, *vīṇā*, *kamaṇḍalu*, etc. The manuscript and the *vīṇā* indicate her association with learning and music, respectively. The **haṁsa* is her mount (Banerjea 2002; Sukumari Bhattacharji 1970; R B Pande 1988; Rao 1985).

Śaśāṅka. Gauḍa k. He appears to be a very powerful ruler, possessed with a burning desire to establish his supremacy over northern India. His antecedents are not known for certain. On the basis of his *alias Narendrāditya*, noticed by Bühler in a copy of the *Harshacharita*, some scholars regard him as a scion of the *Imperial Gupta dynasty; others regard him as related to *Jaya[nāga] on numismatic grounds; still others associate him with the Later Guptas, Varmans of Kāmarūpa, or *Samāchāradeva. That he began his career as a feudatory, is evident from his title *Śrīmahāsāmanta* in the Rohtasgarh seal matrix, although some scholars would place his stint as a feudatory after his defeat at the hands of *Harsha. Bāṇa refers to him as King of Gauḍa in 606 AD; he was ruling independently in 619 AD, as per the evidence of the Ganjam copperplate of Madhavarāja Śailodbhava; Hiuen-tsang, who visited Gauḍa in 737 AD, refers to Śaśāṅka as 'the recent king'.

Though there is no positive evidence to show the extent of his rule in Bengal, it stands to the reason that he would have established his sway over a considerable part of that region before embarking upon his southern and western expeditions. He is identified with the Gauḍa king referred to in the Dubi copperplate as defeating Supratishṭhitavarman and Bhāskaravarman, the two sons of Susthitavarman of Kāmarūpa. Literary and epigraphic sources also show his hold over Karṇasuvarṇa, Tāmralipti, and Kaliṅga. Around 606 AD, when the *Pushpabhūti ruler, *Prabhākaravardhana, was on his death bed, Śaśāṅka entered into an alliance with Devagupta of Malwa, attacked the *Maukhari kingdom of Kanauj, and killed Grahavarman. Prabhākaravardhana's son and successor, Rājyavardhana II, killed Devagupta, but Bāṇa and Hiuen-tsang inform us that he was himself treacherously murdered by Śaśāṅka, an act which overshadows all his brilliant achievements. According to the *Harshacharita*, Harsha, on ascending the throne, vowed to exterminate the Gauḍas, but there is no definite evidence to show that Harsha and Śaśāṅka ever met each other in the battlefield. The suggestion that Harsha and Bhāskaravarman conjointly defeated Śaśāṅka, and shared his territories on either side of the river Ganga, seems untenable in view of the fact that the supremacy of the Gauḍa king was being acknowledged by the Śailodbhava rulers, at least up to 619 AD (Allan 1914; D Devahuti 2001; Pires 1934; Sircar 1970; B N Srivastava 1962; Thaplyal 1985).

Selene. Deity. This Greek lunar goddess was a daughter of the Titan Hyperion and the Titaness Theia, and a sister of *Helios and Eos. But in some accounts, her father is Pallas. Her most famous lovers include Endymion and Pan. *Zeus begat on her a daughter, Pandia, who is believed to be the brightness of the nights of the full moon. In art, Selene is usually represented as a beautiful maiden, wearing a long robe and veil. She is either shown mounted on a horse or a mule, or riding a chariot drawn by a pair of horses, cows, or mules. Although sometimes described as a winged goddess, she is never shown as such on coins. Later, Selene seems to have come to be identified with *Artemis (Bhaskar Chattopadhyay 1977; Graves 1955; Kerenyi 1951; Rose 1958; Prashant Srivastava 2007c).

Serpent. The serpent, which occupies 'a prominent place in ancient Indian legends and folklore', is considered as a common representative of the deities of procreation. In Indian mythology, it is associated with both *Śiva and *Vishṇu, the former as his ornaments, and the latter as his couch, the *śeshaśayyā*. The connection between water and the snake seems to be 'the vital factor in the Nāga-worship', the association becoming evident from the regular appearance of the snakes at the beginning of the rainy season, as pointed out by Vögel. As a water spirit, the snake, on being duly propitiated, granted ample and timely rains for irrigation. Śesha or Ananta, Vāsukī, Takshaka, Dhṛitarāshṭra, Śaṅkha, Maṇi, Elāpatra or Airāvata, Karkoṭa or Karkoṭaka, and Kauravya, are some famous nāgas mentioned in literature. In Indian art, serpents are often represented in human form, the serpentine nature being indicated either by showing a serpent hood as a canopy on top of the head, or by depicting the human being with the coiled body of a snake from the waist downwards [*Undulating line] (Sircar 1971; Vögel 1926).

Śiva. Deity. The history of the worship of Śiva, in one form or the other, goes back to very early times, and it is not unlikely that he was revered even in pre-vedic times. A seal from Mohenjodaro bears the figure of an ithyphallic '*yogin*' surrounded by wild beasts, and this is regarded as the prototype of Śiva-Paśupati of later times. The worship of the phallus, so intimately associated with Śiva in later times, also seems to be prevalent in the Harappan culture. The character of Śiva was apparently formed by the assimilation of the attributes of many deities, and the earliest among them, besides the Harappan 'proto Śiva-Paśupati', seems to be the vedic Rudra. In the *Ṛigveda*, only three hymns are dedicated to the Rudra alone, and his name occurs 75 times in the text, thus showing that he was but a minor deity in vedic times. Most of the scholars derive *Rudra* from the Skt root *rud*, 'to cry', and Rudra is interpreted as 'the roarer'. Some other interpretations like 'bright' and 'ruddy' have also been suggested. In the *Ṛigveda*, the anthropomorphism of Rudra[-Śiva] is 'fairly advanced'. He has hands, arms, and firm limbs, beautiful lips, and wears hair in braids. He is the strongest of the strong, swift, and unaging. He wields the thunderbolt in his hand, besides carrying a bow and arrows. The fusion of diverse ideas that played an important role in providing a concrete form to the deity is mirrored in the various epithets used for him in the later saṁhitās. He is the lord of the beasts as *Paśupati*, auspicious as *Śaṅkara*, dweller on mountains as *Girichara*, blue and red as *Nīlalohita*, blue-necked as *Nīlakaṇṭha* or *Nīlagrīva*, and clothed in a skin as *Kṛittivāsa*. In vedic literature, Rudra is represented 'as a malevolent deity causing death and disease among men and cattle and is therefore prayed to by the hymnists for allaying his wrath towards them, sparing them, their families and cattle, and attacking and damaging their enemies and their belongings'. Initially, he was not accorded a share of the sacrifice, and it was only by the entreaties of *Umā that 'Śiva established for the first time in the *yāga* of Daksha his right to the receive oblations'. Śiva is credited with multiple origins. In the brāhmaṇa texts, he is described as a son of Prajāpati and Ushas. The puranic literature describes him as a son of Brahmā. But, according to one account, he sprang from the frowned brows of *Vishṇu when he grew fiercely angry with Madhu and Kaiṭabha who were trying to kill Brahmā. In the last quarter of the fourth century BC, Megasthenes seems to refer to Śiva under the name of *Dionysos. Patañjali, in the second century BC, mentions devotees and images of Śiva. The gradual rise in the popularity of the worship of Śiva can be seen even in the *Śvetāśvataropanishad*, which describes him as Mahādeva or the great god. By the time of the *Rāmāyaṇa*, Śiva 'had gained a history and founded a family', and the epic describes in a nutshell some of the legends more elaborately dealt with in the *Mahābhārata* and the purāṇas. In the vedic period, Rudra was a malevolent deity, but the awesome vedic Rudra was transformed with the evolution of Śaivism into an 'Infinite Intelligence...Creator of the World...Redeemer of Mankind'. In the Hindu triad of Brahmā, Vishṇu, and Śiva, the last deity was regarded as 'the destroyer of the universe when it requires to be created anew'. But with the rise in the popularity of the Śaiva cult, Śiva came to be regarded as the creator, supporter, and destroyer of the universe. In the purāṇas, Śiva is described thus : 'he carries a discus, trident, a club, an axe, and a sword; he wears a girdle of serpents, ear-ornaments composed of serpents and a *yajñopavīta* of serpents...he has erect hair, looks obscene in his nakedness and has an excited look'. He is further said to have 'braided hair and matted locks'. In the north Indian depictions, Śiva has *triśūla* and *sarpa* as his characteristic attributes. In the purāṇas and later literature, Śiva is described as a *yogin*, who meditates while seated on a lion skin. A crescent moon adorns his *jaṭāmukuṭa*, and from his matted locks flows the river *Gaṅgā. His abode is Mount Kailāsa. A white *bull is his *vāhana*, and this is probably the result of the comparison of Rudra to a white bull in the *Ṛigveda*. With the rise in the popularity of the worship of Śiva, we see a 'bewildering diversity' in his anthropomorphic representations. Rudra is often identified with *Agni, as is evident from sources like the *Ṛigveda*, the *Atharvaveda*, the *Taittirīyasaṁhitā*, the *Śatapathabrāhmaṇa*, and even the *Mahābhārata* (Banerjea 2002; R G Bhandarkar 1928; Sukumari Bhattacharji 1970; Bhaskar Chattopadhyay 1977; S R Goyal 1986; T R R Iyengar 2003; Macdonell 1897; R B Pande 1988; Rao 1985; Prashant Srivastava 1996a; Prashant Srivastava 1996b; Prashant Srivastava and Deepak Tiwari 1994; Tiwari and Sharma 1983; Wilkins 2006; Yaduvanshi 1988).

Skandagupta *Kramāditya*. *Imperial Gupta k. Kumāragupta I was succeeded by his son, Skandagupta. The reason for the silence of the official records about the name of the mother of Skandagupta has been the subject of much debate among scholars, and it has even been suggested that she might not have been the wedded wife of Kumāragupta I. There are indications that he had to face the opposition of other aspirants to the Imperial Gupta throne. While a prince, Skandagupta had proved his calibre by defeating the Pushyamitras [*Kumāragupta I]. His most notable achievement seems to be his victory over the *Hūṇa invaders. The Buddhist text, *Chandragarbhaparipṛichchh ā*, would suggest that this event, too, took place during the reign of his father. But epigraphs, like the Junagarh rock inscription and the Bhitari pillar inscription, while describing this victory, make no mention of Kumāragupta I in this context. A statement in the Junagarh rock inscription is also taken as referring to Skandagupta's victory over the *Nāgas, perhaps in the context of his struggle for succession (Ashvini Agrawal 1989; Nisar Ahmad 1964; Allan 1914; Altekar 1957; R D Banerji 1933; Fleet 1888; S R Goyal 2005; P L Gupta 1998; B C Jain 1960; K P Jayaswal 1933; Sinha 1988; Sircar 1986; Smith 1972; Prashant Srivastava 2004b; Thaplyal, forthcoming; T P Verma 1991).

***Śrīvatsa*.** Some scholars believe that the earliest representation of this symbol occurs outside India, on a Hittite inscription from Boghazkoi, datable to *c* fourteenth century BC. The word *śrīvatsa* occurs for the first time in the *Mantrabrāhmaṇa*, and is conspicuous by its absence in the saṁhitas and the early brāhmaṇas. *Śrīvatsa* as an auspicious symbol was adopted by almost all the major Indian religious creeds, like Jainism, Buddhism, and Vaishṇavism (Bhaskar Chattopadhyay 1977; Savita Sharma 1990).

Strato I. *Indo-Greek k. He is believed to be the son and successor of *Menander. He was a minor when his father died in camp, and for some time, his mother, *Agathokleia, administered the kingdom as regent. During this period, he issued joint coins with his mother, and then he assumed independent charge of his kingdom. He is depicted on his various coins in different stages of life, from a young boy in his teens to an old man 'with toothless jaws and sunken cheeks', and on this basis it was suggested by scholars like Rapson that he had a long reign of around 70 years. But there is no portrait, which might link his middle-aged portrait on the coins bearing the title of **epiphanes*, with those which show him as an old man of around 70 years of age. On this ground, Narain suggests that after he had ruled for about 35 years, Strato I was superseded by other kings for about 15 years, till he could regain authority. He dates the first phase of his reign between *c* 130 BC and 95 BC, and the second phase between *c* 80 and 75 BC. Osmund Bopearachchi, however, ascribes to him a single reign of only about 15 years, from *c* 125 BC to 110 BC. Towards the beginning of his reign, he might have lost some provinces to *Heliokles II who restruck some joint coins of Agathokleia and Strato I. But he seems to have regained most of the lost provinces with the help of his younger brother, *Apollodotos, whom he appointed his subking or joint king. His coins, though relatively few in number keeping in view his long reign, are very widely distributed, being found in western Gandhāra and Takshaśilā, Ghazni, and the Jammu-Sialkot region, thereby showing that, at least in the first phase of his reign, he retained authority over the larger part of the territories he inherited from Menander. But encouraged by his successes, Apollodotos seems to have replaced Strato I, and declared himself an independent king. After a gap of some 15 years, Strato I regained his throne, perhaps with the help of his grandson, *Strato II and also the Śaka-Pahlava ruler, *Maues. During the second phase of his reign, he seems to have appointed Strato II as his co-ruler, and issued joint coins with him. But Strato II apparently predeceased him, leaving him alone to the rule for some time more (Bopearachchi 1993; Bopearachchi and Pieper 1998; Bopearachchi and Rahman 1995; Cunningham 1970; Gardner 1971; A N Lahiri 1965; Marshall 1975; Narain 1957a; Rapson 1906; Rapson 1987; Senior 2001; Sircar 1980a; Prashant Srivastava 1996a; Tarn 1980; Whitehead 1914).

Sūrya. Deity. Worshipped for 'progeny, protection, health, light and joy', Sūrya is celebrated in at least 10 hymns of the *Ṛigveda*. He is 'the most concrete of the solar deities', as he represents 'primarily the orb of the physical sun itself'. As the son of Aditi, he is Āditya, *par excellence*. In various sources, his father is Dyaus, or Vṛitra, or he arose from the eye of Purusha. Several gods, like *Indra, *Vishṇu, Soma, *Varuṇa, Mitra, Ushas, and Dhātṛi, are said to have produced Sūrya, while Aṅgirases 'caused him to ascend the sky'. In the *Rāmāyaṇa*, his wife is Suvarchalā. The triumph of the light of Sūrya over darkness is adored. He lightens the world, and brings pleasure to the hearts of men with his brightness. The path of Sūrya was prepared by Varuṇa. He supports the sky, like a pillar. He is likened to a bird travelling across the sky, to an *eagle (sometimes a golden one), to a *bull, to a white *horse, to a gem, to a brilliant car, and to a *wheel. His car is pulled by one horse, or by seven horses, or by an indefinite number of horses, or by seven mares. The horses of Sūrya represent the sun rays, but when the number seven is associated with them, they may represent the seven colours of the sunbeam as seen through a prism. Allusions to the burning heat of the sun are very rare; mostly, it is the beneficent aspect of Sūrya that is mentioned. He drives away sickness and evil dreams, and prolongs the days of life. The creative function of the sun god is also alluded to. Like other solar gods the world over, he is associated with intelligence. Sūrya is described as the eye of Varuṇa and Mitra, and his own eyes are mentioned quite often. Interestingly, in the *Avesta*, the sun is called *hvare* (the equivalent of the vedic *svar* from which *sūrya* is derived), which is described as the eye of *Ahuramazda (Banerjea 2002; R G Bhandarkar 1928; Sukumari Bhattacharji 1970; Bhaskar Chattopadhyay 1977; S R Goyal 1986; T R R Iyengar 2003; Macdonell 1897; R B Pande 1988; Rao 1985; Wilkins 2006).

Svastika. The name *svastika* seems to be derived from *svasti*, which means welfare, happiness, good luck, etc. In dictionaries, it is explained as "a Sanskrit word signifying happiness, pleasure, goodluck. It is composed of '*su*' (good) and '*asti*' (being) with the suffix '*ka*'." Its use is seen in Mesopotamia, Assyria, Greece, Italy, Lithuania, Denmark, Sweden, Norway, Germany, Spain, Asia Minor, Bactria, Afghanistan, China, Korea, Japan, Australia, New Zealand, America, and several parts of Africa. In India, it has been a popular auspicious symbol, since prehistoric times, in rock art, pottery, sculpture, painting, terracotta art, ivory art, architecture, and numismatic and glyptic art. A number of inscriptions begin with this symbol. In various contexts, it represents the four directions, Gaṇapati, *Lakshmī, *nāda-sṛishṭi*, creation and birth, religious harmony, cycle of seasons, etc, but, primarily, it symbolizes the sun, or, more particularly, the movement of that heavenly body (Bhaskar Chattopadhyay 1977; Savita Sharma 1990; A L Srivastava 2004-2005).

T

Telephos. *Indo-Greek k. He is believed to be a son of *Antialkidas on the basis of the enthroned *Zeus types of his coins, and to have ruled over Takshaśilā in the period between the end of the reign of *Apollodotos *c* 95 BC, and its occupation by *Maues *c* 85 BC. But Tarn regards him as a usurper and even doubts if he was at all a Greek. His rare coins are reported mostly from Gandhāra and Takshaśilā, and one coin even comes from the Hazara region; he might have conquered the Takshaśilā region from *Nikias. There is no evidence to support Tarn's claim that he ruled over Kapiśā or the Kabul valley. He ruled from *c* 95 BC to 80 BC; R C Senior, however, places him *c* 60 BC (Bopearachchi 1993; Bopearachchi and Pieper 1998; Bopearachchi and Rahman 1995; Cunningham 1970; Gardner 1971; A N Lahiri 1965; Marshall 1975; Narain 1957a; Rapson 1987; Senior 2001; Sircar 1980a; Tarn 1980; Whitehead 1914).

Theophilos. *Indo-Greek k. He is believed to belong to the family of *Euthydemos I on the basis of his *Herakles type of coins, and he was, perhaps, a son of *Lysias. Although some of his coins are reported from Rawalpindi and Sialkot, the *provenance* of most of his coins is difficult to establish. Narain suggests that he did not immediately succeed his father, but rebelled and set up an independent kingdom in some regions north of the Hindukush some time in the second decade of the first century BC; R C Senior, however, places his reign between *c* 115 BC and 110 BC. His use of the title of **autokratoros* is unique in Indo-Greek numismatics, and has been taken as suggestive of his rebellion. Shortly afterwards, he seems to have been overthrown by *Amyntas (Bopearachchi 1993; Bopearachchi and Pieper 1998; Bopearachchi and Rahman 1995; Cunningham 1970; Gardner 1971; A N Lahiri 1965; Marshall 1975; Narain 1957a; Rapson 1987; Senior 2001; Sircar 1980a; Tarn 1980; Whitehead 1914).

Tiger. Since primitive times, just as the male herbivorous animals, like the *bull, *elephant, buffalo, etc, were believed to stand for the male fecundative power, the carnivorous animals, like the *lion, tiger, jaguar, etc, irrespective of their sex, came to be associated for the female procreative principle. In her terrible aspect, the goddess may either herself assume the form of a terrifying beast, or 'her terrible aspect may become the animal that accompanies and dominates her'. She may either be a lioness, as in Egypt, or she may be shown enthroned or riding a lion or a tiger. The association of the tiger with the mother goddess seems to be hinted at on an Harappan seal, where the posterior part of a female figure is shown attached to the body of a tiger (Bhaskar Chattopadhyay 1977; Neumann 1955).

Toramāṇa. *Hūṇa (?) chief. He is generally regarded as a Hūṇa chief, who advanced from his base, probably in Gandhāra, and overran a large part of western and northern India. The *provenance* of his coins testifies to his rule over parts of Uttar Pradesh, Rajasthan, Punjab, Kashmir, and as far south as Eran (Madhya Pradesh). The conquest of Eran seems to have taken place shortly after *Budhagupta. According to the Kura inscription, he took the title of *Shāhi Jaūvla*. The Jaina text, *Kuvalayamālā* (778 AD) informs us that he adopted Jainism, and lived at Pavvaiyā on the banks of the river Chandrabhāgā (Chenab) in Punjab. But, after the initial successes, he seems to have been defeated by the Aulikara chief, Prakāśadharman, as per the evidence of the Risthal inscription, and also apparently by *Bhānugupta, and forced to fall back to the west of the river Indus. This appears from the testimony of both Sung-yün, the Chinese ambassador to the court of the Hūṇa king of Gandhāra in 520 AD, and of Kosmas' *Christian Topography* (begun in 535 AD and reaching its final form in 547 AD), which suggests that initially the sway of *Mihirakula, the son and successor of Toramāṇa, was confined to the territories west of the river Indus (Altekar 1986b; Biswas 1973; Cunningham 1962; Cunningham 1967; R C Majumdar 1988; Sircar 1986; Upendra Thakur 1967a; Upendra Thakur 1967b).

Tripod lebes. It was the seat, from which Pythia proclaimed oracles. According to Callimachos, Diodoros Siculus, Apollodoros, Pausanias, Hyginos, and others, once *Herakles entered the Delphic shrine to ask the Oracle as to how he might rid himself of the sin of the murder of his guest, Iphitos. But the Pythoness Xenoklea, refused to reply to his query. Angered at this, Herakles stole the tripod. This led to a dispute between him and *Apollo, which was settled by their father, *Zeus, and Herakles returned the *tripod* to Apollo (Graves 1955; Kerenyi 1951; Rose 1958).

Triton. Deity. He was a son of *Poseidon and *Amphitrite, and a brother of Rhodos. He might have been adopted in Greek mythology from Minoan or Anatolian belief. He is a merman, human from the waist up, and fish-shaped from the waist down. In literature and art, he is often represented as playing a role in the tales of the major sea gods like Poseidon, Pontos, Nereus, and Okeanos. He tried to do violence to some women at Tanagra, while they were bathing for some ritual of *Dionysos. These women appealed to Dionysos for help, and he worsted Triton. Triton is described as very dangerous under provocation. In art, he is often shown as blowing a conch shell (Bhaskar Chattopadhyay 1977; Graves 1955; Kerenyi 1951; Rose 1958; Prashant Srivastava 2007c).

Tyche. Deity. She was one of the 41 daughters that Tethys bore to Okeanos, of whom Styx was the mightiest. But in some accounts, Tyche is a daughter of *Zeus. The name Tyche means 'what may hap', or 'chance'. She is a deity 'of whom no particular stories are told, but whose power... proved stronger than the rule of Zeus'. She is believed to be 'an artificial deity' thought of by the early philosophers, who also redefined Nemesis, 'due enactment', as a 'moral control' on Tyche. Tyche has the power to decide the fortune of men, but is 'altogether irresponsible in her awards'. However, if a man favoured by her becomes boastful, neglects to sacrifice to the gods and alleviate the sorrows of his fellow beings, Nemesis wrecks divine wrath on him (Graves 1955; Kerenyi 1951; Rose 1958; Prashant Srivastava 2007c).

U

Umā. Deity. Umā is usually described as the consort of *Śiva, although some upanishads mention her as his sister. She sometimes has the epithet *Haimavatī*, 'daughter of Himavat', but she is mostly described as the daughter of Daksha. According to the *Brahmavaivartapurāṇa*, her father performed a sacrifice, to which her husband was not invited. Feeling slighted, she entered the sacrificial fire, and immolated herself. Śiva was mad with grief, at which Umā appeared before him, and consoled him by promising to be born again as *Pārvatī, the daughter of Himavat. In the *Kenopanishad*, Umā reveals the identity and nature of *brahman* to Indra, and on this basis, some scholars associated her with divine knowledge, and this seems to be supported by the *Harivaṁśa*, which describes Aparṇā (Umā-Pārvatī) and her two sisters as expounders of divine knowledge (Banerjea 2002; Sukumari Bhattacharji 1970; Bhaskar Chattopadhyay 1977).

V

Vainyagupta *Dvādaśāditya*. *Imperial Gupta k. Vainyagupta is known from three sources—the Gunaighar (District Comilla) copperplate grant, which supplies his only known date, *Gupta era 188 (= 507 AD), the Nalanda seal, and gold coins. The Gunaighar inscription uses the title **mahārāja* for him, but in his Nalanda seal, he is called **mahārājādhirāja*. Besides, in the Gunaighar grant, he is referred to as *Bhagavān Mahādeva pādānudhyāta*, and the seal of this grant bears the Śaiva device of the *bull. But on the Nalanda seal, Vainyagupta is given the title, **paramabhāgavata*. On the basis of these two differences, some scholars suggest that Vainyagupta of the Gunaighar inscription is different from the Vainyagupta of the Nalanda sealing. But the Gunaighar inscription shows that Vainyagupta had under him, *Mahārāja* Rudradatta and *Mahārāja* Vijayasena, who held high offices. From this, it has been inferred that Vainyagupta of this inscription, despite his feudatory title of *mahārāja*, was an independent king. Difference in religious leanings, too, is not an insuperable difficulty in identifying Vainyagupta of the Gunaighar inscription with that of the Nalanda seal. There is overwhelming evidence to show that *Narasiṁhagupta Bālāditya leaned towards Buddhism, yet his Nalanda seal refers to him as *paramabhāgavata*. As such, the two rulers named Vainyagupta may be treated as identical. The name of the father of Vainyagupta is not known for certain. But, on the basis of his Nalanda seal, where the first part of the name of his father is damaged, it has been suggested that he was, perhaps, a son of *Pūrugupta, and ruled after his brother, *Budhagupta. The view, on the evidence of *Āryamañjuśrīmūlakalpa*, that he was a son of *Chandragupta III, does not seem to be convincing. No inscription, coin, or seal of Vainyagupta has been found from the western provinces of the Imperial Guptas, thereby indicating that his authority was confined to the eastern provinces. From coins, he is known to have assumed the title, *Dvādaśāditya*. His subordinate, *Mahārāja* Vijayasena of the Gunaighar inscription, refers to *Mahārājādhirāja* Gopachandra in his Mallasarul copperplate. This seems to show that the Imperial Guptas lost southern and western Bengal in the first half of the sixth century AD. According to the *Āryamañjuśrīmūlakalpa*, Dvādaśa (Vainyagupta *Dvādaśāditya*) ruled for a few months only, before he was murdered (Ashvini Agrawal 1989; Allan 1914; Altekar 1957; R

D Banerji 1933; Fleet 1888; S R Goyal 2005; P L Gupta 1998; K P Jayaswal 1933; Smith 1972; Thaplyal, forthcoming).

Varuṇa. Deity. He is the king of the gods, and called *samrāj*, 'emperor', a position which he attained by performing the *rājasūya* or through chanting the Varuṇa Sāman. The epithet, *asura*, is more closely associated with him than with any other deity. According to the *Ṛigveda*, the worshippers feel like slaves in his presence; this 'awe and an attitude of profound humility is not found in connection with any other Vedic god', and there is a suggestion that Varuṇa is the creation of primitive monotheism which demands 'a supreme deity, wholly beneficent, omnipotent and omniscient'. The power of Varuṇa rests on his supernatural knowledge, his omniscience. He is called *kavi*, 'the seer'. The sun is the eye of Varuṇa. He is *uruchakshasa*, 'many eyed', and *sahasrachakshaḥ*, 'thousand eyed'. These 'many eyes' and 'thousand eyes' of Varuṇa are evidently the stars of the night sky. These eyes enable him to be *viśvadarśata*, 'the all-seeing', the sun acting as his eyes in the daytime, and the stars at night. Besides, he is also assisted by the *spaśas*, his spies, who are placed all around him. Due to this supernatural power of knowledge, he becomes the upholder of *dharma*. But Varuṇa's personality seems to undergo transformation with time. From the judge, the upolder of *dharma*, he becomes the punisher of those who transgress *dharma*. Frequent are the references to the noose of this god. Some scholars feels that Varuṇa-*pāśa* may be a kind of dropsy. Punishments meted out by this 'god of the norm' are usually in the form of some disease, which is abnormal. These include *yakshman*, 'tuberculosis', physical deformity, premature decay, emaciation, and even death. Varuṇa, the 'moral supervisor' of the world, was a grand, awe-inspiring deity; Varuṇa, the punisher of evil doers, was a dark, wrathful, sinister god. From the god of the sky in all its aspects, he becomes increasingly more associated with the night sky with its stars, with the dark fortnight, and, hence, with darkness itself, while the day sky gradually becomes the sole realm of Mitra, the god of sunlight. Reverence for Varuṇa yields place to dread, and he is found being superseded by the warrior god, *Indra. And ultimately, because the deity had exhausted his mythological potentiality, Varuṇa is 'pensioned off' as a *dikpāla*, the guardian of the western quarter in epic and puranic mythology (Sukumari Bhattacharji 1970; Eliade 1958; Eliade 1961; Hillebrandt 1999; Macdonell 1897; Radin 1955; Prashant Srivastava 2007a; Wilkins 2006).

Vāsudeva-Kṛishṇa. Deity. This eighth incarnation of *Vishṇu—a total incarnation (*pūrṇāvatāra*) as against the others who are only partial incarnations (*aṁśāvatāras*), is worshipped as the central cult figure in Bhāgavatism. It is generally believed that Vāsudeva-Kṛishṇa, the son of Vasudeva and Devakī, was the hero of the Yādava-Sātvata-Vṛishṇis, who was deified by his tribe, and his cult gradually became popular. There is, however, a view that a god named Vāsudeva was worshipped before the cult of Vāsudeva-Kṛishṇa became popular, and that the Vṛishṇi hero was identified with this earlier divinity. He seems to be identical with Kṛishṇa Devakīputra, the disciple of Ghora Āṅgirasa, of the *Chhāndogyopanishad*, and the impact of the teachings of Ghora are evident in the doctrines of Bhāgavatism. Initially, four other Vṛishṇi heroes—Saṁkarshaṇa, Pradyumna, Aniruddha, and Sāmba, were also worshipped along with Vāsudeva-Kṛishṇa, but later, the worship of Vāsudeva-Kṛishṇa alone remained in vogue. He occupies the most important position in the *chaturvyūha* doctrine in the Bhāgavata sect. Several elements are found amalgamated together in the personality of Vāsudeva-Kṛishṇa, and we see him as 'a warrior, a preacher, a child-god of some pastoral tribe and a love-god of the popular lore, all blended into one'. The epics and the purāṇas give stories of his killing the demons Dhenuka, Arishṭa, Keśin, Pralamba, Kuvalayāpīḍa, Chāṇūra, and Pūtanā. He destroyed Yamalārjuna, and subjugated Kalīya. But his greatest exploit was his slaying of Kaṁsa. He humbled the pride of *Indra, and assisted and guided the Pāṇḍava brothers in the Bhārata war. According to the *Mahābhārata*, he preached the *Gītā* to Arjuna before the commencement of this war. Some scholars are of the opinion that the *Herakles, who, according to Megasthenes, was revered by the Śūrasena of Mathurā, should be identified as Vāsudeva-Kṛishṇa (Sukumari Bhattacharji 1970; Gonda 1993; S R Goyal 1986; Suvira Jaiswal 1981; Sircar 1971; Wilkins 2006).

Vishṇu. Deity. In the *Ṛigveda*, Vishṇu is celebrated in only five whole hymns, and is mentioned not more than 100 in that text. From this, it has been surmised that he was not very important in the Rigvedic period, and that his rise to prominence in the puranic pantheon was a later development. In the vedic period, his most frequently mentioned achievements are his three steps, and the assistance he provided his friend, *Indra, in slaying Vṛitra. The three steps of Vishṇu have been interpreted variously as referring to the course of the sun—its rising, culminating, and setting, or to the course of the sun through the three divisions of the universe. In the brāhmaṇa texts, his cut off head became the sun. His weapon *par excellence* is the **chakra* (wheel), which represents the sun. His vehicle is the **garuḍa*, which is the *suparṇa garutmat*, the sun bird of the *Ṛigveda*. His breast jewel, *kaustubha*, has been explained as the sun. Thus, the association of Vishṇu with motion and the sun, is well established : he represents the solar motion. With Indra, Vishṇu not only slew Vṛitra, but also destroyed the 99 forts of Śambara, and defeated the armies of Varchin. Interestingly, he is also described in the *Ṛigveda* as a protector of embryos, and promoter of conception. In the brāhmaṇa texts, he is constantly identified with sacrifice. In the post-vedic period, he gained in importance, got identified with the cosmic god Nārāyaṇa and the Vṛishṇi hero *Vāsudeva-Kṛishṇa, and eventually had a cult of his own, named variously as Bhāgavatism or Vaishṇavism. His worshippers are also known as Pāñcharātras, Ekāntins, and Sāttvatas. He is the second god in the puranic triad of Brahmā, Vishṇu, and *Śiva, who are believed to create, preserve, and destroy the universe, respectively. But some texts state that at the time of creation, Vishṇu, desirous of creating the universe, became threefold, and the puranic triad is but the threefold manifestation of Vishṇu himself. The worship of the various incarnations of Vishṇu gained popularity, mostly in the Gupta period, although a germ of the idea of incarnations existed even in the vedic period. In art, Vishṇu is usually depicted as dark complexioned and four-armed, bearing in his hands, *śaṅkha*, *chakra*, *gadā*, and *padma*. He dwells in his heaven, Vaikuṇṭha, and rides his *vāhana*, the *garuḍa*. *Lakshmī and Pṛithivī are the two consorts of Vishṇu. In the early mediaeval and mediaeval periods, there are instances of the worship of the *Ardhanārī* forms of Vishṇu (Banerjea 2002; R G Bhandarkar 1928; Sukumari Bhattacharji 1970; Bhaskar Chattopadhyay 1977; Coomaraswamy 1928-1929; Hillebrandt 1999; Hopkins 1915; Suvira Jaiswal 1981; Macdonell 1897; Rao 1985; Sircar 1971; Sircar 1980f; Wilkins 2006).

Vishṇugupta *Chandrāditya*. *Imperial Gupta k. Vishṇugupta is mentioned as the son and successor of *Kumāragupta [III] in his Nalanda seal. His only known date, *Gupta era 225 (= 543 AD) is mentioned in his Damodarpur copperplate inscription. In the inscription, he has been given the titles of **mahārājādhirāja*, **paramabhaṭṭāraka*, and **paramadaivata*. It is evident from the seal and the inscription that Vishṇugupta had parts of Bengal and Magadha under his rule. In the Damodarpur copperplate inscriptions of the time of *Kumāragupta I, and of *Budhagupta, all the provincial governors of the Puṇḍravardhana-*bhukti* bear *datta*-ending names, which shows that the office had become hereditary. But in the Damodarpur copperplate inscription of Vishṇugupta, the provincial governor was a prince of the Imperial Gupta family, for he bore the title *mahārājaputra devabhaṭṭāraka*. On this basis, it has been suggested that the rule of the Datta viceregal family was brought to an end by the victorious campaign of Yaśodharman, and Vishṇugupta had to appoint a member of his family as the provincial governor. Allan dates the coins of Vishṇugupta between *c* 540 and 560 AD on numismatic grounds. No Imperial Gupta ruler is known after Vishṇugupta (Ashvini Agrawal 1989; Allan 1914; Altekar 1957; S R Goyal 2005; P L Gupta 1998; K P Jayaswal 1933; Smith 1972; Thaplyal, forthcoming).

Y

Yaksha. Semi-divine being. There exists no exact equivalent of the Skt *yaksha*, *geni* perhaps being the nearest. The term *yaksha* occurs for the first time in the *Jaiminīyabrāhmaṇa*, but simply in the sense of 'a wondrous thing'; as a genius, it appears only in the gṛihyasūtras. In the *Mahābhārata*, the yakshas are placed above the pretas and the bhūtas, but below the devas. Originally, they seem to have enjoyed an honourable status for their benevolence towards men. They are believed to be non-Aryan-pre-Aryan deities or 'beneficent powers of wealth and fertility'. It is only in the later period that they were degraded, and often confused with the rākshasas with whom they seem to share a common origin, the main difference being that while the rākshasas as a rule are bloodthirsty, the yakshas as a rule are kindly. The *Dīghanikāya* and the *Mahāvaṁśa* speak of bad yakshas together with good yakshas. But then, in Buddhist literature, the yakshas are generally described as unbelievers, who did not accept the teachings of the *Buddha. They possess the power to assume any shape. They are *puṇyajana*, 'good folks', and apparently countless in number. Their chief is Kubera. They are sometimes grouped with the nāgas and gandharvas. In some works, they are associated with disease. But one of the chief characteristics of yakshas is their role as guardians and supporters. In early Indian art, yakshas may be seen as supporters of buildings and superstructures. Interestingly, in the legend of Vijaya described in the *Mahāvaṁśa*, the aboriginal inhabitants of Srilanka are called yakshas. In art, yakshas are represented both as independent cult images, and as attendants, guardians, and worshippers. As cult images, they are generally shown as standing, with the r hand raised and sometimes holding a flower or a *chāmara* or a weapon, while the l hand rests on hip. The type is 'massive and voluminous', and conveys the sense of energy, and served as the prototype for the icons of *Śiva and the Buddha. The yakshas, thus, played a significant role, not only in the development of Indian mythology, but also of later Hindu and Buddhist iconography (Bhaskar Chattopadhyay 1977; Coomaraswamy 2001; R N Misra 1981).

Yakshī/Yakshiṇī. Semi-divine being. She is the female counterpart of *yaksha, and associated with wealth and fertility. That the worship of yakshiṇīs was very popular in ancient times can be understood from the fact that the *Mahābhārata* speaks of a 'world-renowned' yakshiṇī shrine at

Rājagṛiha. There is a suggestion that the Saptamātṛikās, Śītalā, the Ḍākinīs and the Yoginīs, village divinities, Mīnākshī the consort of *Śiva to whom the famous temple at Madurai is dedicated, and even Durgā, might originally have been yakshiṇīs. In fact, so popular was the yakshiṇī cult, that when the *Buddha promises to Hārīti, on her reform, that she shall receive regular offerings from the Buddhists who shall revere him as a patroness of children and fertility, he is actually providing sanction for a cult 'too strong to be subverted'. Yakshiṇīs are associated with marriage in the *Maṇichūḍāvadāna*. Yakshiṇīs are often associated with trees, and even regarded as born in trees (*vṛikshajā*). In Indian art, the motif of the woman and tree is very significant, and served as the prototype for the three iconographic types of the Buddha's nativity, the *aśoka* tree *dohada*, and the river goddesses. Yakshiṇī *Aśvamukhī*, 'horse-faced', is one of the very few individual yakshiṇīs mentioned by name. She finds mention in the *Padakusalamāṇavajātaka* as a cannibal who gave up her life on separation from her husband and son, and is represented on the medallions of Buddhist railings at Bodhgaya and Pāṭaliputra, and perhaps also in the art of Ajanta (cave no. XVII). A *valavāmukha*, 'mare-faced', yakshiṇī named Chetiyā is mentioned in the *Mahāvaṁśa* in connection with the legend of Paṇḍukābhaya (Banerjea 1938; Banerjea 2002; Bhaskar Chattopadhyay 1977; Coomaraswamy 2001; Cowell 2005; R N Misra 1981).

Z

Zeus. Deity. This foremost among the Greek gods and dweller of the Olympus, was the son of Kronos and Rhea, and brother of Hestia, Hera, *Demeter, *Poseidon, and Hades. He was originally conceived of as a sky god, and corresponds to Dyaus, the Indian sky god. He was born on Mount Lykaion in Arkadia, and bathed in the spring of river Neda. To protect him from Kronos, he was sent to Krete, where he was nursed by Amaltheia, while he was reared by the nine Telchines. He later led his siblings against the Titans, defeated them, and imprisoned them in Tartaros. He established a new divine order, in which he was *Basileus*, 'king'; *Pater*, 'father'; and *Soter*, 'saviour'. His surnames like *Ombrios* or *Hyetios*, 'the ram god', and *Keraunos*, 'the lightning', reveal his character as a 'god of the weather', and seem to establish his identity with the vedic *Indra. The *thunderbolt and lightning of Zeus are the emblem of his power. They are said to have been fashioned by the Kyklopes. These two are the well-known attributes of Indra also. Zeus is closely associated with the *eagle. He had a number of immortal and mortal lovers, and several children. The foremost among his spouses was Hera, his sister-wife, who bore to him Ares, *Hephaistos, Hebe, and Eileithyia. Themis bore to Zeus the three Moirai. In some accounts, Aphrodite is mentioned as his daughter, but at Dodona she was worshipped together with Zeus as his wife. Zeus swollowed Metis, and gave birth to *Athena from his head. Leto bore him *Apollo and *Artemis. He begat *Hermes on Maia, *Dionysos on Semele, and the Charites on Eurynome. His marriage with Mnemosyne resulted in the birth of the nine Muses. *Demeter or Styx bore him Persephone, who later became the queen of Hades. He ravished Europa in the form of a bull, and had three sons by her, namely Sarpedon, the king of Lykia; Minos, the king of Krete; and Rhadamanthys, the king of the Isles of the Blest. He played a significant role in the birth of Orion. The foremost position of Zeus in the Greek pantheon is clearly evident from the prayer of the followers of Orpheus : 'Zeus is the first, Zeus is the last...Zeus is the foundation of the earth and the starry sky. Zeus is male, Zeus is an immortal woman....Zeus is the roots of the sea. Zeus is the sun and moon....' (Bhaskar Chattopadhyay 1977; Foss 1995; Graves 1955; Kerenyi 1951; Pinsent 1969; Rose 1958; Prashant Srivastava 2007b; Prashant Srivastava 2007c).

Zoilos I. *Indo-Greek k. Some coins bearing the name of Zoilos use the title **dikaios*, while others use the title **soter*. On the basis of the *provenance* of these coins, the coins of Zoilos *Dikaios* have been placed to the west of the river Indus, and those of Zoilos *Soteros*, to the east of that river. Scholars like Cunningham did not distinguish between Zoilos *Dikaios* and Zoilos *Soteros*, but the remarkable difference in style of the two series has been taken as evidence of the existence of two Indo-Greek kings bearing the name of Zoilos, the one using the title of *dikaios* being Zoilos I, and the other with the title of *soteros* being Zoilos II. Zoilos I is believed to have belonged to the family of *Euthydemos I on the basis of the use of the *Herakles type by him. He might have been a subking of *Menander, and was appointed in the Swat valley by *Agathokleia when she transferred *Antimachos II from there to northern Arachosia. The presence of his coins in the *Mir Zakah hoard has been taken to suggest that the transfer might have been mutual. Osmund Bopearachchi regards Zoilos I, perhaps as a rival of Menander I, who might have been responsible for the death of the latter. Coins of Zoilos I have been assigned to the Paropamisadae and western Gandhāra. The rarity of his coins shows his brief reign in the eighth decade of the second century BC (Bopearachchi 1993; Bopearachchi and Pieper 1998; Bopearachchi and Rahman 1995; Cunningham 1970; Gardner 1971; A N Lahiri 1965; Marshall 1975; Narain 1957a; Rapson 1987; Sircar 1980a; Tarn 1980; Whitehead 1914).

Select Bibliography

[It is beyond the scope of a work of this nature to give an adequate bibliography of ancient Indian numismatics; for, such an endeavour would require a separate volume of its own. One can have an idea of the volume of work done on the subject, from the *Bibliography of Indian Numismatics* (Ancient Period), and its supplements, published by the Numismatic Society of India. I have included in the Select Bibliography, here, only those books, monographs, and research papers, which had a direct bearing on my writing, and which I had occasion to consult during the course of this work. In cases, where more than one publications of a scholar were available on the same subject, I have usually referred to his latest work, and not burdened the reader with the earlier one(s), unless it was otherwise deemed necessary. As a result, a reader, conversant with the subject, would find many omissions, for which I would crave his indulgence.]

Agrawal, Ashvini 1989. *Rise and Fall of the Imperial Guptas*. Delhi.

Agrawal, Ashvini 1992. The Prakāśāditya Problem : A Reappraisal. *Numismatic Studies* 2, pp. 107-118.

Agrawala, R C 1952. Numismatic Data in the Kharoshṭhī Documents from Chinese Turkestan. *Journal of the Numismatic Society of India* 14, pp. 103-106.

Agrawala, R C 1953a. *Śāṇa* as a Weight Denomination. *Journal of the Numismatic Society of India* 15(2), pp. 151-152.

Agrawala, R C 1953b. Greek *Stater* in Ancient Indian Epigraphs and Literature. *Journal of the Numismatic Society of India* 15(2), pp. 153-154.

Agrawala, R C 1954a. Numismatic Data in the Niya Kharoshṭhī Documents from Central Asia. *Journal of the Numismatic Society of India* 16(2), pp. 219-230.

Agrawala, R C 1954b. Coins, Weights and Measures in the Bakhshali Manuscript. *Journal of the Numismatic Society of India* 16(2), pp. 231-235.

Agrawala, R C 1955. *Dramma* in Ancient Indian Epigraphs and Literature. *Journal of the Numismatic Society of India* 17(2), pp. 64-82.

Agrawala, R C 1958. Numismatic Data in the *Gaṇitasāra*. *Journal of the Numismatic Society of India* 20(1), pp. 38-41.

Agrawala, R C 1967. Six-headed Skanda. *Journal of the Numismatic Society of India* 29, p. 41.

Agrawala, R C 1968. Six-headed Goddess on Yaudheya Coins. *Journal of the Numismatic Society of India* 30, pp. 181-184.

Agrawala, V S 1941. Some Notes on New Pañchāla Coins. *Journal of the Numismatic Society of India* 3, pp. 79-82.

Agrawala, V S 1943a. Coins of Yugasena. *Journal of the Numismatic Society of India* 5, pp. 19-20.

Agrawala, V S 1943b. Goddess Shashṭhī on Yaudheya Coins. *Journal of the Numismatic Society of India* 5, pp. 29-32.

Agrawala, V S 1945. *Prati* as the Name of a Coin. *Journal of the Numismatic Society of India* 7, pp. 32-35.

Agrawala, V S 1950. Presidential Address at the Nagpur Session of the Numismatic Society of India (Hindi). *Journal of the Numismatic Society of India* 12(2), pp. 188-205.

Agrawala, V S 1952. A New Type of *Śāṇa* Coin. *Journal of the Numismatic Society of India* 14, pp. 22-25.

Agrawala, V S 1953. Ancient Coins as known to Pāṇini. *Journal of the Numismatic Society of India* 15(1), pp. 27-41.

Agrawala, V S 1954. An Explanation of the *Chakravikrama* Type Coin of Chandragupta II. *Journal of the Numismatic Society of India* 16(1), pp. 97-101.

Agrawala, V S 1955. *Cornucopiae* in Indian Literature and Tradition. *Journal of the Numismatic Society of India* 17(2), pp. 92-94.

Agrawala, V S 1956. Coin Data in the *Mahābhārata*. *Journal of the Numismatic Society of India* 18(2), pp. 143-156.

Agrawala, V S 1957. Coin Names in the *Aṅgavijjā*. *Journal of the Numismatic Society of India* 19(1), pp. 20-31.

Agrawala, V S 1969. *Pāṇini Kālīna Bhāratavarsha* (Hindi). Varanasi.

Agrawala, V S 1970. *Ancient Indian Folk Cults*. Varanasi.

Ahmad, Nisar 1964. On the Identification of Mahendrāditya and Kramāditya of Repoussé Gold Coins. *Journal of the Numismatic Society of India* 26(1), pp. 31-39.

Ahmad, Nisar 1972. The Vemaka Coins. *Journal of the Numismatic Society of India* 34 (2), pp. 176-188.

Ahmad, Nisar 1977. The Mitras of Punjab. *Journal of the Numismatic Society of India* 39, pp. 52-68.

Ahmad, Nisar 1993. Coins of the Ārjunāyanas. *Numismatic Digest* 17, pp. 15-24.

Ahmad, Nisar 1996. The Coins of the Śibis. *Numismatic Studies* 4, pp. 31-39.

Allan, John 1914. *Catalogue of the Coins of the Gupta Dynasties, and of Śaśāṅka, King of Gauḍa, in the British Museum, London*. London.

Allan, John 1936. *Catalogue of the Coins of Ancient India, in the British Museum, London.* London.

Altekar, A S 1940. The Relative Prices of Metals and Coins in Ancient India. *Journal of the Numismatic Society of India* 2, pp. 1-13.

Altekar, A S 1942a. New Kings and Interesting Coin Types from Kauśāmbī. *Journal of the Numismatic Society of India* 4, pp. 1-16.

Altekar, A S 1942b. Further New Coins from Kauśāmbī. *Journal of the Numismatic Society of India* 4, pp. 133-145.

Altekar, A S 1942c. A Coin of Vaṅgapāla, A King of Kauśāmbī. *Journal of the Numismatic Society of India* 4, pp. 19-20.

Altekar, A S 1946a. Some Rare Indo-Bactrian Coins. *Journal of the Numismatic Society of India* 8(1), pp. 51-59.

Altekar, A S 1946b. New and Interesting Coins and Seals from Madhyadeśa (UP). *Journal of the Numismatic Society of India* 8(1), pp. 7-14.

Altekar, A S 1947. Identity of Kāchagupta. *Journal of the Numismatic Society of India* 9(2), pp. 131-136.

Altekar, A S 1952a. Two Coins of Jyeshṭhapura, Capital of the Śibis ? *Journal of the Numismatic Society of India* 14(1), pp. 5-8.

Altekar, A S 1952b. Two More Coins of Huvishka with Ahura Mazda. *Journal of the Numismatic Society of India* 14, pp. 71-72.

Altekar, A S 1953. Origin and Early History of Coinage in Ancient India. *Journal of the Numismatic Society of India* 15(1), pp. 1-26.

Altekar, A S 1954. *Catalogue of the Gupta Gold Coins in the Bayana Hoard.* Bombay.

Altekar, A S 1957. *The Coinage of the Gupta Empire.* Corpus of Indian Coins, IV. Varanasi.

Altekar, A S 1967. *Rāshṭrakūṭas and their Times.* Poona.

Altekar, A S 1986a. The Punjab, Sindh and Afghanistan. Chapter I, in R C Majumdar and A S Altekar (ed), *The Vākāṭaka-Gupta Age (*c *200-550 AD).* A New History of the Indian People 6, (Delhi, 1986), pp. 13-24.

Altekar, A S 1986b. The Coinage. Chapter XV, in R C Majumdar and A S Altekar (ed), *The Vākāṭaka-Gupta Age (*c *200-550 AD).* A New History of the Indian People 6, (Delhi, 1986), pp. 295-308.

Altekar, A S, and D B Diskalkar 1946. Kasarwad Hoard of Ujjain Coins. *Journal of the Numismatic Society of India* 8, pp. 99-106.

Audouin, R, and P Bernard 1973. *Trésor de Monnaies Indiennes et Indo-Grecques d'Aï Khanoum* (Afghanistan). *Revue Numismatique*, pp. 238-289.

Bachhofer, L 1941. On Greeks and Śakas in India. *Journal of the American Oriental Society*, pp. 223ff.

Badam, G L 1989. Animals, Domestication of. A Ghosh (ed), *An Encyclopaedia of Indian Archaeology* 1, (New Delhi, 1989), pp. 1-5.

Bailey, H W 1943. *Zoroastrian Problems in the Ninth-century Books.* Oxford.

Bajpai, K D 1953. New Pañchāla and Kauśāmbī Coins. *Journal of the Numismatic Society of India* 15(1), pp. 42-45.

Bajpai, K D 1960. New Copper Coins from Kauśāmbī and Vidiśā. *Journal of the Numismatic Society of India* 22, pp. 131-133.

Bajpai, K D 1961. Rāmagupta, A Gupta Kings. *Journal of the Numismatic Society of India* 23, pp. 340-344.

Bajpai, K D 1962. New Pañchāla Coins and the Problem of Pañchāla Chronology. *Journal of the Numismatic Society of India* 24(1), pp. 9-19.

Bajpai, K D 1963. The Joint Issues of the Kshatrapas Hagāna and Hagāmasha. *Journal of the Numismatic Society of India* 25(1), pp. 102-103.

Bajpai, K D 1964. Fresh Light on the Post-Aśokan History of Kauśāmbī. *Journal of the Numismatic Society of India* 26(1), pp. 1-6.

Bajpai, K D 1965. A Seal of King Dhanabhūti and a Coin of Śuṅgavarmā from Kauśāmbī. *Journal of the Numismatic Society of India* 27(2), pp. 188-190.

Bajpai, K D 1966. Anamitra—A New Pañchāla Ruler. *Journal of the Numismatic Society of India* 28(1), pp. 43-44.

Bajpai, K D 1971. A Rare Gupta Coin from Sanchi. *Journal of the Numismatic Society of India* 33(1), pp. 120-121.

Bajpai, K D 1973. Yaudheya Coins—A Critical Study. *Journal of the Numismatic Society of India* 35, pp. 90-94.

Bajpai, K D 1976. *Indian Numismatic Studies*. New Delhi.

Bajpai, K D 1989. Bodhisattva and Buddha: The Early Iconic Forms. *Buddhist Iconography* (Sambhota Series 2, Tibet House, New Delhi), pp. 60-68.

Bajpai, K D 1991. Ancient Indian Numismatics : Symbology and the Decorative Aspect. *Numismatic Studies* 1, pp. 111-120.

Baldev Kumar 1973. *The Early Kuṣāṇas*. New Delhi.

Banerjea, J N 1938. Devices on Some Tribal Coins. *Indian Historical Quarterly* 16.

Banerjea, J N 1950. The Obverse Device of Some *Decadrachms* with Alexandrian Association. *Journal of the Numismatic Society of India* 12(2), pp. 118-120.

Banerjea, J N 1951. The Reading and Interpretation of Some Yaudheya Coin Legends. *Journal of the Numismatic Society of India* 13(2), pp. 160-163.

Banerjea, J N 1968. *Religion in Art and Archaeology*. R K Mookerji Endowment Lectures, University of Lucknow, 1961-1962. Lucknow.

Banerjea, J N 2002. *The Development of Hindu Iconography*. 5th ed, New Delhi.

Banerji, R D 1914. A New Type of Audumbara Coinage. *Journal of the Asiatic Society of Bengal* 10, NS 22 (134), pp. 247-250.

Banerji, R D 1933. *The Age of the Imperial Guptas*. Manindra Chandra Nandi Lectures, 1924, revised by the author in 1929-1930. Varanasi.

Barton, George A 1990. *The Religions of the World*. Reprint, New Delhi.

Basham, A L 1953. A New Study of the Śaka-Kuṣāṇa Period (review of J E van Lohuizen-de Leeuw, *The "Scythian" Period*). *Bulletin of the School of Oriental and African Studies* 15, pp. 80-97.

Basham, A L 1957. The Succession of the Line of Kanishka. *Bulletin of the School of Oriental and African Studies* 20, pp. 77-88.

Bayer, T S 1738. *Historia Regni Graecorum Bactriani*. St Petersbourg.

Beckert, Heinz 1995. *When Did Buddha Live. The Controversy of the Dating of the Historical Buddha*. (English translation of *Die Datierung des Historischen Buddha*, 2 vols. Göttingen, 1991-1992). Delhi.

Bhandare, Shailendra 2007. Not Just a Pretty Face : Interpretations of Alexander's Numismatic Imagery in the Hellenic East. H P Ray and Daniel T Potts (ed), *Memory as History—The Legacy of Alexander in Asia*, (New Delhi, 2007), pp. 208-256.

Bhandarkar, D R 1913-1914. Kshatrapa Coins from Sarvania. *Archaeological Survey of India—Annual Report 1913-1914*, pp. 227-245.

Bhandarkar, D R 1981. *Corpus Inscriptionum Indicarum* 3. Inscriptions of the Early Gupta Kings. Ed by B Ch Chhabra and G S Gai. New Delhi.

Bhandarkar, D R 1984. *Carmichael Lectures in Ancient Indian Numismatics*. Reprint, Patna.

Bhandarkar, R G 1928. *Vaishṇavism, Śaivism and Some Minor Religious Systems*. Poona.

Bhatia, Pratipal 1989. Coins. A Ghosh (ed), *An Encyclopaedia of Indian Archaeology* 1 (New Delhi, 1989), pp. 10-14.

Bhattacharji, Sukumari 1970. *The Indian Theogony*. Cambridge.

Bhattacharya, Sibesh 1992. Ghaṭotkacha : The King Kācha of Coins. B Ch Chhabra, P K Agrawala, Ashvini Agrawal, and Shankar Goyal (ed), *Reappraising Gupta History for S R Goyal*, (New Delhi, 1992), pp. 77-82.

Bhattacharyya, P K 1979. Interesting Coins of Śaśāṅka. *Journal of the Royal Asiatic Society of Great Britain and Ireland*, pp. 153-155, and figures.

Bhattasali, N K 1923. Notes on Gupta and Later Gupta Coinages. *Journal of the Asiatic Society of Bengal, Numismatic Supplement* 37, pp. 54-64.

Bhowmik, S K 1965. Conservation of 1400 Kshatrapa Coins Discovered from Amreli. *Journal of the Numismatic Society of India* 27(2), pp. 197-201.

Biswas, Atreyi 1973. *Political History of the Hūṇas in India*. New Delhi.

Bivar, A D H 1953. The Indo-Greek Victory Medallions. *Spink's Numismatic Circular* 61, cols 201-202.

Bivar, A D H 1954. The Inscriptions of Uruzgan. *Journal of the Royal Asiatic Society of Great Britain and Ireland,* pp. 112-118.

Bivar, A D H 1955. Bactrian Treasure of Qunduz. *Journal of the Numismatic Society of India* 17(1), pp. 37-52.

Bivar, A D H 1956. The Kushāṇo-Sassanian Coin Series. *Journal of the Numismatic Society of India* 18, pp. 13-46.

Bivar, A D H 1965. Indo-Bacrtrian Problems. *Numismatic Chronicle* 1965, pp. 73-108.

Bivar, A D H 1970. The Sequence of Menander's Drachmae. *Journal of the Royal Asiatic Society of Great Britain and Ireland*, pp. 123-136, and plates.

Bopearachchi, Osmund 1993. *Indo-Greek, Indo-Scythian and Indo-Parthian Coins in the Smithsonian Institution*. Smithsonian Institution, Washington D C.

Bopearachchi, Osmund 1994. Recent Discoveries : Hoards and Finds of Ancient Coins from Afghanistan and Pakistan. *Yavanika* (Journal of the Indian Society for Greek and Roman Studies) 4, pp. 3-30.

Bopearachchi, Osmund 1997. Nasten, A Hitherto Unknown Iranian Ruler in India. *Studies in Silk Road Coins and Culture* : Papers in the Honour of Professor Ikou Hirayama. The Institute of Silk Road Studies, Kamakura, pp. 67-74.

Bopearachchi, Osmund 2004. Two Rare Pre-Kushan Coins. *Newsletter of the Oriental Numismatic Society* 178, pp. 18-20.

Bopearachchi, Osmund, and Wilfried Pieper 1998. *Ancient Indian Coins*. Brepols, Turnhout.

Bopearachchi, Osmund, and A U Rahman 1995. *Pre-Kushāṇa Coins in Pakistan*. Islamabad.

Brown, C J 1999. *The Coin of India*. Reprint, New Delhi.

Bühler, Georg 1904. *Indian Palaeography from about BC 350 to about AD 1300*. English translation of *Indische Palaeographie von circa 350 A Chr-circa 1300 P Chr* (Strassburg 1896), by J F Fleet, as an appendix to the *Indian Antiquary* 33.

Bühler, Georg 2001. *The Laws of Manu*. Sacred Books of the East 25. Reprint, Delhi.

Burn, Richard 1906. Some Coins of the Maukharis and of the Thanesar Line. *Journal of the Royal Asiatic Society of Great Britain and Ireland,* 1906, pp. 843-850.

Burn, Richard 1945. Coinage Bearing the Names of Indian Queens. *Journal of the Numismatic Society of India* 7, pp. 69-77.

Burns, Craig Alden 1984. Later Kushan Conflict. *Numismatic Digest* 8, pp. 54-66.

Burns, Craig Alden 1985a. 1984 Yields Two Unique Kushan Coins. *Numismatic Digest* 9, pp. 52-54.

Burns, Craig Alden 1985b. Last Kushāṇ Decades. *Numismatic Digest* 9, pp. 55-71.

Burns, Craig Alden 1990. A New Kushāṇa Find. *Journal of the Numismatic Society of India* 52, pp. 7-8, and figures.

Burns, Craig Alden, and Shafqat Mirza 1990. Topi Hoard of Kushāṇa Dīnāras. *Numismatic Digest* 14, pp. 16-21.

Burrow, T 1940. *A Translation of the Kharoshṭhī Documents from Chinese Turkestan*. London.

Chakrabortty, S K 1931. *A Study of Ancient Indian Numismatics* (Indigenous System) from the Earliest Times to the Rise of the Imperial Guptas. Mymensingh.

Chakravarti, Mahadev 1994. *The Concept of Rudra-Śiva through the Ages*. Delhi.

Chamberlain, C C 1960. *Guide to Numismatics*. London.

Chandra, R G 1960. A New *Chakravikrama* of Chandragupta II. *Journal of the Numismatic Society of India* 22, pp. 261-263.

Chatterjee, C D 1931. Some Numismatic Data in Pāli Literature. B C Law (ed), *Buddhistic Studies* 4 (Calcutta), pp. 383ff.

Chatterjee, C D 1933. Some Numismatic Terms in Pāli Texts. *Journal of the U P Historical Society* 6(1), pp. 156-173.

Chatterjee, C D 1957. Some Unique Gold and Brass Coins of the Imperial Guptas. *Bulletin of the U P Historical Society* 2. Lucknow.

Chattopadhyay, Bhaskar 1967. *The Age of the Kushāṇas—A Numismatic Study*. Calcutta.

Chattopadhyay, Bhaskar 1977. *Coins and Icons—A Study of Myths and Symbols in Indian Numismatic Art*. Calcutta.

Chattopadhyaya, Sudhakar 1955. *The Śakas in India*. Santiniketan.

Chattopadhyaya, Sudhakar 1958. *Early History of North India*. Calcutta.

Chhabra, B Ch 1949. A Unique Gold Coin of Chandragupta I. *Journal of the Numismatic Society of India* 11(1), pp. 15-31.

Chhabra, B Ch 1986. *Catalogue of the Gupta Gold Coins of the Bayana Hoard in the National Museum, New Delhi*. New Delhi.

Coomaraswamy, A K 1927. *History of Indian and Indonesian Art*. London.

Coomaraswamy, A K 1928-1929. Early Indian Iconography 2, Śrī-Lakṣmī. *Eastern Art* 1.

Coomaraswamy, A K 2001. *Yakṣas*, 2 parts. Reprint, New Delhi.

Coomaraswamy, A K 2003. *Buddha and the Gospel of Buddhism*. Reprint, New Delhi.

Cowell, E B (ed) 2005. *The Jātaka or Stories of the Buddha's Former Births*. Translated from the Pāli by various hands, 6 vols. Reprint, Delhi.

Cribb, Joe 1980. Kaniṣka's Buddha Coins—The Official Iconography of Śākyamuni and Maitreya. *Journal of the International Association of Buddhist Studies* 3(2), pp. 79-88, and plates.

Cribb, Joe 1982. The Earliest Gaṇeśa : A Case of Mistaken Identity. *Numismatic Digest* 6, pp. 30-32.

Cribb, Joe 1985a. The Late Kushan Type Gold Coins of Mashra. *Coin Hoards* 7, pp. 306-307.

Cribb, Joe 1985b. Indian's Earliest Coins ? *Coins Haords* 7, pp. 278-281.

Cribb, Joe 1999-2000. Kanishka's Buddha Image Coins Revisited. *Silk Road Art and Archaeology* 6, pp. 151-189.

Cribb, Joe 2005. *The Indian Coinage Tradition : Origins, Continuity and Change*. Nashik.

Cribb, Joe, and Nicholas Sims-Williams 1995-1996. A New Bactrian Inscription of Kanishka the Great. *Silk Road Art and Archaeology* 4, The Institute of Silk Road Studies, Kamakura, pp. 75-142.

Cunningham, Alexander 1962. *Later Indo-Scythians*. Reprinted from *Numismatic Chronicle* 1893-1895. Indian reprint, Varanasi.

Cunningham, Alexander 1967. *Coins of Mediaeval India*. Reprint, Delhi.

Cunningham, Alexander 1970. *Coins of Alexander's Successors in the* East. Reprint, Varanasi.

Cunningham, Alexander 1971a. *Coins of the Indo-Scythians, Sakas, Kushans*. Reprinted from *Numismatic Chronicle* 1888-1892. Indian reprint, Varanasi.

Cunningham, Alexander 1971b. *Coins of Ancient India*. Reprint, Varanasi.

Dani, A H 1983. *Chilas—The City of Nanga Parvat*. Islamabad.

Dani, A H 1992. Greek Monograms. D W Macdowall, Savita Sharma, and Sanjay Garg (ed), *Indian Numismatics, History, Art, and Culture* (Essays in the Honour of Dr P L Gupta), (Delhi, 1992), pp. 99-114.

Dani, A H 1997. *Indian Palaeography*. Reprint, New Delhi.

Dar, M B L 1940. Some Rare Pañchāla Coins from the Site of Ancient Ahichchhatra, Bareilly District. *Journal of the Numismatic Society of India* 2, pp. 115-117.

Darmesteter, J 1974. *The Zend-Avesta*, 3 parts. Sacred Books of the East 4, 23, 31. Reprint, Delhi.

Dasgupta, C C 1958. *The Development of the Kharoṣṭhī Script*. Calcutta.

Dasgupta, K K 1974. *A Tribal History of Ancient India—A Numismatic Approach*. Calcutta.

Davary, G Djelani, and Helmut Humbach 1976. *Die Baktrische Inschrift IDN 1 von Dasht-e Nāwūr (Afghanistan). Akademie der Wissenschaften und der Literatur, Abhandlungen der Geistes- und Sozialwissenschaftlichen Klasse*, Jahrgang 1976, Nr. 1 (Wiesbaden), pp. 3-21.

Deb, H K 1934. Indo-Greek Coin-Types. *Indian Historical Quarterly*, pp. 509-522.

Decourdemanche, J-A 1912. *Note sur Les Anciennes Monnaies de L'Inde Dites 'Punch-Marked' Coins et sur Le Système de Manou. Journal Asiatique* January-February 1912, pp. 117-132.

Devahuti, D 1964. The Coins of Harsha Śīlāditya—A Reappraisal. *Journal of the Numismatic Society of India* 26(1), pp. 40-46.

Devahuti, D 2001. *Harsha—A Political Study*. New Delhi.

Deyell, J S 1984. Indo-Greek and Kshaharāta Coins from the Gujerat Seacoast. *Numismatic Chronicle*, pp. 115-127.

Dhavalikar, M K 1975. The Beginning of Coinage in India. *World Archaeology* 6(3), (London), pp. 330-338.

Diringer, David 2005. *The Alphabet : A Key to the History of Mankind*. Reprint, New Delhi.

Dobbins, K W 1970. The Question of the Imitation Hermaios Coinage. *East and West* 20, pp. 307-326.

Dobbins, K W 1973. *Śaka-Pahlava Coinage*. Memoirs of the Numismatic Society of India 5. Varanasi.

Dobbins, K W 1980. *A Schema of Indo-Baktrian Coinage*. Numismatic Notes and Monographs (Numismatic Society of India) 18. Varanasi.

Durr, Niklaus 1978. New Porus Commemoratives. Translated from the original Swiss by Angelika Ilsch. *Numismatic Digest* 2(1), pp. 4-6, and figures on pp. 8-9.

Eliade, M 1958. *Patterns in Comparative Religion.* Sheed and Ward.

Eliade, M 1961. *Myths, Dreams and Mysteries.* New York.

Feller, Danielle 2004. *The Sanskrit Epics' Representation of Vedic Myths.* Delhi.

Fleet, J F 1888. *Corpus Inscriptionum Indicarum* 3. Inscriptions of the Early Gupta Kings and their Successors. Calcutta.

Foss, Michael 1995. *Gods and Heroes : The Story of Greek Mythology.* London.

Foucher, Alfred 2003. *The Life of the Buddha, according to the Ancient Texts and Monuments of India.* Reprint, New Delhi.

Frey, A R 1973. *Dictionary of Numismatic Names.* Reprint, London.

Furdoonjee, D J Paruck 1976. *Sassanian Coins.* New Delhi.

Fussman, G 1974. *Documents Épigraphiques Kouchans, "I. –Inscriptions et Antiquités du Dašt-e Nāwur". Bulletin de l'Ecole Francaise d'Extreme-Orient* 61, pp. 2-50.

Gadre, A S 1939. Important Coins from Baroda State. *Journal of the Numismatic Society of India* 1, pp. 20-26.

Gardner, Percy 1878. *Catalogue of the Coins of the Seleukid Kings, in the British Museum, London.* London.

Gardner, Percy 1887. New Greek Coins of Bactria and India. *Numismatic Chronicle*, pp. 177-181.

Gardner, Percy 1918. *A History of Ancient Coinage (700 BC – 300 BC).* Oxford.

Gardner, Percy 1971. *Catalogue of the Coins of the Greek and Scythic Kings of Bactria and India, in the British Museum, London.* Indian Reprint, New Delhi.

Ghirshman, Roman 1948. *Begram. Mémoires de la Délégation Archéologique Française en Afghanistan* 13. Cairo.

Ghosh, A 1943. Coins of Varuṇamitra of Ahichchhatrā. *Journal of the Numismatic Society of India* 5, pp. 17-18.

Ghosh, A (ed) 1989. *An Encyclopaedia of Indian Archaeology*, 2 vols. New Delhi.

Gokhale, Shobhana 1976. Ranjangaon Hoard of Kshatrapa Coins. *Journal of the Numismatic Society of India* 38(1), pp. 27-37.

Gonda, Jan 1993. *Aspects of Early Viṣṇuism*. Reprint, Delhi.

Gopal, Lallanji 1989. Kharoṣṭhī. A Ghosh (ed), *An Encyclopaedia of Indian Archaeology* 1 (New Delhi, 1989), pp. 368-369.

Gopal, Lallanji, and T P Verma 1989. Brāhmī and its Derivatives. A Ghosh (ed), *An Encyclopaedia of Indian Archaeology* 1 (New Delhi, 1989), pp. 365-368.

Goyal, S R 1984. *A Religious History of Ancient India* 1. Meerut.

Goyal, S R 1986. *A Religious History of Ancient India* 2. Meerut.

Goyal. S R 1994. *Indigenous Coins of Early India*. Jodhpur.

Goyal, S R 1995a. *The Dynastic Coins of Ancient India*. Jodhpur.

Goyal, S R 1995b. *The Coinage of Ancient India*. Jodhpur.

Goyal, S R 2005. *The Imperial Guptas*. Jodhpur.

Graves, Robert 1955. *The Greek Myths*, 2 vols. Penguin.

Graves, Robert 1960. *Larousse Encyclopaedia of Mythology*. London.

Griswold, H D 1999. *The Religion of the Ṛigevda*. Reprint, Delhi.

Gupta C S 1971. A Coin of the City State of Tagara. *Journal of the Numismatic Society of India* 33(2), pp. 37-40.

Gupta, C S 1982. Foreign Denominations of Early Indian Coins. A M Shastri (ed), *Foreign Elements in Indian Indigenous Coins*. Memoirs of the Numismatic Society of India 8, (Varanasi, 1982), pp. 109-123.

Gupta, C S 1983. Gupta Lead Coins. *Numismatic Digest* 7, pp. 56-59.

Gupta, C S 1993. Repoussé Technique of Minting Coins. *Numismatic Studies* 3, pp. 60-84.

Gupta, L C 1983. Prajapati Akhyasya : A New Name in Kuṇinda Coinage. *Journal of the Numismatic Society of India* 45, pp. 16-19.

Gupta, P L 1950. The Coins of Rāmagupta. *Journal of the Numismatic Society of India* 12(2), pp. 103-111.

Gupta, P L 1954. An Unexplained Archer Type Coin of Samudragupta. *Journal of the Numismatic Society of India* 16(1), pp. 102-104.

Gupta, P L 1958. The City-goddess of Pushkalāvatī. *Journal of the Numismatic Society of India* 20(1), pp. 68-70.

Gupta, P L 1960. Numismatic Data in the Arthaśāstra of Kauṭalya. *Journal of the Numismatic Society of India* 22, pp. 13-37.

Gupta, P L 1969. *Coin Hoards from Gujarat State*. Varanasi.

Gupta, P L 1973. A Kushāṇa Coin with Brāhmī Legend. *Journal of the Numismatic Society of India* 35, pp. 123-126.

Gupta, P L 1977. Coins of the Ārjunāyanas. *Numismatic Digest* 1(1), pp. 14-18.

Gupta, P L 1978. Editor's note on Niklaus Durr, New Porus Commemoratives. *Numismatic Digest* 2(1), pp. 6-7, and figures on pp. 8-9.

Gupta, P L 1980. Western Kshatrapa Coins from Karnataka. *Numismatic Digest* 4(2), pp. 10-12.

Gupta, P L 1987. The Brahmaṇya Coins. *Numismatic Digest* 11, pp. 28-39.

Gupta, P L 1988. *Numismatic History of Himachal Pradesh and the Catalogue of Coins in Himachal Pradesh State Museum, Shimla, and Bhuri Singh Museum, Chamba*. Delhi.

Gupta, P L 1992. Barwani Hoard of Silver Punch-marked Coins. *Numismatic Digest* 16, pp. 6-23.

Gupta, P L 1993. A New Gold Coin Type of Kumāragupta I. *Numismatic Digest* 17, pp. 37-39.

Gupta, P L 1994. Silver Punch-marked Coins of Magadha. *Numismatic Digest* 18, pp. 1-18.

Gupta, P L 1996. Narhan Hoard of Silver Punchmarked Coins. *Numismatic Digest* 20, pp. 1-24.

Gupta, P L 1998. *The Imperial Guptas* 1. Varanasi.

Gupta, P L 2004. *Coins*. Reprint, NBT, New Delhi.

Gupta, P L, and Terry Hardaker 1985. *Ancient Indian Silver Punch-marked Coins of the Magadha-Maurya Kārshāpaṇa Series*. Nasik.

Gupta, P L, and Sarojini Kulashreshtha 2004. *Kuṣāṇa Coins and History*. New Delhi.

Hamid, Maulvi Muhammad, *et al* 1922. *Catalogue of the Museum of Archaeology at Sanchi*. Bhopal State.

Handa, Devendra 2003-2004. Coins of King Magha. *Numismatic Digest* 27-28, pp. 39-42.

Handa, Devendra 2005-2006. Huvishka's Buddha Image Gold Coin. *Numismatic Digest* 29-30, pp. 53-58.

Handa, Devendra 2007a. *Tribal Coins of Ancient India*. New Delhi.

Handa, Devendra 2007b. *Coins and Temples : Numismatic Evidence on the Evolution of Temple Architecture*. Bombay.

Hardaker, Terry 2005-2006. "Punchmarked" Coins with no Punchmarks ? A Puzzling New Find. *Numismatic Digest* 29-30, pp. 1-6.

Hardaker, Terry, and P L Gupta 1985. See under Gupta, P L, and Terry Hardaker 1985.

Haughton, H L 1943. A Note on the Distribution of Indo-Greek Coins. *Numismatic Chronicle*, pp 50-59.

Haughton, H L 1946. Notes on Greek and Kushan Coins from the North-West Frontier of India : (a) The Bajaur Hoard of 1942; (b) Some Rare Copper Coins from the North-West Frontier of India. *Numismatic Chronicle*, pp. 141-145.

Haughton, H L 1948. The Silver Coinage of Strato and of Agathocleia. *Numismatic Chronicle*, pp. 134ff.

Haughton, H L 1958. *Sale Catalogue*. Sotheby London. 1st May 1958.

Head, Barclay V 1906. The Earliest Graeco-Bactrian and Graeco-Indian Coins. *Numismatic Chronicle*, pp. 1-16.

Head, Barclay V 1911. *Historia Numorum*. London.

Head, Barclay V 1932. *A Guide to the Principal Coins of the Greeks*. London.

Herzfeld, Ernst 1932. *Sakastan*. Berlin.

Herzfeld, Ernst 1998. *Kushano-Sasanian Coins*. Memoirs of the Archaeological Survey of India 34. Reprint, New Delhi.

Hill, G F 1906. *Historical Greek Coins*. London.

Hill, G F 1909. *Historical Roman Coins*. London.

Hillebrandt, Alfred 1999. *Vedic Mythology*. Translated from the original German, *Vedische Mythologie* (2nd revised edition, Breslau, 1927, 1929), by S R Sarma, 2 vols. Reprint, Delhi.

Hirano, Shinji 1999-2000. Novel Types of Local Punch-marked Coins. *Numismatic Digest* 23-24, pp. 1-6.

Hirano, Shinji 2005-2006. A Hoard of Early Magadhan Coins from Fatuha (Bihar). *Numismatic Digest* 29-30, pp. 15-26.

Hirano, Shinji, and Sharad Sharma 2007. A Hoard of Early Local Punchmarked Coins of Magadha Janapada. *Numismatic Digest* 31, pp. 1-16.

Holt, Fr 1980. The Euthydemid Coinage of Bactria : Further Hoard Evidence from Ai Khanum. *Revue Numismatique*, pp. 7-44.

Hopkins, E W 1902. *Religions of India*. London.

Hopkins, E W 1915. *Epic Mythology*. Strassburg.

Hopkins, E W 1987. Family Life and Social Customs as they appear in the Sūtras. Chapter X, in E J Rapson (ed), *The Cambridge History of India* 1, (reprint, New Delhi, 1987), pp. 203-223.

Huntington, J C 1993. A Re-examination of a Kanishka Period Tetradrachm Coin Type with an Image of Metrago/Maitreya on the Reverse (Göbl 793. 1) and a Brief Notice on the Importance of the Inscription Relative to Bactro-Gandhāran Buddhist Iconography of the Period. *The Journal of the International Association of Buddhist Studies* 16(2), pp. 355-374.

Huxley, George 1983. Geography in the *Acts of Thomas*. *Greek, Roman and Byzantine Studies* 24, pp. 71-80.

Iyengar, T R 2003. *Dictionary of Hindu Gods and Goddesses*. New Delhi.

Jain, B C 1960. Hitherto Unknown Repoussé Coins of Kramāditya. *Journal of the Numismatic Society of India* 22, pp. 184-187.

Jain, J C 1984. *Life in Ancient India, as Depicted in the Jaina Canon and Commentaries*. 2nd ed, New Delhi.

Jaiswal, Suvira 1981. *The Origin and Development of Vaiṣṇavism*. New Delhi.

Jayaswal, K P 1920. The Statue of Wema Kadphises and Kushan Chronology. *Journal of the Bihar and Orissa Research Society* 6, pp. 12-22.

Jayaswal, K P 1933. *History of India, 150 AD – 350 AD*. Lahore.

Jayaswal, K P 1988. *Hindu Polity*. Reprint, Patna.

Jenkins, G K 1955. Indo-Scythic Mints. *Journal of the Numismatic Society of India* 17(2), pp. 1ff.

Jenkins, G K 1959. The Apollodotos Question : Another View. *Journal of the Numismatic Society of India* 21, pp. 20-33.

Jenkins, G K 1977. Kushan Coins from Iraq. *Numismatic Digest* 1(2), pp. 26-29.

Jenkins, G K, and A K Narain 1957. *The Coin-types of the Śaka-Pahlava Kings of India*. Numismatic Notes and Monographs (Numismatic Society of India) 4. Varanasi.

Jha, Amiteshwar, and Dilip Rajgor 1994. *Studies in the Coinage of the Western Kshatrapas*. Nashik.

Joshi, M C 1962. Kuṇinda Coinage : A Review (with Special Reference to Later Series). *Bhāratīya Vidyā* 22 (1-4), pp. 45-50.

Joshi, M P 1989. *Morphogenesis of Kuṇindas—A Numsimatic Overview*. Almora.

Junge, Ewald 1984. *World Coin Encyclopaedia*. London.

Kangle, R P 2000. *The Kauṭilīya Arthaśāstra*, 3 parts. Reprint, Delhi.

Keith, A B 1987. The Period of the Later Saṁhitās, the Brāhmaṇas, the Āraṇyakas, and the Upanishads. Chapter V, in E J Rapson (ed), *The Cambridge History of India* 1, (reprint, New Delhi, 1987), pp. 102-133.

Kerényi, C 1951. *The Gods of the Greeks*. Translated from the original German text by Norman Cameron. London, New York.

Konow, Sten 1929. *Corpus Inscriptionum Indicarum*, 2(1). Kharoshṭhī Inscriptions with the Exceptions of those of Aśoka. Calcutta.

Konow, Sten 1933. Notes on Indo-Scythian Chronology. *Journal of Indian History* 12, pp. 1-46.

Kosambi, D D 1965. *The Culture and Civilization of Ancient India*. London.

Kosambi, D D 1992. *Indian Numismatics*. Reprint, New Delhi.

Kothari, Narendra 1991. New Kauśāmbī Coins. *Numismatic Digest* 15, pp. 10-17.

Kothari, Narendra, and M Morrison 1990. Coins of Agnimitra of Pañchāla. *Numismatic Digest* 14, pp. 4-9.

Kovalenko S 1995-1996. The Coinage of Diodotus I and Diodotus II, Greek Kings of Bactria. *Silk Road Art and Archaeology* 4, The Institute of Silk Road Studies, Kamakura, pp. 17-74.

Kraay, Colin M 1985. Demetrius in Bactria and India. *Numismatic Digest* 9, pp. 12-30.

Kulashreshtha, Sarojini 1986. Coins of Vāsishka—Historical Implications. *Numismatic Digest* 10, pp. 70-80.

Kulashreshtha, Sarojini, and P L Gupta 2004. See under Gupta, P L, and Sarojini Kulashreshtha 2004.

Kumar, Manmohan 1978. A Unique Gupta Copper Coin from Sanghol. *Prāchya Pratibhā* 6(1), pp. 67-70.

Kundu, Pulak 1982. Indian Deities on Bactrian and Indo-Greek Coins. *Journal of the Numismatic Society of India* 45, pp. 130-135.

Lahiri, A N 1954. Coins of Queen Agathocleia and the Attribution of the Legendless Indo-Greek *Staters*. *Journal of the Numismatic Society of India* 16(2), pp. 189-196.

Lahiri, A N 1965. *Corpus of Indo-Greek Coins*. Calcutta.

Lahiri, A N 1971. Early Indigenous Coins of Northern India. D C Sircar (ed), *Early Indian Indigenous Coins*, (Calcutta, 1971), pp. 48-77.

Lahiri, A N 1973. Archaic Coins from Northern India. *Journal of the Numismatic Society of India* 35, pp. 1-38.

Lahiri, A N 1977. The So-called Joint Coins of the Indo-Greeks. *Journal of the Numismatic Society of India* 39, pp. 69-76.

Lahiri, A N 1995. The Zeus Devices on Indo-Greek Coins : A Religio-Mythical Study. *Yavanikā* 5, pp. 3-12.

Lahiri, Bela 1974. *Indigenous States of Northern India (*circa *200 BC to 320 AD)*. Calcutta.

Lahiri, Bela 1976. India's Earliest Inscribed Coins : The City Issues. *Journal of the Numismatic Society of India* 38(2), pp. 35-54.

Lal, B B 1997. *The Earliest Civilization of South Asia*. New Delhi.

van Lohuizen-de Leeuw, J E 1949. *The "Scythian" Period : An Approach to the History, Art, Epigraphy and Palaeography of North India from the 1st century BC to the 3rd century AD*. Leiden.

Lüders, Heinrich 1961. *Mathura Inscriptions*, edited by K L Janert. Gottingen.

MacDonald, D, and R C Senior 1998. *The Decline of the Indo-Greeks—A Re-appraisal of the Chronology from the Time of Menander to that of Azes*. Hellenic Numismatic Society, Monograph Series 2.

Macdonald, George 1987a. Ancient Greek (Athenian and Macedonian) Coins in India. Appendix to Chapter XV, in E J Rapson (ed), *The Cambridge History of India* 1, (reprint, New Delhi, 1987), pp. 346-350.

Macdonald, George 1987b. The Hellenic Kingdoms of Syria, Bactria, and Parthia. Chapter XVII, in E J Rapson (ed), *The Cambridge History of India* 1, (reprint, New Delhi, 1987), pp. 384-419.

Macdonell, A A 1897. *Vedic Mythology*. Strassbourg.

Macdonell, A A, and A B Keith 1995. *Vedic Index of Names and Subjects*, 2 vols. Reprint, Delhi.

MacDowall, D W 1968. *Soter Megas*, the King of Kings, the Kushāṇa. *Journal of the Numismatic Society of India* 30, pp. 28-48.

MacDowall, D W 2002. The Rabatak Inscription and the Nameless Kushan King, in *Cairo to Kabul : Afghan and Islamic Studies Presented to Ralph Pinder-Wilson* (London), pp. 163-169.

MacDowall, D W 2003-2004. Heliocles I the Greek King of Bactria. *Numismatic Digest* 27-28, pp. 31-38.

Maheshwari, K K 1978. New Tribal and Monarchical Coin. *Numismatic Digest* 2(2), pp. 14-23.

Maity, S K 1970a. *The Economic Life of Northern India, in the Gupta Period (*circa *AD 300 - 550)*. 2nd ed, Delhi.

Maity, S K 1970b. *Early Indian Coins and Currency System*. New Delhi.

Majumdar, N G 1928-1929. Notes on the Coins of Azes. *Archaeological Survey of India—Annual Review* 1928-1929, pp. 169-174.

Majumdar, R C 1960. *The Classical Accounts of India*. Calcutta.

Majumdar, R C 1988. The Disintegration of the Empire. Chapter V, in R C Majmudar, A D Pusalker, and A K Majumdar (ed), *The Classical Age*. The History and Culture of the Indian People 3, (Bombay, 1988), pp. 33-41.

Majumdar, R C, A D Pusalker, and A K Majumdar (ed) 1980. *The Age of Imperial Unity*. The History and Culture of the Indian People 2. Bombay.

Majumdar, R C, A D Pusalker, and A K Majumdar (ed) 1988. *The Classical Age*. The History and Culture of the Indian People 3. Bombay.

Majumdar, R C, and A S Altekar (ed) 1986. *The Vākāṭaka-Gupta Age (c 200 – 550 AD)*. A New History of the Indian People 6. Delhi.

Majumdar, R C, and K K Dasgupta (ed) 1981. *A Comprehensive History of India (AD 300 – 985)* 3(1). New Delhi.

Mani, B R 1978. Determining the Type and Substantival Attribution of *Kāḍasa* Coins. *Journal of the Numismatic Society of India* 40, pp. 9-12.

Mani, B R 1981. New Evidence Concerning Gold Prototype Silver Coins of the Gupta Emperors. *Journal of the Numismatic Society of India* 43(2), pp. 54-59.

Mann, Richard D 2007. Yaudheya Chronology and Coinage : An Analysis. *Numismatic Digest* 31, pp. 47-113.

Marshall, J H 1936. *A Guide to Taxila*. 3rd ed, Delhi.

Marshall, J H 1947. Greeks and Śakas in India. *Journal of the Royal Asiatic Society of Great Britain and Ireland*, pp. 3ff.

Marshall, J H 1960. *The Buddhist Art of Gandhāra*. Memoirs of the Department of Archaeology in Pakistan 1. Cambridge.

Marshall, J H 1975. *Taxila*, 3 vols. Indian Reprint, Delhi.

McCrindle, J W 1896. *Invasion of India by Alexander the Great, as described by Arrian, Q Curtius, Diodoros, Plutarch, and Justin*. New edition, Westminster.

McCrindle, J W 1901. *Ancient India as described in Classical Literature*. Westminster.

Mirashi, V V 1939. Gold Coins of Three Kings of the Nala Dynasty. *Journal of the Numismatic Society of India* 1, pp. 29-35.

Mirashi, V V 1963. Were *Dramma* Coins Issued in Gold ? *Journal of the Numismatic Society of India* 25(2), pp. 238-240.

Mirashi, V V 1973. Dahigaon Hoard of Kshatrapa and Traikūṭaka Coins. *Journal of the Numismatic Society of India* 35, pp. 118-122.

Mirashi, V V 1982. *Sātavāhanoṁ aura Paśchimī Kshatrapoṁ kā Itihāsa aura Abhilekha* (Hindi). Lucknow.

Misra, R N 1981. *Yaksha Cult and Iconography*. New Delhi.

Mitchiner, Michael 1973. *The Origins of Indian Coinage*. London.

Mitchiner, Michael 1975-1976. *Indo-Greek and Indo-Scythian Coinage*, 9 vols. London.

Mitchiner, Michael 1978. *Oriental Coins and their Values* 2 : *The Ancient and Classical World*. London.

Mitchiner, Michael 2001-2002. The Kushan King, Vima Takshuma, Son of Kujula Kadphises : A Discussion of his Name. *Numismatic Digest* 25-26, pp. 43-50.

von Mitterwallner, Gritli 1986. *Kuṣāṇa Coins and Kuṣāṇa Sculptures from Mathurā*. Mathura.

von Mitterwallner, Gritli 1994. The Sargodha Hoard of Late Kuṣāṇa Coins in the Lahore Museum. *Numismatic Digest* 18, pp. 27-68.

Monier-Williams, Monier 2005. *A Sanskrit-English Dictionary*. Reprint, Delhi.

Mookerji, R K 1943. Some Aspects of Gupta Coinage. *Journal of the Numismatic Society of India* 5, pp. 151-152.

Mookerji, R K 1973. *The Gupta Empire*. 5th ed, Delhi.

Mukherjee, B N 1960. The Prototype of an Obverse Device of Kushāṇa Coinage. *Journal of the Numismatic Society of India* 22, pp. 109-112.

Mukherjee, B N 1967. *The Kushāṇa Genealogy*. Studies in Kushāṇa Genealogy and Chronology 1. Calcutta.

Mukherjee, B N 1969a. *An Agrippan Source—A Study in Indo-Parthian History*. Calcutta.

Mukherjee, B N 1969b. *Nana on Lion A Study in Kushāṇa Numismatic Art*. Calcutta.

Mukherjee, B N 1972. *The Pāradas*. Calcutta.

Mukherjee, B N 1978. A Note on Reverse Devices on Coins of Kanishka I and His Successors. *Numismatic Digest* 2(2), pp. 34-43.

Mukherjee, B N 1981. *Mathura and its Society—The Śaka-Pahlava Phase*. Calcutta.

Mukherjee, B N 1982a. Numismatic Art. Appendix to Chapter XXXV, in R C Majumdar and K K Dasgupta (ed), *A Comprehensive History of India (AD 300 – 985)* 3(2), (New Delhi, 1982), pp. 1415-1433.

Mukherjee, B N 1982b. Impact of the Kushāṇa Coinage on Early Indian Indigenous Coins. A M Shastri (ed), *Foreign Elements in Indian Indigenous Coins*. Memoirs of the Numismatic Society of India 8, (Varanasi, 1982), pp. 13-26.

Mukherjee, B N 1983. An Interesting Scytho-Parthian Coin. *Journal of the Numismatic Society of India* 45, pp. 27-30.

Mukherjee, B N 1985. *Art in Gupta and Post-Gupta Coinages*. Lucknow.

Mukherjee, B N 1987. Amitābha on Kushāṇa Coins. *Journal of the Numismatic Society of India* 49, pp. 44-45, and plate.

Mukherjee, B N 1995. The Great Kushāṇa Testament. *Indian Museum Bulletin* 30. Calcutta.

Mukherjee, B N 1997-1998. Vima Taktu, An Alleged Kushana King. *Numismatic Digest* 21-22, pp. 5-10.

Mukherjee, B N 1999-2000. *Śatamāna* and *Kārshāpaṇa*. *Numismatic Digest* 23-24, pp. 13-16.

Mukherjee, B N, and P K D Lee 1988. *The Technology of Indian Coinage*. Calcutta.

Murphy, Paul 2003-2004. A New Punchmarked Hoard from the Mathura Region. *Numismatic Digest* 27-28, pp. 19-29.

Nagar, M M 1949. A Rhinoceros-slayer Type Coin of Kumāragupta I. *Journal of the Numismatic Society of India* 11(1), pp. 7-8.

Narain, A K 1953. Remarkable Discovery of Some Indo-Greek Victory Medallions. *Journal of the Numismatic Society of India* 15(2), p. 213.

Narain, A K 1955. *The Coin-types of the Indo-Greek Kings*. Numismatic Notes and Monographs (Numismatic Society of India) 1. Bombay.

Narain, A K 1957a. *The Indo-Greeks*. Oxford.

Narain, A K 1957b. A Note on *Kārshāpaṇa*. *Journal of the Numismatic Society of India* 19(2), pp. 181-183.

Narain, A K 1973. The Two Hindu Divinities on the Coins of Agathocles from Ai-Khanum. *Journal of the Numismatic Society of India* 35, pp. 73-77.

Narain, A K 1993. Approaches and Perspectives. Presidential Address to the First International Conference of the Indian Society of Greek and Roman Studies, 1991. U P Arora (ed), *Milinda*, (Bareilly, 1993), pp. 5-34.

Narain, Sudha 1956. The Twenty-*Stater* Gold Piece of Eukratides I. *Journal of the Numismatic Society of India* 18(2), pp. 217-218.

Neumann, Erich 1955. *The Great Mother : An Analysis of the Archetype*. London.

Newell, E T 1938. *The Coinage of the Eastern Seleucid Mints*. Numismatic Sudies 1. New York.

Newell, E T 1941. *The Coinage of the Western Seleucid Mints*. Numismatic Studies 4. New York.

Nigam, L S 1987. Numismatography of Repoussé Gold Coins. *Vājapeya* (Prof K D Bajpai Felicitation Volume), (Delhi), pp. 155-159.

Nigam, L S 1988. Rare Silver and Copper Repoussé Coins of Prasannamātra. *Journal of the Numismatic Society of India* 50, pp. 30-32.

Noss, John B 1949. *Man's Religions*. (Macmillan) New York.

O'Flaherty, W D 1975. The Hindu Symbolism of Cows, Bulls, Stallions, and Mares. *Art and Archaeology Research Papers* 8, pp. 1-7.

Oikonomides, A L N 1973. Soter the Great—The Last of the Indo-Greek Kings. *Journal of the Numismatic Society of India* 35, pp. 82-89.

Ojha, G H 1959. *Bhāratīya Prāchīna Lipimālā* (Hindi). Delhi.

Pandey, D B 1957. Six-headed Kṛittikā on Yaudheya Coins. *Journal of the Numismatic Society of India* 29(1), pp. 5-8.

Pandey, D B 1971. The Hydaspese-Battle Commemorative Medal of Alexander the Great—A Fresh Approach. *Journal of the Numismatic Society of India* 33(2), pp. 1-7.

Pandey, D B 1975. A Note on the Hāriṇī in the Śrī-sūkta and the Antelope on the Coins of the Kuṇinda King Amoghabhūti. *Journal of the Numismatic Society of India* 37, pp. 20-24.

Pandey, Rajbali 1953. *Indian Palaeography*. Varanasi.

Pandey, Rajbali 1988. *Hindu Dharmakośa* (Hindi). Lucknow.

Pandya, A V 1965. A Find of Kshatrapa Coins from Deva in Gujarat. *Journal of the Numismatic Society of India* 27(1), pp. 96-97.

Pathak, V S 1986. Motifs on Gupta Coins and Sassanian Wares. *Numismatic Digest* 10, pp. 81-90.

Pathak, V S 1988-1989. Motifs on Gupta Coins and Sassanian Wares – II. *Numismatic Digest* 12-13, pp. 40-62.

Petitot-Biehler, C Y 1975. *Le Trésor d'Aï Khanoum. Revue Numismatique*, pp. 23-57.

Pieper, Wilfried 2005. Achyu Coins of Ahichhatra and Their Late 4th Century Derivatives. *Newsletter of the Oriental Numismatic Society* 184, pp. 13-14.

Pinsent, John 1969. *The Greek Mythology*. London.

Pires, E A 1934. *The Maukharis*. Madras.

Powell-Price, J C 1945. Kuṇindas and Katyuras. *Journal of the UP Historical Society* 18, pp. 214-218.

Prinsep, James 1858. *Essays on Indian Antiquities, Historic, Numismatic, and Palaeographic*. Edited by E Thomas, 2 vols. London.

Puri, B N 1965. *Indian under the Kushāṇas*. Bombay.

Radin, Paul 1955. *Monotheism among Primitive Peoples*. Allen and Unwin.

Rajgor, Dilip 1988-1989. Coin of an Unknown Kshaharāta Kshatrapa. *Numismatic Digest* 12-13, pp. 12-16.

Rajgor, Dilip 1991. Recent Researches in Kṣatrapa Numismatics. *Numismatic Studies* 1, pp. 33-44.

Rajgor, Dilip 1992. An Inventory of Dates known on the Coins and Inscriptions of the Western Kshatrapas. *Numismatic Studies* 2, pp. 87-105.

Rajgor, Dilip 2001. *Punch-marked Coins of Early Historic India*. San Jose (California), USA.

Rajgor, Dilip, and Amiteshwar Jha 1994. See under Jha, Amiteshwar, and Dilip Rajgor 1994.

Rao, Dinkar 1977. Two Unidentified Ancient Coins. *Numismatic Digest* 1(1), pp. 34-38.

Rao, S R 1966. Excavations at Amreli, A Kshatrapa-Gupta Town. *Bulletin of Museums and Picture Gallery* (Baroda) 18, pp. 1-114.

Rao, T A Gopinatha 1985. *Elements of Hindu Iconography*, 2 vols. Reprint, Delhi.

Rapson, E J 1897. *Indian Coins*. Strassburg.

Rapson, E J 1904. Ancient Silver Coins from Baluchistan. *Numismatic Chronicle* 1904, pp. 311-325.

Rapson, E J 1905. Indian Coins and Seals, part 6. *Journal of the Royal Asiatic Society of Great Britain and Ireland*, pp. 783-814.

Rapson, E J 1906. Coins of the Graeco-Indian Sovereigns Agathocleia, Strato I Soter, and Strato II Philopator. *Corolla Numismatica* (Numismatic Essays in Honour of Barclay V Head), (Oxford, 1906), pp. 245-258.

Rapson, E J 1914. *Ancient India, from the Earliest Times to the First Century AD*. London.

Rapson, E J 1975. *Catalogue of the Coins of the Andhra Dynasty, the Western Kṣatrapas, the Traikūṭaka Dynasty, and the "Bodhi" Dynasty, in the British Museum, London*. Indian reprint, New Delhi.

Rapson, E J (ed) 1987. *The Cambridge History of India* 1. Indian reprint, Delhi.

Raven, E M 1994. *Gupta Gold Coins with a* Garuḍa-*Banner (Samudragupta to Skandagupta)*, 2 vols. New Delhi.

Rawlinson, H G 1912. *Bactria, the History of a Forgotten Empire*. London.

Rawlinson, H G 1916. *Intercourse between India and the Western World*. Cambridge.

Raychaudhuri, H C 1972. *Political History of Ancient India*, from the Accession of Parīkshita to the Extinction of the Gupta Dynasty. 7th ed, Calcutta.

Rhodes, Nicholas, and Ujjwal Saha 2006. Two Copper Aśvamedha Coins of Chandra Gupta II (*c* 380-414 AD). *Newsline of the Indian Institute of Research in Numismatic Studies* 51, p. 6.

le Rider, G 1967. *Monnaise de Taxila et d'Arachosie, Une Nouvelle Reine de Taxila. Revue des Études Grecques* 80, pp. 331-342.

Rose, H J 1958. *A Handbook of Greek Mythology, including its Extension to Rome*. London.

Rosenfield, J M 1967. *The Dynastic Arts of the Kushāṇas*. University of California Press.

Rostovtzeff, M 1957. The Social and Economic History of the Roman Empire, 2 vols. Oxford.

Sachau, Edward 1887. *Al-Beruni's India* (English translation of Al-Beruni's *Tahqīq-i-Hind*). London.

Sahai, Bhagwant 1975. *The Iconography of Some Minor Hindu and Buddhist Deities*. Delhi.

Sahni, Birbal 1945. *The Technique of Casting Coins in Ancient India*. Bombay.

von Sallet, A 1883. *Die Nachfolger Alexanders des Grossen in Bactrien und Indien*. Berlin.

Salomon, Richard 1982. The 'Avaca' Inscription and the Origin of the Vikrama Era. *Journal of the American Oriental Society* 102(1), pp. 59-68.

Salomon, Richard 1986. The Inscription of Senavarma, King of Oḍi. *Indo-Iranian Journal* 29, pp. 261-293.

Salomon, Richard 1996. An Inscribed Silver Buddhist Reliquary of the Time of King Kharaosta and Prince Indravarman. *Journal of the American Oriental Society* 116(3), pp. 418-452.

Salomon, Richard 1998. *Indian Epigraphy*. New Delhi.

Saraswati, Swami Omanand VS 2031. *Ancient Seals of Haryana*. Jhajjar.

Saraswati, Omanand VS 2036. *Ancient Mints of Haryana*. Jhajjar.

Sastri, K A N (ed) 1957. *A Comprehensive History of India* 2. Indian History Congress. Place of publication, not mentioned.

Satya Shrava 1981. *The Śakas in India*. New Delhi.

Satya Shrava 1985. *The Kushāṇa Numismatics*. New Delhi.

Schoder, Raymond V (nd). *Masterpieces of Greek Art*. London.

Schoff, W H 2001. *The Periplus of the Erythraean Sea*. Reprint, New Delhi.

Scott, H R 1898-1901. Description of Hoard of 1200 Coins of the Kshatrapa Kings of Dates 203-376 AD found in Kathiawar. *Journal of the Bombay Branch of the Royal Asiatic Society* 20, pp. 201-210.

Scott, H R 1908. The Nasik (Jogelthembi) Hoard of Nahapāna's Coins. *Journal of the Bombay Branch of the Royal Asiatic Society* 22, pp. 223-244.

Seltman, Charles 1955. *Greek Coins*. 2nd ed, London.

Senior, R C 1995. Posthumous Hermaeus Coinage : Transition from Indo-Greeks to Indo-Scythians. *Numismatic Digest* 19, pp. 43-72.

Senior, R C 1996. The Apracharajas and their Coinage. *Numismatic Digest* 20, pp. 33-40.

Senior, R C 2001. *Indo-Scythian Coins and History*, 3 vols. Lancaster, Pennsylvania, London.

Senior, R C 2003. More Unpublished Indo-Greek Coins. *Newsletter of the Oriental Numismatic Society* 175, pp. 9-11.

Senior, R C, and D MacDonald 1998. See under MacDonald, D, and R C Senior 1998.

Shah, U P 1952. Numismatic Data in Early Jaina Literature. *Journal of the Numismatic Society of India* 14, pp. 107-110.

Sharma, Savita 1990. *Early Indian Symbols : Numismatic Evidence*. Delhi.

Sharma, Savita 2007. Sarai Denguri Hoard of Silver Punch-marked Coins. *News Bulletin of the Chandrapur Coin Society* 13, p. 2.

Sharma, Savita, and M N P Tiwari 1983. Śiva on Kushāṇa Coins. *Journal of the Numismatic Society of India* 45, pp. 134-149.

Sharma, Sharad 1981. Early Cast Copper Coins from Kauśāmbī. *Numismatic Digest* 5(2), pp. 4-11.

Sharma, Sharad 2003-2004. A Mixed Hoard of Local Punchmarked Coins from Uziaraghat. *Numismatic Digest* 27-28, pp. 1-18.

Sharma, Sharad, and Shinji Hirano 2007. See under Hirano, Shinji, and Sharad Sharma 2007.

Sharma, Sharad, and B P Verma 2001-2002. A Mixed Hoard of Local Punch-marked coins from Bargama. *Numismatic Digest* 25-26, pp. 1-24.

Shastri, A M 1964. Some Observations on Audumbara Coinage. *Journal of the Numismatic Society of India* 26 (2), pp. 157-161.

Shastri, A M 1967. Coins in *Bṛihatsaṁhitā* of Varāhamihira. *Journal of the Numismatic Society of India* 29(2), pp. 41-45.

Shastri, A M 1971. *Tripurī* (Hindi). Bhopal.

Shastri, A M 1972. Was Mahādeva an Audumbara Chief ? *Journal of the Numismatic Society of India* 34, pp. 15-22.

Shastri, A M 1979. *Kaushambi Hoard of Magha Coins*. Nagpur.

Shastri, A M (ed) 1976. *Coins and Early Indian Economy*. Memoirs of the Numismatic Society of India 6. Varanasi.

Shastri, A M (ed) 1982. *Foreign Elements in Indian Indigenous Coins*. Memoirs of the Numismatic Society of India 8. Varanasi.

Shastri, A M 1984. Interesting Kuṇinda and Yaudheya Coins. *Numismatic Digest* 8, pp. 24-36.

Shastri, A M 1995. Jogalthambi Hoard of Nahapāna Coins : Some Aspects. *Numismatic Digest* 19, pp. 73-95.

Shastri, A M 1999-2000. Silver Coins of Chandra Gupta II : A Chronological Framework. *Numismatic Digest* 23-24, pp. 75-78.

Shukla, K S 1980. A Unique Gold Coin of Bhānugupta and Prakāśāditya. *Journal of the Numismatic Society of India* 42, pp. 120-126.

Simonetta, Alberto M 1957. An Essay on the So-called 'Indo-Greek'Coinage. *East and West* 8, pp. 44-66.

Simonetta, Alberto M 1958. A New Essay on the Indo-Greeks, the Śakas and the Pahlavas. *East and West* 9, pp. 154-183.

Sims-Williams, Nicholas, and Joe Cribb 1995-1996. See under Cribb, Joe, and Nicholas Sims-Wolliams 1995-1996.

Singh, J P 1971. Negama and City Coins. D C Sircar (ed), *Early Indian Indigenous Coins*, (Calcutta, 1971), pp. 101-110.

Singh, O P 1968. Ardhanārīśvara on the Coins of Kanishko (Later Kushāṇa). *Journal of the Numismatic Society of India* 30, pp. 195-198.

Singh, Purushottam 1986. The Narhan Hoard of Punchmarked Coins. *Proceedings of the 19th International Numismatic Congress*, London, pp. 165-169.

Singh, S S 1984. *Early Coins of North India—An Iconographic Study*. Patna.

Singh, Y B 1979. Some Recently found Silver Coins of the Imperial Guptas. *Journal of the Numismatic Society of India* 41, pp. 47-50.

Sinha, B P 1988. King and Queen (?) Coin-Type of Skandagupta. *Journal of the Numismatic Society of India* 50, pp. 84-88.

Sircar, D C 1952. Kauṭilya and Indian Numismatics. *Journal of the Numismatic Society of India* 14, pp. 128-143.

Sircar, D C 1964. The *Viṁśopaka* and its Quarters. *Journal of the Numismatic Society of India* 26(2), pp. 127-130.

Sircar, D C 1965. *Indian Epigraphy*. Delhi.

Sircar, D C 1966. *Indian Epigraphical Glossary*. Delhi.

Sircar, D C 1968. *Studies in Indian Coins*. Delhi.

Sircar, D C 1969. *Ancient Malwa and the Vikramāditya Tradition*. New Delhi.

Sircar, D C 1970. *Religious Life in Ancient India*. Calcutta.

Sircar, D C 1971. *Studies in the Religious Life of Ancient and Mediaeval India*. Delhi.

Sircar, D C 1976. Some Problems of Early Indian History. *Journal of the Royal Asiatic Society of Great Britain and Ireland*, pp. 130-135.

Sircar, D C 1980a. The Yavanas. Chapter VII, in R C Majumdar, A D Pusalker, and A K Majumdar (ed), *The Age of Imperial Unity*. The History and Culture of the Indian People 2, (Bombay, 1980), pp. 101-119.

Sircar, D C 1980b. The Śakas and the Pahlavas. Chapter VIII, in R C Majumdar, A D Pusalker, and A K Majumdar (ed), *The Age of Imperial Unity*. The History and Culture of the Indian People 2, (Bombay, 1980), pp. 120-135.

Sircar, D C 1980c. The Kushāṇas. Chapter IX, in R C Majumdar, A D Pusalker, and A K Majumdar (ed), *The Age of Imperial Unity*. The History and Culture of the Indian People 2, (Bombay, 1980), pp. 136-153.

Sircar, D C 1980d. Northern India after the Kushāṇas. Chapter XI, in R C Majumdar, A D Pusalker, and A K Majumdar (ed), *The Age of Imperial Unity*. The History and Culture of the Indian People 2, (Bombay, 1980), pp. 159-177.

Sircar, D C 1980e. The Śaka Satraps of Western India. Chapter XII, in R C Majumdar, A D Pusalker, and A K Majumdar (ed), *The Age of Imperial Unity*. The History and Culture of the Indian People 2, (Bombay, 1980), pp. 178-190.

Sircar, D C 1980f. Vaishṇavism. Section D of Chapter XIX, in R C Majumdar, A D Pusalker, and A K Majumdar (ed), *The Age of Imperial Unity*. The History and Culture of the Indian People 2, (Bombay, 1980), pp. 431-453.

Sircar, D C 1986. *Select Inscriptions bearing on Indian History and Civilization, from 6 century BC to 6 century AD*. 3rd ed, Delhi.

Sircar, D C (ed) 1970. *Early Indian Indigenous Coins*. Calcutta.

Sivaramamurti, C 1951. *Chakravikrama* Type. *Journal of the Numismatic Society of India* 13(2), pp. 180-182.

Smith, V A 1889. The Coinage of the Early or Imperial Guptas. *Journal of the Royal Asiatic Society of Great Britain and Ireland*, pp. 1-41.

Smith, V A 1893. Observations on Gupta Coinage. *Journal of the Royal Asiatic Society of Great Britain and Ireland*, pp. 17-148.

Smith, V A 1972. *Coins of Ancient India—Catalogue of the Coins in the Indian Museum, Calcutta, including the Cabinet of the Asiatic Society of Bengal* 1. Reprint, Varanasi.

Smith, V A 1999. *The Early History of India*. Third revised and enlarged edition. Reprint, New Delhi.

Sohoni, S V 1942. A Note on Audumbara Temple Coins. *Journal of the Numismatic Society of India* 4, pp. 55-57.

Sohoni, S V 1957. Alleged *Cornucopiae* and Fillet on Gupta Coinage. *Journal of the Numismatic Society of India* 19(2), pp. 162-167.

Spence, Lewis 1949. *Myths & Legends of Ancient Egypt*. Reprint, London.

Srivastava, A L 1975. A Silver Coin of Chandragupta-Kumāradevī Type. *Journal of the Numismatic Society of India* 37, pp. 83-84.

Srivastava, A L 1991. *Nandyāvartya*. Allahabad.

Srivastava, A L 2004-2005. *Svastika : Bhāratīya Jīvana kā eka Apratima Pratīka* (Hindi). Patna.

Srivastava, B N 1962. Śaśāṅka, the King of Gauḍa. *Journal of the U P Historical Society* (New Series) 10, pp. 27-56.

Srivastava, Balram 1964. Economic Significance of Roman Coins found in India. *Journal of the Numismatic Society of India* 26(2), pp. 222-227.

Srivastava, Nidhi 1994. *Pañchāla Mudrāoṁ para Triśūla kā Aṅkana* (Hindi). *Pañchāla* 7, pp. 19-21.

Srivastava, Prashant 1987. The Controversial '*Apratigha*' Coins of Kumāragupta I. *Journal of the Numismatic Society of India* 49, pp. 86-89.

Srivastava, Prashant 1989. Observations on the Joint Issues of Vaṅgapāla and Damagupta of Pañchāla. *Journal of the Numismatic Society of India* 51, pp. 56-57.

Srivastava, Prashant 1990a. *Joint Coin-types of Ancient India*. Numismatic Notes and Monographs (The Numismatic Society of India) 22. Varanasi.

Srivastava, Prashant 1990b. Some Observations on the Hermaios-Kalliope Type. *Journal of the Numismatic Society of India* 52, pp. 45-47.

Srivastava, Prashant 1990c. The Lysias-Antialkidas Coin. *Bulletin of Museums and Archaeology in UP* 45-46, pp. 81-85.

Srivastava, Prashant 1991. Śaka-Pahlava Monetary Elements in Imperial Gupta Coinage. *Bulletin of Museums and Archaeology in UP* 47-48, pp. 53-58.

Srivastava, Prashant 1992a. The Joint Rule of Orthagnes and Gondopharnes : A Numismatic Overview. *K D Bajpai Commemoration Volume*, pp. 215-217.

Srivastava, Prashant 1992b. On an Ayodhya Coin Bearing the Names of Devamitra and Āyumitra. *Kosala Through the Ages*, pp. 159-161.

Srivastava, Prashant 1993a. On the Identification of the 'Female Between Vines' on the Poseidon Type of Coins. *Journal of the Numismatic Society of India* 55, pp. 112-113.

Srivastava, Prashant 1993b. Agni in Ancient Indian Numismatic Art, with Special Reference to Pañchāla Coins. *Pañchāla*, 6, pp. 145-147.

Srivastava, Prashant 1994. The Site of the Buddha's Descent from the Trayastriṁśa Heaven. *Pañchāla*, 7, pp. 95-97.

Srivastava, Prashant 1996a. *Aspects of Ancient Indian Numismatics*. Delhi.

Srivastava, Prashant 1996b. An Iconographic Study of Brahmanical Divinities on Śaka-Pahlava Coins. S D Singh (ed), *Culture Through the Ages* (Professor B N Puri Felicitation Volume), (Delhi, 1996), pp. 343-359.

Srivastava, Prashant 1997. The Art and Iconography of a Kushāṇa Gold Coin. *Numismatic Studies*, 5, pp. 43-46.

Srivastava, Prashant 1998a. Some Seleukid Monetary Elements in Śaka-Pahlava Coinage. V D Misra (ed), *Reconstructing History* (Essays in Honour of Prof V C Srivastava), (Varanasi, 1998) 2, pp. 587-593.

Srivastava, Prashant 1998b. On the Rarity of Busts and of Realistic Portraiture on Indigenous Indian Coins. *Pañchāla* 10, pp. 131-134.

Srivastava, Prashant 1998c. Oesho on Kushāṇa Coins. *Pañchāla* 11, pp. 82-83.

Srivastava, Prashant 2000-2001. The Beginning of Legends on Ancient Indian Coins. *Purāvṛitta* (Journal of the Department of Ancient Indian History and Archaeology, University of Lucknow) 1, pp. 215-220.

Srivastava, Prashant 2001. The Imperial Hunter on Gupta Coins. *Numismatic Studies* 6, pp. 144-152.

Srivastava, Prashant 2004a. *Art Motifs on Ancient Indian Coins*. New Delhi.

Srivastava, Prashant 2004b. Skandagupta and the Nāgas. A K Sinha (ed), *Perspectives in Indian History*, (New Delhi, 2004), pp. 82-86.

Srivastava, Prashant 2005a. The Bearing of the Standing Herakles Device on the History of Arachosia. A K Sinha and A K Singh (ed), *Dialogue Between Cultures : India and Iran*, (New Delhi, 2005), pp. 160-163.

Srivastava, Prashant 2005b. Two Śaka-Pahlava Kings Named Azes ? A K Sinha (ed), *Dimensions of Indian History*, (New Delhi, 2005), pp. 74-79.

Srivastava, Prashant 2005c. The Date of Gondopharnes. *Proceedings of the Indian History Congress* (65th Session, Bareilly, 2004), pp. 159-164.

Srivastava, Prashant 2006a. Rudra-Śiva and Hermes : Some Mythological Parallels. A K Sinha (ed), *Facets of Indian History*, (New Delhi, 2006), pp. 88-96.

Srivastava, Prashant 2006b. Apollo as a Coin Device. *Yavanika* 10 (2000, released in 2006), pp. 112-116.

Srivastava, Prashant 2007a. *The Apracharajas* (A History based on Coins and Inscriptions). Delhi.

Srivastava, Prashant 2007b. Metamorphosis in Mythology : A Case Study of the Indian Sky-god. A K Sinha and A K Singh (ed), *Udayana* (New Horizons in History, Classics and Inter-Cultural Studies, Essays in Honour of Professor Udai Prakash Arora), (New Delhi, 2007), pp. 329-332.

Srivastava, Prashant 2007c. Greek Divinities on Śaka-Pahlava Coins. S P Shukla, *et al* (ed), *History and Heritage* (in Honour of Prof K K Thaplyal), (Delhi, 2007) 1, pp. 237-266.

Srivastava, Prashant 2007d. Asura-Varuṇa *vis-à-vis* Ahura Mazda : Some Observations. A K Sinha and A K Singh (ed), *Cultural Parallels : India and Iran*, (New Delhi, 2007), pp. 77-89.

Srivastava, Prashant 2007e. From *Cornucopiae* to *Bījakosha* (Seedpod) : Indianization of an Exotic Coin Motif. Mahendra Pratap and S Z H Jafri (ed), *Region in Indian History*, (New Delhi, 2008, released in 2007), pp. 68-72.

Srivastava, Prashant 2007f. The *Vajra* of Indra in the Devāsura Conflict. *Bulletin of Museums and Archaeology in UP* 55-56, pp. 41-46.

Srivastava, Prashant 2007g. Indravasu : A New Apracha King. *Proceedings of the Indian History Congress* (67th Session, Calicut, 2006-07), pp. 128-130.

Srivastava, Prashant 2007h. Demeter as a Coin Device in the Ancient World. *Numismatic Studies* 8, pp. 1-9.

Srivastava, Prashant 2007i. The So-called 'Bhagamoya' Inscription of the Time of Vijayamitra, Azes Year 77. *Satata* 1, pp. 177-180.

Srivastava, Prashant 2008a. The Lion-slaying Device on Ancient Greek and Indian Coins : Some Observations. A K Sinha (ed), *Approaches to History, Culture, Art and Archaeology* (Essays in the Honour of Professor Om Prakash), (New Delhi, 2009, released in 2008), pp. 199-202.

Srivastava, Prashant 2008b. Machene, the Śaka-Pahlava Queen : Some Observations. Pratima Asthana and S Z H Zafri (ed), *Transformations in Indian History*, (New Delhi, 2009, released in 2008), pp. 168-173.

Srivastava, Prashant 2008c. Die-striking Mode of Fabrication of Coins : Its Origin in India. *Journal of the Numismatic Society of India* 70, pp. 28-31.

Srivastava, Prashant 2009. On the Problem of the Identity of the Pursuer of Poros in the Battle of Hydaspese. *Yavanika* 12, pp. 42-50.

Srivastava, Prashant 2010. The Theory of the Graeco-Iranian Origin of Indian Coinage : A Reappraisal. Sushma Srivastava (ed), *Socio-Economic Implications of Commercial Pursuits in Ancient India*, (Allahabad, 2010), pp. 146-151.

Srivastava, Prashant, and Deepak Tiwari 1994. Śiva on Ujjayinī Coins. *Journal of the Numismatic Society of India*, LVI, pp. 5-6 (1994) (jointly).

Srivastava, Prashant, and Prachi Srivastava 1993. On the Relationship Between Nikias and Hippostratos. *Milinda*, pp. 97-98.

Srivastava, S K 1989. Fire Worship as Depicted on Ancient Indian Coins. *Journal of the Numismatic Society of India* 51, pp. 74-76.

Stein, M Aurel 1888. Zoroastrian Deities on Indo-Scythian Coins. *Indian Antiquary* 17, pp. 89-98.

Stein, Aurel 1921. *Serindia*. Oxford.

Stein, Aurel 1929. *Kharoshṭhī Inscriptions discovered by Sir A Stein in Chinese Turkestan*, 3 vols. Oxford.

Stutley, Margaret 2003.*The Illustrated Dictionary of Hindu Iconography*. Reprint, New Delhi.

Tarn, W W 1948. *Alexander the Great*, 2 vols. Cambridge.

Tarn, W W 1980. *The Greeks in Bactria and India*. Reprint, New Delhi.

Thakur, Upendra 1961. Mints and Minting in India. *Journal of the Numismatic Society of India* 23, pp. 175ff.

Thakur, Upendra 1967a. The Hūṇa Coinage. *Journal of the Numismatic Society of India* 29(1), pp. 9-21.

Thakur, Upendra 1967b. *The Hūṇas in India*. Varanasi.

Thaplyal, K K 1971. Coin Devices on Clay Lumps. D C Sircar (ed), *Early Indian Indigenous Coins*, (Calcutta, 1971), pp. 127-130.

Thaplyal, K K 1972. *Studies in Ancient Indian Seals*. Lucknow.

Thaplyal, K K 1980-1981. Chandragupta-Kumāradevī Coins. *Purātattva* (Bulletin of the Indian Archaeological Society) 12, pp. 152-154.

Thaplyal, K K 1985. *Inscriptions of the Maukharīs, Later Guptas, Puṣpabhūtis, and Yaśovarman of Kanauj*. Delhi.

Thaplyal, K K 1989a. Die. A Ghosh (ed), *An Encyclopaedia of Indian Archaeology* 1 (New Delhi, 1989), p. 321.

Thaplyal, K K 1989b. Mould. A Ghosh (ed), *An Encyclopaedia of Indian Archaeology* 1 (New Delhi, 1989), p. 329.

Thaplyal, K K 1996. *Guilds in Ancient India*. New Delhi.

Thaplyal, K K 1997. Parentage and Nativity of Dhruvasvāminī, Chief-queen of Chandragupta II. J P Joshi (ed), *Facets of Indian Civilization—Recent Perspectives* (Essays in Honour of Prof B B Lal), (New Delhi, 1997) 3, pp. 884-889.

Thaplyal, K K forthcoming. [Political History of the Imperial Guptas].

Thaplyal, K K, and Prashant Srivastava 1998. *Coins of Ancient India*. Lucknow.

Tiwari, M N P, and Savita Sharma 1983. See under Sharma, Savita, and M N P Tiwari 1983.

Torday, Laszlo 1997. *Mounted Archers—The Beginnings of Central Asian History*. Durham.

Tripathi, R R 1962. Some New and Rare Copper Coins in the Allahabad Museum. *Journal of the Numismatic Society of India* 24(1), pp. 20-23.

Trivedi, H V 1957. *Catalogue of the Coins of the Nāga Kings of Padmāvatī*. Gwalior.

Trivedi, H V 1964. *Western Kshatrapa Coins in the Andhra Pradesh Government Museum*. Hyderabad.

Upadhyaya, D, and S N Chaturvedi 1972. Two Gold Punch-marked Coins. *Journal of the Numismatic Society of India* 34, pp. 153-156.

Valentine, W H 1993. *Sassanian Coins*. Reprint, Delhi.

Vanaja, R 1983. *Indian Coinage*. New Delhi.

Vats, M S 1926-1927. A Gold Coin of Samudragupta of the 'Battle-axe Type'. *Archaeological Survey of India – Annual Report* 1926-1927, pp. 233-234.

Verma, B P, and Sharad Sharma 2001-2002. See under Sharma, Sharad, and B P Verma 2001-2002.

Verma, T P 1991. Notes on Repoussé Coins. *Journal of the Numismatic Society of India* 53, pp. 142-149.

Vogel, J Ph 1926. *Indian Serpent Lore*. London.

Vogel, J Ph 1962. *The Goose in Indian Religion and Art*. E J Brill.

Walsh, E H C 1975. Two Hoards of Silver Punch-marked Coins Found in the Bhiṛ Mound at Taxila. Chapter 40, in J H Marshall, *Taxila* 2 (Indian reprint, Delhi, 1975), pp. 843-852.

Warmington, E H 1928. *The Commerce between the Roman Empire and India*. Cambridge.

Watters, T 1961. *On Yuan Chwang's Travels in India*. Edited by T W Rhys Davids and S W Bushell. Reprint, Delhi.

Wheeler, R E M 1954. *Rome Beyond the Imperial Frontiers*. London.

Whitehead, R B 1914. *Catalogue of the Coins in the Punjab Museum, Lahore* 1. The Indo-Greek Coins. Oxford.

Whitehead, R B 1922. *Period-Mohammadan Coinage of North-West India*. Numismatic Notes and Monographs 13. New York.

Whitehead, R B 1923. Notes on Indo-Greek Numismatics. *Numismatic Chronicle*, pp. 294-343.

Whitehead, R B 1940. Notes on the Indo-Greeks, Part 1. *Numismatic Chronicle*, pp. 89-122.

Whitehead, R B 1943. The Eastern Satrap Sophytes. *Numismatic Chronicle* 1943, pp. 60-72.

Whitehead, R B 1947. Notes on the Indo-Greeks, Part 2. *Numismatic Chronicle*, pp. 28-51.

Whitehead, R B 1950. Notes on the Indo-Greeks, Part 3. *Numismatic Chronicle*, pp. 205-232.

Whitehead, R B 1975. Commentary on Rare and Unique Coins. J H Marshall, *Taxila* 2, pp. 830-842.

Wilkins, W J 2006. *Hindu Mythology : Vedic and Purāṇic*. Indian reprint, New Delhi.

Wilson, H H 1971. *Ariana Antiqua—A Descriptive Account of the Antiquities and Coins of Afghanistan*. Indian Reprint, Delhi.

Wood, A H 1959. *The Gold Coin-types of the Great Kushāṇas*. Numismatic Notes and Monographs (Numismatic Society of India) 9. Varanasi.

Wroth, W 1903. *A Catalogue of the Greek Coins in the British Museum, London*. Coins of Parthia. London.

Yaduvanshi 1988. *Śaivamata* (Hindi). Patna.

Zimmer, Heinrich 1999. *Myths and Symbols in Indian Art and Civilization*. Edited by Joseph Campbell. Indian reprint, Delhi.